FROMMER'S

COMPREHENSIVE TRAVEL GUIDE

NEW ENGLAND '93

by Susan Farewell,
Lisa M. Legarde, and
Dale Northrup

PRENTICE HALL TRAVEL

NEW YORK • LONDON • TORONTO • SYDNEY • TOKYO • SINGAPORE

FROMMER BOOKS

Published by Prentice Hall General Reference
A division of Simon & Schuster Inc.
15 Columbus Circle
New York, NY 10023

ISBN 0-671-84699-X
ISSN 1044-2286

Design by Robert Bull Design
Maps by Geografix Inc.

FROMMER'S EDITORIAL STAFF
Vice President/Editorial Director: Marilyn Wood
Senior Editor/Editorial Manager: Alice Fellows
Senior Editor: Lisa Renaud
Editors: Charlotte Allstrom, Thomas F. Hirsch, Peter Katucki, Sara Hinsey Raveret, Theo-
dore Stavrou
Assistant Editors: Margaret Bowen, Lee Gray, Ian Wilker
Editorial Assistant: Gretchen Henderson
Managing Editor: Leanne Coupe

SPECIAL SALES
Bulk purchases of Frommer's Travel Guides are available at special discounts. The publishers
are happy to custom-make publications for corporate clients who wish to use them as
premiums or sales promotions. We can excerpt the contents, provide covers with corporate
imprints, or create books to meet specific needs. For more information write to Special Sales,
Prentice Hall Travel, Paramount Communications Building, 15 Columbus Circle, New York,
NY 10023.

Manufactured in the United States of America

CONTENTS

LIST OF MAPS

INVITATION TO THE READERS

In researching this book, we have come across many wonderful establishments, the best of which we have included here. We're sure that many of you will also come across appealing hotels, inns, restaurants, guesthouses, shops, and attractions. Please don't keep them to yourself. Share your experiences, especially if you want to comment on places that we have covered in this edition that have changed for the worse. You can address your letters to:

Authors
Frommer's New England '93
c/o Prentice Hall Travel
15 Columbus Circle
New York, NY 10023

A DISCLAIMER

SAFETY ADVISORY

Whenever you're traveling in an unfamiliar city or country, stay alert. Be aware of your immediate surroundings. Wear a moneybelt and keep a close eye on your possessions. Be particularly careful with cameras, purses, and wallets, all favorite targets of thieves and pickpockets.

CHAPTER 1

GETTING TO KNOW
NEW ENGLAND

When it comes to American history and culture, New England is where it all began.

Certainly history is not the only thing to attract you to the six states that make up the region: Connecticut, Rhode Island, Massachusetts, Maine, New Hampshire, and Vermont. Each state has natural beauties worth bragging about, like the beaches of Rhode Island, the windswept dunes of Cape Cod, the rugged coasts of Maine, or the Green Mountains of Vermont. And there's the local cuisine, particularly the seafood: lobster, the freshest you can get; clam chowder, easily the best in the world; Vermont Cheddar cheese; hotcakes with New Hampshire's maple syrup.

New England is not all cities and civilization, either—despite all the talk about the Eastern megalopolises. The Appalachian Trail has its beginning here; the sandy shores of Cape Cod are more than 100 miles long; Vermont alone has over two dozen challenging ski areas; and if these places are too busy for you, head for the untracked wilderness forests of northern Maine. In fact, it's not really the big cities such as Hartford, Providence, and Boston that set the tone of New England community life, but rather the small New England villages—Litchfield, Conn.; Newfane, Vt.; Kennebunkport, Me.—each with its village green surrounded by the church, school, library, and town hall, each village separated from its neighbor by rolling pastures, lush woodland, and glacial lakes.

Although New England is not just history, one soon discovers that New Englanders love the region because of its history and its traditions. Only here can you see Plymouth Rock, climb Bunker Hill, visit the site of the very first Thanksgiving feast. At Connecticut's Mystic Seaport you can see a New England maritime town of the past, re-created and in full operation; and at Sturbridge Village and Plimoth Plantation the crafts of the colonial period are performed as they were centuries ago.

Even in modern Boston the history of New England is everywhere. From the observation deck atop a sleek skyscraper, you can look down upon the charming colonial buildings ranged along gas-lit, cobblestone streets on Beacon Hill. Wander through Faneuil Hall, where American colonists debated the abuses of British rule, then plow through the crowds thronging the renovated Quincy Market, Boston's favorite gathering place. Make an excursion out to the suburban towns of Lexington and Concord, where the first battles of the American Revolution were fought more

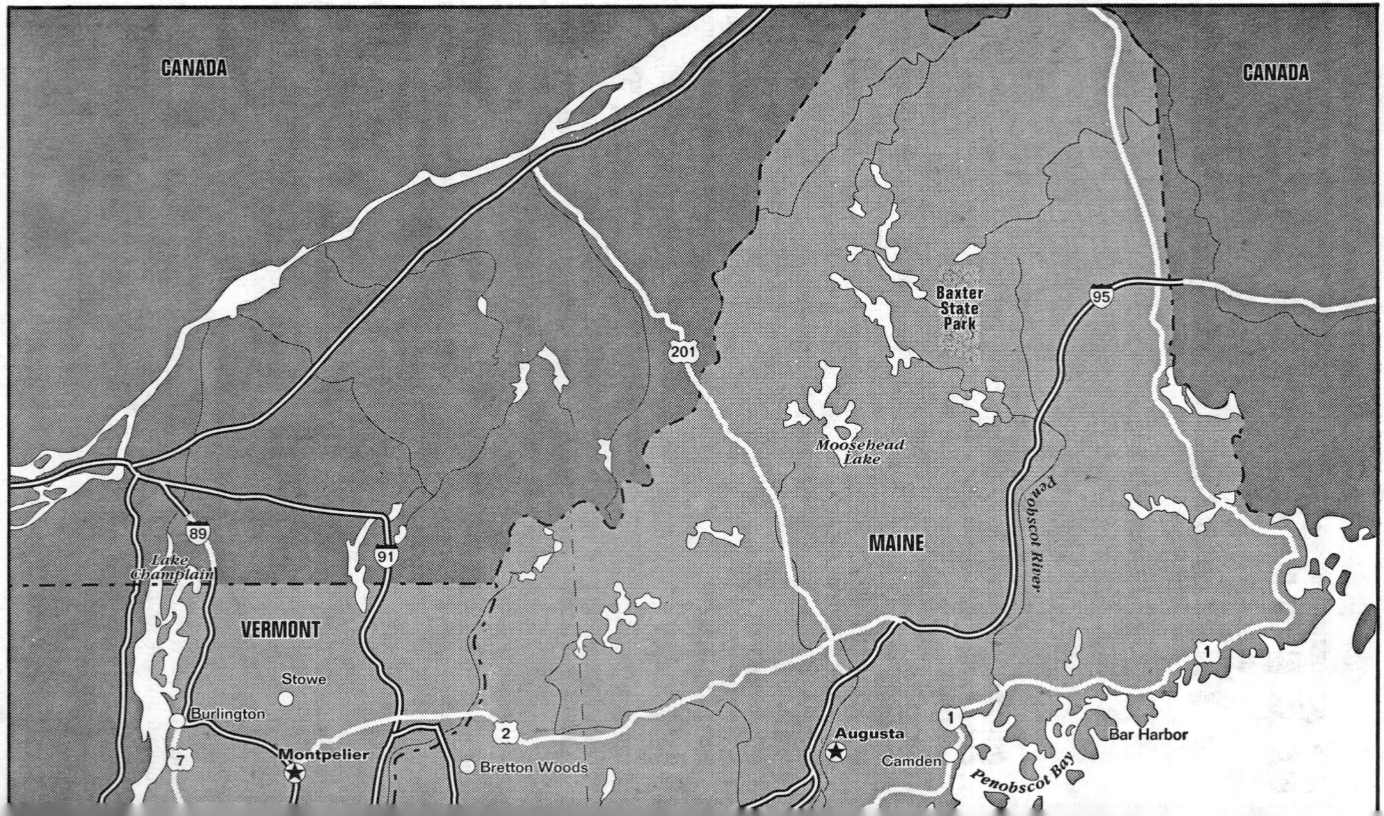

N
0
20 m
32 km
CANADA
CANADA
Baxter State Park
Moosehead Lake
MAINE
Penobscot River
95
201
91
89
1
1
2
7
Lake Champlain
VERMONT
Stowe
Burlington
Montpelier
Bretton Woods
Augusta
Camden
Bar Harbor
Penobscot Bay

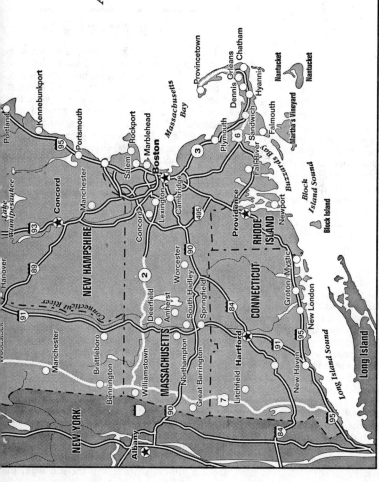

Atlantic Ocean

Kennebunkport
Portland
Portsmouth
95
Rockport
Marblehead
Salem
Massachusetts Bay
Boston
Cambridge
Lexington
Concord
Manchester
Concord
Winnipesaukee
Hanover
93
89
NEW HAMPSHIRE
495
3
Provincetown
Dennis Orleans Chatham
Hyannis
Sandwich
6
Plymouth
Falmouth
Fall River
Nantucket
Nantucket
Martha's Vineyard
Buzzards Bay
Block Island Sound
Newport
RHODE ISLAND
Block Island
90
Worcester
2
Deerfield
South Hadley
Amherst
Northampton
Springfield
Connecticut River
97
Manchester
Brattleboro
Bennington
Williamstown
MASSACHUSETTS
Great Barrington
7
Litchfield
Hartford
84
CONNECTICUT
Groton Mystic
New London
91
95
New Haven
Long Island Sound
Long Island
84
95
NEW YORK
Albany
90

? DID YOU KNOW . . . ?

- Basketball was invented in 1891 by Dr. James Naismith in Springfield, Mass. You can visit the Basketball Hall of Fame there.
- In 1895 William Morgan invented volleyball in Holyoke, Mass.
- The dollar bills in your pocket were probably printed on paper produced by the Crane Paper Co. of Dalton, Mass., main supplier to the U.S. Mint.
- Great Barrington, Mass., was the first town in the world to have electric streetlights, in 1886.
- Sylvester Graham (1794–1851) of Northampton, Mass., advocating a diet of vegetables and coarse-milled grains, invented the Graham cracker.
- Boston is at a latitude similar to Barcelona, Rome, and Istanbul.
- Harvard University is America's oldest institution of higher learning, founded in 1636.
- Of the hundreds of people accused of witchcraft in Salem in 1692, only one confessed—and she claimed others had forced her into evil.
- Mount Washington (6,288 ft.), the highest summit east of the Rockies, holds the record for the highest winds ever recorded: 231 miles per hour. The summit qualifies as an arctic climate zone.
- Boston's subway system was the first built in the western hemisphere.

than 200 years ago, and you'll cross Route 128, the nexus of high-technology research and development for the eastern United States.

New England's paradoxical loves of both tradition and innovation have coexisted peacefully from the very beginning, when men and women came to New England to escape the strictures of Reformation Europe and experiment with new religious and societal frameworks. They built a new way of life on this continent, but they included in it the things they loved best about the old countries they had left behind.

1. GEOGRAPHY & HISTORY

GEOGRAPHY

The New England landscape, as we see it, is left from the age of the glaciers. But long before the ice age, several billion years ago, the earth cooled and shrank, and its crust wrinkled, throwing out towering mountain ranges. The friction and pressure of this "wrinkling" was so intense that sand turned to marble and limestone to gneiss and schist. Molten rock (magma) flowed from the planet's boiling core through faults in the folded crust, but the magma never made it to the surface. Instead it snaked its way into fissures, sometimes reaching a great open "bubble" of air in the crust, filling it. Then the molten rock cooled slowly, insulated beneath the earth's crust, and its liquid minerals slowly took on the crystalline texture we identify as granite.

The results of this geological wonderwork are easily visible throughout New England today—in Vermont's vast quarries of creamy marble, around farmers' fields in the stone fences made of textured gneiss flecked with shiny mica, and in the great domed hills of solid granite (like Mount Monadnock) that were formed deep within the earth.

About eight million years ago, one final geologic upheaval gave us the mountains we know as the **Appalachian range,** which stretches from Maine to Georgia. The lofty mountains formed aeons ago were worn down, subjected to pressure again and again, stretched and mangled, beaten and weathered. Finally they were only a fraction of their former height, yielding today's New England of gentle valleys and easily climbed mountains: New Hampshire's White Mountains, Vermont's Green Mountains, and Massachusetts's Berkshires.

Several hundred million years ago, before the mountains were given their final form, New England was in the midst of a tropical climate rich in plant life. The Connecticut River Valley was a paradise for the **dinosaurs** who thrived here, and who left their footprints—and even their skeletons—in the thick river silt, which later turned to stone. At Dinosaur State Park in Rocky Hill, Connecticut, you can see these remnants of New England's inhabitants from 200 million years ago.

In very recent geological time, about a million years ago in the **ice age,** the

IMPRESSIONS

I think you [in New England] have beyond all question the happiest and best country going.
—ARTHUR HUGH CLOUGH, IN A LETTER TO CHARLES ELIOT NORTON,
AUGUST 29, 1853

New England is a finished place. Its destiny is that of Florence or Venice. . . . It is the first American section to be finished, to achieve stability in its conditions of life. It is the first old civilization, the first permanent civilization in America.
—BERNARD DEVOTO, *NEW ENGLAND: THERE SHE STANDS—*
FORAYS AND REBUTTALS, 1936

---

world's temperature dropped and the polar ice caps thickened. Millions of tons of ice built up on the original ice pack, and the weight of this build-up pushed the edges of the ice pack outward, toward the equator. An enormous blanket of ice slowly moved southward over New England, plowing up the soil, and absorbing dirt and rock into itself by a slow-motion churning. As the climate warmed and the ice retreated, it dumped this debris into long mounds called drumlins, of which Bunker Hill is perhaps the most famous. The ice's bulldozing action also formed thousands of glacial lakes and ponds, including Thoreau's Walden Pond. Across the landscape, huge boulders picked up and carried by the advancing ice were dropped helter-skelter as it retreated. You will come upon these "glacial erratics," as they're called, which stand naked in flat fields where they don't seem to belong.

The glaciers came and went, sculpting the terrain of New England at least four times. When they finally retreated, 10,000 to 20,000 years ago, the sea flooded in to cover much of the region. Melting ice added to the oceans' volume, and the weight of the ice had depressed the low terrain beneath the new sea level. But the land rebounded, reaching the level it has today, the oceans retreated, and New England became the New England we know.

HISTORY

To understand New England and its people, you must take at least a quick look at the region's history. To a surprising extent, today's New Englanders think and do as they do because of how their ancestors thought and acted.

EUROPEAN EXPLORERS Historians think that the Vikings were the first Europeans to explore North America's shores, but there is evidence, none of it conclusive, that the discoverers may have been Irish, Spanish, or Portuguese. But we know that the Norse came to this area about 1000 B.C., and may have founded settlements in the land they called Vinland. Though the land was fruitful, the settlers found it hard going, mostly because the indigenous peoples fought the settlers ferociously. The great Nordic leaders did not judge the land to be worth the deaths of many of their people, so they withdrew to their more easily ruled settlements in Greenland and Iceland.

By the time the intrepid Columbus set out on his epoch-making voyage 500 hundred years later (1492), Europe had become ready to profit from discoveries of new lands. Columbus was followed by other explorers, including Giovanni Caboto (known as John Cabot), who sailed under the English flag in 1497 and claimed all of what

DATELINE

- **9000 B.C.** Immigrants from Asia reach what is now New England.
- **1000 B.C.** Norse mariners explore parts of the New England coast.
- **1497** Giovanni Caboto (John Cabot) lands on the New England mainland and claims it for the king of England.
- **1524** Giovanni da Verrazano sails along the New England coast, naming Rhode Island.
- **1602** Bartholomew Gosnold and
(continues)

DATELINE

colonists arrive in New England, name Cape Cod and Martha's Vineyard, and set up a colony that lasts only 22 days.

1614 Capt. John Smith returns to England with a rich cargo of fish and furs from what he calls "New England," the first use of the region's name.

1620 Pilgrims aboard the *Mayflower* reach the tip of Cape Cod in November, and Plymouth in December.

1636 Harvard College is founded to educate young men for the ministry.

1638–39 Portsmouth, R.I., is founded; Hartford, Windsor, and Wethersfield, Conn., join to form the Connecticut Colony.

1692 Witch trials are held in Salem, Mass.

1765–67 Passage of the Stamp Act and Townshend Acts infuriate American colonists.

March 1770 Boston Massacre heralds the beginning of the American Revolution.

December 16, 1773 Boston Tea Party goads Parliament to pass strict

(continues)

would become New England for his master, King Henry VII.

It took a century before the English monarch was ready to exploit his claims. During the early 1600s, expeditions were sent out under Sir Humphrey Gilbert, Bartholomew Gosnold, Martin Pring, and George Weymouth. These brought back useful intelligence on the new land (and Weymouth brought back a Native American named Squanto, who learned English before returning to his homeland), but it was Captain John Smith who studied the land seriously with an eye to colonization, and who gave it the name "New England."

COLONIAL NEW ENGLAND Before Gilbert, Gosnold, and Smith set out for the New World, several hundred Puritans had already left England for Holland in search of religious freedom. Their stay in Leyden was not a happy one, since they found the morals of the local people to be less than strict; so a number of these Puritan "pilgrims" returned to England and, in late summer of 1620, set sail in the *Mayflower* for the New World. They arrived at what is now Provincetown, on the tip of Cape Cod, in November, and paused there long enough to draft and sign the Mayflower Compact, which would be their governing law. But Cape Cod's sandy terrain and scrubby vegetation, which delight present-day vacationers, were too poor for the Pilgrims' purposes, and the search for more fertile land finally brought them to Plymouth Rock, south of Massachusetts Bay, in the middle of the frigid month of December 1620.

Half of the Pilgrims died that winter of disease and privation. But luck was with the rest: Squanto, George Weymouth's prisoner, found them and persuaded Massasoit, *sachem* (chief) of the Wampanoags, to agree to 50 years of peace between his people and the colonists. In 1621 more colonists arrived, and in a few years Plymouth was a sturdy colony. At first, land was held and worked in common, but this system was abandoned when it was realized that family plots would be worked more diligently.

Land north and south of Plymouth proved to be more fertile, and soon there were several thriving communities nearby ready to welcome new settlers.

The Founders, as they are called, were followed in 1628 by another group of Pilgrims who established the colony of Massachusetts Bay. By 1637 the colony had several thousand inhabitants, and new towns were being founded up and down the coast, and even inland at Concord, Dedham, and Watertown. The Puritan settlers must have seen a bright future, for in 1636 they set up Harvard College to educate young men for the ministry.

By 1640 there were sturdy communities of settlers in Connecticut and Rhode Island as well as in Massachusetts. By 1680 the indigenous peoples who had lived here before the coming of the settlers were reduced to only a few thousand souls through fierce warfare, European-introduced disease, and alcohol addiction.

SPIRIT OF INDEPENDENCE The settlers of New England governed themselves, while paying lip service to the sovereignty of the British crown. They built their own prosperity despite laws promulgated in London that placed burdens and restraints on their economic activities. Governors sent out by the king were universally disliked, and often forced to return home by the cantankerous colonists.

It was King George III (reigned 1760–1820) who forced the issue, refusing to bear the irritation of the Americans' independent spirit any longer. Taxes were imposed on the colonies, even though the colonists had no elected representatives and no voice in Parliament. Resentment grew as the colonists chafed under the burden of taxation without representation. In March 1770, a crowd of Bostonians began taunting royal army sentries, and soon the mob got out of hand. Greatly outnumbered, the soldiers fired into the crowd, killing five citizens in what would be known as the Boston Massacre.

Life in Boston was outwardly peaceful for a few years, but king and Parliament were still determined to rule the unruly colonists, and the colonists were determined not to permit interference with their privileges of self-government, now a century and a half old. As a symbol of London's supremacy, a tax was placed on tea shipped to the colonies. The tax was widely reviled, not so much for its economic impact, which was minimal, but because of its symbolic importance: Virtually everyone drank tea, and thus everyone was forced to pay the tax. The political temperature rose as American patriots formed secret societies, such as the Sons of Liberty and the Committees of Correspondence, and worked out plans of resistance to London's control.

In the autumn of 1773, matters came to a head as the patriotic activists insisted that the king's governor order HMS *Dartmouth,* arriving in Boston with a cargo of taxable tea, to go back where it came from. Governor Hutchinson would not give the order, so on the night of December 16, bands of patriots disguised as Native Americans and blacks emptied the *Dartmouth* and two other ships of their tea cargoes. The tea was dumped into Boston Harbor, and the night's action became known as the Boston Tea Party. When London learned of this rebellious act, laws were passed that were meant to strangle the colonial economy and to teach the nasty colonists a lesson. The political temperature in New England neared the boiling point.

REVOLUTIONARY WAR Seeing war as inevitable, farmers and tradesmen began to stockpile arms, ammunition, and matériel. Boston and other large towns were under the direct control of sizable royal garrisons, but the countryside and its villages belonged to the revolutionists, so this "arms race" went on uninhibited.

In an effort to stop the colonists' arms collecting, a British expeditionary force marched secretly to Concord on the night of April 18, 1775, to make surprise searches of suspected illegal arms caches at dawn the next day. But

DATELINE

laws strangling New England's economy.

• **April 19, 1775** Minutemen of Lexington and Concord battle British regulars, beginning the American Revolution.

• **June 17, 1776** Revolutionary forces inflict heavy casualties on the British at the Battle of Bunker Hill.

• **1777** Vermont declares independence from Great Britain as a republic.

• **1783** In the Treaty of Versailles, Great Britain recognizes the independence of the United States.

• **1790s** Salem shipowner and merchant Elias Hasket Derby becomes America's first millionaire. Eli Whitney's cotton gin provides cheap thread for New England's burgeoning textile industry.

• **1820** Maine, once part of colonial Massachusetts, becomes 23rd state.

• **1845** Thoreau builds his cabin on Walden Pond in Concord, Mass.

• **1852** Harriet Beecher Stowe's book *Uncle Tom's Cabin* inspires Abolitionists.

• **1857** Discovery of petroleum in *(continues)*

DATELINE

Pennsylvania sounds the death knell for New England's whalers and rich whale-oil trade.

- **1929** Stock Market crash signals the end of New England's commercial and industrial greatness.
- **1944** World monetary conference held at Bretton Woods, N.H.
- **1954** USS *Nautilus*, the world's first nuclear-powered submarine, is launched at Groton, Conn.
- **1960–63** John F. Kennedy, of Brookline, Mass., serves as President of the United States.
- **1970s** Computer boom brings renewed prosperity to New England.

American spies learned of the plan, and set up a system to warn their countrymen. If the redcoats departed Boston along the isthmus that linked it to the mainland, one lantern would be hung in the steeple of Boston's Old North Church. If the troops instead boarded boats to row across the water and march on a different route, two lanterns would be hung.

As the British filled the boats, two lanterns appeared in the steeple, easily visible from the far shore where Paul Revere, William Dawes, and Samuel Prescott waited on horseback. These messengers rode into the dark hinterland, sounding the alarm in each village. The American intelligence network was so good that the citizens of Lexington and Concord leapt from their beds long before Major Pitcairn and his royal infantry were anywhere near. As dawn broke on April 19, 70 Lexington Minutemen faced Pitcairn's regiments on Lexington's town green.

The Minutemen were ordered by Major Pitcairn to disperse. They stood their ground. Taunts were exchanged. A shot was fired, and that triggered a battle. When the smoke cleared, eight Minutemen were dead, and the British troops went on a rampage that was stopped only with difficulty by their commanders, who immediately marched them in the direction of Concord.

Word of the Lexington engagement was rushed to Concord, where the local Minutemen retreated across the North Bridge over the Concord River in the face of the powerful British force. The Battle of Concord was fought for command of the bridge. The British forces were unable to take it, which was a victory for the much smaller colonial force. But the redcoats pursued their mission in town, discovering and burning some wooden gun carriages. The smoke rising from the town convinced the Minutemen, holding their position at North Bridge, that their homes were in flames, and they fought all the more fiercely.

The "shot heard 'round the world" was fired from a Minuteman's musket at Concord North Bridge, where this band of farmers held off professional soldiers. But this first battle of the American revolution was actually won by the colonists as the British retreated. Sniping from behind trees and stone walls along the road back to Boston, Minutemen brought the British casualty count up to 200, a grievous and embarrassing loss for the powerful forces of the Crown.

On June 17, 1776, full war broke out when the Americans fortified Breed's Hill, next to Bunker's Hill, in Charlestown, just across the harbor from Boston. General Gage, the British commander, was forced to attack this threat, but from their entrenched positions the Americans shot more than a thousand of his soldiers. As the battle raged, the Americans' ammunition ran low, and their commander, Col. William Prescott, said to his troops, "Don't fire until you see the whites of their eyes," in order to make every shot count. Their ammunition exhausted, the Revolutionary forces abandoned their positions, having won another important victory.

A few weeks later on July 4, in Philadelphia, American leaders signed a Declaration of Independence from Great Britain.

Though many of the most important battles of the revolutionary war were later to be fought in New York and Pennsylvania, New England prides itself on having been the place where it all began. Patriots Day (April 19) is a holiday in Massachusetts, and hundreds of citizens and visitors turn out at dawn to witness reenactments of the battles of Lexington and Concord staged by groups in period uniforms.

By 1781, the revolutionary war was over and the American colonies were free and independent states. But the forging of a strong and effective central government for the former British territories would not be accomplished until 1789. In the meantime, the removal of British legal restrictions on trade meant that New England merchants were at last free to trade with the world as they liked. New Englanders put to sea in ships built in Maine, Massachusetts, Rhode Island, and Connecticut, and were soon returning with the riches of Europe, Africa, China, and India in trade. Whaling ships out of Salem and New Bedford brought back whale-oil wealth of similar greatness. Though the renewal of war with Great Britain (the War of 1812) disrupted New England's progress for a time, the seas were soon open again.

THE INDUSTRIAL REVOLUTION Across the open sea from England, a young man named Samuel Slater had arrived in 1789. Slater had worked in the new cotton-spinning factories of England. Though it was against British law to "export" knowledge of the machines, which were making Great Britain the world's wealthiest textile producer, Slater slipped out of the country and established a cotton-spinning mill at Pawtucket, R.I., based on his knowledge of English machine design. The mill revolutionized the weaving of textiles in the New World, and set the stage for New England's great weaving industry.

Throughout the 19th century, as New England's clipper ships and whalers swept through the world's oceans, land-bound New Englanders exploited the region's waterpower resources to run their new mills, and industrial towns sprang to life along New England's rivers. The textile factories grew and grew, and some, like the gigantic Amoskeag Mills in Manchester, N.H., had many-windowed facades that marched along the riverbank for more than a quarter mile. Next to the factories were new houses for the armies of workers, many of whom were women. Company stores and company-financed civic buildings filled the streets of the new towns, which were founded on the wealth from weaving.

From some of the factories it was not textiles but machinery, firearms, shoes, watches, and instruments that marched out the doors on their way to the markets of the world. New England inventors and New England engineers gained a reputation for ingenuity that survives today, and samples of "Yankee ingenuity" are still proudly displayed.

New England's commercial success brought New Englanders wealth and sophistication. Boston, chief city of the region, was proud to call itself the "Athens of America." But times change, and changing times brought changed circumstances to the region in the next century.

THE TWENTIETH CENTURY After the prosperity of the 1800s, the steamship replaced the New England clipper; natural gas, petroleum, and electricity replaced whale-oil lamps; and textile manufacturers moved their operations to Southern states, where wages were lower. Millions of immigrants who had come from abroad to share in New England's commercial boom were left with minimal skills in a diminishing job market. New England's farms, set on rocky soil in a northern climate, were out-produced and out-sold by the vast farms in other areas of the country.

The stock market crash of 1929 and its aftermath spelled the bitter end of New England's golden age. What had once been America's richest, proudest, and most cultured region was now economically depressed, politically corrupt, and spiritually defeated.

IMPRESSIONS

The Yankee is one who, if he once gets his teeth set on a thing, all creation can't make him let go.
—RALPH WALDO EMERSON, *JOURNALS*, 1842

You can always tell the Irish,
You can always tell the Dutch;
You can always tell a Yankee,
But you cannot tell him much.
—ERIC KNIGHT, *ALL YANKEES ARE LIARS*, BEFORE 1943

But New England was still beautiful, historic, and proud. In the years after World War II, New Englanders realized that their land had other kinds of wealth. New England's hundreds of colleges and universities were leaders in education. The New England landscape was sprinkled with graceful towns and villages. New Englanders were as ingenious as ever, and the chilly waters of the Atlantic still held a wealth of seafood, so New England survived, and even prospered again.

In recent decades, graduates of New England's universities, no matter where they came from, settled here and founded small companies—including Wang Laboratories and Digital Equipment—that became large companies employing tens of thousands. The sturdy old 19th-century textile mills of brick and granite were recycled as computer-company offices and factories. The name of Route 128 became synonymous with the computer industry. New England's picturesque towns and villages found a new vocation as the great old houses were transformed to historic inns, and the more modest houses began to provide bed-and-breakfast to travelers and vacationers.

Today New England is known for its beautiful landscapes and settlements, its rich history, its technical expertise, its medical research, and, well, its "livability" and charm. More than one New Englander will proudly claim that this is America's first and best, and after your visit here, I think you'll agree.

2. FAMOUS NEW ENGLANDERS

Phineas T. Barnum (1810–91) The great American showman began his career by exhibiting Joice Heth, "George Washington's nurse, 161 years old" (she was about 80, and had never laid eyes on George). Barnum traveled widely, but always looked upon his native Connecticut as home.

[John] Calvin Coolidge (1872–1933) "Callow Cal" was the 30th President of the United States. He worked his way up the political ladder as a Massachusetts state senator, lieutenant governor, and governor. Elected vice president in the Harding administration (1920), he assumed the presidency upon Harding's death (1923). His New England honesty and simplicity served him well in politics, and contributed greatly to his popularity. His boyhood home in Plymouth, Vt., is now a museum, and Coolidge descendants run the local cheese factory.

Emily Dickinson (1830–86) Born in Amherst, Mass., she was raised in almost Puritan surroundings by her wealthy lawyer father. At age 23, she withdrew from public view and lived the rest of her life in near seclusion.

Ralph Waldo Emerson (1803–82) A founder of the Transcendentalist movement, Emerson believed in the mystical unity of nature and God. Although such unitarian and ecological beliefs are accepted around the world today, they were quite radical in 19th-century Concord, Mass. Emerson's essays, poems, and lectures had a profound effect on American religion, literature, and society.

Winslow Homer (1836–1910) Among America's greatest landscape painters, Boston-born Winslow Homer began his career as a magazine illustrator of Civil War scenes. When he was 40 years old, he took up painting full-time, and developed a direct, realistic, and very colorful style. Working at Prouts Neck, Me., he rendered the beautiful but tempestuous Maine coast as no other artist has done. His naval and maritime oils and watercolors hold a unique prominence in American art.

John F. Kennedy (1917–63) Born in Brookline, Mass., to a prosperous and politically savvy family, John Kennedy was educated at Harvard before serving as a PT-boat captain in World War II. After serving as a congressman and senator, he was elected 35th President of the United States in 1960, the youngest ever elected, and the first Roman Catholic.

Massasoit (1580–1661) Among New England's most powerful Native American rulers, Massasoit was chief of the Wampanoags when the Pilgrims landed in Plymouth. By signing a treaty with the Pilgrim settlers in 1621, and by faithfully observing its provisions, he guaranteed that the fledgling colony would survive.

Plymouth founding father Edward Winslow, and Roger Williams, founder of Providence, R.I., were among Massasoit's friends and admirers.

Paul Revere (1735–1818) Most Americans remember Revere because of Longfellow's famous poem, *Paul Revere's Ride*. Besides acting as a courier for Massachusetts's secret Committee of Correspondence and participating in the Boston Tea Party, Revere was a noted silver- and goldsmith, printer and engraver, bell-founder, dentist, soldier, and propagandist of the American cause. He even had a profitable business shipping ice from Massachusetts's winter ponds to the torrid West Indies. Revere's house in Boston's North End is now a notable museum.

Harriet Beecher Stowe (1811–96) Born in Litchfield, Conn., she was the daughter of a Puritan minister. A teacher and author, she saw *Uncle Tom's Cabin* (1852) become a best-seller, with 300,000 copies sold within a year of publication. Even though the novel was not specifically antislavery or pro-Abolition, it became an Abolitionist favorite, and was widely translated, published, and read abroad. Stowe raised six children, kept house, wrote novels, poems, essays, and magazine articles, and worked tirelessly for temperance and women's suffrage.

3. ART, ARCHITECTURE, LITERATURE & RELIGION

ART

Early New England art was folk art. Colonial women produced wonderful patchwork quilts that were both practical bed coverings and delightful works of art. Sailors, particularly those on the whaling ships that might be at sea for months at a time, carved household utensils, buttons, letter openers, and corset stays from whale bone and tooth. Often these objects were decorated with etched designs known as scrimshaw. The delicacy of scrimshaw scenes, many of which feature ships and other nautical subjects, is impressive, not merely because the artists were self-taught, but because their tools were sometimes no more refined than a pocket knife.

The Shaker religious communities in Maine, New Hampshire, and western Massachusetts looked upon honest work as a prayer, and each object crafted by hand as an offering to God of one's labor and creativity. Pieces of Shaker furniture, especially the famous Shaker chairs, are valued heirlooms and antiques today.

Metalworking was highly advanced as well. Besides being an active patriot and partisan of the American cause, Paul Revere (1735–1818) was a renowned silversmith. His simple, harmonious design for a silver or pewter bowl ("Revere bowl") is still a favorite among connoisseurs in New England.

Painting was a craft, then an art in New England. The primitive works of untrained daubers decorated many a colonial household. Fine portraits of the great and powerful graced the mansions of the upper class. During and after the revolutionary war, painters turned their efforts to the American cause, turning out patriotic works that are still revered. Archibald Willard (1836–1918), whose famous painting *The Spirit of '76* hangs in Abbot Hall, in Marblehead, Mass., was trained to decorate carriages but soon showed his skill with oil on canvas.

During the mid- and late 19th century, New England's world-class painters had to move to more sophisticated regions in order to prosper and be recognized. James Abbott McNeill Whistler (1834–1903) was born in Lowell, Mass., and though he lived abroad for much of his life, New England still claims him as one of its own. After living in St. Petersburg and Paris, he established himself in London, where his belief in "art for art's sake" was very unconventional. While others were making paintings of almost photographic quality, Whistler held to his credo that a painting was essentially an "arrangement of light, form and color." His most famous painting, of his mother sitting in a chair, is entitled *Arrangement in Grey and Black;* we know it better as

Whistler's Mother. Whistler's *Girl in a White Dress* hangs in the National Gallery in Washington, D.C.

John Singer Sargent (1856–1925) was born in Florence, Italy, and worked mostly in Paris and London, but he also gained a reputation as a painter of portraits of many famous and socially prominent Bostonians and other New Englanders. In the 1890s Sargent did a series of murals depicting *The History of Religion* for the Boston Public Library.

An earlier painter of the same last name, Henry Sargent (1770–1845), was born in Gloucester, Mass., and studied in London with Benjamin West. Two of his most famous works, *The Tea Party* and *The Dinner Party* are in the Museum of Fine Arts in Boston; his famous portrait of Peter Faneuil hangs in Boston's Faneuil Hall.

By the turn of the century, New England had painters content to use local scenes as subject matter. Childe Hassam (1859–1935) was born in Boston, and though he studied in Paris, he returned to his native city to create enchanting impressionist-influenced paintings of Boston Common, the Isles of Shoals, and a church in Gloucester.

Winslow Homer (1836–1910), also a Boston native, began his career as a magazine illustrator of Civil War scenes, but took up painting full time at the age of 40. His direct, realistic, and colorful style was just right for the nautical and coastal scenes he favored, taken mostly from life in Maine.

Though Grandma Moses (Anna Mary Robertson Moses, 1860–1961) did most of her painting in Washington County in New York state, her themes and subjects are familiar to New Englanders. The Bennington Museum in Bennington, Vt., just across the state line from the painter's hometown of Hoosick Falls, N.Y., now holds an outstanding collection of her charming primitives. Most were painted after the artist's 70th birthday, some when she was more than 100.

ARCHITECTURE

COLONIAL STYLE The early colonists who came to New England brought no visions of grand mansions or stately churches. Their homes were simple, as befitted a people of strict religious beliefs. Their public building was usually a simple meetinghouse (what others might call a church). For a look at buildings remaining from the 1600s, visit the Hoxie House (1637) in Sandwich, on Cape Cod, or the Whipple House (1640) in Ipswich, on Boston's north shore. Plimoth Plantation, near Plymouth, Mass., gives perhaps the best glimpse of 17th-century life and architecture. The simple, homespun design and decoration used in early New England has become what we think of as colonial style.

GEORGIAN STYLE America is a rich land of great potential, and it wasn't long before the colonists were prosperous. Along with prosperity came a waning of religious strictures; along with trade came glimpses of how life was lived in other countries, particularly in England. After the great fire of 1666, London had been rebuilt in Palladian style by Inigo Jones and Christopher Wren. This updated classicism, which we call the Georgian style, appealed to colonial New England's builders, who happily used Wren's designs in building some of the regions most famous and stately churches. Harvard University is a riot of Georgian red brick and white cornice. Throughout New England you'll run across the Palladian window, the epitome of the style, in building after building. Georgian houses were built up to the time of the Revolution, and in beautiful Litchfield, Conn., until the end of the 1700s.

FEDERAL STYLE With political independence came even more prosperity. The shipowners and merchants of New England's great maritime ports—Salem, Mass., Portsmouth, N.H., and Providence, R.I., for example—wanted large, comfortable, imposing houses, and local architects gave them just what they wanted in the years following the Revolution. Domestic Federal architecture was straightforward and commodious: large rectangular two-story wooden buildings with rows of windows, chimneys at both ends, and a grandish portal centered in the facade. The famous Charles Bulfinch, who designed the State House (Massachusetts's state capitol), on

Beacon Hill in Boston, is New England's most famous Federalist architect; lesser-known Samuel McIntire of Salem left his indelible imprint on the older streets of his hometown. In Providence, College Hill boasts many handsome Federal-style houses.

GREEK REVIVAL   Spacious domes, soaring columns topped by Ionic capitals, and noble echoes of the Doric order—this is Greek Revival. There are fewer Greek Revival houses and public buildings in New England than in other parts of the United States, but the ones that remain here are particularly fine. Boston's Quincy Market building (1825), now the centerpiece of Faneuil Hall Marketplace, is perhaps the best-known example. The Arcade (1828) in Providence is another. For good specimens of domestic Greek Revival architecture, visit Grafton, Vt., a veritable museum of the style carefully preserved by its sensitive residents.

LATE 19TH- & 20TH-CENTURY STYLES   The great textile mills that were built along the rivers of New England were Federal style, but the mill owners wanted something fancier. As the 1800s wore on, they employed Henry Hobson Richardson, the firm of McKim, Mead and White, and other designers to build worldly fantasies: Egyptian temples, Renaissance palaces, Romanesque temples and Gothic churches. Trinity Church, at Copley Square in Boston, is a fine example of the period. Newport, R.I.'s elegant mansions—many of them actually small palaces—demonstrate how this late-century exuberance would end. Among the "common people," exuberance led to Victorian gingerbread, some of the best of which survives in the town of Oak Bluffs on Martha's Vineyard island in Massachusetts.

During the 20th century skyscrapers began to soar above the quaint old neighborhoods of Boston, Providence, and Hartford. Many were undistinguished, and few had echoes of New England's past. But among the great commercial towers were some of imposing form and striking originality, such as Boston's slender, mirror-covered John Hancock Tower and Hartford's glass ellipse.

LITERATURE

From the Puritan sermons and devotional writings of Increase Mather (1639–1723) and his son, Cotton Mather (1663–1728), New England literature has come all the way to the punchy *Spenser* thrillers of Robert Parker. Along the way, New England has fostered some of America's greatest writers.

The runaway best-seller of the early 1800s was not a book of sermons or a novel or even a history of the late war with England; and the book remains a best-seller to this day. It's the *American Dictionary of the English Language,* by Yale graduate Noah Webster (1758–1843). First published in 1828, Webster's 70,000-word dictionary was bought by hundreds of thousands of Americans every year—and still is.

Among the writers most closely associated with New England is Ralph Waldo Emerson (1803–82). Emerson's beliefs in the mystical unity of nature, and Thoreau's championing of the simple life in tune with nature's laws, were radical in 19th-century Concord, Mass. Along with other writers, Emerson was a founder of the Transcendental movement, and had more effect on American literature than any other New Englander.

Henry David Thoreau (1817–62), a friend of Emerson's, is best remembered for *Walden, or Life in the Woods* (1854). This journal of observations and opinions written during his solitary sojourn (1845–47) on Walden Pond in Concord, Mass., may be the best-known book on New England. Thoreau was also known for *Civil Disobedience,* and his accounts of walking trips, entitled *The Maine Woods* and *Cape Cod.*

Nathaniel Hawthorne (1804–64) was born in Salem, Mass., attended Bowdoin College in Maine, then pursued a career that produced *The Scarlet Letter, Twice-Told Tales,* and *The House of the Seven Gables.* Hawthorne is thought by many to be the writer who established the American short story. His contemporary, Edgar Allan Poe (1809–49), was born in Boston, but pursued his career in Virginia.

Among New England poets, the 1800s belonged to Henry Wadsworth Longfellow (1807–82). Born in Portland, Me., he attended Bowdoin, taught at Harvard, and lived in a big yellow house on Brattle Street in Cambridge that is now a historic landmark. Several of Longfellow's poems are a part of Americana: *Paul Revere's Ride, The Song of Hiawatha,* "The Village Blacksmith," "Excelsior," and "The Wreck of the Hesperus" are among the better-known ones.

Preceding and during the Civil War, New England writers such as abolitionist William Lloyd Garrison (1805–79) and John Greenleaf Whittier (1807–92) contributed their literary and poetic talents to the struggle to end slavery.

Few Americans realize that Samuel Clemens (1835–1910), better known as Mark Twain, settled in Hartford, Conn., at the age of 35. Though Missouri-born, Twain wrote his masterpieces *Tom Sawyer* and *Huckleberry Finn* in Hartford, as well as *The Prince and the Pauper* and *A Connecticut Yankee in King Arthur's Court.* Touring his grand Victorian mansion at Nook Farm is the high point of a visit to Hartford.

In the 1800s, many excellent New England women's colleges produced graduates instilled with a spirit of independence and self-reliance. Harriet Beecher Stowe (1811–96) exposed the injustice of slavery in her novel *Uncle Tom's Cabin* (1852), which sold an amazing 300,000 copies in one year.

Opposite in temperament to the energetic Ms. Stowe was poet Emily Dickinson (1830–86), a native of Amherst, Mass., who lived there in near seclusion most of her life. Only seven of her poems were published during her lifetime, but the posthumous editing and publishing of nearly 1,000 poems established her reputation. Her influence on American poetry is matched only by that of Robert Frost.

Among New England's other famous female poets is Katharine Lee Bates (1859–1929), a native of Falmouth, Mass., and a graduate of Wellesley College. Though much of her work is unfamiliar today, every American knows her patriotic hymn, *America the Beautiful.*

Robert Frost (1874–1963) was born in San Francisco to a New England family. He moved to New England early in life, attended Dartmouth and Harvard without taking a degree, and later returned to teach poetry at Amherst and Harvard. His many books capture the quintessence of New England living and the Yankee soul.

RELIGION

When most people think of New England religion, they think of Puritanism. This strict form of Calvinism sought to "purify" the church of its high-church accretions, and demanded a strict reading of the Bible rather than elaborate interpretations. "Presbyterians" wanted a central church governing system, while Congregationalists thought that each congregation could and should be independent of central control. Though the stern tenets of early American Puritanism suited the colonists' harsh life, religion's influence lessened as life in the colonies improved.

Puritan theologians often found themselves disagreeing with one another. Their disagreements had a profound effect on the history of New England and of the United States as a whole. When two New England preachers couldn't agree, one of them would leave town with his followers and establish a new congregation in a new town. Thus, Thomas Hooker of Cambridge set off to found Hartford, and likewise, Roger Williams founded Providence. Plentiful land allowed differing religious beliefs to thrive in the same region. Soon there was a prosperous synagogue and a tidy Quaker meetinghouse in Newport, and more religious diversity to follow.

Among the most fascinating religions to take shape in New England was the American expression of Shakerism. Ann Lee (1736–84), a mill worker and cook from Manchester, England, had a vision (about 1770) that she was the manifestation of the Second Coming. She came to America in 1775 and established a small religious community in Watervliet, N.Y. Though "Mother Ann" died within a decade at age 48, Shakerism took hold. In 18 Shaker communities more than 6,000 devotees put their "hands to work" and their "hearts to God." Four of the six surviving Shaker communities are in New England, at Hancock and Harvard, Mass.; Sabbathday Lake, Maine; and Canterbury, N.H.

Shakers believed in a closed community, separate from the world, where men and women lived without mutual physical contact, but worked, prayed, and dined in common. Without procreation a sect depends mightily upon proselytization, and the Shakers didn't proselytize much. But the purity and goodness of their lives and their ideals brought adherents in sufficient numbers until the 20th century, when the temptations of modern life led to the slow death of the sect.

One of the best known of New England's religions is Christian Science. In 1866 a devout New England woman experienced quick recovery from a severe accident, attributing her cure to a glimpse of God's healing power as taught and lived by Jesus. Thereafter Mary Baker Eddy devoted the remainder of her long life (1821–1910) to better understanding, practicing, and teaching Christian healing, and to founding and promoting the Church of Christ, Scientist. Today Christian Science, headquartered in Boston, has branch churches in some 68 countries.

4. PERFORMING ARTS & EVENING ENTERTAINMENT

New England's major cities have lively cultural seasons, including symphony and chamber music performances, ballet, and an impressive array of theatrical venues.

Best known of the region's orchestras is the Boston Symphony Orchestra under Maestro Seiji Ozawa. After a more serious winter season, the Boston Pops gives champagne concerts in Symphony Hall and outdoor concerts on Boston's Esplanade. In summer, the BSO moves to Lenox, in Massachusetts's Berkshire hills, for the Tanglewood Music Festival.

Speaking of the Berkshires, several pretty hill towns host important summer seasons of dance, theater, and music. See Chapter 8 for details. If jazz and pop music are more your style, check out what's happening in Newport, R.I., during the summer (Chapter 9).

New England's many colleges and universities attract the performing arts to several small towns in the New England countryside. Williams College in Williamstown, Mass., sponsors an important theater festival (see Chapter 8). The Marlboro Music Festival, held each summer in Marlboro, Vt., is among the region's most famous and well attended (see Chapter 13).

5. SPORTS & RECREATION

Sports opportunities are rich in New England. Whether it's a vigorous climb up Mount Washington in New Hampshire, or sitting back and watching the Red Sox play in Boston's Fenway Park, you'll find lots of activity.

For spectators of professional sports, there's basketball (the Boston Celtics), baseball (the Boston Red Sox), ice hockey (the Boston Bruins), and professional football (the New England Patriots). The college football season is just as important, particularly the long-standing rivalry played out at the annual Harvard-Yale game.

Every New England state except Vermont has a seacoast, and Vermont has the lengthy eastern shore of Lake Champlain. With so much coastline, it's no wonder that water sports are a favorite with New Englanders. Swimming, boating, sailboarding, fishing, and waterskiing are possibilities at many beaches and lakes, including Cape Cod, Martha's Vineyard, Nantucket, and Lake Winnipesaukee.

For mountain climbing and hiking, the favored places are New Hampshire's White Mountains and Vermont's Green Mountains, though Maine has many fine hiking trails as well. The Appalachian Trail starts at Maine's Mount Katahdin (5,267 ft.) and meanders through the Maine wilderness, the White Mountains National Forest, Vermont's Green Mountains, the Berkshires of Massachusetts and Connecticut, before crossing the Hudson River north of New York City. Vermont's Long Trail traces the spine of the state's Green Mountains from Jay Peak (3,861 ft.) in the north to Bennington in the south. For beginners and weekend hikers, New Hampshire's Mount Monadnock (3,165 ft.), near Jaffrey, is the "easy" climb.

Several of New England's rivers are good for canoe trips. The center of the sport is in North Conway, N.H.

Bicycling is done everywhere: along the Charles River in Boston and Cambridge; on special bike paths between Falmouth and Woods Hole, and on Cape Cod and Martha's Vineyard; everywhere on Nantucket and Block Island, and on pretty back roads throughout the region.

6. FOOD & DRINK

FOOD Seafood is New England's strong suit, of course. Many kinds of fish are taken in New England's waters.

In colonial times, the codfish was so important to the region's economy that a stuffed codfish had a place of honor in the Massachusetts State House (capitol). Filets of choice little codfish (or any other whitefish) are called scrod, sautéed in lemon butter or topped with a cheese sauce; it's pretty bland, as is halibut. Bluefish, smoked and served as an appetizer or broiled for a main course, has a fuller flavor. Monkfish sautéed in butter tastes mildly like lobster. Swordfish and fresh tuna steaks are best if grilled over charcoal. Fish chowder, as made in New England, uses bland whitefish, potatoes, corn, and milk.

Shellfish are also important. Everyone knows about Maine lobster, but Massachusetts has a large lobstering fleet as well, and the state supports hatcheries where baby lobsters are raised before being released to sea.

Clams are of several varieties. Soft-shell clams have shells that chip and crack easily. The clams are usually steamed in the shells, which gave rise to their other name, steamers. Hard-shell clams have very hard porcelainlike shells; among the most popular varieties are littlenecks and cherrystones. These can be steamed, baked, or served raw on the half shell with lemon, tomato sauce, or a dab of horseradish. Quahogs (*ko*-hogs) are clams larger than your fist; they're often cut into strips, fried in batter, and served as fried clams at roadside or beachfront snack stands, or minced for use in clam chowder.

New England clam chowder has clams and potatoes in a base of milk or cream. It's quite different from Manhattan clam chowder, which uses tomato instead of milk. Oysters from Chatham, Wellfleet, and Cotuit on Cape Cod are usually eaten raw on the half shell, or served whole in milk-based oyster stew.

Many traditional New England foods are not often served anymore. Boston may

IMPRESSIONS

Those New England States, I do believe, will be the noblest country in the world in a little while. They will be the salvation of that very great body with a very little soul, the rest of the United States; they are the pith and marrow, heart and core, head and spirit of that country.
—FANNY KEMBLE (MRS. BUTLER), *A YEAR OF CONSOLATION*, 1847

No author, without a trial, can conceive of the difficulty of writing a romance about a country [New England] where there is no shadow, no antiquity, no mystery, no picturesque and gloomy wrong, nor anything but a commonplace prosperity, in broad and simple daylight, as is happily the case with my dear native land.
—NATHANIEL HAWTHORNE, *TRANSFORMATIONS, THE MARBLE FAUN*, 1860

be famous for baked beans (navy beans, molasses, salt pork, and onions cooked slowly in a crock), but very few restaurants serve them, and then mostly for sentimental or touristic reasons. New England boiled dinner, a chunk of beef boiled with cabbage, carrots, and potatoes, is also rarely served, and perhaps that's just as well.

Vermont is dairy country, known for Cheddar cheese and delicious Ben & Jerry's full-fat ice cream. All of the New England states produce delicious pure maple syrup in the late winter and early spring. Many inns and some restaurants serve it with breakfast pancakes and waffles.

As for dessert, fresh fruit and fruit pies are the best. Strawberry season is early to mid-June; rhubarb is also ripe then, and if you come across a strawberry-rhubarb pie, don't let it get away whole. Late June to mid-July is blueberry season, when pies of fresh blueberries appear. Autumn brings peaches, plums, and apples, and also gallons of fresh apple cider. Look for it at roadside stands throughout the region.

A New England Clambake   Whether on the beach around a driftwood fire, at a backyard cookout, or in a restaurant, chances are you'll encounter the traditional clambake during your stay in New England. The true clambake takes place on the beach, starting with the digging of the clams, but the backyard and restaurant versions are good substitutes provided you observe the rituals properly.

The three essential courses are steamed soft-shell clams, corn on the cob, and lobsters. Here's a recipe: Take one very large pot, fill with clean seawater, and place on the fire to boil. Put live lobsters in the bottom, then a layer of seaweed, then ears of corn, more seaweed, and finally a layer of "steamers" (soft-shell clams for steaming). When the clams open, they're ready.

Take a clam, open it completely, and lift out the meat. The "neck" is black and covered with a wrinkled black membrane. Shuck the membrane off (you pick up the knack for this by about the fifth clam), hold the clam by the neck, and dip it in "clam broth" (seawater that has had clams steamed in it—even in a restaurant you'll be provided with it). The "broth" is strictly for dipping, not for drinking; the dip washes any sand off the clam. Next, dip in the melted butter provided, and then enjoy.

When you've had your fill of clams, it's on to the buttered ears of corn, and finally to the lobsters. Eating a lobster is an art in itself.

Restaurants will prepare lobsters in any number of elaborate ways, but to a true New Englander there are but three ways to cook a lobster: you boil (steam) it, you broil it, or you grill it. To broil or grill, take a live lobster, make a straight cut underneath from head to tail, and place cut-upward under the broiler, or cut-downward on the grill.

Boiling or steaming is even easier. Put the live lobsters into a pot that has a few inches of boiling seawater in it, cover, bring to a boil again, and let them cook until they turn bright red (10 to 12 minutes, longer for lobsters of several pounds or more). When you take them out, they'll be very hot, and full of hot water, too. Give the lobster a few minutes to cool.

DRINK   New England is as famous for what it doesn't (or didn't) drink as for what it drinks. The town of Oak Bluffs on Martha's Vineyard, and Rockport on Cape Ann (both in Massachusetts) are "dry" towns where alcoholic beverages may not be bought or sold.

Though New Englanders' taste in drinks is largely the same as that of most Americans, there are some specialties. Maine's Poland Spring water is now bottled and shipped throughout the country. In the autumn, fresh apple cider is the beverage of choice throughout the region. Cranberry juice, from berries raised in the bogs of southeastern Massachusetts, is usually mixed with other liquids to ease its tartness.

The urge for better, more distinctive beers led to the rise of Boston's own Samuel Adams lager, and also Schooner, both premium brews.

Despite its rocky soil and uncooperative weather, enterprising New England vintners have identified hospitable microclimates for the culture of hybrid and vinifera wine grapes. You should definitely sample the vintages offered by Rhode Island's

Sakonnet Vineyards, Chicama Vineyards on Martha's Vineyard, Haight Vineyards near Litchfield, Conn., and Hopkins Vineyard on Connecticut's Lake Waramaug. Nashoba Valley Winery, near Concord, Mass., harvests fruit from its own orchards and produces delicious colonial-style fruit wines.

By the way, many New Englanders still call a carbonated soft drink a "tonic," and the neighborhood food shop where you buy a tonic is a "spa."

7. RECOMMENDED BOOKS & FILMS

BOOKS

HISTORY   For a good grounding in New England's history, read Christina Tree's *How New England Happened* (Boston: Little, Brown, 1976). This "historical guidebook" uses landmarks that you can visit along the path of history.

FICTION   Most famous of the books about New England life is perhaps Herman Melville's *Moby-Dick* (1851). Melville was a native New Yorker, but his great novel of ambition, will, and struggle with the sea and its creatures is a New England classic. *Two Years before the Mast* (1840), by Richard Henry Dana, with its descriptions of shipboard life, had an important influence on Melville.

The Bostonians (1886) is Henry James's novel of Boston manners. For more reading on Bostonians, pick up John P. Marquand's *The Late George Apley* (1937), which is stylistically similar.

To get the flavor of 17th-century New England, read Nathaniel Hawthorne's *The Scarlet Letter* (1850), a novel of sin and repentance among the Puritans. *The Last Puritan* (1936), by George Santayana, takes Puritan development to its very end by describing a 20th-century Harvard man, descended from Puritans, who still lives by their ideals.

Though most of Mark Twain's works recall his boyhood in Missouri, *A Connecticut Yankee in King Arthur's Court* (1889), tells of a shrewd Yankee transported back to the days of chivalry who shows the knights a thing or two.

Louisa May Alcott's *Little Women* (1868–69) is a favorite among young visitors to New England, who can even visit the Alcott homestead in Concord, Mass. *Little Men* (1871) and *Jo's Boys* (1886) are sequels.

Henry David Thoreau's *Walden, or Life in the Woods* (1854), is his journal of observations and opinions written during his solitary sojourn (1845–47) on Walden Pond in Concord, Mass. Thoreau wrote several other books of New England observations, including *The Maine Woods* and *Cape Cod*.

For up-to-date thrills set in Boston and New England, pick up any of the Spenser thrillers written by Robert B. Parker. *Jaws*, by Peter Benchley, is the novel from which the popular motion picture was made.

OUTDOORS   Anyone planning to hike the Appalachian Trail or climb the White Mountains will want to order trail guides from the Appalachian Mountain Club, 5 Joy St., Boston, MA 02108.

FILMS

Though New England is not a common setting for commercial cinema, you may recognize scenes from Martha's Vineyard in *Jaws* (1975) and its sequels. *On Golden Pond* (1981), Henry Fonda's last notable performance, is set on New Hampshire's Squam Lake. A more recent movie, *Housesitter* (1992), with Steve Martin and Goldie Hawn, is set in Concord, Mass.

John Huston's *Moby Dick* (1956), with Gregory Peck and Orson Welles, brings Melville's drama of struggle with the sea to life.

CHAPTER 2

PLANNING A TRIP TO NEW ENGLAND

The smoothest trips are those that are properly prepared in advance. Here's the information you'll need to get ready for your New England sojourn.

1. SOURCES OF INFORMATION

There are both public and private sources of information. Each state has a tourism office, which issues brochures, maps, lists of festivals and special events, and other useful materials. Municipal governments often have their own tourism offices as well, but the job of providing information in a town or city is done mostly by the local chamber of commerce or convention and visitors bureau. We've written the names, addresses, and telephone numbers of these chambers and bureaus in the relevant chapters. See also **Travelers Aid** under "Emergencies," in "Fast Facts," later in this chapter.

Here are the addresses and telephone numbers of the state tourism offices: **Connecticut Department of Economic Development,** 865 Brook St., Rocky Hill, CT 06037 (tel. 203/258-4200, or toll free 800/282-6863); **Maine Publicity Bureau,** Box 2300, 209 Maine Ave., Farmingdale, ME 04344 (tel. 207/582-9300, or toll free 800/533-9595 outside Maine); **Massachusetts Office of Travel & Tourism,** 100 Cambridge St., 13th floor, Boston, MA 02202 (tel. 617/727-3201); **New Hampshire Office of Travel and Tourism,** 172 Pembroke Rd., Concord, NH 03301 (tel. 603/271-2666); **Rhode Island Tourism Division,** 7 Jackson Walkway, Providence, RI 02903 (tel. 401/277-2601, or toll free 800/556-2484); **Vermont Department of Travel,** 134 State St., Montpelier, VT 05602 (tel. 802/828-3236).

2. WHEN TO GO — CLIMATE, HOLIDAYS & EVENTS

CLIMATE Without doubt, the best times to tour New England are summer (June through August) and autumn (September and October), unless you're coming for skiing. You can enjoy a visit here any time of year if you prepare for the weather and are wary of the busy times when hotels, restaurants, and transportation are filled to capacity.

Want to know what the weather is right now in New England? From a pushbutton telephone, call WeatherTrak at 900/370-8725, enter the telephone area code of the city or region you want, and a computer will tell you the time, temperature (present, high, and low), humidity, wind, barometric pressure, and tomorrow's forecast; you can even hear an extended forecast if you like. Calls cost 75¢ for the first minute, and 50¢ for each additional minute.

THE SEASONS   Weather in New England is a much-discussed topic, always with a certain fatalism, not so much because there's a lot of bad weather, but because it's so unpredictable. But, after all, Boston does seem to have its own weather: A snowfall may cover practically all New England, but stop short at Route 128; or a summer downpour may drench the city while the sun shines everywhere else. However, there are some generalizations that seem to hold true from year to year, and these may affect your plans on when to visit New England.

Coming very late and staying very briefly, **spring** tends to be a disappointment. The week or two of spring days in the normal year are a delight, with cool temperatures in the evening and just the perfect degree of warmth during the day, in bright, clear sun. In the countryside the thaw brings "mud time," the period between frost and spring planting. Mud time is the slowest season for tourist facilities, coming after ski season and before summer warmth and school vacations bring out the city folk. Thus many country inns, resorts, and amusements close for a few weeks in April or thereabouts.

By mid-June, **summer** is well established and, despite the region's northerly and coastal location, it can be pretty hot and sometimes quite humid. When it's 85°F (or even up to 95°F) and humid, as it often is through mid-September, head for the beaches, the islands, mountains, lakes, and riverbanks. Sailing, along the coast or on the rivers, is a choice activity, as is a hike to the top of Mount Washington, or a week at a beach on Narragansett Bay. A drive through the Berkshires or along the Connecticut coast can also be very satisfying.

Autumn is undoubtedly New England's glory and its finest season, and if you have a choice of vacation times, this is the one to pick. Although you may have to forsake swimming, the famous fall foliage is a worthy substitute; it's at its peak usually in late September and early October, starting in northern Maine, New Hampshire, and Vermont and moving southward and eastward as the weeks pass. Days are still warm and very pleasant, nights a bit chilly but not uncomfortably so. City people load their bikes into the car and head for the country, picking up fresh apple cider, pumpkins, and squash from farm stands on the way home. Fresh cranberries are on sale in the markets all autumn, and although the blueberry-picking season is past, many apple orchards open so you can "pick-your-own," and get the freshest fruit possible at a very low price.

People want to get away for the weekend, no matter where they live. Those who don't want to tangle with the traffic on fall weekends can take special bus and rail foliage tours from the major cities. Most tourist resorts and inns stay open through September and often to Columbus Day. Those that stay open all year sometimes close for 2 weeks or so from mid-October to early December to give the staff a break before the advent of the ski season. By Thanksgiving, everyone's getting in shape for the ski season and shopping for the holidays.

After a period of chilly weather in October, New England usually gets a respite, with a short period of warm weather known as "Indian summer," which can occur in late October or November. It's not dependable, and it may be brief, but it's glorious all the same.

Winter, as they say, depends: In the winter of 1976–77, the region had 6 inches of snow in November, which is very early; for the first flurries usually come in mid-December, when hopes are high that the accumulation will be sufficient for good skiing during the holiday season. Sometimes snow wishes are too well answered, as in the Great Blizzard of 1978, which piled 6 feet of snow on Boston, closing the city for a week. Ski reports appear in newspapers and the broadcast media, and the special skiing-condition phone lines go into operation. January through March is cold and snowy, and the skiing may be quite good through April; gray snowy days alternate with brilliant, crisp, sunny days when the air is very cold but the sun's warmth makes it pleasant. Those who aren't skiing take advantage of the cities' cultural seasons, or perhaps escape to an inn somewhere in the snow-clad mountains for a weekend.

Mount Washington Weather: None of this applies to Mount Washington in New Hampshire, of course. This "highest peak in New England" is said to have the worst weather in all the U.S., and New Englanders delight in exchanging horror stories of the latest report: winds of 150 miles per hour (the record is 211 m.p.h.!), temperatures of minus 40°F, windchill factors that don't seem earthly.

HOLIDAYS & TRAVEL SEASONS January New Year's Day (January 1)
is a holiday, and transportation services are quite busy on the days immediately preceding and following it. Otherwise, the first 2 weeks of the month are not a busy time, travel services are unburdened, and prices are lower. The weekend of the third Monday is when **Martin Luther King Day** (January 15) is celebrated. This is the holiday that begins the ski season in earnest. Ski lodges and inns offer money-saving package deals, especially if you stay on weekdays rather than weekends.

February Ski season continues, though many New Englanders fly to the Caribbean or Mexico for a few weeks of warmth and sun. The third Monday is **Presidents Day,** a holiday honoring the birthdays of Washington (February 22) and Lincoln (February 12). The holiday weekend is particularly busy in ski country.

March Traditional wisdom holds that after St. Patrick's Day (March 17, not a holiday) in the southern New England states (Massachusetts, Connecticut, and Rhode Island), there will be no more big snowstorms—but traditional wisdom is occasionally proved wrong. In any case, ski areas in the northern states (Maine, New Hampshire, and Vermont) have plenty of snow until April.

March and early April are "mud time" in much of New England. Farmers take advantage of the warming weather and rising sap for "sugaring off," tapping their maple trees for sap and boiling it down to make pure maple syrup. Some country inns provide glimpses of the sugaring process.

April **Patriots Day** (April 19) is a holiday in Massachusetts, celebrated on the Monday nearest that date. The day commemorates the first battles of the Revolutionary War, fought in the early hours of April 19 in Lexington and Concord. All state government offices and many local businesses close, though federal government offices and offices of large interstate and international companies remain open. **Easter** often falls in April, and New England's hundreds of colleges empty out for Easter vacation or spring break. Good Friday, preceding Easter, is not an official holiday though some businesses close and many people travel. Ski season is winding down and spring has not really arrived, so many country inns close for all or part of the month.

May Many seasonal services (small museums, campgrounds, flights, etc.) begin operating in May, at least on the weekends. Open hours may be limited, but prices may also be lower. The weekend nearest **Memorial Day** signals the official start of the summer tourism season; the holiday is celebrated on the last Monday in the month. Rooms at inns and resort hotels are in great demand on the holiday weekend, and on weekends through Labor Day (the first Monday after the first Sunday in September), but the demand is much lower during the week.

June Early June is not very busy in New England's vacation areas because most children are still in school. But when school ends in mid-June, many families head out for their summer vacations at the beach or in the mountains. Accommodations, campgrounds, and other services are busy by late June.

July Early July sees the tourist season in full swing. The **Independence Day**

holiday (July 4) is very busy, particularly when it falls on a Friday or a Monday. The 6 weeks from mid-July through Labor Day are the busiest time of the year. The beach resorts and islands are often filled to capacity.

August   The height of the tourism season continues through August to the Labor Day weekend.

September   The **Labor Day** holiday weekend, the first Monday after the first Sunday, signals the official end of the summer vacation season. The weekend is very busy, but the 2 weeks following are a good time to travel since children are back in school, few families travel, services are uncrowded, and some price reductions are offered. Foliage season begins in mid-September in the northern states, late September in the southern states.

October   New England's deservedly famed fall foliage is in full color everywhere in the southern states in early October. Rooms at country inns are in great demand, especially on weekends. The blazing finale to foliage season is the **Columbus Day** holiday weekend, the second Monday in October. Every room in the countryside is reserved in advance. In Boston, hotels are often filled by conventioneers since October is also a popular month for meetings and conferences. Many inns and seasonal services close for the winter after the Columbus Day weekend, and late October is fairly quiet in the countryside, though busy in the cities.

November   This is a slow month for travel. The foliage crowds have departed and the ski crowds have yet to arrive, so many country inns close for part or all of the month. Ski resorts begin to make their own snow if nature has not provided the traditional cover, and some eager skiers take advantage of the **Veterans Day** holiday (November 11, celebrated on the nearest Monday) for a first schuss down the slopes. The big holiday in November is **Thanksgiving,** the fourth Thursday, when transportation services are strained to the breaking point as everyone travels to have Thanksgiving dinner with friends or relatives. The busiest times are the Wednesday before and the Sunday after Thanksgiving, especially the afternoon and evening. Don't plan to travel at these times if at all possible. If you must travel, expect long delays and inconvenience. Throughout the United States, this is the busiest travel time of the entire year.

December   The ski resorts are open, and though they may be fairly busy on weekends, innkeepers offer special low prices during the week to lure vacationers. Until the **Christmas** holiday (December 25), this is not a busy month for tourism. Travel is heavy on the day or two preceding Christmas and the day or two following, then there is a lull until New Year's, when travel intensifies again.

NEW ENGLAND CALENDAR OF EVENTS

For up-to-date information on events throughout New England, buy the Thursday edition of the *Boston Globe,* which carries a separate calendar section with detailed listings on all sorts of happenings.

JANUARY

☐ **First Night.** The arrival of the new year is celebrated with festivities in Boston, Mass.; Providence, R.I.; Stamford, Conn.; Burlington, Vt.; and other cities and towns. New Year's Eve.

☐ **Stowe Winter Carnival.** Stowe, Vt. Ski races, parties, and other festivities, many of them outdoors. Third week.

FEBRUARY

☐ **Dartmouth Winter Carnival.** Hanover, N.H. Dartmouth College's annual snow celebration. Second week.

MARCH

☐ **Maine Maple Sunday.** Maple sugarhouses throughout the state open their doors to visitors. Third Sunday.

APRIL

☐ **Boothbay Harbor Fishermen's Festival.** Boothbay Harbor, Me. Seafood feasts, exhibits, and games. Second weekend.

✪ *PATRIOTS DAY* *Reenactment of the battles between Minutemen and redcoats at Lexington Green and Concord North Bridge, with real musket fire (but no bullets). To do it right, be at Lexington Green by dawn for the Lexington battle, then walk along Battle Road to Concord North Bridge (8 miles) for the Concord one.*

Where: Lexington and Concord, Mass. When: Patriots Day, April 19 (celebrated on the third Monday), a holiday in Massachusetts. How: For information, contact Minuteman National Historic Park (tel. 508/369-6944), Lexington Chamber of Commerce Visitors Center (tel. 617/862-1450), or Concord Chamber of Commerce (tel. 508/369-3120).

☐ **Boston Marathon.** Patriots Day.

MAY

☐ **Brimfield Antiques Fair.** Brimfield, Mass. Up to 2,000 dealers fill several fields near this central Massachusetts town, with similar fairs in early or mid-July and mid-September. Mid-May.
☐ **Lobster Weekend.** Mystic Seaport in Mystic, Conn. Lobster feasts and live entertainment. Late May.

JUNE

☐ **Yale-Harvard Regatta.** On the Thames River in New London, Conn. Early June.
☐ **Blessing of the Fleet.** Provincetown, Mass. Festivities, seafood feasts, dancing, and exhibits. Late June.
☐ **Quechee Balloon Festival.** Near Woodstock, Vt. Balloon races and rides. Late June.
☐ **Block Island Race Week.** Block Island, R.I. Boat races and parties. Late June.
☐ **New Haven Jazz Festival.** On the green in New Haven, Conn. Late June into July.

JULY

☐ **Bar Harbor Music Festival.** Bar Harbor, Me. Classical and popular concerts. July–August.
☐ **Jacob's Pillow Dance Festival.** Beckett, Mass. The region's premier summer dance festival. Contact Jacob's Pillow Dance Festival, P.O. Box 287, Lee, MA 01238 (tel. 413/243-0745). July–August.
☐ **Marlboro Music Festival.** Marlboro, Vt. Among New England's oldest and most renowned. July and August.

✪ *TANGLEWOOD MUSIC FESTIVAL The summer season of the Boston Symphony Orchestra brings symphony and chamber concerts and solo recitals to the Berkshire hills.*
  Where: Tanglewood, near Lenox, Mass. When: July and August. How: Write for a program: Symphony Hall, 301 Massachusetts Avenue, Boston, MA 02115 (tel. 617/266-1492), or call Tanglewood, tel. 413/637-1940 (July and August only).

✪ *HARBORFEST A week of concerts, exhibits, and special events culminates in the famous Boston Pops Fourth of July concert at the Hatch Memorial Shell on the Esplanade: after Tchaikovsky's "1812 Overture" (with real cannons), a mammoth fireworks display goes off over the Charles River.*
  Where: Various locations in Boston. When: Week of July 4. How: For information and schedules, contact the Greater Boston Convention & Visitors Bureau, Prudential Plaza, P.O. Box 490, Boston, MA 02199 (tel. 617/536-4100; fax 617/424-7664).

- ☐ **Great Schooner Race.** Rockland, Me. First or second Friday.
- ☐ **Boothbay Harbor Windjammer Days.** Boothbay Harbor, Me. Boat races and cruises. Second week.
- ☐ **Newport Music Festival.** Newport, R.I. Chamber music concerts are held in the great mansions. Second and third weeks.
- ☐ **Historic Homes Tour.** Litchfield, Conn. One day is your only opportunity to tour this beautiful town's historic houses. Call 203/567-9423 or 203/868-2214 for details. Mid-July.
- ☐ **Barnstable County Fair.** Hatchville, Mass., on Cape Cod. An old-time county fair complete with rides, food, and livestock contests. Late July.

✪ *NEWPORT FOLK FESTIVAL & JVC JAZZ FESTIVAL Thousands of music lovers congregate at Fort Adams State Park on alternate weekends in July and August. Performers include such big names as Suzanne Vega, Judy Collins, Randy Newman, B. B. King, Ray Charles, and Tony Bennett.*
  Where: Newport, R.I. When: Late July (Folk Festival), early August (Jazz Festival). How: For information on schedules and tickets ($24–$40) call the Folk Festival at 401/847-3700, and the Jazz Festival at 401/331-2211. For lodging and general help contact the Newport County Chamber of Commerce, 10 America's Cup Ave., P.O. Box 237TB, Newport, RI 02840 (tel. 401/847-1600).

AUGUST

- ☐ **Maine Lobster Festival.** Rockland, Me. With lobsters on the table everywhere. First weekend.
- ☐ **League of New Hampshire Craftsmen Fair.** Mt. Sunapee State Park, near Newbury, N.H. Crafts displays and demonstrations amid other festivities. Second week.
- ☐ **Bennington Battle Days.** Bennington, Vt. Commemorates the Battle of Bennington (August 11, 1777) with exhibits, speeches, and celebrations. Second week.

SEPTEMBER

- ☐ **Blue Hill Fair.** Blue Hill, Me. A country fair with rides, games, and lots to eat. Labor Day and four days preceding it.
- ☐ **Vermont State Fair.** Rutland, Vt. Agricultural exhibits, games, rides, and entertainment. Labor Day weekend.

☐ **Providence Waterfront Festival.** Providence, R.I. Performances, art exhibits, boat races, and multiethnic feasts. Early September.
☐ **New Haven Fall Antiques Show.** Among the region's largest shows. Mid-September.

✪ *EASTERN STATES EXPOSITION* "The Big E" is New England's largest agricultural fair, with a midway, games, rides, agricultural judgings, lots of eats, and general fun.
   Where: Springfield, Mass. *When:* Mid-September. *How:* Contact the Eastern States Exposition (tel. 413/737-2443), or the Greater Springfield Convention and Visitors Bureau, 34 Boland Way, Springfield, MA 01103 (tel. 413/787-1548).

☐ **National Traditional Old-Time Fiddler's Context.** Barre, Vt. Lots of good music. Late September.
☐ **Northeast Kingdom Fall Foliage Festival.** Hometown church breakfasts, crafts sales, and open-house tours in the towns of Barnet, Cabot, Groton, Peacham, Plainfield, and Walden, Vt. Late September–early October.

OCTOBER

☐ **Festival of Vermont Crafts.** Montpelier, Vt. Crafts both traditional and modern. Late October.

NOVEMBER

☐ **Thanksgiving Celebration.** Plymouth, Mass. Authentic colonial food, dress, and festivities in town and at nearby Plimoth Plantation. Third Thursday.

DECEMBER

☐ **Boston Tea Party Reenactment.** Boston, Mass. At the Tea Party Ship and Museum on Boston's Museum Wharf. Mid-December.
☐ **Christmas Eve and Christmas Day** Special festivities throughout New England. In Newport, R.I., several of the great mansions have special tours; Mystic Seaport in Mystic, Conn., has a special program of Christmas festivities; Nantucket, Mass., features carolers in Victorian garb, art exhibits, and tours of historic houses. December 24–25.

3. WHAT TO PACK

You won't need any exotic gear for New England. You'll want at least one fairly nice outfit of the dress or jacket-and-tie variety for special evenings in fancy restaurants. Few establishments enforce a strict dress code anymore, but you should be prepared

IMPRESSIONS

The most serious charge which can be brought against New England is not Puritanism but February.
—JOSEPH WOOD KRUTCH, "FEBRUARY," *THE TWELVE SEASONS*, 1949

I believe no one attempts to praise the climate of New England.
—HARRIET MARTINEAU, *RETROSPECT OF WESTERN TRAVEL*, 1838

nonetheless. (Newport, R.I., has numerous restaurants requiring jacket-and-tie/dress, and the Ritz-Carlton in Boston also enforces the dress code.)

Rain can come at any time of year. A small umbrella is minimal rain gear in summer; in other seasons a raincoat may be necessary as well.

Summer days can get very hot and muggy, so cool cotton clothing is best, but have a sweater or jacket for cool evenings, cruises, and whale-watching expeditions. In spring and autumn moderately warm clothing, including sweater and windbreaker, is essential. In winter, be prepared for freezing weather and snow. Full woolens and foul-weather gear are required.

If you take prescription medicines regularly, bring a supply of the medicine, not a prescription for it. Doctors are licensed by state, and prescriptions are not accepted in any state except the one in which they are licensed. In other words, a prescription from a California doctor will not be accepted in Connecticut.

Other handy items might include a pair of binoculars, a flashlight, and a travel alarm clock.

4. TIPS FOR THE DISABLED, SENIORS & FAMILIES

FOR THE DISABLED Most of New England's large hotels, museums, large stores, and other large institutions are readily accessible to visitors on wheelchairs or on crutches. However, many of the smaller country inns and bed-and-breakfast houses are not accessible, or not fully accessible. The best plan is to call ahead to determine if the level of accessibility is sufficient.

Two states offer lists of accessible facilities and events. For copies of the lists, contact the Vermont Department of Travel, 134 State St., Montpelier, VT 05602 (tel. 802/828-3236), and the New Hampshire Office of Travel and Tourism, 172 Pembroke Rd., Concord, NH 03301 (tel. 603/271-2666).

Amtrak trains are accessible to the disabled, but not all Amtrak stations are; ask about this when you make your train reservations, and also about help with your baggage, special seating, and other assistance. There's a bonus: Amtrak grants discounts of 25% (off the normal coach fare) to adult disabled travelers, and 50% (off normal children's fares) to disabled travelers aged 2 to 12. For full information, ask for a copy of Amtrak's annual *Travel Planner* from Amtrak, National Railroad Passenger Corp., 400 North Capitol Street NW, Washington, DC 20001 (tel. toll free 800/USA-RAIL).

FOR SENIORS Senior discounts are readily available throughout New England at museums, parks, attractions, some hotels, and on Amtrak trains, so make sure to carry some convincing form of photo identification. It's best to request discounts on hotel rates, train and plane fares, and rental-car fees *when you make your reservation,* not when you're paying for the services. For more information about senior discounts in general, and for a good-as-gold discount card, contact the **American Association of Retired Persons (AARP),** 1909 K Street NW, Washington, DC 20049 (tel. 202/434-2277).

If you are over age 62, pick up a free Golden Age Passport at Bar Harbor National Park, and you'll be admitted free, for life, to all parks and recreations operated by the federal government.

By the way, Boston is the home of **Elderhostel,** 75 Federal St., Boston, MA 02110-1941 (tel. 617/426-7788), with innovative educational programs throughout the world for those 60 years and older.

FOR FAMILIES New England is a favorite destination for families on vacation.

and many price breaks are available. Museums, amusement attractions, whale-watch expeditions, and most other sights offer reduced admission rates for children; many offer even better deals in the form of family plans, whereby one admission price covers an entire family; the price is lower than the sum of two adult and two children's tickets.

Some attractions (outdoor concerts, state parks, beaches, etc.) charge admission "per car," so families on a driving vacation pay as little as solo travelers.

Often a family of four or even five can stay in the same hotel room. Most modern hotels and motels allow children to stay for free with their parents if the parents pay the normal two-person rate (not a special discount rate) and the children use the room's existing beds. In a room with two double beds, a family of four can stay as cheaply as two. If there are three children and a rollaway bed is necessary, there'll be a small charge ($10 to $20) for it. The age permissible for children under the "family plan" varies; for some plans, there is no age limit. Some inns follow the same policy, but at many others children are not accepted.

5. EDUCATIONAL/ADVENTURE TRAVEL

EDUCATIONAL TRAVEL

Do you have some special interest, such as Victorian architecture, colonial history, New England literature, or Italian cuisine? **Uncommon Boston Ltd.**, 437 Boylston St., Boston, MA 02116 (tel. 617/731-6353), can design a special guided tour of Boston just for you. Drawing on a long list of experts in many fields, they'll set you up with a knowledgeable guide for a walking or driving tour of the city.

Elderhostel, 75 Federal St., Boston, MA 02110-1941 (tel. 617/426-7788), offers a great variety of programs for those aged 60 and over. Programs take participants to several parts of New England, to other regions of the United States, and to many foreign countries.

ADVENTURE TRAVEL

The mountains, forests, seacoasts, and rivers of New England are all venues for exciting, memorable outdoor adventures, from biking the back roads of Vermont to braving the bracing waters of the Maine coast in a sea kayak.

WALKING/HIKING   Country Walkers, Inc., P.O. Box 180, Waterbury, VT 05676-9742 (tel. 802/244-1387), organizes 5- to 11-day walking trips in New England (principally Vermont and Maine) and other parts of the world. Walking tours typically cover 4 to 9 miles (6.5 to 14.5km) per day, in 3 to 5 hours. You walk at your own pace with similarly paced participants, who range in age from 30 to 80; luggage is transported in a van. Lodging is in rooms with private baths at nice country inns; all three meals are included. Tours range in price (per person) from 5-day weekends for about $900 to 11-day trips at $2,500.

New England Hiking Holidays, P.O. Box 1648, North Conway, NH 03860 (tel. toll free 800/869-0949), runs 2- to 5-day hiking trips in New England and other areas, providing accommodation at country inns at night. Call or write for a detailed brochure of their offerings.

BICYCLE TOURING   New England Bicycle Tours, 41 South Main St., Box D, Randolph, VT 05060 (tel. 802/728-3261; fax 802/728-4911), organizes 2-, 3-, 5-day, and longer bicycle and canoe tours along many beautiful routes through New England. Different tours are designed for different skill and stamina levels, from novices to fitness freaks, from those who want a leisurely cruise through the countryside to those who want to test their speed and stamina. Prices (per person) range from 3-day (2-night) tours at $230 to 5- and 6-day tours for $700 to $850. The price includes lodging at good inns, breakfast, dinner, maps, and snacks. Bring your own bike, or rent one of theirs for $45 per weekend, $80 per week; canoes are provided on canoe trips.

You can arrange your own bicycle tours on Cape Cod with the aid of *The Cape Cod Bike Book,* which has maps and details on bike paths, rest stops, places to take a break, and where to rent or repair a bicycle. You can buy the book ($2.50) in many stores on the Cape, or order it ($3.25) from Cape Cod Bike Book, P.O. Box 627, South Dennis, MA 02660.

MOUNTAIN BIKING   Touring the backwoods by bike can be exhilarating, especially during New England's autumn foliage season. If you plan to do your biking from mid-September to mid-October, make your reservations well ahead of time.

Mount Snow's **Mountain Bike School** (tel. toll free 800/451-4211) is designed to provide mountain-biking fun to riders from beginner to expert. Run only on weekends in summer, the school provides a welcome reception, 2 days of instruction, bike rental, lunch, and swimming for $140; with lodgings and all meals, the price is $300.

Vermont Mountain Bike Tours, P.O. Box 541, Pittsfield, Vt. (tel. 802/746-8580), runs guided tours for off-road bike enthusiasts. Prices range from $60 to $500 per person per day, plus $25 daily bike rental (if you don't bring your own), and includes guide, lodgings (from camping to country inns), and breakfast.

The **Craftsbury Center,** P.O. Box 31, Craftsbury Common, VT 05827 (tel. 802/586-7767), has a program of mountain-bike tours that includes accommodations and meals at lower prices than most other organized tours. If you bring your own bike and use a room with shared bath as your base, you may pay less than $56 per person per day; for more comfortable accommodations with private bath and all meals, the rate is about $85 per person per day. Tours range in length from 2-day weekend jaunts to 5-day excursions.

SEA KAYAKING & SCHOONER CRUISES   Maine Island Kayak Co., 70 Luther St., Peaks Island, ME 04108 (tel. 207/766-2373), 20 minutes by ferry from Portland, offers ½-day and day-trips by sea kayak among the Diamond Islands, long weekend excursions featuring camping on the islands, and 5- to 10-day expeditions along the most beautiful stretches of the Maine coast. Most trips do not require any previous knowledge or experience of sea kayaking, so beginners are welcome. "If you can walk a few miles," they say, "you can paddle between camps."

Out O' Mystic Schooner Cruises, Inc., 7 Holmes St., P.O. Box 487, Mystic, CT 06355 (tel. toll free 800/243-0416) has been running schooner cruises from Mystic since 1967. You can ship out on the *Mystic Whaler* or *Mystic Clipper* on a 1-, 2-, 3-, or 5-day cruise, spend your time relaxing, photographing, conversing with your shipmates, or lending a hand to shipboard chores, as you like. Prices (per person) include lodging on board and all meals, and depend upon the length of the cruise, the season (May, June, September, and October are cheaper than July and August), and the cabin you choose. One-day overnights (you board the evening before you sail) range from $89 for an off-season bunk in the co-ed "dorm" to $169 for the "Owner's Cabin." For a 5-day cruise, prices range from $519 to $579.

6. GETTING THERE

Three major gateways to New England are New York City, Montréal, and Boston. Most train and bus routes to New England pass through either New York or

Montréal, and a large number of transcontinental and transatlantic flights arrive at the airports in these cities. Many travelers choose to fly directly to Boston, of course. All of these routes are covered below, along with information on how to travel around New England by bus, rail, air, and car.

BY PLANE

FLIGHTS FROM NEW YORK CITY   You can easily catch a connecting flight from New York to Boston. There are several flights daily from each of the three major airports, John F. Kennedy, LaGuardia, and Newark, N.J. Airlines flying between New York and Boston include American, Continental, Delta, Northwest, Trans World (TWA), and USAir.

If you find no convenient connecting flight, consider taking the airport transfer bus to LaGuardia to catch an air shuttle. Some shuttle flights depart every hour on the hour, others on the half hour, between 6am and 9pm. No advance reservations are needed, you are guaranteed a seat. The one-way fare is $119 on weekdays during peak flying times (morning and evening), $89 off-peak (10am to 2pm and from Saturday morning until 5pm on Sunday).

Flights from New York City go daily to these other airports in the region as well: Albany, N.Y.; Bangor, Me.; Bridgeport, Conn.; Burlington, Vt.; Hartford, Conn.; Hyannis, Mass.; Lebanon, N.H.; Manchester, N.H.; Martha's Vineyard, Mass.; Nantucket, Mass.; New Haven, Conn.; New London, Conn.; Portland, Me.; Presque Isle, Me.; Providence, R.I.; and Worcester, Mass.

FLIGHTS FROM CHICAGO   Flights take off from the city's four airports— O'Hare International, Midway, Pal-Waukee, and Merrill C. Meigs—daily for New England and nearby destinations, including Albany, N.Y.; Bangor, Me.; Boston, Mass.; Burlington, Vt.; Hartford, Conn.; Manchester, N.H.; Portland, Me.; Providence, R.I.; and Worcester, Mass. The most active airlines are American, Midway, Northwest, United, and USAair.

FLIGHTS FROM CANADA   Delta Airlines operates routes from Montréal's Dorval Airport to Boston and Hartford; Air Canada's commuter line, Air Alliance, flies from Dorval to Boston as well. Either flight takes just over an hour.

FARES   These days, 90% of all air travelers buy tickets at discounted fares. Very few people pay full fare, which can be surprisingly expensive. At full fare, it can cost as much to make the 2-hour flight from Washington, D.C., to Boston, and return, as it does to fly round-trip from Boston to London, Paris, or Rome on an excursion ticket. The matter of airfares is so complex that only a travel agent with a good knowledge of the airlines' computer reservations systems can get the lowest fare and best flights for you.

DISCOUNT TICKETS   Discount airfares normally have three constraints attached to them. First, you must make your reservations and purchase your tickets in advance. Usually you must close the deal at least a week before you fly, but some airfares require even more time, perhaps 2 or 3 weeks.

Second, you cannot change your plans without paying some sort of penalty. This penalty ranges from 25% to 100% of the price you've paid.

The third constraint is that airlines may offer very few seats on each flight at the lowest fare.

Are there ways around these rules? Yes! Nothing can substitute for good advance planning, so make your plans and talk to your travel agent well in advance of your trip. Find an agent who is willing to "dig" into the plethora of airfares and discover a special fare or a special routing that will save you money. Make your reservations, but don't buy your ticket until you're required to do so. When the time comes to buy your ticket, ask the agent to take another look to see if the situation has changed. The

FROMMER'S SMART TRAVELER: AIRFARES

1. Avoid holiday "blackout" periods, when discount fares are hard to come by.
2. Fly when airline bookings are low: mid-January through March and October through mid-December (except Thanksgiving).
3. Check to see if flying on certain days is cheaper than others.
4. Ask your travel agent if you can save money by splitting your trip into segments or by taking an indirect route.
5. Consider buying a low excursion-fare (round-trip) ticket if you are flying one-way. Some one-way tickets are so disproportionately expensive that this can be cheaper. And you may be able to sell the return ticket.
6. Ask your travel agent to look into alternate airports that are still convenient. Sometimes fares are cheaper if you fly to a less-used airport.

reservations and airfare business is so complex that seats on particular flights may be "reserved" and "released" many times before the plane even leaves the ground, and fares go up and down almost daily.

As for penalties, airlines rarely levy a penalty if you advance your return date, that is, if you come back to your starting point early.

Foreign visitors can sometimes take advantage of special air-travel passes that offer unlimited flying for a period of time (3 weeks, a month, several months, etc.) on a particular airline's routes. You must buy the pass before you leave home (Europe, Japan, etc.), you cannot fly during holiday blackout periods, you cannot backtrack, and there may be a minimum or maximum number of takeoffs. There is also the constraint of the airlines route system: Does it operate flights to the places you want to visit? But these passes provide indisputable bargains when they are offered.

BY TRAIN

Amtrak's schedules are carried in all the major airline systems, and any travel agency with one of the airlines' computerized reservation systems can give you information on Amtrak schedules and fares, and can sell you tickets.

Amtrak's rail passenger service travels coast to coast. From the south, trains speed north along the eastern seaboard to Washington, D.C., the southern end of the "Northeast Corridor" (Washington-Boston route). Most passengers who come to New England by train take this line via New York City.

Amtrak's *Lake Shore Limited* travels nightly **from Chicago** to New England, departing Chicago's Union Station at 6:25pm, arriving in Springfield, Mass., at 12:55pm the next day. Several through cars from the *Lake Shore Limited* continue to Boston, departing Springfield at 1:25pm, arriving in Boston at 4:15pm. From Springfield, you can continue north by bus, east or south by train.

One train daily, the *Maple Leaf*, departs **Toronto** at 9:35am and arrives at Albany-Rensselaer at 6:25pm. From Albany, it's a short hop by bus to the Berkshires or southern Vermont. There is only one train a day, the *Lake Shore Limited* (see above), connecting Albany-Rensselaer with Boston, and this train departs Albany-Rensselaer at 10:40am. If you've come this far on the *Maple Leaf*, you must continue by bus, or stay overnight and catch the *Lake Shore Limited* the next day.

Two Amtrak trains run daily **from Montréal**'s Central Station (beneath the Queen Elizabeth Hotel) to New York City, a distance of 450 miles. The *Adirondack* is a day train (10 hr.) departing Montréal at 8:40am, arriving in New York City at 6:43pm. If you get off the train at Albany, you can take a bus to southern Vermont or to the Berkshires.

The *Montrealer* is a night train (12 hr.), departing Montréal at 5:10pm, arriving at New York City at 7:35am.

Note: Schedules may change, so call Amtrak toll free at 800/USA-RAIL for a current schedule.

Note: Besides Amtrak service from Penn Station, there is **Metro North** train service on the Connecticut Department of Transportation's New Haven Line from New York's Grand Central Terminal to New Haven, Conn., every hour on the hour from 7am until after midnight on weekdays, with extra trains during the peak morning and evening hours. Service on Saturday, Sunday, and holidays is almost as frequent, with a train at least every 2 hours. The trip from Grand Central to New Haven takes 1¾ hours. For exact schedule information, call 212/532-4900 in New York City, or toll free 800/223-6052 in Connecticut.

TRAINS TO CAPE COD During the peak summer vacation season of July and August (through Labor Day weekend), Amtrak operates special weekend trains from New York City to Hyannis on Cape Cod.

The *Cape Codder* departs Washington, D.C., in mid-afternoon on Friday, stops at New York's Pennsylvania Station in late afternoon, departs New Haven at suppertime, and arrives in Hyannis at bedtime. On Saturday, trains from Washington and New York connect with the *Clamdigger* at Providence, R.I., for the final run to Hyannis. Return trips from Hyannis to Providence, New York, and Washington depart Saturday morning and Sunday afternoon.

FARES Amtrak offers the **All Aboard America** fares, special reduced-rate round-trip excursion fares to various points, and seasonal and special reductions. These fares divide the country into three regions: East, from the Atlantic coast to Chicago and New Orleans; West, from the Pacific coast to Wolf Point (Mont.), Denver, Albuquerque, and El Paso; and Central, everything in between, including the boundary cities. For only $199 in summer, $189 the rest of the year, you can make a one-way or round-trip journey within any one of these regions, with three stopovers along the way. To tour within two regions costs only $289 in summer, $249 at other times; freedom to plan a three-region, cross-country return trip with three stopovers costs only $349 in summer, $269 at other times.

Another special deal, subject to certain restrictions, is their **$7 Return Fare,** especially good for short or medium-length journeys: Buy a one-way ticket costing $65 or more (with no change of trains), and the return trip costs only $7.

A **kids' fare** plan allows a 50% discount off the lowest available adult coach fare for children up to age 15.

Only a limited number of tickets are sold at these special fares, so make your reservations as soon as you've decided on your itinerary. For more information, write to the Amtrak Distribution Center, P.O. Box 7717, Itasca, IL 60143, requesting their free travel planner entitled "Amtrak's America." For the latest information on ever-changing fares and schedules, call toll free 800/872-7245, which is 800/USA-RAIL.

Remember that unless you travel first class in a club or sleeping car, meals are not included in Amtrak's prices; you must pay for meals on the train when you receive them, or carry your own food.

BY BUS

New York's main bus station is the **Port Authority Bus Terminal,** Eighth Avenue and 42nd Street (tel. 212/564-8484). From Newark International Airport, shuttle buses go directly to the Port Authority terminal. From LaGuardia Airport or John F. Kennedy International Airport, take a Carey airport bus to Grand Central Terminal, (Park Avenue and 42nd Street) and walk (or take a taxi) 5 blocks west along 42nd Street to the bus terminal.

From the Port Authority Bus Terminal, various lines run to different parts of New England:

Bonanza Bus Lines Bonanza's (tel. 212/564-8484, or toll free 800/556-3815) routes go to Albany, N.Y., via the Berkshires (Great Barrington, Stockbridge, Lee, Lenox, and Pittsfield) from New York City; and from New York City to Cape Cod

(Falmouth, Woods Hole, and Hyannis) via Providence, R.I. During the winter months, service to Falmouth and Woods Hole (for the ferries to Martha's Vineyard and Nantucket) is via connection at Bourne, Mass. Bonanza also operates between New York City and Providence and Newport, R.I., and New Bedford, Mass. Buy your tickets in New York's Port Authority Bus Terminal at the Adirondack Trailways Ticket Plaza.

Greyhound Lines   Greyhound (tel. 212/971-6363) operates buses from New York City to Hartford, Springfield, Worcester, New Haven, New London, and Providence. Service to Cape Cod is provided in conjunction with Bonanza. The Boston service has a few buses daily. The direct trip to Boston takes about 4¾ hours. From Boston, connections are made to points in Maine, New Hampshire, and Vermont.

Vermont Transit Lines   Vermont Transit (tel. toll free 800/451-3292, 800/ 642-3133 in Vermont) operates in conjunction with Greyhound to serve Vermont's ski and vacation regions as well as Montréal and several points in New Hampshire.

The major bus routes to New England **from Chicago and Toronto** enter the region at Albany and Montréal, and you may find yourself changing buses at one of these points to reach your final destination. The distance by road to Boston from Chicago is almost 1,000 miles (1,600km), from Toronto 550 miles (880km).

Vermont Transit buses depart at least three times daily **from Montréal**'s central bus station, the Terminus Voyageur, 505 bd. de Maisonneuve est (tel. 514/842-2281), en route to Boston (9 hr.). In the summer months, Greyhound operates daily service from Montréal to Burlington, Vt.; North Conway, N.H.; Old Orchard Beach, Me.; and Boston. Other Greyhound buses head due south along Canada 15 and I-87 to New York City, stopping in Albany along the way.

FARES   To reach Boston by bus costs $160 from Chicago, $75 from Washington, D.C., $40 from New York City, U.S. $119 from Toronto, U.S. $60 from Montréal if you pay full fare. For long-distance runs like the trip from Chicago or even farther away, discount travel plans often bring the price down substantially. Round-trip fares, by the way, are in some cases only 40% more than one-way fares.

BY CAR

Starting **from New York City,** choose your route according to your destination:

For **northwestern Connecticut, the Massachusetts Berkshires, southern and western Vermont,** follow the Henry Hudson Parkway or I-87 north to the Saw Mill River Parkway, which connects with the Taconic State Parkway north. The Taconic is a beautiful road and trucks are not allowed.

To **southwestern Connecticut, Hartford, central Massachusetts, Boston, eastern Vermont, New Hampshire, and Maine,** take the Henry Hudson Parkway or I-87 north to the Saw Mill River Parkway, and that north to I-684. At the junction with I-84, go east via Danbury and Waterbury to Hartford and beyond.

If you're heading for points along the **Connecticut and Rhode Island coasts** (New Haven, New London, Mystic, Providence, Newport), Cape Cod and the islands, New Bedford, and Plymouth, follow the Henry Hudson Parkway or I-87 north to I-287. Head east on I-287 to the Hutchinson River Parkway north; after a few miles this road enters Connecticut and becomes the Merritt Parkway. Unlike the alternate route, I-95, this scenic toll road is not open to trucks, making it even more pleasant. Beyond Bridgeport, the Merritt Parkway is named the Wilbur Cross Parkway; it continues past New Haven and north to Meriden, where it's best to take I-91 north. To head east along the coast from New Haven take I-95, unless you want to slow down and take the older U.S. 1, an interesting route that goes through many coastal towns—and red lights.

From Chicago Interstate 80 is very heavily traveled to Cleveland, and not particularly pleasant to drive, but it is the most direct route. For scenery and a more relaxed time, take I-94 to Detroit, then cross the border into Canada to follow Highway 401 to Hamilton before heading down via Niagara Falls to Buffalo to pick up I-90, the New York State Thruway, to Albany and Boston. **From Toronto,** the Hamilton-Niagara-Buffalo-Albany route is the logical choice unless you're headed for northern New England, in which case you might want to drive via Montréal (see below).

The most direct route **from Montréal** to Vermont, southern New Hampshire, and the southern New England states is to cross the Pont Victoria and follow Canada 10, the Autoroute des Cantons de l'Est, eastward 22km (13 miles) to Canada 35 south; this is all expressway. Beyond Iberville the route is marked as Québec Highway 133, and is a fairly fast two-lane highway through flat farming country. At the U.S. border, the road becomes I-89 south, and continues via Burlington and Montpelier to White River Junction, Vt., where it intersects with I-91. Continue on I-89 to Concord and Manchester, N.H., and to Boston; take I-91 south to southern Vermont and New Hampshire, central Massachusetts, and central Connecticut around Hartford.

For the western parts of Vermont, Massachusetts, and Connecticut, take the Pont Victoria or Pont Jacques-Cartier east out of Montréal and follow Canada 15 due south to the U.S. border, where the highway becomes I-87. You can leave this road at Exit 39 north of Plattsburgh, N.Y., to catch a ferry from Gordon Landing over to Grand Isle and thence via U.S. 2 to I-89 and Burlington; or you can take an exit farther south to get to Port Kent and the ferry across Lake Champlain directly to Burlington (for details on this service, see "Burlington," Chapter 13). Near Albany, roads go east to Bennington in southern Vermont, Williamstown, Mass., and the Berkshires; just south of Albany, I-87 intersects with I-90, the Massachusetts Turnpike to Boston. If you're headed farther south, follow I-90 east from I-87 to the Taconic State Parkway, a pleasant, fast road open only to cars, not to trucks.

From Montréal to northern New Hampshire and Maine, take the Pont Victoria, follow Canada 10, the Autoroute des Cantons de l'Est, eastward as far as Magog. Turn south here on Canada 55 to the U.S. border. South of the border the highway is I-93, which leads straight to New Hampshire's White Mountains. To get to Maine, you can take U.S. 2 or U.S. 302 eastward from I-93.

Another route to Maine, slower and less scenic, with fewer tourist services, is to continue on Canada 10 east from Magog and through Sherbrooke. Beyond Sherbrooke, the road becomes two lanes and is numbered Québec 112. Follow 112 to the small town of St-Gérard, then follow Québec 161 through Lac-Mégantic to the U.S. border. In Maine, the road is Maine Highway 27, a lonely route through forests and mountains, finally bringing you to Augusta, the state capital.

7. GETTING AROUND

Whether you use your own car or a rental (hired) car, driving is perhaps the best way to see New England. The forested hills, winding river valleys, and historic New England towns and villages are most accessible and best appreciated when seen from a car traveling at moderate speed on secondary roads. But other means of transportation are available as well.

BY PLANE

The larger cities, such as Boston, Providence, Hartford, Portland, and Burlington, all have good air service provided by the larger domestic airlines. Numerous regional "feeder" airlines fly between the larger cities and smaller ones. There are also many connections by regional carrier to New York City.

Almost all of the small regional airlines operate in conjunction with larger national and international airlines. The regional airlines' flights are included in the flight schedules of the larger airlines, including American, Continental, Delta, Pan Am, and USAir. Call these airlines for information on flights, fares, and cities served.

BY TRAIN

Amtrak operates trains connecting Boston with Springfield and Pittsfield, Mass., and Albany, N.Y.; Hartford, New Haven, New London, and Mystic, Conn.; Providence, R.I.; and (via Springfield) Brattleboro, White River Junction, and Montpelier, Vt., and Montréal, Québec. There is no interstate train service northeast of Boston (that is, to Maine or central and eastern New Hampshire), but there are buses that run from Amtrak's terminus at Boston's South Station to Portsmouth, N.H., and to major cities and towns in eastern Maine. Trains on routes between Boston and points south and west are fast and frequent; but to get to points in Vermont from Boston, connections are not good, and service is infrequent.

BY BUS

Bus service is quite good in New England. Here are some of the major companies, their phone numbers, the terminal from which they operate in Boston, and the areas they serve:

American Eagle (tel. 508/990-0000), Peter Pan Terminal, operates frequent buses daily between Boston and New Bedford.

Bonanza Bus Lines (tel. 617/720-4110, or toll free 800/556-3815), Greyhound Terminal, runs from Boston to Cape Cod (Falmouth and Woods Hole) and Fall River, Mass., and Newport and Providence, R.I. Other routes run from Providence to central and western Connecticut and the Berkshires of Massachusetts, and from Providence to Cape Cod.

Concord Trailways (tel. 617/426-8080, or toll free 800/639-3317 in New England) is the line to take to New Hampshire. Buses start at Logan airport and the Peter Pan Terminal in Boston, then head north to Concord, Laconia and North Conway, Plymouth, Waterville Valley, and Franconia. Another route goes to Alton and Wolfboro.

Greyhound (tel. 617/423-5810), with its terminal at 10 St. James Ave. in Boston (any Green Line subway car to Arlington), operates many of the long-distance routes in New England, and connects the region with the rest of the country. Greyhound buses operate from Boston via Hartford and New Haven to New York City; from New York City via New Haven and Hartford to Springfield, Mass., connecting with Vermont Transit buses for points in Vermont, and Montréal, Québec.

Another Greyhound route is from Boston via Portsmouth, N.H., to the Maine coast, stopping at Portland, Freeport, Brunswick, Bath, Wiscasset, Camden, and Bangor (with connecting service to Ellsworth for Bar Harbor); this route connects with Canadian SMT buses headed for New Brunswick and Nova Scotia.

Greyhound also connects New York City via New Haven and New London, Conn., with Providence, R.I., and with connecting service to Hyannis and Province-town on Cape Cod.

Another route is between Islip, N.Y. (on Long Island), via New Haven and Hartford, Conn., and Boston.

Greyhound also operates buses heading due west from Boston, stopping at Worcester, Springfield, Lee, Lenox, and Pittsfield, Mass., and Albany, N.Y., with connecting service to points west in both the United States and Canada.

Peter Pan Bus Lines (tel. 617/426-7838, or toll free 800/237-8747), at the Peter Pan (formerly Trailways) Terminal in Dewey Square, opposite Amtrak's South Station, runs between Boston and Albany, Amherst, Bridgeport, Danbury, Hartford, Holyoke, Lee, Middletown, New Britain, New Haven, New York City, Northampton, Norwalk, Pittsfield, Springfield, Sturbridge, Waterbury, and Worcester. Other routes connect Springfield, Mass., with Bradley International Airport and Hartford, Conn.

Plymouth & Brockton Street Railway Co. (tel. 508/746-0378), Peter Pan

Terminal, is the one to take from Boston to Plymouth, Sagamore, Barnstable, Hyannis, and Provincetown on Cape Cod. P&B also runs from Hyannis to Chatham and Provincetown on Cape Cod. Many P&B runs start at Logan airport, then head into Boston for stops at Park Square, the Peter Pan Terminal, and South Station. You can take any P&B bus from Logan airport, and transfer to another one downtown.

Vermont Transit Lines (tel. 617/292-4700; or toll free 800/451-3292, 800/642-3133 in Vermont), Greyhound Terminal, in collaboration with Greyhound Lines, operates from New York City via Albany to Bennington, Manchester, East Dorset, Rutland (with connecting service to Killington, Woodstock, and White River Junction), Middlebury, and Burlington. Connecting service from Burlington goes on to Montréal.

Another service is from Boston via Manchester, Concord, Mount Sunapee, and Hanover, N.H., to White River Junction (with connecting service to Woodstock, Killington, and Rutland), then to Barre, Montpelier, Burlington, and Montréal.

Vermont Transit also runs buses between Portland, Me.; Burlington, Vt.; and Montréal, stopping at North Conway and Bretton Woods, N.H.; and St. Johnsbury, White River Junction, and Montpelier, Vt.

Another route takes travelers from New York City or Boston to White River Junction for connections to St. Johnsbury and Newport, Vt., and Sherbrooke and Québec City.

To get to Stowe, Vt., you must first go to Burlington or Newport, Vt.

BY CAR

Within New England you will normally drive only an hour or two to your next destination. From Boston, it's only about an hour's drive to Providence, Plymouth, Manchester, or Portsmouth; about 2 hours to Hartford, Portland, Mystic, or Cape Cod; about 3 hours to New Haven, the Berkshires, southern Vermont, Boothbay Harbor, or New Hampshire's White Mountains; and only about 4 hours to New York City or central Vermont. Five hours takes you from Boston to the resort and national park at Bar Harbor, Me., and not much more than 6 hours' driving deposits you in beautiful Montréal.

CAR RENTAL To rent a car in New York or New England you must be 21 years of age, and have a valid driver's license. A credit card is almost always a necessity. Without one you must leave a sizable cash deposit, perhaps $100 per day for the estimated length of the rental, or perhaps a flat $2,000 or more.

Rental rates vary among companies. Most expensive are the well-known **international companies** with car-rental desks right in the major airports; cheapest are small local agencies in major cities. In between are the moderate-sized agencies with airport shuttle buses to take you to their "off-airport" locations.

Cheapest rates are for the smallest cars, rented on "weekends" (Thursday noon through Monday noon), or for an entire week or more with unlimited mileage, and returned to the place of rental, or at least to the city of rental. Always return a rental car to the agency with as much gas in it as when the rental began (usually a full tank). Agencies will charge you if they must refuel the car, and some charge high prices at their pumps.

Among the high charges for car rental are those for insurance. The so-called Collision Damage Waiver or Loss Damage Waiver can cost from $8 to $14 or more per day. These charges are currently the subject of legal debate, and may be abolished or regulated by state governments in the future. For now, you can avoid them several ways. If your own auto insurance covers damage to a rental car, you needn't waste money on CDW or LDW; check with your auto insurance broker to be sure. Otherwise, your American Express card or gold VISA or MasterCard may provide coverage for any rental car rented with the card; check your credit-card agreement to see what coverage is provided. In case of damage, rental-car companies may require not only that you pay for repairs, but that you pay normal rental fees for all the time that the rental car is out of commission for repairs.

If you're under 25, you might also get charged an extra $7.50 a day depending on the company you choose, so be sure to ask. Rental cars from the national companies may be reserved through any travel agent, or by calling a car-rental company directly on its toll-free line. Here are the toll-free numbers of the national companies: **Alamo** (tel. 800/327-9633); **American International** (tel. 800/527-0202); **Avis** (tel. 800/331-1212); **Budget** (tel. 800/527-0700); **Dollar** (tel. 800/421-6868); **Hertz** (tel. 800/654-3131); **National** (tel. 800/227-7368); **Rent-A-Wreck** (tel. 800/535-1391); **Thrifty** (tel. 800/367-2277); **USA Rent-A-Car System** (tel. 800/872-2277).

Besides the large national companies there are many small, **local car-rental companies** in each New England city. Look in the yellow pages telephone directory under "Automobile Renting and Leasing." Though they do not have the national companies' far-flung systems of agents, many of these local companies provide good local service at excellent rates. Most offer free delivery and pickup at the airport or at a hotel, unlimited mileage, and good late-model cars. Since New England is not a large region, you may not be too far from the rental agency if a problem arises.

Following are the names and addresses of a few of the larger local car-rental agencies in Boston, picked at random from the hundreds of small companies doing business in the area. **Agency Rent-A-Car,** 367 Western Ave., Brighton, MA 02135 (tel. 617/783-4470); **Brodie Auto Rentals,** 24 Eliot St. (Harvard Sq.), Cambridge, MA 02138 (tel. 617/491-7600); **Excel Car & Van Rental,** 25 River St. (Central Sq.), Cambridge, MA 02139 (tel. 617/227-7368); **Ugly Duckling Rent-A-Car,** 34 Dudley St., Arlington, MA 02174 (tel. 617/648-3825).

Another source of reasonably priced rentals is **local auto dealerships.** Several Ford dealerships in the Boston area, including Jack Madden Ford (tel. 617/769-4130), 128 Rental (a division of Tom Ford; tel. 617/245-9560), Main Street Ford (tel. 617/899-0300), and York Ford (tel. 617/322-8340), offer rental cars at competitive rates. Chrysler dealers in the area provide similar service.

GASOLINE Unleaded regular (89 octane) gasoline costs $1.30 to $1.50 per U.S. gallon in New England; more if you buy it in the very center of a large city. Smaller cars ("subcompact" and "compact" in car-rental terminology) normally have fuel efficiencies of about 30 to 40 miles per gallon, which means that the cost of fuel works out to about 3¢ or 4¢ per mile (2¢ to 3¢ per km). Thus the cost of fuel to drive between Boston and New York City (205 miles) would be $6.15 to $9.90, depending upon the car and your driving habits.

DRIVING RULES Highway and street speed limits, licensing of drivers, and all other rules governing automobile use are set by each state's legislature. In general, you must be 18 years old to get a driver's license. Maximum speed on most expressways in New England is 55 m.p.h. (89kmph), though many drivers regularly exceed that. A few expressways (mostly in New Hampshire) have speed limits of 65 m.p.h. (105kmph). Fines for speeding are $75 to $100 or more per offense, and after several offenses, your driver's license is revoked for a period of time.

Police use radar to detect speeding drivers, but some drivers use radar detectors to warn them about police speed traps. In Connecticut, it is illegal to mount or to use a radar detector. If you are caught speeding in Connecticut, and if you have a radar detector in your car (whether or not it is connected or in use), fines may total upwards of $300. If you must go very fast, take an airplane; it will cost less than getting caught speeding!

Laws requiring use of car safety belts are uncommon, but every intelligent driver knows that the chances of surviving an accident and avoiding injury are increased greatly if safety belts are worn. Throughout the United States, infants and small children (under 4 years of age) are required by law to be placed in child safety seats secured by seat belts. Child safety seats are available from car-rental firms at a small extra charge.

ROAD MAPS New England maps are sold in the region's bookstores and gas stations for $1 or $2. Maps of each state drawn with greater detail are available, usually for free or for less than $1, from official state tourism departments by mail, or from state roadside information centers located on major highways near state borders. For addresses of the state tourism offices, see "Sources of Information," above.

BREAKDOWNS/ASSISTANCE Several interstate highways have Motorist Aid Call Boxes posted at regular intervals along the side of the roadway. State police officers patrol all major highways to assist travelers with car problems. If your car stops and you can't get it going, wait in your car until a patrol stops. The officer can call a repair or tow truck to help you. If you are driving a rental car, remember to call the rental company before authorizing a mechanic to do more than the most minor repairs.

If you are a member of the **American Automobile Association,** 1000 AAA Drive, Heathrow, FL 32746 (tel. toll free 800/222-4357), the AAA will provide simple towing and breakdown assistance at no charge, although long-distance tows and more expensive repairs are your responsibility. To become a member of the AAA, you join a local AAA-affiliated automobile club near your home, paying that club's normal membership dues. Members of some foreign auto clubs can use AAA. AAA-affiliated clubs offer trip-related financial services and issue road maps and guidebooks at no charge to members. The AAA can also provide foreign visitors to the United States with "Touring Permits" validating your home driver's license for use in the United States.

BY RECREATION VEHICLE

Among the most pleasant ways to tour the country is in a recreation vehicle (RV, motorhome, or camper). RVs come in all sizes and shapes, and dozens of models. They usually sleep four to six people comfortably, include a full kitchen with cooking range, refrigerator, and running water, are air conditioned, and some even come equipped with a shower! Hundreds of campgrounds in New England can provide electrical, water, and sewer hookups for $15 to $20 per night. Some RVs are so self-sufficient that they can operate for several days without hookups. In an RV, you're completely independent, you can save money by cooking your own meals, and you needn't pay for expensive hotel rooms. The advantages to families with young children are obvious. Family travel in a rental RV can be a very cost-effective way to tour New England.

Renting an RV has its disadvantages as well. Rentals are fairly expensive, and you should work out estimated budgets for a trip in an RV versus a trip using a rental car and hotels before making your final decision. When figuring costs, keep in mind that RVs are heavy vehicles, and they use a lot more fuel than do passenger cars. During the busy summer months you may not be able to find the campsite you want in the location you want, since many of New England's choicest campgrounds fill up early in the day. You may have to reserve in advance, which takes some of the fun out of footloose vagabond travel. Finally, New England is a region with many delightful country inns. If you've rented an RV at considerable expense, you may not feel that you can pay to stay in country inns very often.

RV RESOURCES For more information on RVs contact the **Recreation Vehicle Industry Association,** P.O. Box 2999, 1896 Preston White Dr., Reston, VA 22090 (tel. 703/620-6003), and the **Recreation Vehicle Dealers Association,** 3251 Old Lee Highway, Fairfax, VA 22030 (tel. 703/591-7130).

RV RENTAL COMPANIES Companies renting recreational vehicles are listed in yellow pages telephone directories under "Recreational Vehicles—Renting & Leasing," "Motor Homes—Renting & Leasing," and "Trailers—Camping & Travel." (Don't let the word "Trailers" mislead you; this section has lots of listings for RVs, since many businesses rent both trailers and RVs.) Two of the largest national franchisers are **Cruise America** (tel. toll free 800/327-7778, or 617/625-6121 in Boston) and **Bates Rent-a-Motor Home, Inc.** (tel. toll free 800/732-2283).

Several companies in the Boston area rent RVs. The listings below are for your convenience, since RV rentals should be arranged in advance, and you might otherwise find it impossible to learn who rents RVs in Boston. For information on a company's reputation you can contact Boston's **Better Business Bureau,** 20 Park Plaza, Boston, MA 02108 (tel. 617/426-9000). Try **AAT Motor Home Rental & Sales,** 1724 Revere Beach Parkway, Everett, MA 02149 (tel. 508/664-4032); **Trip Makers, Inc.** 401 Providence Highway, Norwood, MA 02062 (tel. 617/255-9810), or P.O. Box C, Foxboro, MA 02035 (tel. 508/543-8941).

HITCHHIKING

Hitchhiking is not a good way to get around New England, either within cities or between cities and towns. It is illegal to hitchhike on expressways. Incidents of robbery and violence by driver or hitcher, though few in number, have left most motorists unwilling to stop for hitchhikers.

SUGGESTED ITINERARIES

Many visitors to New England have specific destinations and activities in mind when they plan their visits: rambling along the Maine coast looking for antiques, or visiting the sites where the American Revolution began in and around Boston, or inn-hopping in Vermont. If you have no such itinerary already in mind, refer to the sections entitled "What's Special About . . ." at the beginning of each chapter. These sections may help you to decide what you want to see and do in the time available to you.

NEW ENGLAND'S HIGH POINTS

Boston   New England's oldest, largest, and most historically significant city should appear on every visitor's itinerary. Within a short drive of the city are many more historic towns such as Salem, Marblehead, Lexington, Concord, and Plymouth. In Plymouth you can revisit the 17th century at Plimoth Plantation.

Cape Cod   With its charming historic towns, Cape Cod National Seashore, beaches, and bike paths, Cape Cod has something for every visitor. The islands of Martha's Vineyard and Nantucket, offshore of the cape, are equally fascinating.

Sturbridge   Central Massachusetts is where you'll find Old Sturbridge Village, a faithful re-creation of a New England town of the early 1800s. A similarly historic site from the 1700s is **Old Deerfield,** not far away.

Berkshires   The hills of western Massachusetts are noted for summer festivals of music, theater, and dance, including the Tanglewood Music Festival and Jacob's Pillow Dance Festival, and the Williamstown Theater Festival.

Newport   Rhode Island's oceanside playground boasts palatial turn-of-the-century mansions that must be seen to be believed, as well as good restaurants and beaches.

New Haven   Besides the lovely campus of Yale University, New Haven, Conn., has several first-rank museums and a lively cultural season during the college year.

Mystic and New London   Connecticut's eastern coast is alive with maritime history at Mystic Seaport Museum, a carefully preserved New England maritime town of the 1800s; and at New London, home of the U.S. Coast Guard Academy, and the Navy submarine base at neighboring Groton.

Portsmouth   New Hampshire's short seacoast is long on attractions. Strawbery Banke, in Portsmouth, is a living museum of the 1700s, with artisans actually making their livings (not just "demonstrating") at their centuries-old crafts.

White Mountains   New Hampshire's White Mountains are perfect for scenic drives, hiking, or camping. North Conway is the outdoor activities capital of the region; Franconia Notch has many natural wonders.

Maine Coast   The southwestern coast of Maine is lined with pretty beach towns, among them Kennebunkport, with its presidential retreat. Bar Harbor is far "down east," but many visitors make the trek to visit this turn-of-the-century summer resort of the wealthy, and neighboring Acadia National Park.

Green Mountains   From gracious Bennington in the south to alpine Stowe in the north, Vermont's Green Mountains are dotted with cozy inns, charming New England villages clustered around their commons, and excellent possibilities for outdoor activities. Drive Vermont Route 100 for a good introduction to the Green Mountain state. Just south of Burlington, the Shelburne Museum has perhaps the best and fullest collection of Americana ever assembled.

PLANNING YOUR ITINERARY

For first-time visitors, here are some sample itineraries covering many of the high points:

BOSTON & VICINITY

IF YOU HAVE 3 TO 4 DAYS   Day 1   Follow the Freedom Trail around Boston's most historic sights, have lunch in or near Faneuil Hall Marketplace, spend some time shopping at Downtown Crossing or along Newbury Street, and have a good dinner in one of the city's better restaurants.

Day 2   Visit one or two of the city's better museums (Museum of Fine Arts, Gardner Museum, Museum of Science, Museum Wharf), then take the subway to Harvard Square for some café-sitting, shopping, and a tour of Harvard University.

Day 3   Drive, or take the suburban train, to Concord for a walk around that historic town and out to Old North Bridge, where the second battle of the revolutionary war was fought. If you're driving, follow the course of Battle Road from Cambridge through Lexington and Concord in the Minuteman National Historic Park. Or, instead of heading west to Concord, drive or take a train north to Salem to explore New England's maritime history at the Essex Institute, Peabody Museum, and Salem Maritime National Historic Site. You can get a look at some of Salem's witch lore as well.

Day 4   With an extra day you can do both of the excursions outlined in Day 3. Or, if Pilgrim lore is fascinating to you, drive or take a Plymouth & Brockton bus south to Plymouth for a look at Plymouth Rock, the *Mayflower II,* and other sites in Plymouth, then spend the afternoon at Plimouth Plantation, south of town.

SOUTHERN NEW ENGLAND

IF YOU HAVE 7 TO 10 DAYS   Here's a loop tour by car that starts at Boston, but that can actually be started anywhere along the loop.

Day 1   Drive west for 90 minutes on the Massachusetts Turnpike (I-90) to Sturbridge for a visit to Old Sturbridge Village. Stay in the area, or continue westward to Amherst or Northampton. Visit Old Deerfield if you have extra time.

Day 2   Head for the Berkshires. Enjoy a picnic, visit the Norman Rockwell Museum in Stockbridge, Chesterwood, or perhaps the Hancock Shaker Village, and take in an evening performance at Tanglewood, Jacob's Pillow, the Berkshire Theater Festival, or some other cultural venue.

Day 3   Drive south to Lake Waramaug and Litchfield for a look at this pristine 18th-century town. Continue south down the Naugatuck River Valley along Connecticut Route 8 to Derby, then east on Route 34 to New Haven for dinner.

Day 4   Explore Yale University and its museums in the morning, and drive east along the Connecticut Turnpike (I-95) to Essex, Ivoryton, and Old Lyme. Choose a place for lunch, and tour these towns at the mouth of the Connecticut River. Continue to New London or Mystic for the night. (If you're starting your tour from New York City, this would be Day 1).

Day 5   Visit Mystic Seaport Museum or, if you prefer, the U.S. Coast Guard Academy and Navy Submarine Base. Spend the night in Mystic, Stonington, or Watch Hill.

Day 6   Drive to Newport to tour the fabulous mansions along Bellevue Avenue, ride bicycles along Ocean Drive, amble along Cliff Walk, and enjoy an excellent seafood dinner.

Day 7   If time is short, head for Plymouth to view Plymouth Rock and visit Plimoth Plantation before heading back to Boston. If you have a few more days, head for Cape Cod. It's best not to attempt the drive all the way to Provincetown today; choose a town on the "lower cape" or "mid-cape" for the night.

Day 8   Enjoy Cape Cod: Tour the national seashore, lunch on fried clams and french fries, take a swim. If you're in the mood for a circus atmosphere, drive out to the tip for a look at Provincetown. Or, from Woods Hole or Hyannis, take a day-trip or an overnight excursion to Martha's Vineyard or Nantucket (going by plane will save time).

Day 9   Continue your explorations of Cape Cod, Martha's Vineyard, or Nantucket.

Day 10   Head back to Boston, stopping at Plymouth for a look at The Rock, and a few hours at Plimoth Plantation.

NORTHERN NEW ENGLAND

IF YOU HAVE 6 TO 10 DAYS   Northern New England has its cultural side, but most people who tour here are looking for outdoor adventure. The following itinerary can also be followed as two shorter trips. Look upon Days 1 through 4 as a short tour of the Maine coast, returning to Boston on Day 4. To make a 6-day tour of New Hampshire and Vermont, drive north from Boston to North Conway, N.H., and pick up the itinerary at that point in Day 5.

Day 1   Head north from Boston on I-93, then I-95, stopping at Portsmouth, N.H., for lunch and a tour of Strawbery Banke. Continue to the Maine coast, staying the night in Ogunquit or Kennebunkport, or, if you prefer, in Portland.

Day 2   Continue northward along I-95, stopping for some shopping in Freeport, home of L. L. Bean and many factory outlets. Just before Brunswick, follow U.S. 1, continuing through Bath. Spend part of the day around Boothbay Harbor, or Camden, or Blue Hill, but plan to stay the night in one of Bar Harbor's sumptuous inns.

Day 3   Explore Acadia National Park and Bar Harbor, with another overnight here.

Day 4   Return to Portland and drive north on the Maine Turnpike and Maine Route 26 via Sabbathday Lake and Poland Spring to Bethel, for the night.

Day 5   Follow U.S. Route 2 west to Gorham, then New Hampshire Route 16 south through Pinkham Notch to Glen and North Conway. Have lunch in North Conway, or buy supplies for a picnic, then drive westward along the Kancamagus Highway, the heart of the White Mountains. Stop for a picnic and a short hike at one of the National Forest areas along the highway. Spend the night at Lincoln, at the western end of the highway.

Day 6   Drive north from Lincoln through Franconia Notch, stopping to see the Old Man of the Mountain and The Flume. Stop for lunch in Littleton, then head southwest on U.S. Route 302. You may want to take a look at the Rock of Ages quarry and Hope Cemetery in Barre. Spend the night in Stowe, Burlington, or Sugarbush Valley.

Day 7   Visit the Shelburne Museum south of Burlington, then follow U.S. Route 7 south through Middlebury and the Middlebury Gap to Hancock, on Vermont Route 100. Drive south on Route 100, perhaps with a detour to Woodstock or Plymouth. Stay the night in Woodstock, Weston, or Grafton.

Day 8   Spend today exploring the beautiful villages of southern Vermont: Manchester, Dorset, Grafton, Newfane, Weston. Spend the night in any one of these.

Day 9   From Manchester, go south along U.S. Route 7 via Arlington to Bennington for a visit to Old Bennington, the Bennington Battle Monument, and Bennington Museum. If you have the time, you can slip across the state line to see Williamstown, Mass., and the wonderful Clark Art Institute. Stay the night in Bennington.

Day 10   Go east along Vermont Route 9, the Molly Stark Trail, via Marlboro to Brattleboro, perhaps with a detour to Newfane for lunch. Continue via Keene, N.H., and Mount Monadnock back to Boston.

8. WHERE TO STAY

In the lodging recommendations, you'll find the full mailing address, with the ZIP (postal) code, so that you can write ahead for reservations. Telephone numbers, and a toll-free reservation number if the hotel has one, are included. The hotel or motel room you rent (but not bed-and-breakfast or country-inn rooms) will normally be air conditioned and will have a private bath and a color cable TV set. The room may have either one or two double or queen-size beds in it (single beds are rare), and note that prices are for the room, not for each bed.

DISCOUNTS   Most large hotels in cities charge less for rooms on weekends, when business travelers are not in town, than for the busy weekdays. If a hotel does not offer simple, **low weekend rates,** it may offer a special mini-vacation deal whereby guests get 2 nights (Friday and Saturday), plus some credit toward meals and drinks in the hotel's restaurants and bars, at one low price. A $180-a-night double might be $110 per night for the 2-day period from 5pm Friday to checkout time on Sunday, with perhaps $30 credit toward drinks and dinners, or maybe a free sightseeing tour of the city. These mini-vacation programs and rates vary from year to year and from hotel to hotel, so it's best to call or write ahead for full details.

   Some city hotels and motels offer **discounts to senior citizens** who have proper identification, such as a membership card in the American Association of Retired Persons (AARP). Ask about this if you qualify. These rates are usually offered at times when business is a bit slack, such as on weekends, in summer, in early January and in late winter.

BED & BREAKFAST GUESTHOUSES   The bed-and-breakfast house, long popular in Europe, is sweeping America as travelers discover that they can get charming accommodations at a B&B. Some houses have a half-dozen rooms, others only one or two; some serve a full, hearty sausage-and-eggs breakfast, others provide home-baked muffins and rolls; some guesthouses provide no breakfast. Rooms can be large or small, with a view or without—in short, nothing is standard. The only sure way to know what you're getting at a B&B is to look at the room yourself. I've chosen the houses recommended in this guide on grounds of general cleanliness, friendliness, price, location, and charm.

COUNTRY INNS   New England is justly famous for its country inns, delightfully cozy and hospitable or elegant and historic places to stay, often with very fine food. You should realize, however, that country inns are no longer the informal roadside "guesthouses" that they were a generation ago. Rather, they are more like small vacation resorts. Prices tend to be fairly hefty, and requirements for a stay can be complex, very much like those at a resort. For instance, one inn in Massachusetts charges $75 for a double room with bath in summer on Monday through Wednesday nights, but $120 for the same room on Thursday through Sunday. To these rates you must add 9.7% room tax, $3 for chamber service (required), and $8 if you use the fireplace in the room. All in all, that comes to over $94 for the "$75" Monday-through-Wednesday room, or $144 for the "$120" Thursday-through-Sunday room.

   You may have to reserve well ahead for a country-inn room, particularly if you wish to stay during foliage season or when there's some big event nearby. The innkeeper may require a minimum stay of 2, 3, 4, or even more days, with payment in cash (see below).

City hotels offer weekend packages, since the business trade disappears on weekends. But for country inns, weekends are the busy time. What you want to do is plan your city visits for weekends (or at least partly so), and spend Monday through Thursday out in the country.

Inn brochures paint rosy pictures of the warm welcome you're bound to receive, and of the friendliness and hospitality of your hosts. But innkeepers are in the lodging business, and they must make a profit, so they make certain stipulations that you must know about. If you make a reservation and put down a deposit, and the inn or hotel accepts your deposit and confirms your reservation, you have made a legal contract. However, it is usually the inn that spells out the terms of the contract, and this can lead to unpleasant—and sometimes costly—surprises.

When making reservations, you can avoid hassles and disappointments by asking the following questions: Is smoking allowed in the inn? Are children welcome? What age? What about pets? Is there a requirement for a minimum stay of 2, 3, 4 nights, or even more? Can you reserve a precise room or sort of room ("with antiques," "in the main inn and not in the annex," "with a canopy bed and full bath," "with a view of the water") or must you take whatever the innkeeper gives you? How many beds does the room have? Real beds or sofa beds? Can you get all this in writing?

Are meals included or required? If breakfast is included, is it store-bought doughnuts and instant coffee, or freshly made French pastries and brewed café au lait? If the inn has no dining room, how close is the nearest restaurant?

Is there a service charge? Is there tax? How much? Are there any other charges, such as for activities or use of a fireplace? They might not tell you if you don't ask.

Are credit cards accepted? Never assume that they are! Many of the most popular inns refuse to accept credit cards, preferring not to pay the 2% to 6% service charge to the credit-card company. They require cash, traveler's checks, or an approved personal check, sometimes for the full amount of your reservation, which might approach $1,000; and sometimes the full amount must be paid upon arrival. Be prepared. (The majority of lodgings listed in this guide do accept credit cards.)

How much deposit must you send, and how soon? Under what circumstances can you ask for, and get, a refund of your deposit? What if you are delayed in transit by car problems, a late train or ferry, or weather conditions impossible for flying?

Does the deposit guarantee you a room at the inn absolutely, or does the innkeeper have the option of finding you "equivalent lodgings nearby" if the inn is overbooked?

If your deposit is to be returned, will a "service charge" of 10% to 25% be deducted? What is the deadline for the innkeeper's return of the deposit? Two weeks? Two years?

Paying attention to details such as these is tedious, but it's necessary if you want to have a hassle-free vacation.

PETS Pets are not allowed in the majority of hotels, inns, motels, and guesthouses recommended in this book. If a hotel or inn does accept pets, we've mentioned this in the text. No mention of pets means that no pets are accepted.

ADVANCE RESERVATIONS At certain times of year, rooms in New England's hotels and inns are in high demand, and you may not be able to get the room you want in the establishment you want unless you reserve it well in advance. The busiest periods are high summer (mid-July through Labor Day), foliage season (mid-September through Columbus Day), Christmas and New Year's Eve, and ski season (late January through March). Low seasons, when business is slack and many inns may be closed, are April, May, and late October through late December.

CAMPING New England has many campsites in local, state, and national parks and forests, and on private land. Often there are private campgrounds near popular public ones; for example, there may be several private campgrounds just outside a state or national park which offers camping. Most campgrounds, both public and private, are open from sometime in May through mid- or late October, and a few private campgrounds stay open all year.

In summer, most campsites, including some fairly remote ones, fill up quickly on weekends, and they may also be full on weekdays during July and August. Reservations can be made at some public and virtually all private campsites; usually you must send a deposit to secure the reservation. If you don't (or can't) reserve in advance, plan to arrive early on a weekday to find and hold a spot. For weekends, arrive by mid-morning Friday, or, even better, Thursday afternoon. It is usually easy to find a vacant campsite on weekdays in late spring and early autumn, but weekends may be as crowded as summer.

Campsites in public parks and forests are usually simple, consisting of a place to park, flat ground upon which to pitch a tent, a picnic table, and a stone fireplace. Some have facilities for hot showers; most have washbasins with hot and cold water, and flush toilets. Some forest campsites are very basic, with just parking places and tent sites, a drinking water tap, and chemical or composting toilets. Fees for using public campsites range from $8 to $18 per site.

Private campgrounds tend to have less open space, fewer shade trees, more facilities, and higher fees. Some "resort" campgrounds have children's playgrounds, swimming pools, games rooms, cable television and VCR movie rooms, lake swimming and boating facilities, and so on. Virtually all private campgrounds provide hot showers and hookups (electrical, sewage, water) for recreational vehicles and trailers (caravans). Fees can range from $15 to $30 or more, depending upon the number of people in your party, and the facilities used.

See also "Recreation Vehicle Rentals" under "Getting Around," above.

 NEW ENGLAND

Banks Most banks are open Monday to Friday 9am to 3pm, and many have extended hours, until 5pm (or even 8 or 9pm on Thursday), and Saturday 9am to 2pm or later. All banks are closed Sunday except currency-exchange booths at Boston's Logan airport. Most banks and supermarkets and shopping malls have Automatic Teller Machines (ATMs) for after-hour transactions. If you have a bank card, you can obtain cash from an ATM that is on the same network (PLUS, Cirrus, etc.). If you have a major credit card (American Express, MasterCard/Access/EuroCard, or VISA) you may be able to obtain cash from an ATM. Ask anyone for the location of the nearest ATM or call one of the major ATM networks: Cirrus (tel. toll free 800/424-7787) or PLUS (tel. toll free 800/843-7587).

Business Hours Business hours in public and private offices are usually Monday to Friday 8 or 9am to 5pm. Most stores are open Monday to Saturday 9:30 or 10am to 5:30 or 6pm; many are also open Sunday 11am or noon to 5pm. All cities and large towns have at least a few "convenience stores" for food, beverages, newspapers, and some household items; many are open 24 hours. In cities, most supermarkets stay open from 8 or 9am to 9 or 10pm, with shorter hours Sunday; some are open almost 24 hours a day. For bank hours see "Banks," above.

Climate See "When to Go," earlier in this chapter.

Crime See "Safety," below.

Driving Rules See "Getting Around," earlier in this chapter.

Emergencies In major cities dial 911 from any telephone (no coin needed at pay telephones/call boxes) to contact the local police, fire department, or ambulance. In areas without 911 service, dial "0" (zero) to reach an operator who will direct your call to the proper emergency service. Local numbers for emergency services are also listed on the inside front cover of most telephone directories.

The Travelers Aid Society, 711 Atlantic Ave. (at 17 East St.), Boston, MA 02111 (tel. 617/542-7286) is non-profit social service agency that is dedicated to helping travelers solve problems large and small. Professional staff members provide crisis intervention counseling, referrals to community resources, and emergency financial assistance to travelers in crisis. Travelers Aid volunteers at Logan airport (tel. 617/567-5385) and the Greyhound Bus Terminal (tel. 617/542-9875) will help you find an address, a hospital, lost luggage, a way to get money from home, or the solution to any other travel dilemma.

Gasoline   See "Getting Around," above.

Health Services   All cities in New England have hospitals; blue signs bearing a white "H" mark the way. Boston is one of the country's most renowned medical centers, with dozens of hospitals and medical facilities. To use most of the facilities, however, you will need health insurance, since prices for services are astronomical. A 3-day stay in a hospital can cost more than $1,000 just for the room and basic services; medical procedures and doctors' fees might cost several thousand more.

Hitchhiking   See "Getting Around," earlier in this chapter.

Holidays   See "When to Go," earlier in this chapter.

Information   See "Sources of Information," earlier in this chapter, and specific chapters for local information offices.

Laundry   Every city and town in New England has several Laundromats where you can wash and dry your clothes in automatic machines for a few dollars. Many are located in small suburban shopping centers. Laundry detergent is usually available from vending machines.

Liquor Laws   In Maine, New Hampshire, and Vermont, liquor is sold in government-operated stores only; in Connecticut, Massachusetts, and Rhode Island, liquor is sold privately. Liquor is not sold on Sunday, though most restaurants and bars with liquor licenses may serve liquor by the drink on Sunday. The minimum age for drinking varies by state, but in most it is 18 years. A few towns in New England, such as Rockport, Mass., are "dry," which means that no shop, restaurant, or hotel may sell liquor, but it is not illegal to bring in your own liquor and drink it. You serve yourself in restaurants.

Restaurants have either a full liquor license (for liquor, wine, and beer), a wine and beer license, or no license. At some restaurants that have no license, you can bring your own liquor. Others do not allow this.

It is illegal to drink alcohol in public areas such as streets, parks, and benches. If you are discreet, you can usually have wine or beer with your picnic.

Mail   See "Post Offices," below.

Maps   See "Getting Around," earlier in this chapter.

Newspapers/Magazines   Each of the larger cities in New England has its own daily newspaper. The *Boston Globe* and the *Boston Herald* are distributed throughout New England, as is the *New York Times*, and, in most cities, the *Washington Post*. The national newspapers *USA Today* and the *Christian Science Monitor* are also available. You can also buy the *International Herald Tribune* at Boston's Logan airport and at some newsstands in larger cities.

Police   In an emergency, dial 911.

Post Offices   Most post offices are open Monday to Friday 8am to 5pm, Saturday 8am to noon or 2pm. A few major post offices stay open until 5:30 or 6pm, and the post office at Boston's Logan airport stays open until midnight. To receive mail at a post office, have it sent to you c/o General Delivery in the town where you would like to pick up your mail. Specify the name of the post office where you would like to pick up your mail; if in doubt, write "Main Post Office." You'll need to show identification, such as a passport or driver's license, to pick up your mail.

Safety   Whenever you're traveling in an unfamiliar city or country, stay alert. Be aware of your immediate surroundings. Wear a moneybelt and keep a close eye on your possessions. Be particularly careful with cameras, purses, and wallets, all favorite targets of thieves and pickpockets.

Taxes   Taxes on hotel rooms, restaurant meals, some transportation services, and purchases in general are levied by each state and by some cities. Taxes on rooms, meals, and other prices (which can be as high as 11% or 12%) are not included in the price, but in this book, most prices include taxes. Here are the current tax rates by state: Connecticut, 8%; Maine, 6% (7% on lodging); Massachusetts, 5% (9.7% on lodging); New Hampshire, 8%; Rhode Island, 7% (12% on lodging); and Vermont, 6% (8% on rooms and meals).

Tipping   Tips are generally 10% to 20% of the price. If service is not particularly good, leave 10%; for very good service, 15% to 20%. Use the following guidelines for tipping: bartender, 10% to 15%; bellhop, 50¢ to $1 per piece; checkroom attendant, 50¢ to $1 per garment; doorman, $1 for calling a cab, getting your car from a parking lot, or other direct service; hairdresser, barber, 15%; chamber service, $2 to $5 for a stay of several days; parking-lot attendant, $1 if car is brought to you; porter, 50¢ to $1 per piece of luggage; restaurant or nightclub, 15% to 20%; taxi driver, 15% of fare.

Tourist Offices   See "Sources of Information," earlier in this chapter, and the specific chapters for local offices.

CHAPTER 3

FOR FOREIGN VISITORS

Although American fads and fashions have spread across Europe and other parts of the world so that America may seem like familiar territory before your arrival, there are still many peculiarities and uniquely American situations that any foreign visitor will encounter.

1. PREPARING FOR YOUR TRIP

For detailed information, see "Sources of Information" in Chapter 2, and specific chapters.

ENTRY REQUIREMENTS

DOCUMENTS   Canadian nationals need only proof of Canadian residence to visit the United States. Citizens of Great Britain and Japan need only a current passport. Citizens of other countries, including Australia and New Zealand, usually need two documents: a valid **passport** with an expiration date at least 6 months later than the scheduled end of their visit to the United States and a **tourist visa** available at no charge from a United States embassy or consulate.

To get a tourist or business visa to enter the United States, contact the nearest American embassy or consulate in your country; if there is none, you will have to apply in person in a country where there is a United States embassy or consulate. Present your passport, a passport-size photo of yourself, and a completed application, which is available through the embassy or consulate. You may be asked to provide information about how you plan to finance your trip or show a letter of invitation from a friend with whom you plan to stay. Those applying for a business visa may be asked to show evidence that they will not receive a salary in the United States. Be sure to check the length of stay on your visa; usually it is 6 months. If you want to stay longer, you may file for an extension with the Immigration and Naturalization Service once you are in the country. If permission to stay is granted, a new visa is not required unless you leave the United States and want to reenter.

MEDICAL REQUIREMENTS   No inoculations are needed to enter the United States unless you are coming from, or have stopped over in, an area known to be suffering from an epidemic, particularly cholera or yellow fever.

If you have a disease requiring treatment with medications containing narcotics or drugs requiring a syringe, carry a valid signed prescription from your physician to allay any suspicions that you are smuggling drugs.

CUSTOMS REQUIREMENTS   Every adult visitor may bring in, free of duty: 1 liter of wine or hard liquor; 200 cigarettes or 100 cigars (but no cigars from Cuba) or 3 pounds of smoking tobacco; $100 worth of gifts. These exemptions are offered to travelers who spend at least 72 hours in the United States and who have not claimed them within the preceding 6 months. It is altogether forbidden to bring into the country foodstuffs (particularly cheese, fruit, cooked meats, and canned goods) and plants (vegetables, seeds, tropical plants, and so on). Foreign tourists may bring in or take out up to $10,000 in United States or foreign currency with no formalities; larger sums must be declared to Customs on entering or leaving.

INSURANCE

Unlike most other countries there is no national health system in the United States. Because the cost of medical care is extremely high, every traveler should secure health coverage before setting out. You may want to take out a comprehensive travel policy that covers (for a relatively low premium) loss of, or theft of your baggage; trip-cancellation costs; guarantee of bail in case you are arrested; sickness or injury costs (medical, surgical, and hospital); costs of accident, repatriation, or death. Such packages (for example, "Europe Assistance" in Europe) are sold by automobile clubs at attractive rates, as well as by insurance companies and travel agencies.

---

2. GETTING TO THE U.S.

Travelers from overseas can take advantage of the **APEX (Advance-Purchase Excursion) fares** offered by all the major United States and European carriers. Aside from these, attractive values are offered by **Icelandair** on flights from Luxembourg to New York and by **Virgin Atlantic** from London to New York/Newark.

Some large American airlines (for example, TWA, American Airlines, Northwest, United, and Delta) offer travelers—on their transatlantic or transpacific flights— special discount tickets under the name **Visit USA,** allowing travel between any United States destinations at minimum rates. They are not on sale in the United States, and must, therefore, be purchased before you leave your foreign point of departure. This system is the best, easiest, and fastest way to see the United States at low cost. You should obtain information well in advance from your travel agent or the office of the airline concerned, since the conditions attached to these discount tickets can be changed without advance notice.

The visitor arriving by air, no matter what the port of entry, should cultivate patience and resignation before setting foot on United States soil. Getting through immigration control may take as long as 2 hours on some days, especially summer weekends. Add the time it takes to clear Customs and you will see that you should make very generous allowance for delay in planning connections between international and domestic flights—an average of 2 to 3 hours at least.

In contrast, for the traveler arriving by car or by rail from Canada, the border-crossing formalities have been streamlined practically to the vanishing point. And for the traveler by air from Canada, Bermuda, and some places in the Caribbean, you can sometimes go through Customs and Immigration at the point of departure, which is much quicker and less painful.

For further information about travel to and around New England, see "Getting There" and "Getting Around" in Chapter 2.

FAST FACTS ~ FOR THE FOREIGN TRAVELER

Abbreviations In printed text you may see the names of the six New England states abbreviated as Ct. or Conn., Ma. or Mass., Me. (Maine), N.H., R.I., and Vt. In postal addresses the proper abbreviations are CT, MA, ME, NH, RI, and VT. By the way, citizens of Massachusetts in general and Bostonians in particular are famous for abbreviating everything when speaking, especially their state's long Native American name. Massachusetts Avenue becomes "Mass. Ave.," Harvard Business School is "The 'B' School," Cape Cod is just "The Cape," and Martha's Vineyard is truncated to "The Vineyard." Even Boston's subway, officially the MBTA Rapid Transit System, becomes merely "The T."

Business Hours   **Banks** open weekdays from 9am to 3pm; although there's 24-hour access to the automatic tellers (ATMs) at most banks and other outlets. Generally, **offices** open weekdays from 9am to 5pm. **Stores** are open six days a week with many open on Sunday, too; department stores usually stay open until 9pm one day a week.

Climate   See "When to Go," Chapter 2.

Currency   The U.S. monetary system has a decimal base: one American **dollar** ($1) = 100 **cents** (100¢).

Dollar **bills** commonly come in $1 ("a buck"), $5, $10, $20, $50, and $100 denominations (the last two are not welcome when paying for small purchases and are not accepted in taxis or at subway ticket booths).

There are six coin denominations: 1¢ (one cent or "penny"); 5¢ (five cents or "nickel"); 10¢ (ten cents or "dime"); 25¢ (twenty-five cents or "quarter"); 50¢ (fifty cents or "half dollar"—rare); and the very rare—and prized by collectors—$1 piece (both the older, large silver dollar and the newer, small Susan B. Anthony coin).

Traveler's checks denominated in U.S. dollars are accepted without demur at most hotels, motels, restaurants, and large stores. But as any experienced traveler knows, the best place to change traveler's checks is at a bank.

Credit Cards are the method of payment most widely used: VISA (BarclayCard in Britain), MasterCard (EuroCard in Europe, Access in Britain, Diamond in Japan), American Express, Diners Club, Carte Blanche, Discover, and Transmedia, in descending order of acceptance. You can save yourself trouble by using "plastic" rather than cash or traveler's checks in 95% of all hotels, motels, restaurants, and retail stores. A credit card can serve as a deposit for renting a car, as proof of identity (often carrying more weight than a passport), or as a "cash card," enabling you to draw money from banks that accept them.

Currency Exchange   **Thomas Cook Currency Services** (formerly Deak International) offers a wide variety of services: more than 100 currencies, commission-free traveler's checks, drafts and wire transfers, check collections, and precious metal bars and coins. Rates are competitive and service excellent. Call toll free 800/582-4496 for information. Many hotels will exchange currency if you are a registered guest.

Note: The "foreign-exchange bureaus" so common in Europe are rare even at airports in the United States and nonexistent outside major cities. Try to avoid changing foreign money, or traveler's checks denominated in other than United States dollars, at small-town banks, or even at branches in a big city; in fact leave any currency other than United States dollars at home—it may prove more nuisance to you than it's worth.

Drinking Laws   See "Fast Facts: New England" in Chapter 2.

Electric Current   The United States uses 110-120 volts, 60 cycles, compared to 220-240 volts, 50 cycles, as in most of Europe. Besides a 100-volt converter, small appliances of non-American manufacture, such as hairdryers or shavers, will require a plug adapter, with two flat, parallel pins.

Embassies/Consulates   All embassies are located in the national capital, Washington, D.C.; some consulates are located in major cities, and most nations have a mission to the United Nations in New York City.

Listed here are the embassies and consulates of the major English-speaking countries—Australia, Canada, Ireland, New Zealand, and the United Kingdom. If you are from another country, you can get the telephone number of your embassy by calling "information" in Washington, D.C. (tel. 202/555-1212).

Australia: The **embassy** is at 1601 Massachusetts Ave. NW, Washington, DC 20036 (tel. 202/797-3000). **Consulates** are located in the following cities: **Chicago**—Quaker Tower, 321 N. Clark St., Suite 2930, IL 60610 (tel. 312/645-9440); **Honolulu**—1000 Bishop St., Penthouse, HI 96813 (tel. 808/524-5050); **Houston**—3 Post Oak Central A.H., 1990 Post Oak Rd., Suite 800, TX 77056 (tel. 713/629-9131); **Los Angeles**—611 N. Larchmont Blvd., CA 90004 (tel. 213/469-4300); **New York**—International Building, 630 5th Ave., NY 10111 (tel. 212/245-4000); **San Francisco**—360 Post St., CA 94108 (tel. 415/362-6160).

Canada: The **embassy** is at 501 Pennsylvania Ave. NW, Washington, DC 20001 (tel. 202/682-1740). **Consulates** are located in the following cities: **Atlanta**—One CNN Center, Suite 400, South Tower, GA 30303 (tel. 404/577-6810); **Boston**—3 Copley Pl., Suite 400, MA 02116 (tel. 617/262-3760); **Buffalo**—One Marine Midland Center, Suite 3550, NY 14203 (tel. 716/852-1247); **Chicago**—310 S. Michigan Ave., Suite 1200, IL 60604 (tel. 312/616-1860); **Cleveland**—Illuminating Bldg., 55 Public Sq., OH 44113 (tel. 216/771-0150); **Dallas**—St. Paul Place, 750 N. St. Paul, Suite 1700, TX 75201 (tel. 214/922-9811); **Detroit**—660 Renaissance Center, Suite 1100, MI 48243 (tel. 313/567-2340); **Los Angeles**—300 Santa Grand Ave., 10th floor, CA 90071 (tel. 213/687-7432); **Minneapolis**—701 4th Ave. South, MN 55415 (tel. 612/333-4641); **New York**—1251 Ave. of the Americas, NY 10020 (tel. 212/768-2400); **San Francisco**—One Maritime Plaza, Golden Gateway Center, CA 94111 (tel. 415/495-6021); **Seattle**—412 Plaza 600, 6th and Stewart, WA 98101 (tel. 206/443-1777).

Ireland: The **embassy** is at 2234 Massachusetts Ave. NW, Washington, DC 20008 (tel. 202/462-3939). **Consulates** are located in the following cities: **Boston**—Chase Bldg., 535 Boylston St., MA 02116 (tel. 617/267-9330); **Chicago**—400 N. Michigan Ave., IL 60611 (tel. 312/337-1868); **New York**—515 Madison Ave., NY 10022 (tel. 212/319-2555); **San Francisco**—655 Montgomery St., Suite 930, CA 94111 (tel. 415/392-4214).

New Zealand: The **embassy** is at 37 Observatory Circle NW, Washington, DC 20008 (tel. 202/328-4800). A **consulate** is located in **Los Angeles**—Tishman Bldg., 10960 Wilshire Blvd., Suite 1530, Westwood, CA 90024 (tel. 310/477-8241).

United Kingdom: The **embassy** is at 3100 Massachusetts Ave. NW, Washington, DC 20008 (tel. 202/462-1340). **Consulates** are located in **Atlanta**—245 Peachtree Center Ave., Suite 912, GA 30303 (tel. 404/524-5856); **Chicago**—33 N. Dearborn St., IL 60602 (tel. 312/346-1810); **Houston**—601 Jefferson, Suite 2250, TX 77002 (tel. 713/659-6270); **Los Angeles**—11766 Wilshire Blvd., Suite 400, CA 90025 (tel. 310/477-3322); **New York**—845 3rd Ave., NY 10022 (tel. 212/745-0202).

Emergencies Call **911** for fire, police, and ambulance. If you encounter such traveler's problems as sickness, accident, or lost or stolen baggage, call **Travelers Aid,** an organization that specializes in helping distressed travelers whether American or foreign. Check the local telephone directory for the nearest office.

Holidays On the following national legal holidays, banks, government offices, post offices, and many stores, restaurants, and museums are closed: January 1 (New Year's Day), third Monday in January (Martin Luther King Day), third Monday in February (Presidents Day), last Monday in May (Memorial Day), July 4 (Independence Day), first Monday after first Sunday in September (Labor Day), second Monday in October (Columbus Day), November 11 (Veterans Day/Armistice Day), fourth Thursday in November (Thanksgiving Day), and December 25 (Christmas Day).

The Tuesday following the first Monday in November, Election Day, is a legal holiday in presidential-election years.

Information See "Sources of Information," in Chapter 2.

Legal Aid If you are stopped for a minor infraction (for example, of the highway code, such as speeding), never attempt to pay the fine directly to a police officer; you may be arrested on the much more serious charge of attempted bribery. Pay fines by mail, or directly into the hands of the clerk of the court. If accused of a more serious offense, it is wise to say and do nothing before consulting a lawyer.

Under U.S. law, an arrested person is allowed one telephone call to a party of his or her choice. Call your embassy or consulate.

Liquor Laws See "Fast Facts: New England," in Chapter 2.

Mail Mailboxes are blue, and carry the inscription "U.S. MAIL." For further details, see "Post Offices," in "Fast Facts: New England," in Chapter 2.

Newspapers/Magazines The *New York Times,* widely available in large cities, and the magazines *Newsweek* and *Time* cover world news. Most magazine racks at drugstores, airports, and hotels stock a selection of foreign periodicals, such as *Stern,* the *Economist,* and *Le Monde.* For more details see "Fast Facts: New England," in Chapter 2.

Radio and Television There are dozens of radio stations (both AM and FM), each broadcasting talk shows, continuous news, or a particular kind of music—classical, country, jazz, pop, gospel—punctuated by frequent commercials. Television, with three coast-to-coast networks—ABC, CBS, and NBC—joined in recent years by the Public Broadcasting System (PBS) and a growing network of cable channels, plays a major part in American life.

Safety Whenever you're traveling in an unfamiliar city or country, stay alert. Be aware of your immediate surroundings. Wear a moneybelt and don't flash expensive jewelry and cameras in public. This will minimize the possibility of your becoming a crime victim. Be alert even in heavily touristed areas.

Taxes In the U.S. there is no VAT (Value-Added Tax) or other indirect tax at a national level. Every state, and each city in it, is allowed to levy its own local tax on all purchases, including hotel and restaurant checks, airline tickets, and so on. These taxes are not refundable.

Telephone, Telegraph, Telex, and Fax Pay phones can be found on street corners, as well as in bars, restaurants, public buildings, stores, and service stations. Local calls in New England cost 10¢.

For **long-distance or international calls,** stock up with a supply of quarters; the pay phone will instruct you when you should put them into the slot. For long-distance calls in the U.S., dial 1 followed by the area code and number you want. For direct overseas calls, first dial 011, followed by the country code (Australia, 61; Republic of Ireland, 353; New Zealand, 64; United Kingdom, 44; and so on), then by the city code (for example, 71 or 81 for London, 21 for Birmingham) and the number of the person you wish to call.

Before calling from a hotel room, always ask the hotel phone operator if there are any telephone surcharges. These are best avoided by using a public phone, calling collect, or using a telephone charge card.

For **reversed-charge or collect calls,** and for **person-to-person calls,** dial 0 (zero, not the letter "O") followed by the area code and number you want; an operator will then come on the line and you should specify that you are calling collect, or person-to-person, or both. If your operator-assisted call is international, ask for the overseas operator.

For local directory assistance ("Information"), dial 411; for long-distance information dial 1, then the appropriate area code and 555-1212.

Like the telephone system, **telegraph** and **telex** services are provided by private corporations like ITT, MCI, and above all, Western Union office (there are hundreds across the country), or dictate it over the phone (a toll-free call, 800/325-6000). You can also telegraph money, or have it telegraphed to you very quickly over the Western Union system.

Most hotels have **fax** machines available to their customers (ask if there is a charge to use it). You will also see signs for public faxes in the windows of small shops.

Time The U.S. is divided into six time zones. From east to west, these are: Eastern Standard Time (EST), Central Standard Time (CST), Mountain Standard Time (MST), Pacific Standard Time (PST), Alaska Standard Time (AST), and Hawaii Standard Time (HST). Always keep the changing time zones in mind if you are traveling (or even telephoning) long distances in the U.S. For example, noon in Boston (EST) is 11am in Chicago (CST), 10am in Denver (MST), 9am in Los Angeles (PST),

8am in Anchorage (AST), and 7am in Honolulu (HST). When it is noon in London (GMT, or Greenwich Mean Time), it is 7am in Boston.

Daylight Savings Time is in effect from 1am on the first Sunday in April until 2am on the last Sunday in October, except in Arizona, Hawaii, part of Indiana, and Puerto Rico.

Tipping   See "Fast Facts: New England," in Chapter 2.

Toilets   Often euphemistically referred to as "restrooms," public toilets are nonexistent on the streets of American cities. They can be found, though, in bars, restaurants, hotel lobbies, museums, department stores, and service stations—and will probably be clean (although ones in the last-mentioned sometimes leave much to be desired). Note, however, that some restaurants and bars display a notice TOILETS ARE FOR USE OF PATRONS ONLY. You can ignore this sign, or better yet, avoid arguments by paying for a cup of coffee or soft drink, which will qualify you as a patron. The cleanliness of toilets at railroad stations and bus depots may be questionable; some public places are equipped with pay toilets that require you to insert one or two dimes (10¢) or a quarter (25¢) into a slot on the door before it will open. In restrooms with attendants, leaving at least a 25¢ tip is customary.

Yellow Pages   The local phone company provides two kinds of telephone directory. The general directory, called the "white pages," lists subscribers (business and personal residences) in alphabetical order. The inside front cover lists emergency numbers for police, fire, and ambulance, and other vital numbers (such as the Coast Guard, poison control center, crime-victims hotline, and so on). The first few pages have community-service numbers, and a guide to long-distance and international calling, complete with country codes and area codes.

The second directory, the "yellow pages," lists all local services, businesses, and industries alphabetically by type, with an index at the back. The listings cover not only such obvious items as automobile repairs by make of car, or drugstores (pharmacies), often by geographical location, but also restaurants by type of cuisine and geographical location, bookstores by special subject and/or language, places of worship by religious denomination, and other information that the tourist might otherwise not readily find. The yellow pages often also include city plans or detailed area maps, often showing postal ZIP codes and public transportation.

THE AMERICAN SYSTEM OF MEASUREMENTS
LENGTH

1 inch (in.)			=	2.54cm		
1 foot (ft.)	=	12 in.	=	30.48cm	=	.305m
1 yard (yd.)	=	3 ft.			=	.915m
1 mile	=	5,280 ft.			=	1.609km

To convert miles to kilometers, multiply the number of miles by 1.61. Also use to convert speeds from miles per hour (m.p.h.) to kilometers per hour (kmph).
To convert kilometers to miles, multiply the number of kilometers by .62. Also use to convert kmph to m.p.h.

CAPACITY

1 fluid ounce (fl. oz).			=	.03 liters		
1 pint	=	16 fl. oz.	=	.47 liters		
1 quart	=	2 pints	=	.94 liters		
1 gallon (gal.)	=	4 quarts	=	3.79 liters	=	.83 Imperial gal.

To convert U.S. gallons to liters, multiply the number of gallons by 3.79.

To convert liters to U.S. gallons, multiply the number of liters by .26.

To convert U.S. gallons to Imperial gallons, multiply the number of U.S. gallons by .83.

To convert Imperial gallons to U.S. gallons, multiply the number of Imperial gallons by 1.2.

WEIGHT

```
1 ounce (oz.)                  =   28.35g
1 pound (lb.)   =   16 oz.  =   453.6g   =   .45kg
1 ton                          =   2,000 lb.  =   907kg   =   .91 metric tons
```

To convert pounds to kilograms, multiply the number of pounds by .45.

To convert kilograms to pounds, multiply the number of kilograms by 2.2.

AREA

```
1 acre                      =   .41ha
1 square mile   =   640 acres   =   259ha   =   2.6km²
```

To convert acres to hectares, multiply the number of acres by .41.

To convert hectares to acres, multiply the number of hectares by 2.47.

To convert square miles to square kilometers, multiply the number of square miles by 2.6.

To convert square kilometers to square miles, multiply the number of square kilometers by .39.

TEMPERATURE

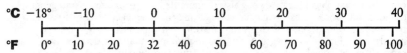

To convert degrees Fahrenheit to degrees Celsius, subtract 32 from °F, multiply by 5, then divide by 9 (example: 85°F − 32 × 5/9 = 29.4°C).

To convert degrees Celsius to degrees Fahrenheit, multiply °C by 9, divide by 5, and add 32 (example: 20°C × 9/5 + 32 = 68°F).

CHAPTER 4

BOSTON

"**B**oston is the Hub of the Universe," or at least that's what many people remembered Dr. Oliver Wendell Holmes as saying. Actually, his statement about his beloved city was less ambitious: "Boston State-house is the hub of the solar system." No matter, because to Bostonians their city is still The Hub, the center of the world. And though outsiders may quibble about its being the Hub of the Universe, they must accept the fact that Boston is and always has been the capital of New England. The Pilgrims settled on the shores of Massachusetts Bay in the 1620s, and the other great cities of the six-state region were offshoots from this early colony: Thomas Hooker, the man who founded Hartford, went there from Cambridge in 1636, and about the same time Roger Williams fled the area to found Providence. The pattern of arriving in Boston and then pushing on into the hills beyond was to be a permanent feature of New England life, and consequently, today the city is a rich mixture of ethnic neighborhoods. Immigrants from all over the world arrived at Boston's docks and established communities of their own within the city. Second-generation immigrants then moved out across the state and across the nation.

What gives Bostonians the idea they're special? Well, theirs was the first large town in the region, first in resistance to British measures that brought on the Revolution, and first in science and culture during the 19th and early 20th centuries. Their city is the home of the Boston Celtics (basketball), the Boston Bruins (ice hockey), the Boston Red Sox (baseball), as well as the Boston Pops Orchestra.

The city of Boston itself is a fairly small area with a population of something over 600,000. But if one adds in the populations of the neighboring cities Cambridge, Somerville, Charlestown, Chelsea, Brookline, and so on, the total population in Greater Boston comes to about three million. And yet Boston is one of the most livable and manageable cities in the world, with the big-city economic and cultural resources, but small-city spirit and pace of life.

1. ORIENTATION

ARRIVING

As major American cities go, Boston is eminently approachable. The airport is less than a 15-minute taxi or subway ride from the center of the city. The train station is

NEIGHBORHOODS:

Back Bay 4
Beacon Hill 5
Boston Common &
 Public Garden 6
Chinatown 7
Downtown Crossing 8
Faneuil Hall Marketplace 9
Financial District 10
Government Center 11
Haymarket 12
Huntington Av. & the Fens 13

Kenmore Square 14
The North End 15
Prudential Center 16
South End 18
Waterfront 17

VISITOR CENTERS:

Boston Common Visitor
 Information Center **1**
Prudential Visitor Center **2**
Visitor Center **3**

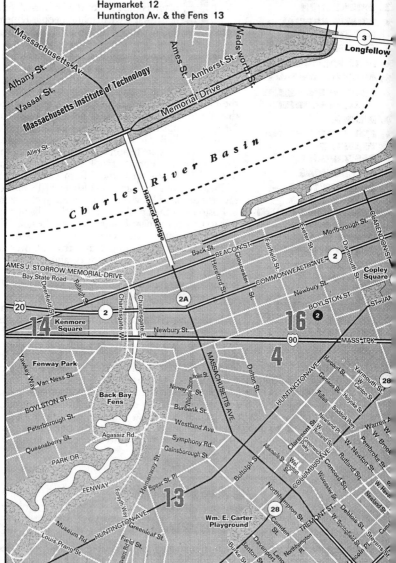

BOSTON ORIENTATION

Playground

New Charles
River Dam & Locks

JOHN F. FITZGERALD EXPWY.

Charlestown
Bridge

COMMERCIAL ST.

Charter St.

Hull St.

Sheafe St.

Prince St.

15

Hanover
Ave.

NASHUA ST.

Lomansey Way

CHARLES ST.

CAUSEWAY ST.

N. WASHINGTON ST.

Thacher St.

Haverhill St.

Canal St.

Friend St.

Portland St.

N. Margin St.

Endicott St.

Salem St.

HANOVER ST.

N. Bennet St.

Garden St.

Richmond St.

Commercial St.

Fulton St.

1A

ATLANTIC AVE.

17

MERRIMAC ST.

New Chardon St.

Sudbury St.

CONGRESS ST.

Stone St.

North St.

12

Chatham St.

STATE ST.

9

Commercial St.

Indian Mill St.

Central St.

Mill St.

E. India
Row

Waterfront
Park

Blossom St.

W.M. Cardinal O'Connell Way

Bank
ound

Fruit St.

Parkman St.

Grove St.

CAMBRIDGE ST.

Irving St.

Russell St.

Ridgeway La.

Hancock St.

Temple St.

Bowdoin St.

Somerset St.

11

COURT ST.

Tremont St.

School St.

Washington St.

King St.

Battery St.

Broad St.

Batterymarch St.

Phillips St.

Revere St.

5

Myrtle St.

Pinckney St.

Joy St.

Mt. Vernon St.

Walnut St.

BEACON ST.

3

Bromfield St.

Franklin St.

River St.

Branch St.

Spruce St.

ut St.

Byron St.

2

CHARLES ST.

Boston Common

6

1

WINTER ST.

Temple Pl.

West St.

Mason St.

Avery St.

Chauncy St.

8

10

SUMMER ST.

Purchase St.

1 **3**

Northern Ave.

93

Public
Garden

Boston
Park Plaza

STUART ST.

Eliot Pl.

ESSEX ST.

Oxford

Edinboro

Beach St.

Lincoln St.

Utica St.

South St.

Kneeland St.

ATLANTIC AVE.

DORCHESTER AVE.

Melcher St.

Fort Point Channel

STON ST.

ARLINGTON ST.

CHARLES ST. S.

HARRISON AVE.

7

93

Wormond
St.

Lawrence St.

Midway St.

Richard St.

EAST BERKELEY ST.

EMONT ST.

Dwight St.

Milford St.

Hanson St.

Waltham St.

SHAWMUT AVE.

Bradford St.

Park

WASHINGTON ST.

Union Park St.

Malden St.

Wareham St.

one

Plympton St.

klin
are

HARRISON AVE.

E. Dedham St.

E. Canton St.

Brookline St.

3

W. 4th St.

W. 1st St.

W. 2nd St.

Athens St.

Silver St.

A St.

B St.

W. 5th St.

Bolton St.

W. 3rd St.

W. BROADWAY

Flaherty Way

Silver St.

right downtown, as are the two bus terminals. But once you get here, Boston's famous twisty colonial streets take over, and Boston's notoriously careless drivers threaten, so read the sections below carefully.

BY PLANE

Boston's **Logan International Airport** (tel. toll free 800/235-6426) is one of the busiest in the country, but it is well organized, and has the advantage of being very near the center of the city, as airports go. After you get your bags, look for the signs to buses, taxis, and "limo," and after a few steps you'll see the stops.

Getting Downtown

BY SUBWAY The **Massport Shuttle Bus** (run by the Massachusetts Port Authority) runs the airport loop, and is free. The bus goes to all the terminals and to the MBTA "Airport" subway stop, where you can take a Blue Line train downtown. The subway into town costs 85¢, and a person in a booth will make change for you except during late-night hours. Trains run every 8 to 12 minutes from 5:30am to 1am; the ride takes only 10 minutes. Some of the hotels recommended in this book are within a few blocks of the Government Center stop, but for most places you'll have to change at Government Center from the Blue Line to Green Line trains bound for Boston College, Cleveland Circle, Riverside, or Arborway (all of which pass near the hotels recommended). For Cambridge, take the Blue Line to Government Center, then the Green Line to Park Street (1 stop), and change to the Red Line for Harvard or Alewife. It's a fairly long haul to Cambridge, with these two subway transfers.

BY WATER SHUTTLE Vehicular traffic through the tunnels connecting the airport to Boston has become very heavy in recent years. One innovative solution to the problem is the **Airport Water Shuttle** (tel. 330-8680) service between the airport's own dock and Rowe's Wharf, on Atlantic Avenue in downtown Boston. A one-way ticket for the 7-minute shuttle boat costs $8 for adults, $4 for seniors, children under 12 free. Trips run every 15 minutes between 6am and 8pm on weekdays, every ½ hour from noon to 8pm on Sunday and holidays. There is no service on Saturday, July 4, Thanksgiving, Christmas, or New Year's Day. From Rowe's Wharf it's only a few blocks to South Station's train, subway, and bus stations.

BY LIMO The **Airways Transportation Company**'s minibuses (160 Ipswich St., tel. 267-2981) will take you from the airport (all terminals) to any downtown hotel for $7.50 per person. The minibuses operate every day from 7am to 7pm running every half hour, 7pm to 10pm running on the hour, and stopping at the "Bus Stop" signs outside each terminal.

    Hudson Bus Lines and **Hudson Limousine Service** (tel. 395-8080) have scheduled service to downtown Boston and to the suburbs.

BY TAXI A taxi from Logan airport to downtown Boston will cost between $8 and $12 for the ride, plus $1 toll, plus excess-baggage charge (if any), plus tip. Figure $10 to $15 altogether.

Getting Beyond Boston

Chances are good that you won't be roaring straight through Boston on your way north, west, or south. But in case you are, you should know about these services to areas outside Boston. If you have questions, you can call the Logan airport information office toll free at 800/235-6426:

    Share-a-Cab: In principle it works like this: Call the Massport Dispatcher (tel. toll free 800/235-6426), or simply pick up one of the special Share-a-Cab phones near the baggage-claim areas. Give your name and destination (any suburban community, but not Boston itself), and within 15 minutes you're on your way, sharing the expense of the cab with several other passengers going to, or near, the same destination. In practice this excellent idea has been languishing of late due to competition from suburban limo companies. You may or may not find that Share-a-Cab works for you. Best time to try is at rush hour, of course.

WHAT'S SPECIAL ABOUT BOSTON

Museums
- ☐ Museum of Fine Arts, one of America's best, noted especially for its collection of impressionist paintings.
- ☐ Gardner Museum, a Renaissance palace imported from Italy and stuffed with precious art by its eccentric owner.
- ☐ Computer Museum, with its amazing machines, old and new.

Parks & Gardens
- ☐ Boston Common, one of the country's oldest public parks.
- ☐ Public Garden, the flowery formal counterpart to the Common.
- ☐ The "Green Necklace," Frederick Law Olmsted's system of parks and verdant thoroughfares.
- ☐ Arnold Arboretum, Boston's "living collection" of plants from around the world.

Architectural Highlights
- ☐ Beacon Hill, its quaint streets lined with 19th-century Federal and Greek Revival town houses.
- ☐ Massachusetts State House (1798), Charles Bulfinch's gold-domed masterpiece.
- ☐ Faneuil Hall Marketplace, Boston's "stomach" in 1825, now restored (1970s) to be its "palate."
- ☐ Old North Church (1723), Boston's oldest, most graceful and historic.
- ☐ Trinity Church (1877), Henry Hobson Richardson's harmonious Romanesque Revival masterpiece.
- ☐ John Hancock Tower (1974), the towering mirror-glass rhomboid designed by I. M. Pei and Partners.
- ☐ Christian Science Center, with its dignified Mother Church, reflecting pool, and clean-lined tower.

Shopping
- ☐ Filene's Basement, the nation's first and best bargain-basement store.
- ☐ Downtown Crossing, Boston's commercial heart, for pedestrians only.
- ☐ Newbury Street, with its elegant and fashionable boutiques.

Events/Festivals
- ☐ Boston Pops concerts on the riverside Esplanade, especially the July 4th concert with cannons and fireworks.
- ☐ First Night, a New Year's Eve festival with ice sculpture, performances, and parades.
- ☐ Boston Marathon, the famous footrace run on Patriots Day (April 19).

Cool for Kids
- ☐ Swan Boat rides on the lake in the Public Garden, setting for the children's classic, *Make Way for Ducklings.*
- ☐ Children's Museum, designed especially for kids of all ages.
- ☐ Museum of Science, with lots of hands-on scientific and technical exhibits.
- ☐ New England Aquarium, a spellbinding undersea world on view.
- ☐ USS *Constitution*, "Old Ironsides," the mighty ship that battled the British in 1812.
- ☐ Boston Tea Party Ship & Museum, where kids can wander around a recreation of a revolutionary war–era ship.

Walking Tours
- ☐ The Freedom Trail, a downtown walking tour, taking you to many spots and sights important to American colonial and Revolutionary history.

LIMOUSINES TO EASTERN MASSACHUSETTS To Lexington, call Hudson Bus Lines or Hudson Limo Service at 617/395-8080; to Concord, call Townsend Limousine Service at 800/698-0006; to Plymouth or Hyannis, call the Plymouth & Brockton Street Railway Co. at 508/746-0378.

BUSES TO RHODE ISLAND   Bonanza Bus Lines (tel. 423-5810, or toll free 800/556-3815) goes from Logan airport right to Providence, a 1½-hour trip, daily every hour on the half hour between 8:30am and 10:30pm, with a final trip at 11:45pm.

BUSES TO NEW HAMPSHIRE   Concord Trailways (tel. 426-8080) will take you to Manchester, Concord, Lake Winnipesaukee, North Conway, Jackson, Glen, and Hanover, right from the airport.

BUSES TO VERMONT   Vermont Transit (tel. 423-5810, or toll free 800/451-3292) operates from the airport to New Hampshire, Vermont, and Montréal.

BY TRAIN

Amtrak trains operate into and out of Boston's **South Station** and/or **Back Bay Station** (tel. 617/482-3660 or toll free 800/USA-RAIL). If you plan to stay downtown or in Cambridge, take the Red Line subway from South Station inbound toward "Alewife." In 2 stops you'll be at Park Street for downtown hotels; if you stay on the Red Line you'll get to Harvard Square. The Back Bay Station is on the Orange Line subway. To reach the Red Line, travel 3 stops to the Downtown Crossing stop.

BY BUS

Boston has three bus stations. Many local, commuter, and regional bus lines operate from a bus area next to Amtrak's South Station. **Peter Pan Bus Lines,** 555 Atlantic Ave. (tel. 617/426-7838, 413/781-3320, or toll free 800/237-8747), is located in its own terminal in Dewey Square, just across the street from South Station. They offer service to and from Maine, New Hampshire, Connecticut, Rhode Island, and Massachusetts. To find your way downtown, look for the towering silver Federal Reserve Bank building, which resembles an enormous truck radiator. It's right in Dewey Square.

    Greyhound Lines has its own terminal at 10 St. James Ave. (tel. 423-5810) right downtown near Park Square, the theater district, the Public Garden, and many hotels. Information on service to Portland, Me., can be obtained by dialing 617/542-3520; to New York City, 617/542-2380; to Hartford, 617/542-2991. At the Greyhound Terminal, you're only 2 blocks from the Arlington (Green Line) subway station.

BY CAR

One of the country's most ambitious construction projects is currently under way right in the heart of Boston. The city's "Central Artery," the John F. Fitzgerald Expressway, is being put underground and a third tunnel is being dug across the harbor to connect Boston with East Boston and Logan International Airport. Construction detours are confusing, and delays may be long. The guidance given below is subject to change as construction progresses.

    The easiest and fastest way to enter Boston by car from the west is via the **Massachusetts Turnpike** ("Mass. Pike"), which goes right through Back Bay to the center of the city; then it connects with the John F. Fitzgerald Expressway, also called the **Central Artery.** There are exits at Prudential Center and Chinatown (Kneeland Street).

    You may approach Boston from the south on Route 3, the Southeast Expressway, as it comes up from the South Shore (Cape Cod and Plymouth). It's the main commuter route from everywhere south of Boston, and is traveled very heavily; at rush hours there are frequent tie-ups.

    From the north, the approach to Boston is by I-93, which crosses the Tobin Bridge to join the Central Artery; or by U.S. Route 1, which comes through East Boston.

    Two divided highways skirt the Charles River toward Cambridge, the faster and busier one being **Storrow Drive** on the southern bank, the more scenic being

Memorial Drive in Cambridge on the northern bank of the Charles. Take either one to go between Boston and Harvard Square. Go all the way to the Larz Andersen Bridge and Cambridge's John F. Kennedy Street, then turn right (north) for Harvard Square.

Once downtown, the Central Artery construction project, and Boston's warren of winding, confusing streets, most of them one way, will try your patience, but once you make your way to a hotel, park the car and try to forget it for the rest of your visit. Driving downtown makes little sense, and driving to Harvard Square even less sense (the parking problem there is even worse). Take the car out to go to Lexington, Concord, or the North Shore, but otherwise leave it parked.

TOURIST INFORMATION

Before coming to Boston, call 617/536-4100, fax 617/424-7664, or write the **Greater Boston Convention & Visitors Bureau,** Prudential Plaza, P.O. Box 490, Boston, MA 02199, and they'll send you an information packet.

The convention and visitors bureau operates the **Prudential Visitor Center,** on the west side of the Prudential Center Plaza (tel. 617/536-4100), open daily from 8:30am to 5pm.

If you call the **Massachusetts Office of Travel and Tourism** at 617/727-3201, and leave your name and address, they'll send you a Massachusetts Vacation Kit.

Much of Boston's historic downtown area is now part of the Boston National Historical Park, and so the National Park Service maintains a **Visitor Center** at 15 State St. (tel. 617/242-5690). Free guided Freedom Trail tours are available in the spring and summer. The information center is open daily from 9am to 5pm. You'll see park rangers here and there at historic spots, ready to help with directions or information.

On Boston Common (Green Line or Red Line to Park Street Station), at the intersection of Tremont and Winter Streets just a few steps from Park Street Station, there's the **Boston Common Visitor Information Center** (tel. 617/536-4100), open year round daily from 9am to 5pm. Come here to get maps and booklets describing the Freedom Trail and other visitor information.

The best calendar of current happenings for free is *Where* magazine, available at visitors' information desks and in hotel lobbies. It's a complete listing of the best plays, sports events, concerts, special exhibits, and programs. The *Boston Globe* has a special "Calendar" supplement each Thursday, listing theater, concert, cinema, and lecture events as well as many other activities, with locations, prices, and telephone numbers.

CITY LAYOUT

In its earliest days Boston was called "Trimountain," for the three hills around which the settlement was built. At that time Trimountain was almost an island, connected to the mainland only by the narrow natural causeway called "Boston Neck."

In the 19th century an ambitious development plan resulted in the leveling of two

---

IMPRESSIONS

Boston State-house is the hub of the solar system.
—OLIVER WENDELL HOLMES, *THE AUTOCRAT OF THE BREAKFAST TABLE*

The Bostonians take their learning too sadly: culture with them is an accomplishment rather than an atmosphere; their 'Hub' as they call it, is the paradise of prigs.
—OSCAR WILDE, "THE AMERICAN INVASION," *COURT AND SOCIETY REVIEW,* MARCH 1887

of the hills and the moving of the dirt to fill in around Boston Neck; the marsh and bogs that were filled in to make the Back Bay quarter soon became a prime residential district with a Manhattan-style grid of streets and a wide, shady central boulevard called Commonwealth Avenue.

From the time when Trimountain had only a few winding pathways, the city has grown to be a maze of twisty streets difficult to get through in a car, easy to get lost in on foot.

MAIN ARTERIES Boston is mostly a city of districts and neighborhoods, with few grand boulevards. The exception is the Back Bay area, which was a planned development built on filled land. **Commonwealth Avenue,** a wide, tree-lined divided boulevard, is the main thoroughfare of Back Bay. **Beacon Street** to the north, and **Boylston Street** to the south, are the other major east-west streets. The shorter north-south streets of Back Bay have been named in alphabetical order. Thus if you go west along Commonwealth Avenue from the Public Garden you'll cross Arlington, Berkeley, Clarendon, Dartmouth, Exeter, and so on.

FINDING AN ADDRESS This can be difficult in Boston, as there are many short streets downtown, and even having the name of a nearby cross street may be of little help. Bostonians are used to giving directions by means of landmarks and neighborhoods: "On Federal Street near South Station in the financial district," "On Hanover Street in the North End near the post office." Remember to get more information than just the address. If you have the telephone number, call and ask for directions by means of neighborhood, landmarks, and subway stops.

NEIGHBORHOODS IN BRIEF

THE NORTH END Starting at the very northeastern tip of Boston's peninsula, this is one of the city's oldest quarters. **Old North Church** is its best-known landmark; **Paul Revere's House,** the city's oldest house still standing, is another. The narrow streets and four-story brick buildings are now home to Italian-American families who preserve much of the old country's daily life in their Italian groceries, butcher shops, cafés, vegetable stands, and restaurants.

HAYMARKET Squeezed in the midst of Government Center, the North End and Faneuil Hall Marketplace, this is where Boston's big open-air food market is held every Friday and Saturday. Most of the costermongers are old-timers from the North End.

FANEUIL HALL MARKETPLACE This phenomenally successful restoration of Boston's historic Quincy Market, North Market, and South Market buildings is not only beautiful and historically important, but also just plain fun. The marketplace, just east of Government Center, deserves its own restaurant guide for the dozens of places to buy the snacks, lunches, or elegant dinners that are provided here.

WATERFRONT East of Faneuil Hall Marketplace and south of the North End is Boston's Waterfront, another area in which restoration has brought new life and vitality. The solid old brick and granite buildings that once served as warehouses for India and China traders, have been modernized and converted to offices, shops, restaurants, and apartments. The **New England Aquarium,** Marriott Long Wharf Hotel, and Boston Harbor Hotel are at the southern end of the "new" Waterfront

GOVERNMENT CENTER All of the districts mentioned above touch on Government Center, a bureaucrats' corral surrounded by striking modern buildings housing city, state, and federal offices, and dominated by the **City Hall,** placed in the midst of a brick-paved plaza that covers several acres. The plaza, with its sunken fountain, is a focus of outdoor activities in summer—free concerts, plays, and exhibits.

FINANCIAL DISTRICT   South of Government Center is the city's Financial District, centered on State Street, Milk Street, Devonshire Street, and the surrounding ways. The skyscrapers tower above several old Boston landmarks as the **Old State House, Old South Meetinghouse,** and the **Old Corner Bookstore.**

BEACON HILL   Due west of Government Center is Beacon Hill, last of the three hills of Trimountain and now an exclusive residential section with a surprisingly old-world ambience. The crown on the hill is Bulfinch's great **State House,** topped by its gold dome; the building is the home of the "Great and General Court of Massachusetts Bay" (the state legislature). Beautiful **Louisburg Square** is famous as the hill's most picturesque collection of houses. The **Charles River Esplanade** is the river's edge of Beacon Hill, on the north side. With its marina, the **Hatch Memorial Shell** for summer concerts, a bikepath, and lots of benches, it is the loveliest part of the Charles's banks.

BOSTON COMMON & PUBLIC GARDEN   South of Beacon Hill is Boston Common, the city's "central park," with its Frog Pond—filled with splashing children in summer and skaters in winter—statues and monuments, walkways, and benches. Park Street Station, at the Common's southeastern corner (intersection of Park and Tremont Streets), is the heart of the "T," Boston's subway system, and also a gathering place for soapbox orators, one-person bands, religious zealots, panhandlers, mimes, and hawkers.

The **Public Garden,** just west of the Common, has flower beds and lawns kept meticulously. The famous **Swan Boats** (run by pedalpower) slowly cruise sightseers around the pond. The Bull & Finch Pub in the Hampshire House, facing the Public Garden on the north, is famous as the inspiration for the television show named **"Cheers."**

DOWNTOWN CROSSING   Southeast of the Common on Washington Street between West and Winter Streets is the city's downtown shopping district, a pedestrian zone called Downtown Crossing. Take the subway to Washington Station, and you can enter either of the two big department stores, **Jordan Marsh** or **Filene's,** directly from the subway station.

CHINATOWN   A few blocks south of Downtown Crossing, packed into the area around Beach Street, Tyler Street, and Harrison Avenue, are dozens of good Chinese restaurants, groceries, businesses, and churches. Like the North End, Chinatown is a place where the language of the old country may greet your ears more frequently than English.

BACK BAY   West of the Public Garden is the large section called Back Bay, with **Commonwealth Avenue** its residential axis, **Boylston Street** its axis of business and pleasure with office buildings, restaurants, clubs, and shops. Walking west on Boylston Street in Back Bay will bring you to **Copley Square,** one of Boston's most genteel areas, bounded by the classic **Boston Public Library,** the elegant **Copley Plaza Hotel,** and Henry Hobson Richardson's famous **Trinity Church,** built in the late 1800s. Modern intruders on this gentility are the striking mirror-glass shaft of the **John Hancock Tower** and the sprawling complex called **Copley Place.**

PRUDENTIAL CENTER   Even farther west along Boylston Street, this was Back Bay's first large-scale redevelopment scheme, with the Prudential Tower ("the Pru") as its centerpiece, flanked by the mammoth **Sheraton Boston Hotel,** several blocks of luxury flats, and stores such as Lord & Taylor. Also in the Pru complex is the **Hynes Convention Center,** the scene of everything from rock concerts to the boat show.

HUNTINGTON AVENUE & THE FENS   After the Pru Center, Huntington

Avenue (which runs along the Pru's southern side) passes the **Christian Science Center, Symphony Hall, Northeastern University,** and the **Museum of Fine Arts** on what might be called Boston's "Cultural Highway." The **Back Bay Fens** sound uninviting, but actually this unappetizing name designates the first links in Frederick Law Olmsted's "Green Necklace," a chain of green parks, copses, and waterways for the residential districts of Back Bay, Roxbury, Jamaica Plain, and Brookline, stretching for miles from the green banks of the Charles River to the **Arnold Arboretum** to the south.

KENMORE SQUARE This is the westernmost part of the city of Boston, at the intersection of Commonwealth Avenue, Beacon Street, and Brookline Avenue. **Boston University** is just a few blocks west of the square, and Kenmore's life is dominated by its student denizens, who flock to its cafeterias, book and record stores, movies, and clubs. On the Boston skyline at night, you can always locate Kenmore Square by the huge red Citgo delta sign.

OUTLYING DISTRICTS Although the city of Boston is fairly large, it is dwarfed by Greater Boston, officially termed the Metropolitan District, which consists of a dozen other cities as well as some outlying sections of Boston proper. **Charlestown,** north of the tip of Boston peninsula, is dominated by the **Bunker Hill Monument** obelisk; the USS *Constitution* (Old Ironsides) is berthed nearby in the old Boston Navy Yard.

    East Boston, northeast of Charlestown, is reached by two tunnels: **Callahan Tunnel** runs north (outbound, no toll); **Sumner Tunnel** runs south (inbound, toll), and the big industry here is Logan International Airport.

    South Boston, southeast of the Financial District, is separated from the city proper by the Fort Point Channel. "Southie" is the city's Irish bastion, and here St. Patrick's Day is the national holiday. (*Note:* If someone mentions the **South End,** they're referring to the residential district just south of Back Bay. The South End and South Boston are, confusingly, completely separate places.)

NEIGHBORING CITIES West of Boston is **Brookline,** a large, mostly residential city and the former hometown of the Kennedy family. On the northern banks of the Charles River, **Cambridge** got most of the riverfront land, while **Somerville** had to be content with a mere foothold. The banks of the Charles from the Charles River Dam (topped by the **Museum of Science**) all the way to **Harvard University** are covered by grass and trees, and in summer the grass is covered with sunbathers and picnickers.

2. GETTING AROUND

BY SUBWAY & BUS

The best way to get around downtown and Back Bay is on the "T" (short for Massachusetts Bay Transportation Authority, or MBTA, which runs Boston's subway and bus network).

SUBWAY INFORMATION The **MBTA Information Booth** is in Park Street Station. For information by telephone, call these numbers: for route information, 617/722-3200, or toll free 800/392-6100; for MBTA commuter railroad schedules toll free 800/392-6099. The central MBTA switchboard number is 617/722-5000.

FARES Fares are 85¢ on the subway and 60¢ on local buses. Buses that go to outlying communities (Salem, Marblehead, Lexington, etc.) charge up to $3.50 one way for the ride. All fares are payable in exact change. On buses and trolleys you must have the exact fare; at subway stations there are change booths open during service hours.

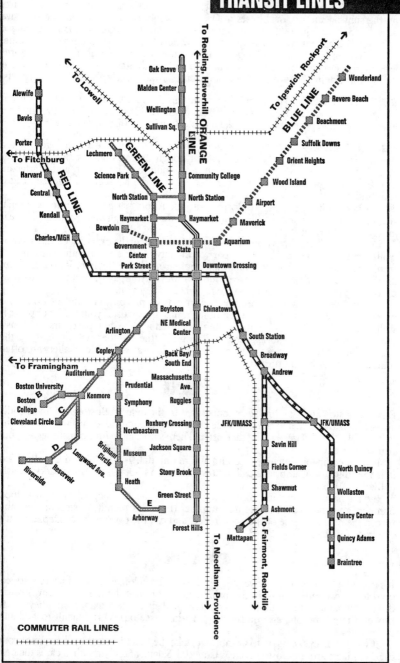

BOSTON MBTA RAPID TRANSIT LINES

N

To Reading, Haverhill

To Ipswich, Rockport

To Lowell

ORANGE LINE

BLUE LINE

Oak Grove
Malden Center
Wellington
Sullivan Sq.

Wonderland
Revere Beach
Beachmont
Suffolk Downs
Orient Heights
Wood Island

GREEN LINE

Alewife
Davis
Porter

To Fitchburg

Lechmere
Science Park
North Station
Haymarket
Bowdoin

RED LINE

Harvard
Central
Kendall
Charles/MGH

Community College

North Station

Haymarket

Government
Center
Park Street

State

Downtown Crossing

Aquarium

Airport
Maverick

Boylston
NE Medical
Center

Chinatown

Arlington

Copley

To Framingham

Auditorium

Boston University
Boston
College

B

Kenmore

C

Cleveland Circle

D

Longwood Ave.

Riverside

Reservoir

Back Bay/
South End

Massachusetts
Ave.

South Station
Broadway
Andrew

Prudential

Symphony

Ruggles

Roxbury Crossing

Brigham
Circle

Northeastern

Jackson Square

Museum

Stony Brook

Heath

E

Green Street

Arborway

Forest Hills

JFK/UMASS

Savin Hill

Fields Corner

Shawmut

Ashmont

Mattapan

To Fairmont, Readville

JFK/UMASS

North Quincy

Wollaston

Quincy Center

Quincy Adams

Braintree

To Needham, Providence

COMMUTER RAIL LINES

Children 5 to 11 pay half fare on subways and buses; children under 5 ride free. Seniors pay 20¢ on the subway, 15¢ on the bus if they have an MBTA identity card.

The MBTA sells a **Tourist Pass** called a "Passport" that allows unlimited travel on the subway and on local buses in Greater Boston. Passes good for 3 consecutive days cost $10 for adults, $5 for children 5 to 11; 7-day passes are $18 for adults, $6 for children. You can buy your Passport at the "Airport" subway station on the Blue Line, at the Baybanks Foreign Exchange booths in the airport's Terminals C (departures level) and E (arrivals level), at North Station and South Station subway stops, and at the Boston Common Visitor Information Center. Many hotels also sell the Passports.

SUBWAY HOURS Times on subway and bus lines vary, but you're pretty sure of being able to take the T any day from 5am up to 12:30am (and up to 1am on some lines). After that, be prepared to take a cab. Hours may vary on Sunday.

SUBWAY LINES Subway lines are color-coded: The **Red Line** goes from Alewife in Cambridge via Harvard Square through Boston's main subway station at Park Street, then on to the suburbs of Quincy, Braintree, Dorchester, and Mattapan. The **Green Line** goes from Lechmere Square near the Museum of Science in East Cambridge through Park Street and downtown, then out to the western suburbs. The **Blue Line** connects downtown Boston with the Airport stop at Logan International Airport; you can also use the Blue Line to reach the New England Aquarium. There is an **Orange Line** as well.

On several subway lines (most notably the Green Line) the cars surface and serve as trolleys after they leave the central part of the city. After an outbound car emerges from underground, passengers boarding aboveground ride for free. If you catch an inbound Green Line trolley above ground, however, you pay the entire fare to your destination (which may cost up to $1.75) when you get on.

Note: Any big-city transportation system has its pickpockets, and Boston is no exception. Be especially careful when riding trains in crowds. If your wallet or purse is stolen, call 722-5000, or one of the numbers listed in the white pages under "Mass. Bay Transportation Authority, Lost and Found" (the number will depend on the subway line or bus you were on); try a few days later as well, since wallets are often found, minus cash, and turned in.

BY TAXI

Fares in Boston and Cambridge are computed by the mile. In Boston, the first ¼ mile costs $1.50, and each additional ⅛ mile costs 20¢. In Cambridge the fare is $1 for the first ½ mile and 25¢ per ½ mile thereafter. There's no charge for normal luggage, but trunks cost extra.

Boston companies include Red and White Cab (tel. 742-9090) and Checker Taxi (tel. 536-7000). In Cambridge call Yellow Cab (tel. 547-3000) or Ambassador Brattle (tel. 492-1100).

If you have a complaint against a driver, get the hackney carriage medallion number, and the driver's name and number (from his permit, posted in the cab), record the date and time of the occurrence, and call the Boston Police Department's Hackney Carriage office at 343-4475.

BY CAR

It's not wise for a visitor to drive much in Boston. Its colonial layout of narrow streets (said to follow cattle paths) is confusing enough on foot, let alone in a car. Boston drivers are famous throughout the country for their careless maneuvers; they act as though there is no one else on the road. Parking (see below) is difficult to find and expensive when you find it.

If you make an excursion to Cambridge, take the Red Line of the subway, not your car. For places around Boston such as Concord, Salem, and Plymouth, a car is the best way to go.

See also "Getting Around" in Chapter 2.

RENTALS   There are car-rental desks at Logan International Airport and at various locations downtown. For more information on renting cars, see "Car Rentals" in "Getting Around," in Chapter 2.

PARKING   Parking meters in downtown Boston charge 25¢ per ¼ hour, and parking lots charge much more, up to $8 for the first ½ hour. Fines for parking illegally are routinely $50 or higher. If you stay for some time in Boston, do not accumulate a backlog of unpaid parking tickets: Cars are towed, or fitted with a "Denver Boot," and held hostage until the tickets are paid.

For the visitor unfamiliar with the city, try the large **Boston Common Underground Garage,** entered from Charles Street between the Common and the Public Garden. Here the rates are moderate, and there's a free shuttle bus to take you to nearby points.

BY BICYCLE

Boston is a good town for bicycling: The hills are gentle, the views are fine, and there are marked bike paths, one running from near the center of town along the beautiful Esplanade and the south bank of the Charles River all the way to Harvard Square. Bring a strong lock or heavy chain to prevent theft. Perhaps the greatest advantage of biking in Boston and Cambridge is the ease and cheapness of parking: Any lamppost will do, and it's free. You can rent bikes in Boston or Cambridge. Rental shops are listed in the "yellow pages" under "Bicycles—Renting." You can also rent mopeds, but these cost about three times as much as a bike, require a hefty deposit, and have more potential for problems than a simple bicycle.

ON FOOT

Walking is the best way to see the sights in Boston. Indeed, if you want to follow the famous Freedom Trail, you've got to do some walking. For suggestions on where to walk, see "Walking Tours," below.

FAST
FACTS   BOSTON

American Express   The company has several travel agencies in the Boston area. The main office is at 1 Court St. (tel. 723-8400; subway: Government Center). There's also an office near Harvard Sq., Cambridge, at 44 Brattle St. (tel. 661-0005; subway: Harvard). To report a lost or stolen American Express charge card, call toll free 800/528-4800; to report lost or stolen American Express traveler's checks, call toll free 800/221-7282.

Area Code   Boston's telephone area code is 617; a number of outlying cities and towns, including Cambridge, Lexington, and Marblehead, are also in the 617 area. Other towns just slightly farther away (Concord, Salem, Cape Ann, Plymouth) have an area code of 508. All telephones on Cape Cod, Martha's Vineyard, and Nantucket are in the 508 area.

Babysitters   Many of the larger hotels can arrange for babysitters; ask about this when you make reservations. Otherwise, nanny and babysitting services are listed in the "yellow pages" telephone directory under "Sitting Services," which includes house-, pet-sitting, and elder-care services as well.

Bookstores   In addition to independent bookstores in Boston and Cambridge, the nationwide chains B. Dalton and Waldenbooks are represented. Among the most interesting stores are the following. Boston's Old Corner Bookstore, a literary gathering place in the 19th century, is now the **Globe Corner Bookstore,** 1 School St. (tel. 523-6658; subway: State or Downtown Crossing), specializing in books and maps for travelers. A few blocks away on Washington St. at Downtown Crossing is the big **Barnes & Noble Bookstore** (tel. 426-5502; subway: Downtown Crossing). There's another Barnes & Noble Bookstore at Copley Sq. (tel. 236-1308). For used and rare books the place to go is the historic **Brattle Book Shop,** 9 West St. (tel. 542-0210; subway: Downtown Crossing). The **Harvard Bookstore Café,** 190 Newbury St. (tel. 536-0095; subway: Copley) serves up good food as well as a good read (see "Where to Dine," below).

Harvard Square in Cambridge has a dozen good bookstores, some quite large. Among the most interesting is **WordsWorth,** 30 Brattle St. (tel. 354-5201; subway: Harvard), with books on all subjects sold at a discount. **Schoenhof's Foreign Books,** 76A Mount Auburn St. (tel. 547-8855; subway: Harvard) has lots of books in dozens of foreign languages, especially French, German, and Spanish. The **Grolier Book Shop,** 6 Plympton St. (tel. 547-4648, or toll free 800/234-POEM; subway Harvard) specializes in poetry books. The **Globe Corner Bookstore** has a branch at 49 Palmer St. (tel. 497-6277; subway: Harvard), with an excellent selection of travel guides, related books, and maps. And a few steps away from the Globe is the entrance to the book department of Harvard's department store, the **Harvard Coop,** 1400 Massachusetts Ave. (tel. 499-2000; subway: Harvard), which has a large bookstore carrying all sorts of general-interest books as well as college textbooks.

Business Hours See "Business Hours" in "Fast Facts: New England" in Chapter 2.

Car Rentals See "Getting Around" in Chapter 2.

Climate See "When to Go" in Chapter 2.

Crime See "Safety" in "Fast Facts: New England" in Chapter 2.

Currency See "Fast Facts: For the Foreign Traveler" in Chapter 3.

Dentist Boston has lots of dentists. If you can't wait to go to your own dentist at home, refer to the "yellow pages" telephone directory under "Dentists" for listings by name, by practice specialty, and by location. You might also ask at your hotel for the name of a dentist who has given satisfactory care to someone on the hotel staff.

Doctor Boston doctors are listed by name and by specialty in the "yellow pages." Most of Boston's hospitals operate physician referral services; if you call the service, they will put you in touch with a doctor who can treat your ailment. Here are several referral services: **Beth Israel Hospital Physician Referral,** tel. 735-5356; **Massachusetts General Hospital Physician Referral Service,** tel. 726-5800; and **New England Deaconess Hospital Physician Referral Service,** tel. 732-8006, 24 hours a day.

Drugstores There is sure to be a drugstore (pharmacy/chemist) nearby. Look in shopping centers and downtown commercial districts, or ask at your hotel. Most pharmacies have business hours from about 8am to 8pm, but times vary. To buy medicines 24 hours a day, 7 days a week, go to **Phillips Drug Co.,** 155 Charles St., Boston (tel. 523-1028 or 523-4372; fax 523-1094; subway: Charles); or **CVS Pharmacy,** Porter Square Shopping Center, Massachusetts Avenue, Cambridge (tel. 876-5519; subway: Porter); or to the emergency room of the nearest hospital.

Embassies/Consulates Boston has consular representatives from many countries. For a full list, see "Embassies/Consulates" in "Fast Facts: For the Foreign Traveler" in Chapter 3. You can also look in the "white pages" telephone directory, in the Government Listing Section (blue pages) at the end of the directory, under "Consulates."

Emergencies Dial 911 from any telephone (no coin needed at pay phones) for police, fire, ambulance, or any other emergency. For information on poisons, call the Poison Control Center at 232-2120. The Rape Crisis Center is at 492-7273. See also "Emergencies" in "Fast Facts: New England" in Chapter 2.

Eyeglasses There are many professional opticians able to fit you with eyeglasses or contact lenses quickly, whether you have a copy of your eyeglass prescription or not (if not, take your glasses, if possible). Look in the "yellow pages" telephone directory under "Opticians." Many opticians promise new glasses "in about an hour."

Some pharmacies (drugstores/chemists) have racks of inexpensive eyeglasses which might solve your problem (at least until you return home), and the cost is a fraction of that for custom-fitted glasses.

Hairdressers/Barbers   Shops are found in commercial districts and shopping centers. Some shops provide simple, moderately priced services, while others are luxurious, meticulous, and expensive. Take a minute to consult with the staff on price and services before sitting down for your cut.

Holidays   See "When to Go" in Chapter 2.

Hospitals   Call 911 from any phone for emergency ambulance service. Boston's many hospitals are listed in the "yellow pages" telephone directory under "Hospitals." Ask at your hotel for the nearest one.

Information   See "Sources of Information" in Chapter 2 and "Tourist Information," earlier in this chapter.

Laundry/Dry Cleaning   Though you can have your hotel do laundry, you'll save money by doing it yourself. Self-service laundries ("Laundromats") are located in residential sections of the city, as are dry-cleaning establishments. They're listed in the "yellow pages" telephone directory under "Laundries," "Laundries-Self Service," and "Cleaners." **Campus Laundry Service** (tel. 247-1005) is at 820 Beacon St., near Boston University; many others are in the North End (subway: Government Center), such as the **Galleria Laundry,** 256 North St. (tel. 227-1925), and **Virgilio Laundromat,** 172 Salem St. (tel. 523-9215).

Liquor Laws   See "Fast Facts: New England" in Chapter 2.

Lost Property   If you have lost or found something on an MBTA bus or subway, call 722-5000.

Police   For police emergency, call 911; for other business, call 247-4200.

Post Office   For general postal information, call 451-9922. Boston's postal center is the General Mail Facility, 25 Dorchester Ave. (tel. 654-5327), next to South Station at Fort Point Channel (subway: South Station). Another convenient post office is the McCormack State Post Office Building at Post Office Sq. (tel. 654-5684; subway: State). For more information on post offices, see "Fast Facts: New England" in Chapter 2.

Religious Services   Consult the "yellow pages" telephone directory under "Churches," "Mosques," "Synagogues," and so on.

Restrooms   See "Toilets" in "Fast Facts: For the Foreign Traveler," in Chapter 3.

Safety   Boston is as safe as any large American city, and safer than many. Follow the general rules: Watch out for pickpockets on subway trains and buses; don't go into parks after dark; don't spend a lot of time in rundown neighborhoods, especially at night.

Shoe Repairs   **Larossa Instant Shoe Repair** has shops at South Station (tel. 345-0656; subway: South Station), in the Faneuil Hall area (tel. 227-8933; subway: Government Center), in Filene's Basement (tel. 338-8656; subway: Downtown Crossing) and at 545 Boylston St. (tel. 424-6881; subway: Arlington).

Taxes   See "Fast Facts: New England" Chapter 2.

Taxis   See "Getting Around," earlier in this chapter.

Transit Info   See "Getting Around," earlier in this chapter.

Weather   Call 936-1234.

3. ACCOMMODATIONS

Boston has a very fine selection of downtown hotels, and each one seems to have something special to recommend it. The best way to get to know this wonderful city is to stay right downtown, where the action is. This can be expensive, however; a double room in one of Boston's fine hotels often costs nearly $200 or more per night, and the city's 9.7% room tax can hike that lofty price to almost $220. To help you see exactly what you'll be spending, **room tax has been included in the prices quoted below.**

MONEY-SAVING TIPS   Visit on a Weekend   First of all, if you want to stay right downtown, by all means plan your visit for a weekend! A double room at any luxury hotel right in downtown Boston may cost $200 during the week. But if you sign up for a 2-night stay on Friday and Saturday, you may get that same room for something like $135, plus a bottle of champagne, breakfast in bed, the morning's newspaper, and free parking. These "weekend specials" are offered by all of the city's luxury hotels, and many are even lower in price. It even makes sense to detour out of town—to Salem and the North Shore, to Cape Cod, or to Old Sturbridge Village—in order to arrive in Boston on Friday afternoon or evening. (By the way, country inns and resorts are most crowded, and highest in price, on weekends; so it makes sense to visit the country places during the week.)

Reserve from a Tourist Information Center   A number of moderate-to-expensive downtown Boston hotels routinely offer special prices to travelers calling from tourist information centers for same-day reservations. For instance, if you arrive at the airport, or train station, or are driving up from Cape Cod or Plymouth and stop at the **Regional Information Complex for Visitors** on Route 3 at Exit 5, and you pick up the hotel's brochure, inside you may find a leaflet offering a special low price. The price may be extremely good, such as $65 to $75 for a room that normally rents for $110 to $125, single or double. What's the catch? You can usually reserve that same day only, you may be limited to a stay of 2 or 3 days, and you must call from the information center and tell the reservations agent the name of the center you are calling from. The offers are based on availability of rooms, and if the hotel is pretty full, they might not grant you the discounted price. Why do hotels do this? They want to fill rooms that may otherwise go empty that night.

Try a Bed-and-Breakfast or a Guesthouse   Another way to save money is to try a bed-and-breakfast room. Several agencies will make reservations and arrangements for you, and they are listed below. By staying in a bed-and-breakfast room, you can pay half or even a third of the downtown hotel price, and make new Bostonian friends in the bargain.

Stay on the Outskirts   Finally, there are the hostelries on the outskirts of town. If you have a car and are willing to stay in Salem, Lexington, Concord, or some other suburban location, you can save 25% to 50% of the cost of a downtown room.

VERY EXPENSIVE

BOSTON HARBOR HOTEL, 70 Rowes Wharf, Boston, MA 02110. Tel. 617/439-7000, or toll free 800/752-7077. Fax 617/330-9450. 230 rms. A/C MINIBAR TV TEL **Directions:** From Central Artery, take "South Station" exit. Hotel is on Atlantic Ave. near intersection of High St. **Subway:** Blue Line to Aquarium.

$ Rates: $253–$308 single; $298–$353 double; $396–$1,560 suite. Weekend packages available. AE, DC, DISC, MC, V. **Parking:** $7 weekends, $18 weekdays, at nearby garage.

Boston's newest luxury hotel (1987) is part of a landmark redevelopment plan that restored the dramatic old buildings at Rowes Wharf into a complex that includes the hotel, offices, condominiums, shops, restaurants, a yacht marina, and a ferryboat terminal—you can spot the striking flat-domed main portal easily if you're driving on the Central Artery.

The hotel is wonderfully luxurious: Each room has its own sitting area separate from the sleeping area, plus a minibar and remote-control television. There are bathrobes, hairdryers, fresh flowers, windows you can open to let in the sea breezes, and top-class luxury furnishings in classic style. Besides the standard rooms, the hotel has deluxe rooms with harbor or city views, plus luxury suites.

The public spaces are classic, conservative, and beautiful, and suggest wealth and richness, from the lavish use of colored marble to the crystal chandeliers, the thick patterned carpets, and the displays of antique maps and charts of Boston and New England. Classical music murmurs in the background, or a piano tinkles in the spacious seaview lounge.

Dining/Entertainment: The Rowes Wharf restaurant features New England seafood and other regional American cuisine and has a sweeping view of Boston harbor. The Rowes Walk Café on the outdoor terrace serves lunch and dinner. The Rowes Wharf bar serves lunch, and the Harborview Lounge serves afternoon tea.

Services: 24-hour room service, free shoeshine service, chamber service twice daily.

Facilities: 60-foot lap pool, whirlpool, sauna, steambaths, massage rooms, exercise equipment, spa-treatment facilities, aerobics classes, weight-training instruction.

BOSTON MARRIOTT HOTEL LONG WHARF, 296 State St., Boston, MA 02109. Tel. 617/227-0800, or toll free 800/228-9290. Fax 617/227-2867. 400 rms. A/C TV TEL **Subway:** Blue Line to Aquarium.

$ Rates: $179–$258 single; $179–$269 double. Weekend packages available. AE, DC, DISC, MC, V. **Parking:** $20 on property.

This seven-story luxury hotel has a modern design done along traditional lines to help it fit into the waterfront cityscape. Located right on the waterfront, off Atlantic Avenue near the New England Aquarium and Faneuil Hall Marketplace, the hotel has a decor that is up-to-date and quietly dramatic, with lofty public spaces and a second floor lobby reached by escalator. Many guest rooms have views of the wharves and the water.

Dining/Entertainment: The spacious Harbor Terrace Sea Grill offers a grand harbor view, and Rachael's Lounge is a popular watering hole.

Services: Valet parking.

Facilities: Indoor swimming pool with outdoor terrace deck, exercise room and sauna, games room.

BOSTONIAN HOTEL, Faneuil Hall Marketplace, Boston, MA 02109. Tel. 617/523-3600, or toll free 800/343-0922. 152 rms and suites. A/C MINIBAR TV TEL **Subway:** Green or Blue Line to Government Center or Haymarket.

$ Rates: $231–$292 single; $259–$320 double. Children under 12 stay free. AE, CB, DC, MC, V. **Parking:** Valet parking $20 per night.

⭐ "What a perfect place for a hotel!" That's how the Bostonian introduces itself. It's true: Next to Faneuil Hall, Government Center, the weekend fruit-and-vegetable market, the North End's Italian shops and restaurants, the Bostonian is in the midst of the action. Modern with colonial accents, the hotel boasts tiny balconies overlooking Faneuil Hall on most rooms. It's a small, low-rise (four-floor) luxury hotel. Honeymoon rooms with Jacuzzi tubs and fireplaces cost somewhat more.

COLONNADE HOTEL, 120 Huntington Ave., Boston, MA 02116. Tel. 617/424-7000, or toll free 800/962-3030. Fax 617/424-1717. 288 rms and suites. A/C MINIBAR TV TEL **Subway:** Green Line to Prudential or Symphony.

$ Rates: $150–$195 single; $160–$195 double. Weekends $159 single or double (including breakfast and parking). AE, CB, DC, MC, V. **Parking:** $18 per day on premises.

Located near the Christian Science Center, and not far from the Prudential Center and Copley Place, Colonnade concentrates on modern luxuries and European-style personal service in a location near Symphony Hall, Copley Place, the Hynes Convention Center, and the Prudential Center. The rooms in this family-owned hotel have many thoughtful touches, as well as all the luxuries.

Dining/Entertainment: Two restaurants with European influence, plus an outdoor café and Zachary's Bar and Jazz Club (open Wed–Sat, $4.50 cover.

Services: Multilingual staff, 24-hour room service, Hertz car rental in lobby.

Facilities: Covered parking, outdoor rooftop swimming pool.

.5 mi
.8 km
N

Boston Harbor Hotel 20
Bostonian Hotel 18
Boston Marriott Hotel Long Wharf 21
Boston Park Plaza Hotel & Towers 10
Colonnade Hotel 5
Copley Plaza Hotel 9
Copley Square Hotel 7
57 Park Plaza Hotel 11
Four Seasons Hotel Boston 13
Holiday Inn Boston Brookline 2
Holiday Inn Government Center 16

Hotel le Meridien Boston 19
Howard Johnson Hotel Kenmore Square 1
Howard Johnson Lodge Fenway 3
Lenox Hotel 6
Omni Parker House 17
Ritz-Carlton Hotel 14
Royal Sonesta Hotel 15
Sheraton-Boston Hotel and Towers 4
Tremont House 12
Westin Hotel Copley Place 8

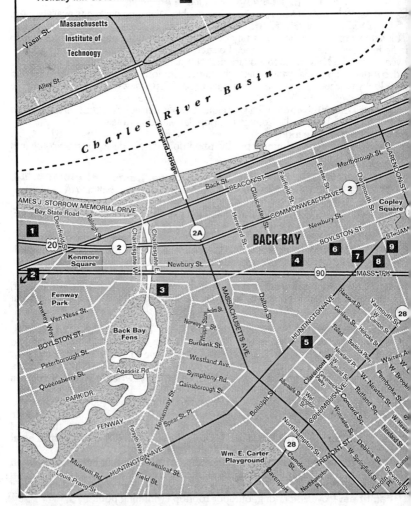

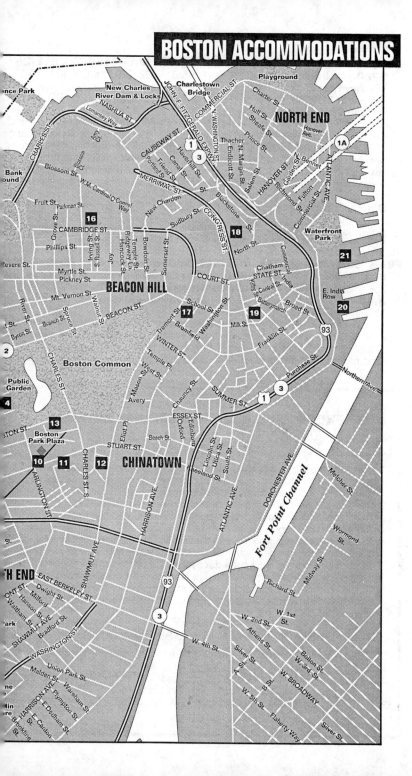

BOSTON ACCOMMODATIONS

COPLEY PLAZA HOTEL, Copley Sq., Boston, MA 02116. Tel. 617/267-5300, or toll free 800/826-7539. Fax 617/267-7668. 370 rms. A/C MINIBAR TV TEL **Amtrak:** Back Bay Station. **Subway:** Green Line to Copley.

$ **Rates:** $127–$287 single or double; $243–$513 suite. AE, CB, DC, MC, V. **Parking:** $16 nearby, $20 valet.

The Copley Plaza Hotel, facing Copley Square, is a wonderful grand old Boston hotel. The attractions are the hotel's grand style and original touches: a quiet cocktail lounge that is, in fact, a comfy club library, complete with oil portraits and brass-nailed leather chairs; the striking, ornate, elegant Plaza dining room, in which the ceilings are heavily gilded, the mantelpieces are marble, and the maître d' a soft-spoken and very suave man in a tuxedo; and Copley's, a mirror-laden brass-rail bar serving drinks and sandwiches, with trompe l'oeil paintings on the mirrors and doors.

Dining/Entertainment: The Plaza Dining Room serves French cuisine with 700 wine cellar selections. Copley's Restaurant offers New England fare and serves breakfast, lunch, and dinner.

Services: 24-hour room service.

FOUR SEASONS HOTEL BOSTON, 200 Boylston St., Boston, MA 02116. Tel. 617/338-4400, or toll free 800/332-3442. Fax 617/426-7199. 288 rms. A/C MINIBAR TV TEL **Subway:** Green Line to Arlington.

$ **Rates:** $210–$360 single; $250–$400 double; $1,481 suite. AE, DC, ER, JCB, MC, V. **Parking:** $20 on premises.

Four Seasons hotels are noted for their quiet whispering of elegance and status, and this one is no exception. This one, opened in June 1985, is an impressive addition to Boston's lineup of luxury hotels. On the south side of the Public Garden, near Back Bay and its chic shopping, a block from the theater district, and a short walk across

---

 FROMMER'S SMART TRAVELER: HOTELS

VALUE-CONSCIOUS TRAVELERS SHOULD
TAKE ADVANTAGE OF THE FOLLOWING:

1. Suburban motels, the best bargains in big-city lodgings. Though it is often most convenient to have your own car for these, it is sometimes possible to reach them easily and economically by public transportation.
2. Bed-and-breakfast services and guest houses in residential areas.
3. The Friday through Sunday rates. Special weekend package deals can save you even more money.
4. A little discreet bargaining if you're planning to stay for more than two nights. It can often bring the per-night room rate down. Ask what the room rate is for one night, then ask, "Do I get a discount if I stay three (or more) nights?" If the hotel is not heavily booked, you're likely to get a positive response.
5. "Local" special rates and packages that are sometimes not available through a hotel's toll-free reservations center. Call the hotel's regular number to inquire.

QUESTIONS TO ASK IF YOU'RE ON A BUDGET

1. Is there a parking garage? How much does it cost? Can I park and remove my car as often as I want, or am I charged for every exit?
2. Is there a service charge? Is there a sales and/or room tax? Are these extras included in the room rates quoted? (They're usually not.)
3. If breakfast is included, is it continental (rolls and coffee), a full breakfast, or a buffet?

Boston Common to the central shopping and financial districts, the Four Seasons couldn't have a better location. Facilities are extremely well thought out for guests' comfort and are very plush in an up-to-date style inspired by tradition. Many rooms, by the way, have views of the Public Garden.

Dining/Entertainment: Aujourd'hui is one of Boston's finest French restaurants. The Bristol Lounge offers lighter fare, a bar menu, and live piano music nightly.

Services: Massage, babysitting, secretarial services, 24-hour room service, twice-daily chamber service.

Facilities: No-smoking floors.

HOTEL LE MERIDIEN BOSTON, 250 Franklin St., Boston, MA 02110. Tel. 617/451-1900, or toll free 800/223-9918. Fax 617/423-2844. Telex 940194. 305 rms, 21 suites. A/C MINIBAR TV TEL **Subway:** Orange or Blue Line to State.
$ Rates: $215–$250 single; $225–$275 double. AE, DC, DISC, ER, MC, V. **Parking:** $17 per day Mon–Fri, free on weekends.

This elegant hotel is housed in the handsome former headquarters of the Federal Reserve Bank of Boston, in the heart of downtown Boston, overlooking the park at Post Office Square. This stately Renaissance-revival built in granite and limestone, has rich, monumental public rooms, but the rooms are modern in style and very comfortable in appointments.

Dining/Entertainment: Julien, the restaurant, is plush, hushed, elegant, satisfying, and expensive with a choice of prix fixe or à la carte for lunch and dinner. The less-formal Café Fleuri has the ambience of a bistro. In the hotel's bar are two patriotic murals by N. C. Wyeth (father of Andrew Wyeth) done in 1923.

Services: 24-hour room service, concierge.

Facilities: Indoor swimming pool and health club, business center.

OMNI PARKER HOUSE, 60 School St., Boston, MA 02108. Tel. 617/227-8600, or toll free 800/843-6664. Fax 617/742-5729. 535 rms. A/C TV TEL **Subway:** Park Street or Government Center.
$ Rates: $165–$215 single; $185–$235 double. AE, DC, DISC, MC, V. **Parking:** $22 valet.

Anyone who's ever come to Boston has considered staying at the Omni Parker House at the corner of School and Tremont streets, midway between Park Street Station and Government Center. It's a traditional beauty that capitalizes on its antiquity, showing off its wood paneling, ornate gilded ceilings, and leather-upholstered furniture. The rooms, although fairly small, are decorated very tastefully with reproductions of antiques.

Dining/Entertainment: The dining room, Parker's, is a haven of quiet, shining crystal and silver, heavy mirrors, and thick carpets. Lunch here might be $20 to $30, and dinner about $40 to $50 per person. Downstairs from the lobby is the Last Hurrah Bar and Grill, an eye-catching collection of Tiffany-style lamps, 1890s bars and booths, brass globe-top lamps, pictures of turn-of-the-century prize fighters, and the like. The Last Hurrah is where many office workers and local politicians in the nearby government and financial districts come for lunch or after-five cocktails that are served with hot and cold hors d'oeuvres (on the house).

RITZ-CARLTON HOTEL, 15 Arlington St., Boston, MA 02117. Tel. 617/536-5700, or toll free 800/241-3333. Fax 617/536-9340. 237 rms, 41 suites. A/C MINIBAR TV TEL **Subway:** Green Line to Arlington.
$ Rates: $220–$340 single; $260–$380 double; $495–$735 suite. AE, DC, DISC, MC, V. **Parking:** Valet parking $20 per night.

This is Boston's grande dame in the luxury class, with careful service and a prime location facing the Public Garden. Guest rooms are very comfortable and classically styled. The location puts you near the upscale boutiques and trendy nightlife of Newbury Street and Back Bay. There are two sections, the older, original building with the lobby and Ritz Dining Room, and the newer, more modern addition. Many guests prefer the charm of the older rooms.

Dining/Entertainment: The Dining Room overlooking the Public Garden serves excellent continental cuisine with impeccable service, while the Ritz Café, on Newbury Street, serves equally good fare in simpler surroundings at lower prices. Sipping tea in the Lounge or martinis in the dignified Ritz Bar are well-practiced Boston customs.

Services: Complimentary limousine, twice-daily chamber service, 24-hour room service, concierge, babysitting, multilingual staff, guest privileges at a nearby spa.

Facilities: Fitness center.

ROYAL SONESTA HOTEL, 5 Cambridge Pkwy., Cambridge, MA 02142.
Tel. 617/491-3600, or toll free 800/766-3782. Fax 617/421-5402. 400 rms. A/C TV TEL **Directions:** Follow Route 3 across the Charles River Dam on the Msgr. O'Brien Hwy., pass the Museum of Science, and turn left onto Commercial Ave. **Subway:** Green Line to Science Park or Lechmere.
$ Rates: $140–$185 single; $160–$205 double; $250–$635 suite. AE, CB, DC, MC, V. **Parking:** $12 per day.

Although it's in Cambridge, the Royal Sonesta Hotel is actually closer to downtown Boston than to Harvard Square. A short trundle from the hotel across the Charles River Dam by the Museum of Science brings you right to Beacon Hill. Located right on the Charles River, the rooms have spectacular views of the Boston Skyline. Original artwork is displayed throughout public spaces as well as in some guest rooms. Across the street from the hotel is the new CambridgeSide Galleria, which houses many shops and restaurants.

Dining/Entertainment: Davio's Ristorante and Café is the hotel's Italian restaurant and is more formal than the hotel's other restaurant, the Charles Bar and Grille.

Services: Room service is available from 6am to 1am.

SHERATON-BOSTON HOTEL AND TOWERS, 39 Dalton St., Boston, MA
02199. Tel. 617/236-2000, or toll free 800/325-3535. Fax 617/236-1702. 1,250 rms. A/C TV TEL **Subway:** Green Line to Prudential or Hynes Convention Center/ICA.
$ Rates: $180 single; $195 double. AE, DC, DISC, MC, V. **Parking:** $16 on premises.

New England's largest convention hotel, right in the Prudential Center, has all the facilities imaginable. The Sheraton Towers, an exclusive 103-room hotel-within-a-hotel, features private registration and a lounge with butler service where you can enjoy free continental breakfast, afternoon tea, and evening hors d'oeuvres.

Dining/Entertainment: The Massachusetts Bay Company restaurant serves seafood, A Steak in the Neighborhood has American cuisine, and The Boylston Park Café serves breakfast and lighter meals until 2:30pm daily.

Services: 24-hour room service.

Facilities: Indoor/outdoor swimming pool, fitness equipment.

WESTIN HOTEL COPLEY PLACE, 10 Huntington Ave., Boston, MA
02116. Tel. 617/262-9600, or toll free 800/228-3000. Fax 617/424-7483. 804 rms and suites. A/C TV TEL **Subway:** Green Line to Copley or Prudential.
$ Rates: $195–$220 single; $220–$245 double. AE, CB, DC, DISC, MC, V. **Parking:** $20 valet at the hotel.

You'll find this large luxury hotel within the business-shopping-hotel complex named Copley Place, its 36 floors rising above the complex to afford some good views (get a room on the 12th floor or above). Guest rooms here have all the luxuries. On rainy or snowy Boston days you can browse a beautiful upscale shopping mall without ever going outdoors; a covered elevated walkway connects Copley Place with the Prudential Center, where there are more shops and restaurants.

Dining/Entertainment: Three restaurants, several bars and lounges; others within the complex as well.

Services: Small pets accepted (inquire in advance), multilingual staff, valet parking, car rental, 24-hour room service.

Facilities: Health club, indoor swimming pool.

EXPENSIVE

Lower in price than the luxury hotels, these upper-bracket places still offer all the services, such as air conditioning, parking garages, color television, room service, restaurants and bars, and downtown locations. Many also have those marvelous weekend-special rates. Be sure to ask about them when you call for information or reservations.

BOSTON PARK PLAZA HOTEL & TOWERS, 64 Arlington St. at Park Plaza, Boston, MA 02117. Tel. 617/426-2000, or toll free 800/225-2008, 800/462-2022 in Massachusetts. Fax 617/426-5545. 977 rms. A/C TV TEL **Subway:** Green Line to Arlington.

$ Rates: $118–$170 single; $138–$190 double. Children stay free with parents. AE, DC, MC, V. **Parking:** $19 on premises.

Built as the great Statler Hilton in 1927, the hotel is proud of its history, but equally proud of its renovations. The nice old features such as the spacious lobby with crystal chandelier, lots of gilt trim and red-carpeted corridors have been kept, but the rooms have been updated with many of the modern comforts. Clientele includes many groups as well as thrifty families, both domestic and foreign. The location is very central, a scant block from Boston Common and only a block or so from the theater district and the Greyhound terminal.

Dining/Entertainment: Guests can enjoy themselves at the Fox & Hounds formal dining room, with continental cuisine; a branch of Boston's famous Legal Seafood restaurant; the Café Rouge bistro, Captains piano bar, and Swans café in the Grand Lobby. There are many other restaurants in the neighborhood, as well.

Services: Foreign-currency exchange, 24-hour room service, travel agency, hairdresser, airport shuttle.

Facilities: Health club with pool, cabaret theater featuring *Forever Plaid,* Amtrak and many airline ticket offices.

57 PARK PLAZA HOTEL, 200 Stuart St., Boston, MA 02116. Tel. 617/482-1800, or toll free 800/468-3557. Fax 617/451-2750. 350 rms. A/C TV TEL **Subway:** Green Line to Boylston or Arlington.

$ Rates: $115–$160 single; $125–$175 double. Extra person $15. Children under 18 stay free with parents. AARP discounts available to those with ID. AE, DC, MC, V. **Parking:** Free on premises.

This well-located, upper-range hotel is only 2 blocks from Boston Common and the Public Garden and is right near the Greyhound bus terminal, in a multipurpose complex of buildings that includes a parking garage, two cinemas, two lounges, and two restaurants. Business meetings provide a big part of its clientele, both because of the facilities and because of its central location.

Facilities: Year-round swimming pool, sauna.

HOLIDAY INN GOVERNMENT CENTER, 5 Blossom St., Boston, MA 02114. Tel. 617/742-7630, or toll free 800/465-4329. Fax 617/742-4192. 301 rms. A/C MINIBAR TV TEL **Subway:** Government Center.

$ Rates: Mid-Apr to mid-Nov, $149–$159 single; $156–$165 double. Mid-Nov to mid-Apr, 20% to 30% discount. Children under 18 stay free with parents. AE, DC, DISC, JCB, MC, V. **Parking:** Covered parking adjacent to the hotel, $7.50 per day.

Just off Cambridge Street, between Government Center and the Longfellow Bridge over the Charles River, is a high-rise haven slightly out of the center of things. It's several blocks from Government Center, and then several blocks again from Government Center to the Boston Common. But prices are not too bad in this modern building, and facilities are good.

Dining/Entertainment: The James Michael Bar & Deli off the lobby serves all meals, but for more atmospheric dining go to the rooftop Lobster Trap dining room. The Reflections Lounge has piano music nightly.

Services: No-smoking rooms, TV movie channel, privileges at nearby health club.

Facilities: Outdoor pool (summer months only), two cinemas, supermarket, and rows of shops in the same complex.

HOWARD JOHNSON HOTEL KENMORE SQUARE, 575 Commonwealth Ave., Boston, MA 02215. Tel. 617/267-3100, or toll free 800/654-2000. 179 rms. A/C TV TEL **Subway:** Green Line to Kenmore.

$ Rates: $85–$160 single; $90–$170 double. Children under 18 stay free with parents. Senior discounts and special packages available. AE, MC, V. **Parking:** Free, on premises.

You'll find this comfortable, modern hotel near Kenmore Square perfectly situated if you're visiting Boston University, and well placed for many other Boston pursuits, as the location allows you to hop right on a Green Line train for the short ride to Park Street Station on Boston Common.

Dining/Entertainment: Guests can relax in the Profiles Café restaurant and Box Seat Lounge.

Services: Freedom Trail audiocassette tapes for walking tours.

Facilities: Indoor rooftop heated pool.

LENOX HOTEL, 710 Boylston St., corner of Exeter, Boston, MA 02116. Tel. 617/536-5300, or toll free 800/225-7676 outside Massachusetts. Fax 617/267-1237. 222 rms. A/C TV TEL **Subway:** Green Line to Copley.

$ Rates: $135–$215 single; $155–$235 double. Extra person $15. Children under 18 stay free with parents. AE, DC, DISC, ER, MC, V. **Parking:** $14.

Enjoy the pleasures of the Prudential Center and Copley Place by staying at the Lenox, where you're right on the same block as the Pru. Guest rooms have French provincial, Chinese, or colonial decor, big closets, and soundproofed walls; some rooms even have fireplaces. Besides being right in the Prudential Center, the Lenox is right next to the Boston Public Library, and only a block from Copley Square.

Dining/Entertainment: An English-style pub is open for lunch, supper, and late-night snacks (till 2am); Diamond Jim's Piano Bar is good for drinking and singing; and the Upstairs Grill serves everything from prime rib to seafood.

Services: *USA Today* room delivery, babysitting, airport shuttle service.

Facilities: Exercise room.

TREMONT HOUSE, 275 Tremont St., Boston, MA 02116-5694. Tel. 617/426-1400. Fax 617/482-6730. 281 rms. A/C TV TEL **Directions:** Take the Chinatown/Kneeland St. exit from the Mass. Pike or I-93, follow Kneeland to Tremont and turn left. **Subway:** Green Line to Boylston or Orange Line to New England Medical Center.

$ Rates: $105–$120 single; $120–$135 double. Children under 12 stay free with parents. AE, CB, DC, MC, V. **Parking:** $15, valet.

Built in 1925 as the headquarters of the Benevolent Protective Order of Elks, this well-located downtown hotel 3 blocks south of Boston Common was later called the Bradford, and as such hosted live radio broadcasts from its rooftop nightclub. Later a favorite stopping place for actors and artists, it has been extensively (and expensively) redone recently from top to bottom. The elegance of the original neoclassical architecture shines through, and is delightful. Guest rooms, tastefully done in Early American with prints of works in Boston's Museum of Fine Arts, are small but comfortable, with queen-size beds.

Dining/Entertainment: The Stage Deli is a branch of the New York operation;

the Roxy is a popular dance club with Big Band and more contemporary sounds; the NYC Jukebox is a disco.

Services: Room service, Gray Line tours office, concierge, no-smoking floor, handicapped accessible, drycleaning.

MODERATE

COPLEY SQUARE HOTEL, 47 Huntington Ave., at Exeter St., Boston, MA 02116. Tel. 617/536-9000, or toll free 800/225-7062. Fax 617/267-3547. 153 rms. A/C TV TEL **Transportation:** Airport shuttle service $7.50 per person. **Subway:** Green Line to Prudential.
$ Rates: $105–$125 single; $120–$145 double; $10 per extra person up to four. Children under 18 stay free with parents. Special winter rates and package plans available. AE, DC, DISC, MC, V. **Parking:** $12, next door.

⑤ This is perhaps the best bargain in the area of the Prudential Center, Symphony Hall, and the Christian Science Center. Like most of the older hotels in Boston, its rooms have been carefully refurbished and maintained, and are very comfortable. Though much less fancy than the big places, this is a full-service hotel. Rooms are pleasantly decorated, have coffee-makers, hair dryers, alarm clock radios, safes, as well as cable TVs with movie channels.

Dining/Entertainment: Café Budapest restaurant, a Boston tradition, serves continental cuisine; Pop's Place is the informal café-bistro; the Original Sports Saloon is a great place for a light meal.

HOLIDAY INN BOSTON BROOKLINE, 1200 Beacon St., Brookline, MA 02146. Tel. 617/277-1200, or toll free 800/465-4329. 208 rms. A/C TV TEL **Directions:** Go west on Beacon St.; the hotel is just across the city line in Brookline. **Subway:** Green Line "Cleveland Circle" train.
$ Rates: May–Oct $135 single; $145 double. Nov–Apr, $125 single; $135 double. AE, DC, DISC, JCB, MC, V. **Parking:** $5 per day.
The rooms in this residential neighborhood motel are clean, comfy and fairly quiet, and are equipped with clock radios as well as TVs. There's an indoor swimming pool and a whirlpool bath to ease out muscles stretched in sightseeing. Public transportation will take you the several miles into town fairly easily.

Dining/Entertainment: The hotel has a moderately priced restaurant serving traditional American cuisine, and a lounge with live entertainment on Friday and Saturday evenings.

HOWARD JOHNSON LODGE FENWAY, 1271 Boylston St., Boston, MA 02215. Tel. 617/267-8300, or toll free 800/654-2000. 94 rms. A/C TV TEL **Subway:** Green Line "Riverside" train to Fenway.
$ Rates: $75–$115 single; $85–$130 double. Children under 18 stay free with parents. Senior discounts and special packages available. AE, MC, V. **Parking:** Free.
This Howard Johnson's is off U.S. 1, near Fenway Park, home of the Boston Red Sox during baseball season. The Museum of Fine Arts and the Gardner Museum are also close by, and public transportation easily gets you to the city's other sights.

BUDGET

MOTELS ON THE OUTSKIRTS

Although it's preferable to stay downtown and not get snarled in city traffic, you may want to know that Boston has several representatives of the budget-priced **Susse Chalet** motel chain. Prices generally run in the range of $45 to $60 for a single and $50 to $65 for a double. If you're not sure where exactly you'd like to stay in relation to the city, call one of the toll-free numbers (tel. 800/258-1980; 800/572-1880 in

N.H.; 800/858-5008 in eastern Canada), because they handle all the Susse Chalets in the area. If you'd rather call directly to the location of your choice, there are two in Neponset—one at 800 Morrissey Blvd. (tel. 617/287-9100), and the other at 900 Morrissey Blvd. (tel. 617/287-9200); there's also one in Newton at 160 Boylston (617/527-9000), which is accessible by subway; and there's one in Braintree at 125 Union St. (tel. 617/848-7890), which is about 11 miles south of downtown Boston and is also accessible by subway. All of the hotels listed above have outdoor swimming pools (except for the one at 900 Morrissey in Neponset—its guests use the pool at the Susse Chalet at 800 Morrissey) and coin-op laundries, as well as color TVs.

BED & BREAKFAST SERVICES

Bed-and-breakfast services will take your reservation, describe accommodations and prices, and give directions to your lodging. All this is best done in advance, but don't be afraid to call one of the following services if you arrive in town without a reservation.

Bed and Breakfast Associates Bay Colony, Ltd., P.O. Box 57166, Babson Park, Boston, MA 02157-0166 (tel. 617/449-5302 from 10am to 12:30pm and 1:30 to 5pm; fax 617/449-5958), will send you brochures describing hundreds of rooms, studios, suites, and apartments located throughout eastern Massachusetts. Prices range from $50 to $85 single, $60 to $125 double, continental breakfast included.

Host Homes of Boston, P.O. Box 117, Waban Branch, Boston, MA 02168 (tel. 617/244-1308; fax 617/244-5156), will find you a room in Newton, Brookline, Cambridge, Boston, or another community for about $44 to $85 single, $54 to $110 double, breakfast included. They will send you a free descriptive directory of their B&Bs. They accept AE, MC, V.

Greater Boston Hospitality, P.O. Box 1142, Brookline, MA 02146 (tel. 617/277-5430), makes reservations for private homes, private city clubs, small inns and condominiums in Boston, Brookline, Cambridge, Needham, Newton, Wellesley, Quincy, Scituate, Gloucester, and Marblehead. You can write, or call from 8:30am to 5:30pm. They accept AE, MC, V.

Beacon Inn Guest Houses, 248 Newbury St., Boston, MA 02116 (tel. 617/262-1771 or 266-7142; fax 617/266-7276), will arrange a daily or weekly room rental for you, with private bath and kitchenette with utensils, for $55 per day, $300 per week single; $70 per day, $400 per week double, tax included. All of their rooms are in renovated brownstone apartment buildings located in Back Bay, on Newbury Street near the Prudential Center and the Hynes Convention Center.

A Bed & Breakfast in Brookline

ANTHONY'S TOWN HOUSE, 1085 Beacon St., Brookline, MA 02146
Tel. 617/566-3972. 10 rms (none with bath or shower). TV **Directions:** From downtown Boston, follow Beacon St. west and south, cross the city limit into Brookline, and look for the guesthouse on the left-hand side of the street.
Subway: Green Line "Cleveland Circle" train.
$ Rates: $30–$60 single or double. No credit cards. **Parking:** Free, on premises.
This turn-of-the-century brownstone town house offers various rooms, most of which tend to be plain rather than fancy, but it's safe and affordable.

4. DINING

Dining possibilities in Boston are virtually limitless. The city's array of restaurants includes at least one representative of every notable cuisine in the world, and usually more than one—in the Boston area there are more than 150 Chinese restaurants alone. Most of Boston's restaurants take advantage of the fresh seafood that comes to the docks daily, whether the specialty is seafood or not.

For our recommendations, we've chosen favorites, places that we've found satisfactory in every way. Remember that the many very fine hotel restaurants, lounges, and coffee shops are covered along with the hotel itself in the preceding section. The good restaurants and coffeehouses in Cambridge are described in Chapter 5, "Around Boston"; remember that most of them are within walking distance of the Red Line's Harvard subway station, and the trip can be made from central Boston in 10 or 15 minutes. The good restaurant in the Museum of Fine Arts, the best place for lunch if you're seeing the MFA or the Gardner Museum, is described along with the museum itself in the sightseeing section.

In the more expensive establishments, it's good to call ahead for reservations if they'll take them—many Boston places do not. This is true especially on weekends and holidays, of course. And when you call, ask whether they honor your credit card, and what parking arrangements there are.

Massachusetts has a meal tax of 5% added to every meal check over a minimal amount.

EXPENSIVE

ANOTHER SEASON, 97 Mt. Vernon St. Tel. 367-0880.
Cuisine: CONTINENTAL. **Reservations:** Recommended. **Subway:** Red Line to Charles or Red or Green Line to Park Street.
$ Prices: Appetizers $4.50–$6.50; main courses $14–$20; dinner $37; fixed-price meals $19. AE, MC, V.
Open: Lunch Tues–Fri 11:45am–2:15pm; dinner Mon–Sat 6–10pm.
Another Season, on Beacon Hill just east of the Charles subway station, is small and friendly, with a marvelous feeling of informal elegance; chef Odette Bery puts her personal touch on classic recipes (the menu changes monthly), then makes the rounds of the tables to see how diners have liked them. The wine list is very fine, the cuisine even finer, the service just as good. You'll find the experience worth far more than the price of a full dinner. Monday through Thursday there are excellent four-course prix-fixe menus.

BAY TOWER ROOM, 60 State St. Tel. 723-1666.
Cuisine: CREATIVE AMERICAN. **Reservations:** Recommended. **Subway:** Orange or Blue Line to State.
$ Prices: Appetizers $4–$8; main courses $15–$28; dinner $50. AE, DC, MC, V.
Open: Dinner Mon–Thurs 5:30–10pm, Fri–Sat 5:30–11pm.
Every table in this restaurant, which is right next to Boston's Old State House, has a marvelous view of the Custom House Tower, Boston Harbor, Logan airport, and the hills beyond (because it's located atop a skyscraper). A cocktail lounge with a band for dancing (Friday and Saturday) is on the mezzanine level (open 4:30pm to 1am Monday to Thursday, to 2am on Friday and Saturday). A jacket is required in the dining room. The menu is long and inclusive, expensive but not outrageous. You can start with lobster ravioli with ginger and basil, or a simple soup. Fish and shellfish, fowl, and grilled meats are all featured; specialties are roast rack of lamb with rosemary, garlic, and cracked pepper in a zinfandel sauce, and a seafood mixed grill of lobster, swordfish, and sea scallops. The menu changes seasonally.

BIBA FOOD HALL, 272 Boylston St. Tel. 426-7878.
Cuisine: AMERICAN. **Reservations:** Required. **Subway:** Green Line to Arlington.
$ Prices: Appetizers $8–$13; main courses $11–$28; full meal $25–$60; wines $25 and up.
Open: Lunch Mon–Fri 11:30am–2:30pm, Sun 11:30am–3pm; dinner daily 5:30–10pm (Fri–Sat to 11pm).
Biba is disconcerting, expensive, and lots of fun. Enter past the valet parking attendant to the high-ceilinged bar where the flashy decoration is on the people, not the walls. Located in the building called Heritage on the Common, to the right of the Four Seasons, this is among Boston's trendiest places for the young and

NEW
ENGLAND

Boston

0   .5 mi
    .8 km
N

Du Barry French Restaurant ⑥
Durgin-Park Market Dining Room ⑳
Hamersley's Bistro ⑦
Hampshire House ⑬
Harvard Bookstore Cafe ④
Imperial Tea House ⑪
Legal Seafoods ⑨
L'Espalier ②
Maison Robert ⑯
Pizzeria Regina ㉑
Rebecca's ⑭
Ritz-Carlton Dining Room ⑧
The Salty Dog ⑱
Seaside Restaurant and Bar ⑲
Travis Restaurant ⑤

Acapulco ③
Another Season ⑮
Bangkok Cuisine ①
Bay Tower Room ⑰
Biba Food Hall ⑩
Commonwealth Brewing
     Company ㉒
Cornucopia ⑫

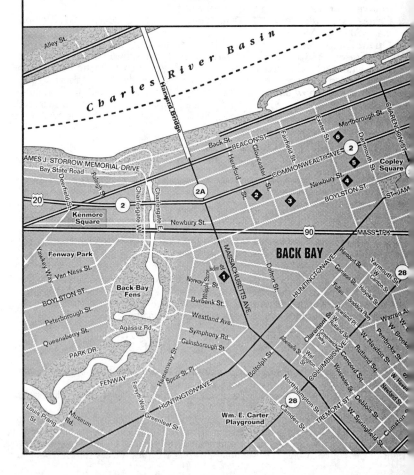

well heeled to drink and dine. Upstairs past the wine racks is the large low-ceiling dining room done in an eclectic, spare style with hints at art deco and the Southwest. Chef-owner Lydia Shire's menu is unlike anything you've ever seen, but the food is excellent. Categories are Fish, Offal, Meat, Starch, Legumina, Specials, and Sweets. Order two or three appetizers if you like or split a main course or two—anything goes. You might see silken tuna over crisp potato chips, macaroni and cheese with oxtail pieces, or spring baby lamb with panzarotti of sheep's-milk cheese and wild leeks. Lunch, equally original, costs $15 to $30. Waiters are friendly and well informed, clientele is youngish and professional, and there's no dress code.

CORNUCOPIA, 15 West St. Tel. 338-4600.
> **Cuisine:** AMERICAN. **Reservations:** Not required. **Subway:** Red or Green Line to Park Street, or Red or Orange Line to Downtown Crossing.
> **$ Prices:** Appetizers $4–$8; main courses $7–$20.50; lunch $14–$18; dinner $30–$40. AE, DISC, MC, V.
> **Open:** Lunch Mon–Fri 11:30am–2:30pm; dinner Tues–Sat 5:30–10pm.

Cornucopia is in an odd but engaging place. Soft muted colors and hanging lamps with diamond-shaped stained-glass shades greet you as you enter; there's an enclosed terrace at the rear, and an attractive upstairs room as well. Original art hangs on the walls, and several black-marble café tables with intricate white veining stand waiting near the sidewalk window.

A meal might begin with chilled artichoke and prosciutto with hazelnuts and a balsamic vinaigrette, then go on to a main course of grilled trout and shrimp with steamed asparagus in a saffron-cream sauce, or roast leg of lamb. Next to each course on the menu, the proprietors have suggested a wine. The dessert selection changes daily, but is as wonderful as the heartier fare. Remember the café menu if you need a pick-me-up after shopping or before a night at the opera. West Street runs from Tremont Street near the Boston Common Visitor Information Center to Washington Street.

HAMERSLEY'S BISTRO, 578 Tremont St. Tel. 267-6068.
> **Cuisine:** NEW AMERICAN. **Reservations:** Required. **Subway:** Orange Line to Dover; the station is about 7 blocks from the restaurant. **Parking:** Valet daily.
> **$ Prices:** Appetizers $7–$12; main courses $18–$25; full meal $45–$65.
> **Open:** Dinner Mon–Sat 6–10pm, Sun 6–9:30pm.

 Gordon and Fiona Hamersley have converted two storefronts on a wide residential boulevard in the South End near the corner of Upton into one of Boston's most fashionable bistros. A spare, clean decor of black and white, venetian blinds, black bentwood chairs, and simple table settings make the mood, and Gordon makes the food, which is outstanding. Starting with seemingly simple dishes like fried chicken, Chef Hamersley performs his magic with marinades and spices to make it unforgettable. The seafood is similarly done: a traditional start ending in an original creation.

HAMPSHIRE HOUSE, 84 Beacon St. Tel. 227-9600.

Ⓕ FROMMER'S SMART TRAVELER: RESTAURANTS

1. If you want to sample Boston's fancy restaurants but don't want to pay the lofty prices, go at lunchtime. Many of the same dishes are served in slightly smaller portions at considerably lower prices.
2. If you find it difficult to make up your mind about what to order, opt for the daily special dishes. They're always fresh, and the chef probably chose to make them because he or she especially enjoys preparing them.

Cuisine: CONTINENTAL. **Reservations:** Recommended. **Subway:** Arlington.
$ **Prices:** Appetizers $4–$9; main courses $17–$30. AE, DC, DISC, MC, V.
Open: Lunch daily noon–3pm; dinner daily 5:30–10pm.

Boston's most famous restaurant faces the Public Garden between Arlington and Charles Streets. While the restaurant is noted for its location in a fine early 20th-century Georgian Revival mansion, its elegant decoration, and its good cuisine, it is far more famous for its Bull & Finch Pub (tel. 227-9605) in the basement, which inspired the setting for the television comedy show called **"Cheers."** Every day, countless visitors pose by the entrance to have their pictures taken, then descend the stairs to take a look and perhaps to buy a Cheers T-shirt. Be forewarned: The pub looks nothing like the set for the show—it is not spacious but rather cozy and crowded. The comfy booths are always crowded with a lively, happy, young, attractive crowd taking in the very English pub atmosphere. The drink to order here is Samuel Adams lager, Boston's own top-quality beer, or Harpoon ale, brewed only a mile or two away on Northern Avenue.

Upstairs is another bar, the Oak Room, as sedate and Beacon Hill–ish as you could imagine. Tall arched windows framed by formal drapes let lots of light into the high-ceilinged room, bringing a glint to the polished glasses and a shine to the grand piano. Dignified gents and ladies, properly dressed, murmur quietly to one another while sipping classic concoctions and munching free hors d'oeuvres. The menu is interesting without being overly exotic, with some classics such as fettuccine Alfredo, New England clam chowder, and French onion soup gratinée as first courses, then lots of steaks, and also chicken. There is live jazz Tuesday to Sunday evenings, and there is free parking in the Boston Common garage every evening.

L'ESPALIER, 30 Gloucester St. Tel. 262-3023.
Cuisine: CONTEMPORARY FRENCH. **Reservations:** Required. **Subway:** Green Line to Copley.
$ **Prices:** Fixed-price dinner $56 per person; dinner for two $150–$200. AE, MC, V.
Open: Dinner Mon–Sat 6–10pm.

Many Bostonians would agree that L'Espalier is one of the finest restaurants in town. For the city's ultimate dining experience, it may be equaled but can't be beat. This is an elegant restaurant in a turn-of-the-century Back Bay town house off Commonwealth Avenue. Reservations are sometimes difficult to get. You enter through a vestibule and walk up a flight of stairs to reach one of three formal dining rooms. Waiters in black and white attend to you immediately, and are professional, polished, and friendly in their work. The menu lists the chef's latest creations of contemporary French cuisine, which, though sometimes exotic, are really inspired and delicious. The wine list is extensive, offering more than 200 bottles. You won't soon forget a meal here.

MAISON ROBERT, 45 School St. Tel. 227-3370.
Cuisine: FRENCH. **Reservations:** Recommended. **Subway:** Red or Green Line to Park Street.
$ **Prices:** Appetizers $3–$15; main courses $8–$30; fixed-price lunch $9.50–$12.75; fixed-price dinner $16–$23. AE, DC, MC, V.
Open: Lunch Mon–Fri noon–2:30pm; dinner Mon–Sat 5:30–9:30pm.

Among Boston's restaurants of long-standing high quality, few can equal the record of Maison Robert. In summer, tables are set outside near the statue of Benjamin Franklin for Ben's Café, where you can have a large salad, cold plate, or main dish for lunch, but dinner is the main event here. Chef Andrée Robert, daughter of the restaurant's founder, creates nouvelle cuisine with American touches. You might start on oysters with raspberry vinegar, or pâté of leeks; go on to lobster with champagne sauce, or sliced breast of duck with apples and blueberries, or perhaps flamed rib of beef for two. Desserts are, of course, sumptuous, from crêpes Suzette through the house gâteau (chocolate), to various soufflés. Surroundings are formal and attractive; the service is impeccable. Maison Robert is located in the Old City Hall building behind King's Chapel, around the corner from the Parker House Hotel.

RITZ-CARLTON DINING ROOM, 15 Arlington St. Tel. 536-5700.

Cuisine: CONTINENTAL. **Reservations:** Recommended. **Subway:** Green Line to Arlington.

$ Prices: Appetizers $5–$70 (caviar); main courses $28–$35; dinner $65–$75. AE, DC, DISC, MC, V.

Open: Lunch daily noon–2:30pm; dinner Sun–Thurs 5:30–10pm, Fri–Sat 5:30–11pm; brunch Sun 10:45am–2:30pm.

The genteel atmosphere here makes a good place for a fine lunch or dinner, where diners look onto the Public Garden, its trees and flowers, or snow scenes as the case may be. Elegance is all around: gold tracery on the cream-colored ceiling, lofty many-paned windows surrounded by blue-and-white print drapes, crystal chandeliers, and sconces, potted plants, a tinkling piano, and impeccable service. The menu changes daily, but a typical luncheon might offer you roast duckling with cherries, a thin veal cutlet in chive butter, or perhaps a selection from the cold buffet. At dinner, start with lobster bisque with cognac, or Louisiana shrimp, and then go on to a roast leg of spring lamb, or lobster prepared with whisky, or médaillons of venison with cranberries and chestnuts. For dessert, have one of the several dessert soufflés, which are first a dream, then ambrosia, then a fond memory. The dress code is enforced at all times.

MODERATE

ON BEACON HILL

REBECCA'S, 21 Charles St. Tel. 742-9747.

Cuisine: NEW AMERICAN. **Reservations:** Recommended. **Subway:** Red or Green Line to Park Street.

$ Prices: Appetizers $4.50–$8; main courses $17–$20; lunch $9–$14; dinner $32–$45. AE, MC, V.

Open: Lunch Mon–Sat 11:30am–4pm; dinner Sun–Thurs 5:30–10:45pm, Fri–Sat 5:30–11:45pm; Sun brunch 11am–4pm.

Rebecca's, just north of Boston Common, is a wonderful eatery convenient to downtown shopping areas and tourist attractions. The cuisine is creative, carefully prepared, and beautifully presented—a rarity for a moderately priced restaurant in any city. There's paella valenciana, chicken stuffed with chèvre cheese and spinach, and, if you're interested in something lighter at lunch, they have great soups and quiches of the day. The desserts are as good as they look—maybe even better. It's doubtful that you'll find one disgruntled soul in the restaurant.

FANEUIL HALL MARKETPLACE & THE WATERFRONT

DURGIN-PARK MARKET DINING ROOMS, North Market Building, 340 Faneuil Hall Marketplace. Tel. 227-2038.

Cuisine: TRADITIONAL AMERICAN. **Reservations:** Not accepted. **Subway:** Green or Blue Line to Government Center.

$ Prices: Appetizers $1.50–$3.75; main courses $7.95–$15.95. AE, MC, V.

Open: Mon–Sat 11:30am–10pm, Sun 11am–9pm.

Durgin-Park, a Boston institution for many years, boasts that it was "established before you were born," and adds that "Your grandfather and great-grandfather may have dined with us, too." As you mount the stairs to the dining room, it crosses your mind that you must have taken the wrong stairway and entered some "employee only" door, for there before you is all the dishwashing machinery and hardworking kitchen help, and right next to this, the kitchen itself, with cooks and waitresses scurrying here and there. To left and right are large, plain rooms with steam pipes running about on the ceiling, and several sets of long tables covered with checkered cloths. The menu, plainly printed with notices of daily specials stapled to it, bears pithy reminders and warnings such as "washroom downstairs" and "We are not responsible for any steak ordered well done." Try the huge prime rib (while it lasts, for this is the specialty), or the *fresh* lobster stew (emphasis theirs), roast stuffed duck, or lowly "frankfort and beans." Clams, oysters, and fish are served as well, as are cocktails. Perhaps the best time to go is at lunch, when crowds are thinner, portions are more manageable, and prices are lower.

SEASIDE RESTAURANT AND BAR, 188 South Market Building, Faneuil Hall Marketplace. Tel. 742-8728.
    Cuisine: SEAFOOD/AMERICAN. **Reservations:** Not required. **Subway:** Green or Blue Line to Government Center.
$ Prices: Appetizers $1.95–$6.95; main courses $4.95–$7.95 at lunch, $9.95–$16.95 at dinner. AE, DC, MC, V.
    Open: Daily 11:30am–10pm.
Lunch is the time to dine, see, and be seen, although Seaside is busy all day. Elaborate sandwiches, complex salads, omelets, and quiches make up the midday bill of fare. Besides the natural-wood tables, Seaside has a bar at which you can sit to have a drink, or a sandwich, or both. At dinnertime, Seaside features steaks, lots of seafood, the chef's daily specialties, and on Wednesday, Thursday, and Sunday, there's live entertainment.

NEAR HARVARD SQUARE

DALI RESTAURANT AND TAPAS BAR, 415 Washington St., Somerville. Tel. 661-3254.
    Cuisine: SPANISH. **Reservations:** Not required. **Directions:** Take the red line to Harvard Square. Walk through Harvard yard, exiting at Kirkland St. Follow Kirkland for several blocks, until it turns into Washington St. The restaurant is on Washington at Beacon St.
$ Prices: Tapas $2.50–$6; main courses $10–$20. AE, MC, V.
    Open: Dinner Mon–Sat 5pm–midnight.
Even though it's a little out of the way (about 15 minutes from Harvard Square), Dali (easily seen because of its purple exterior) is worth the aggravation of getting there. Don't bother to drive out there, it's primarily a residential area and parking places are scarce.
    Upon entering, you'll realize immediately that you're in Boston's most authentic Spanish restaurant. You'll find hams, dried flowers, ropes of garlic, and copperware hanging above the bar; murals, smaller paintings, beautiful tiles, and a small "clothesline" of various types of underwear hanging between the front and back dining rooms—you really have to see it to believe it. Just about everyone orders several tapas dishes—like garlic potatoes, garlicky chicken, baked goat cheese, and veggie puffs—instead of just one main dish, but if you'd rather order a single dish, you can choose from among several kinds of paella available, as well as the house specialty—red snapper baked in a crust of salt. A dessert of crêpes filled with strawberries and topped with chocolate sauce and Grand Marnier is the best way to end a meal here.

INEXPENSIVE

Dining inexpensively does not mean resigning yourself to fast food. This city has hundreds of wonderfully atmospheric and satisfying eating places charging very little.

FANEUIL HALL MARKETPLACE

THE SALTY DOG, basement of Quincy Market. Tel. 742-2094.
    Cuisine: SEAFOOD. **Reservations:** Not accepted. **Directions:** Take Green or Blue Line to Government Center. Face the front of Quincy Market, back to Faneuil Hall, walk to the right of the market facade. Just under the southwest corner of the market is the stairway down to the Salty Dog.
$ Prices: Main courses $4.95–$18.95; blackboard specials $8.95–$12.95. AE, DISC, MC, V.
    Open: Daily 11:30am–11pm.

Good seafood in congenial surroundings is the formula at this seafood "grille and bar" where you can have fish-and-chips, clams on the half shell, or any one of several fried or baked fish plates. In recent years owner Roland Prevost has upgraded service and decor, and has added interesting specialties (Cajun, barbecue) to the menu. The oyster stew seems expensive, but you'll find at least a half dozen whole, succulent oysters in each bowlful. The double tall Bloody Mary comes with a shrimp. There is a sidewalk café and open-air oyster bar for those who prefer eating outside.

NORTH END

COMMONWEALTH BREWING COMPANY, 138 Portland St. Tel. 523-8383.

Cuisine: GERMAN/AMERICAN. **Reservations:** Not required. **Subway:** Green Line to Haymarket or North Station.

$ Prices: Appetizers $2.50–$7; main courses $8–$15; meals $15–$25. AE, CB, DC, DISC, MC, V.

Open: Sun–Thurs 11:30am–midnight, Fri–Sat 11:30am–1am.

Through the huge windows of this working brewery and restaurant near North Station and Boston Garden, the antique copper brewing equipment gleams and shines. In the high-ceilinged main dining room are long brass-clad tables and a long stand-up bar running the length of the back wall. There's a spirit of conviviality, inspired by the decor but forcefully encouraged by the Commonwealth's forte: golden ale, amber ale, bitter, and stout, brewed right here and served live. If you descend to the basement (where there are more tables, and another long bar), you can witness the brewing. The menu is long and satisfying: open-face steak sandwich, shrimp salad, baby back pork ribs, and smoked seafood sampler are a few examples. Come for lunch, dinner, a late-night snack, or just a glass or two of real beer.

NEWBURY & BOYLSTON STREETS

The two principal shopping and business streets in the Back Bay have a tremendous number of places to nosh, snack, eat, lunch, or dine. Keep this section in mind when you make the rounds of Newbury Street galleries.

ACAPULCO, 266 Newbury St. Tel. 247-9126.

Cuisine: MEXICAN. **Reservations:** Not accepted. **Subway:** Green Line to Hynes Convention Center/ICA.

$ Prices: Appetizers $2.50–$6.95; main courses $6.95–$12.90; meals $8.50–$15. AE, DC, MC, V.

Open: Mon–Sat 11:30am–11pm, Sun 2–11pm.

Mexican food on Newbury Street? Yes, in this attractive little restaurant done in brick, butcher block, and Mexican crafts. A typical meal might consist of gazpacho, a tostada, flan for dessert, and a glass of guava juice to drink. Or you could order taquitos, crispy buñuelos for dessert, and drink Dos Equis Mexican beer, and pay somewhat more. Have just a combination plate, which is very filling. You can order meatless meals, or dishes put up to take out. In summer, enjoy the outdoor patio tables.

BANGKOK CUISINE, 177a Massachusetts Ave. Tel. 262-5377.

Cuisine: THAI. **Reservations:** Not accepted. **Subway:** Green Line to Hynes Convention Center/ICA.

$ Prices: Appetizers $2–$4.50; main courses $8–$13.25; meals $20–$25. AE, DC, MC, V.

Open: Lunch Mon–Sat 11:30am–3pm; dinner daily 5–10:30pm.

This small, attractive place near Boylston Street is always busy serving Thai classics clear soups made with scallions, shrimp, and hot peppers; savory dishes of duck with pineapple, spices, and Asian vegetables and mushrooms—once you've tried the food here, you may indeed want to take off for Bangkok. Have soup or an appetizer, a main course based on seafood, pork, beef, or chicken, a dessert, and a bottle of Thai beer

A warning: Soups are marked "moderately hot," but they are very spicy-hot (and very good).

DU BARRY FRENCH RESTAURANT, 159 Newbury St. Tel. 262-2445.
Cuisine: FRENCH. **Reservations:** Recommended. **Subway:** Green Line to Copley.
$ Prices: Appetizers $1.75–$11; main courses $6–$8 at lunch, $13.50–$22 at dinner; dinner $25–$35. AE, DC, DISC, MC, V.
Open: Lunch daily noon–2:30pm; dinner daily 5:30–10pm.
This is Newbury Street's Gallic eatery of long standing (since 1936). Chef René Rubaud's dinner main courses are classics: filet of sole, daube of tournedos rossini, frogs' legs Provençale, rabbit sautéed in dijon mustard, and beef tongue in a Madeira sauce. At lunch, numerous platters are offered. In good weather the outdoor patio and enclosed terrace are the choice places to dine—walk through the restaurant to reach them. Du Barry is between Dartmouth and Exeter.

HARVARD BOOKSTORE CAFE, 190 Newbury St. Tel. 536-0097.
Cuisine: AMERICAN/MEDITERRANEAN/EUROPEAN/NORTH AFRICAN.
Reservations: Not required. **Subway:** Green Line to Copley.
$ Prices: Appetizers $2.50–$5.50; sandwiches $6–$8; main courses $8–$13.50. AE, MC, V.
Open: Mon–Wed 8am–10pm, Thurs 8am–11pm, Fri–Sat 8am–midnight, Sun noon–10pm.
This is one of the nicest locations in the Back Bay, a shady street corner with lots of interesting sidewalk and street activity. If you can grab a sidewalk table, do so; then settle in with coffee and pastry, or order from their menu of fairly substantial luncheon fare, including salads and sandwiches. It's sure to satisfy, for the chef here is none other than Moncef Meddeb, formerly of nearby ultra-pricey L'Espalier.

LEGAL SEAFOODS, 35 Columbus Ave. Tel. 426-4444.
Cuisine: SEAFOOD. **Reservations:** Recommended for lunch. **Subway:** Green Line to Arlington.
$ Prices: Appetizers $2.25–$8; main courses $6–$22; meals $22–$36. AE, DC, DISC, MC, V.
Open: Mon–Thurs 11am–10pm, Fri–Sat 11am–11pm, Sun noon–10pm.
This Boston institution, located in the Boston Park Plaza Hotel, is a no-nonsense operation that prides itself on freshness and reasonable prices. The light and attractive restaurant is big, but nicely arranged into cozy sections. The menu is encyclopedic, listing close to 100 items, but this is for reference: When fresh stocks run out, that's it for any particular fish. Start with a shrimp cocktail or oysters on the half shell, go on to scrod, bluefish, mako shark, trout, lobster, salmon, or scallops. Note that there is often a wait for a table, especially long on weekends.

CHINATOWN

IMPERIAL TEA HOUSE, 70 Beach St. Tel. 426-8439.
Cuisine: CHINESE. **Reservations:** Not required. **Subway:** Orange Line to Essex.
$ Prices: Appetizers $2–$4.25; main courses $8–$13.50; dim sum meal $10–$20. AE, MC, V.
Open: Daily 9am–2am (dim sum served 9am–3pm).
This restaurant in the heart of Boston's small Chinatown has been around for a long time, but has only recently been recognized for what it is: the best place in town for dim sum yum chai. The best time to go for the classic meal of Chinese hors d'oeuvres is between 10 and 11am, or after 1:30pm on weekdays. Other times the crowd is dense. Most of the patrons here are Chinese Bostonians who know a good thing or, rather, things: spareribs, water chestnuts in gelatin, pork dumplings, tofu, green sugarcane leaves stuffed with sweet rice, pork, and quail eggs, even fried duck feet. Sit in the upstairs room for dim sum. The à la carte restaurant downstairs is not as good. The system is this: You pick what you like from the carts, which appear in a

steady stream throughout the morning and afternoon. Each plate on the cart has about three portions of the item (so it's good to do dim summing with two friends). When you've had enough, the waiter counts up the plates and gives you the bill, which will be very low considering the amount and quality of the food.

SOUTH BOSTON

JIMMY'S HARBORSIDE, 242 Northern Ave. Tel. 423-1000.
  Cuisine: SEAFOOD. **Reservations:** Recommended. **Subway:** Red Line to South Station, then no. 7 bus, "City Point-South Station" (taxi is preferable).
$ Prices: Appetizers $2.75–$19; main courses $7.95–$22.95 at lunch, $10.50–$26.95 at dinner. AE, CB, DC, MC, V.
  Open: Mon–Sat noon–9:30pm, Sun 4–9pm.
Jimmy's, "Home of the Chowder King," located at the end of Northern Avenue or Fish Pier, due east of downtown Boston across the Fort Point Channel, has a dress code, lots of nautical memorabilia, plush carpets and chairs, and a boat-shaped bar surrounded by little cocktail tables. The lunch special includes chowder or lobster bisque, main course, salad, potato, dessert, and coffee, for about $12. At dinner, have two "chicken" lobsters (weighing about a pound apiece), with french fries and salad for $24.25, jumbo shrimp for $16.75, swordfish shish kebab for $13.75, or one of the pasta specialties. The wine list runs to almost 115 items.

BROOKLINE

SOL AZTECA, 914a Beacon St., Brookline. Tel. 262-0909.
  Cuisine: MEXICAN. **Reservations:** Not accepted. **Subway:** Take a Green Line "Cleveland Circle" train and get off at the first stop aboveground.
$ Prices: Appetizers $2.25–$5; main courses $9.35–$14.50; dinner $20–$25. AE MC, V.
  Open: Dinner Mon–Thurs 5–10:30pm, Fri–Sat 5–11pm, Sun 5–10pm.
The word got around quickly among devotees of Mexican food that the guacamole enchiladas (rojas, verdes, or Suizas), tacos, and tostadas at Sol Azteca were authentic delicious, and moderately priced. In fact, it is now considered by many to be the best Mexican food in Boston. Dinner starts with chips and salsa, and maybe a margarita or a bottle of Dos Equis. Appetizers include the standard nachos as well as other expected dishes, but also more exotic fare, such as cactus, which is quite good. If you want a little of everything, try one of the combination platters—they're a best buy. On Friday and Saturday, especially during college term, it's very crowded, so get there early.

BUDGET

It's not difficult to dine inexpensively in Boston. The variety and cuisine make it possible to eat pleasantly for $10 per day, or less. But the restaurants recommended below are not just for those on a very slim budget—no one wants haute cuisine at every meal. For those times when you just want a quick and inexpensive meal, but one that's wholesome and delicious, try one of these places.

NEWBURY STREET

TRAVIS RESTAURANT, 135 Newbury St. Tel. 267-6388.
  Cuisine: AMERICAN. **Reservations:** Not required. **Subway:** Green Line to Copley.
$ Prices: Appetizers $2–$4; main courses $5–$9. No credit cards.
  Open: Daily 7am–4:30pm.

Here you can get a slice of pie à la mode and a cup of coffee, or a hamburger, or perhaps a large salad plate (with tuna, ham, etc.). The small tables on the sidewalk out front are good for an espresso or cappuccino, the interior is the familiar lunch counter and stools (with some tables as well), and it's serve yourself, inside and out.

NORTH END

PIZZERIA REGINA, 11½ Thacher St. Tel. 227-0765.
   Cuisine: PIZZA. **Reservations:** Not required. **Subway:** Orange Line to Haymarket.
$ **Prices:** Pizza $5–$13. No credit cards.
   Open: Mon–Sat 10am–10pm.

If you have trouble finding Boston's most famous pizza place, located at the corner of Thacher and North Margin Streets, just ask anyone in the North End. Old dark-wood booths with Formica tables, and a small bar for the solitary lunchers make up the interior. The decor is simple but the pizzas are fancy, for the cooks know the secret of making a good one: the best imported cheese and tomato sauce, and a few dashes of real olive oil. A small, simple 10-inch cheese pizza feeds two moderately hungry people for lunch. You pay somewhat more with mushrooms, anchovies, sausage, or other toppings. The elaborate 16-inch Giambotta easily feeds a party of three or four. Beer and wine are served.

5. ATTRACTIONS

SUGGESTED ITINERARIES **If You Have 1 Day** The best way to get the flavor of Boston both old and new is to walk the **Freedom Trail.** Besides leading you to many of the city's historical sites, the trail takes you past the financial and government districts to fun-filled Faneuil Hall Marketplace and the picturesque North End. Have lunch in Faneuil Hall Marketplace or the North End. To enjoy the trail fully will take a full day; if you cut it short, you may have time in the afternoon for a visit to one of the top museums—the **Museum of Fine Arts** or the **Gardner Museum** for the aesthetic-minded, the **Museum of Science** or the **Computer Museum** for those of a scientific bent. The kids are sure to like the **New England Aquarium,** the **Children's Museum,** and the **Boston Tea Party Ship & Museum.**

If You Have 2 Days Start your second day with a walk through **Boston Common,** the **Public Garden,** and **Back Bay.** Be sure to see some of the wonderful old houses along **Commonwealth Avenue** and the shops, cafés, and boutiques along **Newbury Street.** In the afternoon, pick another of the top museums, or do some shopping and café-sitting. For nightlife, look into the current roster of musical events (there are dozens each night), or see what's doing in the Theater District.

If You Have 3 Days On your third day it's time to cross the river for a look at **Harvard Square** and Harvard University in Cambridge. You can easily spend a full morning sightseeing, shopping and café-sitting around the square. In the afternoon, head for Boston's **Downtown Crossing.** Take the Red Line subway from Harvard Square, get off at Downtown Crossing, and you can exit the station directly into **Filene's Basement.** For more shopping tips, see "Savvy Shopping," below.

If You Have 5 Days With 5 days to spend you can really get to know Boston. You'll have time to visit the **Kennedy Library,** the **Boston Athenaeum, Arnold**

Arboretum, and the Mapparium in the **Christian Science Center.** If you prefer spend a day on an excursion to **Salem, Gloucester, Rockport, Concord,** o **Plymouth** (see Chapter 5, "Around Boston," for details.)

ORGANIZED TOURS A guided **bus tour** is the easiest way of all to ge acquainted with the city and its landmarks, and the price for such an introduction i reasonable. The **Gray Line,** 275 Tremont Street (tel. 617/426-8805), offers 16 tour of New England, one a tour of Boston and Cambridge. Their Tour No. 1 takes hours, covers 18 miles, and includes many Freedom Trail sights, Beacon Hill, Bunke Hill, and Old Ironsides. **Harvard and MIT Tours** leave every day at various time and cost $18 for people 13 years and older; free if you're 12 or under. They also offer Boston Freedom Trail shuttle tour that uses open-air double decker buses. Fares ar $14 for adults, $5 for children. Contact them by phone or at the sightseeing desk o one of the larger hotels.

A novel way to get acquainted with Boston is by taking a **cruise** in the harbor an Massachusetts Bay. **Bay State Cruise Company,** 67 Long Wharf, Boston, M, 02110 (tel. 617/723-7800; fax 617/720-5738) operates vessels that tour the waters o Boston from early spring to late fall. Cruises take 1½ hours (three cruises a day); th price is $5 for adults, half price for children under 12. A 55-minute cruise of Boston' Inner Harbor is also available with the option of going ashore at the Charlestow Navy Yard. There's another cruise to Nantasket Beach, and whale watch sailings a well. In addition to these cruises, short trips at lunchtime (12:15 to 12:45pm) are refreshing break from city life and cost only $1 per person. Sandwiches and beverage are for sale on board. Call for exact schedules. These boats depart from the red ticke office at 67 Long Wharf, opposite the Chart House Restaurant, near the Aquariun (Blue Line) subway station. Offices are at 66 Long Wharf.

The **M/V** *Provincetown II,* also operated by Bay State, journeys to Province town from Boston daily in late June, and throughout July and August, with one trip day sailing from Boston about 9:30am, arriving in Provincetown at about 12:30pm then departing P-town at about 3:30pm to arrive back in Boston before 6:30pm. Th M/V *Provincetown* also makes the voyage on weekends in May, early June September, and October. For more details, see Chapter 6, "Cape Cod."

WALKING TOURS The **National Park Service** (tel. 617/242-5642) organize daily free walking tours of historic sights in downtown Boston.

The **Black Heritage Trail** is a walking tour of Beacon Hill and other Bosto locales which figured prominently in the lives and careers of Bostonian African Americans. For information and trail pamphlets, contact the National Park Servic (tel. 617/242-5642) or the Museum of Afro-American History, 46 Joy Street, o Beacon Hill (tel. 617/742-1854).

The **Boston Women's Heritage Trail** publishes a guidebook ($4) detailin walks that highlight the accomplishments of Boston women. The guidebook is sold a several stops on the Freedom Trail, including Old South Meeting House, the Pau Revere House, Old North Church, and the Globe Corner Bookstore. You can order by mail ($5) from Boston Women's Heritage Trail Guidebook, 22 Holbrook Stree Jamaica Plain, MA 02130 (tel. 617/522-2872).

THE TOP ATTRACTIONS
THE FREEDOM TRAIL

The sights of Revolutionary Boston are linked together by the Freedom Trail, marke by a red line or double row of red bricks on the sidewalk. The trail leads past almos all the important sights in 1½ miles; the outer loop of the trail goes to the Bunker Hi Monument and the USS *Constitution* (*Old Ironsides*), across Boston's Inner Harbo in Charlestown, 2½ miles from Boston Common.

The Freedom Trail does, however, leave out many other important things to se The Freedom Trail has been divided into two walking tours here, so you can see mor without retracing your steps. If you follow "Beacon Hill & Downtown Boston" an

THE FREEDOM TRAIL

1. The Boston Common
2. Statehouse
3. Park Street Church
4. Granary Burying Ground
5. King's Chapel
6. Site of the First Public School
7. Statue of Benjamin Franklin
8. Old Corner Bookstore
9. The Old South Meeting House
10. Benjamin Franklin's Birthplace
11. The Old State House
12. Site of the Boston Massacre
13. Faneuil Hall
14. The Paul Revere House
15. Pierce-Hichborn House
16. James Rego Square
17. St. Stephen's Catholic Church
18. Old North Church
19. Copps Hill Burial Ground
20. USS *Constitution*
21. USS *Cassin Young*

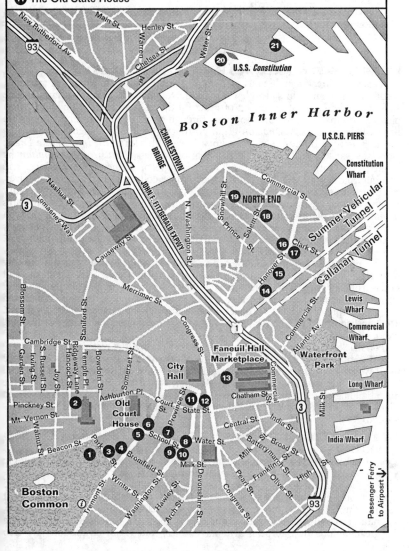

"North End & Charlestown," you will have seen most of the sights along the Freedom Trail, and many others besides.

If you'd rather not walk all of the Freedom Trail, you can ride the red **Beantown Trolley** (tel. 617/236-2148), operated by Brush Hill Tours (tel. 617/986-6100). Schedules for the trolleylike bus vary with the seasons, summer being the time when service is most frequent (about every 45 minutes from 9am to 5pm). Fare is $14 per adult ($10 for seniors), $6 per child 11 and under (kids under 5 ride free). Your ticket entitles you to hop on and off the buses as often as you like all day, or you can stay on for the 90-minute lecture tour. Trolleys run from 9am to 5pm in summer, about every 15 minutes. Buy your ticket right on the trolley, or at the Sheraton Boston Hotel, Westin Hotel, at the Charles Street crosswalk between Boston Common and the Public Garden, or at the Boston Common Visitor Information Center. See above for offerings by Gray Line Bus Tours.

The **Boston Common Information Center** (tel. 800/858-0200), on Boston Common near the Park Street Station, also hands out maps of the Freedom Trail.

MUSEUMS

MUSEUM OF FINE ARTS, 465 Huntington Ave. Tel. 267-9300.

This great Greek temple houses one of the world's finest collections of artworks, second in the country only to New York's Metropolitan. Boston's Museum of Fine Arts is a wonder, a vast collection of beautiful things in a beautiful building. Many pictures you may have admired for years through prints and photos in art books are here: Gilbert Stuart's *Athenaeum Head* portrait of George Washington; Renoir's *Le Bal à Bougival*; Burne-Jones's *The Love Song*; Whistler's *Girl in a White Dress*; works by van Gogh, Gauguin, Degas, lots of Monets; *Death of Maximilian* by Manet; and works by Japanese, Chinese, European, medieval, Renaissance, and baroque masters are all well represented. A fine collection of Paul Revere silver, several rooms taken from French châteaux, a full-size Japanese temple, a 9th-century Spanish chapel, Egyptian mummies, Assyrian seals—the list goes on to the treasures of almost 200 galleries. The way to find what you want is to pick up a floor plan as you enter; you can't possibly see even a fraction of it all, so pick out a few areas or rooms to concentrate on, and enjoy. To find out about special exhibits, call 267-9300, ext. 363.

The museum's restaurant is located in the west wing. Lunch is served Tuesday through Sunday from 11:30am to 2:30pm; dinner, on Wednesday, Thursday, and Friday from 5:30 to 8:30pm. Surrounded by glass, the dining room is ultramodern and attractive. The menu is often keyed to special exhibits—Chinese dishes predominated when the impressive Chinese bronzes were on display—and the prices are moderate. You can figure $10 to $12 for lunch, $18 to $22 for dinner. The wine list is short, good, and fairly priced.

For snacks and pick-me-ups, head for the café below the restaurant.

Admission: $6 adults, $5 seniors and college students, $3 for youths 6–17; free to all Wed 4–6pm; if you visit when only the new West Wing is open, the fee is $1 less.

Open: Tues and Thurs–Sun 10am–4:45pm, Wed 10am–9:45pm. Thurs–Fri the main building closes at 5pm but the west wing stays open till 10pm. **Subway:** Green Line "E" train ("Arborway" or "Huntington Avenue") to the second stop aboveground.

ISABELLA STEWART GARDNER MUSEUM, 280 The Fenway. Tel. 566-1401.

After visiting the Museum of Fine Arts, try to spend at least a few hours at the Isabella Stewart Gardner Museum nearby. "Mrs. Jack" Gardner early developed a love of art, and with her considerable wealth and the services of Bernard Berenson she set about to build an outstanding collection, which now includes almost 300 paintings, almost as many pieces of sculpture, close to 500 pieces of furniture, and hundreds of works in textiles, ceramics, and glass. Most of the holdings are from the great periods of European art, but classical and Asian civilizations are also represented. Not the least of the exhibits is the house itself, which she had built to hold the collection in 1902. "Fenway Court" is not much to look at from the outside, but inside it is Mrs. Gardner's vision of a 15th-century Venetian palace, with many doors, columns, windows, and the like, which were brought from Europe and assembled around an open court topped by a glass canopy. The court is always planted with flowers, in bloom summer and winter, and several fountains bubble merrily at one end. Upstairs in one room is a dramatic portrait of "Mrs. Jack" herself, displayed with various masterpieces above a floor covered in tiles from Henry Mercer's Moravian tile and pottery works in Pennsylvania. Along a corridor nearby, look for mementos of Mrs. Gardner's years, including letters from many of the great and famous of the turn of the century.

In March 1990, this lovely museum suffered a tragedy when art thieves dressed as police officers tricked the guards and made off with 12 masterpieces, including paintings by Degas and Rembrandt and a rare Chinese vase, worth hundreds of millions of dollars. These irreplaceable works will probably end up in a vault somewhere, unavailable to the public, because of some thieves' greed and selfishness.

Except during July and August, free concerts of chamber music are given Thursday at 12:15pm, Sunday at 3pm, and Tuesday at 6pm; they're usually very well attended, so go early and claim a seat (for information, call 734-1359). The museum has a nice café where light meals are served.

Admission: $6 adults, $3 students and seniors.

Open: Tues–Sun 11am–5pm. **Directions:** Walk west from the Museum of Fine Arts around its parking lot to the Fenway; turn left and walk 2 short blocks.

MUSEUM OF SCIENCE, Science Park. Tel. 723-2500.

Nobody ever has a bad time when they visit Boston's famous Museum of Science because there are so many things to see and do, and of such a variety. Children are especially delighted here, for they can, for example, pat a reptile, confront a live owl or porcupine eyeball to eyeball, "stop" a drop of water in mid air, weigh themselves in moon measurements, or climb into a space module. Exhibits run the gamut from a giant chicken egg incubator to a life-size replica of a tyrannosaurus, to a gargantuan magnifying glass.

There is also the Thomson Theater of Electricity, where artificial lightning is produced twice daily, and an exhibit on the human brain, where you can test your brain's reactions to different stimuli. The museum also hosts national and international traveling exhibitions and special events. You should call to see what's featured while you're in town.

Don't miss the adjoining Mugar Omni Theater where the movie screen actually wraps around the entire theater and you might be surrounded by penguins under Antarctic icebergs or whizzing through outer space.

Across from the Omni Theater is the Charles Hayden Planetarium (there is an extra charge for the planetarium, and you should buy your ticket when you enter the museum, even if it's quite some time before the performances, since the shows sell out early), which puts on daily star shows. On weekends the planetarium hosts rock 'n' roll laser programs.

Parking in the museum's own garage costs $2 an hour with a maximum of $10 a

IMPRESSIONS

Boston prides itself on virtue and ancient lineage—it doesn't impress me in either direction. It is musty, like the Faubourg St. Germain. I often want to ask them what constitutes the amazing virtue they are so conscious of.
—BERTRAND RUSSELL, LETTER TO MARGARET LLEWELLYN DAVIES, APRIL 12, 1914

I have learned enough never to argue with a Bostonian.
—RUDYARD KIPLING, FROM SEA TO SEA, 1889

Boston Architectural Center ❻
Boston Athenaeum ❿
Boston Children's Museum ⓮
Boston Tea Party Ship & Museum ⓯
Christian Science Church Center ❹
Computer Museum ⓭
Fenway Park ❸
The Freedon Trail (see separate map) ❾
Institute of Contemporary Art ❺
Isabella Stewart Gardner Museum ❶
John Hancock Observatory ❽
Museum of Fine Arts ❷
Museum of Science ⓫
New England Aquarium ⓬
Prudential Tower ❼

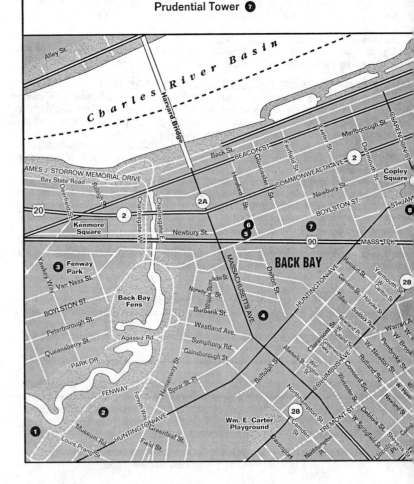

BOSTON ATTRACTIONS

New Charles River Dam & Locks

Charlestown Bridge

Playground

ce Park ⑪

NASHUA ST

Lomansey Way

CHARLES ST

Bank und

Blossom St

Blossom Ct

W.M. Cardinal O'Connel Way

CAUSEWAY ST

JOHN F. FITZGERALD EXPWY

N. WASHINGTON ST

COMMERCIAL ST

Charter St

Hull St

Sheafe St

Prince St

NORTH END

Hanover Ave

N. Bennet

Garden Ct St.

Richmond St

Fulton

Commercial St

ATLANTIC AVE

1A

Haverhill St

Portland St

Friend St

Cond St

Thacher St

Endicott St

N. Margin St

Salem St

HANOVER ST

1

3

MERRIMAC ST

Fruit St

Parkman St

New Chardon St

Blackstone St

Waterfront Park

Grove St

CAMBRIDGE ST

Phillips St

Myrtle St

Pickney St

evere St.

Temple St

Ridgeway La.

Hancock St

S. Russell St

Irving St

Anderson St

Joy

Bowdoin St

Somerset St

Sudbury St

CONGRESS ST

North St

Chatham

STATE ST

Commercial St

India

12

E. India Row

BEACON HILL

Mt. Vernon St

Walnut St

Spruce St

Branch St

River St

Byron St

BEACON ST

10

Tremont St

School St

Washington St

Central St

Batterymarch

Broad St

Milk St

Franklin St

Pearl St

Congress St

Purchase St

93

2

CHARLES ST

Boston Common

9

WINTER ST

Temple Pl

West St

Mason St

Avery

Chauncy St

SUMMER ST

1

3

Northern Ave

Public Garden

TON ST

Boston Park Plaza

STUART ST.

ESSEX ST

Oxford

Edinboro

Beach St

Eliot Pl

CHARLES ST. S.

CHINATOWN

Lincoln St

Utica St

South St

Kneeland St

HARRISON AVE

ATLANTIC AVE

15

13

14

Melcher St

ARLINGTON ST

Lawrence St

SHAWMUT AVE

DORCHESTER AVE

Fort Point Channel

Wormond St

END

EAST BERKELEY ST

Dwight St

Milford

Hanson St

Waltham St

Bradford St

SHAWMUT AVE

WASHINGTON ST

ark

ne

lin re

Union Park St

Malden St

Wareham St

HARRISON AVE

E. Dedham St

Plympton St

Canton

Brookline

93

3

W. 4th St

Richard St

W. 1st St

W. 2nd St

Athens St

Silver St

A St

B St

W. BROADWAY

Bolton St

W. 3rd St

W. 5th St

Flaherty Way

Silver St

Midway St

day. Besides the rooftop Skyline Cafeteria, there's a Friendly's snack shop within the museum.

Admission: $6.50 adults, $4.50 children 4–14 and seniors, free for children under 4.

Open: Sat–Thurs 9am–5pm, Fri 9am–9pm. **Subway:** Green Line Lechemere train to Science Park.

BOSTON CHILDREN'S MUSEUM, 300 Congress St. Tel. 426-8855.

A short walk from Faneuil Hall and South Station, the Children's Museum is a great destination for families. Cultural exhibits allow families to explore the lifestyles of kids around the globe. Children can discover the world of science with exhibits featuring unusual physical science experiments; or they can set out on an adventure in the climbing exhibits that will take them up, up, and away. Some 30 current exhibits include "Teen Tokyo," where kids can ride an authentic Japanese subway car, grapple with a sumo wrestler, and sing karaoke. The "Kids Bridge" is an interactive video tour that teaches children to value their own race and work against discrimination. With a series of rotating physical science exhibits (including Tops, Salad Dressing Physics, and Bubbles) kids can play on the "Science Playground." "Playspace" is where toddlers can climb a castle, drive a car, and make a rainbow.

Admission: $7 adults, $6 children 2–15, $2 1–year olds, free for infants. Friday 5–9pm $1.

Open: June 22–Labor Day, Sat–Thurs 10am–5pm, Fri 10am–9pm. Labor Day–June 21, Tues–Sun 10am–5pm, Fri 10am–9pm. **Subway:** Red Line to South Station; follow the signs to Museum Wharf.

COMPUTER MUSEUM, Museum Wharf. Tel. 423-6758 or 426-2800 (for museum offices).

"What?" you may say. "Computers aren't old enough to have a museum!" But they are. The calculating and computing devices on display at the Computer Museum on Museum Wharf go back centuries. It seems that we've always had a passion for number-crunching, but have been unable fully to realize that passion until today. The abacus has been used in China for a millennium; Scottish mathematician John Napier (1550–1617), inventor of the logarithm, came up with a calculator called "Napier's Bones"; French army officer Amedée Mannheim invented the slide rule in 1850. In 1893, in Zurich, a "direct-multiplying machine" called The Millionaire came on the market, and sold 4,655 units in the years following.

A $1 million interactive exhibit, "People and Computers: Milestones of a Revolution," opened in 1991. A walk through the exhibit gives you an excellent briefing on how computers came to affect our lives so deeply. A new exhibit, "Tools & Toys," allows visitors hands-on experience with 35 different exhibits, including a flight simulator.

In addition, the museum has 75 other hands-on, interactive exhibits. You can do everything from designing a car on a graphics terminal to flying an airplane, launching a rocket, or haggling over the price of strawberries with a computerized "vendor." Perhaps most fascinating of all is the Walk-Through Computer, a gigantic working personal computer you can use by trying out its 25-foot-long keyboard; results are displayed on a 108-square-foot monitor. Walk through the computer, past the giant chips, to find out how it all works.

The Computer Museum is right next door to the Children's Museum, and just across Fort Point Channel from the Boston Tea Party Ship.

Admission: $6 adults, $5 students and seniors, free for children under 5; half price for all Sat 10am–noon.

Open: Labor Day–June 21, Tues–Sun 10am–5pm. June 22–Labor Day, daily 10am–6pm, until 9pm Fri. **Closed:** Mon in winter. **Subway:** Red Line to South Station.

MORE ATTRACTIONS

NEW ENGLAND AQUARIUM, Central Wharf. Tel. 973-5200.

It seems fitting that a sea-conscious city such as Boston should have a major aquarium, and it has exactly that in the New England Aquarium, on Central Wharf off Atlantic Avenue and 2 blocks from Faneuil Hall Market in the newly redeveloped waterfront area (look for the twin Harbor Towers apartment buildings). Pride of the aquarium is the largest cylindrical, glass-enclosed saltwater tank in the world, and this and other exhibit tanks are stocked with more than 600 species of marine life, from electric eels to sharks. In the ship *Discovery,* moored next door, sea lion presentations are put on daily for aquarium visitors (call for current show times). The variety of fishes is truly astounding, and the shapes, colors, and forms that evolution and adaptation have produced in these creatures really give one a sense of the richness of the marine environment. The price of admission covers all exhibits, including the newly renovated "Edge of the Sea" hands-on tide pool exhibit, plus daily films, and multimedia presentations.

Admission: $7.50 adults, $3.50 children aged 3–11, $6.50 seniors; Thurs 4–8pm $1 off for all.

Open: Mon–Wed, Fri–Sun, and holidays 9am–6pm; Thurs 9am–8pm. Call for extended summer hours. **Subway:** Blue line to Aquarium.

BOSTON TEA PARTY SHIP AND MUSEUM, Congress Street Bridge. Tel. 338-1773.

The events recalled here are very much a part of colonial Boston's struggle for independence. What you see here is the brig *Beaver II,* a full-size replica of one of the merchant ships emptied by the "Indians" on the night of the tea-party raid, and a museum with exhibits outlining the "tea party." At the nearby Tea Party Store you can buy some tea. Complimentary Salada tea is served—iced in summer, hot in winter.

Admission: $5 adults, $2.75 children 5–14, free for children under 5.

Open: Ship and museum, Mar–Dec, daily 9am–dusk (about 7pm in summer, 5pm in winter). **Closed:** Major holidays. **Directions:** Take the Red Line to South Station, walk north on Atlantic Ave. 1 block past the Federal Reserve Bank (which looks like a mammoth space-age radiator), turn right onto Congress St. and walk a block to the water, and there's the ship at Congress Street Bridge. A shuttle van operates daily May–Oct from the rear of the Old State House on the Freedom Trail corner of Devonshire and State Sts).

BOSTON ATHENAEUM, 10½ Beacon St. Tel. 227-0270.

Tucked away atop Beacon Hill, facing the State House, is the Boston Athenaeum, near Boston Common, an independent research library founded in 1807. The Athenaeum's collections are strong in the history and literature of Boston and New England; its picture and sculpture collections were once, de facto, Boston's premier art museum. This grand old Boston institution is owned by 1,049 "Proprietors" who can pass right of ownership by heredity, and its neoclassical 19th-century reading rooms are used by members, their guests, and other approved researchers (you must have references). You can visit the Athenaeum's second-floor gallery to view the current exhibition, or call and reserve a place on a guided tour (Tuesday and Thursday at 3pm) of the building.

Admission: Free.

Open: Mon–Fri 9am–5:30pm, plus Sat Oct–May 9am–4pm. **Subway:** Red or Green Line to Park Street.

INSTITUTE OF CONTEMPORARY ART, 955 Boylston St. Tel. 266-5151 recording, 266-5152 person.

Located across the street from the Prudential Center, the institute is a beautifully modern place inside a historic Richardsonian structure. Shows may be anything from an exhibit of New England photographers' work to works in various media by British artists, or perhaps a show of the outstanding works by modern artists that are in Boston private collections. Special events include video programs, musical concerts, and evening lectures. All exhibitions change about every 6 to 10 weeks. The institute never has works for sale.

Admission: $4 adults, $1.50 seniors and children under 16, $3 students; free Thurs 5–8pm.

Open: Wed and Sun 11am–5pm, Thurs–Sat 11am–8pm. **Subway:** Green Line's "Boston College," "Riverside," or "Cleveland Circle" car to Hynes Convention Center/ICA Station.

BOSTON ARCHITECTURAL CENTER, 320 Newbury St. Tel. 536-3170.

There's often an interesting exhibit in the lobby of the Boston Architectural Center, at the corner of Hereford Street. The show will be connected in some way with architecture, whether it be the life and work of Henry Mercer, the turn-of-the-century Pennsylvania tile maker, or a collection of neon signs from many cities and many decades.

Admission: Free.

Open: Mon–Thurs 9am–9pm, Fri–Sat 9am–5pm, Sun (winter) noon–5pm. **Subway:** Green Line to Hynes Convention Center/ICA.

THE KENNEDY LIBRARY, Columbia Point, Dorchester. Tel. 929-4523.

The nation's memorial to JFK is the museum at the John F. Kennedy Library. This dramatic chalk-white building, designed by the distinguished architect I. M. Pei, sits on a peninsula on Dorchester Bay. The landscaping of Cape Cod roses, sea grass, and weeping willows serves to harmonize the building with the peninsula, harbor islands, and sea. The library features an exhibition that is introduced by a 30-minute movie on the late president's life. Then, arranged in chronological order, it displays JFK memorabilia from his christening dress, PT-109 uniform, and flight jacket worn when president, to papers relating to the Bay of Pigs and Cuban Missile Crisis. There is a re-creation of the Oval Office as it was when he was president, and his desk and rocking chair.

Admission: $3.50 adults, $2 seniors, free for children under 16.

Open: Daily 9am–5pm. **Closed:** Thanksgiving, Christmas, and New Year's Day. **Subway:** Red Line to JFK/U Mass Station.

ARNOLD ARBORETUM, 125 Arborway, Jamacia Plain. Tel. 524-1717.

Ever since this 265-acre park was given to the city by Harvard, Bostonians have been coming here to enjoy the peacefulness of the park and the more than 14,000 trees, plants, and shrubs from various parts of the world that make up the arboretum's "living collection." Spring is a fine time to catch the first blossoms like the lilacs, early summer brings the rhododendrons, and all through the warm months the scents here will bring back any nose dulled by the city air.

The Arnold Arboretum of Harvard University, designed by Charles Sprague Sargent and Frederick Law Olmsted, is maintained jointly by Boston's park department and Harvard University, which uses it as an open-air classroom in botany.

Admission: Free.

Open: Daily dawn–dusk. **Subway:** Orange Line to Forest Hills, or Green Line to Arborway (the Orange Line's probably faster).

THE CHRISTIAN SCIENCE CHURCH CENTER, 175 Huntington Ave. Tel. 450-2000.

In 1866 a devout New England woman experienced quick recovery from a severe accident, attributing her cure to a glimpse of God's healing power as taught in the Bible and lived by Jesus. Thereafter Mary Baker Eddy devoted the remainder of her long life (1821–1910) to better understanding, practicing, and teaching Christian healing; to founding the Church of Christ, Scientist; and establishing the church' periodicals, including the renowned international daily newspaper, the *Christian Science Monitor*.

Today the Christian Science religion has branch churches in some 68 countries with headquarters in Boston, site of the denomination's Mother Church, built in 1894. Next to the church stands the Christian Science Publishing Society, home of the *Monitor* and other Christian Science publications. Two new church office buildings and the Sunday School complete the Church Center. The whole complex, near Symphony Hall at the intersection of Huntington and Massachusetts avenues is a new

Boston landmark, and it's right between two other landmarks, Symphony Hall and the Prudential Center.

The main points of interest are the plaza and reflecting pool, the exterior of The Mother Church and its grand extension where services are held, and the Publishing Society's Mapparium and elegant Sales Room. You can take a 15- to 30-minute tour through the Mother Church, or just take the elevator up to see the auditorium. This huge chamber is the main inner space of the church, which is built on the plan of a Byzantine church with its great dome and two semidomes.

The church's newest addition is a multimedia Bible Exhibit, located in the Broadcasting Building, displaying rare Bibles and a giant Plexiglas map.

Admission: Tours are arranged for free, or you can visit the various buildings on your own. Free parking is available while visiting the Church Center.

Open: Church, Mon–Sat 9:30am–4pm, Sun 11:15am–2pm; Mapparium, Mon–Sat 9:30–4pm; Bible Exhibit, Mon and Wed–Sat 10am–5pm, Sun 11am–5pm.

Subway: Green Line's "Boston College," "Riverside," or "Cleveland Center" to Hynes Convention Center/ICA or Symphony.

OBSERVATORIES

Take the Green Line (any car you see except "North Station" or "Lechmere") to the Copley Station for the **John Hancock Observatory,** 200 Clarendon St. at Copley Square (tel. 572-6429). The ticket office entrance is on the corner of Trinity Place and St. James Avenue. This, the tallest building in New England, has landmarks picked out for visitors with special telescopelike viewers. Several audiovisual shows outline Boston history and the makeup of the modern cityscape. Hours are Monday through Saturday from 9am to 10pm year round. On Sunday, summer (May through October) hours are 10am to 10pm; in winter, noon to 10pm. Adults pay $2.75; seniors, $2; children 5 to 15, $2.

The **Prudential Tower,** 800 Boylston St. (tel. 236-3318), centerpiece of the Prudential Center, has a **Skywalk** on the 50th floor with a full-circle panorama of the city. It's open from 10am to 10pm Monday through Saturday, and noon to 10pm on Sunday. Admission is $2.75 for adults, $1.75 for children (5 to 15) and seniors. Two floors above is the Top of the Hub restaurant and cocktail lounge, and you can see the city for free when you buy a drink or a meal. To get to the Pru, take a Green Line "Arborway" car to Prudential Station, or "Boston College," "Cleveland Circle," or "Riverside" cars to Hynes Convention Center/ICA Station or Copley Station.

WALKING TOUR 1 —— Beacon Hill & Downtown Boston

Start: Boston Common (subway: Red or Green Line to Park Street).

Finish: Faneuil Hall Marketplace.

Time: 2 hours; more if you tour several buildings; the distance is about 1 mile (1.6km).

Best Time: Sunday morning is most peaceful, but any morning will do. (Note that the State House is closed on the weekend.)

From Park Street station, exit at the easternmost corner of:

1. **Boston Common,** the colonial town's "common pasture land," to which any citizen's cows could be brought. Though this is now the city's most popular park, the pasture ordinance is still in effect. No one seems to take advantage of it—as if with all the picnickers, sunbathers, soapbox orators, street buskers, and pitch persons there'd by any room left for a cow to graze! The entrance to Park Street Station is Boston's unofficial "speaker's corner," where ideologues hold forth on their political, social, and religious beliefs.

Stroll through the Common as you like, making your way up the slope to the:
2. **Massachusetts State House,** which dominates Beacon Hill and the Boston Common, its gold dome shining and visible for miles. It was designed by Charles Bulfinch, Boston's most famous and best-loved architect, and built at the end of the 1700s. This is where the Massachusetts General Court (legislature) sits today; in its Archives (which you can visit) are curious and famous documents relating to the history of the colony of Massachusetts Bay and the early republic. The State House (tel. 727-3676) is open Monday to Friday 10am to 4pm.

From the rear (north) side of the State House, turn left and walk along:
3. **Mount Vernon Street,** the prettiest street on Beacon Hill, Boston's prettiest residential neighborhood. The brick Federal-style houses (see "Architecture" in Chapter 1) are all superbly kept. In a few minutes you'll come to:
4. **Louisburg Square,** laid out in the 1840s with its tiny private park. The square is Beacon Hill's architectural gem, and its most prestigious address. The park is owned in common by the residents of the houses facing the square. Continue down the hill on Mt. Vernon to West Cedar Street and turn left. The next street on the left is:
5. **Acorn Street,** a short street that is so picturesque it is almost synonymous with Beacon Hill. If you see a photograph of a Beacon Hill street, it's probably Acorn Street. Continue to the next corner and turn right onto Chestnut Street, like Mount Vernon Street, lined with fine Federal brick row houses. At the top of Chestnut Street turn left, then right on Mt. Vernon, then left on Joy Street. Descend the hill on Joy to the corner with Myrtle, near which you'll see the:
6. **African Meeting House,** 46 Joy St., at Smith Court (tel. 723-8863), built in 1806 and now the nation's oldest African-American church building. Though it's now set up as a museum, it was once the venue for speeches by abolitionists William Lloyd Garrison and Frederick Douglass. Equally interesting, is the:
7. **Museum of Afro-American History,** also at 46 Joy St. (tel. 742-1854), open Tuesday to Friday 10am to 4pm for free.

Walk back up Joy Street, around to the front of the State House and down Park Street, back to the intersection of Park and Tremont Streets. Directly across Park Street from the subway station entrance is the:
8. **Park Street Church,** the tall-steepled, graceful church designed by Peter Banner and built in 1809. William Lloyd Garrison thundered against slavery from the pulpit here in 1829, and thus began his long abolitionist campaign. Take a look inside, so you can compare this early 19th-century church with the earlier churches farther along the Freedom Trail. The church (tel. 523-3383) is open to visitors from late June to late August, Tuesday to Saturday, 9:30am to 3:30pm; closed July 4; Congregational services are held all year on Sunday at 10:30am and 6pm.

Go out of the church, turn left and walk along Tremont Street a few steps to the:
9. **Old Granary Burying Ground,** last resting-place for some of the American Revolution's most famous figures, including Samuel Adams, Peter Faneuil, John Hancock, and Paul Revere. Crispus Attucks and the other victims of the Boston Massacre (March 1770; see "History" in Chapter 1) were laid to rest here, as were Benjamin Franklin's parents The cemetery took its name from a nearby granary, now long gone. Take a walk through—you'll constantly be surprised and delighted by the names, dates, and mottoes on the finely carved headstones.

Continue northeast on Tremont Street to the intersection with School Street and:
10. **King's Chapel,** which dates from 1754. Once the Anglican church of the royal governors, then the Episcopalian church of Boston's great personages, this dark mass of granite is now a Unitarian meetinghouse. The bell was cast by Paul Revere, and is the largest he ever made. In the **Burying Ground** next to the chapel are the graves of John Winthrop (1588–1649), first governor of the Massachusetts Bay colony, and many of his family, as well as other Boston notables.

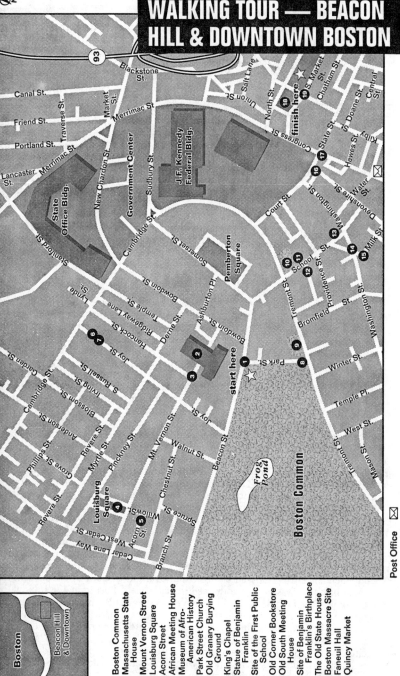

WALKING TOUR — BEACON HILL & DOWNTOWN BOSTON

N

93

Blackstone St.

Salt Lane

finish here

19 N. Market St.

Chatham St.

Canal St.

Union St.

North St.

18

Central St.

Friend St.

Merrimac St.

Market St.

Traverse St.

Congress St.

State St.

Doane St.

Kilby St.

Portland St.

Merrimac St.

17

Haves St.

Lancaster St.

Sudbury St.

J.F. Kennedy Federal Bldg.

16

Water St.

Devonshire St.

State Office Bldg.

New Chardon St.

Government Center

Court St.

13

Mill St.

Stanford St.

Cambridge St.

Somerset St.

Pemberton Square

14

15

Washington St.

Cambridge St.

Bowdoin St.

10 11

School St.

Providence St.

12

Lynde St.

Temple St.

Ridgeway Lane

Derne St.

Ashburton Pl.

Tremont St.

Bromfield St.

7

Hancock St.

2

9

Joy St.

S. Russell St.

Irving St.

Bowdoin St.

start here

Park St.

8

Winter St.

3

1

Cambridge St.

Anderson St.

Blossom St.

Revere St.

Myrtle St.

Pinckney St.

Mt. Vernon St.

Walnut St.

Joy St.

Beacon St.

Temple Pl.

West St.

Garden St.

Phillips St.

Grove St.

Revere St.

Louisburg Square

4

Willow St.

Chestnut St.

Spruce St.

Frog Pond

Boston Common

Tremont St.

Mason St.

Cedar Lane Way

West Cedar St.

Acorn St.

5

Branch St.

Post Office ⊠

Walk down School Street to the:

11. Statue of Benjamin Franklin. Most Americans remember the story o
Franklin getting off the boat in Philadelphia with very little money and two loave:
of bread for sustenance to begin his famous career, but some people forget tha
he was coming from Boston, his birthplace (1706) and childhood home; he wa:
born in a house on nearby Milk Street (see below). This statue by Richaro
Greenough (1856), in front of Boston's old city hall, pays tribute to Boston':
famous son, who is buried in Philadelphia.

Near the statue (follow the red line) is the:

12. Site of the First Public School to be established in the American colonie:
(1635), which boasted Cotton Mather, Benjamin Franklin, and Samuel Adam:
among its alumni. Though the building is gone, the school survives as Bosto•
Latin School, the city's most prestigious high school, located now in the western
part of the city.

Continue down School Street to the corner of Washington Street and the:

13. Old Corner Bookstore. The building dates from 1718, but its fame begar
when it became a gathering place for famous American authors in the 19th
century. At that time bookstores were also publishers, and Messrs. Ticknor &
Fields, who ran the Old Corner Bookstore, published and drank coffee with th•
outstanding literary men of the age, including Emerson, Hawthorne, Holmes
Longfellow, and Whittier. Now called the Globe Corner Bookstore (tel
523-6658), at 3 School Street, it specializes in books about travel and adventure

Turn right and walk a block to the:

14. Old South Meeting House, at 310 Washington Street, at the corner of Mill
Street. New England congregations call their buildings meetinghouses rathe
than churches, and it's from this that the Old South Meeting House gets it
name, although it was used for town meetings as well. (Old North Church, from
which the lanterns hung to signal Paul Revere, is a different building farther alon;
the Freedom Trail.) Built in 1729, the meetinghouse saw its most famous meetin;
on December 16, 1773, when a group of colonials in Native American dress se
out from here to throw the Boston Tea Party. Today the building is a museur
with exhibits of historical documents, currency, furniture, and a scale model o
Boston in 1775, which gives you a very clear idea of the size and layout of th
town. An audiovisual show recounts Old South's history. Admission to Ol•
South (tel. 482-6439) costs $2 for adults, $1.50 for seniors, 75¢ for children 6 t•
18; open April through October 9:30am to 5pm; November through Marc•
10am to 4pm (to 5pm on weekends).

Around the corner on Milk Street is the:

15. Site of Benjamin Franklin's Birthplace, marked by an obscure plaque o:
the side of a skyscraper. Though Franklin (1706–90) made his fame and fortun
in Philadelphia, he was a Boston native who learned his printing trade here in th
shop of his half brother, James.

Backtrack on Washington Street, past the Old Corner Bookstore, to find:

16. The Old State House. The charming brick building at 206 Washington Stree
dates from 1713, and was built to house the colonial government; after th
Revolution it was known as the State House, and after the present State Hous
was built in 1795, this one became the Old State House. The Declaration c
Independence was first read to Bostonians from its balcony in 1776. From tha
same balcony, Washington addressed the citizens of Boston in 1789. Now th:
the building is hemmed in by giant buildings on all sides, much of the dignity
must have held for colonial and Revolutionary Americans is lost. Inside,
museum has changing exhibits. Historical talks are given on the hour. There's a
entry fee to the museum (tel. 720-1713) of $1.25 for adults, 75¢ for senic
citizens, 50¢ for children. Summer hours are 9:30am to 5pm every day, but th
building is undergoing renovation, with reopening scheduled for sometime i
1992, so call to confirm these hours.

Walk east down Court and State Streets 2 short blocks to the:

17. Boston Massacre Site, near the corner of State and Congress streets, where colonists protesting the excesses of the royal government confronted some British soldiers who then fired (March 5, 1770) into the crowd, killing five men. The incident served to enflame anti-British feeling in the colonies which led, 5 years later, to the outbreak of the revolutionary war.

Turn left and go down Congress Street ½ block to:

18. Faneuil Hall, (*fan*-yool or *fan*-l), the "Cradle of Liberty," so called because of citizens' meetings which were held here before and during the Revolution. The handsome brick building was erected by the Town of Boston in 1742 with money given by Peter Faneuil; designed by John Simbert, it was later enlarged by Bulfinch (1805). The ground floor was originally a food market, and is now filled with shops; the second floor was—and is—used for public meetings; and the third floor houses the headquarters of Boston's most famous chowder-and-marching society, the Ancient and Honorable Artillery Company. Entrance to the second-floor meeting hall is from the east side; National Park Service guides are on hand to tell you all about the building: The huge painting dominating the front of the hall, they will tell you, is of Daniel Webster speaking on the virtues of a close union of states (as opposed to states' rights). The speech was given in Washington in 1830, not in Faneuil Hall, but the painting must have inspired hundreds of less talented, although perhaps equally long-winded, orators. Entrance to the hall is free.

Facing Faneuil Hall is the stout gray granite facade of:

19. Quincy Market, named for Boston Mayor Josiah Quincy who had it erected in 1826, along with the large Greek Revival market buildings on either side. Quincy Market was Boston's larder for a century before the changing patterns of commerce and provisioning led to its decline. Its restoration in the 1970s, along with the North Market and South Market buildings, has created the booming Faneuil Hall Marketplace you see today. (For details on shopping in the marketplace, see "Savvy Shopping," below.)

REFUELING STOPS Faneuil Hall Marketplace is filled with snack shops, chowder houses, cafés, delis, bakeries, and restaurants. If you only want a snack or light lunch, wander through Quincy Market and pick up freshly baked bagels, bags of dried apricots, nuts or Turkish figs, fragrant French bread, Italian salads, Chinese finger food, or any of a hundred other treats. For restaurant suggestions, see "Boston Dining," above. If it's raw clams or oysters you crave, drop in for a dozen at the **Union Oyster House,** Boston's oldest restaurant (see "Walking Tour 2").

WALKING TOUR 2 — North End & Charlestown

Start: Faneuil Hall Marketplace (subway: Green Line to Government Center).
Finish: USS *Constitution* (Old Ironsides) in Charlestown.
Time: 2 hours; more if you tour several buildings; the distance is about 2 miles (3km).
Best Time: Anytime; the open-air market is on Friday and Saturday; Old North Church has services Sunday morning.

From Faneuil Hall Marketplace, cross North Street and walk up Union Street past the:

1. Union Oyster House, at 41 Union St. (tel. 227-2750), Boston's oldest restaurant still in operation; it's been here since 1826. Continue walking north, then turn right and if it's Friday or Saturday you'll be in the midst of:

2. Haymarket, the name by which Boston's open-air produce market is generally known. Every Friday and Saturday, this area is thronged with costermongers selling fresh fruits and vegetables in Boston's weekly outdoor market. To get to the North End, look for the pedestrian passage beneath the Central Artery (Fitzgerald Expressway). (*Note:* The massive Central Artery construction project may have changed the face of this area by the time you arrive. Watch for Freedom Trail signs, or signs for Paul Revere's House.)

On the northeastern side of the Central Artery is the North End, Boston's "Little Italy." The first street you'll see is:

3. Salem Street, the narrow street lined with Italian groceries, butchers, fish stores and other shops. Turn right and walk 1 block to:

4. Hanover Street, the "main street" of the North End, lined with Italian-style cafés and stores. Walk 2 blocks up Hanover to Prince St. and turn right to reach North Square and the:

5. Paul Revere House, at 19 North Sq. (tel. 523-2338), a small clapboard dwelling surrounded by crooked cobbled streets. It's the only house left in downtown Boston that was built in the 1600s. Paul Revere moved in about a century after the house was built, and he lived here during the Revolutionary period. The house would be interesting even if the great patriot had never set foot in it, with its quaint weathered exterior, small windows, and wide floorboards. But furnished in colonial style and admirably furnished with explanatory materials, the house is better than an hour's history lecture. Admission costs $2 for adults, $1.50 for seniors and college students, 75¢ for children 5 to 17, under 5 free. No photography is allowed inside the house. Hours are 9:30am to 4:15pm in winter, to 5:15pm in summer; closed Monday January through March.

Walk back down Prince Street to Hanover Street, turn right, and walk a few very short blocks to:

6. Paul Revere Mall, with its equestrian statue of the Revolutionary hero. The church at the southeastern end of the mall and across Hanover Street is St. Stephen's, built by Boston's favorite architect, Charles Bulfinch. At the northwest end of the mall stands:

7. Old North Church, at 193 Salem St. (tel. 523-6676). You can see by the church's location why it was a good place from which to give a signal. The code, as every schoolchild knows, was "one if by land, two if by sea," and it was two lanterns hung in the tower that started Paul Revere on his fateful night ride to warn the Colonials that British troops were heading out from Boston to search for hidden arms. It's the oldest church building in Boston (1723), and is today officially known as Christ Church in the City of Boston. A walk around inside turns up many curiosities that bear on the history of Boston and the United States: memorial plaques to famous men, nameplates on the very high pews. The tall graceful windows of Old North Church are exceptionally fine.

Although it's hemmed in by houses and shops on all sides, Old North Church does have a set of tiny terraces and gardens on its north side, open to the public. The small formal garden and the fountain are good to refresh your spirit on a hot day, and the memorial plaques set into the walls are, in some cases, delightful. Donations are appreciated. It's open daily 9am to 5pm; visitors are also welcome for Sunday services at 9 and 11am, and 4pm.

Walk uphill on Hull Street past no. 44, the narrowest house in Boston, to find:

8. Copps Hill Burying Ground, the second-oldest cemetery (1660) in the city. Among the cemetery's permanent inhabitants is fiery Puritan preacher Cotton Mather. Some of the tombstones were marked by British musket balls during the Revolution. You can visit daily from 9am to 4pm. While you're up on Copps Hill look across to Bunker Hill, with its obelisk monument, and the old Charlestown Navy Yard to see the tall masts and complicated rigging of the USS *Constitution*. To reach the ship you must walk over a mile, across the Charlestown Bridge and to the right; you might want to take a taxi instead.

9. Bunker Hill. The 200-foot granite obelisk that towers above Charlestown marks the spot where Colonel William Prescott of the Continental army stood with his small force and held off wave after wave of attack by British regulars on June 17

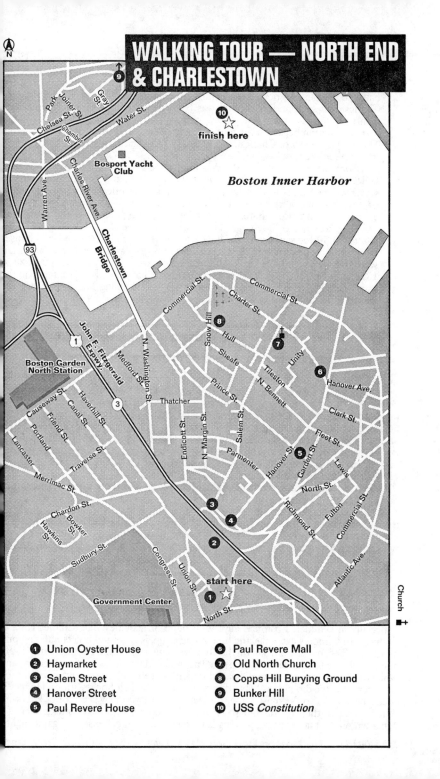

WALKING TOUR — NORTH END & CHARLESTOWN

N

Park
Joiner St.
Gray St.
Chelsea St.
Chamber St.
Water St.

Bosport Yacht Club

Boston Inner Harbor

finish here

Warren Ave.

93

Charles River Ave.

Charlestown Bridge

John F. Fitzgerald Expwy.

Boston Garden North Station

N. Washington St.

Medford St.

Commercial St.

Commercial St.

Charter St.

Snow Hill

Hull

Sheafe

Prince St.

Tileston

N. Bennett

Unity

Hanover Ave.

Clark St.

Thatcher

Causeway St.

Haverhill St.

Canal St.

Friend St.

Portland

Traverse St.

Lancaster

Merrimac St.

Endicott St.

N. Margin St.

Salem St.

Parmenter

Hanover St.

Garden St.

Fleet St.

Lewis

North St.

Richmond St.

Fulton

Commercial St.

Chardon St.

Bowker St.

Hawkins St.

Sudbury St.

Congress St.

Union St.

Atlantic Ave.

start here

Government Center

North St.

Church

❶ Union Oyster House	❻ Paul Revere Mall
❷ Haymarket	❼ Old North Church
❸ Salem Street	❽ Copps Hill Burying Ground
❹ Hanover Street	❾ Bunker Hill
❺ Paul Revere House	❿ USS *Constitution*

1775. Their ammunition running low, Colonel Prescott cried to his men, "Don't fire until you see the whites of their eyes" in order to make each shot count. When their ammunition was exhausted the Americans were forced to retreat, but the battle had caused grievous casualties to Boston's British garrison. Most of Charlestown surrounding the hill was burnt by the British during the engagement.

Construction began on the monument in 1828, a half-century after the battle. There's a fine view of Charlestown, the navy yard, and Boston from the top, 295 steps up (no elevator!).

Down the hill, docked in the decommissioned Navy Yard is the:

10. **USS** *Constitution* (*Old Ironsides*) (tel. 242-1797), still commissioned in the service of the U.S. Navy. The ship still gets under way once a year, on the Fourth of July, when it's taken a short distance out into the harbor to fire a 21-gun salute. Sailors in 1812 period uniforms will take you through the ship and explain its workings to you free of charge. The nearby **museum** (tel. 242-5670; $2.50 for adults, $1.50 for seniors, $1 for kids 6 to 16, free for children under 6) houses many artifacts dealing with the *Constitution*'s history and its 40 battles at sea (all won), besides a "Life at Sea" exhibit, showing what shipboard life was like in 1812. The Boston Navy Yard National Historic Site also offers programs on the yard and the American Revolution every hour in Building No. 5 (between the ship and the museum).

6. SPECIAL/FREE EVENTS

Lots of **films** are shown for free in Boston, or very nearly for free—the college film series at many Boston colleges often charge as little as $1 for admission. Newspaper listings may or may not have information about college film series, and indeed the movie to be shown, place of screening, and even date and time may change without notice except for a few mimeographed flyers stuck up here and there on the campus. Still, try calling one of the college switchboards and asking about "the film series." For Harvard, check the *Gazette,* a weekly (less often when classes are not in session) newspaper about the university available for free in the University Information Office Holyoke Center, Harvard Square.

More dependable and predictable than the college film series are the films shown fairly regularly by these institutions, all for free. **Boston Public Library** (tel. 536-5400), shows various films in the lecture hall and at the library's branches throughout the city. Take the Green Line to Copley. The **Institute of Contemporary Art,** 955 Boylston St. (tel. 266-5151), screens various films usually having to do with modern art or artists; see "More Attractions," above, for transportation details.

7. SPORTS

Especially in summer, Boston is alive with outdoor activities: The Charles River is dotted with sailboats every day the breeze comes up, joggers and bikers huff and puff along the Esplanade, the roar of the Red Sox fans rises from Fenway Park. Every autumn, tickets to the Harvard-Yale game are grabbed up like passes into heaven, and while the aristocrats are urging Harvard to fight fiercely, the Boston Bruins and their opponents for the day are probably doing just that with their hockey sticks. Hockey is such a part of Boston's cold-weather life that in winter you may see a lot of kids with schoolbooks in their hands, but you'll see a lot more with hockey sticks. Here's a rundown on the major sports; parking is tough to find and expensive on game nights.

BASEBALL   The **Boston Red Sox** play at Fenway Park (subway: Green Line)

"Riverside" car to Fenway Station, then follow the crowd!), and if you buy your tickets a few days before the game, you can get them at the nearest ticket agency (Ticketron, Bostix, and the like). Call 267-1700 for Red Sox information.

BASKETBALL   The famous **Boston Celtics** play in Boston Garden (subway: Green Line to North Station), a large hall that has nothing to do with Boston's Public Garden. Call 523-6050 for the latest info.

FOOTBALL   The **New England Patriots,** affectionately called "The Pats" in these "pahts," play at Schaefer Stadium, Route 1 in Foxboro, Mass., some 30 miles southwest of Boston. Several Boston bus companies run special buses to the games; try calling Bonanza (tel. 423-5810) or Peter Pan (tel. 482-6620). For information on Patriots games, call 262-1776.

HOCKEY   The famed **Boston Bruins** battle it out with all comers at Boston Garden (same as basketball, above), and tickets are often sold out very early. Catch 'em when they take on Montréal and you've got a spectacle. Call 227-3200 for information.

8. SAVVY SHOPPING

Like New York, Washington, and other great American cities, Boston has its special places to buy things, whether you're in the market for the mundane or the exotic. Here are some of the prime locales for getting rid of money.

DOWNTOWN CROSSING   The two Boston giants are **Jordan Marsh Company** and **Filene's,** located cheek-by-jowl in the downtown pedestrian shopping district on Washington Street (subway: Red Line or Orange Line to Washington) called Downtown Crossing. Jordan's is a large department store with a vast assortment of items for sale, everything from baubles to bar stools. "Jordan's Great Basement Store" is admittedly great in terms of size, but it is outdone in popularity by neighboring Filene's Basement, which has become a New England legend. Tales circulate about women changing clothes right between the dress racks to try things on, of the crowds one must fight, of the "automatic reduction" policy, which dictates that if an item is not sold in a certain amount of time, it is simply given away just to get rid of it.

Well, the basement has become a bit more refined now that it's famous, and the prices in many cases are similar to those in any of the big new suburban discount stores. As for the automatic reductions, they're still in operation; but few items reach the date when they're given away, and if they do it's usually because they're too torn or ugly or useless to be bought, and even so they're given away to charity (Goodwill Industries, for example) as a tax write-off, and not to you. But the basement is still busy, often crowded, and it's because people know that there's a good chance they'll run into something that suits them at a very good price. Don't go to Filene's Basement to buy a pair of shoes, but rather go to dig around in the shoe bins and see what there is in your size, and at a good price—you may find something that makes good sense to buy. And look through the other clothes departments, accessory counters, and various sections—a $400 outfit with a marked-down $40 price tag could very well be waiting there for you.

Surplus merchandise from famous stores such as Lou Lattimer's in Houston and Saks in New York comes frequently to Filene's Basement, with such classy labels as I. Magnin and Yves Saint Laurent. Don't be disappointed if you don't find anything. Come back in a few days, for the stock moves incredibly fast and new shipments arrive daily.

Also at Downtown Crossing is **Lafayette Place,** a vast shopping mall with a central courtyard for sipping and dining, a 500-room hotel, and hundreds of shops.

Washington Street, the pedestrian thoroughfare of Downtown Crossing, has its own lineup of shops. Across from Filene's, at 333 and 387 Washington St., for instance, are entrances to the **Jeweler's Building,** a warren of little shops in a homely building. The building may not look like much, but the display cases in each shop are laden with fortunes in gold, diamonds, rubies, and emeralds. If you're at all interested in jewelry, take a stroll through here. Prices can be very good.

FANEUIL HALL MARKETPLACE The Faneuil Hall Marketplace is a whole complex of buildings including **Faneuil Hall** and **Quincy Market,** flanked by the **North and South markets** on either side.

Quincy Market is the centerpiece of this imaginative and fantastically successful redevelopment venture by the Rouse company with the guidance of Cambridge architect Benjamin Thompson. For years the area was a rundown waterfront slum, with only the 19th-century-style butchers' shops and provisioners to provide life. The early plan was to have the buildings razed to the ground and replaced with a modern shopping center, but architect Thompson changed the thinking to conservation, and the result is a beauty. Behind Faneuil Hall, the market is busy with crowds of customers from sunrise to sundown every day of the week. A granite block pavement is spread between Faneuil Hall and the market's pillared classic Greek facade, and inside, the long main hall stretches for a city block on two floors.

Downstairs are **food shops,** where you can buy everything from take-out snacks to a full picnic-style meal, to a pound of Camembert for the kitchen at home. On a recent stroll through Quincy Market I noted the following items for sale (partial list): a dozen kinds of bagels right out of the oven on the premises, an infinite array of deli sandwiches, southern fried chicken, shish kebab, subgum chow mein, Baby Watson cheesecake, German Blutwurst, French Brie, Châteauneuf-du-Pape, live lobsters, mixed nuts, cold cuts (domestic and imported), rumpsteak, fresh doughnuts, and, at the clam bar, half a dozen cherrystone clams opened and ready to eat.

The wings of the market are of glass, and shelter **restaurants, drinking places,** and **singles' hangouts** patronized by the good-looking and well-to-do from the business, financial, and government offices nearby. In the basement are various shops selling fish, meat, health foods, and imported delicacies.

On the second floor the emphasis is on **crafts and exotic imports**—rugs from Persia, jewelry from India, baskets from China and Mexico. There's a fine **flower shop** in a very handsome all-glass building in front, on the granite pavement, and benches set out under the trees between the market and the adjoining buildings.

About the best purchase you can make here at Faneuil Hall Marketplace is **tickets** to the theater, concerts, ballet, shows, and so on. **Bostix** (tel. 723-5181) in a kiosk right next to Faneuil Hall itself, sells half-price seats for today's performances, and this is the only place in the city where you can buy them. Plan your nightlife while you're here, rather than coming all the way back. Cash only for same-day, half-price seats—that's the policy.

Street buskers and musicians are always on hand to entertain in the market promenades, and a genial mounted police officer draws scores of children, all wanting to pat his mount's nose. The whole complex is an all-year, day-and-night carnival you shouldn't miss, open for free. For restaurant details, see the restaurant section, above. To get to Faneuil Hall Marketplace, take the Green or Blue Line to Government Center, or the Blue or Red Line to State Street.

NEWBURY STREET Boston's famous street of boutiques, galleries, and café runs from fashion to funk. It starts at the intersection of Arlington and Newbury, right next to Burberrys' and the Ritz-Carlton Hotel, and the shoppers' and strollers' delights continue for half a dozen blocks. Shops sell everything from the sublime (and expensive) to the ridiculous (and expensive); galleries can be chic or somewhat traditional. Cafés are good and bad, expensive and cheap, and all possible permutations of those four qualities.

Serious shoppers and gallerygoers should pick up two useful brochures, available at information booths (City Hall, Boston Common, Boston Public Library) entitled *The Newbury Street League Map,* which gives a list of most of the shops and some of

IMPRESSIONS

When I got into the streets [of Boston] upon this Sunday morning, the air was so clear, the houses were so bright and gay; the signboards were painted in such gaudy colours; the gilded leters were so very golden; the bricks were so very red . . . that I almost believed the whole affair could be taken up piecemeal like a child's toy, and crammed into a little box.
—CHARLES DICKENS, *AMERICAN NOTES*, 1842

the cafés along the street, their specialties, addresses, and phone numbers; and *Map of the Newbury Street Art Galleries,* which gives brief descriptions of the 30 galleries on the street, times of operation, special services, and so forth.

Newbury Street starts at the Ritz, and the shops in the first few blocks are, naturally, the most expensive. All of the shops mentioned below are along the first 6 blocks or so of Newbury Street, starting at Arlington.

If you're shopping for classic and high-fashion clothing, look for big names such as **Burberry's, Brooks Brothers, Bonwit Teller's** (in the old Boston Museum of Natural History Building), **Cartier, Giorgio Armani, Ann Taylor, Laura Ashley,** and **Guy Laroche,** as well as Boston-based designers **Charles Sumner, Louis-Boston,** and **Robert Todd.** For furs, there's **Kakas.** For more contemporary wear, seek out **Joseph Abboud, Martini Carl, In Wear Martinique, The Gap, Banana Republic, Reebok, Claire Williams,** and **Agnes B.** For outrageous fashions, try **Alan Bilzerian.** Jewelry crafters include **Body Sculpture,** at no. 127, and **Silver & Gold-The Finest Hour,** at no. 274. **F.A.O. Schwarz,** the famous New York toy store, has two branches in Boston, at 40 Newbury and in the Prudential Center.

Streets in the Back Bay were laid out in a grid and the cross streets that run north-south were given names with initial letters running from A to H—Arlington, Berkeley, Clarendon, Dartmouth, and so on—so it's easy to know how far you are from the start of Newbury Street at Arlington Street. The second cross street, then, is Berkeley.

COPLEY PLACE   Just off Copley Square is Copley Place, a vast ultramodern shopping, dining, lodging, and entertainment complex. **Neiman-Marcus** is the big store here, but there are dozens of shops as well. **Ralph Lauren, Williams-Sonoma, Saint Laurent Rive Gauche, Jaeger, Gucci,** and **Godiva,** among others, all have outlets. Hours are normally 10am to 9pm Monday through Friday, to 7pm on Saturday, and noon to 5pm on Sunday. The hotels in the complex are the Boston Marriott Copley Place and the Westin Hotel Copley Place.

9. EVENING ENTERTAINMENT

Forget everything you've ever heard about things being "banned in Boston," for at night in this big city it seems as though anything goes. The opportunities for evening activities are bewildering in their variety, and because of all the students in town, nightlife is very active, available, and—in many cases—not all that expensive. This section will give you some idea of what's going on, with details on a selection of the better things to see and do.

Bostonians have been known to call their city "The Athens of America"—they did this even before the city had a sizable Greek population. The reason, of course, is Boston's lively cultural and artistic life. It could fairly be said that on any given day of the year one could take a pick of a dozen or more lectures, concerts, or dance and theater offerings, and at least a few of these would be free of charge.

The best way to find out what's on is to buy the *Boston Globe* on Thursday; that issue includes a free "Calendar" guide to happenings in Boston and vicinity, with locations and phone numbers.

Another useful publication is *Boston By-Week* (a brochure arts schedule at information booths, hotel desks, and depots), or the tabloid "alternative" weekly newspaper, the *Boston Phoenix,* which is especially good for youth and student events, movies, and concerts.

Harvard University publishes its own *Gazette* weekly during the fall and spring semesters and sporadically at other times. It's available for free from the Harvard University Information Office, Holyoke Center, Harvard Square. The paper includes listings of a great many films, lectures, discussions, gallery shows, plays, and concerts taking place at Harvard, many of which are open to the general public. The other great universities in the area also publish similar calendars, yours for the asking.

An outfit called **Bostix** (tel. 723-5181 for a recording) sells all kinds of tickets to all sorts of events in Boston and beyond. Buy a ticket to almost anything in eastern Massachusetts here. You'll pay the regular price plus a small service charge. This is a useful service.

But the real excitement at Bostix is the sale of tickets at half price on the day of performance. Theater, concerts, shows, and so on are put on a "daily list" of half-price offerings, and you must stop by the Bostix kiosk next to Faneuil Hall in Faneuil Hall Marketplace (subway: Green or Blue Line to Government Center) to read the list—they won't give it to you over the telephone. For same-day, half-price seats you must pay in cash, no refunds or exchanges; for advance bookings you may pay with a check drawn on a Massachusetts bank. No credit cards are accepted.

THE PERFORMING ARTS

MAJOR PERFORMING ARTS COMPANIES

BOSTON SYMPHONY ORCHESTRA, 301 Massachusetts Ave. Tel. 266-1492.

The Boston Symphony Orchestra preserves a reputation for excellence and innovation that it has had for over a century. The formal symphony season runs from October through April, with performances in Symphony Hall. The hall was designed in 1900 by McKim, Mead, and White, who carried out one of the earliest-known scientific acoustical studies for such a structure, and their careful work has been an outstanding success for nearly a century.

To get to Symphony Hall by subway, take the Green Line ("Brigham Circle" car also called the "E" train) to Symphony; or any other Green Line train to Hynes Convention Center/ICA. Turn left as you leave the station, and walk down Massachusetts Avenue. Bus no. 1 runs from Dudley to Harvard Square down Massachusetts Avenue and right by Symphony Hall.

For the latest information on current symphony programs, call 617/266-2378 (that's 617/C-O-N-C-E-R-T). Symphony tickets range in price from $19.50 to $55. Normal ticket sales are at the Symphony Hall Box Office, open from 10am to 6pm Monday through Saturday, and 1 through 6pm on Sunday, and also during concerts through the first intermission. To reserve seats and order tickets by phone, call SymphonyCharge at 617/266-1200; there's a handling fee of $2.25 per ticket ordered by phone. To order tickets by mail, send your payment and a stamped, self-addressed envelope to Symphony Hall Box Office, 301 Massachusetts Avenue, Boston, MA 02115. You can pay for tickets by credit card, check, or cash.

There are ways to enjoy the Boston Symphony Orchestra without paying full price: **rush seats and open rehearsals.**

A limited number of tickets for each BSO concert (Tuesday and Thursday evening, Friday matinee—and sometimes Friday evening, and Saturday evening) are held back to be sold only on the day of the concert, one to a customer, in the Massachusetts Avenue lobby of Symphony Hall. These rush seats go on sale Friday at 9am, Tuesday and Saturday at 5pm, and cost a mere $6 each. You must buy them in person, not by phone or mail, and there's a limit of one ticket per customer.

During the symphony season, open rehearsals are held on six Wednesday evenings at 7:30pm (doors open at 6:15pm, with a lecture at 6:30pm), and four Thursday mornings at 10:30am (complimentary coffee and pastries are served between 9:15 and 9:30am). The rehearsals, preceded by a ½-hour lecture on the musical program, are almost the same as a full-fledged concert, but tickets cost only $10.50.

Tanglewood: In July, the indefatigable members of the orchestra move out to the Berkshire hills in western Massachusetts for the Tanglewood Music Festival in Lenox. The Tanglewood season runs from July through August to Labor Day weekend. Chamber music concerts, recitals, and full symphony concerts fill each week, and a jazz festival ends the season on Labor Day weekend. Again, these performances are very heavily attended, and it's best to go early to get a good seat (you can sit inside the "Music Shed" or on the lawn outside, depending on how much you want to spend for a ticket); even more important than going early to the concert is to get a room reservation nearby, unless you plan to drive out (2½ to 3 hours) and back the same day.

Special excursions to Tanglewood concerts are offered by various tour companies, including, in New York City, Biss Tours (tel. 718/426-4000) and Parker Tours (tel. 718/428-7800). From Boston, K & L Tours (tel. 617/267-1905) will take you there, or you can catch a bus run by Peter Pan Bus Lines (tel. 617/426-7838).

For more information on Tanglewood, refer to "Lenox" in Chapter 8.

THE BOSTON POPS, Symphony Hall, 301 Massachusetts Ave. Tel. 266-1492 for general information, 266-2378 (April–June) for the latest program information, 266-1200 for tickets.

The Boston Pops concerts of light classical works, music from the cinema and Broadway, and catchy orchestral arrangements of popular tunes run from early May through mid-July. The floor in Symphony Hall is cleared of seats, and café tables and chairs are brought in, and light refreshments, beer and wine are served to those on the floor (but not in the balconies).

Tickets: The rules are similar to those for buying symphony tickets (see above). Pops concert ticket prices range from $10 to $34.50, with a $2 service charge.

In the first week in July, the Boston Pops performs several free concerts in the Hatch Memorial Shell, on the Charles River Esplanade (subway: Red Line to Charles). Highlight of the series is the traditional Fourth of July performance, which always ends with Tchaikovsky's *1812* Overture, accompanied by a battery of cannons and followed by a mammoth display of fireworks over the river.

OTHER CONCERTS

Two well-known music schools offer frequent concerts by students, faculty, and visiting groups of performers.

THE NEW ENGLAND CONSERVATORY OF MUSIC, 30 Gainsborough St. Tel. 262-1120, ext. 257.

The conservatory has frequent concerts, many of them free, in its performance halls, which include Jordon Hall. It is located 1 block from Symphony Hall, on Gainsborough Street at Huntington Avenue, close to the Boston YMCA and Northeastern University (Green Line's "Arborway" or "Northeastern U" cars to Symphony Station, or to the first stop aboveground; or take the Orange Line to Massachusetts Avenue; or take bus no. 39, "Forest Hills," from Copley Square and Back Bay). A monthly calendar of events is available on request.

BERKLEE COLLEGE OF MUSIC, 136 Massachusetts Ave. Tel. 266-7455 for a recorded schedule, or 266-1400 for a human being.

The Berklee Performance Center, on Massachusetts Avenue (near the corner of Massachusetts Avenue and Boylston Street) is for larger groups, while the Recital Hall, at 1140 Boylston Street, is for small ensembles. There's also the Berklee Concert Pavilion, an urban amphitheater, for outdoors events. Take the Green Line's "Boston College," "Cleveland Circle," or "Riverside" cars to Hynes Convention Center/ICA Station for both places. Both halls are fairly near the Prudential Center.

HANDEL AND HAYDN SOCIETY, 295 Huntington Ave. Tel. 266-3605.

Few Boston institutions predate the society, which has been giving concerts in Boston since 1815. The society's season runs year round, with a Symphony Hall Series, a Chamber Series, a Jordan Hall Chamber Series, and a Summer Series. The society, older even than the Boston Symphony Orchestra, has a closely guarded reputation for high excellence in its performances.

DANCE

BOSTON BALLET, 19 Clarendon St. Tel. 695-6950.

Some may not know it, but the Boston Ballet is the fourth-largest dance company in the America. For almost 30 years it has maintained a high standard of artistic excellence and vision. Under Artistic Director Bruce Marks, Boston Ballet's repertory is an eclectic mix of classic story ballets, contemporary ballets, and avant-garde works. Watch for notices and times in the papers, then go to the Wang Center Box Office, 270 Tremont St., Monday through Saturday, 10am to 6pm to purchase tickets.

THEATERS

Boston's taste in theater runs the gamut from previews of Broadway musicals to the most experimental of experimental. The offering is so rich and varied it would be impossible in this small space even to give an idea of the range available: Groups will pop up here and there, struggle to survive, and in the meantime put on fine performances, and then fail financially and disperse, having left many theatergoers with a lasting impression. I would stress that people interested in the theater should not limit themselves to the possibilities outlined below, but should take the trouble to seek out the new groups performing in odd places, for they're often at the frontier.

Nevertheless, if you have only a little time to spend in Boston and you'd like to take in a play or a musical, the following are some hints. Besides these, the universities have a great many drama offerings, usually at fairly low prices; and during the summer the city of Boston and other organizations sponsor outdoor performances in City Hall Plaza, other public squares, and along the Charles River Esplanade. (See also "Cambridge" in Chapter 5.) Note that the old-line theaters with musicals and plays slated for Broadway are all downtown near the Green Line's Boylston Station.

NEXT MOVE THEATER, 1 Boylston Place. Tel. 423-5572.

The Next Move Theater is perhaps the city's most interesting and talented theater group. For all its technical excellence, it's a homey sort of place where the actors stand near the door as you enter and as you leave, greeting the audience and exchanging comments on the plays. Boylston Place is a tiny alley off Boylston Street, midway between Tremont and Charles Streets, across from Boston Common. By subway, take the Green Line to Boylston.

WANG CENTER FOR THE PERFORMING ARTS, 270 Tremont St. Tel. 931-2000.

With almost 4,000 seats, the Wang Center, formerly the Metropolitan Theater was known as Boston's most important landmark of the Roaring Twenties. The Wang

---

IMPRESSIONS

We really are 15 countries, and it's really remarkable that each of us thinks we represent the real America. The Midwesterner in Kansas, the black American in Durham—both are certain they are the real America. And Boston just knows it is
—MAYA ANGELOU, *TIME* MAGAZINE, APRIL 24, 1978

On another occasion a guest at a White House reception eased up to the President and remarked: 'Mr President, I'm from Boston.' His blue eyes rested only briefly on her as he said: 'You'll never get over it.'
—ISHBEL ROSS, *GRACE COOLIDGE AND HER ERA*, 1962

presents a variety of performing arts to the Boston communities, as well as providing educational and outreach programs like "young at Arts." The theater, declared a historical landmark, is currently being restored to its original glory.

CHARLES PLAYHOUSE, 74 Warrenton St. Tel. 426-6912.

Good drama is the rule at the Charles Playhouse, located right down behind the Shubert and Wilbur theaters and the Tremont House Hotel (subway: Green Line to Boylston; Warrenton is parallel to Tremont 1 block west, but it's only a block long).

THE CLUB & MUSIC SCENE

The Boston area's more than 75 colleges and universities give downtown nightlite a particularly lively character; a lot of graduates get to like the town so much they settle down here, and so Boston's crew of "young professionals" is also very large and very conspicuous in the clubs.

The Department of Commerce says that Boston is the most expensive city in the country except for Anchorage, and yet a night on the town won't kill your budget: Drinks are mostly $4 to $6; beer or a glass of wine, $3 to $4.

CLUBS & SINGLES' BARS

Boston is covered with clubs, from the North End waterfront to Kenmore Square. Boston's all-time success story, the Faneuil Hall Marketplace (subway: Green or Blue Line to Government Center) is a riot of activity morning, afternoon, and evening, with buskers and street musicians outside (in good weather), and a host of clubs and restaurants. Here are just a few of them.

DAISY BUCHANAN'S, 240a Newbury St. Tel. 247-8516.

Daisy Buchanan's at Fairfield (subway: Green Line to Copley or Hynes Convention Center/ICA) is a favorite with the professional-sports set and young Newbury Street sophisticates, making for an interesting mixture in the closely packed room. The music is recorded, the action is live. Drinks and light meals.

LIV'S, Quincy Market Building. Tel. 227-4242.

For happy hour, you can't beat the crowd that gathers at the Piano Bar here. Sometimes it's hard to find a place at the bar or at one of the tables, but then again, asking to share a table is the perfect icebreaker. Happy hour (5 to 7pm) and after is the time when Lily's is most closely packed, with a piano player to provide accompaniment for the social action. Take the Blue or Green Line to Government Center.

T.G.I. FRIDAY'S, 26 Exeter St. Tel. 266-9040.

The music at Friday's is recorded, but the people are very much alive and sociable. You can have a full meal here, a sandwich, or just a drink in the sumptuous Victorian atmosphere. The routine is to cluster at the small bar under the glass canopy—which will be pretty crowded—and when you inevitably bump into someone interesting, move on to one of the small tables in the dusky interior. Friday's stays open till midnight weeknights, till 1am on Friday and Saturday. Take the Green Line to Copley.

TOP OF THE HUB LOUNGE, Prudential Center. Tel. 536-1775.

The view at the top of the lofty Prudential Tower in Prudential Center is panoramic, breathtaking, wonderful. The combo is cool, as are the drinks, as are the patrons. If you don't succeed in meeting someone interesting here, no matter—the view is worth it. Dinner is served in the adjoining Top of the Hub restaurant, for about $35 to $50 per person, tax, tip, and wine included. Take the Green Line to Hynes Convention Center/ICA or Prudential.

JAZZ, FOLK & ROCK

Modern music is all over Boston, but except for a few clubs downtown and a few coffeehouses in Cambridge, performers do a gig here or there and then disappear. The very big names usually play in the Wang Center for the Performing Arts, 270 Tremont

St. (tel. 931-2000; subway: Green Line to Boylston or Orange Line to New England Medical Center); in the Hynes Convention Center (tel. 424-8585) at the Prudential Center (subway: Green Line to Hynes Convention Center/ICA); in the Boston Garden (tel. 227-3200), below North Station (subway: Green Line to North Station); or in one of the university halls.

MORE ENTERTAINMENT

CONCERT MUSIC CRUISES

Young Bostonians are crazy for both boats and serious music, and a firm called **Water Music, Inc.,** 12 Arrow St., Cambridge (tel. 876-7777), has put the two together to make the "Concert Cruise." Twice each evening boats leave for a twilight tour of Boston Harbor and Massachusetts Bay, with its own prominent local or national musical group on board. Cruises operate in summer only, and the musical group is different each week. Food such as quiches, pâté, salads, and sandwiches can be purchased on board, as can wine, beer, and cocktails. Call for current schedules, musical programs, prices, and boarding information.

MOVIES

Movies are a big part of Boston's nighttime entertainment picture, and the hot-topic big releases are always crowded during the first few weeks. But besides major releases, silent movies, golden oldies, and best-sellers of the recent past are always available. Prices range from $7 per seat to free admission.

The local listings will let you know what's on tonight. What you may find of help is directions on how to get to the principal movie theaters. Remember to check out Cambridge movies as well, listed separately in the Cambridge section. Here are the prime movie houses in Boston:

BEACON HILL, 1 Beacon St., at Tremont St. Tel. 723-8110.
Near King's Chapel and the Parker House Hotel. Take the Green or Red Line to Park Street, or Green or Blue Line to Government Center.

CHARLES, 195a Cambridge St. Tel. 227-1330.
Next to the Holiday Inn near the corner of Cambridge and Blossom streets. Take the Green or Blue Line to Government Center, or Red Line to Charles.

CHERI, 50 Dalton St. Tel. 536-2870.
Next to Hynes Convention Center in the Prudential Center complex. Take the Green Line's "Boston College," "Cleveland Circle," or "Riverside" cars to Hynes Convention Center/Auditorium, turn left out of the station, left again down Boylston and look right.

CINEMA 57, 200 Stuart St. Tel. 482-1222.
In the tall 57 Park Plaza Hotel–Howard Johnson, in Park Square. Take the Green Line to Boylston, then walk along the edge of the Common on Boylston Street to the intersection with Charles Street and turn left—it's right in front of you.

COOLIDGE CORNER, 290 Harvard St., in suburban Brookline. Tel. 734-2500.
Take the Green Line's "Cleveland Circle" car along Beacon Street to the junction with Harvard Street, called Coolidge Corner. This is the place to go for offbeat movies and foreign films.

COPLEY PLACE, 100 Huntington Ave. Tel. 266-1300.
In the new Copley Place complex next to Copley Square and the Prudential Center. Take a Green Line subway car to Copley or Prudential.

NICKELODEON CINEMAS, 606 Commonwealth Ave., near Kenmore Sq. Tel. 424-1500.
This is actually slightly off Commonwealth, behind Boston University's College of

Communication, but you'll see the cinema's big sign as you walk west along Commonwealth from Kenmore Square.

PARIS CINEMA, 841 Boylston St. Tel. 267-8181.
Very near Prudential Center. Take the Green Line to Copley, Hynes Convention Center/ICA, or Prudential.

WANG CENTER FOR THE PERFORMING ARTS, 270 Tremont St. Tel. 931-2000.
Near Stuart Street in the Theater District; this is often booked with theater, dance, and concerts, but it does have several subscription film series too. Take the Green Line to Boylston, then walk south (away from the Common) 2 blocks on Tremont Street. The Wang Center is on the left.

MUSEUM OF FINE ARTS, 465 Huntington Ave. Tel. 267-9300, ext. 306.
The M.F.A. has many film programs, with screenings most Thursday and Friday evenings. Call for details, times, and prices.

THE COMBAT ZONE

Police hate it, politicians want to get rid of it, some citizens revel in it—the several blocks of Washington Street between Avery and Stuart Streets (subway: Green Line to Boylston or Orange Line to Essex) are perhaps the most "un-Bostonlike" part of Boston. No grand old traditions are here except that of "the oldest profession"; no lofty artistry unless one can call nude dancing art. The Combat Zone, as it is known to all, is Boston's tenderloin: several blocks of prime downtown real estate full of strip shows, "naked college girl revues," porno films, and generally sleazy diversions.

Despite its sinister name and gamy appearance, the Combat Zone is not a wildly dangerous place to stroll through, and many of the bars and clubs and movie houses are safe enough to enter if you follow a few simple rules. First, don't go late at night; things are hopping by early evening, and you might as well see this part of the world around 8 or 8:30pm, rather than later. It's brightly lit and there are lots of police around. Second, don't go alone; anything's better than being a loner, whether you go with a date, a threesome, or a small group. In most places women are as welcome as men. Third, watch your wallet or purse. And finally, if you want to try out a place, go by gut feeling: Some places are fairly attractive and seem safe enough; others look pretty bad, with all sorts of types hanging around. Walk around for a while until you find an acceptable place. And if all this seems terrifying, remember that the people who own the Combat Zone places are interested in selling you movie tickets and drinks, not in ripping you off so you never come back again; they'd rather not have any trouble that'll bring the police.

CHAPTER 5

AROUND BOSTON

The towns around Boston can be neatly divided into three full-day excursions. Cambridge, Lexington, and Concord are to the west; Salem, Marblehead, Gloucester, and Rockport are to the north, known as the North Shore; and Plymouth, New Bedford, and Fall River are to the south.

WEST OF BOSTON As Paul Revere sped through the countryside along another road, William Dawes made a famous midnight ride that took him from the banks of the Charles through the communities of **Cambridge** (once called Newtown), **Lexington,** and **Concord.** Boston's expansion, like America's, was westward toward the mountains, and these important communities west of the city were large enough to play a significant role in the Revolution.

Today Cambridge, Lexington, and Concord are linked by Battle Road, a designation given by the National Park Service, which harks back to that historic day when Revere and Dawes rode out, followed by troops of Redcoats. The story of Battle Road and the events of that day in 1775 is clearly told in the exhibits at Minuteman National Historic Park in Lexington and Concord, but before looking at Revolutionary history, you should visit the home city of Harvard College, which is much older than the Revolution. Cambridge is easily reached from Boston by bus or subway. Buses run to Lexington, and commuter trains go from Boston's North Station and the Red Line's Porter Square station in Cambridge directly to Concord.

THE NORTH SHORE North of Boston are many of the towns that brought great wealth to the North Shore of Massachusetts Bay in the 18th and 19th centuries. Ships from these Essex County towns would sail to Asia and Africa and return several years later with cargoes so rich that everyone involved in the voyage became wealthy overnight.

The gracious houses and public buildings constructed during this era are still here to be seen, and **Salem**'s museums hold a treasure of mementos and artifacts from the maritime boom. **Marblehead** and **Rockport** are still important as yacht harbors and excursion points, but all three towns now make their living primarily from the land: as "bedroom" communities for Boston, and as vacation stops for Bostonians and those who come from farther away. Commuter trains run frequently from Boston's North Station to Salem and **Gloucester;** Marblehead and Rockport can be reached by commuter train, then bus.

THE SOUTH SHORE Of the many communities on the South Shore of Massachusetts Bay, **Plymouth** is easily the most famous. Crowds of visitors make the pilgrimage every summer to see one of the places where this country began.

Though Plymouth makes a logical day-trip, you would probably want to visit the

WHAT'S SPECIAL AROUND BOSTON

Museums

- ☐ Harvard's University Museums, with everything from glass flowers to Mayan ruins.
- ☐ Harvard's art museums, with treasures of European, Middle Eastern, and Asian art.
- ☐ Concord Museum, where a colonial town comes alive.
- ☐ Peabody Museum & Essex Institute in Salem, exhibiting the riches and exotica of the China trade.
- ☐ New Bedford Whaling Museum, showing how New England lit its lamps before electricity.
- ☐ Plimoth Plantation, a "living museum" re-creating the life of the Pilgrims in the 1600s.

Architectural Highlights

- ☐ Harvard University's campus, especially historic Harvard Yard.
- ☐ Pretty town greens in Lexington and Concord, surrounded by historic buildings.
- ☐ Handsome 19th-century ship captains' houses in Salem.
- ☐ New Bedford's restored historic district.
- ☐ The great granite mill buildings of Fall River.

Shopping

- ☐ Rockport's boutiques and artists' galleries, especially along Bearskin Neck.
- ☐ Fall River's huge factory outlets, selling everything from haberdashery to housewares.

Events/Festivals

- ☐ Patriots Day (April 19), when the first battles of the Revolutionary War are reenacted at Lexington and Concord.
- ☐ St. Peter's Festival in Gloucester, with games, rides, and the blessing of the fleet.

Cool for Kids

- ☐ *Mayflower II* in Plymouth, an authentic replica of the original *Mayflower*.
- ☐ Canoeing down the Concord River to Old North Bridge, where the Minutemen fought the Redcoats.
- ☐ Whale-watch expeditions out of Gloucester.

Literary Shrines

- ☐ Ralph Waldo Emerson's house in Concord, the birthplace of Transcendentalism.
- ☐ Site of Thoreau's cabin on Walden Pond in Concord.
- ☐ Orchard House in Concord, home of Louisa May Alcott and her family.
- ☐ Longfellow's house in Cambridge.
- ☐ The Old Manse in Concord, where Nathaniel Hawthorne lived and worked.
- ☐ House of the Seven Gables in Salem, setting for one of Hawthorne's most famous novels.

19th-century whaling port of **New Bedford** and the old textile center of **Fall River** on your way to Cape Cod, Providence, or Newport. Car is the best way to go, but buses travel from Boston to all three towns.

1. CAMBRIDGE

3 miles (5km) W of downtown Boston, 6 miles (8km) SE of Lexington, 15 miles (24km) SE of Concord

GETTING THERE By Subway The MBTA's Red Line connects Harvard Square to Park Street Station on Boston Common. The Red Line is the fastest, most

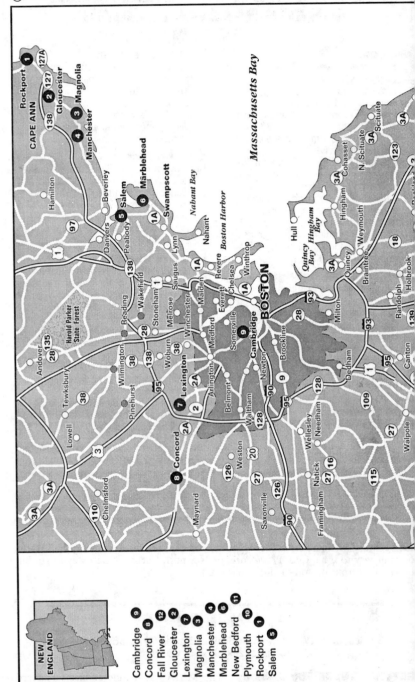

26 mi
0 ━━━━━━━ 41.6 km

N

Massachusetts Bay

CAPE ANN
Rockport ❶ 127A
❷ 127 Gloucester
138 ❸ Magnolia
❹ Manchester

Beverley
Hamilton

Marblehead ❻
Salem ❺ Swampscott
1A
Danvers Peabody
Nabant Bay
97
Lynn Nahant
Boston Harbor
1 138
Wakefield Saugus
1 1A Revere
Reading
28 Stoneham Melrose Winthrop
Harold Parker State Forest Winchester Malden Chelsea 1A
Andover 28 35 Woburn 38 Medford Everett **BOSTON**
38 138 Somerville ❾
Wilmington 28 Cambridge 28
Tewksbury 38 95 Arlington Brookline
Pinehurst Lexington ❼ 2A Newton 93
38 2A Belmont Milton
Lowell 2 Waltham 90 93
110 Chelmsford 3 128 95 Dedham ⓫ 95
Concord ❽ 128 Needham 109 Canton
3A Weston Wellesley 27
3A 126 20
Maynard 27 Natick 27 ⓰ Walpole
126 Saxonville 115
90 Framingham

Hull
Quincy Bay
Hingham Bay
Cohasset 3A N.Scituate 3A
3A Scituate 3A
Hingham 123
Weymouth
3A Quincy 18
Braintree
Randolph 139
Holbrook
Milton

NEW ENGLAND

Cambridge ❾
Concord ❽
Fall River ⓬
Gloucester ❷
Lexington ❼
Magnolia ❸
Manchester ❹
Marblehead ❻
New Bedford ⓫
Plymouth ❿
Rockport ❶
Salem ❺

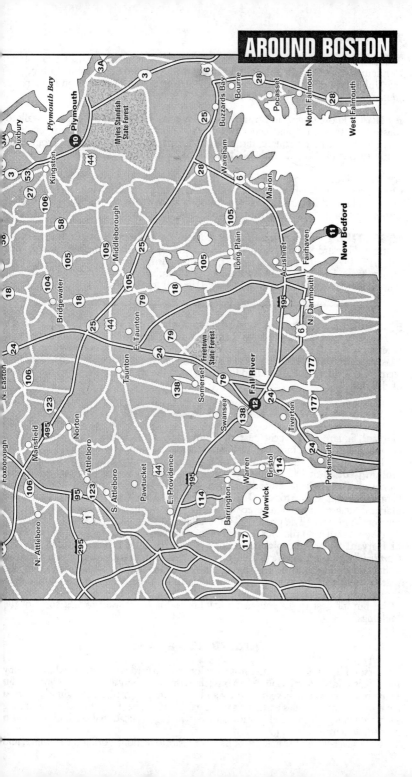

frequent, and most comfortable in the system, and the journey normally takes about 15 minutes from turnstile to turnstile. Going from Harvard Square into Boston, take any "Inbound" train; all trains stop at Park Street Station. From Boston to Harvard Square, take an "Outbound" train marked "Alewife" or "Harvard."

By Bus   Those staying in Boston's Back Bay section might find it easier to walk to Massachusetts Avenue and catch bus no. 1 ("Harvard-Dudley"), which goes past MIT, through Central Square, directly to Harvard Square, the last stop. From areas nearer to Boston Common, the Red Line subway is faster than the bus.

By Car   From Boston, take Storrow Drive westbound along the south bank of the Charles River, or Memorial Drive westbound along the north bank, and follow the signs to Harvard Square. You can also follow Massachusetts Avenue from Boston across the Charles River and all the way to Harvard Square.

ESSENTIALS   The **area code** is 617. There's an **information kiosk** right in the center of Harvard Square, maintained and staffed by **Cambridge Discovery, Inc.** (tel. 617/497-1630), open Monday through Saturday from 9am to 6pm and on Sunday from 1 to 5pm. Walking tours of Old Cambridge leave from the kiosk four times daily between late June and Labor Day; call for details.

Cambridge means Harvard to most visitors who come to Boston, and although Harvard is not the only thing in the city of Cambridge (MIT's there too, after all), it is certainly the city's most important institution. Harvard Square, at the intersection of Massachusetts Avenue, Brattle Street, and John F. Kennedy Street, is a crossroads that teems with evidence of a hundred lifestyles, from the stuffily academic to the loosest of dropouts.

WHAT TO SEE & DO

Harvard Square is the heartbeat of Cambridge, a place where all styles of life commingle in a wild, busy carnival atmosphere.

The Cambridge Historical Commission and Cambridge Discovery, Inc. sponsor **walking tours** of Old Cambridge four times daily from late June through Labor Day. Call **Cambridge Discovery** (tel. 617/491-1630) for details. You can also climb aboard a trolley for an **Old Town Trolley Tour** (tel. 269-8137). They leave Harvard Square on the hour every day from 9am to 4pm for a 1-hour fully narrated tour of Cambridge. The price is $14 for adults, $10 seniors, and $5 for children.

If you'd rather do the tour on your own, go to the information kiosk in the center of Harvard Square and pick up a copy of the fine little brochure called the *Old Cambridge Walking Guide* ($1). The brochure has a map and a description of the 30 sights and buildings to be seen along the walk, each marked with a sign giving the place's name and the number corresponding to it in the brochure. You could walk through the tour route in about an hour if you didn't stop to look closely at any one place, but it's best to plan at least a few hours, for you'll want to visit some of the buildings.

HARVARD UNIVERSITY

The first college founded in the British colonies, Harvard was established in 1636 by the Great and General Court of Massachusetts Bay, the colonists' assembly. John Harvard, a clergyman, gave his library and a sum of money to the fledgling college, a generous gesture that has earned his name worldwide fame. From that early beginning Harvard College grew into Harvard University, a huge educational establishment with an endowment of over $4.2 billion.

The university sponsors tours of its most historic sections during the summer, and during the school year when school is in session (that is, no tours during Christmas recess, spring vacation, etc.). Most of the tours depart from the **Harvard University Information Center,** 1350 Massachusetts Ave. (tel. 617/495-1573), in Holyoke Center, the tallest building in the square. During the months when school is in session, tours depart Monday to Friday at 10am and 2pm and on Saturday at 2pm from the Harvard University Information Center. Additionally, the University Admissions Office conducts tours daily. Saturday tours leave from the information center at 2pm. From June through August tours are at 10 and 11:15am and 2 and 3:15pm Monday through Saturday, 1:30 and 3pm on Sunday, all from the information center. The tours last about 1 hour and are free.

HARVARD UNIVERSITY NATURAL HISTORY MUSEUMS, 24 Oxford St. Tel. 495-1910.

The Harvard University Natural History Museums are a quartet of museums located in one building. There are entrances at 24 Oxford St. and 11 Divinity Ave. Here are the high points of each:

Botanical Museum: The world-famous collection of glass flowers is the big attraction here. The incredibly delicate and detailed glass replicas of flowers that grow all over the world were made in the days before color photography allowed a botanist to make teaching aids easily and cheaply with only a camera. The variety of "flowers" on view and the artistry that it took to make them are truly amazing.

The Botanical Museum has other displays and dioramas on the stair landing as you enter the building. These change from time to time, but may include such things as an exhibit of crossbreeding in the cultivation of corn, or the various narcotic substances used by primitive peoples in different parts of the world.

Museum of Comparative Zoology: Despite its forbidding name, this museum is a favorite with children, for it's loaded with stuffed animals of all kinds, from a tiny hummingbird to a towering giraffe. Sharks, ostriches, hippopotamuses, and zebras abound, as do the exotic beasts from exotic places: tapirs, lemurs, quetzals, and aardvarks. The museum is a product of the 19th-century rage for natural history, which sent Harvard men all over the world in search of specimens to use in scientific teaching. Don't miss the full-size whale skeletons, in the same high-ceilinged room that houses the giraffe.

Peabody Museum of Archeology and Ethnology: The collections here were gathered by adventurers, explorers, archeologists, and scholars. The museum's strong suit is the indigenous peoples of North America; its great hall of the North American Indian reopened in 1990 after having been closed for 10 years. The Maya civilization is particularly well represented, with statues (authentic as well as fiberglass copies), wall-size photographs of jungle scenes, copies of the giant stelae and zoomorphs from Quirigua, Guatemala, and Copan, Honduras, gold jewelry, and household artifacts. Notes and extracts from diaries posted here and there give you an idea of what it was like being one of the first archeologists to discover and study these fascinating works of art.

Other exhibits cover the tribal art of Oceania, and 19th-century photographs and objects from Japan. The Peabody Museum Shop is one of Cambridge's most fascinating places. Handcrafts and folk art from all over the world are on display and on sale, at reasonable prices.

Mineralogical and Geological Museum: This museum houses an internationally important collection of rocks, minerals, ores, and meteorites. Exhibits include an unusually comprehensive systematic mineral collection, minerals from New England, gems, and meteorites.

Admission: $3 adults, $2 seniors and students, $1 children 5-15.

Open: Mon-Sat 9am-4:30pm, Sun 1-4:30pm. **Directions:** Ask your way to the Science Center and Memorial Hall, then walk between these buildings to get to Oxford St. Walk north on Oxford; the third building on your right is the University Museums.

BUSCH-REISINGER MUSEUM, 32 Quincy St. Tel. 495-9400.

The Busch-Reisinger Museum specializes in the arts of German-speaking Europe.

It showcases one of North America's leading collections of German Expressionist art, with famous pieces by Klee, Nolde, Kandinsky, Beckmann, and others. It also houses an impressive collection of Constructivist, Vienna Secession, and Bauhaus pieces. The museum is located in the recently completed Werner Otto Hall, which adjoins the Fogg Art Museum.

Admission: (also good for Fogg Art Museum and Arthur M. Sackler Museum): Sat morning free; Sun–Fri $4 adults, $2.50 students and seniors, free for children up to 18.

Open: Tues–Sun 10am–5pm. **Subway:** Harvard.

FOGG ART MUSEUM, 32 Quincy St. Tel. 495-9400.

The Fogg Art Museum ranks as one of the more important collections of painting and sculpture in the Boston area. Founded in 1891, the Fogg has long served as the center of art study at Harvard. The Fogg is on Quincy Street between Harvard Street and Broadway, east of Harvard Yard. As you enter, the mood for your visit to the galleries is set by the interior court, copied in Italian travertine from an Italian building. Sometimes exhibits are set up in the court. The museum's permanent collections include a fine collection of English silver, drawings, photographs; Italian, Dutch, and American art; and 19th- and 20th-century Parisian art. Shows of other works from the museum's holdings are set up periodically, and are very well done. You can get recorded information on current offerings by dialing 495-9400.

Admission (also good for Busch-Reisinger Museum and Arthur M. Sackler Museum): $4 adults, $2.50 students and seniors, free for children up to 18.

Open: Tues–Sun 10am–5pm. **Subway:** Harvard.

ARTHUR M. SACKLER MUSEUM, 485 Broadway. Tel. 495-9400.

The Arthur M. Sackler Museum opened late in 1985. Housed here are the university's collections of ancient, Asian, and Islamic art, including the world's most extensive collection of ancient Chinese jades, plus important collections of Persian miniatures and Japanese prints. You can get recorded information on current offerings by dialing 495-9400.

Admission (also good for Busch-Reisinger Museum and Fogg Art Museum): Sat morning free; Sun–Fri $4 adults, $2.50 students and seniors, free for children up to 18.

Open: Tues–Sun 10am–5pm. **Subway:** Harvard.

HISTORIC HOUSES

LONGFELLOW NATIONAL HISTORIC SITE, 105 Brattle St. Tel. 876-4491.

Those interested in 19th-century Cambridge will want to see this house, which is now a National Historic Site. Although the house was built by Maj. John Vassall in 1759, and was for a time Washington's headquarters (he and Martha celebrated their 17th wedding anniversary here), most of the furnishings are left from the time of Henry Wadsworth Longfellow, who lived here for 45 years. Mrs. Andrew Craigie took in boarders (mostly Harvard professors), and Longfellow was one, starting in 1837. Soon after he and Fanny Appleton were married, Fanny's father bought the house for the young married couple, and the poet lived here until his death in 1882. Virtually all of his belongings and furnishings are still here, as he left them when he died, for the house was occupied by his descendants until the early 1970s. It's an elegant and beautiful house, and yet still warm and homey, a treat to walk through. The National Park Service guides who take you through are friendly and knowledge-able.

Longfellow House sponsors concerts every 2 weeks on Sunday afternoons in summer, on the lawn, free, and open to the public. Other special events include the February birthday anniversary celebration, and the Christmas open house.

Admission: $2 adults, free for children under 16 and senior citizens.

Open: Daily 10am–4:30pm. **Directions:** From Brattle Sq. (a few steps from

Harvard Sq.), take Brattle St., and after about 5 blocks look for the big yellow house on the right-hand side.

WHERE TO STAY

Guidelines for Cambridge hotels are similar to those for Boston. There is no reason you shouldn't plan to stay in Cambridge during the length of your Boston visit. Keep in mind that bed-and-breakfast organizations serving the Boston area serve Cambridge, as well. See the Boston hotel section for details.

Note: Unless otherwise specified all of the rates below include tax.

EXPENSIVE

CHARLES HOTEL AT HARVARD SQUARE, 1 Bennett St., Cambridge, MA 02138. Tel. 617/864-1200, or toll free 800/882-1818. Fax 617/864-5715. 296 rms. A/C MINIBAR TV TEL **Subway:** Harvard.
$ Rates: $207–$240 single; $207–$262 double. Weekend discounts available; call for details. AE, CB, DC, MC, V. **Parking:** Covered parking on premises, $14 a day.

Just steps away from Harvard Square, the Charles Hotel is located in the complex called Charles Square, off Mount Auburn Street and Brattle Square. All the guest rooms have contemporary furnishings softened by the hotel's down quilts. From the upper floors there are wonderful panoramic views of Boston and Cambridge. In addition to being a full-service luxury hotel, the Charles has extra-special touches, such as three phones in each guest room (including one in the bathroom), a second TV in the bathroom, a bathroom scale, terry bathrobe, hairdryer, and a service whereby guests can buy books and have them delivered to their rooms.

Dining/Entertainment: The restaurant called Rarities is elegant, epicurean, and pricey. The Regattabar is among the Boston area's best jazz clubs, with top-name artists. Bennett St. Café (see below) is open for breakfast, lunch, dinner, and Sunday brunch. On each table, there's a glass filled with crayons to be used on paper tablecloths. The best artwork of the month gets displayed on a bulletin board.

Services: 24-hour room service, concierge, valet parking, twice-daily chamber service, currency exchange, teleconferencing, personal-computer rental, laundry and valet (same-day service), room-service books.

Facilities: Pool, sauna, whirlpool, exercise room, use of Le Pli Health Spa and Salon in same complex.

GUEST QUARTERS SUITE HOTEL, 400 Soldiers Field Rd., Boston, MA 02134. Tel. 617/783-0090, or toll free 800/424-2900. Fax 617/783-0897. 310 suites. A/C MINIBAR TV TEL **Directions:** From Storrow Dr. westbound (coming from Boston), follow signs for Newton and Arlington. Take Central Sq./Mass. Pike exit. At set of lights, take a wide left U-turn. From Harvard Sq., take Storrow Dr. eastbound (toward Boston); take Mass. Pike exit, but instead of turning right to Mass. Pike entrance, go straight on, to the hotel.
$ Rates (including continental breakfast): $163–$240 suite Mon–Thurs; $108–$240 suite Fri–Sat. AE, CB, DC, DISC, MC, V. **Parking:** $12, free on weekends.

The Guest Quarters Suite Hotel is a good choice if you're in search of more space and convenience for the same money as a standard hotel room. Though the address is Boston, this 15-story building is as close to Harvard Square and MIT as it is to Boston University and downtown. Each suite consists of a bedroom with king-size bed, AM/FM radio, writing desk, living room with full-size sofa bed, and dining table. Weekend guests enjoy free continental breakfast and a manager's reception with hors d'oeuvres and discounted drinks.

Dining/Entertainment: Scullers Grille serves breakfast, lunch, and dinner and specializes in New England seafood. Scullers, the hotel's jazz club, is one of the city's best.

Services: Free van shuttle service to Cambridge and Boston for weekend guests, room service.

Facilities: Indoor pool, whirlpool, and sauna.

HYATT REGENCY CAMBRIDGE, 575 Memorial Dr., Cambridge, MA 02139. Tel. 617/492-1234, or toll free 800/233-1234. 469 rms. A/C MINIBAR TV TEL **Directions:** Take Memorial Drive eastbound from Harvard Square about 2 miles.

$ Rates: $108–$207 single; $108–$229 double; $411–$603 suite. Weekend discounts (as low as $110) available. AE, CB, DC, MC, V. **Parking:** $12 per day, on premises.

The most dramatic hotel in town is the Aztec-pyramid Hyatt Regency Cambridge. True to the Hyatt design tradition, it has a grand interior space rising from ground floor to top floor, planted with trees and hanging vines and surrounded with mezzanine walkways to the guest rooms. It's not easily reached by public transportation, so plan to use taxis, bicycles, or your car. There is a complimentary shuttle to local points of interest, as well.

Dining/Entertainment: Of the several restaurants in the hotel, Jonah's Seafood Café is on the mezzanine one flight up from ground level, and diners thus can enjoy the atmosphere of the central space. The Pallysadoe Bar, just off this mezzanine, has a good view of the Charles River, as does Sally Ling's, the fancy Chinese restaurant. Take one of the crystal-shaped glass elevators that slide up the wall to reach the Spinnaker Italian restaurant on the top floor. Open for lunch and dinner, the restaurant affords a panoramic view of Boston, Cambridge, and the Charles. Once you're seated, take in the view at once, because the entire dining area is on a revolving disc, which moves very slowly so that the perspective is always changing.

Services: Free shuttle van to Harvard Square and downtown Boston.

Facilities: Health club and children's playground.

THE INN AT HARVARD, 1201 Massachusetts Ave., Cambridge, MA 02138. Tel. 617/491-2222, or toll free 800/528-0444 (Doubletree Central Reservations). Fax 617/496-5050. 113 rms. A/C TV TEL **Subway:** Harvard.

$ Rates: $159 single or double. Ask about special packages. AE, DC, DISC, MC, V.

Step into the lobby of the red-brick Inn at Harvard and you'll feel as if you've stepped into a university library. Indeed, Cambridge's newest hotel has a very academic air about it, and feels as if it's an extension to the university. The main lobby—which is called the atrium—is four-stories high, surrounded by guest rooms and balconies, not unlike a Renaissance palazzo. There are several shelves lined with books that were very skillfully "Selected by the Harvard Book Store." Individual guest rooms are very simply, but tastefully, decorated in earth tones. Each one has a computer data port, two telephones connected to Harvard University's Centrex system, and voice-mail message service. The inn is adjacent to Harvard Yard, at the intersection of Massachusetts Avenue, Harvard Street, and Quincy Street.

Dining/Entertainment: Breakfast, snacks, light meals, and bar service is available in the atrium lounge.

Services: Valet parking, concierge, complimentary shoe shine, room service from 6am to 11pm, library stocked with current periodicals, books, and Harvard University Press publications.

SHERATON COMMANDER, 16 Garden St., Cambridge, MA 02238. Tel. 617/547-4800, or toll free 800/325-3535. 176 rms. A/C TV TEL **Subway:** Harvard.

$ Rates: $108–$152 single; $119–$163 double; $220–$383 suite. Children under 18 stay free in parents' room. AE, CB, DC, MC, V. **Parking:** Free.

The Sheraton Commander is a renovated hotel, not far from Harvard Square. Garden Street runs from Harvard Square past Cambridge Common to Radcliffe, and the Commander is just about equidistant (a 10-min. walk) from either campus. The decor in the public rooms tends to the high-brow colonial—the "commander" for whom the hotel was named is George Washington, and a bronze statue of General

Washington stands in the entry garden, to the right of the doors. Although there is free parking at the hotel, the lot is small and you may have to leave your keys at the desk so the doorman can jockey the cars around to best advantage.

MODERATE

DAYS INN, 1234 Soldiers Field Rd., Boston (Brighton), MA 02135. Tel. 617/254-1234, or toll free 800/325-2525. Fax 617/254-1234. 113 rms. A/C TV TEL **Directions:** From Harvard Sq., take John F. Kennedy St. to Soldiers Field Rd. (which is the westward continuation of Storrow Dr.). Follow Soldiers Field Rd. 1 mile to the motel, on the left-hand side.

$ Rates: $82–$115 single; $93–$126 double. Children under 12 stay free in parents' room. Weekend discounts available. AE, DC, DISC, MC, V. **Parking:** Free.

At the Days Inn, you get a small swimming pool (open from Memorial Day to Labor Day) and a large restaurant, plus views of the Charles River. The waterfront park across from the hotel has biking and jogging paths and a childrens' play area. Harvard Square is 1 mile away.

HOWARD JOHNSON HOTEL, 777 Memorial Dr., Cambridge, MA 02139. Tel. 617/492-7777, or toll free 800/654-2000. 205 rms. A/C TV TEL

$ Rates: $82–$137 single; $91–$148 double. Weekend discounts available with advance notice. AE, MC, V. **Parking:** Free.

The Howard Johnson Hotel is a 14-story establishment, and the height of your room determines its price, since the higher rooms have better views; some rooms have small balconies. Views are of Boston and the Charles, straight across the Charles, up the Charles River to Harvard, and a city view of Cambridge. The hotel has a year-round swimming pool, a restaurant and bar, and a pleasant brick-and-dark-wood interior. Harvard special events (freshmen registration, Harvard-Yale game, homecoming, graduation, and the like) can fill the hotel, and rooms should be reserved well in advance. The hotel is 1 mile east of Harvard Square; car or taxi must be used to get to and from Harvard Square or downtown Boston.

BUDGET

DAYSTOP, 1800 Soldiers Field Rd., Boston (Brighton), MA 02135. Tel. 617/254-0200, or toll free 800/325-2525. Fax 617/782-8002. 55 rms. A/C TV TEL **Directions:** From Harvard Sq., take John F. Kennedy St. to Soldiers Field Rd. (which is the westward continuation of Storrow Dr.). Follow Soldiers Field Rd. several miles to the motel, on the left-hand side.

$ Rates (including continental breakfast): $66 single; $77 double. Children under 12 stay free in parents' room. AE, DISC, MC, V. **Parking:** Free.

Formerly the Charles River Motel but now a unit of the Days Inn chain, Daystop is not in Cambridge, strictly speaking, but it offers advantages to visitors to Cambridge who have their own cars. Larger-than-average recently refurbished rooms and buses to Cambridge and downtown Boston are among the advantages. The motel has a lounge open from 2pm to 2am, and there are several restaurants within walking distance. Although Daystop is several miles from Harvard Square, Soldiers Field Road allows you to speed to the center of town in only 10 minutes.

SUSSE CHALET, 211 Concord Tpk. (Rte. 2 east), Cambridge, MA 02140. Tel. 617/661-7800, or toll free 800/524-2538. 79 rms. A/C TV TEL **Directions:** From Boston, cross the Charles River to Cambridge and follow Memorial Dr. (Mass. Rte. 2) westward 4 miles; pass the motel on the left, exit and return on the eastbound side to the motel. From I-95/Rte. 128, take Rte. 2 east to the motel. **Subway:** Alewife, then a 15-minute walk.

$ Rates (including continental breakfast): $55–$76 single; $59–$76 double. AE, DC, MC, V. **Parking:** Free, on premises.

Another clean, simple motel offering good value, this one is on the outskirts of

Cambridge, and is easily reachable by subway from downtown Boston and Harvard Square. In the past, some readers have complained about noise, but since the disco next door has closed, the situation has improved. Continental breakfast is available; other restaurants are about a mile from the motel.

Services: Loan of hairdryer and iron.

Facilities: Coin-operated laundry.

WHERE TO DINE

Cambridge, in its woolly way, is even more cosmopolitan than Boston, and this is well demonstrated in its restaurants. Cannelloni to couscous, wonton to Weisswurst, Cambridge has it. Some of the best places to have a good, inexpensive lunch or a light supper are Cambridge's coffeehouses, almost all of which serve food as well as a wide selection of hot and cold coffee and tea drinks. And finally, there are the ice-cream shops of Harvard Square, worthy of a list unto themselves.

The half-dozen restaurants in the Harvard Square Garage, a sort of mall bounded by J.F.K., Mount Auburn, and Dunster Streets, are all moderate to inexpensive in price. **Souper Salad** is an attractive lunch or light-supper place, with interesting spaces in which to sit, an upbeat menu, and prices to suit any appetite or budget. Nearby is **Baby Watson,** whose cheesecake is Boston's best known.

EXPENSIVE

BENNETT ST. CAFE, in the Charles Square complex, 1 Bennett St. Tel. 864-1200.

    Cuisine: AMERICAN. **Reservations:** Recommended. **Subway:** Harvard.

$ **Prices:** Lunch $12–$15; dinner $15–$30. AE, DC, MC, V.

    Open: Daily 7am–11pm.

The Bennett St. Café, located in the Charles Hotel, just out of Brattle Square, is among the area's most attractive and interesting restaurants. In fair weather you can dine outdoors in the court; otherwise, the indoor dining room is plush and attractive. The selection of luncheon salads, sandwiches, and light main courses (the menu changes constantly) is among the finest and most interesting I've seen among Harvard Square's plethora of upscale dining places. The café also serves Sunday brunch.

HARVEST, 44 Brattle St. Tel. 492-1115.

    Cuisine: AMERICAN. **Reservations:** Required on weekends, not accepted in café. **Subway:** Harvard.

$ **Prices:** Appetizers $6–$14; main courses $23–$30; lunch $20; dinner $40–$60; café $6–$17. AE, DC, DISC, MC, V.

    Open: Lunch daily 11:30am–2:30pm; dinner daily 6–10pm; Sun brunch 11:30am–3pm.

In the top price range, first place goes to Harvest, hidden away down the passageway that penetrates the four-story glass building that houses Crate and Barrel on Brattle Street. The restaurant's location allows it to have the most pleasant outdoor luncheon area in all Cambridge. Harvest offers meticulously prepared dishes: at lunch, a four-liver pâté to start, then venison Stroganoff, and for dessert a chocolate marquise, for example. For dinner you might have creole okra gumbo or a game terrine, a grilled pharaoh quail salad, and a main course of sautéed rock shrimp and sea scallops served with garlic fettuccine, fennel, and plum tomato. The menu in the section called Ben's Corner is less expensive than the main dining room, but equally interesting. Sunday brunch is fancy and satisfying.

UPSTAIRS AT THE PUDDING, 10 Holyoke St. Tel. 864-1933.

    Cuisine: CONTINENTAL/NORTHERN ITALIAN. **Reservations:** Recommended, especially on theater evenings. **Subway:** Harvard.

$ **Prices:** Appetizers $7–$11; main courses $16–$23; dinner $40–$50. AE, DC, MC, V. Ask about the pre-theater meal.

    Open: Dinner daily 6–10pm; Sun brunch noon–3pm.

Located on the third floor of the building that houses Harvard's famous Hasty

Pudding Club, this is about as "Harvardy" a place can get. There's always a low hum of satisfaction in the grandly accoutred main dining room (complete with brass service plates) and Secret Garden terrace (during fair weather months). The menu—which changes daily—includes a fine selection of Northern Italian dishes and desserts that can be counted on to elicit a whole string of oohs and aahs.

MODERATE

BORDER CAFE, 32 Church St. Tel. 864-6100.
Cuisine: MEXICAN/CAJUN. **Reservations:** Recommended on weekends. **Subway:** Harvard.
$ Prices: Appetizers $3.25–$7; main courses $5–$11; meals $16–$20. MC, V.
Open: Mon–Thurs 11am–1am (Fri–Sat to 2am), Sun noon–1am.

The Border Café is a mock-stark Mexican cantina with rough wood tables and naive murals of favorite Mexican bottles, but also a chic black-clad hostess to seat you (she'd never survive in a real cantina). The café is popular partly because of its tongue-in-cheek decor, but more because the food is surprisingly inexpensive. The cuisine here borrows from Mexican, Cajun, fajita, and mesquite-grill cooking, and you'll love it. Not only that, but you can have a sandwich and Corona (beer), or more elaborate and delicious plates of shrimp, fajitas (shredded fried meat or chicken), or blackened redfish. The restaurant is at the corner of Church and Palmer Streets.

COTTONWOOD CAFE, 1815 Massachusetts Ave. Tel. 661-7440.
Cuisine: SOUTHWEST. **Reservations:** Required. **Subway:** Porter.
$ Prices: Appetizers $3–$7; main courses $12–$19; lunch $12–$16; dinner $20–$25. MC, V.
Open: Lunch daily 11:45am–3:30pm; dinner Mon–Thurs 5:45–10pm, Fri–Sat 5:45–11pm.

Located in the renovated Sears, Roebuck building at Porter Square, the Cottonwood is a cozy, attractive upscale Mexican place with an inventive menu that might best be described as "New Latin American Cuisine": Although Mexican-inspired, the dishes are original creations. Many are pretty spicy, so ask. Authentic, carefully chosen crafts enliven the decor.

GRENDEL'S RESTAURANT AND BAR, 89 Winthrop St. Tel. 491-1160.
Cuisine: INTERNATIONAL. **Reservations:** Recommended. **Subway:** Harvard.
$ Prices: Appetizers $1.95–$5.25; main courses $5–$18. AE, DC, DISC, MC, V.
Open: Sun–Thurs 11am–11pm, Fri–Sat 11am–midnight.

Every college student reads about Grendel, the dragon that threatens the hero of the ancient English epic *Beowulf*, but anyone in Harvard Square—student or not—can frequent Grendel's, a restaurant noted for its reasonable prices and large portions. Grendel's is behind a tiny patch of grass off John F. Kennedy Street at Mount Auburn Street, 1 block south of Harvard Square toward the Charles River: A huge sign on the roof leads the way. The cellar of the redbrick building is the bar, furnished with a fireplace for cold winter nights, and dark-wood tables. Upstairs is the restaurant, with two fireplaces and a glassed-in terrace overlooking busy John F. Kennedy Street. The menu tells of international specialties, such as spinach pie, fettuccine, chicken curry, shish kebab, quiche, omelets, burgers, and sandwiches. There's a good salad bar. Alcoholic beverages are served. As for the desserts, they're a list in themselves, but suffice it to say that they include chocolate fondue.

IRUÑA, 54 and 56 John F. Kennedy St. Tel. 868-5633.
Cuisine: SPANISH. **Reservations:** Recommended. **Subway:** Harvard.
$ Prices: Appetizers $4.50–$6; main courses $9–$14; lunch $9–$12. AE, DISC, MC, V.
Open: Lunch Mon–Sat 11:30am–2pm; dinner Mon–Sat 6–10pm.

Iruña is Harvard Square's best-kept secret. Though it's been here for years, only locals know about Iruña's good, hearty Spanish food, low prices, and pretty outdoor patio in the rear (summer only). Come for lunch and you can have soup, *carne guisada* (chunks of beef in a sauce of wine, mushrooms, and carrots), and salad for a refreshingly low price. *Arroz con pollo* (chicken and rice) is another staple here. You can spend even less by ordering only the main course. Prices at dinner are similarly pleasant. Wine and beer are served.

LEGAL SEA FOOD, INC., 5 Cambridge Center. Tel. 864-3400.

Cuisine: SEAFOOD. **Reservations:** Recommended. **Subway:** Kendall Square.

$ Prices: Lunch $5.95–$12.95; dinner $11.95–$29.95. AE, DISC, DC, MC, V.

Open: Mon–Sat 11am–10pm, Sun 4–10pm.

This nationally known restaurant needs no introduction. Along with its sister restaurant in Boston, it has a reputation for spanking fresh seafood and fish and, in fact, NBC news called it "the best seafood restaurant in America." Do yourselves a favor and make reservations. Otherwise, you'll have to take a number and wait in line.

BUDGET

ELSIE'S FAMOUS SANDWICHES, 71a Mount Auburn St. Tel. 864-0461.

Cuisine: DELI. **Reservations:** Not accepted. **Subway:** Harvard.

$ Prices: Sandwiches $3.25–$5.75. No credit cards.

Open: Daily 8am–8pm.

Though nothing fancy, Elsie's deli has never been surpassed for good prices, and good food in both quantity and quality. The mainstay is the Roast Beef Special, which comes with Bermuda onion and "Elsie's Special Russian Dressing"; the Turkey Deluxe, the Elsieburger (a double hamburger), and the thick-cut Romanian pastrami-filled Landsman are other favorites. From the Harvard subway station walk east on Massachusetts Avenue to Holyoke Street, turn right; Elsie's is 1 block down at the corner of Mount Auburn Street.

SPECIALTY DINING

Coffeehouses

An intellectual center will have its coffeehouses, dedicated to serving the beverage that stimulates thought and aids conversation. Harvard Square has a good selection of coffeehouses, all of which serve light meals, desserts, ice cream, and beverages besides coffee. Each draws a special clientele, and you can spend a very pleasant day or two hopping from one to another of these, testing them to find the one that suits you best. Here is a rundown of the best places:

AU BON PAIN, 1360 Massachusetts Ave. Tel. 497-9797.

Cuisine: CAFE. **Reservations:** Not accepted.

$ Prices: Coffee and soft drinks 90¢–$2.25; soups and pastries $1–$5; sandwiches $3.70–$6. No credit cards.

Open: Daily 7am–10pm.

Harvard Square's most visible café is Au Bon Pain, a branch of the chain café, located outside the Harvard subway station in the Holyoke Center across the street from Harvard Yard. In summer the little square in front of the café is filled with tables and chairs; in winter you can see all the tasty croissants, baguette sandwiches, and pastries through the huge plate-glass windows. Buy your breakfast, lunch, or supper at the counter, and then find an unoccupied table. The menu includes plain croissants, those stuffed with spinach or ham and cheese, muffins, and a variety of upscale sandwiches.

BLACKSMITH HOUSE BAKERY AND CAFE, 56 Brattle St. Tel. 354-3036.

Cuisine: CAFE. **Reservations:** Not required. **Subway:** Harvard.

$ Prices: Beverages 90¢–$3.50; desserts $1.20–$3.75; salads and sandwiches $4.95–$7.95; main courses $4.95–$7.95. MC, V (with $10 minimum).
Open: Mid-Sept to mid-June, Mon–Wed 8am–5pm, Thurs–Sat 8am–8pm, Sun brunch 11am–3pm. Mid-June to mid-Sept, Tues–Sat 8am–8pm, Sun brunch 11am–3pm.

It is said that Longfellow, who lived only 6 blocks away, wrote his famous poem about a Cambridge blacksmith whose shop was on Brattle Street: "Under the spreading chestnut tree/The village smithy stands/The smith, a mighty man is he,/With large and sinewy hands." The spot the smithy occupied is now taken by the Blacksmith House, a café and bakery, just 1½ blocks up Brattle Street from Harvard Square. In summer the large terrace in front of the house is set with tables; in winter coffee lovers have to settle for a nice upstairs room in the house, furnished with small wood tables and spindle-back chairs. Hot main dishes include Nasi Goreing (sautéed shrimp and chicken tossed with rice, peanuts, raisins, spices, and herbs) and Mussel Pasta (steamed mussels in white wine, garlic, and cream sauce with linguine and parmesan cheese) when available. There's also a selection of salads and cold dishes. Coffee is good, and refills cheap, but the stars of the show are the German- and Austrian-style pastries, such as Wiener torte, Sacher torte, Mozart torte, Linzer torte, and apple torte. Other types of Kuchen, and also brioche and croissants, are made daily, too. The Blacksmith House does as big a business selling cakes (especially wedding cakes) and pastries to go as it does selling coffee to stay.

CAFE PAMPLONA, 12 Bow St. No phone.

Cuisine: CAFE. **Reservations:** Not accepted. **Subway:** Harvard.
$ Prices: Coffee $1–$3; pastries and sandwiches $2.50–$5. No credit cards.
Open: Mon–Sat 11am–1am, Sun 2pm–1am.

Harvard Square's woolliest of intellectual coffeehouses is the Café Pamplona. Nothing disturbs the current of conversation here, for there's no telephone, no music, and no live entertainment. Various kinds of coffee are served, from the inexpensive espresso to the mocha, a rich coffee-and-chocolate blend topped with real whipped cream. Most coffees start from a very dark-roast bean, and are therefore quite strong. From 11am to 3pm, gazpacho, toasted sandwiches, and other light-lunch items are prepared, and in summer the tiny terrace beside the Pamplona's entrance stairway is furnished with tables, chairs, and umbrellas (the indoor café is in a basement). In winter the atmosphere is that of a group of high-brow troglodytes, and invariably the table next to yours will be occupied by someone writing poetry, or music, or translating some abstruse language. The Pamplona is tiny, and you may have to wait for a seat.

COFFEE CONNECTION, 36 John F. Kennedy St. Tel. 492-4881.

Cuisine: CAFE. **Reservations:** Not accepted. **Subway:** Harvard.
$ Prices: Coffee $1.25–$4; pastries $2–$5. AE, MC, V.
Open: Sun 9am–6pm, Mon–Wed 7am–7pm, Thurs–Fri 7am–9pm, Sat 8am–9pm.

It is generally agreed that the finest and most delicious coffee in Harvard Square—and the widest selection—is to be had at the Coffee Connection. Although light meals are served here, such as breakfast of fresh-squeezed juice, granola, and coffee, the star of the show is the coffee. The different characteristics of the various brews are described in the menu. Some coffees are very strong and hearty, others are smooth and mild—but the flavor in all is well rounded and delicious. The cheapest way to have good coffee here is to order the coffee of the day; cappuccino and other coffee specialty drinks are more expensive. Black and herbal teas are also available. Surroundings here are modern and attractive, light and airy, with a raised sitting area and a nearby counter where coffee beans and teas can be bought in bulk to take home.

PASSIM, 47 Palmer St. Tel. 429-7679.

Cuisine: CAFE. **Reservations:** Not accepted. **Subway:** Harvard.

$ Prices: Coffee $1.50–$3; pastries $2–$5; light lunch $4–$9. MC, V.
 Open: Lunch Tues–Sat noon–4:45pm.
Passim is a Harvard Square institution, known in the world of jazz, blues, and folk music as a place where numerous nationally known performers first thrilled an audience. Drop in for a beverage, snack, tea, and cake, or a light meal, then spend some time at the small gallery, which displays the work of local artists, or look for a bauble among the glass cases of interesting objets d'art from all over the world that are on sale here. While you're here, check out the schedule of performers, then come back in the evening in plenty of time to get a good seat. Palmer Street runs between the Harvard Coop's main store and bookstore. The gift shop is open Tuesday to Saturday from noon to 5:30pm.

Ice Cream

From a short study of Harvard Square shops, it might appear that the two most valued commodities hereabouts are the photocopy and the ice-cream cone. Ice cream, at $1.65 to $2.50 for a "small" (actually, huge) cone, is almost a cult food in Cambridge, and the virtues of the various shops and their selections of flavors are a frequent topic of debate, and even fierce loyalty. The eating of ice cream is by no means limited to the summer months, and in fact only one or two people thought it unusual that cones should be seen along Massachusetts Avenue during the bitter days of the blizzard of 1978. Herewith, a guide for the discriminating cone-oisseur:
      Once upon a time, a local fellow decided to open an ice-cream parlor that served only ice cream made from cream and things like vanilla beans, fruits, and other natural ingredients. He set up shop in Somerville, and the lines of passionate devotees soon stretched around the block.
      That's the legend behind the legendary Steve Herrell, founder of Steve's Ice Cream. He later sold the business and retired to the mountains for a breather, but then returned to franchise a new line of stores called **Herrell's,** with one at 15 Dunster Street (tel. 497-2179), along similar lines. Just around the corner from the Cambridge Savings Bank in Harvard Square, Herrell's is the ultimate of Harvard Square ice-cream shops. It's located in a former bank building, and you can devour your cone or dish in the vault, now walled with mirrors. Flavors change somewhat from day to day, and all cost the same. Take special note of Chocolate Pudding, a supercharged chocolate ice cream that leaves chocoholics in ecstasy. There's also their own frozen yogurt, made right here, and "No-Moo," a nondairy ice cream, as well as Vitari, another ice-cream alternative. Herrell's is open until 1am on Friday and Saturday during the summer months.
      Steve's Ice Cream is now famous from coast to coast, still producing top-quality treats, still attracting hordes of faithful devotees. The Harvard Square location, at 31 Church St. (tel. 491-0254), has been added to the original shop at 191 Elm Street (Davis Square) in neighboring Somerville. The solution to unhappiness on any hot summer day is a cone from Steve's; winter days too, for that matter.
      Baskin-Robbins Ice Cream Store, 1230 Massachusetts Ave. (tel. 617/547-3131), at the corner of Bow Street, several blocks east along Massachusetts Avenue from Harvard Square proper, sells good ice cream in 48 flavors, plus frozen-yogurt cones. They'll make you an ice-cream cake, sundae, shake, banana split, freeze, or ice-cream sandwich if you like, anytime from 6am to 12:30am.

EVENING ENTERTAINMENT

THEATER

HARVARD'S LOEB DRAMA CENTER, 64 Brattle St. Tel. 547-8300.
      The touchstone of theater in Cambridge is Harvard's Loeb Drama Center, located at the corner of Hilliard, home of the American Repertory Theatre. This resident

professional company performs a variety of works year round in a rotating repertory. For 6 weeks in the autumn and spring, the ART steps aside as Harvard/Radcliffe undergraduates take the stage.

Prices: $10–$38, depending upon the show.

CINEMA

Although Boston has a lively movie nightlife, Cambridge has its own group of movie theaters, many of which tend to be slightly more "far out" than some of the mass-market houses downtown. If you're staying in Boston but want to go to a cinema in Cambridge, take the Red Line to Harvard. Check the *Boston Globe* for listings of what's currently being shown. Here are Cambridge's major movie houses:

Brattle Theater, 40 Brattle St. (tel. 876-6837), 1 longish block from the Harvard subway station, specializes in nostalgia and American and foreign classics.

Janus Cinema, 57 John F. Kennedy St. (tel. 661-3737), 2 blocks from the Harvard subway station down toward the river, usually has one of the hotter big films of the season, playing to a packed house.

Harvard Square, 10 Church St. (tel. 864-4580), is right around the corner from the subway station. In this multiscreen complex, two screens are reserved for first-run showings, and the others feature the most popular films with the college crowd that have been released in the past few years; they're repeated at intervals of a few weeks. This is where you go to see it if you missed it two or three years ago, or didn't want to pay the high price when it was a first-run hit. Seats are low priced, especially before 6pm (call for exact screening times).

To find out about **free films,** get hold of a copy of the *Harvard Gazette* (free) from the Harvard University Information Office (tel. 495-1000), Holyoke Center, just across the street from Harvard Yard. The Gazette, published regularly when Harvard is in its fall and spring semesters, sporadically at other times, lists all the university activities, including quite a few films for free or for a very low price.

JAZZ CLUBS

The big names show up in the plush atmosphere of the **Regattabar** at the Charles Hotel (tel. 864-1200), in the complex called Charles Square, off Eliot and Mount Auburn Streets, just steps from Harvard Square. The club has hosted Stephane Grappelli, Ahmad Jamal, the Ritz, and many other big names, at prices ranging from $15 to $30, parking in the hotel's garage included. You can book through CONCERTIX (tel. 617/876-7777) for an additional fee. Warning: The big names produce big crowds, and if you don't reserve seats in advance, you may have to wait in line for standing-room-only tickets—and you may not even get those.

---

2. LEXINGTON

6 miles (8km) NW of Cambridge, 9 miles (13km) NW of downtown Boston,
6 miles (8km) E of Concord

GETTING THERE   Public transportation to Lexington is good, but note that it is not possible to go directly between Lexington and Concord by public transportation.

By Train   You can take a commuter train from Boston's North Station or Cambridge's Porter subway station to Waltham (every 20 min. during rush hours, every 1½ hr. during the day, every hour in the evening, every 2 hr. or more on weekends), and then bus no. 525, "Lexington-Waltham," to your destination—buses run every hour during the day (no evening or Sunday service).

By Bus   To Lexington from Cambridge, the easiest way is bus no. 528, "Hanscom

Field-Harvard," which leaves Harvard Square on the 45-minute ride every hour during the day, every ½ hour during rush periods (no night or Sunday service).

By Car   Coming from Boston in a car, take U.S. 3 to Mass. 2, then a road with two route numbers, 4/225, into the center of Lexington. An alternative route subject to tolls is the Mass. Pike west to I-95 (Rte. 128) north, exiting at Exit 44, "Bedford Street," for Lexington.

ESSENTIALS   The **area code** is 617. First thing to do is to go to the **Chamber of Commerce Visitors' Center,** 1875 Massachusetts Ave. (tel. 617/862-1450), just off the Green near the Minuteman statue and next door to Buckman Tavern. Here, every day between the hours of 9am and 5pm (10am and 4pm October to June), you can pick up a sketch map of the town, and brochures and information on the sights. More important, you can inspect the diorama, or scale model, of the Battle Green and the events of April 19, 1775: the Minutemen in their farmers' clothes scattering before the long files of crack troops dressed in brilliant colors. The diorama is well worth seeing (it's free, too); historical accounts and explanations of the battle accompany the display.

The National Park Service has organized most of the interesting historical sites in Lexington and Concord into Minuteman National Historical Park, and those with their own car can pick up the park service's Minute Man brochure, which has a sketch map of Battle Road and most of the sights to see.

Lexington was the home of the first Minutemen to die from British bullets in the Revolutionary War. Although they were not the first Americans to die for their country (victims of the Boston Massacre hold that honor), nor even the first to offer spirited resistance as the Minutemen of Concord did, the eight Minutemen who fell on Lexington Green served their country well. For without the battle at Lexington, the Concord Minutemen might not have been determined to offer strong resistance to the British force.

Americans in the colonies had always had virtually total control over their own destinies, and so, when the government in London tried to levy taxes of which the colonists did not approve, their anger was aroused. To show who was boss, the government sent troops from England and quartered them in the homes of the colonists, further stirring up their anger. As it looked more and more likely that a head-on collision might occur, the colonists, led by Samuel Adams and John Hancock, began stockpiling arms and ammunition, especially cannons. Hearing rumors of these stockpiles, General Gage, the British commander in Boston, prepared to send out a body of troops to scour the countryside and destroy the stockpiles so as to nip any armed resistance to London in the bud. But the colonists' spy network found out about the plan, and as the troops mustered late at night in preparation for the expedition, Paul Revere and William Dawes galloped through the darkness to alert the patriots.

The "alarm system" was so efficient that the Lexington Minutemen, led by Capt. John Parker, turned out shortly after Revere arrived at midnight, but there were no British troops in sight. The patriots returned home or retired to the Buckman Tavern near Lexington Green, ready to appear again the minute they heard the sound of the drum.

About daybreak, the British column finally arrived in Lexington, and the 100 or so Minutemen drew themselves up in soldierly order on the Green. Nobody knew what would happen. The Minutemen knew only that a much larger force of some 600 soldiers was coming to search their homes, and although it would have been folly to try to stop them, they could still show that they didn't like it and perhaps worry the British a little. The British soldiers knew only that men with rifles were waiting in a position of defiance to keep the soldiers from doing their duty. When the forces finally came face to face at Lexington Green, officers on both sides seemed to think it would be just as well if everybody kept calm—everybody had a lot to lose—and not a shot was fired. Captain Parker, perhaps fearing capture of his men, ordered them to disperse peaceably; but this only encouraged the British to try and round them up, and some of the soldiers took after the Minutemen. Somehow the running added a sense of alarm to the situation, and a shot rang out. Whether it was a patriot defending himself and his friends, or a British soldier "out to get the rebels" and excited by the chase, the identity of the man who fired the first shot is still a mystery. But other shots followed, of course, and soon eight Minutemen lay dead, and 10 others were wounded.

The "battle" was more like a troop riot, and once the British officers regained control of their troops, they started marching them out of town. The Minutemen took their wounded to Buckman Tavern to treat them. It all took less than ½ hour. Word was rushed to Concord, where Minutemen assembled for the later events of the day, knowing that they might be the next martyrs.

WHAT TO SEE & DO

When you approach Battle Green and come up to the Minuteman statue (erected in 1900), you'll feel the great historic significance of the spot. Battle Green is really where it all began: The ivy-covered monument on the southwest part of the Green marks the burial spot of seven of the eight Minutemen killed on the memorable day, April 19, 1775. The boulder that sits incongruously on the soft grass of the Green marks the place where the Minutemen drew up in a double rank to face the British grenadiers.

The Lexington Village Green looked much different then than it does today. The meetinghouse, or church building, was located near where the Minuteman statue stands; since it was mid-April, and the Green was in the center of town traffic, it may have been pretty muddy rather than "green." The best time to visit Lexington's historic sights is, of course, at dawn on April 19, when the townfolk reenact the famous confrontation with festivities, real musket fire, and fife-and-drum corps. But any day after April 19, until the end of October, will do; note that most of the happenings and places mentioned below are closed between November 1 and April 18.

Besides the Battle Green, several early buildings figured significantly in the battle, and they are today maintained by the **Lexington Historical Society** (Buckman Tavern, Munroe Tavern, and Hancock-Clarke House), Lexington (tel. 617/861-0928).

Of the houses, **Buckman Tavern** (1709), facing Lexington Green, is the most important. Here, in the taproom, many of the Minutemen waited out the time between that first midnight call to muster and the final arrival of the British forces at daybreak. After the battle, the wounded were brought here and laid out on the tables for treatment. The tours are given by young women well versed in their subject, which not only encompasses the events of the battle, but ranges much more widely, covering a great number of topics on life in the colonies at the time of the Revolution. They'll tell you about the construction of the tavern; about the people who came there to stay, or to have a drink, or for a reception or tea; what and how they ate and drank, how they cooked, slept, and kept warm in unheated rooms. The tavern has an excellent collection of utensils, tools, and implements from the period, "time- and labor-saving devices" that show a good deal of Yankee ingenuity. The tour is well worth the price of admission. The tavern is located opposite the Common and has a gift shop.

The **Munroe Tavern** (1695), 1332 Massachusetts Ave., was to the British what Buckman Tavern was to the colonials: a headquarters and a place to care for the wounded after the battle. Today it's furnished with antiques and battle mementos and is open to the public on the same basis as Buckman Tavern. It's a walk (or a short drive) from Battle Green, about 7 blocks southeast along Massachusetts Avenue; the tavern will be on your right.

The third significant house is the **Hancock-Clarke House** (1698), 36 Hancock St., which was the parsonage of the Reverend Jonas Clarke at the time of the battle, and it was with Clarke that John Hancock and Sam Adams, the two "rabble-rousers" most wanted by the British authorities, hid themselves during the uncertain days before the battle. Clarke's house was the first place Paul Revere headed for when he heard of the British plan to march out into the countryside. Revere actually came to Clarke's house twice to warn Adams and Hancock: on April 15, just after hearing that the British were about to do something, and again on April 18, the night the British troops moved out. It's located only about a block north of Battle Green.

Admission and a guided tour cost $2.50 for adults, 50¢ for children aged 6 to 16 (children under 6 free), at each house; an adult combination ticket, good for all three houses on weekends, can be purchased at Buckman Tavern gift shop for $5. It's open mid-April through October Monday to Saturday from 10am to 5pm, Sunday from 1 to 5pm.

Several other sights in Lexington are worth a look. Gravestone-rubbers will want to head for **Ye Olde Burying Ground,** just off Battle Green by the church, on its western side. The oldest stone dates from 1690. Another way to get into the spirit of the day of battle is to visit **Cary Memorial Hall,** several blocks southeast of the Green along Massachusetts Avenue, between the town offices and the police station. Here you can see Sandham's famous painting *The Battle of Lexington,* and also statues of John Hancock and Samuel Adams.

Lexington has a handsome, modern gallery for historical displays of Americana, the **Museum of Our National Heritage.** Built by the Scottish Rite Masons in 1975, there are four galleries exhibiting photograph collections, documents, artifacts, and works of art and industry. Lectures and films are scheduled frequently as well. An exhibit entitled "Let It Begin Here: Lexington and the Revolution," explains the town's crucial role in the American quest for independence. Call for details of current exhibits. The museum is at 33 Marrett Rd. (tel. 617/861-6559), near the intersection of Routes 2A and 4/225, a short way from the center of Lexington on the road to Boston. It's open Monday through Saturday from 10am to 5pm, on Sunday from noon to 5pm. Admission and parking are free.

WHERE TO STAY

Although Lexington will most likely be a day-trip for you, here is a lodging suggestion in case your itinerary indicates a night in the Minutemen's town.

BATTLE GREEN MOTOR INN, 1720 Massachusetts Ave., Lexington, MA 02173. Tel. 617/862-6100, or toll free 800/343-0235, 800/322-1066 in Mass. 96 rms (all with bath). A/C TV TEL

$ Rates: Summer, $57 single; $65 double. Winter, rates are 15% lower. AE, DC, DISC, MC, V. **Parking:** Free.

Whether driving or busing, the Battle Green Motor Inn, located 3 blocks east of Lexington Green, is a convenient place to stay. The modern and comfortable units are grouped around a long central court dotted with young trees and potted plants. Room cable TVs have HBO, and you can park your car in a covered lot. From the inn, you can easily walk to the Green and to all the historic sites.

WHERE TO DINE

PEKING GARDEN, 27 Waltham St. Tel. 862-1051.
  Cuisine: CHINESE. **Reservations:** Recommended. **Directions:** From Massachusetts Ave. in the center of the commercial district, turn onto Waltham St. and the restaurant is 1 block away, on the right.
$ Prices: Appetizers $3.50–$10.50; main courses $5.95–$15; lunch buffet $5.25; dinner buffet $10.50 adults, $6 children under 10; Special House Dinner $14.95 per person. AE, MC, V.
  Open: Sun–Thurs 11:30am–9:30pm, Fri–Sat 11:30am–10:30pm.

The best value in a full restaurant is, believe it or not, Chinese. It's the Peking Garden, several doors down from the intersection of Massachusetts Avenue and Waltham Street, right in the main shopping district. The special bonus is the Chinese buffet served Monday through Thursday evening from 6 to 9pm, and the food is delicious and varied. Two or more can order the Special House Dinner at other times, and receive a varied and bounteous selection of dishes. Besides the evening buffet, the

Peking Garden hosts a luncheon buffet Monday through Friday from 11:30am to 2:30pm. Wine, beer, and drinks are served. Special Mandarin dim sum is served every Saturday and Sunday from 11:30am to 2:30pm.

3. CONCORD

18 miles (29km) NW of Boston, 15 miles (24km) NW of Cambridge, 6 miles (8km) W of Lexington

GETTING THERE By Train On weekdays, 20 trains a day leave Boston's North Station for the 40-minute trip to Concord; on Saturday there are 12 trains, and on Sunday, 8. The train can also be boarded at the Porter Square subway station in Cambridge. Call 617/722-3200 for the latest detailed schedule information. The train arrives at Concord's Depot, which is about 5 blocks from Monument Square.

By Bus By public transportation, there's no way to travel along Battle Road unless you're in a sightseeing tour bus.

By Car The most interesting route is via Lexington along Route 2A, following the signs reading "Battle Road;" this is the route taken by the British troops going out to Concord to search for arms stockpiled illegally by the colonials. The fatest route, however, is Mass. Route 2. At the traffic signal at the bottom of the steep hill, the highway turns left; continue straight on along Cambridge Turnpike to reach the center of Concord.

ESSENTIALS The **area code** is 508. The Minuteman National Historic Park's **Battle Road Visitors' Center** (tel. 508/369-6944) is just off Marrett Road (Rte. 2A) a mile or two west of I-95 (Rte. 128). This is the place to get a map and brochure of Battle Road.

The **Concord Chamber of Commerce** (tel. 508/369-3120) operates an information booth on Heywood Street (follow the signs), 1 long block southeast of Monument Square, just off the road to Lexington and Cambridge. It's open on weekends, mid-April through May, and every day from May through October, from 9:30am to 4:30pm. They have brochures and maps.

Once strictly a farming town, Concord today is part Boston suburb, part farm town. It's a beautiful place filled with old trees, graceful houses, and a rich history that goes beyond the events of the Revolution. Besides the historical sites encompassed by Minuteman National Historical Park, Concord offers a look at the lives and times of America's great 19th-century writers and philosophers: Emerson, Thoreau, Hawthorne, and Louisa May and Bronson Alcott.

WHAT TO SEE & DO

Begin your walk around Concord at the town green, officially called Monument Square, complete with obelisk inscribed FAITHFUL UNTO DEATH. The little church facing Main Street, **St. Bernard's** (Roman Catholic), is particularly pretty when seen from a short distance down Main Street. Of the other buildings on the green, the most historically noteworthy is the **Wright Tavern,** which, being right on the road from Boston, was one of the first places the British stopped to search for arms. Several shops and firms' offices are located in the tavern today, and you're welcome to walk in and look around during business hours. The **Colonial Inn** has been facing the square since colonial times; it's a good place to stop for a refreshing drink, a meal, or a bed for the night.

MINUTE MAN NATIONAL HISTORIC PARK

The Minute Man National Historic Park, North Bridge Unit, Monument Street, (tel. 369-6993), encompasses many of the most important sites having to do with the first

Revolutionary War battle at Concord. There's a visitors center located in the Buttrick Mansion, north of the center of Concord, on the other side of North Bridge. A large parking lot near North Bridge is often full during the summer, and if you have a good parking spot in town, and a few extra minutes, walk the ½ mile to the bridge and admire Concord's lovely old houses as you go.

After the events in Lexington, the British officers headed their men quickly off to Concord, afraid—no, certain—that since shots had been fired and men killed, there'd be a great deal more trouble coming. Of course, the Minutemen in Concord knew of the Lexington battle shortly after it happened and long before the British troops arrived at 7am. The Minutemen kept an eye on the British as they entered the town, waiting for whatever was to happen. When a force of regulars was sent to stand guard over Concord's North Bridge, the Minutemen retreated before them, crossing the bridge and taking up a position on a hilltop nearby, where they awaited reinforcements from nearby towns.

Meanwhile, in Concord a polite and not-too-thorough search was being carried out; some arms were found, in particular a number of gun carriages, which were brought out and burned. The Minutemen saw the smoke, assumed the British were burning the town, and began to advance in revenge. The regulars retreated across the bridge and began firing at the Minutemen, who fired back and pursued them until they fled. It was here at the North Bridge, then, that the Minutemen fired the "shot heard 'round the world."

Soon afterward the British troops began the return to Boston, but Minutemen kept up a constant sniper fire on them all the way back to Boston, which enraged the regulars and goaded them to murder some of the innocent persons they met along the way of their march. The bitterness left on both sides by the events of April 19, 1775, would soon bring war to all the British colonies in North America.

Walk across the placid Concord River on the Old North Bridge (a modern reproduction of the kind of bridge that spanned the river in colonial times), and it is easy to imagine, even to half see, the way things happened on the day of the battle. At the far (western) end of the bridge is Daniel Chester French's famous *Minuteman* statue, the pediment inscribed with Emerson's famous poem. On the near (east) side of the bridge, take a look also at the plaque on the stone wall commemorating the British soldiers who died in the revolutionary war.

Admission to the park is free, and it is open daily from April to November.

THE OLD MANSE

After visiting the bridge and the visitor center on the far side, turn back toward town. Right next to North Bridge, slightly nearer to the center of town, is The Old Manse, Monument Street at the North Bridge (tel. 369-3909), Concord's most famous house. It was built in 1769 by the Reverend William Emerson and was lived in by his descendants for 169 years, except for a 3-year period when young Nathaniel Hawthorne and his bride, Sophia, lived here. Hawthorne's residence here gave him material for several later stories. The house today is filled with the spirit and the mementos of their short stay, and those of the Emerson clan. Admission includes a guided tour and costs $4 for adults, $3.50 for seniors, $1.50 for children aged 6 to 16. The Old Manse is open from mid-April through May on Saturday from 10am to 4:30pm, Sunday and holidays from 1 to 4:30pm. June through October it's open Monday, Thursday, Friday, and Saturday from 10am to 5pm, Sunday and holidays from 1 to 5pm.

SIGHTS OF THE TRANSCENDENTALISM MOVEMENT

Concord was the center of a philosophical and social movement that, although small in scope, had important effects on American thought and literature. Emerson, Thoreau, Bronson Alcott, and others were all friends living in Concord from about 1836 to 1860. They were aware of the philosophical upheaval going on in Europe at this time, and were encouraged to break away from the Unitarianism that had been their belief. Although they never published a manifesto detailing their beliefs, their creed at this time was that each person has a part of God within himself, and by being sensitive to the dictates of that part, can do what is good and right. Nature had a large share in this belief as well, for the Transcendentalists thought true harmony in life could only be achieved by communing closely with nature and coming to understand it. This, perhaps, was the basis for Thoreau's period of retreat at Walden Pond.

The transcendentalists got together and tried out their beliefs by buying a farm and living with nature there (1841–47). The Brook Farm experiment, although it failed, has been an example down to our own times. (The farm was in West Roxbury, now a suburb of Boston.) Hawthorne lived on Brook Farm for a while, and he and his friend Herman Melville were both affected by transcendentalism.

The best way to learn about the transcendentalist movement is to read Ralph Waldo Emerson's works. While you're here in Concord, you can visit his house and those in which other adherents of the movement lived, and also go out to **Walden Pond** and see the place where Thoreau had his cabin from 1845 to 1847. Drive out Walden Street (Route 126), which leaves the center of Concord from Main Street near Monument Square. After crossing Route 2, look for signs on the right not far from the intersection; park and walk to the site of his hut, marked by a pile of stones. The path circling the pond provides an interesting and refreshing walk; fires and alcoholic beverages are not permitted at any time. The main parking lot by the public beach (which you are required to use) costs $5 per carload in summer; the beach itself is free.

On your way back from the Old Manse, by Old North Bridge, take a detour up the hill, east off Monument Street before you reach the town green, to get to **Sleepy Hollow Cemetery.** Author's Ridge, on top of the hill, has the graves of Hawthorne, Thoreau, the Alcotts, and Emerson. Emerson's grave, you'll notice, is marked by a great uncarved boulder, very natural and without religious symbolism.

Starting from Monument Square, most of the transcendentalists' homes are east along Lexington Road; Thoreau sites and memorabilia are, appropriately, off by themselves, in another direction.

HOUSE OF RALPH WALDO EMERSON, 28 Cambridge Tpk. Tel. 369-2236.

Located at the intersection of Lexington Road and Cambridge Turnpike, a 10-minute walk from the green, the house was a center for meetings of Emerson and his friends, and still contains original furniture and Emerson's memorabilia.
Admission: $3.50 adults, $2 children aged 6–17, free for children under 6.
Open: Mid-Apr to Oct, Thurs–Sat 10am–4:30pm, Sun 2–4:30pm.

CONCORD MUSEUM, Lexington Rd. and Cambridge Tpk. Tel. 369-9609.

The Concord Museum, across the street from Emerson's house, transports the visitor back in time to the early 17th century, when the town of Concord was founded. The museum contains numerous period rooms and galleries, and vividly depicts the growth and evolution of Concord. The collections of documented decorative arts and domestic artifacts were either owned by Concord-area residents or made by Concord-area artisans.

Permanent exhibits include the lantern that hung in the spire of the Old North Church in Boston on the night of Revere's famous ride, Ralph Waldo Emerson's study, Henry David Thoreau's belongings used at Walden Pond, and a collection of early powder horns including the one worn by A. Hosmer, one of two minutemen killed at the Old North Bridge. There are changing exhibitions in the New Wing throughout the year. A guided tour lasts about 45 minutes, or you can wander around on your own if you like.
Admission: $5 adults, $4 seniors, $3 students, $2 children 15 and under, $12 families.
Open: Tues–Sat (plus Mon holidays) 10am–5pm. Closed: New Year's Day, Easter, Christmas Day.

ORCHARD HOUSE, 399 Lexington Rd. Tel. 369-4118.

Continuing east along Lexington Road, a short drive will bring you to home of the Alcotts during the period 1858–77. Bronson Alcott's life passion was the reform of traditional education methods. His open and natural approach to education was not appreciated in cosmopolitan centers like Boston, but was perfectly congenial to transcendentalist Concord. Here he was ultimately commissioned as superintendent of schools, and he opened a "School of Philosophy" in a building in his backyard. This house is also the house in which Louisa May Alcott wrote *Little Women*.

Admission (including the requisite tour): $4 adults, $3.50 seniors and students, $2.50 children 6–12, free for children under 6.

Open: Early Apr to mid-Sept, Mon–Sat 10am–4:30pm, Sun and holidays 1–4:30pm. Mid-Sept to late Oct, daily 1–4:30pm. Nov–Apr, groups by appointment only.

WAYSIDE, 455 Lexington Rd. Tel. 369-6975.

One mile east of Monument Square and just a few steps east of Orchard House is the house described by Louisa May Alcott in her famous book, although today most of the furnishings are those of Margaret Sidney, who wrote *Five Little Peppers*. There are several exhibits dealing with the house's famous former residents; Hawthorne also lived here.

Admission: 30-minute guided tour, $1 adults, free for children 16 and under.

Open: Mid-Apr to Oct, Tues–Sun 9:30am–5:30pm; last tour starts at 5pm, and tours are limited to 10 persons.

THOREAU LYCEUM, 156 Belknap St. Tel. 369-5912.

This Thoreau "learning center" includes a library, museum with artifacts dealing with his life, and a replica of Thoreau's Walden cabin. There is also a bookstore carrying old as well as new books by or about Thoreau.

Admission: $2 adults, $1.50 students, 50¢ children in grades 1–8.

Open: Mon–Sat 10am–5pm, Sun 2–5pm. **Closed:** Mon Jan–Mar and on national holidays.

CANOEING ON THE CONCORD RIVER

After you've taken the standard walking tour of Concord, see the town again, adventurously, by renting a canoe for a paddle up the Concord River. The **South Bridge Boat House** (tel. 369-9438), west of the center of town at 496 Main St. (Route 62), will rent you a canoe for $6 per hour, $26 per day on weekdays, or $8 per hour, $35 per day on weekends (students get lower rates). In 2 hours or so you should be able to make your way down to Concord North Bridge and back, depending on the strength of your paddling muscles. The grand houses and gardens that grace the riverbanks alternate with patches of field and wild shrubbery to make a serene and lovely landscape. You can also rent a small boat with an outboard motor for $20 an hour. The boat house is open from the beginning of April into November until the first snowstorm. Payment can be made with MasterCard, VISA, or the Discover card.

A VISIT TO A WINERY

You've heard of Concord grapes, a variety developed here by Ephraim Bull and now used to make grape juice, jelly, and sweet wines. You might think the **Nashoba Valley Winery**, 100 Wattaquadoc Hill Rd., Bolton, MA 01740 (tel. 779-5521), only a dozen miles west of Concord, would use Concord grapes. But you're in for a delightful surprise. Nashoba pursues the old New England tradition of making delicious wines from fruits other than grapes: apples, peaches, pears, blueberries, cranberries. They've taken this art one step further, and now make premium varietal dry table wines from fruit. The wines are intriguing, satisfying, and delightful. The tart, dry Cranberry-Apple goes especially well with Thanksgiving turkey, and the After Dinner Peach has an exquisite sweet-dryness like good sauterne. Clear your palate and drop in for a free tasting any day of the week, until 6pm. Winery tours cost

$1 and are conducted on Friday, Saturday, and Sunday from 11am to 5:30pm. Leave time for a self-guided walking tour through the orchards, with a picnic at one of the tables, all of which enjoy fine country views. June through October, come out and "pick-your-own" fruit.

To get here, take Route 62 west from Concord through Maynard to Stow, then Route 117 west to Bolton, just west of I-495 (Exit 27). Take Route 117 west to the blinking yellow light in the center of Bolton. Turn left onto Wattaquadoc Hill Road; the winery is ¼ mile up the hill, on the left-hand side.

LONGFELLOW'S WAYSIDE INN

The country inn made famous by Henry Wadsworth Longfellow's poem, "Tales of a Wayside Inn," is still serving the public, and is still an interesting place to visit. For details on this historic inn in the neighboring town of Sudbury, see "Where to Stay," below.

WHERE TO STAY

CONCORD INNS

COLONIAL INN, 48 Monument Sq., Concord, MA 01742. Tel. 508/369-9200, or toll free 800/370-9200. Fax 508/369-2170. 60 rms (all with bath). A/C TV TEL
$ Rates: Main inn $109–$142 single or double; Prescott wing $82–$120 single or double. Weekend discounts available. AE, DISC, MC, V. **Parking:** Free.
The main building of the Colonial Inn dates from 1716, and is a smallish, colonial-size hostelry, but several new and modern additions have been unobtrusively added, giving the inn a lot more room. Only 12 original colonial-era rooms are available to guests, and these are the ones most in demand. If you call or write ahead for reservations, you might ask for one of these; the manager will do his best to put you in one, but cannot guarantee any particular room to any guest. Housekeeping rooms are also available should you be planning to stay a while. The inn faces Monument Square in the center of Concord.

THE HAWTHORNE INN, 462 Lexington Rd., Concord, MA 01742. Tel. 508/369-5610. 7 rms (all with bath). TV **Directions:** From Monument Sq., follow Lexington Rd. east 1 mile to the inn, on the right.
$ Rates (including continental breakfast): $82–$164 single; $102–$181 double. Extra person $15. No credit cards. **Parking:** Free, on premises.
Concord's coziest place to stay is the Hawthorne Inn, located directly across the road from "The Wayside," Nathaniel Hawthorne's house. The location is convenient to Orchard House, the Alcotts' home, as well. The inn has pleasant gardens with a tiny fountain, and the rooms are decorated with period pieces, antique beds, original works of art, and nice homey touches like hooked rugs. Only seven rooms here, so reserve early.

LONGFELLOW'S WAYSIDE INN

WAYSIDE INN [1700], Wayside Inn Rd., South Sudbury, MA 01776. Tel. 508/443-1776. 10 rms (all with bath). TEL **Directions:** Drive 13 miles along Sudbury Rd. (which starts from Main St. in Concord), and U.S. 20 West will take you to the inn.
$ Rates (including full breakfast): $71 single; $82 double. AE, DC, MC, V. **Parking:** Free.
The Wayside Inn was made famous by Longfellow's "Tales of a Wayside Inn," and now boasts that it is the oldest operating inn in the country. Bought by Henry Ford in the early 1920s, it is now a private, nonprofit operation, and all

proceeds from the guest rooms and restaurant are put toward its upkeep and restoration. Rooms 1 through 8 are of modern construction and traditional decor; Rooms 9 and 10 are in the old, original part of the inn, and are very quaint. These latter two rooms are the ones most in demand, particularly from April to December. Should you want to stay at the inn, it's wise to make reservations as far in advance as possible, even a month or two; but if you can't make them, call up in any case and see what vacancies they might have.

A fire around 1955 caused heavy damage to the inn (as you can see in the old kitchen), but restoration work was done well and the rooms are worth seeing even if you don't plan to stay for the night. A short tour of the inn is available for $1 per person or by following the self-guided tour, or for free if you drop in for a meal. Lunch is served from 11:30am to 3pm, dinner, from 5 to 9pm; Sunday dinner, from noon to 8pm.

Besides the inn itself, you should explore the grounds and surroundings: the beautiful formal garden near the inn, the reconstructed barn across the road, and the Grist Mill, a short (15-minute) walk away, farther down the road. The Grist Mill, a pretty and romantic stone building, is a replica of the mills that used to dot the New England rivers and streams. It is in a beautiful spot, with a copse of pines nearby, and although it's not 100% authentic (the mill wheel is made of heavy-gauge steel instead of wood), it is worth a look and a walk around. The flour ground here is used in the Wayside Inn's kitchens, and is for sale at the inn's shop. By the way, the Martha-Mary Chapel, on the road between the inn and the Grist Mill, is a typical New England meetinghouse that Ford had built to be rented out for weddings. The chapel and the Wayside Inn are very popular with wedding parties and honeymooners.

WHERE TO DINE

LONGFELLOW'S WAYSIDE INN, Wayside Inn Rd., South Sudbury. Tel. 443-1776.
   Cuisine: NEW ENGLAND. **Reservations:** Recommended. **Directions:** Drive 13 miles along Sudbury Rd. (which starts from Main St. in Concord), and U.S. 20 West will take you to the inn.
$ Prices: Lunch $7.50–$14.50; dinner $12–$27. AE, DC, MC, V.
   Open: Mon–Sat 11:30am–3pm and 5–9pm, Sun and holidays noon–8pm.
If you can't stay in this historic inn (see "Where to Stay," above), at least have a meal here. In addition to a main dining room, there are four smaller dining rooms, all beautifully furnished with antiques. Absolutely every inch is filled with history. There are wood beams, old brick fireplaces, even the bar that has been welcoming wayfarers since 1716. Specialties include roast duckling, Indian pudding, and a deliriously good deep-dish apple pie.

4. SALEM

17 miles (27.5km) NE of Boston, 4 miles (6.5km) NW of Marblehead,
16 miles (26km) SW of Gloucester, 22 miles (35.5km) SW of Rockport

GETTING THERE   By Train   Commuter trains run from Boston's North Station to Salem, Beverly, Gloucester, and Rockport. The trip to Salem takes about 30 minutes; trains run about every 20 minutes during rush hours, every ½-hour during the day, every hour at night and on weekends. Call toll free 800/392-6099 for schedules.

By Bus   Salem is served by MBTA bus no. 450, which leaves from the parking garage next to Haymarket subway station in Boston; the trip, under good traffic conditions, takes 40 minutes. Buses leave every 15 minutes during rush hours, every hour during the day Monday through Saturday, every 90 minutes on Sunday.

By Car   The fastest way from Boston to Salem is the least direct: Take I-93 north to I-95 north (Rte. 128 east), and take the exit marked for Route 114 and Salem. A more direct route, via U.S. 1, is not faster. The most direct route, via Mass. Route 1A, is slowest because it passes through many towns (and many traffic signals) along the way. Route 1A North becomes Lafayette Street in Salem.

Note that street and highway signs on the North Shore are particularly bad. Routes are filled with turns, and signs are confusing or missing—you will probably find yourself lost more than once. Resign yourself to stopping and asking the way, not once but several times.

ESSENTIALS   The **area code** is 508. The **Salem Chamber of Commerce,** 32 Derby Sq. (tel. 508/744-0004), maintains two information booths around the city. One is in Riley Plaza (Rte. 114E), near the station for commuter trains from Boston, and one is in Old Town Hall, 32 Derby Sq. Both are open Monday through Saturday from 9am to 5pm, on Sunday from noon to 5pm. The **National Park Service** (tel. 508/745-1470) maintains a visitor information center in the Museum Place Mall on Essex Street. That center is open daily from 9am to 5pm; 9am to 6pm during summer months.

Think of Salem, think of witches. Although the fame of Salem's witch trials has spread around the world, the town's place in New England history comes from its maritime industries—shipbuilding, warehousing, chandlery, and trade. In the late 1700s, ships from Salem sailed the world, many dealing in trade from the Far East, especially spices, silks, and other luxury goods. The wealth of the Indies brought great prosperity to the town, which enabled its citizens to build and decorate fine mansions and impressive museums.

As for the witches, it has never been proven that there were any in Salem. The witch-hunt took place in only 1 year (1692), and the score of people executed met that fate because they would not admit to being witches—many of the less courageous "admitted" being witches so that they wouldn't be executed. The whole witch-calling affair reached the point of absurdity and then fizzled out. Salem would like to forget it all, no doubt, but the rest of the world enjoys remembering this bizarre episode.

WHAT TO SEE & DO

Salem today is a very interesting town, with many of its old houses (dating back to the 1600s) and 19th-century mansions intact and in good repair. Try to visit at least one of the 17th-century houses to see what life was like in one of the earliest towns in the United States. Part of the downtown section has been restored and closed to traffic as a fine pedestrian mall. Additionally, the waterfront area—Pickering Wharf—has been restored and colonized by several restaurants, gift shops, antiques shops, crystal shops, a new-age bookstore, and the like.

Though you could keep yourselves busy for days seeing the town's most celebrated historical sights below, do take time to visit some of its newer attractions, including **Harbor Sweets,** 85 Leavitt St. (tel. 745-7648), where you can buy sailboat-shaped almond-butter–crunch chocolates right where they are made (you get to sample the selections). Tours of the chocolate factory are offered, but it's necessary to call for an appointment. By the way, if you plan to take home boxes of these outrageously good chocolates, they'll pack them in cold packs. How convenient!

Crows Haven Corner, 125 Essex St. (tel. 745-8763), is another must-see nonhistorical attraction in Salem. This tiny witch shop is owned by Laurie Cabot, Salem's most illustrious witch. Here you can buy all sorts of herbs, powders, and seeds to ward off evil or attract love, luck, and money. Also for sale are gargoyles and unicorns, witch books, crystals, moon stones, black cat candles, crystal balls (just like the one in the Wizard of Oz), magic wands—you get the picture. You can also make an appointment to have a tarot card reading with Laurie Cabot.

Finally, while poking around the shops on Pickering Wharf, make a point of going into the **Pickering Wharf Antiques Gallery** (tel. 741-1797). When you first step in, it looks like any other antiques shops. Wander around to the back, turn the corner, and all of a sudden, you'll find yourself in an enormous theater-in-the-round where 35 dealers display their collections. So much for "a quick look around" an antiques gallery.

THE SALEM WITCH MUSEUM, 19½ Washington Sq. Tel. 744-1692.

Many houses in Salem from the 1600s have been preserved and are open to public view, but before you visit them, you should stop in at the Salem Witch Museum, next to Salem Common at the intersection of Brown Street and Hawthorne Boulevard. The museum's Gothic, churchlike building houses an audiovisual re-creation of the witchcraft trials of 1692 using life-size figures, a sound track, and special lighting. Shows begin every 30 minutes.

Admission: $4 adults, $3.50 seniors, $2.50 children aged 6–14, free for children 5 and under.

Open: Year-round, daily 10am–5pm.

WITCH HOUSE, 310½ Essex St. Tel. 744-0180.

The home of Magistrate Jonathan Corwin, one of the judges in the witch trials, stands at the corner of Essex and North Streets. Preliminary examinations of those accused of witchcraft were held in the house, which is now nicely restored.

Admission: $4 adults, $1.50 children 5–16.

Open: Mid-March to June, daily 10am–4:30pm. July–Labor Day, daily 10am–6pm. Labor Day to Dec 1, daily 10am–4:30pm.

HOUSE OF THE SEVEN GABLES, 54 Turner St. Tel. 744-0991.

The House of the Seven Gables, which served as the setting for Nathaniel Hawthorne's novel of the same name, is the centerpiece of a historic site with period gardens on Salem Harbor. The attractions here include the House of the Seven Gables (1668), Hooper-Hathaway House (1682), Hawthorne's birthplace (ca. 1750), and Retire Becket House (1655). The Garden Coffee Shop is open from May through October. Parking is free.

Admission: Guided tours of the Gables and Hawthorne's birthplace $6.50 adults, $4 children ages 13–17, $3 children 6–12.

Open: July–Labor Day, daily 9:30am–5:30pm. Labor Day–June, daily 10am–4:30pm.

PIONEER VILLAGE: SALEM IN 1630, Forest River Park. Tel. 745-0525, or 744-0991.

For a look at 17th-century Salem, tour this "living history museum" built in 1930 and recently restored. Costumed "interpreters" will guide you through the village, past dugout hoses, wigwams, thatched cottages, and the governor's house, through

---

 FROMMER'S COOL FOR KIDS: ATTRACTIONS

Salem Willows Amusement Park Follow Derby Street northeast out of the center of town, or, if you are pressed for time, take the **Salem Trolley.** This re-created old-time vehicle makes tours of the town and stops at Salem Willows every day (Apr–Dec 10am–4pm) on the hour. Tours leave from Riley Plaza; you can buy tickets on board the trolley.

Witch Dungeon Museum At 16 Lynde St., near Washington Street (tel. 741-3570), just ½ block from the western end of East India Marine Mall, live reenactments of a witch trial, a re-created dungeon, and a replica of Old Salem Village are among the exhibits. It's open daily from 10am to 5pm. Admission costs $4 for adults, $2.50 for children.

gardens such as the colonists might have cultivated and past species of animals that they may have raised. Demonstrations of yarn spinning, building, and open-hearth cooking are here to see; you can even learn how to use a match-lock musket. Pioneer Village, adjacent to a beach and picnic area, is off West Street.

Admission: $4 adults, $3.50 children ages 13–17, $2.50 children ages 6–12, $3.50 seniors.

Open: Late May–Oct, Mon–Sat 10am–5pm, Sun noon–5pm.

THE ESSEX INSTITUTE, 132-134 Essex St. Tel. 744-3390.

The Essex Institute is a museum and historical society dedicated to the preservation, study, and exhibition of historical works and artifacts dealing with Essex County. The collection of artifacts ranges from rare early newspapers to entire houses, restored and furnished with authentic antiques. Just about anyone who comes to Salem finds something of interest here: The historian of American trade and culture uses the library, nautical buffs want to see the relics of the China trade, and those interested in architecture and decoration take the tour through one or more of the institute's half-dozen Salem houses, which date as far back as 1684. Children are fascinated by the unique collection of dolls, doll furniture, and toys from earlier times.

There's a lot more here than one can see on a day-trip to Salem, but an hour spent in one of the institute's 13 buildings, particularly in the main building and the adjoining houses, is a must for any Salem visitor. Here is a list of some of the special collections you can look over: clocks, ceramics, military uniforms and weapons, dolls and toys, glassware, buttons, silver and pewter, lamps and lanterns, sculpture, tools, costumes from earlier centuries, and bits and pieces from the China trade, as well as a very good collection of Massachusetts works of art including paintings and furniture. Several galleries and exhibition rooms have changing shows, so the return visitor should check to see what's new.

Note: At press time, The Essex Institute and the Peabody Museum of Salem had just merged. For the time being, each will continue to charge its own admission fees and keep its own hours. The name will be changing. Call to verify times.

Admission: Museum, library, and houses combination ticket $6 adults, $5 senior citizens, $3.50 children aged 6–16.

Open: Mon–Wed and Fri–Sat 10am–5pm, Thurs 10am–9pm (library 1–9pm), Sun noon–5pm.

PEABODY MUSEUM OF SALEM, East India Sq., Essex Street Mall. Tel. 745-1876.

When a group of Salem sea captains and world travelers formed the East India Marine Society in 1799, their charter included provisions for "a museum in which to house the natural and artificial curiosities" brought back from their worldwide travels. This was the genesis of the Peabody Museum, America's oldest museum in continuous operation, located on the Essex Street pedestrian mall, at the corner of New Liberty Street.

In 1824, the society and its collections moved to grand new headquarters in East India Marine Hall. Since then, five annexes have been added. The most recent, the highly acclaimed Asian Export Art Wing, is dedicated to decorative art pieces made in Asia for Western use from the 14th to 19th centuries.

The museum's other major collections are in New England maritime history; the practical arts and crafts of the East Asian, Pacific Islands, and Native American peoples; and the natural history of Essex County. Maritime collections include portraits of captains, pictures of ships, scale models, figureheads, old navigation instruments and tools, scrimshaw, prints, and gear from the whaling era, plus porcelain, paintings, furniture, and silver from Salem's China trade. There's even a reproduction of the saloon (main cabin) of America's first oceangoing yacht, *Cleopatra's Barge,* built in 1816 by a member of the East India Marine Society. The Ethnology Department has superb collections of objects from everyday life in primitive Polynesia, Micronesia, and Melanesia. A similar collection from preindustrial Japan is rated the best in the world.

Note: At press time, the Peabody Museum of Salem had just merged with The Essex Institute. For the time being, each will continue to charge its own admission fees and keep its own hours. The name will be changing. Call to verify times.

Tours: A free guided tour is held daily at 2pm.

Admission: $6 adults, $5 students and seniors, $3 children ages 6–18, free for children under 6, $12 families of four (1 or 2 adults and children 18 or under).

Open: Mon–Sat 10am–5pm, Sun noon–5pm. **Closed:** Thanksgiving, Christmas, and New Year's Day.

SALEM MARITIME NATIONAL HISTORIC SITE, 174 Derby St. Tel. 745-1470.

In 1938, the National Park Service took over the **Custom House,** where Nathaniel Hawthorne once worked, and nearby Derby Wharf, one of the city's busiest trade centers, as a basis for the maritime site. First thing to do is to pick up free copies of the National Park Service's materials about the site, which have a sketch map and directory of the buildings as well as short histories of the prominent Derby merchant family and of the adventures of several famous Salem vessels, both merchantmen and privateers. These accounts are very well written, and are just the thing to get you in the mood for a tour of the Custom House, wharves, and warehouses.

The site also contains the **Derby House,** built in 1762 for the shipping magnate Elias Derby by his father, Capt. Richard Derby, and the **West India Goods Store,** right next to Derby House, open for business and selling teas, coffee (beans and brew), spices, and other treasures from the East.

Tours: Daily tours of the Derby and Narbonne-Hale House are given; hours vary.

Admission: Free.

Open: Daily 8:30am–5pm. **Closed:** Thanksgiving, Christmas, and New Year's Day.

WHERE TO STAY

COACH HOUSE INN, 284 Lafayette St., Salem, MA 01970. Tel. 508/744-4092, or toll free 800/688-8689. 11 rms (9 with bath). TV

$ Rates (including continental breakfast): $82–$93 double. AE, MC, V. **Parking:** Off-street.

A 10-minute walk from the center of town and 2 blocks from Salem State College, the Coach House Inn is a large Victorian house built in 1879 by E. Augustus Emmerton, sea captain, merchant, and banker. The Victorian decor (some rooms even have antique fireplaces) has been updated with private bathrooms; several rooms have kitchenettes. The higher prices are for rooms with baths.

HAWTHORNE HOTEL, 18 Washington Sq. West, Salem, MA 01970. Tel. 508/744-4080, or toll free 800/833-2008. Fax 508/745-9842. 89 rms (all with bath). A/C TV TEL

$ Rates: $88–$139 double; $213 suite. Extra person $12. Children under 16 stay free in parents' room. AE, DC, DISC, MC, V. **Parking:** Free, on premises.

The Hawthorne Hotel, on Salem Common, a major Salem landmark in the middle of town, is within easy walking distance of all the sights in town. It's a good-size hotel, restored with lots of fine wood paneling, brass chandeliers, and new paint. The lobby and public rooms (including the Tavern and the restaurant, called Nathaniel's) use these elements to achieve a simple but very elegant atmosphere; it's echoed in the rooms with the use of smaller brass chandeliers and wingback chairs. Otherwise, the rooms are modern and decorated in solid colors.

Dining/Entertainment: In the restaurant (open for breakfast, lunch, and dinner daily), a good luncheon costs $8 to $12, dinner about $30 to $40. The hotel serves traditional Sunday brunch until 2:30pm; there's live entertainment in the Tavern Thursday through Saturday from 9pm.

SALEM INN, 7 Summer St., Salem, MA 01970. Tel. 508/741-0680, or
toll free 800/446-2995. Fax 508/744-8924. 21 rms (all with bath). A/C TV TEL
$ Rates (including continental breakfast): $93–$115 single or double; $115–$137
2-room suite with kitchenette. Extra person $16. AE, DC, DISC, MC, V. **Parking:**
Free, 2 blocks away at city lot with validation.

The Salem Inn, near the intersection with Essex Street, is only a ½ block from the
Witch House and 2 blocks from the Peabody Museum. It's a lovely old restored brick
mansion with large, beautiful, and comfortable rooms. Rooms have queen- or
king-size beds and fireplaces. The price differential for rooms depends on plumbing:
All rooms have private bathrooms, but the baths for the less expensive rooms are
across the hallway from the rooms themselves. Some rooms have Jacuzzis.

**STEPHEN DANIELS HOUSE, 1 Daniels St., Salem, MA 01970. Tel.
508/744-5709.** 4 rms (shared baths).
$ Rates (including continental breakfast): $66–$88 single; $92–$100 double; $155
(with this travel guide) quad. AE. **Parking:** Free.

Those who are traveling in a group of four or six will find the Stephen Daniels House
ideal; smaller parties will enjoy its comforts as well. The house, located in the center
of Salem, several blocks from the Hawthorne Hotel, was built in 1667, with a wing
added in 1756. It is owned today by Katherine Gill, who has furnished it with antiques
of the period and has virtually turned it into a time machine that takes you back to the
Salem of witch-hunting and sea-captain days. Canopied four-poster beds, working
fireplaces (three wood-burning), low-beamed ceilings, and a delightful little terrace
garden make it a real showpiece. Be sure to call or write ahead for reservations.

WHERE TO DINE

THE GRAPEVINE RESTAURANT, 26 Congress St. Tel. 745-9335.
  Cuisine: NORTHERN ITALIAN/AMERICAN GRILL. **Reservations:** Recommended, especially on weekends.
$ Prices: Appetizers $1.75–$5.50 at lunch, $3–$8.95 at dinner; main courses
  $5.95–$9.50 at lunch, $11–$19 at dinner; dinner $20–$40. AE, DISC, MC, V.
  Open: Mon–Sat 11:30am–10pm, Sun 5:30–10pm.

This place is cloud nine. During the warm-weather months, choose to sit in the
courtyard out back and you'll feel as if you've been transported to Tuscany.
Both lunch and dinner menus include a wonderful selection of Italian dishes
along with some creative American dishes. If you don't want to settle in for a long
drawn-out meal, you can always sit at the bar and order a bowl of linguine tossed with
pesto and topped with sautéed vegetables, or, for that matter, anything else from the
menu. You'll undoubtedly find yourself sitting next to a local in for their weekly
Grapevine fix.

LYCEUM, 43 Church St. Tel. 745-7665.
  Cuisine: AMERICAN. **Reservations:** Recommended.
$ Prices: Appetizers $3–$6; main courses $9–$16; dinner $28–$40. AE, DISC,
  MC, V.
  Open: Lunch Mon–Sat 11:30am–3pm; dinner Mon–Sat 5:30–10pm; Sun brunch
  11am–3pm.

One block from the pedestrian mall, near the corner of Church and Washington
Streets, the Lyceum was once at the center of the city's cultural life, and Alexander
Graham Bell, who once lived in Salem, gave the first public demonstration of the
telephone in its halls. Today the Lyceum is an attractive restaurant-bar and grill. The
menu is heavy with local seafood, plus grilled meats and poultry. In good weather,
find your way to the terrace out back in the courtyard.

RED'S SANDWICH, 15 Central St. Tel. 745-3527.
  Cuisine: DINER. **Reservations:** Not accepted.

$ Prices: Breakfast $1.25–$3.40; lunch $1.45–$4.45. No credit cards.
Open: Mon–Sat 5am–3pm, Sun 6am–1pm.

Here you'll find the townies crowded around two horseshoe-shaped bars and in adjacent tables and booths every morning from 5am (6am on Sun). It's the kind of place where you sit down for breakfast and the waitress immediately plunks down a heavy mug and asks, "Coffee?" It's also the kind of place where you can fill up on all the vacation kinds of breakfast foods like Belgian waffles piled high with whipped cream and the fattest French toast you've ever seen. For lunch you'll find all your dinner favorites, including burgers and club sandwiches. It's next to the police station.

VIVA, Museum Place. Tel. 744-9633.
Cuisine: ITALIAN. **Reservations:** Recommended.
$ Prices: Appetizers $2.95–$5.50 at lunch, $1.95–$5.95 at dinner; main courses $5.95–$9.95 at lunch, $7.95–$13.95 at dinner. AE, DC, MC, V.
Open: Daily 11:30am–9pm.

You may have to plan two visits to Viva—one to sample their gourmet pizzas at lunch and one to settle in for a leisurely Italian dinner. The pizzas are "to die for," as one local put it. You can take your pick of more than a dozen varieties, from the Genovese (calamari, pesto sauce, tomato, and mozzarella cheese) to the Giudia (smoked salmon, onions, capers, and mascarpone cheese). For dinner, start with a mouth-watering scampi all'olio (large shrimp baked with garlic, olive oil, and paprika), and move on to Scrod Livornese (scrod sautéed in white wine, capers, olives, and garlic, in a tomato sauce). Viva is a huge restaurant with floor-to-ceiling windows, several dining areas (including patio seating), and an all around festive atmosphere. It's located opposite the Peabody Museum, along the Essex Street Mall.

5. MARBLEHEAD

4 miles (6.5km) SE of Salem

GETTING THERE   By Bus/Train   The commuter trains between Boston and Salem (see "Salem," above) stop at Lynn, and buses no. 441 and 442 run between Marblehead and Boston's Haymarket Square about every ½ hour during rush hours, every hour other times, but note that only bus no. 442 runs in the evening and on Sunday.

By Car   See "Getting There," under "Salem," above. From Route 1A North, take Route 129 in Swampscott, and follow it right into Old Town, Marblehead.

ESSENTIALS   The **area code** is 617. For information contact the **Marblehead Chamber of Commerce,** 62 Pleasant St. (P.O. Box 76) Marblehead, MA 01945 (tel. 617/631-2868).

What Salem was to merchant ships a century ago, Marblehead is to yachts today. Summer and winter, the beautiful, perfectly sheltered harbor is full of white boats bobbing on the water, or in dry dock, or heading out to sea. But it's not only yachters who come to Marblehead. This is without doubt one of the prettiest and best-kept towns in the country, and people love to come up from Boston on the weekend just to walk the streets and window-shop, or have a bowl of chowder in one of several good restaurants. They also come for a look at *The Spirit of '76*, the famous painting made even more famous during the Bicentennial celebrations, which is hung in Abbot Hall, Marblehead's Town Hall. If you plan to go to Salem, make the detour to Marblehead for at least an hour or two, or for a meal or even overnight.

WHAT TO SEE & DO

Walking around, window-shopping, and admiring the buildings and the rugged coast are the best things to do in Marblehead's Old Town section. Here are some landmarks to seek out as you go.

DOWNTOWN

ABBOT HALL, Washington St. Tel. 631-0000.

Abbot Hall dominates the town from a hilltop, readily visible as you ride into Marblehead—you can hardly miss its brick clock tower. Go to the hall and ask the way to the Selectmen's Meeting Room (town council) to find that marvelous patriotic painting, *The Spirit of '76*. While you're there, take a look at the deed by which the Native Americans transferred ownership of the land to the European newcomers in 1684.

Admission: Donations appreciated.

Open: Nov–May, Mon–Fri 9am–4pm. June–Oct, Mon, Wed, and Fri 9am–4pm, Tues and Thurs 9am–9pm; Sat 9am–6pm; Sun and holidays 11am–6pm.

JEREMIAH LEE MANSION, near the intersection of Hooper and Washington Sts. Tel. 631-1069.

Down in the center of the Historic District, this is one of two old Marblehead mansions open to the public for a fee. The Jeremiah Lee Mansion, owned by the Marblehead Historical Society, was built by a wealthy maritime merchant and furnished with the best things money could buy in 1768—before the Revolution. The style is Georgian, of course, and the period furnishings—including hand-painted wallpaper and paneling—are from all over the world.

Admission: $4 adults, $3 seniors and students, $2 children ages 10–16.

Open: Mid-May to mid-Oct, Mon–Fri 10am–4pm, Sat–Sun 1–4pm. **Closed:** Holidays.

KING HOOPER MANSION, 8 Hooper St. Tel. 631-2608.

The King Hooper Mansion, located more or less across the street from the Lee Mansion, is a smaller house and older—built in 1728, with a Georgian extension added in 1747. Now owned by the Marblehead Arts Association, it offers tours of four floors. Art exhibits change each month.

Tours: $1.

Admission: Free for exhibits in gallery and ballroom.

Open: Tues–Sun 1–4pm.

THE WATERFRONT & CROCKER PARK

After a walk in the "downtown" part of the Historic District, make your way down to the waterfront and **Crocker Park,** on a hill at the western end of Front Street. Relax on one of the benches and admire the panoramic view of the harbor and the town. Bring or buy a sandwich, and have a picnic here. The view is unforgettable.

From Crocker Park, walk east along Front Street, past its little restaurants, boatyards, and houses built on the rocks, to **Fort Sewall.** The fort is an earthwork fortification built in the 1600s and "modernized" in the late 1700s to include barracks and half-buried buildings, which still remain. The fort is right at the mouth of the harbor and offers a commanding view of the water and of Marblehead Neck, at the other side of the harbor's mouth, dominated by a light. This is another good picnic place, and it's great for children, who will love playing within the fort (where there is little risk of falling into the water).

When you're ready to leave Fort Sewall, walk back along Front Street, turn right on Franklin, then right again on Orne Street to get to **Fountain Park** and **Old**

Burial Hill, where the town's first church meetinghouse was built (it's gone now) and where ancient gravestones mark the places of many of Marblehead's earliest inhabitants and revolutionary war dead. Orne Street east of Fountain Park leads to the beach.

If you're traveling by car, be sure to drive the loop around **Marblehead Neck.** This quiet residential community is made up of several grand ocean- and harbor-front homes surrounded by handsome lawns and gardens. Along the way, there's an **Audubon Bird Sanctuary** (on Ocean Avenue), **Castle Rock** (from which the ocean views are staggeringly beautiful), and—at the tip—**Chandler Hovey Park,** which is home to the Marblehead Light and several benches where you can sit and look out at the boat-filled harbor. This is one day not to leave the camera in your hotel room.

WHERE TO STAY

Should you really want to get into the spirit and soul of this beautiful seacoast town, you'll have to spend the night. Possibilities are limited, but very attractive. I suggest that you try to plan your visit for a weekday, and that you call ahead for reservations, especially in July and August.

HARBOR LIGHT INN, 58 Washington St., Marblehead, MA 01945. Tel. 617/631-2186. 12 rms (all with bath). A/C TV TEL **Directions:** Take Washington St. into historic district, until you see yellow Old Town Hall on its own little "island" in middle of road; just behind town hall is corner of State St., and just beyond that, on Washington St., is the inn.
$ Rates (including continental breakfast): $84–$127 double; $158–$185 suite. AE, MC, V. **Parking:** Free, on premises.
Located between Pearl and Pickett Streets, the Harbor Light Inn is an 18th-century Marblehead house right in the center of the historic district. The house is pretty from the outside, but even better inside. Each of the guest rooms has either a four-poster or a canopy queen-size bed; some have views of the harbor, some have television sets. One room has its own large private deck with a fine view, others have working fireplaces, and all have antique furniture and modern private baths. The three large suites have canopy beds, fireplaces, and Jacuzzis. There's a beautiful formal parlor, and an observation deck on the roof. Here you're only steps from shopping and 2 blocks from the waterfront.

THE NAUTILUS, 68 Front St., Marblehead, MA 01945. Tel. 617/631-1703. 6 rms (none with bath). **Directions:** Take Washington St. into historic district, until you see yellow Old Town Hall on its own little "island" in middle of road; just behind town hall, turn right on State St., follow it to waterfront, and turn right. The Nautilus is on the right.
$ Rates: $52 single; $70 double. No credit cards. **Parking:** Free.
The recommendable guesthouse on the waterfront is the Nautilus, run by Ethel Dermody. This small Marblehead house is in great demand because of its waterfront location, so it's advisable to call ahead for reservations, particularly on weekends in summer. Bathrooms are not in the rooms but are nearby, and a small fridge is in the hall for guests' use. One or two rooms have sea views. Parking is a problem downtown, but Mrs. Dermody will recommend places without danger of towing or tickets. The Nautilus is right across the street from the Driftwood Restaurant, which is by the municipal parking lot on the water at the end of State Street.

WHERE TO DINE

DRIFTWOOD RESTAURANT, 63 Front St. Tel. 631-1145.
Cuisine: DINER. **Reservations:** Not required. **Directions:** Take Washington St. into historic district, until you see yellow Old Town Hall on its own little "island" in middle of road; just behind town hall, turn right onto State St., follow it to waterfront, and you'll see the Driftwood.

$ Prices: Breakfast $1.50–$4.95; lunch $1.50–$7.50. No credit cards.
Open: Summer, daily 5:30am–5pm. Winter, daily 5:30am–2pm.

In spite of its magnet-for-tourists location, the Driftwood is a piece of the real Marblehead full of hearty fishers and boatbuilders. Its barn-red clapboard exterior is matched inside with red-and-white–checked tablecloths and a long lunch counter. At 5:30am, the fishers troop in for coffee, eggs, and ham; later in the day, they may return for a bowl of chowder or a portion of "fried dough," a Driftwood specialty served with butter and maple syrup. Breakfast, clam chowder, sandwiches, and fish or seafood plates are the hot items here.

KING'S ROOK, 12 State St. Tel. 631-9838.

Cuisine: CAFE. **Reservations:** Not required. **Directions:** Take Washington St. into historic district, until you see yellow Old Town Hall on its own little "island" in middle of road; just behind town hall, turn right onto State St., and look for King's Rook on the left.
$ Prices: Appetizers $2.50–$5.50; main courses $7–$12. MC, V.
Open: Tues–Fri noon–2:30pm and 5:30–11:30pm, Sat–Sun noon–11:30pm.

The literary-minded in Marblehead who have a free hour in the evening spend it at the King's Rook, a European-style coffeehouse and wine bar, located not far from the intersection with Washington. Coffee drinks are in the $1.50 to $4 range, and the atmosphere—provided by captain's chairs, small wood-plank tables, low-beamed ceiling, tin lamps, and watercolors on the walls—is yours at no extra charge. Beers, wines by the glass, sandwiches, and a long list of desserts are also served. Many couples find it a romantic place.

THE LANDING, on Clark's Landing off Front St. Tel. 631-1878.

Cuisine: SEAFOOD. **Reservations:** Recommended. **Directions:** Take Washington St. into historic district, until you see yellow Old Town Hall on its own little "island" in middle of road; just behind town hall, turn right on State St., follow it to waterfront, and you'll see The Landing.
$ Prices: Appetizers $2.75–$5.95 at lunch, $2.75–$7.95 at dinner; main courses $6.95–$14.95 at lunch, $13.95–$25 at dinner. AE, DC, DISC, MC, V.
Open: Lunch daily 11:30am–4pm; dinner daily 5–11pm.

The Landing, about the largest and most elaborate of Marblehead's restaurants, caters to the boating crowd—which includes early-morning amateur scallop and lobster hunters. Here you'll find an English-style pub and dining rooms with a view of yacht-filled Marblehead Harbor. Come for a simple lunch of fish-and-chips ($10), or something fancier. At dinnertime, there's mesquite-smoked duck, lobsters cooked with Pernod, and mahi-mahi fish. The setting, a semiformal dining room right over the water, is excellent. The Landing's Pub section, popular with the younger boating set, offers burgers and beer.

ROSALIE'S, 18 Sewall St. Tel. 631-5353.

Cuisine: ITALIAN. **Reservations:** Recommended.
$ Prices: Appetizers $3–$8; main courses $7–$21; dinner $30–$40. MC, V.
Open: Dinner daily 5:30–9:45pm; Sun brunch (off-season only) 10:30am–2:30pm.

Year after year Marblehead's most popular place to dine is Rosalie's, at the corner of School Street. Enter the front door of the unprepossessing three-story brick factory building and climb the stairs to the small bar. Behind the bar booths is a large, high-ceilinged dining room where polite and friendly waiters glide professionally among the small tables. The decorations are eclectic, from 19th-century touches to Roman columns, but the overall effect is upbeat and elegant. There's another dining room at the top of the stairs, with its own kitchen visible at the back, and yet another one in the basement; but the maître d' is near the bar, so go there first.

The menu changes daily, but always has various antipasti, such as snails and garlic butter in mushroom caps, or shrimp with prosciutto in a mustard-butter sauce. Then comes the pasta (made here): lobster ravioli, cannelloni, and fettuccine pomodoro.

Main courses include veal, chicken, and shrimp prepared in interesting ways. There's pollo francesca, sautéed chicken breast in a light egg batter, with mushrooms in Grand Marnier; veal marinara with eggplant, prosciutto, and mozzarella; and seafood posillipo of shrimp, mussels, littleneck clams, and fish poached in marinara-clam sauce, on linguine.

6. MANCHESTER & MAGNOLIA

10 miles (6km) NE of Salem, 7 miles (11km) SW of Gloucester

GETTING THERE **By Train** Boston's MBTA Commuter Rail trains (tel. 617/722-3200), leave the downtown North Station 12 times a day (eight a day on weekends) for Manchester, Harbor Station, Gloucester, and Rockport. The ride takes about 1 hour to Gloucester. Children's, seniors', and family fares can save you money, as can travel during off-peak hours (basically, that's before 4:30pm from Boston, and after 8am from Rockport, on weekdays; all weekend trains are off-peak).

By Bus CATA, the Cape Ann Transportation Authority (tel. 508/283-7916), runs local buses among the towns and villages of Cape Ann.

By Car For a visit to Cape Ann, I'd suggest you tour by private car. Coming from Boston, take I-93 north to I-95 north (Rte. 128 east), and take the exit for Manchester. From Salem, follow Route 1A to Beverly, then Route 127 north to Manchester. The drive up the coast on Route 127 from Salem is of exceptional beauty.

ESSENTIALS The **area code** is 508. Contact the **Cape Ann Chamber of Commerce,** 33 Commercial St., Gloucester, MA 01930 (tel. 508/283-1601 or toll free 800/321-0133).

When Bostonians tell you they're taking a trip to the Cape, they mean they're heading south to Cape Cod. But there is another cape that attracts weekend and summer visitors from the metropolis: Cape Ann, just over an hour's drive or train ride north of the city.

Though few out-of-towners are familiar with Cape Ann, many have heard of Gloucester and Rockport, the picturesque seaport towns with a fascinating, almost legendary, history of struggle and communion with the sea.

If you look closely at the map, you'll notice that Cape Ann is in fact an island connected by bridges to the mainland, as is Cape Cod (since construction of the Cape Cod Canal). The bays, inlets, harbors, and coves of Cape Ann lend a variety to the landscape and shoreline which has long attracted vacationers, especially in the summertime. The best way to appreciate the scenic beauties of the North Shore and Cape Ann is to drive north along the coast through Manchester and Magnolia to Gloucester.

Manchester is a tidy little North Shore town peopled by old New England types and many professionals who commute into Boston by train. Should you visit during the summer, you can take advantage of **Singing Beach,** ½ mile from the train station (center of town) along Beach Street. If you drive, you'll have to pay a parking fee. If you walk, you swim for free. **White Beach,** off Ocean Street, has the same arrangement and the same facilities: bathhouse and snack bar.

A drive 3 miles northeast of Manchester along Route 127 brings you to **Magnolia.** Once a humble fishing village, Magnolia is now a lush and wealthy town. Lavish "summer cottages" built by the rich during the 19th century have been insulated, and heating installed, so that they can be used as year-round principal residences. The scenery is wonderful.

The town center is quite pretty, and less than a mile past it lie two natural features you may want to inspect: **Rafe's Chasm,** a dramatic cleft in the shoreline rock, is just opposite the reef of **Norman's Woe,** which figured in Longfellow's poem "The Wreck of the Hesperus." Should you want to spend some time in this lovely setting, there's a good place to stay the night.

WHAT TO SEE & DO

North of Magnolia along Route 127, signs will point to the right, down Hesperus Avenue, to the ✪ **Hammond Castle Museum,** 80 Hesperus Ave. (tel. 283-2080 recording; 283-7673 person). The castle-mansion was built by inventor, electrical engineer, and collector Dr. John Hays Hammond, Jr. (1888–1965), whose creations included radio remote control, and aspects of radar and sonar, including torpedo-guidance systems. Despite his name and his interest in things electric, J. H. Hammond, Jr., was not related to Laurens Hammond, inventor of the electric organ.

The castle builder's father, John Hays Hammond (1855–1936), was a mining engineer who helped Cecil Rhodes open up South Africa's hugely rich gold mines. He took part in the Boer War, was captured, ransomed, and returned to the United States.

His son grew up in a cosmopolitan and wealthy household, and did a lot of traveling himself, as you will see from exhibits in the castle. The younger Hammond grew rich on government defense contracts and the proceeds from his inventions, became a director of RCA, and spent his wealth on his obsession: European history. His castle is built in four sections, each made to epitomize a distinct period of European architecture. The Great Hall is Romanesque, the interior courtyard is fitted out as a medieval town square, and the living quarters are Gothic and Renaissance French. The guide who takes you on the obligatory 45-minute tour will explain Dr. Hammond's passion for collecting, and his macabre sense of humor. You come away from the tour marveling at the house's lovely setting, amused by its half-treasure-chest, half-gimcrack planning and construction, and puzzled by Hammond's genius, romanticism, and sheer weirdness. In any case, you don't want to miss it.

While you're waiting for the tour, you can explore the Tower Galleries, with various exhibits and artifacts, and you can pick up a flyer listing the museum's many concerts, lectures, and special programs. There are recitals on the Great Hall's fabulous 8,200-pipe organ, which got a brand-new console in 1987. Other concerts have included Scott Joplin rags, chamber music, and guitar music. There are special theme evenings as well (call for details).

The museum costs $5.50 for adults, $4.50 for seniors and students, and $3.50 for children aged 6 to 12. It's open daily from 9am to 5pm.

WHERE TO STAY

OLD CORNER INN, 2 Harbor St., Manchester by the Sea, MA 01944. Tel. 508/526-4995. 9 rms (6 with bath). **Directions:** From Rte. 128, take Manchester's Pine St. exit, turn left at end of ramp. Follow that road approximately 3 miles. Turn right onto Rte. 127. Go ½ mile, and inn is on left.
$ Rates: $55 double without bath, $98 double with bath. AE, MC, V.

This aptly named inn is, indeed, on a corner and is, indeed, old; the building was erected back in 1865. It's also the only inn in Manchester, so reservations made well in advance are a must. Guest rooms are located on three floors; the lower-level rooms are the loveliest. Room numbers one and two have four-poster feather beds and working fireplaces. Room number one also has a ball-and-claw bathtub. The inn is within easy reach of beaches (including Singing Beach) and the village.

WHITE HOUSE, 18 Norman Ave., Magnolia, MA 01930. Tel. 508/525-3642. 16 rms (13 with bath). TV **Directions:** Norman Ave. is Rte. 127, and the White House is at the corner of Lexington Ave., near the town's shops.
$ Rates (including continental breakfast): High season, $82–$88 double. DISC, MC, V. **Parking:** Free, on premises.

Centerpiecing a stately lawn and surrounded by gardens and rhododendrons, the White House is a fine old Magnolia Victorian house with an unobtrusive residential wing attached. In the house are six charming rooms, three with private bath; in the wing are 10 motel-style rooms with complete facilities: private bath, TV set, air conditioning. Guests receive passes for the use of a private beach; Rafe's Chasm, Norman's Woe, and Hammond Castle (see above) are all close by. Right across Route 127 is Lexington Avenue, a short and interesting street of shops, ice-cream parlors, and small café-restaurants.

WHERE TO DINE

THE MAGNOLIA BEACH CAFE, 35 Fuller St., Magnolia. Tel. 525-2008.
   Cuisine: CAFE. **Reservations:** Not required.
$ **Prices:** Breakfast $1.25–$4.75; lunch $3.25–$6.95. No credit cards.
   Open: Tues–Sun 6am–3pm.
This small café is the perfect spot for breakfast or lunch. The interior is full of conversation pieces; there's a marble-tiled floor in one room and an antique soda fountain bar. Daily specials include pasta salads, seafood, and Italian dishes. Several homemade desserts, such as mud pie, grapenut custard, and brownie à la mode, are worth saving room for.

7. GLOUCESTER

33 miles (53km) NE of Boston, 16 miles (26km) NE of Salem,
7 miles (11km) S of Rockport

GETTING THERE By Train Commuter trains run from Boston's North Station to Salem, Beverly, Gloucester, and Rockport. The trip to Salem takes about 30 minutes; trains run about every 20 minutes during rush hours, every ½ hour during the day, every hour at night and on weekends. Call toll free 800/392-6099 for schedules. From the station in Gloucester, it's about a mile to the "Man at the Wheel" statue. The beaches and some other attractions are several miles away.

By Bus CATA, the Cape Ann Transportation Authority (tel. 508/283-7916), runs local buses among the towns and villages of Cape Ann.

By Car Leaving from Boston and heading directly for Cape Ann, you'll save time by taking I-93 north to I-95/Route 128. Follow I-95 North/Route 128 east, and when the highway divides, stay on Route 128 (I-95 will head north, toward Maine) all the way into Gloucester. For the scenic coastal drive, follow Route 128 to the exit for Manchester. In Manchester, take Route 127 north.

ESSENTIALS The **area code** is 508. The **Cape Ann Chamber of Commerce** (tel. 508/283-1601, or toll free 800/321-0133) provides information at two locations. The downtown headquarters at 33 Commercial St., Gloucester, MA 01930, has a spacious information center furnishing maps, brochures, special-events bulletins, listings of accommodations, rest rooms, and a rack of restaurant menus. Not far from the statue of the Gloucester Fisherman, across the drawbridge, at the intersection of Routes 127 and 133, is the chamber's little tourist information booth. Guides at either of these locations will be happy to provide information on any town on Cape Ann.

The Pilgrims founded Plymouth in 1620, and three years later fishermen founded Gloucester. The marvelous natural harbor and the plentiful fishing grounds made that early settlement a fishers' paradise. Almost four centuries later, it still is.

Gloucester, at one time an important shipbuilding town, prides itself on being the birthplace of the schooner (1713). Like many others on the New England coast, it profited from the wealth of forests inland, the plentiful fish, and the richness of trade. Over the years, Gloucester lost so many of its sons to the ravages of the sea that the town thought it fitting to set up a memorial to them. The *Gloucester Fisherman* (also known as "The Man at the Wheel") is one of New England's most famous statues, with a plaque that reads "They That Go Down to the Sea in Ships, 1623–1923."

The sea is still Gloucester's provider, and the "fishing boats out of Gloucester" still head for open water early each morning. You'll see some of these sturdy little boats, festooned with all sorts of nets and rigging, down in the harbor. Fish-packing plants at quayside process the catch as soon as it's brought in.

Another maritime industry has become important in recent years: whale-watch tours (see below). You might want to take yours from here.

WHAT TO SEE & DO

Signs direct motorists along Gloucester's **Scenic Tour,** covering the Harbor Cove, Inner Harbor, and Fish Pier, as well as to the famous statue of the Gloucester Fisherman by Leonard Craske.

If you're lucky enough to be in Gloucester late in June, ask about the **Festival of St. Peter,** the high point of which is the Blessing of the Fleet. Several hundred boats make up Gloucester's important fishing fleet, and the blessing pays tribute to them.

A great "summer cottage" turned museum, **Beauport,** the Sleeper-McCann House, is at 75 Eastern Point Boulevard (tel. 283-0800), on Eastern Point, the peninsula across the bay from downtown Gloucester. The house, now under the care of the Society for the Preservation of New England Antiquities, was built by Henry Davis Sleeper, a prominent interior decorator and antiquarian of the 1920s. Sleeper worked for 27 years to make Beauport a showplace. It still is. You can take the hour-long tour Monday through Friday, May 15 to October 15, from 10am to 4pm; also on weekends from mid-September through mid-October, 1 to 4pm. Admission costs $5 per adult, $2.50 for children aged 6 to 12, $4.50 for seniors.

On your excursion down to Beauport, you'll want to stroll through East Gloucester's **Rocky Neck Art Colony.** The winding streets offer interesting glimpses of the harbor, and every other house seems to be an artist's studio. You'll see signs asking you to park *before* you enter the narrow streets. Take advantage of the lot next to the signs.

BEACHES

Gloucester's favored place for a hot summer afternoon is **Good Harbor Beach** in East Gloucester, on Route 127A toward Rockport. It may be crowded if the day is really hot, and parking will be tight. Alternatives are **Long Beach** and **Pebble Beach,** just a bit farther along 127A, within the boundaries of Rockport. **Wingaersheek Beach** is on Ipswich Bay to the northwest (head back down Route 128 south and watch for signs). **Coffin Beach** is just northwest of Wingaersheek.

WHALE-WATCH CRUISES

There are a number of boats offering whale-watching cruises out of Gloucester Harbor from April to November. Cruises usually last between 4 and 5 hours, and thus take up a full morning or afternoon. Bring warm clothing, even on a warm day, because the maritime breezes out on the water will make the ambient temperature at least 10° cooler than on land, and the windchill factor might make it feel even colder. Also remember your sunglasses to ward off the glare from the water; and sunscreen, because that same glare, combined with the bright sun, can really give you a burn. Wear rubber-soled shoes if you have them. You can buy soft drinks and snacks on board.

Once out on the water, keep your eyes peeled for humpback whales, 30-ton creatures usually about 50 feet long which seem to love their briny habitat, breeching and playing for hours, accompanying themselves with their own curious songs. A cousin of the humpback is the finback, about twice as heavy and up to 80 feet long, making it second in size to the great blue whale. Long and slender, it's a super-fast swimmer, propelling its great bulk through the deep at speeds of 20 knots or even more. The minke whale is "small," weighing only 11 tons, and growing to 30 feet in length. Minke whales have a well-developed sense of curiosity, and may snoop around your boat just to see what's up. In addition, you may see right whales, dolphins, pilot whales, seals, sharks, and seabirds such as petrels, shearwaters, gannets, and gulls.

Capt. Fred Douglass and his sons pioneered whale-watch cruises out of Gloucester with their Daunty Fleet of boats, and now they operate **Cape Ann Whale Watch** (tel. 508/283-5110), with daily departures at 8:30am and 1:30pm from Rose's Wharf, at 415 Main St., across from the Old Colony gas station. A research naturalist accompanies every cruise. Whale sightings are guaranteed (Capt. Douglass has had a 99% record since 1979); if you don't see a whale, you'll receive a free pass for a future cruise. Reservations are requested, and tickets can be purchased from the ticket office on Rose's Wharf daily from 7am to 6pm. Daytime cruises cost $20 for adults, $12 for children under 16, $14 for seniors over 60, and other discounts are given for AAA members, military personnel, and college students.

Seven Seas Whale Watch, Seven Seas Wharf (tel. 508/283-1776, or toll free 800/238-1776), operates daily cruises at similar prices. Continental breakfast is available on board ship. In high summer, there are also sunset cruises with entertainment.

WHERE TO STAY

GRAY MANOR, 14 Atlantic Rd. (Bass Rocks), Gloucester, MA 01930. Tel. 508/283-5409. 9 rms (all with bath). A/C MINIBAR TV TEL **Directions:** Exit 9 off Rte. 128 North, turn left onto Bass Ave., then right onto Atlantic.
$ Rates: Summer, $61–$64 double; $466 efficiency apartment per week. Spring and fall, discounts available. No credit cards. **Parking:** Free, on premises. **Closed:** Winter.

Robert and Madeline Gray have converted a nice big summer house into a guesthouse; the Gray Manor is up the hill behind the Blue Shutters and is only a few minutes' walk from Good Harbor Beach. Guest rooms have private baths and some even have their own decks.

TWIN LIGHT MANOR, Atlantic Rd., Gloucester, MA 01930. Tel. 508/283-7500, or toll free 800/528-1234. Fax 508/281-6489. 63 rms (all with bath). A/C TV TEL **Directions:** Exit 9 off Rte. 128 North to Rte. 127A East. Turn right onto Atlantic Rd. and travel 1 mile.
$ Rates: Mid-May to mid-Oct, $105–$175 single or double. Mid-Oct to mid-May, rates about 10% less. AE, CB, DC, DISC, MC, V. **Parking:** Free, on premises.

First choice, without a doubt, is Twin Light Manor. Atlantic Road is the shore road on the eastern side of the East Gloucester peninsula and forms part of the ring road around the peninsula. Twin Light Manor is a complex of buildings centered on an attractive English Tudor mansion, set on a highland overlooking the ocean from 7 acres of well-kept grounds. Six buildings hold the guest rooms, which come in all shapes and sizes. The most delightful ones are in the ivy-covered, granite, stucco, and half-timbered mansion with its gracious large public rooms, big fireplaces, dark wood, and even a Victorian billiards room. The vast original manor bedrooms each have a king-size bed or two double beds, and some have fireplaces; they go for $165 in high season. The smaller "guest" bedrooms have king-size beds and rent for $148 double in high season. The other buildings have modern motel-style rooms, most with either king-size beds or two double beds, all with ocean views, and many with private balconies overlooking the grounds and the sea. Twin Light has its own dining room.

Services: Free harbor cruise; complimentary wine and cheese and cookies in the living room; free use of bicycles.

Facilities: Living room, where movies are shown frequently on wide-screen TV; in-room video rentals available; two swimming pools (one heated); badminton, volleyball, croquet, shuffleboard courts; free access to Bass Rocks Golf Club (greens fees are charged).

WHERE TO DINE

THE GULL, 75 Essex Ave. (Rte. 133). Tel. 283-6565.
    Cuisine: SEAFOOD. **Reservations:** Recommended. **Directions:** Take Rte. 133 less than 2 miles west of the "Man at the Wheel" statue or approach along Rte. 133 eastbound from Rte. 128.
$ **Prices:** Appetizers $3.95–$5.45; main courses $5.95–$10.95 at lunch, $6.95–$18.95 at dinner. MC, V.
    Open: Daily 5:30am–9pm.

Ⓢ Among our favorite dining places in Gloucester is the Gull, located at the Cape Ann Marina on Route 133, a mile or so from the center of town right next to where the Yankee Whale Watch boats depart. The Gull is a big, friendly, fairly simple but attractive restaurant overlooking the Annisquam River, usually packed with boaters, whale watchers, families, couples, and sailors. Seafood is the forte here, and you can have the huge, succulent lobster sandwich or a full clambake with steamers, corn on the cob, coleslaw, and a lobster, or settle for fish-and-chips. The Gull has a bar and serves alcoholic beverages.

HALIBUT POINT, 289 Main St. Tel. 281-1900.
    Cuisine: SEAFOOD. **Reservations:** Not accepted.
$ **Prices:** Appetizers $2.50–$4; main courses $6–$11. DISC, MC, V.
    Open: Daily 11am–midnight.
Halibut Point is the name of a state park near Rockport, and also of this publike restaurant in downtown Gloucester. The atmosphere is of a friendly neighborhood tavern, not fancy but fun. The menu is short and to the point, with sandwiches, salads, burgers, and several popular seafood items, but the blackboard always bears interesting special dishes. Swordfish is usually a good bet. The soup-and-sandwich special, with a mug of beer, is a particularly good bargain.

THE RUDDER RESTAURANT, 75 Rocky Neck Ave., East Gloucester. Tel. 283-7967.
    Cuisine: SEAFOOD/INTERNATIONAL. **Reservations:** Required for weekends.
$ **Prices:** Appetizers $3.95–$10.95; main courses $12.95–$19.95. MC, V.
    Open: Summer only, daily noon–10pm.

✪ A meal at the Rudder is not just a meal—it's a party! This wildly imaginative restaurant—smack dab on the water in the heart of the Rocky Neck Art Colony—not only has some adventurous cooks in the kitchen (try the wing dings for an appetizer), but is literally floor-to-ceiling crammed with gadgets, gizmos, colored lights, antiques, cards, photos, menus from around the world, and other collectibles. On top of that, there's entertainment, including a woman who does an invisible flaming baton twirling act. Brunch is served Friday to Sunday.

WHITE RAINBOW RESTAURANT, 65 Main St. Tel. 281-0017.
    Cuisine: NEW AMERICAN. **Reservations:** Recommended.
$ **Prices:** Appetizers $4–$8; main courses $18–$30; dinner $35–$50. AE, MC, V.
    Open: Dinner Tues–Fri and Sun 5:30–9:30pm (and Mon in summer), Sat 6–10pm.
Gloucester's fanciest and best is the White Rainbow Restaurant in the basement of a 19th-century brick office building (go by the street numbers, as the sign is small and difficult to spot). There are two places to dine here: the formal dining room and the less formal café. Both have dusky brick walls, low lights, and modern paintings. Waiters and waitresses are dressed in black and white, friendly but professional, and after you've been seated they will take your order for an opener like lobster stew,

grilled shrimp, or baked Brie; then you can go on to roast duck, tournedos of beef, or a grilled prime veal chop. Desserts are heavily biased in favor of chocolate. The wine list gives you plenty of room for making your selection, and bottles are just slightly higher than the moderate range.

---

8. ROCKPORT

40 miles (64.5km) NE of Boston, 7 miles (11km) N of Gloucester

GETTING THERE By Train Commuter trains run from Boston's North Station to Salem, Beverly, Gloucester, and Rockport. The trip to Rockport takes about 1¼ hours; trains run about every 20 minutes during rush hours, every ½ hour during the day, every hour at night and on weekends. Call toll free 800/392-6099 for schedules.

By Bus CATA, the Cape Ann Transportation Authority (tel. 508/283-7916), runs local buses among the towns and villages of Cape Ann.

By Car Between Gloucester and Rockport are two loop roads. Route 127 takes you to Rockport through the middle of Cape Ann, then loops around the northern and western shores to return to Gloucester. Route 127A, on the other hand, takes you up the eastern shore of the cape before reaching Rockport. If you get lost, don't worry. In a short while some loop will bring you back to one or the other town.

ESSENTIALS The **area code** is 508. The **Rockport Chamber of Commerce** (tel. 508/546-6575) maintains a year-round information booth on Upper Main Street (Rte. 127) on the outskirts of town, coming from Gloucester. In season, you'll get help finding a room for the night—if there's a room available. Stop at the booth for this free service.

    Parking conditions downtown are sure to be very tight any time in summer, so, if you drive, find a nice back street, or use the town-supported parking lot on the outskirts rather than getting snarled in the press of traffic downtown. The town lots charge several dollars per day for parking, but they offer a free shuttle bus from the lot to downtown Rockport. This isn't a bad deal, considering the gasoline and frustration you'll waste trying to find a legal spot to park downtown.

North of Gloucester is the small seacoast town of Rockport, famed as an artists' colony and, well, just as a very picturesque place. Winslow Homer, Childe Hassam, and Fitz Hugh Lane came here to paint the fishermen working on their vessels and the quarrymen cutting and moving granite.

    It's been a long time since Rockport was a village of hearty, independent fishermen and their families, living by their daily struggle with the sea, and today you're likely to see ten times as many day-trippers as you are to see colorful village types. But the Rockport Art Association is active—the town is dotted with galleries holding paintings and crafts both pleasing and awkward, and amateur daubers test their skill at capturing daily life all over town. The Rockport Art Association's headquarters is also the venue for musical performances during the month-long annual Rockport Chamber Music Festival.

    Rockport's popularity means that there are lots of good places to stay and to dine, and if you decide to remain overnight here, you'll notice that as the evening wears on, the streets become calmer and the village resumes something of its slow, antique pace.

WHAT TO SEE & DO

First thing every visitor does after arriving in Rockport is take a stroll down **Bearskin Neck,** the narrow peninsula jutting into the water off Dock Square, the town's main square. Here you'll find lots of quaint shops and art galleries to draw your attention, and many good views of the water and of the town.

Other strolls in town are also rewarding, and local brochures will urge you to take a photograph of the red fisherman's shack called "Motif No. 1," apparently named for its popularity among the first picture painters who moved to Rockport. Actually it should now be named "Motif No. 2," as the original shack was swept away in the great storm of 1978 and a new one was built from scratch. In the interest of originality, try to be the first person to visit Rockport *without* seeing this unimportant landmark; frankly, the thing is now famous because it's famous.

Rather, spend your time looking at the **local granite.** It was cut at the town's Swan Quarry (now flooded), and shipped out, giving the town its name. Curbstones, markers, pavements, foundations, piers, even whole buildings were made of the durable stone during the town's quarrying heyday. Now, if "Motif No. 1" were a fisherman's shanty made of granite, that would be something to see!

For swimming, walk along Beach Street north to Front Beach and Back Beach, or wander (in your car or on your bike) north along the coast to **Pigeon Cove,** about 2 miles north (a ½-hour walk).

You can go farther than Pigeon Cove by car or bike. In fact, you can make a loop of Cape Ann on Route 127 via Pigeon Cove, Folly Cove, Plum Cove, Annisquam, and Lobster Cove, ending in Gloucester.

If you love chamber music, plan your visit to coincide with the **Rockport Chamber Music Festival.** Recitals are given Thursday through Sunday during the month of June. For exact dates and details, call 508/546-7391.

WHERE TO STAY

IN TOWN

ADDISON CHOATE INN, 49 Broadway, Rockport, MA 01966. Tel. 508/546-7543, or toll free 800/649-7543. 10 rms (all with bath). **Directions:** Coming from Gloucester on Rte. 127, you enter Rockport on Broadway; the inn is on the right, several blocks south of Dock Sq.

$ Rates (including continental breakfast): $95 double; $110 stable house for two; $120 suite. MC, V. **Parking:** Free.

Rockport's most charming place to stay is the Addison Choate Inn. Rooms in the tidy old house (built in 1851) have been meticulously restored, and are equally well maintained. There's a feeling of authenticity bred of fine taste; nothing in the decor is overdone, but neither is it spare. It is not "chock full of antiques"; it's tastefully furnished with them. Guests can enjoy the pretty swimming pool, and the center of town is within easy walking distance.

CAPTAIN'S BOUNTY MOTOR INN, 1 Beach St. (P.O. Box 430), Rockport, MA 01966. Tel. 508/546-9557. 24 rms (all with bath). TV **Directions:** From Dock Sq., go east on Rte. 127 toward Annisquam, but turn right onto Beach St.

$ Rates: High season, $99–$110 double or efficiency. Off-season, rates are as much as 30% less. DISC, MC, V. **Parking:** Free, on premises.

The Captain's Bounty Motor Inn is right on the beach near the center of town, with modern rooms and efficiencies facing the sea, on two levels. If modern motel conveniences and a prime location are what you're looking for, this is the place to look.

INN ON COVE HILL, 37 Mount Pleasant St., Rockport, MA 01966. Tel. 508/546-2701. 11 rms (9 with bath). TV **Directions:** From Dock Sq., follow Rte. 127A east for 100 yards; inn is on left.

$ Rates (including continental breakfast): $52 double without bath, $66–$105 double with bath. No credit cards. **Parking:** Free, on premises. **Closed:** Late Oct–early Apr.

The Inn on Cove Hill is only a few steps from the center of town on Route 127A. The charming house was built in 1791 with the proceeds (so they say) from cashing in some pirate gold found on Cape Ann. Today the house is as neat as a pin, old-fashioned in feel but modern in comforts. Breakfast is served to your room or by the garden during comfortable weather. No smoking is allowed in the inn.

LINDEN TREE INN, 26 King St., Rockport, MA 01966. Tel. 508/546-2494. 18 rms (16 with bath). MINIBAR
$ Rates (including continental breakfast): $66 single; $88–$105 double. Folding bed $11. MC, V. **Parking:** Free, on premises. **Closed:** Dec to mid-Apr.

The Linden Tree Inn, located on a quiet street in the center of town, 3 blocks from the train station, is a tidy inn run by friendly innkeepers Larry and Penny Olson. The yard is shaded by an enormous old linden tree, as you'd expect. The inn has rooms in various sizes and styles; efficiencies have minibars. All rooms in the main house have private bath; half have air conditioning. The two rooms in the annex share a bath. In the modern Carriage House, each room has a double and twin bed, air conditioning, color television, and a private deck. This is a nice place—homey, convenient, and friendly.

PEG LEG INN, 2 King St., Rockport, MA 01966. Tel. 508/546-2352, or toll free 800/346-2352. 33 rms (all with bath). TV **Directions:** From Rte. 127, turn left onto Railroad Ave. at the five-road intersection, then take first right onto King St.
$ Rates (including continental breakfast): Mid-June to Oct, $88–$120 double. Off-season, discounts available. MC, V. **Parking:** Free, on premises. **Closed:** Late Nov to mid-Feb.

Serenely situated on the edge of the sea, the Peg Leg Inn has been a haven for Rockport visitors for many years now. The original inn has been expanded to include five buildings, and most of the rooms have views of the water. The decor varies from room to room and building to building, but as the houses of the inn are a century or two old, emphasis is on Early American, with modern luxuries added. The rooms are kept as neat as the white clapboard houses they're in, and the rates depend on the size of the room and the view it has of the water. The Peg Leg Inn is a short walk from the center of town, but the location makes it a good deal quieter than most in-town lodgings. The inn's full-service restaurant is next door.

ON THE OUTSKIRTS

OLD FARM INN, 291 Granite St., Rockport, MA 01966. Tel. 508/546-3237. 9 rms (all with bath). TV **Directions:** Follow Rte. 127 north and west from Rockport toward Annisquam, and watch for inn on right.
$ Rates (including continental breakfast): Summer, $86–$118 double. Apr–June and Nov. lower rates available. MC, V. **Parking:** Free. **Closed:** Dec–Mar.

North and west of Pigeon Cove is Folly Cove, on the way to Annisquam, just past the road to Halibut Point. It's here you'll find the Old Farm Inn. It may be old but it is kept pretty as a picture. Set on 5 acres of grounds very near Halibut Point State Park, the farmhouse has four guest rooms, and there are another four rooms in the barn guesthouse. All have such country touches as rustic antiques and homey quilts. The highest-priced room is a two-room suite, which sleeps four.

RALPH WALDO EMERSON INN, Phillips Ave., Pigeon Cove, Rockport, MA 01966. Tel. 508/546-6321. Fax 508/546-7043. 36 rms (all with bath). A/C TEL **Directions:** Follow Rte. 127 north and west from Rockport toward Annisquam for 2 miles, and watch for sign on right.
$ Rates: Summer, $66–$121 single; $91–$128 double. Add $23 per person for breakfast and dinner. DISC, MC, V. **Parking:** Free, on premises. **Closed:** Dec–Mar and weekdays in Apr and Nov.

Among the best things about the Ralph Waldo Emerson Inn is its location: a block in from the road, on a bluff overlooking the sea. The grand white inn actually did host Emerson at one time. Since then a new section has been added (1912), but the porch is still fine for sitting and taking in the view. The gracious and airy public rooms hold lots of good paintings. For fun, there's a heated saltwater pool, whirlpool bath, sauna, and recreation room.

SANDY BAY MOTOR INN, 173 Main St., Rockport, MA 01966. Tel. 508/546-7155. 46 rms (all with bath). A/C TV TEL **Directions:** The motel is on the left-hand side of Rte. 127 as you approach from Gloucester.

$ Rates: Summer, $94–$129 double; Fall–spring, lower rates available. AE, DC, MC, V. **Parking:** Free.

For a modern hotel on the outskirts, try the Sandy Bay Motor Inn. The colorful rooms here, all with the luxury features, are only the beginning of the story. Besides these, the motel has an indoor swimming pool, a whirlpool bath, saunas, tennis courts, and a breakfast room. It's a good idea to make reservations in the busy summer months.

YANKEE CLIPPER INN, 96 Granite St. (P.O. Box 2399), Rockport, MA 01966. Tel. 508/546-3407, or toll free 800/545-3699. Fax 508/546-9730. 27 rms (all with bath). TEL **Directions:** Take Rte. 127 toward Pigeon Cove and the outskirts of town.

$ Rates (including breakfast): Summer, $109–$207 double. Midweek and extended-stay packages available. AE, DISC, MC, V. **Parking:** Free, on premises.

Two of the inn's three buildings occupy a waterfront site with excellent views; the third is a fine old house designed by none other than Charles Bulfinch, architect of the Massachusetts State House in Boston and (in part) of the Capitol in Washington. Grounds include several shady nooks and a heated saltwater swimming pool. The Bulfinch House is up the hill a bit and across the road.

Dining/Entertainment: The oceanfront dining room is open to the public, but reservations are essential. Main dishes, classic American and European, are $13.95 to $25 at dinner.

WHERE TO DINE

The first thing you should know is that Rockport is a dry town. No liquor, wine, or beer is served in its restaurants or sold in its inns or shops. You can drink in Rockport if you BYO, and the restaurants will provide setups, corkscrews, ice buckets, and the like. But you must plan ahead and buy your booze in Gloucester, or in Lanesville, on Route 127 west of Rockport.

This all came about in 1856 when one Hannah Jumper, an outspoken leader of the temperance movement in Rockport, led a raid on the town's liquor supplies. In the four preceding years, sale of ardent spirits in Rockport had more than doubled, and many a fisherman and quarry worker spent wages on rum which should have gone for family needs.

The town's Fourth of July bash in 1856 had gotten out of hand as usual, and on July 8, Hannah and other good citizens went to work. Casks and bottles stored in shops and warehouses—and even in private homes—were breached and broken, and though some people cried "Foul!" most people supported this radical solution. Hannah's early-morning direct action changed the history of Rockport, and it has been dry, by the active consent of a majority of its citizens, ever since.

BLACKSMITH SHOP RESTAURANT, 23 Mount Pleasant St. Tel. 546-6301.

Cuisine: SEAFOOD/TRADITIONAL AMERICAN. **Reservations:** Recommended.

$ Prices: Appetizers $4–$11; main courses $9–$18; dinner $25–$40; early bird specials available all afternoon up until at least 7pm. AE, CB, DC, MC, V.

Open: May–Oct, daily 7am–10pm.

Just off Dock Square, in the center of Rockport, the Blacksmith Shop Restaurant has something that Bearskin Neck restaurants don't have: lots of space and some sense of elegance. And yet the views of the harbor and of Motif No. 1 from the Blacksmith Shop are as good as any in town, and better than most. There is so much space here that you enter through various old-time kitchen exhibits and memorabilia, then step down into the spacious waterside dining rooms to order from a menu heavy in seafood and traditional American favorites.

ELLEN'S HARBORSIDE, just off Dock Sq. on T-Wharf. Tel. 546-2512.
  Cuisine: SEAFOOD. **Reservations:** Not accepted.
$ Prices: Breakfast $1.25–$4; main dinner courses $7–$15; meals $12–$20. MC, V.
  Open: Daily 5:30am–10pm. **Closed:** Dec–Apr.

⑤ Ellen's Harborside next to the firehouse is a tiny, crowded, but pleasant place that specializes in budget seafood, "authentic" pit barbecue cooking, and homemade desserts and packs 'em in every night of the summer. Ellen's is especially popular with thrifty seniors, who like the freshness of the seafood, the hardworking waitresses, and the delicious and abundant desserts. The seafood special usually costs about $6.95. The dining room and lunch counter are simple and functional, and the hours of service are long enough to please anyone—they close when things calm down after dinner.

THE HANNAH JUMPER, Tuna Wharf, Bearskin Neck. Tel. 546-3600.
  Cuisine: SEAFOOD. **Reservations:** Not accepted. **Directions:** Walk out Bearskin Neck, glancing to the right until you see the restaurant.
$ Prices: Appetizers $3–$7; main courses $12–$14; dinner $20–$25. MC, V.
  Open: Apr–Oct, daily 11:30am–8:30pm. Mar and Nov, lunch daily 11:30am–3pm.

Bearskin Neck, the center of Rockport's tourist industry, has numerous restaurants, including the Hannah Jumper. Its sign bears a huge axe—in gold leaf, no less—such as Hannah used to break casks during her noble endeavors to rid the town of Demon Rum. Though you can't get a glass of wine here, you can bring your own, and get a table with one of the best views of the harbor, especially good at sunset. Come for a lunch of sandwiches, chowder, salads, or seafood plates, or return in the evening for dinner. The chef offers baby gulf shrimp, fried for just a few seconds to retain the delicate flavor; and chicken Kiev, the breast wrapped around a luscious stuffing of butter and flavorings. Of course, there's boiled lobster. You can sit in the narrow dining room with its simulated rough-board walls, brick floor, and hanging ferns, or out on the shaded Harbor Deck, with the best harbor view of all.

LOBSTER POOL, 329 Granite St. (Rte. 127), in Folly Cove. Tel. 546-7808.
  Cuisine: SEAFOOD. **Reservations:** Not accepted. **Directions:** Follow Rte. 127 toward Lanesville and Annisquam; about 1 mile past Old Farm Inn, look for Lobster Pool on right, overlooking the sea.
$ Prices: Main courses $8.50–$15 (lobsters priced according to size). No credit cards.
  Open: May, Wed–Sun 11:30am–8:30pm. June, Tues–Sun 11:30am–8:30pm. July–Aug, daily 11:30am–8:30pm. Sept, call for hours.

If you've never dined at an authentic, informal seaside fried-clam house, make the short drive to Folly Cove. The Lobster Pool, known locally as Tommy's, serves food that's simple and good, in spare but cheery surroundings. Besides the dining rooms, there are outdoor picnic tables overlooking the sea. Order a lobster roll of solid lobster meat (Tommy's doesn't use celery as filler). Portions are gargantuan, and it's not unusual for two semihungry people to share, say, one bowl of chowder and one clam plate, which comes with french fries and coleslaw. You can get your food to take out, if you like.

MY PLACE-BY-THE-SEA, 68 Bearskin Neck. Tel. 546-9667.
  Cuisine: SEAFOOD. **Reservations:** Recommended for dinner. **Directions:** Walk out to top of Bearskin Neck; it's on left.

$ Prices: Appetizers $2.75–$7.50; main courses $2–$6 at lunch, $11–$18 at dinner; lunch $9–$13; dinner $20–$30. AE, CB, DC, MC, V.
Open: May–Columbus Day, daily noon–9:30pm.

At the very end of Bearskin Neck is My Place-by-the-Sea, a small cedar-shingled building with the best outdoor ocean-front dining on Cape Ann. The moderately priced lunch menu features soups, salads, omelets, and sandwiches. Dinner—which is available throughout the day—features lots of fresh fish and seafood, including lobster prepared about half a dozen ways. My Place-by-the-Sea also boasts a wide selection of nonalcoholic drinks, which make perfect accompaniments for watching the sun set. Setups are also available at a small charge if you prefer to bring your own spirits.

PORTSIDE CHOWDER HOUSE, Bearskin Neck. Tel. 546-7045.
Cuisine: SEAFOOD. **Reservations:** Not accepted. **Directions:** Walk out Bearskin Neck, and look to the left.
$ Prices: Chowders and appetizers $2–$7; sandwiches $2.50–$7.50; platters $6.50–$9.60. No credit cards.
Open: Late June–Labor Day, daily 11am–8pm. Labor Day–late June, daily 11am–3pm. **Closed:** Thanksgiving and Christmas.

Just want a bowl of chowder? The place to go is the Portside Chowder House, to the left off the main street on the Neck, a tiny hole-in-the-wall of a place with low ceilings, wood beams, and a few tables in the back with partial views of the water. Chowder made from various seafoods is the specialty here, and it comes by the cup, the bowl, or the quart. Salads, sandwiches, and platters of fish, lobster, and crab are served, and there are also a few beefy items from the grill.

EASY EXCURSIONS

HALIBUT POINT

Head north out of Rockport on Route 127, toward Lanesville and Annisquam, and after a few miles you'll see a sign pointing off to the right (north) to **Halibut Point State Park,** just before the Old Farm Inn. Drive to the parking lot, leave your car, and then follow the path through the forest for 10 minutes, and you will come to an old granite quarry, now flooded with water. The park interpretive center, still being furnished at this writing, is in the building that dominates the quarry. Exhibits demonstrate the flora and fauna of the reservation, and how granite quarrying contributed to the culture and economy of the region. A weird World War II concrete observation tower has been grafted onto the building, a typical clapboard Cape Ann house. From the tower during the war, sharp eyes kept a lookout against enemy submarines. The entrance fee is $5.

Continue along the path to reach the Observation Point atop a cliff of granite quarry rubble. Far beneath, the Atlantic's waves roll in and crash on the smoothed granite bedrock below. You can make your way down to the water. Some people go swimming here, although it's not an ideal spot: The water is always chilly, the rocks difficult and slippery, the waves sometimes perilous. For additional information, write to Halibut Point Association, P.O. Box 710, Rockport, MA 01966.

CASTLE HILL

Not far from Rockport is Castle Hill, the fabulous hilltop mansion built by Richard Teller Crane, Jr., who made a fortune in plumbing and bathroom fixtures early in this century. The house is a Stuart-style mansion designed by David Adler. It is open four Sundays during the year and Tuesdays during July and August for tours. The Castle Hill Summer Festival begins in June with a Father's Day event and continues through August; it includes an Independence Day Celebration, Jazz Ball, Reggae, and

Dressage. Contact Castle Hill for information at P.O. Box 563, Ipswich, MA 01938 (tel. 508/356-4351).

9. PLYMOUTH

39 miles (63km) SE of Boston, 38 miles (61km) NE of New Bedford, 37 miles (60km) NE of Fall River, 35 miles (56.5km) NW of Hyannis

GETTING THERE By Bus   Plymouth is served from Boston and Hyannis by buses of the Plymouth & Brockton (P&B) Street Railway Company (tel. 508/746-0378). About two dozen buses a day run in each direction between Plymouth and downtown Boston and/or Logan airport; about the same number of buses run from Hyannis to Plymouth and back. In Boston, buses leave from Park Square at Broadway or from the Peter Pan (Trailways) bus terminal, 555 Atlantic Avenue (tel. 617/482-5510), across the street from South Station.

Buses serving Logan airport pick up and take on passengers at all airline terminals.

In Plymouth, the P&B Terminal is in the Industrial Park, Route 3, Exit 7, North Plymouth (tel. 508/746-0378), but buses stop downtown in Plymouth as well. The express trip between Boston and Plymouth takes about an hour; the local route, stopping in downtown Plymouth and at Plimoth Plantation, takes 1¼ hours. From Plymouth to Hyannis is a 45-minute ride. In Hyannis, the P&B terminal (tel. 508/775-5524) is at 17 Elm Street.

By Car   From Boston, follow the Southeast Expressway and Route 3 south. You might want to stop at the **Regional Information Complex for Visitors** on Route 3 at Exit 5.

ESSENTIALS   The **area code** is 508. The town of Plymouth maintains an **information booth** (tel. 508/746-4779) and accommodations service in the Village Landing Marketplace. From the highway (Rte. 3), take exit 6, turn east onto Route 44. After crossing Route 3A at the traffic lights, turn left for the Plymouth 5 Bank. Look for the booth on your right in the marketplace. The guides will help you find a room if you don't have a reservation or if you'd like to see what's available. They also have a current list of events and attractions for the area.

There is a **Regional Information Complex for Visitors** on Route 3 at Exit 5. For information, call 508/746-1150.

Plymouth is famous because of a small and rather unimpressive boulder. But when visitors come to Plymouth Rock, they are coming not because the rock is much to look at—its only notable features are a crack and the date "1620" engraved on it—but because Plymouth, as the landing place of the Pilgrims, is a symbol for the ideal of religious freedom and the quest for a better life.

Besides the rock, which will take you about 5 minutes to inspect, Plymouth has lots of other sights and exhibits dealing with Pilgrim and Early American history: a collection of historic houses, a full-size replica of the Pilgrim ship *Mayflower*, an authentic re-creation of an entire Pilgrim village complete with living inhabitants, a wax museum, and still more. Many people make Plymouth a day-trip, stopping here on their way from Boston to the Cape or vice versa, but should you want to stay overnight in the Pilgrims' town, there are several attractive lodging possibilities.

WHAT TO SEE & DO

Sightseeing in Plymouth means Pilgrim lore: what the early settlers looked like, how they dressed, how they lived from day to day. The many exhibits here make it possible to get a very clear picture of what arrival in America meant to these pioneers.

At 5pm on Fridays in August, a group of Plymouth citizens dressed as Pilgrims honor the memory of their ancestors by re-creating the **pilgrims' procession to church.** The number of persons, their sexes, and ages have been matched to the small group of Pilgrims who survived the first winter in the New World. When you see the procession, you may be amazed at the small size of the group that started it all.

After taking in the attractions and exhibits about the Pilgrims' life in Plymouth, visit **Cranberry World Visitors Center,** 225 Water St. (tel. 747-2350), and learn about these tart, juicy berries, the bogs where they are grown, and the products made from them. The Pilgrims found cranberries in abundance when they arrived, and cranberry harvesting and processing is still a big industry in and around Plymouth, on Cape Cod, and on the islands. Admission is free, and you can sample free cranberry refreshments. The center is open May to November daily from 9:30am to 5pm, until 9pm on weekdays in July and August.

PLYMOUTH ROCK, Plymouth Rock State Park. Tel. 866-2580.

From anywhere in Plymouth, road signs and residents will guide you to the rock on the waterfront.

Plymouth Rock is an American icon, a symbol of intrepid discovery, liberty, and freedom of conscience. The stone itself is granite, probably from a formation known as the Dedham granite, formed 680 million years ago (give or take a few million years). The rock was picked up from this formation at a spot south or west of Boston and transported by a glacier to Plymouth about 20,000 years ago. The spot it left was somewhere in the terrane (specific geologic area) called Atlantica, which surrounds Boston.

Geologists who study plate tectonics say that many millions of years ago there was a huge continent called Pangaea, which split into eastern and western parts, the eastern becoming Europe and Africa, the western part North America. The Dedham granite is found mostly in Africa, so it is surprising to consider that Plymouth Rock came over from another continent just as the Pilgrims did, only millions of years before.

When the Pilgrims arrived, they may or may not have stepped on the rock. If they did, they never mention it in their letters and written accounts. In any case, the rock was much larger in 1620, but erosion by sea and wind has reduced it to a mere fraction of its former self. Nature did havoc to the rock, but humans did worse, chipping off small pieces for patriotic souvenirs, taking large pieces to put on display to build patriotic fervor, even using it as part of a wharf at one time. In 1774, 20 yoke of oxen came to move the rock, and it split in the process. Half of the rock was put on display at Pilgrim Hall from 1834 to 1867, but was then brought back here. In November 1989, the rock was repaired and strengthened to withstand the blows from the sea and the laserlike gazes of a million affectionate visitors.

Today the rock is sheltered by a monumental enclosure, designed by McKim, Mead & White and built in 1921, which stands in Plymouth Rock State Park.

Just as the rock marks the beginning of the Pilgrims' adventure in America, so it can serve as the beginning point for your tour of Plymouth. After your look at it, head for the attractions nearby.

Right next to Plymouth Rock is a replica of the sort of house the Pilgrims first built in the New World. Though there's not much to the interior, you can best imagine what it'd be like to live in so tiny a house by stepping inside. Remember that in the 1600s people were not as tall as average Americans today.

PLIMOTH PLANTATION. Tel. 746-1622.

Mention Saddam Hussein or even Michael Jackson to one of the roof-thatchers at Plimoth Plantation's Pilgrim Village and you will get a totally baffled look. This is the year 1627.

In this Pilgrim village, all the buildings were built—and are always being improved upon by rebuilding—as they were in the 17th century. Houses have thatched roofs, wooden-frame chimneys, hand-hewn wood beams, and dirt floors. Well versed in the history and culture of the time, role-players talk about life as it was after arriving on the *Mayflower.*

Adjacent to the Pilgrim Village is a Wampanoag Indian Settlement complete with houses made from bent saplings. And moored in nearby Plymouth Bay, is the *Mayflower II*, a meticulously detailed, full-sized replica of the *Mayflower*, with sails made of flax and sewn by hand (see below for complete details on the latter).

In 1992, a brand new exhibit center called the Crafts Center opened at Plimoth Plantation. Also a living exhibit, it explores the manufacture of goods as well as international trade relationships during the early 17th century. Visitors can watch artisans weave woolen cloth, create redware pottery, perform basketry, and demonstrate the crafting of fine furniture as it was done in England for export. Reproductions are for sale in the gift shop.

Admission (including Pilgrim Village, Wampanoag Indian Homesite, Carriage House Crafts Center, and *Mayflower II*): $20 adults, $12 children aged 5–12, free for children under 5. (Tickets for *Mayflower II* only, $6 adults, $4 children.)

Open: Apr–Nov, daily 9am–5pm. Extended hours July–Aug.

MAYFLOWER II. Tel. 746-1622.

The suffering that the Pilgrims underwent to get to America will be brought home more forcefully when you tour *Mayflower II*, a reproduction of the original ship built in England in 1955, which sailed across the Atlantic to Plymouth in 1957. How, you are sure to ask yourself, was it possible for 102 passengers—even small ones—to fit themselves and all their baggage for setting up a new town into the tiny rooms and onto the tiny decks of this little ship? And how could they stay on it for 2 months? The only answer that comes to mind is "by courage and dedication," and it's for those virtues that the Pilgrims are admired and remembered. Guides on *Mayflower II* will tell you about the boat's workings and will answer questions; display panels on the dock and an excellent leaflet given to you as you enter will explain other details of nautical lore. *Mayflower II* is only a few steps from Plymouth Rock. A museum shop, restaurant, and picnic area are here as well.

Admission: $6 adults, $4 children 5–12, free for children under 5. This includes free parking, a visit to the ship, an audiovisual show at the theater, and indoor exhibits on early Pilgrim life. A special combination ticket ($20 adults, $12 children 5–12, free for children under 5) admits you to *Mayflower II* and to Plimoth Plantation.

Open: Apr–Nov, daily 9am–5pm. Extended hours July–Aug.

PILGRIM HALL MUSEUM, 75 Court St. Tel. 746-1620.

Seeing how the Pilgrims lived in the earliest period of America's colonization is what Plymouth is all about. You can see exhibits like *Mayflower II* and the early huts to give you an idea, or you can see the actual Pilgrim furniture and huge oil paintings featured in Pilgrim Hall, at the corner of Chilton and Court Streets (Court, Main, and Sandwich are all names for different sections of the same street).

The oldest continually operating public museum in the United States, Pilgrim Hall was built in 1824 to house artifacts the Pilgrims used, a library for research into Plymouth's early history, and galleries for the monumental paintings depicting important events in Pilgrim history. In the main hall the visitor may see 19th-century paintings interpreting the Pilgrim story, the remains of the 17th-century ship *Sparrowhawk*, Wampanoag artifacts, and books and maps of the Pilgrims. The Lower Hall houses domestic possessions, tools, furniture, and decorative pieces of Plymouth Colony. Highlights of the collection include the wicker cradle of the first English child born in New England, Captain Myles Standish's sword, and chairs that belonged to Elder William Brewster and Governor William Bradford.

Admission: $5 adults, $4.50 seniors and students, $2 children aged 6–15.

Open: Daily 9:30am–4:30pm.

PLYMOUTH NATIONAL WAX MUSEUM, 16 Carver St. Tel. 746-6468.

Even more lifelike than Pilgrim Hall's paintings are the tableaux at the Plymouth National Wax Museum, at the top of the hill across the street from Plymouth Rock. The hill is Cole's Hill, where the first Pilgrim cemetery was established and where the first victims of the frigid New England winter were laid to rest. The museum's scenes trace the history of the Pilgrims from persecution in England through the move to Holland to the trip across the Atlantic and the foundation of the settlement at Plymouth. Sound tracks add to the vividness of the scenes.

Admission: $5 adults, $2 children aged 5–12, $4 seniors.
Open: Mar–Nov, daily 9am–5pm.

THE FOREFATHERS' MONUMENT. Tel. 746-1790.

The National Monument to the Forefathers is the sort of grand statue-and-pedestal one would expect to see on a central boulevard in a world capital. Instead it stands in a small park on Allerton Street, off Samoset (U.S. 44) near the junction with Route 3A—follow the signs on the road. First proposed in 1820, the monument was designed by Hammet Billings of Boston in 1855 and dedicated in 1889.

The composition is figurative, with a great granite statue of Faith surrounded by smaller figures of Liberty (with Peace and Tyranny Overthrown), Law (with Justice and Mercy), Education (with Wisdom and Youth), and Morality holding the Decalogue (Ten Commandments) in the left hand and the scroll of Revelation in the right. Between the statues, bas-reliefs remember the most significant events of Pilgrim history: the departure from Delft Harbor in the Netherlands, the signing of the Mayflower Compact at Provincetown, the landing at Plymouth Rock, and the treaty with Massasoit, sachem of the Wampanoags.

The monument, 81 feet high, is impressive, and it's interesting to speculate about the times and people's thoughts through its history: when it was planned (only 44 years after the signing of the Declaration of Independence), when the cornerstone was laid (1859, on the eve of the Civil War), and when it was dedicated (a year after invention of the Kodak box camera and the electric motor). The view from the little park, by the way, is very fine; a small cast-iron outline map near the base of the monument traces the outline of Cape Cod, which you can see on a clear day.

RICHARD SPARROW HOUSE, 42 Summer St. Tel. 747-1240.

Built in 1640, this is the oldest house in Plymouth; in 1990 it celebrated its 350th anniversary. The house overlooks Town Brook Park, and there is a craft gallery with pottery made on the premises; the gallery stays open through Christmas, so you can pick up some Plymouth crafts as holiday presents.

Admission: Donation requested.
Open: Thurs–Tues 10am–5pm.

HOWLAND HOUSE, 33 Sandwich St. Tel. 746-9590.

Howland House dates from 1667 and is the only Plymouth house still standing that was known to have been occupied by Pilgrims. The parents of Jabez Howland, builder of the house, came over on the *Mayflower,* and it's presumed that they spent their last years with their son.

Admission: $2.50 adults, 50¢ children aged 6–16, free for children under 6.
Open: Late May–Oct, daily 10am–5pm.

PLYMOUTH ANTIQUARIUM SOCIETY. Tel. 746-0012.

At three historical homes, interpreters trace three centuries of Plymouth life. These include **Harlow Old Fort House,** 119 Sandwich St., which was built in 1677 and offers a hands-on look at life for Plymouth's second generation of settlers; **Spooner House,** 27 North St., which was built in 1747 and occupied by the Spooner family of Plymouth for over 200 years (there's a wealth of original furnishings and heirlooms); and **Hedge/Antiquarium House,** 126 Water St., a handsome Federal building that was built by the prosperous ship-owning Hedge family in 1809 and furnished with objects from around the world.

Admission: $2.50 adults, 50¢ children under 16, free for children under 6.
Open: June, Sat–Sun 11am–5pm. July–early Sept, Tues–Sun 11am–5pm. Early Sept–early Oct, Wed–Thurs and Sat 11am–5pm.

MAYFLOWER SOCIETY MUSEUM, 4 Winslow St. Tel. 746-2590.

The Mayflower Society Museum was once the elegant home of Edward Winslow. Part of the house was built in 1754, and the other part in 1898. Besides the furnishings, a primary attraction is a daring, flying staircase which looks as though it really should fall down, but doesn't. It's double the size it was in 1754. The formal gardens are nice as well.

Admission: $2.50 adults, 25¢ children.

Open: July–early Sept, daily 10am–5pm. June and early Sept to mid-Oct, Fri–Sun 10am–5pm. Also open two weekends prior to Thanksgiving, Thanksgiving Day, and the Fri and Sat that follows it.

WHERE TO STAY

MOTELS

Right downtown are two motels: the Governor Bradford Motor Inn and the John Carver Inn. Both are about the same distance—2 blocks—from Plymouth Rock.

BLUE ANCHOR MOTEL, 7 Lincoln St., Plymouth, MA 02360. Tel. 508/ 746-9551. 4 units (all with bath). A/C TV **Directions:** From center of town, go south on Sandwich St. from post office. Third street on left is Lincoln.

$ Rates (including morning coffee): $49–$60 single or double. MC, V. **Parking:** Free, on premises.

The tiny Blue Anchor Motel has only four units; thus there's a good chance it'll be full in busy periods, but it's worth considering because the motel is on a quiet street next to Plymouth's town hall and only a short walk from the center of town. It's very much a ma-and-pa place, informal and friendly, with comfy rooms. The rates depend on the unit and the number in your party.

COLD SPRING MOTEL, 188 Court St. (Rte. 3A), Plymouth, MA 02360. Tel. 508/746-2222. 31 units (all with bath). A/C TV TEL **Directions:** From the north, take Rte. 3 south to Exit 9, turn right on Rte. 3A. The motel is 3 miles south on right.

$ Rates: $56–$67 single; $56–$72 double. AE, DISC, MC, V. **Parking:** Free, on premises. **Closed:** Winter (exact dates vary from year to year).

One of the better bargains is to be found at the Cold Spring Motel. Although a bit out of the center of town—it's about ½ mile to the Rock—the surroundings of grass lawns and large trees make up for the small distance. Some 31 rooms and cottages, many paneled in pine, are for rent. All have electric heat and parking at the door. A picnic area is provided for guests' use. The motel has no restaurant, but there's one almost across the street in the small shopping plaza.

PILGRIM SANDS MOTEL, 150 Warren Ave. (Rte. 3A), Plymouth, MA 02360. Tel. 508/747-0900. 64 rms (all with bath). A/C TV TEL

$ Rates: Mid-June to Sept, $88–$119 double. Off-season, $53–$90 double. AE, DC, DISC, MC, V. **Parking:** Free, on premises.

Down near Plimoth Plantation, 2½ miles south of the center of Plymouth, is the Pilgrim Sands Motel. The bonus here, besides proximity to the plantation, is the private beach, which you'd normally enjoy for $3 weekdays, $5 weekends; it's free for motel guests. There are also two pools. All rooms have two double or queen-size beds, and some have refrigerators; the higher rates are for oceanfront rooms. After a day's walking in the sun, it's great to take a swim and then sit looking out to sea, before going to bed to be lulled asleep by the sound of the surf. The Sands is open year round.

GUESTHOUSES

You can find a room in a private home in Plymouth, "America's Home Town." Prices will be about $44 to $55 single, $66 to $137 double (including tax). Breakfast is included, of course. **Be Our Guest,** P.O. Box 1333, Plymouth, MA 02362 (tel. 617/837-9867), will find you a room in or near Plymouth, Boston, and Cape Cod.

HALL'S BED & BREAKFAST, 3 Sagamore St., Plymouth, MA 02360. Tel. 508/746-2835. 2 rms (neither with bath).
$ Rates (including breakfast): $60 single or double. DISC, MC, V. **Parking:** Free.
Call and see if there's a room at Hall's Bed & Breakfast, then head south along the waterfront from Plymouth Rock and take a left onto Route 3A south. Turn right on North Green Street, continue on Jefferson to Sagamore, and turn right. You'll see the Halls' tidy white clapboard house perched on the hillside at no. 3. This little B & B is within walking distance of Plymouth Center and the Historic Waterfront and is 1 mile away from Plimoth Plantation and the beach.

WHERE TO DINE

Plymouth has a number of snack places, sandwich shops, and restaurants, and although it's not noted for a wide range of culinary styles, the town will be able to fill your needs.

LOBSTER HUT, on the Town Wharf. Tel. 746-2270.
Cuisine: SEAFOOD. **Reservations:** Not accepted.
$ Prices: Lunch $4.50–$6.75; main courses $5.50–$11.50. No credit cards.
Open: Summer, daily 11am–9pm. Winter, daily 11am–7pm.
A favorite self-service place on the waterfront is the Lobster Hut, which serves up steaming bowls of clam chowder, lobster bisque, fried clams, fish-and-chips, and lobsters, plus wine and beer (with your meal only). Order a huge portion of fish-and-chips, or fried clams, and with a soft drink you'll pay less than $10. Dine inside, or at one of the picnic tables overlooking the bay. It's north of Plymouth Rock.

STATION ONE, 51 Main St. Tel. 746-6001.
Cuisine: AMERICAN/CONTINENTAL. **Reservations:** Recommended.
$ Prices: Appetizers $2–$4; main courses $7–$15; lunch $5–$18; dinner $15–$25. MC, V.
Open: Daily 11:30am–12:30am.
Among Plymouth's most popular restaurants is Station One, up the hill from the waterfront in the center of town. Station One started life as the town's Central Fire House in 1904, but has been utterly transformed into an elegant space paneled with mahogany and glistening with brass and crystal. Have lunch or dinner either inside or on the patio out front. The menu is exhaustive, with something for any mood or taste, from lobster bisque to ziti with chicken and broccoli. Liquor is served.

10. NEW BEDFORD

57 miles (92km) S of Boston, 32 miles (51.5km) SE of Providence, 38 miles (61km) SW of Plymouth, 15 miles (24km) E of Fall River

GETTING THERE By Bus American Eagle (tel. 508/990-0000), operates frequent buses daily between New Bedford and Boston's Peter Pan Bus Terminal, 555 Atlantic Ave., across from South Station.

By Car New Bedford is 1 mile south of I-195, on U.S. Route 6. From Boston, take Mass. Route 128 to Mass. Route 24 south, then Mass. Route 140. From Plymouth, take Mass. Route 3 south to U.S. 6 south and west, but pick up I-495 and I-195 when possible to save time.

DEPARTING The Ferry to Martha's Vineyard MV *Schamonchi,* operated by **Cape Island Express Lines, Inc.,** P.O. Box 4095, New Bedford, MA 02741 (tel. 508/997-1688), carries passengers (no cars) from New Bedford to the town of Vineyard Haven on the island of Martha's Vineyard four times daily in summer for $8.50 one-way, $15 round-trip for adults; for kids under 12, $4.50 one-way, $7.50 round-trip. Call for up-to-date schedules and information (tel. 508/997-1688).

ESSENTIALS The **area code** is 508. Right in the middle of the restoration area is the **New Bedford Visitors Center,** 47 North 2nd St., New Bedford, MA 02740 (tel. 508/991-6200). Here you can pick up brochures, maps, and other information on the area. There are also hour-long guided walking tours of the historic area ($1 per person) daily in the summer (tours at 9:30am, 11:30am, and 3pm Monday to Saturday; at noon on Sunday). The office is open from 10am to 4pm Monday through Saturday and from noon to 3pm on Sunday.

Due south of Boston on Buzzards Bay is New Bedford, one of the region's best-known towns during the whaling era. The whaling museum and the ferry to Martha's Vineyard are the big attractions in New Bedford today.

New Bedford, like Fall River, owed part of its living to textiles, but its fame rests on its history as a whaling port. Herman Melville set his American classic, *Moby-Dick,* in New Bedford as the logical spot to begin a whaling epic, and so it was. During the heyday of whale-oil lamps, New Bedford had about 400 ships out scouting the seas for the monster denizens. A ship might be at sea for several years, and when it returned to port it could have thousands of barrels of whale oil in its hold. The story of what whaling was all about—how the ships were staffed and equipped, how the search was carried out, how the men pursued and killed the whale, and then butchered and rendered it to get the oil—is all told in New Bedford's famous **Whaling Museum** on Johnny Cake Hill.

New Bedford's historic waterfront downtown section has undergone extensive renovation and restoration. The centerpiece of the restoration is Melville Mall, a pedestrian shopping street complete with trees, benches, and music in the air. East of the mall, going down to the water's edge along cobbled streets, the Custom House and many merchants' buildings are being restored. The center of the city is taking on an appearance much like it had during its 19th-century heyday.

WHAT TO SEE & DO

WHALING MUSEUM, 18 Johnny Cake Hill. Tel. 997-0046.

⭐ In the heart of the Historic Waterfront District, the New Bedford Whaling Museum is a complex of seven buildings which form the block between William and Union streets. The museum is dedicated to the history of New Bedford, with particular emphasis on the story of whaling in the age of sail.

The first exhibit to confront you is the largest ship model in the world: a replica of the bark *Lagoda* made to exactly one-half the ship's original size. Rigging, tryworks, whaleboats, and other equipment are all in place, and you can walk about the model at will. On the wall of the *Lagoda* room is a 100-foot-long mural showing sperm whales. The family who owned and operated the *Lagoda* donated the model, and the building to house it, to the museum. Around the walls of the museum are old photographs and drawings explaining the whaling industry, and many other rooms in the museum hold collections of other whaling lore: cooperage and chandlery; records of the countinghouse, brokerage, banking, and insurance; and articles of glass, china, and pewter manufactured in the New Bedford area, or owned by leading citizens.

Perhaps the most beautiful exhibit besides the *Lagoda* is the scrimshaw, the delicate, intricate articles of carved whalebone and tooth which the whalesmen made to while away the long hours at sea. The artistry displayed is almost breathtaking, and the ingenuity very revealing of quick and sensitive minds. It wouldn't be far wrong to say that without understanding whaling, one couldn't understand 19th-century New England; and the place to find out about whaling is certainly New Bedford.

Admission: $3.50 adults, $3 seniors, $2.50 children aged 6–14, free for children under 6.

Open: Mon–Sat 9am–5pm, Sun 1–5pm.

SEAMEN'S BETHEL, Johnny Cake Hill. Tel. 992-3295.

Across the street from the Whaling Museum, the Seamen's Bethel is a chapel (still functioning) constructed in 1832 "for the moral improvement of sailors," and immortalized in *Moby-Dick*. And several blocks away, at Pleasant and William, the **Public Library** has displays of whaling books and pamphlets.

Admission: Donations requested.

Open: May–Columbus Day, Mon–Sat 10am–4pm, Sun noon–4pm.

NEW BEDFORD FIRE MUSEUM, Bedford St. at 6th St. Tel. 992-2162.

Anyone interested in the history of firefighting in America will want to take a look at the New Bedford Fire Museum. The museum's beginnings date back to 1890, and it is situated appropriately next to New Bedford's Fire Station No. 4, a building that dates from 1867 and is still in active use. Come any day in summer to see the restored antique fire trucks and other firefighting equipment, displays of old uniforms, working models of pumps and fire poles, and other memorabilia.

Admission: $2 adults, $1 children aged 6–16, free for children under 6.

Open: Summer daily 9am–3:30pm.

ROTCH-JONES-DUFF HOUSE AND GARDEN, 396 County St. Tel. 508/ 997-1401.

A beautiful example of Greek Revival architecture as practiced by New Bedford's wealthy whaling merchants, the Rotch-Jones-Duff House was designed in 1834 by Richard Upjohn, founder of the American Institute of Architects. The period gardens include a wildflower walk.

Admission: $4 adults, $2 children.

Open: Tues–Fri 10am–4pm; also June–Aug Sat 10am–4pm, Sun 1–4pm.

WHERE TO STAY

DURANT SAIL LOFT INN, 1 Merrill's Wharf, New Bedford, MA 02740. Tel. 508/999-2700, or toll free 800/752-9649. 16 rms (all with bath). A/C TV TEL **Directions:** Go south on Union St., cross expressway, and turn right just before gates of New Bedford State Pier (don't enter pier area). The inn is a short distance along this road, on left.

$ Rates (including breakfast): $85–$92 twin or double. Extra person $7. AE, DC, DISC, MC, V. **Parking:** Free, on premises.

The Durant Sail Loft Inn is located right in the waterfront district, which is half commercial and half industrial. The inn is in a restored granite countinghouse, now refurbished with simple rooms, and has its own Portuguese restaurant, called Lisboa Antiga.

---

11. FALL RIVER

51 miles (82km) S of Boston; 17 miles (27.5km) SE of Providence, R.I.; 15 miles (24km) W of New Bedford; 24 miles (39km) N of Newport, R.I.

GETTING THERE   By Bus   Bonanza Bus Lines (tel. 617/423-5810 in Boston) operates frequent daily buses between Boston's Greyhound Terminal and Fall River, and runs buses between Fall River and other points as well.

By Car   Fall River is easy to reach, as it stands at the confluence of several major highways, including I-195, Mass. Route 24, and U.S. 6.

ESSENTIALS   The **area code** is 508. For information contact the **Bristol**

County Convention and Visitors Bureau, 70 N. Second St. (P.O. Box 976), New Bedford, MA 02741 (tel. 508/997-1250 or toll free 800/288-6263). There is also an information center in **Heritage State Park** at Battleship Cove (tel. 508/675-5759) where you can pick up maps and brochures. The office is open Monday through Saturday, 9am to 5pm and noon to 8pm on Sunday.

In the mid-19th century, Fall River was a boom textile town. Because of its natural harbor, ample waterpower, and a moist climate ideal for working thread, it became a world textile-weaving center. Huge mills made from blocks of the local granite were built everywhere, making an awesome scene of industry and wealth. But in the 20th century, the textile business began moving to the southern states, and Fall River's industry foundered.

Prosperity has returned to Fall River, and now many of the impressive granite mills produce finished apparel; others turn out rubber products, foods, and paper. The town's Government Center, built on the airspace over I-195, is a symbol of Fall River's resurgence and adds its impressive appearance to that of the great mills. Today most visitors come to Fall River to shop in the many factory outlet stores, and to visit the battleship and submarine docked at Battleship Cove.

Fall River's other claim to fame is the celebrated Lizzie Borden murder trial of 1892, in which Lizzie, a young Fall River girl, was tried for chopping up her parents with an axe. It's good to remember that the poor girl was acquitted. The guilty party was never found.

WHAT TO SEE & DO
SIGHTS

BATTLESHIP COVE. Tel. 678-1100.

Most people pass through Fall River on their way from Providence to Cape Cod or from Boston to Newport, and when they do, the sight they stop to see is Battleship Cove, permanent berth of a number of impressive craft. The USS *Joseph P. Kennedy, Jr.,* a World War II destroyer, is here, as are wooden PT boats and the submarine USS *Lionfish.* But the star of the exhibit is the mighty USS *Massachusetts,* the battleship berthed here as a memorial to Massachusetts men and women who were killed in World War II. You can tour both above and below decks on all the ships and have a meal or a snack in the wardroom.

Admission: $8 adults, $4 children aged 6–14.
Open: May–Oct, daily 9am–5pm. Nov–Apr, daily 9am–5pm.

MARINE MUSEUM AT FALL RIVER, 70 Water St. Tel. 674-3533.

The Marine Museum at Fall River, past the battleship and the State Pier, on the left, has a number of fascinating shipping exhibits, including lots of *Titanic* lore. Certainly the most popular is the 1-ton, 28-foot-long scale model of the *Titanic,* created in 1952 for 20th Century–Fox's movie about the *Titanic* tragedy. Other beautiful ship's models and maritime artifacts detail the history of the Fall River Line, which ran luxury steamers between Fall River and New York from 1847 to 1937. Yet another exhibit follows the history of steam power at sea. Nautical buffs from around the world, many of them famous collectors, have donated exhibits to the museum.

Admission: $3 adults, $2 children aged 6–14, free for children under 6.
Open: Mon–Fri 9am–5pm, Sat–Sun 10am–5pm.

SHOPPING

Fall River is a mecca for those who love **factory-outlet shopping,** because the revival of apparel manufacture here has led to the opening of dozens of huge factory-outlet stores. Billboards on I-195 trumpet that it is the "largest factory-outlet center in New England!" Signs lead you off the highway to the "Heart of Fall River's Factory-Outlet District," with more than 70 outlet stores. If you follow the signs, will you really save money? Yes, a definitive yes!

What can you find here? When it comes to clothing, everything! Shoes, sweaters, raincoats, accessories, designer labels, coats, handbags, jewelry, children's clothing, cosmetics, luggage. Branch out a bit and you'll find kitchenware, gifts, furniture, braided rugs, curtains, crystal, candy and nuts, greeting cards and giftwrap, toys, towels, linens, baskets, brass—even wallpaper. This is definitely a town in which you can shop till you drop.

CAPE COD

Cape Cod is a world of its own. This 70-mile-long arm of sand curled into the Atlantic was formed by glacial action, and was given its name by an early (1602) visitor to the New World, Bartholomew Gosnold. The Pilgrims landed in the New World at Provincetown and drew up the Mayflower Compact before heading on to the mainland at what would become Plymouth.

Strictly speaking, Cape Cod is an island, separated from the rest of Massachusetts by the Cape Cod Canal, a deep waterway built from north to south across the base of the Cape in the early part of this century. Two graceful bridges span the canal—one at Bourne to the south (Route 28), one at Sagamore to the north (Route 6)—and both are very busy in the warm months. Just before crossing either bridge, look for the little information sheds established by the Cape Cod Chamber of Commerce, open from 9am to 7pm every day during the summer. Maps, booklets, motel brochures, and tabloid newspaper "current listings" are all yours for free. The chamber of commerce will also help you make room reservations.

SEEING CAPE COD

GETTING THERE Cape Cod was once a seafarers' domain, and although it's still possible to get there by boat, the rail, bus, air, and road routes make it easy to get there any way you choose.

By Plane **Business Express** (tel. 203/222-1000, or toll free 800/345-3400), a Delta Connection carrier, provides service to Hyannis and Nantucket from Bridgeport, Ct., Baltimore, Boston, New York, and Philadelphia; **Cape Air** (tel. toll free 800/352-0714) has service to Hyannis from Boston and Martha's Vineyard and also to Provincetown from Boston several times a day throughout the year; **Colgan Air** (tel. toll free 800/272-5488) has three flights a day between Newark, N.J., and Hyannis; **Island Airlines** (tel. 508/775-6606, or toll free 800/248-7779) flies between Nantucket and Hyannis several times a day; **Nantucket Airlines** (tel. 508/790-0300) has daily service between Nantucket and Hyannis; and **Northwest Airlink,** a regional airline associated with Northwest Airlines (tel. toll free 800/225-2525) flies between Boston and Hyannis three times a day throughout the year.

By Train **Amtrak** (tel. toll free 800/USA-RAIL) runs trains to the Cape during the summer months only. The trains operate Friday through Sunday between New York and Hyannis, stopping at major New England cities (Stamford, New Haven,

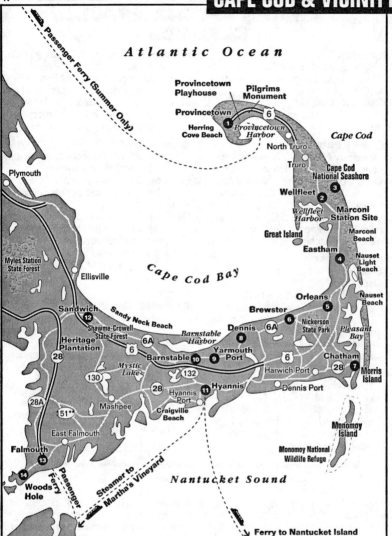

0   5 mi
        8 km

Atlantic Ocean

Passenger Ferry (Summer Only)

Provincetown
Playhouse

Pilgrims
Monument

Provincetown

Herring
Cove Beach

*Provincetown
Harbor*

6

1

Cape Cod

North Truro

Truro

Cape Cod
National Seashore

3

Wellfleet

2

Marconi
Station Site

*Wellfleet
Harbor*

Great Island

Marconi
Beach

Eastham

4

Nauset
Light
Beach

Plymouth

Myles Station
State Forest

Ellisville

Cape Cod Bay

Orleans

5

Nauset
Beach

Brewster

6

Sandwich

12

Sandy Neck Beach

Shawme-Crowell
State Forest

Dennis

8

6A

Nickerson
State Park

*Pleasant
Bay*

Heritage
Plantation

28

6

6A

*Barnstable
Harbor*

**Yarmouth
Port**

9

6

Chatham

28

7

Morris
Island

Harwich Port

Barnstable

10

130

*Mystic
Lake*

132

Dennis Port

28

Hyannis
Port

Hyannis

11

Craigville
Beach

Steamer to
Martha's Vineyard

28A

51**

Mashpee

East Falmouth

*Monomoy
Island*

Monomoy National
Wildlife Refuge

Falmouth

13

Nantucket Sound

14

Passenger
Ferry

**Woods
Hole**

Ferry to Nantucket Island

WHAT'S SPECIAL ABOUT CAPE COD

Museums
- ☐ Heritage Plantation of Sandwich, a 76-acre estate with outstanding collections of Americana.
- ☐ Sandwich Glass Museum, where the town's renowned glass industry lives on.

Nature Reserves
- ☐ Monomoy National Wildlife Refuge, south of Chatham, rich in bird life.
- ☐ Cape Cod Museum of Natural History in Brewster, with its own nature walks.
- ☐ Cape Cod National Seashore, with miles of hiking and bike trails, and excellent beaches.

Pretty Towns
- ☐ Sandwich, "the prettiest town on Cape Cod."
- ☐ Falmouth, with a picture-perfect New England Village Green.
- ☐ Chatham, with its graceful old trees and sturdy lighthouse.
- ☐ Provincetown, with whole neighborhoods of cozy inns.

Cool for Kids
- ☐ Cape Cod Aquarium in West Brewster, for a look at Cape Cod's denizens.
- ☐ New England Fire and History Museum in Brewster, with 35 highly polished fire engines.

- ☐ Railroad Museum in Chatham, with a wonderful wooden caboose.
- ☐ Schooner cruises out of Provincetown, for a real taste of life at sea.
- ☐ Whale-watch cruises from Provincetown, with their excellent record of whale sightings.

After Dark
- ☐ Provincetown Playhouse, an old-time favorite, active all summer.
- ☐ Cape Cod Melody Tent in Hyannis, featuring top-name popular vocalists in concert.
- ☐ Cape Playhouse in Dennis, with famous actors in timely productions.
- ☐ Falmouth Playhouse, with a playbill of musicals, June through October.
- ☐ Monomoy Theater in Chatham, with a stock company from Ohio University.

Historic Monuments
- ☐ Pilgrims Monument, Provincetown, near where the Pilgrims first stepped on American soil.
- ☐ French Cable Station Museum, Orleans, where the first transatlantic telephone cable came ashore.
- ☐ Marconi Station site, near South Wellfleet, where the great Italian physicist established a transatlantic wireless station in 1902.

Providence) and several Cape destinations along the way. The Friday afternoon *Cape Codder* leaves New York's Penn Station in the afternoon and arrives approximately six hours later in Hyannis. Connections to the *Cape Codder* are available on trains from Washington and Philadelphia. On Sunday afternoon, the *Cape Codder* leaves Hyannis, also meeting up with connecting trains to other destinations. The round-trip fare is $99 (one-way is $59). Reservations are required. The railroad has arranged with Plymouth & Brockton Street Railway Company for dedicated connecting bus service from Hyannis to Chatham, Dennisport, Eastham, Harwich, Orleans, South Yarmouth, Wellfleet, and Provincetown, which means that you can buy an Amtrak ticket in New York City for the trip all the way to the tip of the Cape. The service is funded in part by the Commonwealth of Massachusetts. Such special contracts are subject to governmental budgetary ups and downs, so call Amtrak to see if the service is still running when you want it. Other times of year, take Amtrak to Boston and connect with an Amtrak bus to Hyannis. The round-trip fare is $90.

By Bus   Bus service to the Cape from New York, Providence, and Boston is good, fast, and frequent.

From New York: Bonanza (Adirondack Trailways ticket counter in Port Authority terminal; tel. toll free 800/556-3815) runs buses via two routes, along the coast and via Waterbury and Hartford. In high summer there are three buses a day from New York all the way to Provincetown at the tip of the Cape, and a good number of other buses going as far as Hyannis, where you can transfer for other points.

From Providence/Newport: From Providence, catch the Bonanza bus (about six a day) to Hyannis, or to Provincetown (about four a day). The trip takes less than 2 hours to Hyannis. The Bonanza Bus Line Terminal is off exit 25 from I-95 North or South. For information, call toll free 800/556-3815.

From Boston: Plymouth & Brockton Street Railway Company has buses which leave from the Greyhound Terminal (tel. 617/423-5810) and the South Station (Amtrak) Terminal (tel. 617/482-3660). The trip to Hyannis takes 1½ hours.

By Car   Coming from New York or Providence, take I-195 to Mass. Route 25/28 South, and cross the Bourne Bridge if you're heading for Falmouth and Woods Hole; if you're going to Sandwich, Hyannis, or other Cape points, don't take the Bourne Bridge, but take U.S. 6 East just before the Bourne Bridge, and this will take you north and east to the Sagamore Bridge, where you cross the canal.

Coming from Boston, the Southeast Expressway (I-93) will take you right to Mass. Route 3, which goes straight to the Sagamore Bridge. If you're on your way to Falmouth and Woods Hole, stay on I-93 past the intersection with Route 3 and take Exit 66 for Route 24 South, then I-495 South to Mass. Route 28, before taking you right over the Bourne Bridge.

Keep in mind that as wonderful as the Cape may be, driving there during the summer months can be a bit trying at times. Do yourself a favor: Before setting out, study the map well. You'll find there are quite a few rotaries (traffic circles) on the Cape, where you will be forced to make direction decisions quickly. These rotaries, which work perfectly well when everyone knows which way they are going, can be dangerous for confused out-of-towners.

By Boat   Bay State Cruises (tel. 617/723-7800) operates the MV *Provincetown II* on a run from Boston to P-town every day from late June through Labor Day and on Saturday and Sunday between Memorial Day and Columbus Day. There's one daily sailing, which leaves Boston's Commonwealth Pier at 9:30am and arrives in P-town at about 12:30pm; it returns from P-town (at 3:30pm) to Boston (arriving about 6:30pm). A round-trip ticket for an adult costs $25, or $18 for seniors and kids under 12; the one-way fare is $15; for seniors and kids, $13.

GETTING AROUND THE CAPE   Route 6, the Mid-Cape Highway, is the fastest way to travel from the "Upper Cape" (the part you first come to by land) to the "Lower Cape" (the narrow portion north of Orleans to Provincetown). But Route 6 is not necessarily the prettiest way to go; if you have the time, travel one of the smaller, scenic roads instead.

Bus transportation on the Cape is provided by **Plymouth & Brockton Street Railway Company,** Elm & Centre Streets, Hyannis (tel. 508/775-5524). You can take a Plymouth & Brockton bus from Hyannis to Provincetown via Orleans, Eastham, and Wellfleet.

Transportation to the islands of Martha's Vineyard and Nantucket is covered in the sections on Woods Hole and Hyannis.

A Suggested Route   You will need several days to tour the Cape, a week to explore it thoroughly. The northern and western shores, facing Cape Cod Bay, are the more peaceful and bucolic ones. The southern shore has the more commercial towns; the eastern shore is mostly in the Cape Cod National Seashore.

On **Day 1,** drive leisurely along Mass. Route 6A through Sagamore, Sandwich, Barnstable, Yarmouth Port, Dennis, Brewster, and Orleans, staying the night in one of these towns. On **Day 2,** explore Cape Cod National Seashore, Wellfleet, and

Provincetown, returning to your first night's lodging for the night. (Off-season, you can safely plan a second-night stay in Provincetown, but call ahead for reservations.) **Day 3** can be spent along Route 28 west, enjoying Chatham and the towns on the way to Hyannis. On **Day 4,** make your way to Mashpee, Falmouth, and Woods Hole; or make a day-long excursion from Hyannis to Nantucket, or from Woods Hole to Martha's Vineyard.

BED & BREAKFAST INFORMATION Bed & Breakfast Cape Cod, P.O. Box 341, West Hyannisport, MA 02672 (tel. 508/775-2772), will find you a room on Cape Cod (and on Martha's Vineyard or Nantucket for that matter) in one of 80 historic inns and host homes for $39 to $66 single, $50 to $203 double, breakfast and tax included. Write in plenty of time, and you'll be sent a free catalog listing homes and inns that might interest you.

1. FALMOUTH

37 miles (60km) S of Plymouth, 37 miles (60km) SE of
New Bedford, 15 miles (24km) S of the Bourne Bridge,
23 miles (37km) SW of Hyannis, 50 miles (81km) SW of Provincetown

GETTING THERE See "Getting There" at the beginning of this chapter.

DEPARTING Ferry From Falmouth to Martha's Vineyard Falmouth's own *Island Queen,* Falmouth Heights Road (tel. 508/548-4800), operated by Island Commuter Corp., carries passengers and bicycles only (no cars) from Falmouth Harbor to Oak Bluffs on the island. The ferry does not operate year round, but sails twice a day in each direction during early June and mid-September (five times a day on weekends), and seven times a day in each direction from mid-June through the first week in September. Adults pay $9 round-trip ($5 one-way); children under 13 pay $4.50 round-trip. Bicycles are taken at a charge of $6 round-trip. The voyage takes about ½ hour, and is usually quite smooth and comfortable. A refreshment bar on board serves snacks, sandwiches, soft drinks, beer, and cocktails.

For car-ferries to the islands, you'll have to go to Woods Hole or Hyannis (see those sections for details).

ESSENTIALS The **area code** is 508. The **Falmouth Chamber of Commerce,** P.O. Box 582, Falmouth, MA 02541 (tel. 508/548-8500, or toll free 800/526-8532), operates an information office downtown off Main Street in the Lawrence Academy building. Look for a short street called Academy Lane. If the chamber can't answer your question, it's probably not about Falmouth.

Falmouth is a pretty town that has grown rapidly in recent years but has managed to preserve a lot of the charm of a rural New England community. A city park next to the library, a well-preserved village green, and magnificent tall trees along Main Street make the downtown section attractive, and manicured lawns and white clapboard houses dress up the side streets. The town has a few pleasant historical inns, several good beaches, and daily ships to Martha's Vineyard.

A few miles past Falmouth to the south is Woods Hole, home of world-famous Woods Hole Oceanographic Institute; car-ferries depart from Woods Hole for Martha's Vineyard several times daily in summer.

WHAT TO SEE & DO

Walks along Falmouth's beaches, through the older sections of town, and across the Village Green are a must. For a detailed map, or for other information, send for the

80-page brochure from the **Falmouth Chamber of Commerce,** P.O. Box 582, Falmouth, MA 02541 (tel. 508/548-8500, or toll free 800/526-8532).

A prime Falmouth activity is to **rent a bicycle** and to follow the Shining Sea Bicycle Path down to Woods Hole (see below). The **Bikeways Committee of Falmouth** publishes a pamphlet-map that shows bike routes and beaches and gives the addresses of shops that rent bicycles. Ask at the information office mentioned above, or call the chamber of commerce toll free at 800/526-8532. By biking to a beach, you avoid paying the several dollars for parking.

Besides bike trips down to Woods Hole, Falmouth's greatest outdoor attraction is its coastline. The **Town Beach** is down at the end of Shore Street (best to walk, as parking can be a problem). The water can be very chilly except in July and August, but otherwise the beach is fine, and it has a view of Martha's Vineyard in the distance.

The best **swimming and sunning** spot in the area is **Old Silver Beach,** several miles northwest of downtown Falmouth. If you have more energy than money, bicycling is the way to go, even though it's a distance, as the entrance fee at Old Silver is $10 per car for the day. If you drive and pay the fee, just consider that the money goes toward keeping the beach clean and safe.

A headland and several jetties set the beach off into sections; the town runs a clam bar, which sells sandwiches, fried clams, and soft drinks, and offers changing rooms. The crowd at Old Silver is spirited, young, and sun-hungry.

The town of Falmouth sponsors free **band concerts** down at Falmouth Marina on Thursday evening at 8pm during the months of July and August. Try to make it to at least one concert; it's a real old-time event. Bring your own chair.

Falmouth also has its own summer theater, the **Falmouth Playhouse** (tel. 563-5922), with a playbill of musicals that begin in June and go right through the end of September. Tickets for performances are $17 Sunday through Friday, $19 for the 5pm show and $20 for the 9pm performance on Saturday.

The Falmouth Historical Society has interesting displays pertaining to Falmouth's history in its lovely old mansion, the **Julia Wood House,** 55-65 Palmer Ave. (tel. 548-4857), located just off the Village Green. For the price of admission ($2 for adults, 50¢ for children under 12), you also get to see the adjacent Hallett Barn, with displays of early tools and farm implements, and the historical society's shop, as well as Conant House, next door, with more historical collections. The Katharine Lee Bates Room holds memorabilia of Falmouth's poet, who wrote the words to "America the Beautiful." The cordial staff at the historical society will be sure to point out that the white Congregational church on the green is equipped with a bell cast by Paul Revere. It's open mid-June to mid-September Monday to Friday 2 to 5pm.

WHERE TO STAY

Although Falmouth has dozens of motels, mostly expensive and somewhat sterile (though modern and comfortable), the best way to spend a week or two by the sea, at moderate cost, is to rent a room in a private home—or in one of the small inns or guesthouses. During off-season, when inquiring about room prices, be sure to ask about reductions for stays of a few days or more. A room costing $60 for one night may well cost $55 per night if you stay 2 or 3 days.

Lots of houses in **Falmouth Heights,** southeast of the center of Falmouth proper, are devoted to renting rooms for about $40 to $50 double, with a shared bathroom. If you request it, your room may have a view of the sea. You should also be aware that this is the most boisterous section of town.

We've also included descriptions of the best of the larger places.

DOWNTOWN

ELM ARCH INN, 26 Elm Arch Way, Falmouth, MA 02540. Tel. 508/548-0133. 24 rms (12 with bath).

$ Rates: Summer, $55 twin or double without bath, $65–$71 twin or double with bath. Off-season, rates are lower. No credit cards. **Parking:** Free.

The Elm Arch Inn, located off Main Street, was originally a private house, but it has been taking paying guests for over a century—more than 65 years under the present management. The location couldn't be better: right in the center of town, a few steps from the green, and yet back off Main Street in peace and quiet. The inn's rooms are furnished with colonial-style pieces, many handmade, and are just plain charming. Several have private baths; others have running water and share a bath. In Richardson House, the addition to the inn, there are private baths and air conditioning throughout. No meals are served, but the inn offers free coffee in the mornings, in season. Although you're a 15-minute walk from the beach here, the inn has its own small pool, bordered by a lush lawn and large trees, and a big screened patio for summer evenings.

MOSTLY HALL BED & BREAKFAST INN, 27 Main St., Falmouth, MA 02540. Tel. 508/548-3786, or toll free 800/682-0565. 6 rms (all with bath). A/C

$ Rates (including breakfast): $88–$115 double with bath. MC, V. **Parking:** Free, on premises.

Mostly Hall is only steps from Falmouth Green and the beginning of the bicycle path to Woods Hole. The plantation-style house was built in 1849 as a wedding present for the New Orleans bride of Capt. Albert Nye. Rates include the use of bicycles. For getting the real flavor of Falmouth, Mostly Hall can't be beat. Do note that it is a no-smoking bed-&-breakfast inn.

THE PALMER HOUSE INN, 81 Palmer Ave., Falmouth, MA 02540. Tel. 508/548-1230, or toll free 800/472-2632. 8 rms (all with bath).

$ Rates (including breakfast): Peak season, $104–$126 double. Off-season, from $82 double. Discounts available for midweek stays. AE, DISC, MC, V. **Parking:** Free. **Closed:** Jan.

A few steps from the Falmouth Historical Society near Falmouth Green, is the Palmer House Inn, located very near the center of town. The innkeepers, Ken and Joanne Baker, have decorated each of the guest rooms in this turn-of-the-century Victorian house with antiques and authentic period pieces. The Bakers serve a wonderful gourmet breakfast (pain perdu with orange cream, Finnish pancake, and strawberry soup). If the perfect location doesn't get you, the stained glass, wicker, and doilies will. Bikes are available to guests at no charge.

VILLAGE GREEN INN, 40 West Main St., Falmouth, MA 02540. Tel. 508/548-5621. 5 rms (all with bath). **Directions:** From Rte. 28 heading south, turn left at Queen's Byway, right on Hewins St. and right on Main St.

$ Rates (including full breakfast): $82–$98 double; $98–$120 suite. **Parking:** Free, on premises.

Located on the Village Green, this stately white house is a small inn with just five lovely guest rooms (including a two-room suite), each with its own fireplace. All the rooms are large and thoughtfully decorated in soft colors. There's a formal parlor stocked with books, magazines, and games, as well as a front porch lined with white wicker chairs. One of the highlights of every stay is the breakfast: a tasty selection of dishes, including a tangy ambrosia and apple-plum crumble plus homemade muffins.

ALONG GRAND AVENUE

The guesthouses on Grand Avenue in Falmouth Heights differ only slightly from one another in price, accommodations, sea views, and charm. During the summer season, your selection may well have to be made on the basis of availability.

Head down Falmouth Heights Road, which skirts the eastern side of Falmouth Harbor, and soon you'll see Grand Avenue bearing off to the right. It then makes a loop south and east, running along Falmouth Heights Beach before heading back to rejoin Falmouth Heights Road.

GLADSTONE INN, 219 Grand Ave. S., Falmouth Heights, MA 02540. Tel. 508/548-9851. 16 rms (none with bath). **Directions:** From Rte. 3, exit on Rte. 6 west to Bourne Bridge Circle (a rotary). Take Rte. 28 over the Bourne Bridge

and south into Falmouth. Go left on Jones Rd. to Worcester Court, then right on Grand Ave.
$ Rates (including full breakfast): $33 single; $55 double; $77 garage apartment. No credit cards. **Parking:** Free, on premises. **Closed:** Mid-Oct to mid-May.
The Gladstone Inn, owned by Jim and Gayle Carroll, is at the corner of Montgomery Avenue, across the street from the beach. A glassed-in veranda shares the sea view, and this is where you have your buffet breakfast or cool afternoon drink. The apartment over the garage has been newly renovated.

GRAFTON INN, 261 Grand Ave. S., Falmouth Heights, MA 02540. Tel. 508/540-8688, or toll free 800/642-4069. Fax 508/540-1861. 11 rms (all with bath). Directions: From Rte. 3, exit on Rte. 6 west to Bourne Bridge Circle (a rotary). Take Rte. 28 over the Bourne Bridge and south into Falmouth. Go left on Jones Rd. to Worcester Court, then right on Grand Ave.

$ Rates (including breakfast): Peak season, $87–$120 double. MC, V. **Parking:** Free, on premises. **Closed:** Jan.
The Grafton Inn is right across the street from the main beach area, with snack stands and restaurants located conveniently nearby. Rates include a fine buffet breakfast, an enclosed porch, sufficient parking, use of bicycles, and a very comfortable, simple atmosphere. No smoking, no children, and no pets.

PEACOCK'S INN ON THE SOUND, 313 Grand Ave. (P.O. Box 201), Falmouth, MA 02541. Tel. 508/457-9666. 10 rms (all with bath). Directions: From Rte. 3, exit on Rte. 6 west to Bourne Bridge Circle (a rotary). Take Rte. 28 over the Bourne Bridge and south into Falmouth. Go left on Jones Rd. to Worcester Court, then right on Grand Ave.

$ Rates (including breakfast): Peak season, $93–$126 double. Off-season, discounts available. AE, CB, DC, DISC, MC, V. **Parking:** Free.
Romantically poised on a bluff overlooking Vineyard Sound, Peacock's has hosted many a honeymoon couple. It's also been the setting for a couple of weddings. Most of the 10 rooms have spectacular views of the ocean and tasteful country furnishings (two have fireplaces). A full gourmet breakfast—homemade breads and coffee cakes, fresh fruits, and specialties, such as banana-stuffed French toast and Peacock's own Egg Florentine—is served daily from 8 to 10am.

OUT OF TOWN CENTER

COONAMESSETT INN CAPE COD, Jones Rd. and Gifford St., Falmouth, MA 02540. Tel. 508/548-2300. 25 rms (all with bath). A/C TV TEL

$ Rates: $98–$126 sitting room/bedroom combo; $115–$142 living room/2-bedroom combo; $126–$153 cottage. Lower rate applies to midweek, higher rate, weekend. AE, DC, MC, V. **Parking:** Free, on premises.
A venerable red farmhouse, barn, and sheds make up the Coonamessett Inn Cape Cod. It may sound like a farm, but what you see whan you arrive is a beautifully maintained resort hotel with extensive grounds. The rear of the property is landscaped beautifully and slopes gently down to a lake, where a gaggle of geese makes its home. Favored by a mature clientele, the Coonamessett is also noted for its dining room (see below). You'll find it on Jones Road at the corner of Gifford Street.

WHERE TO DINE

COONAMESSETT INN DINING ROOM, Jones Rd. and Gifford St. Tel. 548-2300.

Cuisine: NEW ENGLAND. **Reservations:** Recommended.
$ Prices: Appetizers $2.75–$6.95; main courses $10.95–$19.95; meals $35. AE, DC, MC, V.
Open: Lunch Mon–Sat 11:30am–2:30pm, Sun noon–3pm; dinner daily 5:30–9pm.
This restaurant, at the corner of Gifford Street, has casual elegance, traditional New

England cuisine, and service that's attentive yet not overbearing. Start with chilled oysters on the half shell or the popular quahog chowder, then proceed to a delightful seafood Newburg in casserole. Save room for a side of homemade fresh pasta of the day, and then linger over coffee and the inn's deservedly famous Indian pudding.

Eli's, a separate dining area that is a more casual alternative, serves the dining-room lunch menu throughout the day; try a chicken club ($7) or seafood Newburg ($10). Before you leave, check out the *Legend of the Mermaid* paintings that hang in the dining room.

DOMINGO'S OLDE RESTAURANT, 856 Main St. (Rte. 28A), West Falmouth. Tel. 540-0575.

Cuisine: SEAFOOD. **Reservations:** Recommended. **Directions:** Follow Rte. 28A to West Falmouth.

$ Prices: Appetizers $1.25–$6.50; main courses $9.50–$17.25; dinner $20. AE, DC, MC, V.

Open: Dinner daily 4–11pm.

Domingo's Olde Restaurant serves excellent, moderately priced seafood (with Italian overtones) in an unassuming converted old home. Choose from lobster, swordfish, seafood kebab, and veal marsala. For a light meal, you might have bouillabaisse chock-full of shrimp, haddock, oysters, scallops, and mussels, a side order of garlic bread, and a simple dessert. Check the daily specials for the freshest fish.

REGATTA OF FALMOUTH BY THE SEA, 217 Clinton Ave. Tel. 548-5400.

Cuisine: FRENCH/AMERICAN. **Reservations:** Recommended.

$ Prices: Appetizers $5–$9.50; main courses $16.50–$25; meals $50. AE, MC, V.

Open: Dinner daily 5:30–10pm. **Closed:** Mid-Sept to late May.

Falmouth's finest place to dine from late May through Mid-September is undoubtedly the Regatta, located at the corner of Scranton and Clinton Avenues, overlooking the mouth of Falmouth's long harbor. You'll want to be dressed neatly, if informally. Start with Chesapeake Bay soft-shell crab pancetta, or grilled shrimp with three-mustard sauce; then proceed to the palette of two fish, each with its own sauce, or boneless rack of lamb en chemise with sauce Cabernet, and finish up with the chocolate seduction cake and raspberry sauce.

2. WOODS HOLE

6 miles (10km) SW of Falmouth

GETTING THERE See "Getting There" at the beginning of this chapter; see below for information on ferries to Martha's Vineyard.

DEPARTING Ferry From Woods Hole to Martha's Vineyard The Woods Hole, Martha's Vineyard and Nantucket **Steamship Authority,** P.O. Box 284, Woods Hole, MA 02543 (tel. 508/540-2022), operates car-carrying ferries between the points listed in its name, and also Hyannis. Schedules change several times a year, so it's best to call in advance for full current information. In fact, if you plan to ship your car, you must have a car reservation. You can get one by calling the number above. Ferries from Woods Hole to Vineyard Haven or Oak Bluffs on Martha's Vineyard leave about six times a day in winter, 14 times a day in summer, on the 45-minute trip. Fares are $9 round-trip for adults, half price for kids 5 to 12, free for kids under 5. Bikes go for $2.75 one-way. Autos cost $36 one-way in season. You can't get to Nantucket from Woods Hole or Falmouth, but you can from Hyannis (see below).

Parking Fees at the Docks If you don't plan to ferry your car over, and you don't ride a bike or take the bus to Woods Hole, figure on paying $7 to park your car for each *calendar* day ($14 if you leave your car overnight). It is virtually impossible to find a free, legal parking place in Woods Hole in summer or for overnight unless you stay at a motel and use its lot. The Steamship Authority has a dockside lot charging these fees, and also two large lots in Falmouth (if one is full you'll be directed to the other), with free shuttle-bus service to the Woods Hole docks. In late July and all of August the dockside lot is almost always full, so you'll save yourself some time by planning to park in a Falmouth lot. The Woods Hole ferry docks are served by Bonanza lines to Boston, Providence, and New York.

Note: Although bus schedules leaving Woods Hole are designed to work in conjunction with ferry arrivals, connections are not guaranteed because weather can make the ferry late, and *the bus does not wait*. Do not take the last ferry of the day from the islands to Woods Hole (or to Hyannis) and count on getting the last bus out—you may in fact be able to do it, but it's not dependable. Take an earlier ferry.

ESSENTIALS The **area code** is 508. The nearest **visitors center** is the Cape Cod Chamber of Commerce, at Routes 6 and 132, Hyannis, MA 02601 (tel. 508/362-3225).

When Emperor Hirohito of Japan visited the United States in 1976, the only scientific center he wanted to visit was Woods Hole. Being a marine biologist himself, he was interested in seeing one of the world's great centers for the study of sea life, especially the **Marine Biological Laboratory.** Besides the laboratory, Woods Hole is home to the **Woods Hole Oceanographic Institution (WHOI),** the **Northeast Fisheries Science Center,** and the **U.S. Geological Survey's Branch of Atlantic Geology.** Marine science is the lifeblood of the town, for the scientific buildings take up most of the space at the tip of a tiny peninsula, leaving room for only a few streets of fine old houses, a few small boatyards, a handful of restaurants, and the car-ferry dock to Martha's Vineyard.

The oceanographic institution has no exhibits open to the public, but the **U.S. Department of Commerce's National Marine Fisheries Service** maintains an aquarium (tel. 548-5123), on Water Street (the town's main street) down at the end of the peninsula. Follow Water Street through the town; just after it turns right, the aquarium is on your left. It's open mid-June to mid-September from 10am to 4pm daily; from 9am to 4pm the rest of the year; admission is free. During summer months, they feed the seals at 11am and 3pm daily.

WHERE TO STAY

SANDS OF TIME MOTOR INN, Woods Hole Rd. (P.O. Box 106), Woods Hole, MA 02543. Tel. 508/548-6300. Fax 508/457-0160. 33 rms (all with bath). A/C TV TEL **Directions:** Turn right onto Woods Hole Rd. from Rte. 28 in Falmouth and the Sands will be on your right as you enter Woods Hole.
$ Rates: Summer, $93–$115 double. Off-season, discounts available. Children under 18 half price. AE, DC, DISC, MC, V. **Parking:** Free. **Closed:** Nov–Mar.
The Sands of Time Motor Inn, just out of town on the road to Falmouth, has a fine view of the harbor and is only a short walk from the ferry docks. Rooms are in a modern motel unit and a grand Victorian house, which both overlook the harbor. A small garden and swimming pool are fitted into the hillside between the two. Rooms have two double beds. Those in the motel are modern and comfortable; the ones in the house have nice old touches like crystal doorknobs, fireplaces, bright new paint, and sparkling bathrooms. A grandfather clock inhabits the pretty entranceway.

WHERE TO DINE

FISHMONGER'S CAFE, 56 Water St. No phone.
  Cuisine: SEAFOOD. **Reservations:** Not accepted.

$ Prices: Appetizers $3.25–$4.50 at lunch, $3.95–$6.50 at dinner; main courses $3.50–$12.95 at lunch, $5.95–$14.95 at dinner; breakfast specials $3.20–$6.25. MC, V.
Open: Wed–Mon 7am–11pm, Tues 11:30am–11pm.

We recommend a light lunch at the Fishmonger's Café, on Woods Hole's main street just before the little bridge on the left. Lunch and dinner specials are written on the blackboard and sandwiches are available anytime. There are also many burgers and vegetarian main courses from which to choose, but most people go for the fish-and-chips and the good clam chowder. Wine and beer are served with meals. The atmosphere is rustic, with rough wood tables, board floors, and sea breezes wafting in through the windows. Heavily patronized by local people and visitors to the institute, the café may echo with Japanese or Spanish as foreign biologists discuss their countries' marine problems and opportunities. Service is fast (there's a take-out window, too), which is what you need if you have to catch a ferry.

SHUCKERS, 91 A Water St. Tel. 540-3850.
Cuisine: SEAFOOD. **Reservations:** Not accepted.
$ Prices: Appetizers $3.50–$6.95; main courses $9.95–$14.95. AE, MC, V.
Open: Daily 11am–11pm.

Located right on the docks, Shuckers is famed for its raw bar and its home-brewed beer, Nobska Light. Try to get one of the tables outside, where you can sit under an umbrella and watch the boating activity on Eel Pond. In addition to the raw bar, you'll find a satiating selection of seafood offerings including broiled scrod, haddock au gratin, and mesquite-grilled swordfish. Their lobster roll ($9.95) is almost prohibitively good.

3. SANDWICH

4 miles (6.5km) SE of the Sagamore Bridge, 22 miles (35.5km) SE of Plymouth, 16 miles (26km) NW of Hyannis, 15 miles (24km) W of Yarmouth Port, 62 miles (100km) SW of Provincetown

GETTING THERE   See "Getting There" at the beginning of this chapter.

ESSENTIALS   The **area code** is 508. For information contact the **Cape Cod Chamber of Commerce,** Jct. Rtes. 6 and 132, Hyannis, MA 02601 (tel. 508/ 362-3225).

Sandwich, calling itself "the oldest town on the Cape" (incorporated 1639), is certainly one of the most beautiful and serene. Much of the vacation traffic to the Cape rushes past it on the way to Provincetown, leaving Sandwich to those few who appreciate it. The town holds its appeal both winter and summer, for although it has beaches, its antiques stores and gracious old houses also draw visitors. Other attractions are Heritage Plantation, Dexter's Mill, and the Sandwich Glass Museum, which holds a fine collection of the interesting glassware once made here.

WHAT TO SEE & DO

Sandwich is an old-fashioned town true to its traditions, a very pleasant place to live or visit. A walk downtown will give you clues to its character right away: backyard shops for artisans working in wood, leather, wrought iron, clay, or oil-on-canvas; graceful church steeples; small, well-groomed parks; comely old houses, many with the date of construction posted over the front door.

The town's beaches include **Town Beach,** the most westerly, and then, in order heading east, **Spring Hill Beach, East Sandwich Beach,** and over the line in Barnstable, **Sandy Neck Beach.** They all have toilets and places to park, and the bay side of the Cape has generally warmer swimming than the ocean side. Look for signs to the beaches on the side roads left (north) off Route 6A between Sandwich and Barnstable.

DEXTER GRIST MILL, near Main & River Sts. Tel. 888-4910.

Dexter Mill is located at the end of a lovely mill pond (complete with ducks), and next to a cool, splashing mill race and an old pump. The mill (1654) was fully restored in 1961, and is not just a picturesque attraction, although you can go in and see the wooden mechanisms at work; the mill actually grinds corn, and you can buy bags of fresh meal the same day it's ground.

Admission: $1.50 adults, 75¢ children aged 12–16, free for children under 12.
Open: Memorial Day–Columbus Day, Mon–Sat 10am–4:45pm, Sun 1–4:45pm.

HERITAGE PLANTATION OF SANDWICH, Grove St. Tel. 888-3300.

Perhaps the most famous local attraction is the Heritage Plantation of Sandwich, 1 mile from town on Grove Street. Another of the museums in which New England abounds, Heritage Plantation does not specialize in any one era but has exhibits from all periods of American history. The automobile collection, 34 cars dating from 1899 to 1936, is one of the most popular sights in town.

Another collection features firearms and military miniatures, and still others show American crafts and the tools used to perform them. The buildings and grounds of the plantation are an attraction in themselves: All are reproductions of early-style buildings set in gardens and nature areas covering 76 acres.

There are picnic areas as well as a café where you can have continental breakfasts, light lunches, or snacks.

Admission (grounds, exhibits, shows, concerts, etc.): $7 adults, $6 seniors, $3.50 children 6–18, free for children 5 and under.
Open: Mid-May to late Oct, daily 10am–5pm.

HOXIE HOUSE, Rte. 130. Tel. 888-1173.

Sandwich has several old houses open to the public for a fee. The best known is Hoxie House, located along the shore of Shawme Pond (the millpond). The house dates from the end of the 1600s and has been restored and furnished with articles of that period.

Admission: $1.50 adults, half price children; combination ticket good for Hoxie House and Dexter Mill (see above) available.
Open: Mid-June to Sept, Mon–Sat 10am–5pm, Sun 1–5pm.

PAIRPONT CRYSTAL, Rte. 6A, Sagamore. Tel. 888-2344, or toll free 800/899-0953.

In nearby Sagamore, on the shores of the Cape Cod Canal, you'll find Pairpont Crystal, America's oldest glass works. Here you can watch skilled glassblowers create exquisite crystal items using tools and techniques that were developed over a century ago.

Admission: Free.
Open: Glassblowing demonstrations, Mon–Fri 8:30am–noon and 1–4:30pm. Gift shop, daily 8:30am–6pm.

SANDWICH GLASS MUSEUM, 129 Main St. Tel. 888-0251.

Across from Sandwich's Greek Revival town hall is the Sandwich Glass Museum. Sandwich was a major glass-producing town from 1825 to 1888, and although it specialized in the new process of pressing glass in a mold, it also produced blown, cut, etched, and enameled works as well. A brilliant collection of this American glassware is on display, and dioramas, videos, and pictures show how it was made. Glassmakers' tools and other articles of Sandwich memorabilia are also part of the museum's collection. The glass museum is the only one of its kind on the Cape. Special exhibits are installed each year.

Admission: $3 adults, 50¢ children aged 6–12, free for children under 6.

Open: Apr–Oct, daily 9:30am–4:30pm. Nov–Dec and Feb–Mar, Wed–Sun 9:30am–4pm. **Closed:** Jan.

YESTERYEAR'S DOLL AND MINIATURE MUSEUM, Main and River Sts. Tel. 888-1711.

Sooner or later your walk will bring you by Yesteryear's Doll and Miniature Museum, in what was once the First Parish Meetinghouse. Literally hundreds of fascinating antique dolls, dollhouses, and toys as well as many other domestic articles are on display, and exhibits change from time to time. The museum is nonprofit, but charges admission to defray expenses.

Admission: $2.50 adults, $2 seniors, $1.50 children under 12.

Open: Mid-May to Oct, Mon–Sat 10am–4pm.

WHERE TO STAY

CAPTAIN EZRA NYE HOUSE, 152 Main St., Sandwich, MA 02563. Tel. 508/888-6142, or toll free 800/388-2278. 7 rms (5 with bath). Directions: At fork at Rte. 30 and Main St., go right onto Main St. House is fourth on the right.

$ Rates (including full breakfast): June–Oct, $55–$71 double without bath, $82–$93 double with bath. AE, DISC, MC, V. **Parking:** Free. **Closed:** Nov to late May.

The Captain Ezra Nye House is lovely little place. Choose your bedroom according to color preference—green, yellow, blue, or a calico mix—and admire the hand-stenciling upstairs on the floors and walls. The two common rooms have a piano, TV, VCR, and fireplace.

DAN'L WEBSTER INN, 149 Main St. (P.O. Box 1849), Sandwich, MA 02563. Tel. 508/888-3622, or toll free 800/444-3566. Fax 508/888-5156. 47 rms (all with bath). A/C TV TEL

$ Rates: $75–$191 double. Extra person $11. Children under 12 stay free in parents' room. AE, DC, DISC, MC, V. **Parking:** Free, on premises.

Ask anyone how to get anywhere in Sandwich and they'll inevitably include the Dan'l Webster Inn in their directions. "Go past the Dan'l Webster . . ." Indeed, it is one of the town's most significant landmarks. Its 47 rooms (including nine suites) are decorated in a colonial motif. Many have canopy beds and more than half a dozen offer whirlpool tubs. In addition to the rooms in the main building, suites with working fireplaces are available in the Quince Tree House just down the street. The Dan'l Webster Inn is a good choice if you want all the conveniences of a fine hotel, such as room service, pool, gift shop, meeting rooms, and health club privileges. There are four dining rooms at the inn, all serving the same menus (see "Where to Dine," below). On Friday evening, there is usually a live band and dancing.

ISAIAH JONES HOMESTEAD, 165 Main St., Sandwich, MA 02563. Tel. 508/888-9115, or toll free 800/526-1625. 5 rms (all with bath).

$ Rates (including continental breakfast): Summer, $93–$130 double. Winter, $71–$120 double. AE, DISC, MC, V. **Parking:** Free.

The Isaiah Jones Homestead in the center of town is a small, no-smoking bed-and-breakfast. The rooms (one with a whirlpool) have a rather formal feel to them, but not uncomfortably so. Plush carpeting, chintz fabrics, alcove sitting areas, triple sheeting on the beds, and fresh flowers are all the norm here. Each room is named after an important local person from the town's early days. A candlelit continental breakfast set at one long table, and afternoon tea are included in the room rates.

SETH POPE HOUSE 1699, 110 Tupper Rd., Sandwich, MA 02563. Tel.

508/888-5916. 3 rms (all with bath). **Directions:** From Sagamore Bridge, take Rte. 6A to Sandwich Cooperative Bank (Tupper Rd.), turn right, go ¼ of a mile to Moody, turn right. Driveway is on left.

$ Rates (including full breakfast): $60–$82 double. Two-night minimum stay on weekends. No credit cards. **Parking:** Free, on premises.

Propped up on a knoll overlooking a salt marsh, the Seth Pope House is listed on the Sandwich Town Hall Square National Register of Historic Homes. It's a very welcoming bed-and-breakfast lovingly run by Beverly and John Dobel, two transplanted midwesterners. Throughout, you'll find the couple's collection of antiques, wonderful stenciling on the walls, and a total of seven fireplaces. Guest rooms include the Victorian Room, which has a queen-size bed piled high with pillows, and marble-topped furniture; the Pineapple Room, with two four-poster twin beds and braided rugs; and the Colonial Room, with exposed beams, wide wood floors, and a queen-size pencil-post bed. Each morning a full breakfast is served by candlelight in the dining room.

THE SUMMER HOUSE, 158 Main St., Sandwich, MA 02563. Tel. 508/ 888-4991. 5 rms (1 with bath). **Directions:** From Sandwich Village off Rte. 130 north bear right onto Main St. for ¼ mile.

$ Rates (including full breakfast): June–Oct, $55–$71 double without bath, $82– $93 double with bath. AE, DISC, MC, V. **Parking:** Free.

Built around 1835 in the Greek Revival style popular at that time, the entire whimsical front of the house is set aside for guests. One double room, on the first floor, has a private bath, and the four bedrooms on the second floor share two baths. English-style afternoon tea is included in the room rates. You'll enjoy the porch, lawn, patio, and garden here.

WHERE TO DINE

CONSERVATORY AT THE DAN'L WEBSTER INN, 149 Main St. Tel. 888-3622.

Cuisine: CONTINENTAL. **Reservations:** Recommended.

$ Prices: Appetizers $4–$8; main courses $13–$20; early-evening special starts at $9.95. AE, DC, DISC, MC, V.

Open: Breakfast daily 8–11am; lunch daily noon–3:45pm; dinner daily 4:45– 9:30pm.

Those who are not watching their budgets but who still value their dollar will want to know about the Conservatory at the Dan'l Webster Inn, located right in the middle of town. The dining room here is run by a family with a long history of restaurant success. The Conservatory is a grand solarium with a high ceiling, views of the grounds, potted indoor trees, servers in period costume, and a bounteous menu, with lots of beef and seafood choices. For the early-evening special, you must be seated by 6:15pm. On Thursday and Saturday evenings and at Sunday brunch there is live music.

MARSHLAND, Rte. 6A. Tel. 888-9824.

Cuisine: DINER/BAKERY. **Reservations:** Not required.

$ Prices: Breakfast special $2.75–$4.95; dinner special $5.95–$6.95.

Open: Mon 6am–2pm, Tues–Sat 6am–8pm, Sun 7am–noon.

⑤ Marshland is almost always packed—both with local regulars and visitors who crowd around the twin horseshoe-shaped bars or into the surrounding booths. Here you'll find a mainstream menu, plus several blackboards full of "specials" that are more creative and health-conscious. Best are the breakfasts where you can take your pick of homemade muffins (orange poppyseed, blueberry, corn with peaches, dark bran—you name it). If you want dinner, try to arrive before 6pm to avoid waiting in line.

SAGAMORE INN, 1131 Rte. 6A, Sagamore. Tel. 888-9707.

Cuisine: ITALIAN/SEAFOOD. **Reservations:** Not accepted. **Directions:** Take Rte. 6A, just past the Sagamore Bridge.

$ Prices: Appetizers $2–$9; main courses $7–$16. AE, MC, V.

Open: Apr–late Nov, Wed–Mon 11am–9pm.

The Sagamore Inn is not fancy—wooden booths, a stamped-tin ceiling—but neither are its prices. The waitresses are all local women, the clientele are local families, and the food is hearty, savory, and delicious, with huge portions and low prices. The cook's inspiration is Italian cuisine; you can find spaghetti, seafood, sandwiches, and that hot summer–weather favorite, an antipasto plate. Everyone here is friendly and pleasant, and out to make you happy.

---

4. HYANNIS

16 miles (26km) SE of Sandwich, 23 miles (37km) NE
of Falmouth, 50 miles (81km) SW of Provincetown

GETTING THERE   By Plane   Hyannis's Barnstable Municipal Airport is the busiest airport on Cape Cod, with regular flights to Boston, Nantucket, and Martha's Vineyard, and connecting flights through those points. For details, see "Getting There" at the beginning of this chapter. The airport is just on the northern outskirts of town, a short taxi ride from the bus stations or the center. Several companies based here offer small planes for charter.

By Train   See "Getting There" at the beginning of this chapter.

By Bus   See "Getting There" at the beginning of this chapter.

By Car   See "Getting There" at the beginning of this chapter.

By Boat   Hyannis has two main docks, at the foot of Ocean Street for **Hy-Line passenger ferries** to Nantucket, and at the foot of Pleasant Street for the passenger and car-ferries operated by the **Steamship Authority** (tel. 508/771-4000). The docks are about 5 blocks from the bus stations. (Many buses connecting with ferries take passengers right to the dock.) For details on both these ferries, see below.

DEPARTING   Ferries from Hyannis to Martha's Vineyard and Nantucket   Two companies operate ferries from Hyannis to the islands of Martha's Vineyard and Nantucket, and each sail from a different dock. Here are the details.

The Woods Hole, Martha's Vineyard, and Nantucket **Steamship Authority** (tel. 508/540-2022 for car reservations) runs car and passenger ferries from Hyannis's Pleasant Street docks (follow the signs in town). No direct service is run between Hyannis and Martha's Vineyard by this firm—you have to go via Nantucket or, preferably, direct from Woods Hole to Martha's Vineyard. The Steamship Authority's boats run six times daily to Nantucket in summer, less frequently off-season; the trip takes less than 2½ hours and costs $9.75 for adults, half fare for kids 5 to 12, one-way. Car-ferry space must be reserved in advance; in high summer it costs $83 to ship a car one-way from Hyannis to Nantucket. In high summer, one passengers-only boat is run in each direction daily between Martha's Vineyard and Nantucket, taking about 2 hours and costing $9.75 per adult (kids pay half fare). The ferries are large, comfortable, and equipped with lunch counters and bars. Note that if you park in the dockside lots you'll have to pay $7 per calendar day for the privilege, and that you should arrive at the lot 45 minutes prior to the ferry's departure time.

Note: When returning to Hyannis from Nantucket, don't plan on taking the last ferry of the day and meeting the bus to Boston or New York, for the ferries are often delayed and *the bus does not wait.* To be safe, catch a ferry well ahead of the last bus trip scheduled from Hyannis. If you find yourself in a jam because of ferry mixups, you can always take another line (see below) or fly.

The Hy-Line (tel. 508/778-2600) has several swift (2-hr.) passengers-only boats which depart from Hyannis's Ocean Street docks for Nantucket or Martha's Vineyard; fare is $10.50 for an adult, half price for a child, to either island. Although no cars are carried on the Hy-Line's boats, you can take your bicycle over for $4.50 one-way. These boats operate May through October only. By the way, if you sign up for a same-day round-trip, you'll have to decide which boat you plan to return on, and your ticket will be stamped with the boat's departure time. Reservations are accepted with an additional nominal charge (tel. 508/778-2602). Otherwise, parking is $7 per calendar day.

ESSENTIALS   The **area code** is 508. For information, contact the **Cape Cod Chamber of Commerce,** Routes 6 and 132, Hyannis, MA 02601 (tel. 508/362-3225), open Monday to Friday 8:30am to 5pm (July and August also Saturday and Sunday 9am to 4pm).

Hyannis gained national fame during the presidency of John F. Kennedy because of his summer home in nearby Hyannisport. Some of the town's growth and perhaps a good portion of its honky-tonk dates from that time, and although curious or devoted fans of the late president still stop to look at the town or to visit its memorial to J.F.K., the attractions in Hyannis these days are commercial. Should you need the services of an airline or a department store, supermarket, or foreign auto-parts warehouse while on the Cape, Hyannis is the place to come. If you don't need these things, there are many nicer places on the Cape to spend precious vacation time.

WHAT TO SEE & DO

Many visitors to Hyannis stop to see the **memorial to President Kennedy,** a stone monument bearing the presidential seal and a small fountain, on Ocean Street right along the water. Hyannisport and the "Kennedy compound," noted in news stories while the late president vacationed here, are not far from the monument. The Kennedy compound is not visible from the street and is not open to the public.

Also along Ocean Street are **Kalmus Park** and **Veteran's Park,** with their respective beaches, bathhouses, and snack bars. Go down to the south end of Sea Street for none other than **Sea Street Beach.** Besides swimming facilities, Sea Street Beach has a little platform on top of a dune from which you can take a look at the sweep of the beach.

Big-name stars and bands are booked into the **Cape Cod Melody Tent,** at the West Main Street Rotary in Hyannis (tel. 775-9100). The season goes from late June through Labor Day, and runs the gamut—from Bill Cosby to Olivia Newton John. Tickets are priced differently depending on the show, but most run in the $18 to $35 range, with selected Tuesday and Thursday matinees and weeknight performances. Children's shows are Thursday mornings at 11am. Tickets can be charged by calling the box office.

WHERE TO STAY

BOUCHARD'S TOURIST HOMES AND APARTMENTS AND COTTAGES, 83 School St., Hyannis, MA 02601. Tel. 508/775-0912. 18 rms (10 with bath).

$ Rates: Last week of June–Labor Day, $27 single without bath; $38 twin without bath; $60 twin with bath; $104 suite for four. MC, V. **Parking:** Free.

Bouchard's Tourist Homes and Apartments and Cottages, off Main Street near the beach, has several buildings and therefore a larger number of rooms at tourist-home prices, plus some apartments for long-term stays. Lowest price is for a room with running water which shares a tub-and-shower bathroom with one other room. For slightly more, two people can have a room with twin beds, running water, cable TV, and shared bath. The more expensive rooms have cable color TV, air conditioning, twin beds, private tub-and-shower bath, even a private entrance. A suite of two adjoining rooms and bath sleeps four, and is a good choice for families. Celina Bouchard has been running this place since 1935, and she'll charge you only $5 a day to keep your car here if you're heading to the islands.

ELEGANCE BY THE SEA, 162 Sea St., Hyannis, MA 02601. Tel. 508/775-3595. 6 rms (all with bath).

$ Rates (including breakfast): $66–$95 double with bath. AE, MC, V. **Parking:** Free on premises.

What's in a name? Well, Mary and Clark Boydston, innkeepers at the turn-of-the-century bed-and-breakfast off Main Street named Elegance by the Sea would certainly answer "everything" to that question. With only six guest rooms in this huge Victorian house, bedrooms, common rooms, and even bathrooms are quite spacious. Upstairs are pineapple-post beds, other period antiques, and black-and-white-tiled floors in the old-fashioned bathroom. The room downstairs has a working fireplace. The price includes a hearty breakfast; theme weekends are hosted throughout the winter months. If you come during the holidays, you'll be in for special treats. The inn (which is no-smoking) accepts guests 16 years old and older.

INN ON SEA STREET, 358 Sea St., Hyannis, MA 02601. Tel. 508/775-8030. 9 rms (7 with bath).

$ Rates (including breakfast): $76–$98 double. AE, DISC, MC, V. **Parking:** Free.

The Inn on Sea Street is the kind of place guests return to year after year. It consists of two Victorian buildings, one a Greek Revival house that was built in 1849, the other a grand Victorian (built in 1899) with a French mansard roof and a wraparound porch. Between the two, there are nine guest rooms, all crisply decorated. Those in the newer building have remote-control TVs (discreetly hidden away in armoires). Every morning, breakfast—a feast of fruit, eggs, cheese, cake, granola, and the usual hot drinks—is served in the sun porch. The inn is full of thoughtful details, such as goosedown pillows and umbrellas (in the event of rain) in guest rooms.

SEA BREEZE INN, 397 Sea St., Hyannis, MA 02601. Tel. 508/771-7213. 13 rms (all with bath). TV **Directions:** From Main St. take Sea St. toward ocean; inn will be on right.

$ Rates (including breakfast): $48–$102 double. AE, MC, V. **Parking:** Free.

If being near the beach is a top priority, the Sea Breeze Inn is a good choice. It's a 3-minute walk away. It's also a good choice if you're planning to take a ferry over to one of the islands; the docks are about 15 minutes away by foot. All 13 rooms here have TVs, several are air conditioned, and a couple of them have ocean views.

WHERE TO DINE

Hyannis is full of restaurants specializing in cuisines from around the world. So whether you crave a slice of oven-baked pizza, a chimichanga, or a bowl of sesame noodles, you're sure to find it here. You'll also find a good selection of restaurants specializing in dishes that the Cape is famous for, such as chowders dense with clams, lobsters, and fish 'n' chips. Oh, and keep in mind, there's also a Ben & Jerry's (352 Main St. (tel. 790-0910).

MILDRED'S CHOWDER HOUSE, 290 Iyanough Rd. Tel. 775-1045.
Cuisine: SEAFOOD. **Reservations:** Recommended.
$ Prices: Lunch $2.15–$7.95; dinner $4.95–$16.95. AE, MC, V.
Open: Mon–Sat 11:30am–9pm, Sun buffet 9am–1pm. **Closed:** Thanksgiving Day, Christmas Day.

For the ultimate bowl of chowder, you have to go to Mildred's. This famed chowder house first opened in 1949 and to this day uses Mildred's original recipe. It's a busy spot, all decked out in nautical decor. In addition to chowder, there are seafood and other popular New England dishes.

THE PADDOCK, West Main St. at West End Rotary. Tel. 775-7677.
   Cuisine: NEW ENGLAND. **Reservations:** Recommended.
$ Prices: Lunch $5–$12; dinner $14–$23. AE, DISC, MC, V.
   Open: Daily noon–2:30pm and 5–10pm. **Closed:** Mid-Nov to Apr.
For fine dining, The Paddock is a good choice. It's located beside the Melody Tent, which makes it the perfect place for a pre-show dinner or after-show dessert. Attractively furnished in Victorian decor, The Paddock has been owned and run by the same family for nearly 25 years. Popular menu items are scrod, sole, lobster, steak au poivre, and tournedos of beef.

UP THE CREEK, 36 Old Colony Rd. Tel. 771-7866.
   Cuisine: AMERICAN. **Reservations:** Recommended. **Directions:** Turn left off Sea St. onto Gosnold St., then take first left (you can't miss the jammed parking lot).
$ Prices: Appetizers $2–$6; main courses $4–$8 at lunch, $7–$14 at dinner; brunch $7.50. AE, DC, DISC, MC, V.
   Open: Lunch Mon–Sat 11:30am–2:30pm; dinner daily 4:30–10pm; Sun brunch 11am–2:30pm.
Follow your nose and the locals' toes to Hyannis's value-for-money eatery: Up the Creek. Expect a cozy, tasteful, dark interior. Try a fish, chicken, or sirloin lunch for $5 to $6. For dinner, choose chicken Simone at $9.95 or the special seafood strudel (lobster, shrimp, scallops, crab, and cheese wrapped in pastry) at $8.50.

5. BARNSTABLE

3.5 miles (6km) N of Hyannis, 2.5 miles (4km) W of Yarmouth Port

GETTING THERE   See "Getting There" at the beginning of this chapter.

ESSENTIALS   The **area code** is 508. The nearest **visitors center** is the Cape Cod Chamber of Commerce, at Routes 6 and 132, Hyannis, MA 02601 (tel. 508/362-3225).

The stretch of Route 6A between Sandwich and Dennis is a lush panorama of bogs and marshes, distant views of dunes and the sea, birds calling and fluttering, the winding road dotted with antiques shops, craft shops, art galleries, and other businesses including lots and lots of real estate offices. The road leads through the villages of Barnstable, Cummaquid, Yarmouth Port, Yarmouth, and Dennis before heading eastward to Brewster.

Visitors may be surprised to know that Barnstable, the largest incorporated town on the Cape, actually includes within its boundaries the busy commercial center of Hyannis, its airport, and several small historic villages on the wide salt marshes along the shores of Cape Cod Bay. The village of Barnstable proper is little more than a namesake for the much larger township.

As you wend your way eastward along Route 6A, the village of Barnstable offers several good choices for lodging. In Barnstable, as well as Yarmouth Port, Route 6A becomes Main Street, also called the Old King's Highway.

Whale-watch excursions depart from Barnstable Harbor three times a day during July and August. On these excursions, you are taken to the feeding grounds of the great baleen whales. Sightings have included 40- to 60-ton humpback whales with their calves, finbacks, minke, and sei whales as well as other marine mammals. Summer sailings depart at approximately 8:30am, 1:30pm, and 5:15pm during the week; Saturday and Sunday sailings are at 9am and 2pm. In the spring and fall, a daily sail leaves about 11:45am. All cruises are narrated by a naturalist. Summer rates are

$22 for adults, $10 for children aged 4 to 12, free for children under 3. Spring and fall rates are $20 adults, $10 for children aged 4 to 12, and free for children under 3. There are also senior discounts. Advance reservations are necessary. Write Hyannis Whale Watcher Cruises, P.O. Box 254, Barnstable Harbor, Barnstable, MA 02630, or call 508/362-6088. VISA and MasterCard are accepted.

WHERE TO STAY

ASHLEY MANOR, 3660 Old Kings Hwy. (P.O. Box 856), Barnstable, MA 02630. Tel. 508/362-8044. 6 rms (all with bath). **Directions:** Head east on Rte. 6A; it's on your left.
$ Rates: $110–$137 single or double; $160–$181 suite. AE, MC, V. **Parking:** Free.
A stay at Ashley Manor is a lesson in leisurely living. Innkeepers Donald and Fay Bain will encourage you to linger over afternoon cocktails, evening conversations, and a full breakfast on the backyard brick terrace, enjoying the inn's 2-acre grounds. The six spacious suites and guest rooms in the main manor house (all with Oriental carpets, and antiques, and all but one with a working fireplace). The cottage has a freestanding fireplace and an efficiency. Ashley Manor has its own tennis court, as well as bicycles, beach chairs, and croquet. Children 14 and older are welcome at the inn.

BEECHWOOD, 2839 Main St., Barnstable, MA 02630. Tel. 508/362-6618. 6 rms (6 with bath). **Directions:** Head east on Rte. 6A; it's on your right.
$ Rates (including breakfast): $115–$153 double. AE, MC, V. **Parking:** Free.
This Victorian house takes its name from the big old beech trees that shade the veranda. Don't let the staid parlor mislead you; it's not at all in keeping with the light and airy guest rooms. Period antiques, colored glass, marble-topped dressers, unique bathrooms, and tall shuttered windows make this place special. The garret room in the attic is very private and has angled walls and eaves. Beechwood is set on Old Kings Highway (a.k.a. Route 6A and Main Street) within walking distance of the beach, antiques and art galleries, restaurants, and hiking and biking trails.

CHARLES HINCKEY HOUSE, Old Kings Hwy. (P.O. Box 723), Barnstable Village, MA 02630. Tel. 508/362-9924. 4 rms (all with bath). **Directions:** Head east on Rte. 6A; it's on your left.
$ Rates (including breakfast): $130–$163 double. No credit cards. **Parking:** Free, behind the inn.
With only four rooms (all with working fireplaces), the Charles Hinckey House is very special and welcoming. This Federal-colonial house is a historic landmark and has been painstakingly renovated. Flowers from the profuse bank of wildflower gardens fill the interior. The innkeepers keep their distance, but will spoil you if you give them half a chance.

6. YARMOUTH PORT

2.5 miles (4km) E of Barnstable, 4.5 miles (7km) SW of Dennis

GETTING THERE See "Getting There" at the beginning of this chapter.

ESSENTIALS The **area code** is 508. The **Cape Cod Chamber of Commerce** is at Jct. Rtes. 6 and 132, Hyannis, MA 02601 (tel. 508/362-3225).

Yarmouth is a town with a serious split personality. In the south, along Route 28, there are one motel and fast-food store after another built along crowded beaches.

In the north, in the area of the Old King's Highway, is the Cape just as you pictured it: dignified old Cape Cod houses, lofty trees, and the calm waters of Cape Cod Bay. You won't find any neon lights in the latter. Nor will you find malls, movie theaters, and motels.

Yarmouth Port, though very old (incorporated 1639), has managed to preserve its history beautifully. You can glimpse its beauty by driving along Route 6A, which started life as an Indian path and later became known as the King's Highway before Massachusetts declared its independence. Today, it is known as Main Street and nicknamed the Captains' Mile due to its profusion of captains' houses. At one point, over three dozen sea captains lived in the town.

WHAT TO SEE & DO

One of the highlights of any visit to Yarmouth Port is following the **Nature Trails of the Historical Society of Old Yarmouth.** The trails are open during daylight hours 7 days a week year round; 50¢ admission for adults, 25¢ for children. Note that these are not formal "botanical gardens," but rather trails through particularly beautiful wild areas of Yarmouth's land and marshes. Local flowers and trees, plants, and geological features are on view, and maps and trail booklets available at the gatehouse where you pay admission will tell you all about what there is to see.

Down Centre Street lies **Grays Beach** right on Bass Hole, a small cove. Here you'll find a boardwalk which stretches across a marsh (a rewarding spot for birdwatching) and a lovely patch of beach. According to legend, the Norsemen landed in this very spot back in 1003. The beach is free and open to the public.

Back on Main Street, at the corner of Summer Street, you'll find the **village pump and watering trough,** which dates back to 1866. Nearby is the **Parnassus Book Store** in a building that started life as a church and later became the local incarnation of the A & P grocery chain. Shelves of used books always stand outside, even when the store is closed. Feel free to help yourself by putting the posted price in the box.

BANGS HALLET HOUSE, Rte. 6A. Tel. 362-3021.

The Captain Bangs Hallet House, built by a captain in the China trade, is the headquarters of the Historical Society of Old Yarmouth. This Greek Revival house museum is furnished in the manner in which a prosperous 19th-century sea captain would have lived. Ship models, ship paintings, and other maritime memorabilia are on display.

Admission: $1 adults, 25¢ children.

Open: June–Labor Day, Wed–Fri and Sun 2–4pm. Labor Day–May, call for an appointment.

WINSLOW CROCKER HOUSE, 250 Main St. Tel. 362-4385.

The Winslow Crocker House is owned and maintained by the Society for the Preservation of New England Antiquities. The rooms in this Georgian house are furnished with 17th- to 19th-century collections.

Admission: $4 adults, $2 children aged 5–12.

Open: June to mid-Oct, Tues, Thurs, and Sat–Sun noon–5pm.

WHERE TO STAY

Many of the former sea captains' homes of Yarmouth Port have become bed and breakfasts. Here, you'll find our favorites. For a complete list, contact the **Yarmouth Area Chamber of Commerce,** Box 479, South Yarmouth, MA 02664; tel. 508/398-5311.

LIBERTY HILL INN, 77 Main St., Yarmouth Port, MA 02675. Tel. 508/362-3976, or toll free 800/821-3977. 5 rms (all with bath).

$ Rates (including breakfast): Summer, $104–$137 double. AE, MC, V. **Parking:** Free.

Atop Liberty Hill, set back from Route 6A at the corner of Willow Street, is the Liberty Hill Inn. The classical pillars are a giveaway: Greek Revival architecture, built in 1825. The Liberty Hill is perhaps Yarmouth Port's best bargain: You get a double room (private bath) in the lovely house furnished with authentic Early American pieces, a full breakfast, and a convenient location. Innkeepers Beth and Jack Flanagan see to it that your stay is an enjoyable one. You save money if you come in spring or fall, especially on a weekday.

ONE CENTRE STREET INN, 1 Centre St. Yarmouth Port, MA 02675. Tel. 508/362-8910. 5 rms (all with bath). TEL
$ Rates (including breakfast): double $71–$98. AE, DISC, MC, V. **Parking:** Free.
Despite its name, the One Centre Street Inn is on Old King's Highway; the entrance is around to the side, on Centre Street, right in the middle of Yarmouth Port. For simple good taste, the inn is first choice in this town. Innkeepers Stefanie and Bill Wright have five guest rooms; baths are private or semiprivate. This is my favorite sort of hostelry: small, congenial, thoughtfully and finely furnished with taste but without pretension, walking distance to the activities of the town, friendly owners. Need I say more?

WEDGEWOOD INN, 83 Main St., Yarmouth Port, MA 02675. Tel. 508/362-5157. 6 rms (all with bath). A/C **Directions:** Head east on Rte. 6A; it's on your right.
$ Rates (including breakfast): Peak season, $115–$159 double. Off-season, 20% discounts available. AE, DC, MC, V. **Parking:** Free.
Poised on a knoll right on the Old King's Highway, the Wedgewood Inn is as pretty as a picture. Indeed, this nearly 200-year-old house did grace the cover of *Colonial Homes* magazine in April 1992. Here you'll find half a dozen guest rooms, all individually decorated in a formal country mood except one which is very Victorian. Four rooms have their own working fireplaces; two have screened-in sun porches. Throughout the inn, there are conversation-piece antiques, some hand-stenciled floors, and an overall make-yourselves-comfortable feel.

WHERE TO DINE

ABBICCI, 43 Main St. (Rte. 6A). Tel. 362-3501.
   Cuisine: CONTEMPORARY ITALIAN. **Reservations:** Recommended.
$ Prices: Appetizers $3.75–$6.95 at lunch, $4.50–$10.50 at dinner; main courses $8.95–$12.95 at lunch, $10.95–$23.95 at dinner. AE, CB, DC, DISC, MC, V.
   Open: Daily 11:30am–2:30pm and 5:30–10pm.
If you're looking for something "Cape-y," Abbicci is not it. This sophisticated Italian restaurant is far more urban. Try the sautéed shrimp (with lemon, oil, and garlic) or the roast duck (with a honey, vinegar, and apricot sauce) and you'll have to agree. There is a quartet of small dining areas, each set up with fresh white linens and sturdy bottles of Pellegrino water. A map-mural of the Mediterranean area graces the walls. The restaurant is near the corner of Willow Street and Route 6A.

7. DENNIS

4.5 miles (7km) NE of Yarmouth Port, 5.5 miles (9km) W of Brewster

GETTING THERE   See "Getting There" at the beginning of this chapter.

ESSENTIALS   The **area code** is 508. Write or call the **Dennis Chamber of**

Commerce, Route 28 (P.O. Box 275), South Dennis, MA 02660 (tel. 508/398-3568, or toll free 800/243-9920).

The town of Dennis is much like Yarmouth. Here, it is claimed, the commercial cranberry-harvesting industry began, and salt works flourished for a period.

As you enter the center of Dennis, start looking for a cemetery and a white church, and as you come to them look for Old Bass River Road. Turn right onto this road and follow signs for eight-tenths of a mile to the Scargo Hill Tower. Park at the base of this stone structure surrounded by oak and pine, and climb the iron staircase inside to the top (not far) for a view that will tell you what the Cape is all about. On a clear day you can easily see Provincetown, the white blade of the Cape beaches cutting the deep blue of Cape Cod Bay. The Cape itself appears as a huge green scimitar, a sea of green trees with little white or silver-gray shingled houses poking through here and there. At the foot of the hill that holds the tower is Scargo Lake, and west is the outline of Barnstable Harbor. The tower was given to the town of Dennis in 1929 by the Tobey family, who had had ancestors living in Dennis since 1678. Follow the same road back to Route 6A.

More pretty scenes, including those cranberry bogs and salt marshes, await you in Dennis. If you get off of Route 6A to wander and explore, expect to get lost. This is a confusing, if beautiful, place. For instance, though the village of East Dennis is actually east of Dennis, the village of South Dennis is due north of West Dennis, and these two are due south of East Dennis . . . got it?

WHAT TO SEE & DO

The **Cape Playhouse,** Route 6A (tel. 385-3838), is the place to go on the Cape if you want to see a famous actor or actress in a well-known play. The plays (and actors) usually change every week, so call to see what's current. The season runs from early July through Labor Day, with performances on Monday to Saturday evenings at 8:30pm, plus matinees on Wednesday and Thursday at 2:30pm. Tickets are priced from $13 to $25. The playhouse has its own restaurant, open for lunch on matinee days, dinner, Sunday brunch, and after-theater snacks. Also here is the **Cape Cinema,** which specializes in foreign and independent American films. It's open from Memorial Day through the third weekend in September. For information, call 508/385-2503.

WHERE TO STAY

FOUR CHIMNEYS INN, 946 Main St. (Rte. 6A), Dennis, MA 02638. Tel. 508/385-6317. 9 rms (7 with bath). **Directions:** From end of Union St. (Exit 8 off Rte. 6), take a right onto Rte. 6A. Inn is nearly 4 miles down on the left.
$ Rates (including continental breakfast): Summer, $48–$81 single or double without bath, $82–$98 single or double with bath. Off-season, $38–$54 single or double without bath, $60–$77 single or double with bath. Extra person $15. AE, DISC, MC, V. **Parking:** Free, on premises.

The Four Chimneys Inn has some of the most spacious guest rooms on the entire Cape. Ceilings are high, floors painted, and common rooms (one with a VCR, one with a fireplace) relaxing. Seven of the nine impeccable rooms in this Victorian house have private baths; continental breakfast included in the rates is served in the dining room and on the porch.

ISAIAH HALL B&B INN, 152 Whig St., Dennis, MA 02638. Tel. 508/385-9928, or toll free 800/736-0160. 11 rms (10 with bath). **Directions:** Take Rte. 6 to exit 8, go left 1¼ miles to Rte. 6A, turn right and go 3½ miles to Hope Lane (opposite church and cemetery). Turn left onto Hope Lane, at the end turn right on Whig St. The inn is a short distance on the left.

$ Rates (including breakfast): Mid-June to Labor Day, $57 double without bath, $75–$103 double with bath. Off-season, discounts available. AE, MC, V. **Parking:** Free.

The Isaiah Hall B&B Inn is a gem of a bed-and-breakfast run by Marie and Dick Brophy. Good old-fashioned, homespun country comforts prevail in this 1857 Greek Revival farmhouse. The newly converted barn, with cathedral ceiling and white wicker, sports rooms with small balconies. The living room, dining room, and quilted guest rooms in the main house are filled with solid antiques and are very unpretentious. The house abuts a cranberry bog, is a 10-minute walk to Corporation Beach, and is right behind the Cape Playhouse.

8. BREWSTER

5.5 miles (9km) E of Dennis, 5 miles (8km) W of Orleans

GETTING THERE   See "Getting There" at the beginning of this chapter.

ESSENTIALS   The **area code** is 508. Contact the **Cape Cod Chamber of Commerce** at Jct. Rtes. 6 and 132, Hyannis, MA 02601 (tel. 508/362-3225).

B rewster is another of the picturesque little towns along Route 6A. A country store, several fine churches, and a Town Hall make it look like many other pleasant Cape towns, but Brewster's different in the number of noteworthy museums and exhibitions situated in the town or nearby. It also has one of the best French restaurants on the East Coast.

WHAT TO SEE & DO

Brewster is proud of its **Old Grist Mill** and **Herring Run** at the Stoney Brook Mill Sites, on Stony Brook Road near the intersection with Satucket and Run Hill roads. The water wheel, still in good working order, powers the grinding machinery inside the mill. You can watch the whole process at work, and buy freshly ground cornmeal, from 2 to 5pm on Wednesday, Friday, and Saturday afternoons in July and August. Upstairs there's a small museum with artifacts from the "Factory Village" which occupied this site more than 100 years ago.

The mill is now part of a park owned by the town of Brewster. Wander around the millpond, certainly one of the most romantic and picturesque locales on all of Cape Cod. If your visit falls during mid-April to early May, watch for the run of alewives (herring) which surges upstream from the ocean to freshwater spawning grounds.

CAPE COD AQUARIUM, 281 Main St. Tel. 385-9252, or toll free 800/367-6372.

Set alongside Cape Cod Bay, this facility is a sanctuary for rescued seals, sea lions, and sea turtles. There are several exhibits showcasing regional marine life, including fish, sharks, crabs, and sea turtles. The aquarium prides itself on its hands-on marine science programs, including full scuba-diving services. Seal and sea lion presentations take place daily at 10am, noon, 2pm, and 4pm.

Admission: $4 adults, $2 children ages 2–6, free for children under 2.

Open: July–Aug, daily 9:30am–5pm. Sept–June, Mon–Fri 9:30am–4pm, Sat-Sun 9:30am–5pm. **Closed:** Thanksgiving, Christmas, and New Year's Day. Call to confirm hours, fees, and program schedules.

NEW ENGLAND FIRE AND HISTORY MUSEUM, 1439 Rte. 6A. Tel. 896-5711.

The New England Fire and History Museum has one of the world's largest (35 engines) and most varied collections of early firefighting equipment and memorabilia, plus gardens both herbaceous and ceremonial, and a picnic area. Firefighting paraphernalia dates as far back as the 17th century and includes the world's only known 1929 Mercedes-Benz fire truck. Other exhibits include the Arthur Fiedler memorabilia collection, a historic apothecary, and a blacksmith shop. Guided tours are given; related movies are shown.

Admission: $4.50 adults, $2.50 children aged 5–12, free for children under 5.

Open: Memorial Day to mid-Sept, daily 10am–3pm. Mid-Sept to Columbus Day, Sat–Sun 10am–3pm.

CAPE COD MUSEUM OF NATURAL HISTORY, Rte. 6A. Tel. 896-3867.

Those interested in Cape Cod's flora, fauna, and ecology will want to visit the Cape Cod Museum of Natural History. The museum organization was founded in 1954 to preserve the wildlife and plant life in the area around Stony Brook and its marshes, to study this land, and to teach others about it. Nature walks, a lecture program, and children's classes are held year round. In summer museum naturalists lead trips to Monomoy Island to observe birds and wildlife.

Admission: $3.50 adults, $1.50 children aged 6–14, free for children under 6.

Open: Wed–Sat 10am–4:30pm, Sun 12:30–4:30pm.

WHERE TO STAY

OLD MANSE INN, 1861 Main St. (P.O. Box 839), Brewster, MA 02631. Tel. 508/896-3149. 9 rms (all with bath). A/C TV **Directions:** At the end of Rte. 134, take Rte. 6A; the inn is 4½ miles down on the left side.

$ Rates (including breakfast): $65–$98 double. AE, DISC, MC, V. **Parking:** Free, on premises.

Just west of the intersection of Routes 6A and 124 South in Brewster is the Old Manse Inn, a lovely old white building surrounded by tall trees. Like so many other gracious Brewster houses, this one was built in the early 1800s by a captain in the China trade, one William Knowles. If you just want to relax and not wander out for meals, you'll be happy to know that both lunch and dinner (which have been highly praised by several food and wine writers) are served in the inn's dining room (reservations are required).

OLD SEA PINES INN, 2553 Main St., Brewster, MA 02631. Tel. 508/896-6114. 21 rms (16 with bath). **Directions:** Head east on Rte. 6A; the inn is on your left.

$ Rates (including full breakfast): June–Oct, $48 double without bath; $72–$108 single or double with bath; $150 suite with fireplace. Nov–May, 12%–15% discounts available. Extra person $18. AE, DC, MC, V. **Parking:** Free.

The Old Sea Pines Inn is a pleasant surprise. Built in 1907 as the Sea Pines School of Charm and Personality for Young Women, it retains its turn-of-the-century grace beneath the shade of several old oaks. The spacious, comfortable common rooms have hardwood floors and a working fireplace, and the wraparound porch is furnished with green cane rockers. The highest-priced room comes with a fireplace and four-poster bed. The family suite is for four people; the suite with a fireplace can accommodate two, three, or four people, and a bottle of champagne is included.

WHERE TO DINE

THE BRAMBLE INN & RESTAURANT, Rte. 6A. Tel. 896-7644.

Cuisine: NEW ENGLAND. **Reservations:** Required.

$ Prices: Fixed-price 4-course dinner $36–$44. AE, MC, V.

Open: Apr–Jan 1, dinner Tues–Sun 6–9pm.

Located in a building that dates back to 1861, The Bramble Inn & Restaurant, located just east of the intersection of Routes 6A and 124, is a wonderful old Cape Cod restaurant. There are five small dining rooms, each decorated with antique furnishings and unmatched vintage place settings. The restaurant is very conscientiously run and owned by the Manchester family, who do everything from wait tables to prepare the feasts in the kitchen. For a memorable feast, try the seafood stew. It is a sensationally delicious concoction of cod, lobster, shrimp, scallops, littlenecks, and mussels in a sherry rum tomato fumé with bay leaf, cumin, and allspice.

BREWSTER FISH HOUSE, Rte. 6A. Tel. 896-7867.

> **Cuisine:** SEAFOOD. **Reservations:** Not accepted. **Directions:** Head east on Rte. 6A; it's on your right.
>
> $ **Prices:** Main courses $5.75–$9 at lunch, $9.50–$17 at dinner; meals $18–$30. MC, V.
>
> **Open:** Mid-Apr to mid-Nov, daily 11:30am–"closing."

One look at the lunch or dinner menu at the Brewster Fish House and you're thrown into a tizzy. They offer all the standard seafood dishes, from grilled sea scallops to steamed lobster, but with their own special twists. For example, the grilled Atlantic salmon is prepared with a plum tomato and fresh herb sauce. The cod is served with a cranberry-and-ginger relish. The "Sautéed Cornmeal Flounder" is with lime, olive oil, capers, and salami. For non-seafood eaters, there are usually some lamb, veal, beef, and duck specials available. The Brewster Fish House is a good casual choice for a leisurely lunch or dinner. If you happen to pass it between meals, however, you can always stop in for a filling bowl of chowder.

CHILLINGSWORTH, 2449 Main St. Tel. 896-3640.

> **Cuisine:** CONTEMPORARY FRENCH. **Reservations:** Required. **Directions:** Go 1 mile east of the intersection of Routes 124 and 6A; it's on the left.
>
> $ **Prices:** Appetizers $3.50–$6 at lunch; main courses $6.75–$10.50 at lunch; dinner for two $100–$120; lunch $15–$20. AE, DC, MC, V.
>
> **Open:** Late June–early Sept, lunch Wed–Sun 11:30am–3pm; dinner Tues–Sun 6–6:30pm or 9–9:30pm. Memorial Day weekend–late June and mid-Sept to Nov, lunch Fri–Sat 11:30am–3pm; dinner Fri–Sat 6–6:30pm or 9–9:30pm; Sun brunch 11am–4pm.

Chef-owner Robert Rabin's Chillingsworth is one of the loveliest restaurants on the Cape. The fare is contemporary French cuisine; the atmosphere is a delightful blend of modern and traditional, cozy and spacious. There are two seatings for the seven-course dinner: 6 to 6:30pm and then again at 9 to 9:30pm. If you have a special celebration for a party of two to four, request the separate "library room."

9. CHATHAM

9.5 miles (15km) S of Orleans, 19 miles (31km) E of Hyannis

GETTING THERE See "Getting There" at the beginning of this chapter.

ESSENTIALS The **area code** is 508. During the summer season, there's an **information booth** at 533 Main St. in the center of town (tel. 508/945-0342). It's run by citizens who know the town inside and out, and offers brochures on places to stay, copies of menus from local restaurants, and information on activities. You can write to them at **Chatham Chamber of Commerce,** P.O. Box 793, Chatham, MA 02633. Public restrooms are next door, in the rear of the Town Hall.

Chatham was once the railhead for Cape Cod, and the trains that brought vacationers in and took fish, salt, and shoes out also brought the opportunity for wealth. Chatham is therefore a graceful community with many big old houses and inns, an easy pace, friendly people, and pleasant vistas all around.

WHAT TO SEE & DO

Chatham Light is the first place to go. Go east on Main Street and turn right (south) on Shore Road to the Light. The lighthouse is right next to the Coast Guard Station; on the other side of the street is a place to park while you look at the view through some coin-operated telescopes, and down below, a fine beach. The first light was erected on this point of land in 1808, and the present lighthouse dates from 1878.

The view is very pleasant, looking out to sea across Nauset Beach (the sand bar, actually a peninsula, you see out in the water). The cool sea breeze in summer and the nautical blast in winter make it incredible that Rome is at almost exactly the same latitude (but 4,200 miles away) as Chatham. To get to the **Fish Pier,** take Main Street east to Shore Street, then go left (north). The pier is operated by the town for licensed Chatham fishers. Chatham is very proud of its fishing fleet of small boats, which the townspeople boast brings in the freshest fish around. The boast has some truth to it, for the use of little boats means that the catch must be brought home every day; larger boats often stay out to sea for several days, refrigerating their catch on board.

The time to go down to the pier is between 3 and 6pm (aim for 4). You'll see the fleet come in and unload, and you can buy the day's catch right after it comes off the boat. Those who like to do it themselves can rent a boat at Fish Pier for a day's hunting for bass, bluefish, and tuna out at sea.

The town of Chatham has **public beaches** ($6 a day, $30 a week, $50 the season) at Oyster Pond, only a few blocks from the center of town south on State Harbor Road from Main Street; and a bit farther out at Harding's Beach—follow Main Street (Route 28) west from the center of town for about 2 miles, and turn left (south) onto Barn Hill Road to Harding's Beach Road. Lifeguards and toilets are at both beaches, but no bathhouses.

Chatham is a particularly good place for seeing birds, for **Monomoy Island,** south of the town, has been a National Wilderness Area since 1970. More than 300 different species of birds have been spotted on Monomoy. May is the best time to see birds in their mating plumage, and starting in late July many birds begin to be seen in winter plumage. The only way to get to Monomoy is by boat from Chatham. Full details on current offerings are available from the town's information booth on Main Street (tel. 508/945-0342). For wildlife-tour information, call 349-2615.

One of the nicest things about Chatham in July and August is the schedule of **band concerts** (every Friday evening at 8pm) in Kate Gould Park, just past the Wayside Inn on Main Street. Everybody comes to the concerts, and on a typical Friday evening the crowd may reach into the thousands. Most of the musicians in the town band are year-round residents of Chatham who live and work in the town and enjoy providing a little free entertainment for their fellow citizens and visitors once a week.

The **Monomoy Theater,** 776 Main St. (tel. 945-1589), not far west of the intersection with Old Harbor Road, is the summer-stock operation of Ohio University and offers a different play each week from mid-June through August. Performances are given Tuesday through Saturday (curtain rises at 8:30pm), and the current play is advertised on flyers around town and in the local newspapers. Season tickets are available, should you be spending the summer in Chatham.

ATWOOD HOUSE AND MUSEUMS, 347 Stage Harbor Rd. Tel. 945-2493.

Chatham has its share of antique buildings open to the public, each highlighting a separate part of the town's interesting past. The Atwood House and Museums are run by the Chatham Historical Society and feature more than 2,000 exhibits, including an outstanding shell collection, a good number of pieces of Sandwich glass, and a crewel bedspread which took townspeople 6 years to make. Also on display at the house is a set of French lighthouse lenses used in the Chatham Light from 1923 until recently.

Admission: $3 adults, $1 students, free for children accompanied by adults.

Open: Mid-June to Sept, Wed and Fri 2–5pm. **Closed:** Holidays.

RAILROAD MUSEUM, Depot Rd. No phone.

Chatham's Railroad Museum is located in the old station on Depot Road (take

Old Harbor Road north off Main Street, and Depot Street is a short distance up on the left). The station was built in 1887 by the Chatham Railroad Company and was turned into a museum in 1960. Among the railroading exhibits is a completely restored 1910 wooden caboose, used by the New York Central until that company gave it to the museum. The museum is staffed by volunteer guides.

Admission: Donations accepted.

Open: Mid-June to mid-Sept, Tues–Sat 10am–4pm.

GRIST MILL, Shattuck Place. No phone.

Chatham also has an old Grist Mill open to the public. Sometimes corn is ground between the mill's stones if the wind is sufficient. To find it, take Cross Street south off Main Street to Shattuck Place, which winds down to the mill.

Admission: Donations accepted.

Open: July–Aug, Sat–Sun 10am–4pm.

WHERE TO STAY

A RESORT HOTEL

CHATHAM BARS INN, Shore Rd., Chatham, MA 02633. Tel. 508/945-0096, or toll free 800/527-4884. Fax 508/945-5491. 150 rms and cottages (all with bath). TEL **Directions:** Take Rte. 6 East to Rte. 137, proceed 3 miles and turn left onto Rte. 28 South. Go 3 more miles, through the traffic circle, to the end of Main St. Take a left on Shore Rd. and the inn is ½ mile down on the left.

$ Rates (including breakfast, dinner, and service): Summer, $330–$550 double; without dinner $165–$385 double. AE, DC, MC, V. **Parking:** Free, on premises.

The Chatham Bars Inn is a true bit of old Chatham, a huge, rambling, gracious resort complex with 26 attractive cottages (no kitchens) on the property. Approach the inn by the motor entrance, bear to the right, and you'll enter the parlor, with its high-arched ceiling, lots of windows looking onto a shady veranda, and wicker furniture for cool sitting on warm summer days. The lobby is also grand, large, and spacious, and a stairway out the front door tumbles down the hillside to the road and beyond it to the inn's private beach.

The staff is large, friendly, well trained, and soft-spoken. If the rates look high, remember that, on the average, a luxury inn or motel room costs around $140, plus two breakfasts and two good dinners, which often brings a normal vacation day's expenses to around $300 per couple daily. The Chatham Bars Inn is a bit of history brought up to modern standards of comfort and service.

Dining/Entertainment: Proper dress is required in the cocktail lounge and in the main dining room in the evening: jacket and tie for men; summer cottons or cocktail dress for women.

Services: Children's program in July and August; Guest Services Director on hand.

Facilities: Private beach, outdoor heated pool, five outdoor tennis courts, nine-hole golf course.

INNS

Expensive

BRADFORD INN AND MOTEL, 26 Cross St. (P.O. Box 750), Chatham, MA 02633. Tel. 508/945-1030, or toll free 800/562-4667. Fax 508/945-9652. 25 rms (all with bath). A/C MINIBAR TV TEL **Directions:** From town center, take Main St., turn right onto Cross St.

$ Rates (including full breakfast): Summer, $126–$197 double. Winter, $87–$170 double. AE, DISC, MC, V. **Parking:** Free.

The Gray family's Bradford Inn and Motel is right at the center of town. This extremely neat and tidy complex has 25 guest rooms (11 in a motel annex), a patio, outdoor heated pool, and silk flowers everywhere. Rooms and suites come with a basket of amenities, and some have refrigerators and kitchen facilities. This should be your first motel choice in Chatham. The restaurant, Champlain's, serves dinner nightly in season. It's open on weekends off season.

CAPTAIN'S HOUSE INN, 369-377 Old Harbor Rd., Chatham, MA 02633. Tel. 508/945-0127. 16 rms (all with bath). A/C TEL
$ Rates (including continental breakfast and afternoon tea): Summer, $108–$202 single or double. AE, MC, V. **Parking:** Free.

For my money, Chatham's most perfectly charming inn is Cathy and Dave Eakin's Captain's House Inn. Located ½ mile from the center of town on Route 28 going toward Orleans, the Captain's House, on a private 2-acre estate, has plenty of space for green lawns and flower gardens. It was in fact built by Capt. Hiram Harding in 1839, with various additions later. The guest rooms all have period furnishings, which include some wing chairs, canopy beds, and braided rugs. Three rooms have fireplaces. The Carriage House has five bedrooms, the Cottage has three bedrooms—the best choice for large families or small groups. A continental breakfast and afternoon tea are served.

CHATHAM TOWN HOUSE INN, 11 Library Lane, Chatham, MA 02633. Tel. 508/945-2180, or toll free 800/242-2180. Fax 508/945-3900. 26 rms (all with bath). A/C MINIBAR TV TEL
$ Rates (including continental breakfast): Summer, $137–$202 double with bath; $1,837 cottage, rented by the week (up to 5 persons). Extra person $25. AE, DC, MC, V. **Parking:** Free.

Another downtown inn, at the corner of Library Lane and Main Street, the Chatham Town House has 26 rooms, plus a six-room lodge and several cottages. All the rooms are decorated differently, but with taste and thoughtfulness; hand-hooked rugs rather than wall-to-wall carpeting are used, so that the beautiful old floors can be seen. All have individual thermostats.

The Two Turtles restaurant serves lunch and breakfast during the high summer season only. Reservations are not required. The inn has a swimming pool and a spa.

CHATHAM WAYSIDE INN, 512 Main St., Chatham, MA 02633. Tel. 508/945-1800, or toll free 800/545-4667. 30 rms (all with bath). A/C TV TEL
$ Rates: Summer, $104–$120 double. AE, DC, MC, V. **Parking:** Free.

The Chatham Wayside Inn is owned by Guenther Weinkopf of the Queen Anne Inn. His extensive renovations have brought this old 19th-century hostelry up to—and beyond—current standards for comfort and charm. The guest rooms are located in the cottages surrounding the inn; decor is Early American, but the bathrooms are modern. You won't find an inn more centrally located than the Wayside, on Main Street right next to Kate Gould Park (where the band concerts are held in summer).

The inn's dining room, Sam Bellamy's Tavern, specializes in seafood and pub grub; in the fine summer weather, the Bandstand Café takes over the large porch overlooking Main Street. The inn has a swimming pool.

MULBERRY INN, 44 Cross St. (P.O. Box 212), Chatham, MA 02633. Tel. 508/945-2020, or toll free 800/562-4667. Fax 508/945-9652. 3 rms (all with bath). A/C TV TEL **Directions:** From town center, take Main St., turn right onto Cross St.
$ Rates (including full breakfast): Summer, $170 double. Winter, $126 double. AE, DISC, MC, V. **Parking:** Free.

Right next door to the Bradford Inn and Motel (see above) is the Mulberry Inn, also managed by the Gray family. They've restored this historic house with turn-of-the-century furnishings, including canopy beds, and have added new private bathrooms, and other modern amenities.

QUEEN ANNE INN, 70 Queen Anne Rd., Chatham, MA 02633. Tel. 508/945-0394, or toll free 800/545-4667. Fax 508/945-4884. 30 rms (all with bath). TEL **Directions:** Take Rte. 6 East to Rte. 137 South to Rte. 28 toward Chatham. At your first traffic light bear right onto Queen Anne Rd. and the inn will be in sight immediately on your right.

$ Rates (including continental breakfast): $126–$265 double. AE, EU, MC, V. **Parking:** Free.

The Queen Anne Inn is just a few blocks from the center of Chatham and has been a favorite hostelry here for well over a century. The graceful, shingled, gabled inn is authentic 19th-century Cape Cod, but has many of the amenities of a resort hotel. Several of the rooms have fireplaces, private balconies (some look onto the Oyster Pond), and whirlpool baths (but no TVs). Guests can also enjoy the excursions to Monomoy Island to see the seals, shore birds, and deer. Guenther Weinkopf, the innkeeper, is also a licensed boat captain, so the excursions are easy and reliable.

Elegant dinners are available Wednesday to Monday at the inn's Earl of Chatham restaurant from 6:30 to 10pm. Facilities include tennis courts (with a resident pro for lessons and clinics), bicycles, an indoor spa, and boats for waterskiing.

Moderate

CRANBERRY INN AT CHATHAM, 359 Main St., Chatham, MA 02633. Tel. 508/945-9232, or toll free 800/332-4667. 18 rms (all with bath). A/C TV TEL

$ Rates (including continental breakfast): Summer, $122–$164 single or double. Off-season, $96–$137 single or double. AE, MC, V. **Parking:** Free. **Closed:** Jan to mid-Mar.

A few minutes' walk from downtown is the Cranberry Inn at Chatham operated by Richard Morris and Peggy DeHan, two self-proclaimed "old house enthusiasts." The two—who have a combined innkeeping experience of nearly 20 years—have been very successful in restoring the inn to its original grandeur. The Cranberry Inn is a Chatham landmark, having stood here since 1830. Its 19th-century guests might still feel at home by the fireplace in the restaurant, or among the antique and reproduction furnishings of the guest rooms, but today's travelers appreciate the modern amenities. Children 12 or older are welcome.

CYRUS KENT HOUSE INN, 63 Cross St., at Kent Place, Chatham, MA 02633. Tel. 508/945-9104, or toll free 800/338-5368. 10 rms (all with bath). TV TEL

$ Rates (including breakfast): $71–$120 single; $82–$126 double; $93–$159 suite. Extra person $22. AE, MC, V. **Parking:** Free, on premises.

Located within steps of Chatham's restaurants and shops, and within walking distance of the water, this former sea captain's house is ideally situated. Guests can stay in the main house in an antique brass or canopy bed or in a fireplaced suite in "The Carriage House." Common rooms include a large inviting living room stocked with all the latest area brochures and local newspapers, a sundeck out back, and a breakfast room, where homemade goodies are served by candlelight every morning. Between Labor Day and Memorial Day, complimentary afternoon tea is also served. In every corner, you'll see innkeeper Jodie's touch; she used to be a florist. All the rooms are freshly decorated with thoughtfully selected fabrics and furniture.

A GUESTHOUSE

BOW ROOF HOUSE, 59 Queen Anne Rd., Chatham, MA 02633. Tel. 508/945-1346. 6 rms (all with bath). **Directions:** Take Rte. 6 East to Rte. 137 South to Rte. 28 toward Chatham. At your first traffic light bear right onto Queen Anne Rd. and the house is on the left.

$ Rates (including breakfast and based on a stay of 3 or more nights): $55–$60 double. No credit cards. **Parking:** Free.

⑤ The Bow Roof House has been run by the Mazulis family for 18 years now. It's a pleasant guesthouse out toward the water and also only a few minutes' walk from the center of town and a shopping center. The main house is that of an old sea captain, and many rooms still have the original fireplaces (not working now). A large living room with rough-timbered ceiling and large fireplace is here for guests' use, and just through the door from it is a terrace with tables and umbrellas for a glass of wine (BYO) or tea in the evening. If you go in summer, the bank in front of the house will be a riot of wildflowers, and the two yuccas by the door may be in bloom.

MOTELS

THE MOORINGS MOTOR LODGE, 326 Main St., Chatham, MA 02633. Tel. 508/945-0848. 20 rms (16 with bath). TV
$ Rates (including continental breakfast): $44–$71 carriage-house room; $82–$115 guesthouse or motel room. MC, V. **Parking:** Free.

Close to the downtown area and just steps to the beach, this grand old Chatham house has a carriage (or coach) house with a motel annex, efficiency apartments, and cottages. The complex once belonged to a retired admiral and now serves well as a hostelry, owned by Jan and Earl Rush. Furnishings and styles of rooms vary with the building you stay in: The guesthouse is traditional Victorian, the motel annex is modern but decorated in colonial style.

PLEASANT BAY VILLAGE RESORT MOTEL, Rte. 28 (P.O. Box 772), Chatham, MA 02633. Tel. 508/945-1133. 58 rms (all with bath). A/C TV TEL **Directions:** Turn left onto Rte. 137 from Rte. 6 and then after a short distance, turn left onto Pleasant Bay Rd. Continue to the end until you reach Rte. 28. Turn right, and Pleasant Bay Village is 1 mile ahead.
$ Rates: $104–$115 single; $126–$170 double; $213–$268 suite. AE, MC, V. **Parking:** Free.

The Pleasant Bay Village Resort Motel, on Route 28 several miles north of town, in the section called Chathamport, is accessible only by car. The motel is about as pleasant as you'll find, located on 6 acres of very skillfully landscaped grounds, with evergreen hedges, trees, bushes, and roses, plus a waterfall and pond. The motel's buildings are scattered through the grounds, and there's a heated pool, shuffleboard, and Ping-Pong, besides just lounging in the sun, to keep you occupied. The motel has a breakfast room (light lunches served as well). Rooms are modern with wall-to-wall carpeting.

WHERE TO DINE

IN CHATHAM

BREAK-AWAY CAFE, 201 Main St. Tel. 945-5288.
  Cuisine: AMERICAN. **Reservations:** Recommended for parties over 6. **Directions:** From Chatham center, head towards the sea on Main St. At intersection of Shore Rd. and Main St., turn right. Restaurant is on right just before Hallett Lane.
$ Prices: Menu items $1.95–$10.95. MC, V.
  Open: Mon–Sat 7:30am–8:15pm, Sun 7:30am–4pm.

You can't help but notice this little café as you walk by; it's a tiny shingled building with bright pink-and-white trim. Window boxes crowded with blossoms spill over in front. Inside, there are ceiling fans, wood beams, and checkered tablecloths. The daily specials are listed on the blackboard, but you can count on finding some reliable favorites, such as burgers, quiches, tuna melts, and chef salads. Dinner main courses include a selection of seafood, beef, veal, and chicken dishes. The café will prepare box lunches for those heading out to the beach or taking day-trips. As of this printing, the café does not serve alcohol, but this may change by the time you visit.

CHRISTIAN'S, 443 Main St. Tel. 945-3362.
  Cuisine: AMERICAN. **Reservations:** Required downstairs.
$ Prices: Appetizers $5–$8; main courses $18–$22; meals downstairs $35–$40; meals upstairs $10–$15. AE, DC, DISC, MC, V.
  Open: Summer, daily 11:30am–10pm.

Lodged in an old Chatham house in the middle of town, Christian's has a cocktail bar and light menu served upstairs on a pretty deck (open at 4pm), and several dining rooms within the house itself. The dinner menu is original: crab buerrecks (flaky pastry filled with crabmeat and a bit of curry), seafood mélange (lobster, shrimps, and scallops), or filet mignon prepared any of three ways. In the summer there's entertainment nightly; in spring and fall the music is on weekends only.

COOKIE MANOR, 499 Main St. Tel. 945-1152.
  Cuisine: ICE CREAM/FAST FOOD. **Reservations:** Not required.
$ **Prices:** Main courses $3–$5. No credit cards.
  Open: Memorial Day–Labor Day, daily 7am–10pm. Labor Day–Memorial Day, daily 7am–5pm.
When you get a craving for ice cream, make your way to the Cookie Manor, located right in the center of town. Here, you'll find more than 18 flavors plus a great selection of sandwiches (try the honey-baked ham and cheese, $3.95), pizza, and house specialties like homemade carrot cake and chocolate zucchini cake, which has been featured in food magazines. The Cookie Manor also serves breakfast from 7 to 11am, for under $5.

IMPUDENT OYSTER, 15 Chatham Bars Ave. Tel. 945-3545.
  Cuisine: INTERNATIONAL. **Reservations:** Recommended.
$ **Prices:** Main courses $6.50–$9.50 at lunch, $16–$23 at dinner; dinner $30–$40. AE, MC, V.
  Open: Lunch Mon–Sat 11:30am–3pm, Sun noon–3pm; dinner daily 5:30–10pm.
  Closed: Thanksgiving Day, Dec 24–25.
The Impudent Oyster, located just off Main Street, has a long and eclectic menu. Chinese, French, Italian, and Mexican-style dishes, each with a different local touch; sandwiches and elegant main courses; seafood and meats—all share the menu. The oysters, by the way, are freshly shucked. Dress neatly, but not formally.

SEA IN THE ROUGH, 1077 Main St. (Rte. 28). Tel. 945-1700.
  Cuisine: SEAFOOD. **Reservations:** Not accepted. **Directions:** Take Rte. 28 toward Harwich.
$ **Prices:** Appetizers $2–$7; main courses $7.50–$15. DISC, MC, V.
  Open: Apr–Oct, daily 11:30am–9pm.
If you don't mind driving 10 minutes from the center of town, head out to Sea in the Rough. It's a good, hearty, informal, family place with red vinyl chairs, basic service, and generous servings. In nice weather, sit outside on the side patio under the shade of umbrellas. The entire menu is available all day. Dinner specials on the blackboard start at 5pm and might be fresh salmon or tuna, or any number of chicken dishes.

IN HARWICH PORT

CAFE ELIZABETH, 31 Sea St. Tel. 432-1147.
  Cuisine: CLASSIC FRENCH. **Reservations:** Recommended. **Directions:** Take Rte. 28 6 miles south of Chatham.
$ **Prices:** Appetizers $5–$12.50; main courses $19.50–$33; dinner $40–$50. DC, MC, V.
  Open: Mid-May to Columbus Day, dinner daily 6–9pm.
Café Elizabeth has the atmosphere of an auberge, a French country inn. The owner, Marguerite, will greet you with a French accent and show you to a table in one of the small, cozy dining rooms. For an appetizer, try shrimp quickly sautéed in butter, cayenne pepper, and fresh ground pepper, then flambéed with cognac. As a main course, try an assortment of four médaillons: shrimp with sauce Bonifacio, veal with wild mushrooms, lamb with fresh tarragon, filet with béarnaise; as dessert, a special chocolate truffle. If you prefer a strawberry tarte, put your name on one when you walk past the dessert tray; they disappear rapidly. For those interested in classical French cuisine in a less formal setting, Café Elizabeth has recently opened "Le Petit Café" at the same location. Prices for appetizers range from $2.75 to $3.95; main courses, $7.75 to $12.95. The hours are the same.

10. ORLEANS & EASTHAM

Orleans: 8 miles (13 km) S of Wellfleet
Eastham: 10 miles (16 km) S of Wellfleet

GETTING THERE   See "Getting There" at the beginning of this chapter.

ESSENTIALS   The **area code** is 508. You can contact the **Orleans Chamber of Commerce,** P.O. Box 153, Orleans, MA 02653 (tel. 508/255-1386), or the **Eastham Chamber of Commerce,** P.O. Box 1329B, Eastham, MA 02642 (tel. 508/255-3444).

ORLEANS

Orleans is the midpoint between Cape Cod Canal and Provincetown and is a good place to stop for a meal or a night's rest. Nearby, Eastham has a few attractions worth stopping for.

Orleans owes its name and its fame to French connections. Known as Nauset since its earliest settlement in 1644, the town was renamed Orleans in 1797 when it was separated from neighboring Eastham and incorporated. The duke of Orléans had made a visit to Cape Cod, and the townspeople chose the name in the French nobleman's honor.

Orleans's other French connection was as close as can be without moving continents. In 1879 Orleans was physically connected by underwater telegraph cable with the town of Brest in France, almost 4,000 miles away. You can still see the telegraph station where the cable came ashore before continuing overland to New York.

In its day Orleans has made its living through fishing and shellfishing, clothing manufacture, agriculture, and the production of salt from seawater, not to mention trade in contraband. During the revolutionary war, Orleans sent men and supplies to aid the colonial forces. In the War of 1812, the town refused to pay $1,000 "protection money" demanded by the British enemy. A landing force was sent ashore from HMS *Newcastle,* and the town militia quickly convinced the Redcoats that it was probably a good idea to return to the ship, which they did. Needless to say, Orleans kept its $1,000. When a German submarine broke the surface off Nauset Beach during World War I, the townspeople again demonstrated their coolness in the face of danger. The sub released a few torpedoes at some coal barges, and everybody turned out to watch the show.

WHAT TO SEE & DO

Orleans has a rare sight: a museum in the building erected to house the American terminus of a transatlantic cable from Brest, France. Laid in 1879, the cable came to Orleans in 1891, and the **French Cable Station Museum,** Route 28 and Cove Road (tel. 240-1735), remains much as it was when the cable was still in use. Among other important messages, the cable, which remained in use until 1959, transmitted word of Lindbergh's arrival in Paris. Admission costs $2 for adults, $1 for children aged 12 to 18, and is free for children 12 and under. It's open from early June through Labor Day, 10am to 4pm, Monday through Saturday.

Several good beaches are a short distance from Orleans. Remember that Atlantic-side beaches will invariably be cooler for swimming than the beaches on Cape Cod Bay.

Nauset Beach, a stretch of wide, flat sand 10 miles long, is a town beach of Orleans, and therefore subject to an $8 daily parking fee ($14 off-season); the use of bathhouse and other facilities is included. Permits for a week or more are also available at reduced prices. The surfing's not bad at Nauset, and a section of the beach is reserved for it.

Skaket Beach, on Cape Cod Bay, has less surf, but warmer water and a gently sloping beach. It's operated by the town, with lifeguards, parking places, and a bathhouse, and there's a $6 charge. This is an especially good beach for families with young children.

A short detour to Fort Point off Route 6A will reveal a breathtaking **view** of the surrounding marshlands. There are also some nice trails you can take down to Nauset Marsh.

Orleans is home to a store that's quickly becoming a major Lower Cape attraction. The **Bird Watcher's General Store** (Route 6A; tel. 508/255-6974) is exactly as its name implies: a general store devoted to birds for bird lovers. Here you'll find birds on everything from postcards to mailboxes, as well as bins of corn, thistle, and sunflower and a good selection of birdhouses. Our favorite find: a mallard duck phone that quacks when it rings ($49.95).

WHERE TO STAY

THE COVE, Rte. 28 (P.O. Box 279), Orleans, MA 02653. Tel. 508/255-1203, or toll free 800/343-2233. 47 rms (all with bath). A/C TV TEL
$ Rates: Summer, $97–$174 double. AE, DC, DISC, MC, V. **Parking:** Free.
The Cove is a motel . . . and then some. What separates it from the average motel is its landscaped grounds (complete with gardens, patios, and a heated pool) and its attention to detail. You'll find all rooms have the customary motel amenities, but they also have special extras, such as small refrigerators and coffee makers, and all are individually decorated. All guests are treated to a cruise on The Cove's float boat and to a cookout on the beach.

NAUSET HOUSE INN, Beach Rd. (P.O. Box 774), East Orleans, MA 02643. Tel. 508/225-2195. 14 rms (8 with bath).
$ Rates: $65–$77 single or double without bath, $98–$115 single or double with bath. MC, V. **Parking:** Free. **Closed:** Nov–Mar.
Absolutely every inch of the Nauset House Inn seems to have been touched by somebody with good taste. From the gardened grounds to the antique-furnished rooms, this family-owned inn is obviously very loved. One of the highlights of every stay is the country breakfast prepared by innkeeper Diane Johnson (so many guests have asked for the recipes, she has printed them up in a booklet). Another highlight is taking time out to relax in the Conservatory, a greenhouse garden centerpieced by a weeping cherry tree. Each room is a conversation piece, with hand-painted stenciling, hooked rugs, and truly unique antiques. On top of all that, the Nauset House Inn is just ½ mile from the beach.

ORLEANS HOLIDAY MOTEL, Rte. 6A (P.O. Box 386), Orleans, MA 02653. Tel. 508/255-1514, or toll free 800/451-1833, 800/451-1818 in Mass. 46 rms (all with bath). A/C MINIBAR TV TEL
$ Rates (including continental breakfast): $49–$93 single; $51–$104 double. AE, DC, DISC, MC, V. **Parking:** Free.
The Orleans Holiday, just past the intersection of Routes 6A and 28 as you head northeast, has contemporary motel rooms, all with tile bath and shower, picture windows, and a balcony-walkway. There's a fine large pool surrounded by lounge chairs and equipped with a slide and backyard garden and picnic area. Several rooms in the unit behind Joseph's Lighthouse (open for breakfast, lunch, and dinner) are larger than normal, newer, and a bit more luxurious.

SHIP'S KNEES INN, 186 Beach Rd. (P.O. Box 756), East Orleans, MA 02643. Tel. 508/255-1312. Fax 508/240-1351. 22 rms (11 with bath).
Directions: Take Exit 12 off Rte. 6. Turn right at bottom of ramp onto Eldredge Pkwy., and go 1 mile to the second set of traffic lights at Main St. Turn right and go 1½ miles and bear left at the fork in the road onto Beach Rd. The inn is 1 mile ahead.
$ Rates (including continental breakfast): May–Oct $60–$88 double without bath; $107–$110 double with bath. Off-season, rates lower. MC, V. **Parking:** Free.

Propped up on a sunny knoll 5 minutes from Nauset Beach, the Ship's Knees is a restored 170-year-old sea captain's house. The name "Ship's Knees" comes from the fact that when the house was built, it was held together by ship's knees—the blocks of wood that connect deck beams to ship frames. The inn's rooms are done in a colonial decor, some with water views, and with either private or shared bath; the nearby Cove House has more rooms, each with private bath, color cable TV, and water view. Two rental cottages and one efficiency rent for $713 to $850 per week from May through October (off-season rates are available). They are right at the water's edge, with private bath and color cable TV. A tennis court and swimming pool are on the grounds.

WHERE TO DINE

THE ARBOR, Rte. 28. Tel. 255-4847.
  Cuisine: ECLECTIC. **Reservations:** Required.
$ **Prices:** Main courses $12–$20. MC, V.
  Open: May–Oct, dinner daily 5–10pm. Nov–Apr, dinner Fri–Sun 5–10pm.
Serving creative cuisine in more eclectic surroundings, the Arbor combines just the right ingredients to make a person relax. Perhaps it's the yellow toy truck and the antique tins, or maybe it's the sincere service. At any rate, for starters you'll get an extensive assortment of vegetables, dips, and crackers, followed by homemade biscuits. Proceed to a main course of veal, beef, fowl, or fish. In the adjacent Binnacle Tavern, fare is less formal and more family-oriented, and includes rich and elaborate pizzas. Binnacle Tavern stays open until 11:30pm. If you dine before 6:25pm and pay cash, your dinner will cost 20% less.

JOSEPH'S LIGHTHOUSE RESTAURANT, Rte. 6A. Tel. 255-2266.
  Cuisine: SEAFOOD/NEW AMERICAN. **Reservations:** Recommended.
$ **Prices:** Appetizers $4.95–$8.95; main courses $4.95–$7.95 at lunch, $9.95–$15.95 at dinner. CB, DC, MC, V.
  Open: Sun–Thurs 6am–10pm, Fri–Sat 6am–11pm.
One of Orleans's newest restaurants, Joseph's offers a wide selection of healthy and innovative dishes. For lunch, consider the seafood fettuccine (with shrimp, scallops, clams, and lobster, served in a basil cream, $7.95). For dinner, try the Maryland deviled crab cakes and lemon salsa ($13.50), the chicken and shrimp stir fry ($12.95), or anything else, and you'll not be sorry. Joseph's is an attractive restaurant with lots of hanging plants and windows.

KADEE'S LOBSTER & CLAM BAR, 212 Main St., East Orleans. Tel. 255-6184.
  Cuisine: SEAFOOD. **Reservations:** Not accepted. **Directions:** Follow Beach Rd. east toward East Orleans; Kadee's will be on the left.
$ **Prices:** Appetizers $2.50–$13; main courses $7–$17. MC, V.
  Open: Daily 11:30am–9:30pm.
A food writer recently called Kadee's Lobster & Clam Bar "as delightful a find as the Steuben glass bowl you always hope to unearth at a flea market." The seafood here is fresh (and wonderfully affordable) thanks to the fact that the restaurant is owned by the owners of the next-door East Orleans Fish Market. Favorites include the Kadee's Clambake (a 1¼ lobster served with steamers and cobbed corn), char-grilled swordfish, and a selection of fruity drinks (try the cranberry bog or the apricot sunset). You can sit outside in the sun or under a shady umbrella, or step inside to one of the cheery dining areas hung with fish nets and buoys. Kadee's also has a take-out window (where you can get everything from chowder to boiled lobster) and a gift shop full of T-shirts, visors, and other items emblazoned with the restaurant's logo.

LOBSTER CLAW, Rte. 6A. Tel. 255-1800.
  Cuisine: SEAFOOD. **Reservations:** Not accepted.
$ **Prices:** Main courses $8–$14; meals $9–$16; lobsters $15–$17; daily specials $12. AE, MC, V.
  Open: Apr–Nov, daily 11:30am–9pm.

If you're itching to have the experience of rolling up your sleeves, wearing a bib, and feasting on lobster, the Lobster Claw is the place to do it. Though unquestionably geared for tourists and downright kitschy, this place is a lot of fun. The atmosphere is family-friendly with buoys, fishnets, and lobster traps, with marine murals providing the backdrop. The menus, in the shape of lobster claws, list fish and seafood plates, lobsters, and daily specials, such as soft-shell crabs with French fries and coleslaw. The lobster rolls here are the fattest and tastiest you'll find in the area.

EASTHAM

Eastham's main attraction is the **Salt Pond Visitor Center** of the Cape Cod National Seashore (see below). Right across the street from the center is the quaint and attractive **Eastham Historical Society Museum.** Look for the curious gateway, made from the jawbones of a huge whale. The museum, once a schoolhouse, dates from 1869.

Just south of the Salt Pond Visitor Center on U.S. 6 is the **oldest windmill** on Cape Cod (1793), a favorite place to stop and take a photo. From the windmill, take a side trip west to **First Encounter Beach,** where the Pilgrims first met the Native American inhabitants of the Cape back in 1620. A plaque on a boulder up the hill just north of the parking lot commemorates the meeting, which apparently was anything but cordial. You can visit the boulder plaque for free, but if you want to park and use the beach during the summer, you'll have to pay the town's beach-use parking fee ($5 daily, $15 weekly).

---

11. CAPE COD NATIONAL SEASHORE

ESSENTIALS The National Seashore includes virtually all of the eastern shore of Cape Cod, from Chatham to Provincetown. For information, send a stamped, self-addressed, business-size envelope to: Superintendent, Cape Cod National Seashore, South Wellfleet, MA 02663, or call 508/349-3785. Once in the area, you'll find two extremely efficient visitors centers: the **Salt Pond Visitor Center,** on Route 6 in Eastham (tel. 508/255-3421), and **Province Lands Visitor Center,** on Race Point Road in Provincetown (tel. 508/487-1256). Each contains exhibits, an audiovisual presentation, maps, pamphlets, and information services. There are several activities that take place throughout the summer including guided walks, talks, and evening programs. The centers are open daily from spring until early winter from 9am to 4:30pm.

Established by President Kennedy in 1961 to protect the area from commercialization, the Cape Cod National Seashore encompasses nearly 44,000 acres. It protects much of the Cape's "forearm," including some of its most beautiful ocean beaches. In addition to the beaches (six are run by the Federal government and have lifeguard services and related facilities, and several towns also have public beaches), there are picnic areas, bicycle trails, bridle paths, and self-guided nature trails. Visitors may surf and windsurf outside lifeguarded beaches and surf-fish from many of the beaches away from swimmers. Within the National Seashore area, which stretches 40 miles from the southern tip of Nauset Beach all the way to Provincetown, there are four developed areas for visitors. (Keep in mind that there is a $5 parking fee at all the beaches.)

NAUSET AREA If you're driving out on the Cape, this is the first part of the National Seashore you'll reach. Stop at the **Salt Pond Visitor Center** on Route 6A in Eastham. Here, you can pick up maps and pamphlets and get an overall orientation to the seashore. Inquire about the summer evening programs.

There are two beaches in the Nauset Area, including **Nauset Light Beach** (at the end of Cable Road in Eastham), which is one of the Outer Cape's most attractive. The other beach is **Coast Guard Beach,** which has taken somewhat of a beating from winter storms. Parking is restricted at the latter, but a free shuttlebus is provided from a parking lot near Nauset Light Beach. The bus runs from late June to early September.

In addition to the beaches, there are several nature trails, including the mile-long **Nauset Marsh Trail** that takes you around Salt Pond and Nauset Marsh, and **Buttonbush Trail,** a ¼-mile-long trail that's part boardwalk. Both originate at the visitors center. The **Nauset Bike Trail** (1½ miles) winds its way from the visitors center to Coast Guard Beach.

MARCONI STATION AREA Here's where you'll find the seashore's headquarters (in South Wellfleet). There's also an interpretive shelter at the site of Marconi's wireless station, the first in the United States. **Marconi Beach** is a lovely stretch of sand located behind the National Seashore headquarters. There are two self-guided nature trails to follow, including the **Atlantic White Cedar Swamp Trail** (1¼ miles long) and the **Great Island Trail,** a 4-mile-long (one-way!) trail that takes you through some of the seashore's most densely scenic shoreline.

PILGRIM HEIGHTS AREA This area between North Truro and Provincetown on the Outer Cape has an interpretive shelter dealing with the Pilgrims and Native Americans, a picnic area, several nature trails, a bike trail, the **Head of the Meadow Beach** (follow Head of the Meadow Road in Truro to the end), and the picturesque **Highland Light** (also known as the Cape Cod Light). Do make a point of seeing the lighthouse. It was the very first one in Cape Cod, built in 1797 to warn sailors of the notorious stretch known as "the graveyard of ships." It was rebuilt in 1857 and converted to electric power in 1932.

Nature trails in the Pilgrim Heights area include the **Cranberry Bog Trail,** a ½-mile-long path that is part boardwalk, **Small Swamp Trail** (¾ mile), and **Pilgrim Spring Trail** (¾ mile), which leads to the site of a spring where Pilgrims may have drunk their first water in the New World. The **Head of the Meadow Bike Trail** spans a 2-mile distance from the bay side to the ocean side of the Cape.

PROVINCE LANDS AREA A **visitors center** outside Provincetown on Race Point Road provides information and exhibits on the seashore. There are audio visual programs, an amphitheater, and evening programs in summer months. There are two excellent beaches in the area. **Race Point** (at the end of Race Point Road in Provincetown) is a spectacularly scenic beach backed by dunes that look like whipped egg white. **Herring Cove** (on Province Lands Road in Provincetown) is a bayside beach and *the* place to go to watch the sunset.

Throughout the Province Lands area there's a webwork of bicycle paths that take you over dunes, through pine groves, and alongside the sea. These include the **Loop Trail** (5¼ miles), **Herring Cove Beach** spur (1 mile), **Race Point Beach** spur (½ mile), **Bennett Pond** spur (¼ mile), and **Race Point Road** spur (¼ mile).

Beech Forest Trail is a 1-mile-long self-guided nature trail that takes you through a consistently scenic part of the Province Lands scenery. There's also a picnic area.

12. WELLFLEET

10 miles (16 km) N of Eastham, 12½ miles (20 km) SE of Provincetown

GETTING THERE See "Getting There" at the beginning of this chapter.

ESSENTIALS The **area code** is 508. The **Wellfleet Chamber of Commerce,** P.O. Box 571, Wellfleet, MA 02667 (tel. 508/349-2510), operates an information booth just off Route 6 on the way into town. Hours are 9am to 6pm daily from late June through Labor Day; off-season, it's open Friday through Sunday from 10am to 4pm.

Cooking lobsters and corn on the cob at a beach picnic, meeting friends downtown at the lunch counter for a mid-morning's lazy second cup of coffee, running errands barefoot or in rubber thongs—if you've enjoyed that sort of an easy summer atmosphere, Wellfleet will bring it back to you. Although a number of motels on U.S. 6 take in travelers heading for Provincetown, Wellfleet is mostly a town of "steadies," people who come every summer for the whole summer. But it does have a few inns and restaurants worth a look should you find it good to stop here.

WHAT TO SEE & DO

As most of Wellfleet's crowd is permanent for the summer, not as many things are available for the transient visitor. Note the **town clock** in the steeple of the First Congregational Church, which, Wellfleetans proudly say, is the only church clock in the world that rings ship's time.

Most **beaches** are reserved for permanent or all-summer residents (you need two different permits to swim there, and if you're passing through it's not worth getting them), but White Crest Beach and Cahoon's Hollow Beach, off U.S. 6 on the Atlantic coast, are open to day visitors for $10. And you can always go south on U.S. 6 a short distance from Wellfleet and turn left (east) to the **Marconi Beach** in the national seashore. At the beach is an ocean overlook and an interpretive shelter explaining the activities of the **Marconi Wireless Station,** the first in the United States, which was on this site. The Atlantic White Cedar Swamp nature trail starts from here as well.

The Massachusetts Audubon Society operates the **Wellfleet Bay Wildlife Sanctuary,** P.O. Box 236, South Wellfleet, MA 02663 (tel. 349-2615), 1,000 acres of woods, salt marshes, moors, freshwater pond, and sandy beach. A year-round program of hikes, birding trips, canoe expeditions, boat cruises, workshops, and speakers is offered. There are also birding tours to **Monomoy National Wildlife Refuge.** In July and August, there's a natural-history daycamp for children. From July through September, there are field schools for adults. Trails are open year round from 8am to dusk. Sanctuary admission is $3 for adults and $2 for children.

A REFUELING STOP IN TRURO If you want to head straight to the beach, but you're starving from the long drive and don't want to deal with traffic in P-town, turn off Route 6A into downtown Truro for a quick stop. **Jams, Inc.** (tel. 349-1616), in addition to carrying standard grocery items, stocks an impressive assortment of pâtés, spreads, meats, cheeses, breads, imported crackers, and the like (even an authentic baklava). They also have a cappuccino bar, where you can get a latte, ice cappuccino, or some other delectable drink to go. If you need a beach umbrella, a picnic basket, or a pair of flip-flops, you'll find them all here as well. It's open long hours from Memorial Day through Labor Day.

WHERE TO STAY

HOLDEN INN, Commercial St. (P.O. Box 816), Wellfleet, MA 02667. Tel. 508/349-3450. 28 rms (16 with bath). **Directions:** From Rte. 6, take a left at Wellfleet Center sign, another left at sign to the pier; inn is on right.

$ Rates: $58 double without bath, $69 double with bath. No credit cards. **Parking:** Free. **Closed:** Oct–Apr.

Not far from the center of Wellfleet, the Holden Inn consists of three buildings of very nicely kept rooms, all different, some with water views, and with double or twin beds. One room, for instance, is paneled all in cedar, and is very handsome. No meals are served, and rates vary with the plumbing. Several of the rooms are furnished with antique pieces.

WHERE TO DINE

AESOP'S TABLES, Main St. Tel. 349-6450.
Cuisine: NEW AMERICAN. **Reservations:** Recommended.
$ Prices: Appetizers $3–$7; main courses $14–$20; dinner $35–$45. AE, DC, MC, V.
Open: Late May to mid-Oct, dinner daily 5:30–9:30pm.

For fine New American cuisine, Aesop's Tables is the place to go. Once the summer mansion of a Massachusetts governor, it now has six welcoming dining rooms, all busy on any summer night, so call for reservations. You might start dinner with poached médaillons of scallop mousse wrapped in salmon filet, or a salad of exotic greens and sun-dried tomatoes, then go on to herb-roasted duck with brandy-walnut sauce and cranberry-orange relish, grilled paillards of veal, or any of the daily seafood specials. There's always a vegetarian dish offered as well. Finish with Aesop's trademarked Death by Chocolate dessert, and watch your diet pass away happily. The second-floor lounge is an enjoyable place for a pre- or postprandial drink (you can take dessert here, too).

BAYSIDE LOBSTER HUTT, Commercial St. Tel. 349-6333.
Cuisine: SEAFOOD. **Reservations:** Not accepted. **Directions:** From Rte. 6, take road to Wellfleet Harbor and look for giant lobster on old oyster shack.
$ Prices: Main courses $6–$13. No credit cards.
Open: Memorial Day–Sept, dinner daily $6. July–Aug, lunch noon–3pm.

You can't miss the Bayside Lobster Hutt; on the roof of this big white building there's a lobster dory complete with a statue of a lobsterman, a net, and an enormous lobster. Wellfleet regulars and visitors come into this old oyster shack for a summer picnic-style self-service dinner consisting of live boiled lobster—you pick 'em from the tanks—corn on the cob, steamed clams, and the like. A 1½-pound lobster, easily a plentiful meal for one person, comes with corn on the cob; or have a huge plate of fried clams. Informal, fun, and good food. The Lobster Hutt is on the way to the town dock. Bring your own wine or beer.

CAPTAIN HIGGINS' SEAFOOD RESTAURANT, Commercial St., Wellfleet. Tel. 349-6027.
Cuisine: SEAFOOD. **Reservations:** Recommended.
$ Prices: Appetizers $3.75–$6.95; main courses $6.95–$12.95 at lunch, $10.95–$20.95 at dinner; meal for two $55. MC, V.
Open: Mid-June to Sept, daily noon–9:30pm.

Down by the town dock is Captain Higgins' Seafood Restaurant, with views of the pier and the harbor. A daily evening special of Wellfleet bluefish is $10.95; many main courses are in that price range. You can get a half dozen Wellfleet oysters on the half shell and a bottle of wine. There is a children's menu ($5.95).

WELLFLEET OYSTER HOUSE, E. Main St. Tel. 349-2134.
Cuisine: SEAFOOD. **Reservations:** Required.
$ Prices: Appetizers $3–$8; main courses $13–$20. AE, DC, MC, V.
Open: Apr–Nov, dinner daily 6–10pm.

The Wellfleet Oyster House takes its name and its menu from the renowned Wellfleet oyster. The restaurant is in an early Cape house (built 1750) with wide-board floors and old paintings on the walls. Have oysters as an appetizer, or as a main course, broiled, in a stew, casino, or Rockefeller. The menu lists a dozen other seafood items, including curries, paella, shrimp, sole, and lobster. For meat eaters, there's prime rib, sirloin, and steak tartare. The price of the main course includes a relish tray, salad, vegetable, potato or rice, garlic bread, and coffee or tea, so your tab will essentially be the main-course price plus tax, tip, and cost of drinks.

13. PROVINCETOWN

62 miles (100km) NE of Sandwich, 50 miles (81km) NE of Hyannis

GETTING THERE   By Plane   Cape Air has daily service year round between Provincetown Airport and Boston's Logan Airport. Call toll free 800/352-0174, or 508/771-6944 for more information.

By Train   See "Getting There" at the beginning of this chapter.

By Bus   In summer, **Bonanza Bus Lines** (tel. toll free 800/556-3815) has regularly scheduled service between New York's Port Authority and Hyannis. From Hyannis, it is necessary to transfer to a **Plymouth & Brockton** bus (tel. 508/775-5524) to reach Provincetown. The complete trip takes about 8 hours from Manhattan, 3½ hours from Providence.

Bonanza also runs buses from Albany and Springfield, Mass., to Hyannis, where you connect for P-town. Plymouth & Brockton runs four buses daily in summer from Boston to Provincetown. Connections are arranged for buses coming from Montréal via Boston to the Cape (two buses daily in summer, with additional services on weekends). Note that the bus will drop you off near or right at your hotel, if it's out of the center of town, if you ask the driver to do so. This is a normal service, so feel free to ask.

By Car   U.S. 6 is divided highway all the way to P-town, where it ends and brings you face to face with a parking problem. Don't try to park in the center of town. Get a space in one of the municipal lots (follow the signs) if you can.

By Boat   You can take a delightful cruise to Provincetown aboard the MV *Provincetown II*, operated by **Bay State Cruises,** 66 Long Wharf, Boston, MA 02110 (tel. 617/723-7800). The 3-hour cruise costs $15 one-way ($13 for seniors and children under 12), or $25 round-trip ($18 for seniors and kids) if you make the round-trip all in 1 day. The ship leaves from Boston's Commonwealth Pier: Take the subway's Blue Line to Aquarium Station, or the Red Line to South Station, and then cross the Fort Point Channel. Ask for Northern Avenue, and walk southeast along it for a few blocks; Commonwealth Pier will be on your left. The walk from either subway stop takes about 15 minutes.

Here's the schedule: Leave Commonwealth Pier at 9:30am, arrive at P-town's MacMillan Wharf right in the middle of town at 12:30pm. The return trip leaves MacMillan Wharf at 3:30pm to arrive at Commonwealth Pier by 6:30pm. Breakfast, lunch, snacks, cocktails, and refreshments are on sale aboard; a band provides music, and the captain describes the landmarks and sights in passing. The 1,100-passenger, 195-foot *Provincetown II* has three decks providing open, covered, and enclosed seating areas.

By the way, MacMillan Wharf is where intercity buses begin and end their runs, and where the Provincetown Chamber of Commerce operates its information office.

ESSENTIALS   The **area code** is 508. The **Provincetown Chamber of Commerce** operates an information office (tel. 508/487-3424) at 307 Commercial St. on MacMillan Wharf, open April through December. Boats from Boston arrive at this wharf, and the chamber's office is also the stop for intercity buses from New York, Providence, and Boston. Bus and boat schedules are posted here. You can also get information on the new shuttle bus (50¢ for senior citizens, $1 for everyone else) that takes you to different points in P-town.

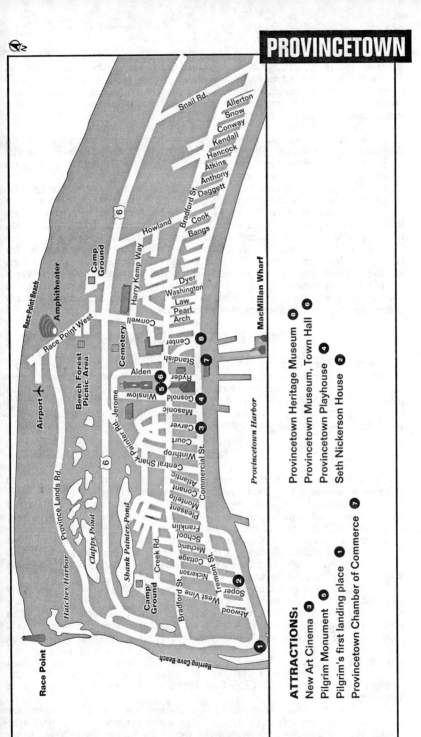

PROVINCETOWN

ATTRACTIONS:

New Art Cinema ❸
Pilgrim Monument ❺
Pilgrim's first landing place ❶
Provincetown Chamber of Commerce ❼

Provincetown Heritage Museum ❽
Provincetown Museum, Town Hall ❻
Provincetown Playhouse ❹
Seth Nickerson House ❷

Provincetown is separated from the rest of the Cape by sand, forest, and marsh, and thus has something of an island ambience, a feeling accentuated by the town's compact size. Out of season, the inhabitants are mostly fishers, descendants of hardy Portuguese sailors who came here for the whaling trade a century ago. In season Provincetown is a carnival constantly alive with all sorts of people from all around: New York, Boston, Montréal, Québec, and also Podunk. Artists and writers, the successful and the hopeful, college sophomores and sophisticates, dowagers and down-at-heelers all mix and mingle in the evening along P-town's narrow streets. The town is at the same time quaint and sophisticated, elegant and tawdry, depending on where you look and how you look at it.

Of all things, the most important when planning a visit to P-town in late July and August is to *have a room reservation without fail*. It is just not possible to find a room in Provincetown for the 6 weeks of hectic high season unless you reserve ahead. If you have no reservation, it's best to plan to stay in Orleans or Wellfleet, or along U.S. 6 some distance from P-town, and to drive up for the day.

Like San Francisco and Key West, Provincetown hosts a large **gay community** on vacation during the summer. The great majority of establishments—hotels, inns, guesthouses, restaurants, cafés, bars, and nightclubs—welcome all customers regardless of sexual orientation, regardless of whether the proprietor is gay or straight. But in a few places, you'll definitely feel out of place if your sexual preference doesn't match that of the proprietor and the majority of customers.

WHAT TO SEE & DO

Provincetown is an interesting small town to browse around. Although people watching could keep you amused for days, below are some of P-town's other highlights. *Provincetown* magazine hits the streets every Thursday; it's free and it has plenty of suggestions for things to do. Or drop in at the chamber of commerce's information office and pick up the Provincetown Historical Society's pamphlet (25¢), which tells you all the historical sights in town.

SIGHTS

For the best view of the town in both physical and historical terms, head to the **Pilgrim Monument** and **Provincetown Museum,** High Pole Hill (tel. 487-1310). The museum is an interesting potpourri of old firefighting gear, costumes, a whaling-ship captain's quarters on board, primitive portraits, World War I mementos, arctic lore, and a sequence of displays on the activities of the Pilgrims in Provincetown, for this is the first place they touched land in the New World. After seeing these you can continue with the Wedgwood, the model of a Thai temple, antique dolls, and other arcana. You can also view the current exhibit on the treasures of the pirate ship *Whydah.* Then head for the tower.

The Pilgrim Monument is copied from the Torre del Mangia in Siena, Italy, and is all granite and 252½ feet high. The cornerstone was laid in 1907 with Pres. Teddy Roosevelt in attendance, and the structure was completed 3 years later, when President Taft did the dedicating. You may think that there's an elevator in it. Well, there's not, and you'll have to c-l-i-m-b to the top, the equivalent of going up the steps in a 20-story building, to see the view. Most of the climb is on a ramp, not steps, and you can take your time and read the commemorative plaques from New England cities, towns, and civic groups which line the granite walls. The view is worth the climb: Provincetown and all Cape Cod spread out like the maps you've been following.

Admission costs $5 for adults and $3 for children aged 4 to 12. It's open year round (except Christmas Day); between July and September, from 9am to 9pm; in the winter, from 9am to 4pm; the rest of the year, from 9am to 5pm. *Note:* Tower climbing stops ½ hour before closing.

Check out the **Pilgrims' first landing place,** the monument commemorating the signing of the *Mayflower* Compact (America's first democratic "constitution"), and the 12-room **Seth Nickerson House,** the oldest dwelling in town (1746), at 72 Commercial St. It is now the home of artist-photographer John W. Gregory and his wife, who will be happy to show you around and explain how it was built by a shipwright from heavy oak posts and beams salvaged from shipwrecks. Admission costs $2 for adults and 50¢ for children. The house is open from June to October daily from 10am to 5pm.

The **Provincetown Heritage Museum**—actually the municipal museum—at Commercial and Center Streets (tel. 487-7098), preserves the town's heritage in its wide-ranging displays. Relics of the fishing industry, Victoriana, and many other items capture Provincetown's history. Especially exciting for children are the antique fire engine and the *Rose Dorothea,* the world's largest half-scale fishing schooner model. Admission costs $2 for adults and is free for children under 12. The museum is open from mid-June to September daily from 10am to 6pm.

GALLERIES, CINEMAS & THEATER

The latest schedules for galleries, cinemas, and theater are published in the local newspaper, the *Provincetown Advocate.* Galleries dot the downtown streets (especially on the east end of town), often open until late in the evening. The **Province-town Playhouse** (tel. 487-0955) is active all summer. Call for current information. The **New Art Cinema** (tel. 487-9222), across from the post office downtown at 212 Commercial St., plays both foreign and domestic first-run films.

WHALE-WATCH CRUISES

It's a great thrill when you see one of the monster denizens break the surface, spout, sport, and play. You can sight whales from the Coast Guard Station on Race Point Beach, and even with the naked eye you can see them spouting and rolling. But to see them up close is something else, and for that you need to sign up for a whale-watch cruise. Several boats leave on morning and afternoon runs, and give you several hours in which to find and watch the whales. Call the **Dolphin Fleet** (tel. 255-3857, or toll free 800/826-9300), which by the way has a 99.7% sighting record; **Portuguese Princess Excursions** (tel. 487-2651, or toll free 800/442-3188); or the **Ranger V** (tel. 487-1582 or 487-3322, or toll free 800/992-9333) for times, prices, and reservations. Boats leave from MacMillan Wharf and charge about $20 per person. By the way, the whales—which seem to perform expressly for the appreciative crowds on the boats—enjoy the trip as much as you do.

OTHER ACTIVITIES

Bicycling in the Provincetown area is perhaps the best way to get around—especially in mid-summer in town, when traffic can be dense. In addition to exploring the town's warren of narrow streets, you'll find a wonderful webwork of paved trails that take you through the dunes of the national seashore. Even these can get congested, however, so take care in riding. Avoid speeding, keep to the right, and be careful not to brake abruptly when you hit sand. In town, it is necessary to be 100 percent alert at all times—there are lots of pedestrians, roller skaters, cars, and other bicyclists moving about. **Arnold's Bicycle Shop,** 329 Commercial St. (tel. 487-0844), rents bikes by the hour, the day, and the week. They also provide free maps of the national seashore trails.

If you want to try something new and exciting, consider taking a **beach buggy tour** through the National Seashore area. **Art's Dunes Tours** (tel. 487-1950, or 487-1050) runs trips throughout the day, from 9am to sunset. The trip starts at the head of Town Wharf in a comfortable "Dunes Mobile," and wends its way through the streets to the dunes. In addition to the astonishingly beautiful dune scenery, it takes in several highlights of the area, including the stretch of coast called the "Graveyard of the Atlantic" and Pilgrim Lake (where the Pilgrims got their water supply). The 1¼-hour narrated tour costs $8 for adults and $6 for children under 12.

You can also take an **aerial tour** of the seashore. **Cape Air** offers both helicopter and small plane sightseeing flights. Call 508/487-0240 for rates and reservations.

Another way to enjoy the area is to take a sail on a **schooner.** The 73-foot-long *Bay Lady II* has four 2-hour sailings every day in the summer months including a sunset cruise. You'll find the *Bay Lady II* berthed at the end of MacMillan Pier in the heart of town. Tickets vary according to which sail you take but range from $9 to $12 for adults and $5 for children under 5. Reservations are recommended, call 508/487-9308 or write to: Captain Bob Burns, c/o Schooner *Bay Lady II*, 584 Commercial St., Provincetown, MA 02657. Those who want more action on their cruise can go out with one of the two daily deep-sea fishing voyages that leave from MacMillan Wharf; whale-watching boats also leave from here, especially from mid-April to mid-June.

Should you want to do nothing more active than sit, you can have a local artist do your portrait in pastels while you're sitting. Shops are along Commercial Street and inside Whalers' Wharf near the town wharf (MacMillan Wharf), and prices start at $70 for a front view, $40 for the side, $40 and $20 if it's to be charcoal; frames and glass are extra and cost $35 and up. The portrait can be done, framed, and wrapped to take home in a surprisingly short time.

You can also sit back and see the sights of Provincetown by taking a narrated sightseeing tour aboard the **Provincetown Trolley** (tel. 487-9483). Tours leave from the Town Hall on Commercial Street every half hour from 10am to 4pm and also from 5, 6, 7, and 8pm. The 40-minute trip costs $6 for adults, $5 for senior citizens, and $4 for children.

But biking, schooner sails, deep-sea fishing, and portrait sitting can't equal the sense of freedom you get if you sail your own boat out onto Cape Cod Bay. You don't have to own a boat, of course, because Provincetown has **Flyer's Boat Rental**, 131A Commercial St. (tel. 487-0898), behind Gallerani's restaurant. Little Sunfish, larger (18- to 20-foot) sailboats, dinghies with outboard motors, and dinghies with just a pair of oars are all for rent. Flyer's will even teach you how to sail if you don't already know. It's open 8am to 6pm, May 1 to Columbus Day. Major credit cards are accepted.

WHERE TO STAY

Provincetown's streets are lined with guesthouses and inns and motels, and in the 6 weeks from mid-July to Labor Day every room in every one will be rented. Outside of that time you have a chance of finding a room by arriving in town by late morning or early afternoon.

A special note is in order concerning credit cards. Demand for services is so great here that very many hotels and restaurants do not accept credit cards. Also, most lodging places require some minimum stay during the peak season period, usually from 3 or 4 days (at least, on weekends) to a full week. And you won't be able to fudge it: You'll probably have to pay the full amount for your stay when you check in.

When you set out to hunt for accommodations, or to find your reserved room, remember that P-town is about 3 miles long from one end of Commercial Street (the main street) to the other.

WEST END GUESTHOUSES & INNS

The West End—west of MacMillan Wharf, that is—has the richest concentration of inns and guesthouses.

CAPTAIN AND HIS SHIP, 164 Commercial St., Provincetown, MA 02657. Tel. 508/487-1850. 8 rms (6 with bath). A/C TV

$ Rates: (including continental breakfast in high season): Summer, $70–$75 single

or double without bath, $101–$141 single or double with bath. Apr to mid-June and mid-Sept to Oct, from $48 single or double. 4-night minimum stay Memorial Day weekend; 5-night minimum stay for visits that include a Fri or Sat night; 7-night minimum stay July 4. MC, V.
Parking: $5 per day, 2 blocks from inn. **Closed:** Nov–Mar.

The Captain and His Ship sounds like the title of a Cape Cod novel, but in fact it's a handsome guesthouse located just far enough from the heart of town to keep the noise level low. Provincetown's shipboard tidiness characterizes the house. Its small front lawn is complete with bench. Each room is different, furnished with Victoriana, and each has a different price: The more expensive ones are those with water views.

CAPTAIN LYSANDER INN, 96 Commercial St., Provincetown, MA 02657. Tel. 508/487-2253. 13 rms (7 with bath), 1 efficiency, 1 apartment, 1 carriage house.
$ Rates: (including continental breakfast): High season $70 room without bath, $82 room with bath. Off-season, room rates $10–$20 less. Extra person $15. Minimum stay 4 nights required over holidays and 3 nights required on weekends. MC, V.
Parking: Free.

The ancestral home of Dr. Vannevar Bush, the Captain Lysander Inn was built by Capt. Lysander Paine in 1852. The rooms feature a blend of antique and traditional-style furnishings. Enjoy breakfast in the front parlor or outside on the spacious front deck or sun porch.

1807 HOUSE, 54 Commercial St., Provincetown, MA 02657. Tel. 508/487-2173. 8 rms (5 with bath).
$ Rates: Summer, $50 single; $61–$90 double. Off-season, $38 single; $49–$64 double. 3-day minimum stays required on Memorial Day, July 4th, and Labor Day weekends. MC, V. **Parking:** Free.

Bright, cheerful, comfortable, and well equipped—that describes the 1807 house. The cedar-shingled main house faces the street, and behind it are several other buildings that hold rooms, studios, and apartments. Each is tastefully and attractively done, many have kitchens, and all share the quiet location and grassy lawns. The owners will be happy to describe each room for you.

MASTHEAD, 31-41 Commercial St., Provincetown, MA 02657. Tel. 508/487-0523, or toll free 800/395-5095. 21 rms (all with bath). TV TEL
$ Rates: July–Labor Day, $69–$152 single or double; $949–$1,468 cottage, suite, or efficiency for two per week. Labor Day–June, rates are lower. AE, DC, DISC, MC, V. **Parking:** Free, limited off-street, valet.

The Masthead lists cottages, apartments, and motel rooms among its accommodations, but you must see the place to appreciate it. All these overnight possibilities are contained in a collection of cozy little cottages that look across flawless green lawn to a private boardwalk, a beach, and the water. Write for the descriptions of the 21 types of accommodations, from modern rooms through efficiency studios to cottages for up to seven people. If you can't find the sort of room you want at the Masthead, you're probably looking for a tent.

EAST END GUESTHOUSES & INNS

The eastern reaches of Provincetown, along Commercial Street, Bradford Street, and the small cross streets between them, hold dozens of small inns and a few guesthouses. Generally speaking, these are more expensive than the majority of West End places. The location is roughly the same in terms of convenience.

ASHETON HOUSE, 3 Cook St., Provincetown, MA 02657. Tel. 508/487-9966. 3 rms (1 with bath).
$ Rates: Summer, $81 double without bath; $102 suite with bath. Off-season, rates 20 percent lower. No credit cards. **Parking:** Free.

Absolutely every inch of Asheton House is attractive—from the double staircase that leads to the front door to the imaginatively decorated guest rooms. Guests can choose

"The Suite," which has a fireplace and a view of the harbor, "The Captain's Room," with a grand four-poster bed, or "The Safari Room," decorated with artifacts from Africa. Out back, there's a deck where you can sit among the Japanese Temple trees. Asheton House is ½ mile from the center of town.

BRADFORD GARDENS INN, 178 Bradford St., Provincetown, MA 02657. Tel. 508/487-1616. 17 rms including cottages (all with bath). TV
$ Rates: (including breakfast): Summer, $114–$131 inn double; $101–$160 cottage double. Extra person $15. AE, MC, V. **Parking:** Free.

The Bradford Gardens Inn is near the corner of Miller Hill Road and is certainly one of Provincetown's most charming and serene places to stay. Every room in the century-and-a-half-old inn is different, and each has a name rather than a number. Alternative arrangements include two apartments, a Swiss chalet–type cottage, and a six- to eight-person lodge. Rates include a big breakfast and (for rooms with facilities to use it) firewood as well. And speaking of gardens, the Bradford has 'em, spreading around the house, set with benches, chairs, and even a garden swing.

WHITE HORSE INN, 500 Commercial St., Provincetown, MA 02657. Tel. 508/487-1790. 12 rms (8 with bath), 6 apartments.
$ Rates: Peak season, $33–$38 single; $66–$71 double without bath, $77 double with bath; $715 studio apartment per week. Off-season, discounts available. Extra person $15. No credit cards. **Parking:** Free.

Located in the quiet East End of town, the White Horse Inn is a lovely 150-year-old captain's house. Inside, lots of quaint old pieces picked up in the area are used in decoration to keep the period feeling and every room seems to contain at least five original paintings. The beach is right across the street (guests have beach rights), and the inn has backyard lawn chairs.

WHERE TO DINE

Wander around the streets of Provincetown and you'll smell garlic, fish, bread—you name it. Here you'll find a wonderful selection of restaurants, from Portuguese-owned bakeries to fine restaurants that have been featured in magazines such as *Gourmet* and *Bon Appétit*. Seafood, of course, is a big specialty. Keep in mind that during the summer months (and weekends during off-season), it's imperative to have a reservation at most restaurants.

IN TOWN

FRONT STREET, 230 Commercial St. Tel. 487-9715.
    Cuisine: CONTINENTAL/ITALIAN. **Reservations:** Recommended.
$ Prices: Appetizers $4.25–$7.50; main courses $5.95–$24.95; dinner for two $60–$75.
    AE, MC, V.
    Open: Apr–Dec, dinner daily 6–11pm (bar remains open until 1am). **Closed:** Tues from mid-Sept to mid-May.

In the very hub of Provincetown is Front Street, located in the lower level of a Victorian house. It has a loyal clientele that, when asked, will recommend the smoked duck or the herb-crusted rack of lamb. Both dishes are offered regularly along with a very pleasing selection of seafood and continental dishes, plus an extensive wine list. During the off-season (April through June and September through December), Front Street offers a full Italian menu.

GRUBER'S, 229 Commercial St. Tel. 487-0765.
    Cuisine: SEAFOOD/CONTINENTAL. **Reservations:** Recommended.
$ Prices: Appetizers $4.26–$7.95; main courses $5.25–$6 at lunch, $14.95–$20 at dinner; breakfast $3.25–$7.50. AE, MC, V.

Open: Breakfast and lunch Fri–Tues 9am–2pm; dinner daily 6–11pm. **Closed:** New Year's Day–Easter.

Down a narrow alleyway just off Commercial Street (about 1 block west of the Town Hall), you'll find this small, dimly lit restaurant. Try the she-crab stew or the roasted pepper stuffed with goat cheese and ricotta for an appetizer and pan-fried sole with citron butter, or homemade fettuccine piled high with lobster, shrimp, and clams for a main course. Save room for the key lime pie, the crème brûlée, or the peanut butter—mousse pie.

SAL'S PLACE, 99 Commercial St. Tel. 487-1279.

Cuisine: ITALIAN. **Reservations:** Recommended.
$ Prices: Appetizers $2.50–$8; main courses $9–$18; meals for two $50–$60. MC, V.
Open: Summer, dinner daily 6–10pm. Spring and fall, dinner Fri–Sat 6–10pm.

Want to have a good dinner at some small, very intimate candlelit spot with particularly interesting and delicious food at moderate prices? The place to go is Sal's Place, where the food is Italian, and all cooked to order. It has tiny wooden tables, Chianti bottles hanging from the ceiling, and a small dining room both simple and romantic; there is also a new, larger room on the water, and outdoor dining. Specialties are brodetto (served on Friday); Wellfleet mussels, scallops, clams, and fish in a wine broth; and bistecca alla pizzaiola, prime rib-eye steak with mushrooms and olives in a red-wine marinara sauce. Try one of the homemade desserts like chocolate mousse pie. On Tuesday several special veal dishes are featured. Sal's has been here since 1963. Sal's is past the Coast Guard station in the West End.

OUT OF TOWN, ON THE MOORS

MOORS RESTAURANT, Bradford St. Extension. Tel. 487-0840.

Cuisine: PORTUGUESE/SEAFOOD. **Reservations:** Required on weekends.
$ Prices: Appetizers $2–$6; main dinner courses $9–$19; fixed-price dinner $14–$15. AE, DC, DISC, MC, V.
Open: Apr–Oct, lunch daily noon–3pm; dinner daily 5:30–10pm.

At Moors Restaurant, at the end of the Bradford Street Extension at the junction with Route 6A, the dining rooms are positively fraught with nautical paraphernalia—on the walls, on the ceiling, adorning the bar. The cuisine is Provincetown seafood with Portuguese accents. At lunchtime you can eat for as little as $7 if you can be contented with a *linguica* roll (a mildly spicy Portuguese sausage in pastry) and a beer; or you can spend a few dollars more for sea-clam pie or broiled Cape scallops. The daily special dinner includes soup, salad, dessert, and coffee. Besides the standard fresh fish and lobster casserole, you might find *carangueijo vieira a moda de peniche* (scallops and crabmeat in a casserole, made with wine, brandy, and tomato sauce). There's live entertainment most evenings in the Smugglers' Lounge.

SPECIALTY DINING

Outdoor Cafés

CAFE BLASE, 328 Commercial St. Tel. 487-9465.

Cuisine: INTERNATIONAL. **Reservations:** Not accepted.
$ Prices: Appetizers $3.50–$7.50; main courses $5.50–$12 at lunch, $9–$14 at dinner. AE, MC, V.
Open: Memorial Day–Sept, daily 9am–1pm.

Located just east of the center of town, Café Blasé is a fine perch from which to watch the steady parade of Provincetown characters. Dishes include burgers, quiches, pasta, pizzas, salads, and sandwiches, plus a selection of dinner specials and a clambake (a 1¼-pound lobster, steamers, and sweet corn for $13.95). If you just want to sit and sip, you can take your pick of an astounding array of drinks, including several nonalcoholic specialties. There's also a selection of beers and wine by the glass, half-liter, liter, or bottle.

EURO ISLAND GRILL AND CAFE, 258 Commercial St. Tel. 487-2505.
   Cuisine: CAFE/ITALIAN/CARIBBEAN. **Reservations:** Recommended.
$ **Prices:** Appetizers $3.75–$7; main courses $4.50–$17. AE, DC, MC, V.
   Open: Early May–early Oct, daily 8am–1am.
During the day, the al fresco Euro Island Grill and Café serves a good selection of café dishes. Come night, however, it turns into a full-blown dinner restaurant with Sicilian and Caribbean specialties (including conch chowder and conch fritters). Day and night, you can get the stone-hearth baked pizza, which is to die for. There's always a good selection of local seafood, plus homemade desserts, including a delectable key lime pie. The Euro Island Grill and Café is next to the Town Hall, upstairs.

Breakfasts

For not just fresh coffee in the morning, but also fresh bread and rolls, find the **Portuguese Bakery,** right down by MacMillan Wharf at 299 Commercial St.—follow the coffee and fresh-bread smells. Not only is breakfast the freshest here, it's the cheapest. Put it together yourself, take it out to the wharf to consume, and you can do it for $2.50 easily.

   Two other favorite breakfast spots are **David's,** 401 Commercial St. (tel. 487-6405), where you can start the day with a muffin, a bowl of granola, or fresh fruit, and **Café Edwige,** 333 Commercial St. (tel. 487-2008), which has a strong emphasis on natural healthy foods, including a wide selection of vegetarian dishes.

Quick Meals

A real institution in P-town for a do-it-yourself lunch or quick dinner is the **Cheese Market,** 225 Commercial St. (tel. 487-3032), which offers a multitude of different sandwiches, both hot and cold, and soups and salads from $3 to $7. Open from 9am to 11pm daily Memorial Day through October and until 7pm the rest of the year.

EVENING ENTERTAINMENT

Throughout the summer months, the hub of Provincetown (along Commercial Street, the Town Hall being the center) always has a sparkly air of carnival. But nighttime is when it's at its most glittery. Start with a satiating seafood dinner in one of the many restaurants or a sunset picnic on the beach at Herring Cove and then do as everyone who goes to Provincetown does: Stroll along Commercial Street. Within the span of 1 or 2 blocks, you are likely to see more characters (and character) than some people see in a lifetime. Among them will be cabaret barkers, portrait artists, female impersonators, salty old fishermen with toothy grins, and spandex-clad roller skaters whizzing through the crowds at alarmingly high speeds.

   Many of P-Town's shops remain open late into the evening—especially on weekends. Among them you'll find several selling very hip clothes, one that specializes in kites and wind socks, another devoted to cat things (cat mugs, cat bumper stickers, cat earrings), and a couple selling fudge and penny candy. At **Penny Patch,** 279 Commercial St., you can fill a basket with Mary Jane's, Tootsie Rolls, fire balls, and all your other favorite candies and pay at the counter.

   Most of P-town's galleries also stay open late (to 10 or 11 pm). In many of them, you'll find excellent works by contemporary Provincetown and Lower Cape artists.

   If you feel like resting your feet a bit, take time out to people-watch from Café Blasé, 328 Commercial St., a centrally located outdoor café. Later, dance till you drop at the **Surf Club,** 315A Commercial St. (tel. 487-1367), to the lively tunes of the Provincetown Jug Band or another band that happens to be spotlighted.

   If you're interested in hearing some great jazz, reggae, or perhaps Gospel music, check who's performing at **Club Euro at Euro Café.** This nightclub is located in a 152-year-old Congregational Church. Tickets are sold at the door or at nearby Strawberries (the record store). For schedules and tickets, call 487-2505 or 487-2511 (major credit cards are accepted).

Many Provincetown restaurants also spotlight musicians in their lounges, including **Ciro and Sal's,** 41 Kiley Court (tel. 487-0049), and the **Mews Restaurant,** 359 Commercial St. (tel. 487-1500).

A word of warning to motorists: If you're planning to drive into town at night, be prepared to move as if in a marching parade. The traffic, as one local put it, is "traffic, but 'friendly' traffic."

CHAPTER 7

MARTHA'S VINEYARD & NANTUCKET

Martha's Vineyard and Nantucket are among the eastern seaboard's most attractive and visited resorts. There's something special about vacationing on an island, a particular feeling of isolation, of being apart from the schedules and worries of city life, and this is truly relaxing and therapeutic.

MARTHA'S VINEYARD

To Bostonians and denizens of Cape Cod, it is simply "the Vineyard." The island got its odd name in the early 1600s, when mariner and explorer Bartholomew Gosnold stopped here. It's said he found wild grapes, and it's thought he had a daughter named Martha. Voilà! Today the island actually has a commercial vineyard and a winery producing fine vintages that you can sample and buy.

Although it is in the same legislative district, the Vineyard is not a part of Cape Cod. Vineyard residents are proud that the island is the County of Dukes County, not part of some mainland county, and they guard the anachronistic redundancy of that title very closely. For a long time the Vineyard had its own representative in the General Court (state legislature), and when redistricting made the island a part of Cape Cod legislative district, the islanders threatened to secede from Massachusetts and become part of another state, one that would allow them their own representative.

Islanders get their exceptional sense of independence from a history of struggle with and mastery of the sea, from the days when whaling brought great wealth to an otherwise poor island. And just about the time the whaling industry declined, the tourist industry began, and Martha's Vineyard found its place in the modern world. Today the big ferries that ply the waters of Vineyard Sound are packed with visitors every day in summer, and are also crowded on weekends in spring and fall.

You will undoubtedly learn it for yourself when you disembark from the boat, but let me be the first one to tell you: The best value on the Vineyard is a $1.79 homemade ice-cream cone at Mad Martha's. Prime locales in Vineyard Haven, Oak Bluffs, and

Edgartown will assure that no matter where you are, a Mad Martha's will never be very far. Keep your eyes peeled for the wild antique ambulance that zips between stores.

SEEING MARTHA'S VINEYARD

GETTING THERE   By Plane   Year round, there are scheduled flights to Martha's Vineyard Dukes County Airport from Boston, Hyannis, Nantucket, and New Bedford. The airport is located in the center of the island within easy reach of all points. There are plenty of taxis available for scheduled arrivals.

Cape Air flies between Boston, Hyannis, Nantucket, New Bedford and Martha's Vineyard throughout the year. For information and reservations, call 800/352-0714. **Direct Flight, Inc.** provides charter service for up to five passengers from airports all over New England. Call 508/693-6688 for more details.

By Ferry   For ferries to Martha's Vineyard, see the information in the sections on Woods Hole, Falmouth, Hyannis (all in Chapter 6, "Cape Cod"), and New Bedford (in Chapter 5).

Hy-Line Cruises, Ocean Street Dock, Hyannis (tel. 508/778-2600), operates three daily passenger boats (morning, noontime, and afternoon) in each direction between Martha's Vineyard and Nantucket islands from mid-June to mid-September. The voyage takes 2¼ hours and costs $10.50 for adults, half price for children 5 to 12 (under 4 travel free). Buy tickets (for cash, traveler's checks, master Card, or VISA) in Oak Bluffs, Martha's Vineyard (tel. 508/693-0112) and on Straight Wharf, Nantucket (tel. 508/228-3949).

ORIENTATION & INFORMATION   The island's three principal towns are **Vineyard Haven,** the commercial center where many of the mainland ferries dock; **Oak Bluffs,** a Victorian resort community of ornate "gingerbread" houses, a marina, and a few grand old wooden hotels; and **Edgartown,** the county seat and main tourist attraction—clearly the prettiest town on the island. The more rural, less populated area is referred to as Up Island; these are the towns in the southwestern third of the island.

In high season—July and August—you need reservations for everything: space for your car on the ferry, for a rental car on the island, for a hotel room, for a weekend mainland-to-island flight. You can't reserve passenger space on the ferry, so the thing to do is get to the docks at least 15 or 20 minutes early, buy your ticket, and get in line. If the ferry's passenger capacity is reached, the remaining passengers in the line will have to wait for the next boat. If you don't have a room reservation in an island hotel, use the direct-line telephone in the Steamship Authority ticket office in Woods Hole for island hotels. On weekends in high season, chances of finding a room are not good; on weekdays you may find a room for a few nights because of a cancellation, or a gap between reservations. If all else fails, plan to visit the island for the day, and return to the mainland in the evening.

The **Martha's Vineyard Chamber of Commerce,** Beach Road (P.O. Box 1698), Vineyard Haven, MA 02568-1698 (tel. 508/693-0085), is located a few doors down from the Tisbury Inn off Main Street. The chamber publishes a very helpful and complete visitor's guide, as well as a list of summer events, and can also help you with accommodations. The island's **area code** is 508.

GETTING AROUND   By Rental Car   Summer driving on the Vineyard can be a bit challenging at times with vacationers traveling by bike, moped, on horseback, or on foot, on generally narrow, winding roads. On top of that, there are no stop lights on the island and, with the crowds (as many as 80,000 people visit every year), four-way intersections can be tricky. Parking can also be challenging during the summer months. Whatever you do, don't leave a car in a lot longer than you've put coins in the meter for; you'll instantly be ticketed. Also, pay attention to speed limits; they're strictly enforced on the island.

WHAT'S SPECIAL ABOUT MARTHA'S VINEYARD & NANTUCKET

Island Ambience
☐ That particular feeling of "being away from it all" on a breezy island out to sea

Museums
☐ The Thomas Cooke House in Edgartown, dating from the 1760s, now a historical museum of Vineyard life
☐ The Nantucket Historical Association's fascinating museums, including one on whaling, another on Nantucket history, and a still-functioning windmill built in 1746

Outdoor Activities
☐ Bicycling on both islands—bike paths are well maintained, and rentals are reasonably priced

☐ The many beaches, some very suitable for children
☐ Schooners, sloops, and a variety of other sailing vessels available for excursions

Pretty Towns
☐ Oak Bluffs, once a tent camp for summer Methodist church meetings, with lots of fine Victorian gingerbread architecture
☐ The stately ship captains' houses of Edgartown, many of which are now inns
☐ The beautiful town and fine buildings of Nantucket—thanks to the great wealth brought to the island by whalers

---

Two of the big names are here: **Hertz** (tel. 508/627-4728) in Edgartown (closed Sunday) and at the airport, open daily (tel. 508/693-2402); and **Budget** (tel. 508/693-1911) in Oak Bluffs and Vineyard Haven.

Adventure Rentals of Martha's Vineyard (tel. 508/693-1959 and also a direct line from the Woods Hole Ferry Terminal) specializes in offbeat equipment, such as dune buggies, vans, mopeds, four-wheel-drive vehicles, and trucks, but it does rent cars as well. Other firms are **Atlantic Auto Rentals** (tel. 508/693-0480) in Vineyard Haven and **All-Island Rent-a-Car** (tel. 508/693-6868) at the airport.

By Bus   Island Transport Bus Service (tel. 693-0058) operates school bus–type vehicles between the Vineyard's various settlements every ½ hour or so, with stops near the various ferry docks. (Trips to Gay Head from Vineyard Haven are much less frequent, though.) Prices vary according to distance traveled; round-trip tickets are always sold at a discount over the normal two-single-trip fare, so ask for a round-trip if that's what suits your needs. The cheapest fare is Vineyard Haven to Oak Bluffs, and fares can be several dollars for longer trips. Don't plan on being in a hurry, as the buses frequently run behind schedule.

By Bicycle & Motorbike   Rental agencies abound, and you can barely descend from the ferry without coming across one. Prices are all competitive, and a 10-speed mountain bike should cost in the range of $10 to $15 for a day's rental (plus a $10 deposit); motorbikes and mopeds are a good deal more, anywhere from $20 to $55 (singles and doubles), and entail greater responsibility, possible destination limitations, and more chance of breakdowns. The island and the bicycle were made for each other, and islanders have even helped this relationship along: There's a fine bike path between Oak Bluffs and Edgartown, right along the beaches. No need to reserve bikes in advance, for there are always plenty to go around.

1. WHAT TO SEE & DO ON MARTHA'S VINEYARD

The most delightful thing about Martha's Vineyard is that it is its own entertainment, and one can often be fully satisfied just strolling along past picket-fenced houses, swimming at the many beaches, or biking past the marshes, forests, and island heath. But should you wish a little directed, purposeful activity, you will not be at a loss. First thing to do is to find out what's on currently in the way of festivities and special events. There's an information desk in the Steamship Authority's dockside ticket office in Woods Hole, so you can find out some things even before getting to the island. But once on the Vineyard, pick up a copy of *This Week on Martha's Vineyard* (a pull-out section of the paper). Here you'll discover a list of the church-sponsored white-elephant sales, music concerts (many free), lectures, dances, movies, tournaments (kite flying, fishing, table tennis), community sings, and the like. Two other free papers, *Island Light* and *Vineyard Summer,* can be picked up in most shops. The island's most important to-do is the annual Regatta and Around-the-Island Race, held on a weekend in late July (hotels are extra-full then).

The **Gay Head Sightseeing Company** (tel. 693-1555) operates daily sightseeing bus tours of the island, including the Vineyard's six towns and two villages, the sea captains' houses (from the outside), and even a stop at the multicolored cliffs at Gay Head. The trip takes about 2 hours, covers 56 miles, and costs $9.50 for adults and $4 for children. Tours leave the ferry wharves after the arrival of the ship, and tickets may be purchased on board the ship or on the sightseeing bus.

SPORTS & RECREATION   Beaches and Bike Trips   The **State Beach** on the road between Oak Bluffs and Edgartown is probably the first beach you'll see. It's a fine long stretch of white sand, free and open to the public, with parking along the road. South of Edgartown the County Beach at Katama Bay, also called South Beach, has surf swimming, and is likewise free. The three major towns all have town beaches open to everyone, but the smaller towns and villages reserve their beaches for local property owners, or charge a beach-use fee. Two other public beaches are **Menemsha Beach** in Chilmark (a good sunset point) and **East Beach** on Chappaquiddick (a 5-minute ferry ride from Edgartown).

Bicycle riding is one of the most enjoyable ways to get around Martha's Vineyard since the island is fairly flat. The island maintains many miles of paved bike paths between Vineyard Haven, Oak Bluffs, Edgartown, and West Tisbury. Keep in mind that Massachusetts law requires riding on the right-hand side of the road in single file. For after-dark bicycling, your bike must be equipped with a working headlight and rear and side reflectors. At all times, hand signals are required.

In addition to cycling to the Vineyard's beaches and attractions, consider taking a bike over to the island of Chappaquiddick ("Chappy" to locals). The 5-minute ferry ride from the docks in Edgartown costs $2.50 for both the bike and rider, round-trip.

There are several **wildlife preserves** you can cycle to, including Felix Neck Wildlife Sanctuary between Edgartown and Vineyard Haven (woods, salt marshes, and meadows); Cedar Tree Neck (more than 250 acres of headlands on the island's north shore); Long Point (a 580-acre preserve on the Atlantic shore); Manuel F. Correllus State Forest (a 4,000-acre preserve of forests in the center of the island); and Cape Poque Wildlife Refuge and Wasque Reservations, two adjacent wilderness areas on the island of Chappaquiddick.

You can also ride out to **Gay Head** to see the cliffs that plunge into the sea. Make certain you're up for the journey; it could take up the better part of the day. You can view the cliffs for free (although you must pay 25¢ to use the nearby public toilets). As with all tourist spots, you'll find a colony of souvenir and snack shops crowning the cliffs, where you can buy the customary postcards, T-shirts, and, a Mad Martha's ice cream cone. If you're not up for peddling out to Gay Head, you can drive or take a bus tour.

On the way to or from Gay Head, take time to visit **Menemsha Harbor** (take Cross Road at Beetlebung Corner in Chilmark up to North Road, turn left, and you'll run right into it). This tiny working harbor is about as picturesque a harbor as you'll find, complete with shingled boathouses crowded around the water's edge, buoys and fishing nets, soaring seagulls, and boats with names like "*Wannakum II*." There's not exactly anything "to do" except stroll and roll away a couple of hours. Take time out to have a lobster roll ($7) on the back porch of the Galley (tel. 645-9819), a snack shack from which you can watch the harbor activity and hear nothing but the sound of mastheads clinking as boats rock with the tide.

Boating   One of the best ways to enjoy Martha's Vineyard is to get out on the water in a boat. After all, as a fishing and whaling center, this is an island with a long seafaring history. You can take your pick of boating options from small "Sea-Doos" (like ski-mobiles, but you ride on the water) to multimasted schooners. You'll find a variety of charter boats available in Vineyard Haven, Oak Bluffs, Edgartown, and Menemsha; sailboats for rent in Vineyard Haven and Edgartown; power boats in Edgartown and Oak Bluffs; and windsurfers in Vineyard Haven.

For those who want to see the sea in grand style, two especially impressive sailboats set sail from Vineyard Haven. The clipper schooner *Shenandoah* is a majestic beauty, measuring 108 feet along the rail. Going all out at better than 12 knots, the *Shenandoah* has all nine sails gusting in a classic square topsail rig. For $700 per person (family discounts are available), you can sail aboard the ship for a week—adventure, food, and lodging all included. Passengers board on Sunday evening, set sail on Monday, and return the following Saturday afternoon (mid-June into September) from the Union Street Wharf. For more information, call 508/693-1699. The *Violet*, built in 1911 and recently restored to perfection, is a spectacularly handsome sailboat available for charter trips for groups and individuals. Call 508/693-5597 for more details.

EDGARTOWN

One of the most rewarding ways to explore Edgartown is to take a **guided walking tour** through its historic streets. Along the way, you'll visit churches, some 18th-century houses, the Dukes County Historical Society, the Whaling Houses on North Water Street, and other historical sites. Hour-long tours begin at the visitors center on Church Street across from the Old Whaling Church at 10am and 4pm Thursday to Tuesday during the summer. In the spring and fall, tours are given at 10am and 3pm on Saturday and 2pm on Sunday. For more information, call 627-8619.

DUKES COUNTY HISTORICAL SOCIETY, Cooke and School Sts. Tel. 627-4441.

Here you'll find a collection of buildings devoted to preserving the island's history. The Captain Francis Pease House (ca. 1845) has an exhibition called "Early Man on Martha's Vineyard" on permanent display, along with temporary exhibitions. The Gale Huntington Research Library and Francis Foster Museum contain a maritime exhibition. A replica watch tower houses the Fresnel First Order lens that was used in the Gay Head lighthouse from 1856 to 1952. The Carriage Shed houses a collection of antique vessels and vehicles. The Thomas Cooke House (ca. 1765) is a 12-room home used as a museum of Vineyard history (tours are held daily).

Admission: Mid-June to mid-Sept, $4 adults, $2 children under 16. Mid-Sept to mid-June, $2 adults, $1 children under 16.

Open: Mid-June to mid-Sept, Tues–Sat 10am–4:30. Mid-Sept to mid-June, Wed–Fri 1–4pm, Sat 10am–4pm. The Thomas Cooke House is open during the summer only.

OAK BLUFFS

THE FLYING HORSES CAROUSEL, 33 Oak Bluffs Ave. Tel. 693-9481.

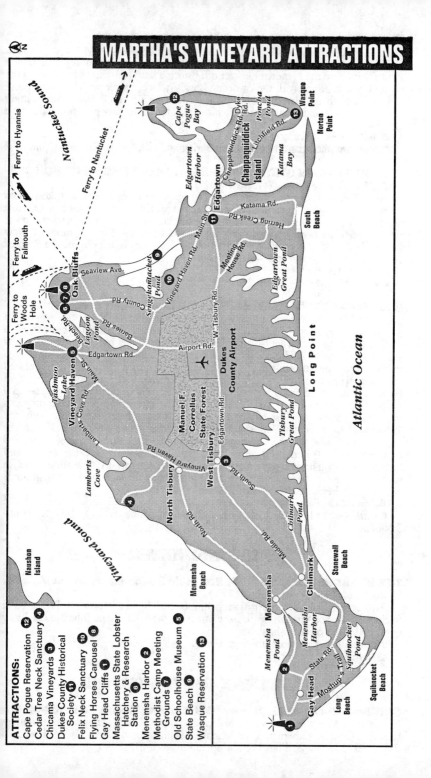

MARTHA'S VINEYARD ATTRACTIONS

N

Nantucket Sound

Ferry to Hyannis

Ferry to Nantucket

Ferry to Falmouth

Ferry to Woods Hole

Vineyard Sound

Atlantic Ocean

Naushon Island

Cape Pogue Bay

Cape Pogue

Dyke Rd.

Poucha Pond

Wasque Point

Chappaquiddick Rd.

Chappaquiddick Island

Litchfield Rd.

Norton Point

Katama Bay

Edgartown Harbor

Edgartown

Katama Rd.

Herring Creek Rd.

Meeting House Rd.

South Beach

Seaview Ave.

Oak Bluffs

County Rd.

Sengekontacket Pond

Vineyard Haven Rd.–Main St.

Edgartown Great Pond

Long Point

Barnes Rd.

Lagoon Pond

Beach Rd.

Edgartown Rd.

Airport Rd.

Dukes County Airport

W. Tisbury Rd.

Tashmoo Lake

Vineyard Haven

Main St.

Lambert's Cove Rd.

Manuel F. Correllus State Forest

Tisbury Great Pond

Lamberts Cove

North Tisbury

West Tisbury

Vineyard Haven Rd.

Edgartown Rd.

South Rd.

Chilmark Pond

Menemsha Beach

North Rd.

Middle Rd.

Chilmark

Stonewall Beach

Menemsha

Menemsha Pond

Menemsha Harbor

State Rd.

Squibnocket Pond

Squibnocket Beach

Gay Head

Long Beach

Moshup's Trail

ATTRACTIONS:

Cape Pogue Reservation **12**
Cedar Tree Neck Sanctuary **4**
Chicama Vineyards **3**
Dukes County Historical Society **11**
Felix Neck Sanctuary **10**
Flying Horses Carousel **8**
Gay Head Cliffs **1**
Massachusetts State Lobster Hatchery & Research Station **6**
Menemsha Harbor **2**
Methodist Camp Meeting Grounds **7**
Old Schoolhouse Museum **5**
State Beach **9**
Wasque Reservation **13**

Whether you're traveling with or without children, a visit to this antique carousel is a must. Listed on the National Register of Historic Places, this merry-go-round is the nation's oldest. Along with the cavorting horses (which, by the way, have real horse hair and were hand-carved in New York back in 1876), you'll find a combination platter of video games and pinball machines plus the customary popcorn-and cotton candy vendors.

Admission: $1 for carousel rides.
Open: Summer, daily 10am–10pm. Spring and fall, Sat–Sun 10am–10pm.

MASSACHUSETTS STATE LOBSTER HATCHERY AND RESEARCH STATION, Shirley Lane. Tel. 693-0060.

Here thousands of tiny lobsters are raised on pieces of shrimp meat to keep them from devouring one another until they are judged capable of fending for themselves in the chilly waters of the Atlantic. This is the oldest operating lobster hatchery in the world, and a fascinating stop for anyone interested in the life and times of New England's tastiest crustacean. The State Lobster Hatchery is just outside the town of Oak Bluffs on Lagoon Pond.

Admission: Free.
Open: Mon–Fri 1–3pm.

METHODIST CAMP MEETING GROUNDS, off Circuit Ave. No phone.

Walk around this web of gaily painted cottages and you'll feel as if you're at an amusement park—without the rides, the cotton candy, and the crowds. It's a carnival spirit that pervades this community of summer residences that began as a religious retreat in 1835. Back then, many groups would come and camp out in tents summer after summer, returning to the same spot each year. Eventually they replaced the tents with wooden cottages modeled after the Victorian styles popular in Newport, but added many Revival elements. Today, more than 300 cottages—in a unique "Carpenter Gothic" style (gabled roofs and filigree trim) stand like contestants in a beauty contest just off Circuit Avenue. The cottages radiate out from the **Tabernacle,** where singalongs, concerts, and religious services are held. On the grounds, you'll also find the **Cottage Museum** (1 Trinity Park), a cottage decorated as it would have been 100 years ago, with hooked rugs, rocking chairs, and bric-a-brac. If you happen to be on the island in July, don't miss Illumination Night, in which hundreds of paper lanterns from Asia are hung throughout the campgrounds and in the Tabernacle.

Admission: Free.
Open: Grounds, daily 24 hours. Museum, mid-June to Sept, daily 10:30am–3:30pm.

VINEYARD HAVEN

THE OLD SCHOOLHOUSE MUSEUM, Main St. (on the corner of Main St. and Colonial Lane). Tel. 627-8017.

This is a small and informal museum owned by the Historical Preservation Society. It's full of Vineyard artifacts, many from the whaling era. It has an especially good collection of scrimshaw.

Admission: Donations are appreciated.
Open: Summer, Mon–Fri 10am–2pm.

ELSEWHERE ON THE ISLAND

CHICAMA VINEYARDS, Stoney Hill Rd., West Tisbury. Tel. 693-0309.

Martha's Vineyard has its own real vineyard, the 33 acres are planted in vinifera varieties such as Cabernet, Chardonnay, Chenin Blanc, Cape Cod White, and Zinfandel. The vineyard has been in operation since 1971.

Admission: Free.
Open: June–Oct, Mon–Sat 11am–5pm, Sun 1–5pm. **Closed:** July 4 and Labor Day.

---

2. WHERE TO STAY ON MARTHA'S VINEYARD

Martha's Vineyard has a wide range of staying places available including basic motel-like accommodations, country inns and bed-and-breakfasts, and resort hotels. The highest concentration of accommodations is in Edgartown, Vineyard Haven, and Oak Bluffs.

EDGARTOWN

EXPENSIVE

CAPTAIN DEXTER HOUSE, 35 Pease's Point Way (Box 2798), Edgartown, MA 02539. Tel. 508/627-7289. 11 rms (all with bath).
$ Rates: Summer $104–$164 double. Winter, $60–$115 double. **Parking:** Free, on premises.
The Captain Dexter House (ca. 1840) is the kind of inn you discover and then hesitate to tell anyone about for fear of it's becoming too popular. Evidently the word is out. A flip through the guestbook revealed that visitors from around the globe (New Zealand, Sweden, Japan) have had the pleasure of staying here. Its rooms are thoughtfully decorated with the kind of big comfortable beds you never want to leave (in several rooms, you have to climb bed steps to get into bed). Some of the rooms have air conditioning, and some have working fireplaces. Common areas include a garden and a parlor complete with a fireplace and the daily papers. The continental breakfast includes homemade muffins and breads. The Captain Dexter House in Edgartown is the sister inn to the well-established Captain Dexter House in Vineyard Haven.

CHARLOTTE INN, 27 S. Summer St. (P.O. Box 1056), Edgartown, MA 02539. Tel. 508/627-4751. 24 rms (all with bath).
$ Rates: (including continental breakfast Mon–Sat): Mid-June to mid-Oct, $192–$323 double. Mid-Oct to Apr, $93–$159 double. May to mid-June, $137–$225 double. AE, MC, V. **Parking:** Free public parking across the street.
The Charlotte Inn is a unique complex combining the services of an inn, a fine art gallery, and a very good French restaurant. Rooms are decorated with fine antique furnishings. The best way to select a room is to see several, although this is often difficult, as many are sure to be occupied. Fifteen rooms have air conditioning; twelve, television; and nine, telephone. Even if you decide not to stay at the Charlotte Inn, stroll by some evening to admire the graceful house and the very good gallery, and perhaps enjoy the garden-terrace dining at L'Etoile (see "Where to Dine on Martha's Vineyard," below).

COLONIAL INN, 38 N. Water St. (P.O. Box 68), Edgartown, MA 02539. Tel. 508/627-4711, or toll free 800/627-4701. Fax 508/627-5904. 42 rms (all with bath). A/C TV TEL
$ Rates: (including continental breakfast): $94–$190 double. Extra person $16. Children under 16 stay free in parents' room. Off-season and mid-week rates available. AE, MC, V. **Parking:** Free. **Closed:** Nov–Apr.
This inn in the center of town looks like Edgartown's answer to the huge rambling Victorian hotels of Oak Bluffs and elsewhere, although to keep with tradition on

North Water Street, this one is covered in cedar "shake" (shingles), and many windows have shutters like those of the sea captain's houses. The advantages at the Colonial, besides its central location, recent renovations, shops, hairstylist, and sea views, are its large number of rooms and varied rates—rooms with harbor views are more expensive. The Colonial has two restaurants. The Café serves light dishes. The main restaurant, Decoys, serves continental cuisine; main dinner courses are $12 to $19, and reservations are accepted.

DAGGETT HOUSE, 59 N. Water St. at Daggett St. (P.O. Box 1333), Edgartown, MA 02539. Tel. 508/627-4600. 18 rms, 8 suites (all with bath). A/C TV TEL **Directions:** Take Main St. down to water, turn left on N. Water, then go 3 blocks on right.

$ Rates: (including continental breakfast): $143–$175 double; $252–$493 suite. AE, MC, V. **Parking:** Free, on premises.

The rooms are tastefully furnished with numerous antique pieces; several are of very good size and some have good water views—the larger rooms and those with views are the more expensive ones. All rooms have king-size, queen-size canopy or four-posters, double, or twin beds, and private bath; some rooms, good for groups of friends or large families, are arranged in suites. There are even lodgings with kitchen facilities, and a garden cottage with three double rooms down by the water. Some rooms have air conditioning, television, and telephone. A continental breakfast is included in the rates, but a full country breakfast is available at an additional cost. The main house has its own dock, and a Chimney Room (ca. 1660), said to have been Edgartown's oldest tavern, now used as a dining room for breakfast and dinner (open to public). The Cap'n Warren House is across the street, and is equally nice, and guests at either house may use the lawns and beach.

GOVERNOR BRADFORD INN, 128 Main St., Edgartown, MA 02539. Tel. 508/627-9510. Fax 508/693-8611. 16 rms (all with bath). **Directions:** Follow signs to Edgartown Center, head down Main St., and watch for sign.

$ Rates: (including full breakfast and afternoon tea): In-season, $114–$192 double. Off-season, $72–$126 double. Two-night minimum stay. AE, MC, V. **Parking:** Free, on premises.

This is a handsome white clapboard New England Gothic house with high-peaked roofs and bright windows. The atmosphere in the common rooms is one of restrained elegance rather than frilliness—a very satisfying feeling. Many of the rooms have televisions. The inn recently started serving dinner to guests and the public Friday through Sunday nights in two small dining rooms. Reservations are required. Main courses (which run from $15.95 to $24.95) include Baked Stuffed Shrimp, Pasta Primavera, and the inn's signature dish—Fillet Mignon Bradford. The inn i handicapped accessible.

MODERATE

EDGARTOWN INN, N. Water St. (P.O. Box 1211), Edgartown, MA 02539. Tel. 508/627-4794. 20 rms (16 with bath).

$ Rates: In-season, $93–$160 inn single or double; $82–$120 barn; $76–$153 Garden House. Off-season, $71–$92 inn single or double. Extra person $22. No credit cards. **Parking:** Free. **Closed:** Nov–Mar.

The Edgartown Inn has been hosting famous guests for well over a century, including Daniel Webster, Nathaniel Hawthorne (who wrote *Twice Told Tales* here), and John F. Kennedy (during his days in the Senate). The inn is thus a place of contrasts: In the rooms, 19th-century decor competes with the modern tile baths, and in the parlor, a portrait of Hawthorne hangs glowering at the color TV. In season, the main inn may not take reservations of fewer than 3 days. Two rooms in the newly remodeled Garden House have king-size beds, TV, balconies, and private baths; another room shares a bath with an employee. Also, there are rooms in the barn on the grounds. The Edgartown Inn serves country breakfasts in its quaint, cozy breakfast room, old-fashioned and neat as a pin: a deer head, a fine ship's model, and "colonial" ceiling

MARTHA'S VINEYARD ACCOMMODATIONS & DINING

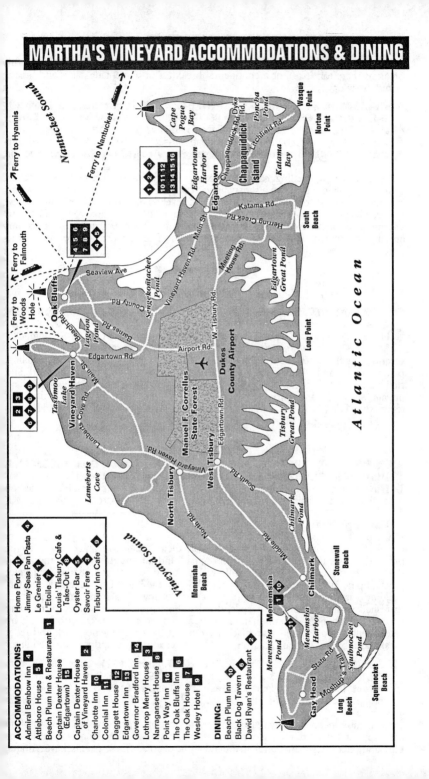

ACCOMMODATIONS:

Admiral Benbow Inn **4**
Attleboro House **5**
Beach Plum Inn & Restaurant **1**
Captain Dexter House (Edgartown) **15**
Captain Dexter House of Vineyard Haven **2**
Charlotte Inn **11**
Colonial Inn **11**
Daggett House **12**
Edgartown Inn **13**
Governor Bradford Inn **14**
Lothrop Merry House **3**
Narragansett House **8**
Point Way Inn **6**
The Oak Bluffs Inn **7**
The Oak House **9**
Wesley Hotel **16**

DINING:

Beach Plum Inn **10**
Black Dog Tavern **6**
David Ryan's Restaurant **2**
Home Port **11**
Jimmy Seas Pan Pasta **4**
Le Grenier **1**
L'Etoile **7**
Louis' Tisbury Cafe & Take-Out **5**
Oyster Bar **3**
Savoir Fare **3**
Tisbury Inn Cafe **9**

fans add to the decor. Whether a guest at the inn or not, you can have the full breakfast here for $6.50, or a continental breakfast of homemade cakes and breads baked every day for $3.75.

POINT WAY INN, 104 Main St. (P.O. Box 128), Edgartown, MA 02539. Tel. 508/627-8633, or toll free 800/942-9569. 15 rms (all with bath). **Directions:** Take Main St. to corner of Pease's Point Way.
$ Rates: (including continental breakfast): In-season, $104–$235 double. Off-season, $71–$126 double. Extra person $22. AE, MC, V. **Parking:** Free, on premises.

Once a 14-room whaling captain's house, this has been converted to a cozy, charming, 15-room inn with a satisfying variety of accommodations. You'll know it's nice as you walk through the garden, past the gazebo and croquet lawn, and into the house, which has a real family feel to it. There are small rooms, large rooms, 11 rooms with fireplace or deck, even a luxury two-room suite, all with private bath; four rooms are air conditioned. The inn has a complimentary convertible available to guests to tour the island.

OAK BLUFFS
EXPENSIVE

THE OAK HOUSE, Seaview Ave., Oak Bluffs, MA 02557. Tel. 508/693-4187. 10 rms (all with bath).
$ Rates: (including continental breakfast and Victorian tea): $119–$240 room. DC, MC, V. **Parking:** Free, on street. **Closed:** Mid-Oct to mid-May.

Overlooking the water, the Oak House is full of oak ceilings, oak floors, oak paneling, oak furniture, and oak bannisters. The living rooms and dining rooms are dark and rich in contrast to the white, glass-enclosed sun porch. Three of the rooms have private balconies and two are suites. A few rooms have air conditioning and televisions. There is a 3-night minimum stay on summer weekends. The Oak House is located on the Corner of Seaview and Pequot Avenues.

MODERATE

ADMIRAL BENBOW INN, 508 New York Ave. (P.O. Box 2488), Oak Bluffs, MA 02557. Tel. 508/693-6825. 7 rms (all with bath).
$ Rates: (including full breakfast): $60–$142 double. Extra person $21. Children ages 5–12 are charged $16; children under 5 stay free in parents' room. AE, MC, V.
Parking: Free. **Closed:** Jan.

Innkeeper Lynn Gaylen likes to think of the Admiral Benbow as a retreat for city people. She says with pride, "Guests arrive with their shoulders up and strained. By the time they leave, their shoulders have dropped." Indeed, the Admiral Benbow Inn is the kind of place where you can fully relax. Dating back to the 1870s, the former private home (now owned by the people who own the Black Dog Tavern) is a stately building within walking distance of the center of town. Its rooms are attractively furnished with big, climb-into beds, floral wallpapering, some antique pieces, and cooling ceiling fans. Common areas include a parlor (complete with a TV, an assortment of books, and a fireplace surrounded by intricate woodwork and relief tiles) and a breezy veranda so attractive that it once was the setting for a wedding.

THE OAK BLUFFS INN, Circuit Ave. (P.O. Box 2477), Oak Bluffs, MA 02557. Tel. 508/693-7171, or toll free 800/955-6235. 9 rms (all with bath).
$ Rates: (including continental breakfast): Summer, $109–$159 double. Fall-spring, discounts of 20% to 30% available. AE, MC, V. **Parking:** Free, on premises.

Conveniently located in town at the corner of Pequot Avenue, within minutes of all the shops, restaurants, and ice cream parlors, the Oak Bluffs Inn is a notice-me blue-and-pink Victorian building topped by a cupola. Guest rooms have antique furnishings. The breezy front porch with its white wicker furniture is a perfect place to settle in and watch the world. For a 360-degree view of town and surrounding environs, climb the ladder up to the window's walk.

WESLEY HOTEL, 1 Lake Ave. (P.O. Box 2370), Oak Bluffs, MA 02557. Tel. 508/693-6611. Fax: 508/693-2216. 82 rms (62 with bath). **Directions:** From the Steamship Authority docks, walk straight inland toward marina; the Wesley is a few blocks down on the left.
$ Rates: $66 double without bath, $120–$142 double with bath; $153 suite. Extra adult $27 in summer, $16 in winter. AE, MC, V. **Parking:** Free.

This big, rambling wooden place dominates the lodging market in town and in recent years it has experienced a make-over. The lobby is country formal and the hallways are papered with a pretty floral design. The rooms, while not in keeping with the gracious common area, are still clean and boast standard motel furnishings; most have televisions. A big plus here is the harbor view from the old-time rocking chairs on the wraparound porch.

INEXPENSIVE

ATTLEBORO HOUSE, 11 Lake Ave. (P.O. Box 1564), Oak Bluffs, MA 02557. Tel. 508/693-4346. 8 rms (none with bath). **Directions:** From the Steamship Authority docks, walk straight inland toward marina; the Attleboro is a few blocks down on the left.
$ Rates: (including continental breakfast): $49–$77 double. MC, V. **Parking:** Free, on street. **Closed:** Oct–May.

This is in that marvelous row of gingerbread houses, next to the old Wesley Hotel, that faces the sheltered harbor. If you arrive by Hy-Line boat, you'll be able to spot Attleboro House even before you debark. The wide verandas are well furnished with rockers and fine views. Many rooms have porches overlooking the harbor. The rooms are Spartan but tidy, and fully in the spirit of Oak Bluffs; in fact, the house is on land owned by the Methodist Campmeeting Association, so guests must agree to refrain from "rude or loud behavior." Only a few rooms have washbasins; none has private bath; and though there are plenty of clean sheets and towels, chamber service is strictly do-it-yourself. Here, and at the Wesley, you're living right within Oak Bluffs' history.

NARRAGANSETT HOUSE, 62 Narragansett Ave. (P.O. Box 2478), Oak Bluffs, MA 02557. Tel. 508/693-3627. 12 rms (all with bath).
$ Rates: (including continental breakfast): In-season, $55–$92 double. Off season, $44–$77 double. MC, V.
Parking: Free, on street. **Closed:** Mid-Oct to mid-Apr.

Built at the turn of the century, the Narragansett House is an eye-catching gingerbread house with arched windows, gables, and other Victorian details painted hot pink, blue, and white. It's situated on a quiet, tree-lined street within walking distance of everything. Rooms, though on the small side, are all very imaginatively decorated with stenciling on the walls throughout. Furnishings are simple and comfortable. The front porch—with its rocking chairs, window boxes spilling over with blossoms, bird-feeders, and wind chimes—is a glorious spot to perch for a while.

VINEYARD HAVEN

CAPTAIN DEXTER HOUSE OF VINEYARD HAVEN, 100 Main St., Vineyard Haven, MA 02568. Tel. 508/693-6564. 8 rms (all with bath).
$ Rates: (including breakfast): Summer, $104–$164 double. Winter, $60–$115 double. AE, MC, V. **Parking:** Free, on premises.

This is one of those rare finds: meticulously restored and exquisitely furnished in the colonial period, yet surprisingly unpretentious. Each of the rooms (one is actually a suite) has a private bath, and some have working fireplaces and four-poster beds with white lace canopies. From the fresh flowers to the fresh-squeezed orange juice served with the "expanded" continental breakfast, you'll notice attention to detail which makes this one of the loveliest inns on the island. If you're walking from the boat, it's 2 blocks away. There is a partner inn in Edgartown.

LOTHROP MERRY HOUSE, at Owen Park (Box 1939), Vineyard Haven, MA 02568. Tel. 508/693-1646. 7 rms (4 with bath). **Directions:** Turn off Main St. toward the ocean at Owen Park.

$ Rates: (including breakfast): In-season, $107–$118 double without bath, $150–$174 double with bath. Off-season, $74–$107 double without bath, $126–$148 double with bath. MC, V. **Parking:** Free, on premises.

Protected on both sides, the lawn slopes gently down to a little beach on the quiet side of the harbor, which makes the location of John and Mary Clarke's Merry House special. It's a 3-minute walk along the shoreline right to the boat dock. And if that's not enough, the sunrise sends reflections from the bay waters into most of the guest rooms. The ambience in this 18th-century house is country comfortable, with braided rugs and uneven door frames. There are doubles with private baths and working fireplaces on the first floor, and smaller doubles, two of which have harbor views, all share baths on the second floor. You can while away the morning with the complimentary breakfast served on the patio overlooking the harbor. Ask about a sail on the innkeepers' 54-foot alden ketch *Laissez Faire*. There's also a canoe and a Sunfish (small sailboat) for guests' use. The Lothrop Merry House is open all year.

UP ISLAND

The best place to get away from the crowds and to begin to feel the serenity of island living is to spend time "up island"—in the towns and areas around West Tisbury, Chilmark, Menemsha, and Gay Head. The scenery here resembles parts of the English countryside; you'll find stone walls, forested roads, and plenty of space.

BEACH PLUM INN AND RESTAURANT, North Rd. (P.O. Box 98), Menemsha, MA 02552. Tel. 508/645-9454. 12 rms (10 with bath). TEL

$ Rates: (including full breakfast): Mid-June to mid-Sept, $164–$274 double. May to mid-June and mid-Sept to Oct, $82–$192 double. AE, DISC, MC, V. **Parking:** Free, on grounds. **Closed:** Nov–Apr.

A long dirt road leads to this inn, which is propped up on a hill overlooking Menemsha Harbor, Vineyard Sound, and the Elizabeth Islands. The grounds are scenic with flowers and a patio where several weddings have taken place (ask to see the inn's photo album). Rooms are located in the main house (several with views of the water), in cottages, and in a three-bedroom farmhouse (available for groups or families). Three rooms have air conditioning. The inn has a tennis court, an ocean beach, a pond stocked with bass and perch, and a living room complete with cable TV (including the Disney channel for kids). The Beach Plum restaurant is highly regarded both for its cuisine and its sunset views (see "Where to Dine on Martha's Vineyard," below). The inn can provide full-time nanny service.

3. WHERE TO DINE ON MARTHA'S VINEYARD

The dining situation is both helped and hurt by Vineyard Haven's status as a "dry" town. You don't have the convenience of ordering wine with dinner, but if you remember to bring your own from Edgartown or Oak Bluffs, you'll save the normal (substantial) restaurant markup on beverages. Plan ahead and save.

EDGARTOWN

Edgartown—like the island in general—can boast a large number of eateries, plain and fancy. I couldn't possibly list them all in the limited space here, and in fact an all-inclusive list would be more bewildering than helpful. Although I can heartily recommend the establishments below as delivering good value for the money, you will no doubt want to do some exploration of your own. By the way, Edgartown is one of the Vineyard's two "wet" towns.

DAVID RYAN'S RESTAURANT, 11 North Water St. Tel. 627-4100.

Cuisine: CONTEMPORARY AMERICAN/ITALIAN. **Reservations:** Required for parties of 6 or more on weekends.

$ Prices: Appetizers $3.95–$8.25; main courses $5.95–$14.95 at lunch, $13.95–$18.95 at dinner. MC, V.

Open: Lunch daily 11:30am–5:30pm; dinner daily 5:30–10pm. Bar stays open until 12:30am.

Walk into David Ryan's and you feel as if you've found the hippest place in town. You've also found a good, casual dining choice for both lunch and dinner. On the street level, you'll find a bar area with good jazz music playing and tanned vacationers crowded around the high tables and stools. Upstairs is more sedate with quiet tables and booths. You can have your meal in either place. For lunch, there's a good selection of pita pizzas, burgers (with guacamole, cheddar cheese, or other toppings), and sandwiches. Dinner main courses include grilled rosemary chicken, fresh grilled swordfish, and some creative pasta dishes.

L'ETOILE, in the Charlotte Inn, 27 S. Summer St. Tel. 627-5187.

Cuisine: CONTEMPORARY FRENCH. **Reservations:** Required.

$ Prices: Fixed-price dinner $48; Sun brunch $22. AE, MC, V.

Open: Summer, dinner daily 6:30–9:45pm; Sun brunch 10:30am–12:30pm. Spring and fall, dinner Fri–Sun 6:30–9:45pm; Sun brunch 10:30am–12:30pm.

Closed: Jan–Feb 14.

In the garden and glassed-in terrace of the Charlotte Inn, the white tables and chairs set out among the trees, vines, and flowers on a patio surrounded by trelliswork provide the perfect place for a warm-weather evening's repast; in bad weather the terrace room is just as good, with lots of windows and skylights. The menu reads like a list of ambrosias: roasted French pheasant with a sauce of oysters, mushrooms, warmed figs, thyme, and cognac; rack of lamb with warm goat cheese, balsamic vinaigrette, and herbed vegetable julienne; grilled swordfish steak with a trio of American caviars, champagne, and chive beurre blanc. You can order wine to accompany your meal, and the Sunday brunch is equally scrumptious-sounding. Call for reservations, and ask what the day's special will be.

SAVOIR FARE, 14 Church St. Tel. 627-9864.

Cuisine: TRADITIONAL TUSCAN. **Reservations:** Required for dinner, not accepted at lunch. **Directions:** In the courtyard behind the Dukes County Court House.

$ Prices: Appetizers $5.95–$7.95; main courses $5.95–$7.95 at lunch, $9.50–$21.50 at dinner. MC, V.

Open: Lunch daily 11:30am–2:30pm; dinner daily 6–10pm. **Closed:** Nov–Apr.

Follow your noses to Savoir Fare if you're in the mood for some good Italian food. This all-white restaurant (white tables, walls, floors, linens, and candles) has been featured in *Gourmet* and several other magazines, and deservedly so. The food (and wine list) is nonpareil. Top dinner choices on our list include the seared black bass with sweet onion, tomato, and anchovies; and the pan-roasted veal chop with lemon, prosciutto, and fontina. The wine list boasts a large selection of California and Italian wines (including some super Tuscans).

OAK BLUFFS

JIMMY SEAS PAN PASTA, 14 Kennebec Ave. Tel. 693-2948.

Cuisine: ITALIAN. **Reservations:** Not accepted.

$ Prices: Appetizers $4.75–$6.75; main courses $11.75–$16.75. No credit cards.

Open: Daily 8am–11pm.

One whiff of the garlic outside Jimmy Seas, and you know the food is good. Young chef/owner Jimmy Cipolla is a master in the kitchen, whipping up all sorts of flavorful Italian meals. All hot dishes are generously proportioned and served in a pan (the Linguine Puttanesca was delicious). The decor is bare and budget-minded (concrete walls have paintings of the sea on them, floors are blue-painted cement), but it is more than compensated for by the celestial food. By the way, don't even think of asking Jimmy to change the Frank Sinatra music; it's his passion.

OYSTER BAR, 162 Circuit Ave. Tel. 693-3300.
   Cuisine: SEAFOOD. **Reservations:** Recommended.
$ Prices: Appetizers $4–$15; main courses $13–$35; dinner $45–$50. MC, V.
   Open: May–Nov, dinner daily 6pm–12:30am.

The Oyster Bar is very trendy and upscale, something you'd expect to find in New York or San Francisco. The solitary strip of hot-pink neon, high on the back wall, sets the tone. General decor is pink and green with soft lighting; the ceiling is high (it's tin, so the noise level is a bit high, too), and the Doric pillars are green painted to look like marble. The dinner menu (as well as the wine and dessert menu) is quite extensive: Oysters galore from the raw bar or as a cooked appetizer, striped bass or mahi-mahi, and a Belgian chocolate pie with white and dark chocolate sauces make a superb supper.

VINEYARD HAVEN

BLACK DOG TAVERN, Beach St. Extension. Tel. 693-1991.
   Cuisine: AMERICAN. **Reservations:** Not accepted. **Directions:** Go to the water end of Beach St., right down next to the yacht marina.
$ Prices: Appetizers $2.25–$5.95 at lunch, $3.95–$9.95 at dinner; main courses $2.95–$8.95 at lunch, $17.95–$20.95 at dinner; Breakfast dishes $1.95–$6.95. AE, DISC, MC, V.
   Open: May–Oct, breakfast Mon–Sat 7–11am; lunch daily 11:30am–2:30pm; dinner daily 5–10pm; Sun brunch 7am–1pm. Nov–Apr, breakfast Wed–Sat 7–11am; lunch Wed–Sun 11:30am–2:30pm; dinner Wed–Sun 5–10pm; Sun brunch 7am–1pm.

Ask anyone on the Vineyard what restaurants they recommend and they'll inevitably include the Black Dog Tavern in their response. Set on the water, it's famed for its food, especially breakfast and dinner. It's always a lively spot, with crowds of fanatical regulars as well as visitors seated in a screened porch overlooking the harbor and in the rustic dining room. There's always a great selection of innovative dishes, such as fresh sea scallops sautéed with roasted red peppers and capers; and fresh flounder sautéed with bananas, almonds, and rum. For lunch, try steamers with broth and butter, chili, hamburgers, or a B.L.T., or treat yourself to a red caviar sandwich with cream cheese and red onion. The nearby Black Dog Bakery is the place to go for take-out sandwiches and homemade desserts.

LE GRENIER, Main St. Tel. 693-4906.
   Cuisine: FRENCH. **Reservations:** Recommended. **Directions:** Walk up the street from the ferry, turn right, to the cobble-studded porch of Le Grenier.
$ Prices: Appetizers $4.25–$8.95; main courses $16–$27; dinner $25–$35. AE, DC, MC, V.
   Open: Mar–Dec, dinner daily 6–10pm.

The menu, as you might guess, tends toward classical French, but stresses local ingredients. Try the stuffed mushrooms to start and the shrimp Pernod flambé with cream sauce for a main course.

LOUIS' TISBURY CAFE & TAKE-OUT, 102 State Rd. Tel. 693-3255.
   Cuisine: AMERICAN/ITALIAN. **Reservations:** Not accepted.
$ Prices: Appetizers $9–$12; main courses $9–$18. AE, MC, V.
   Open: Mon–Sat 11:30am–9pm, Sun 4–9pm.

Not quite a mile out on State Road toward Gay Head is Louis'. The name of the game here is pasta, great homemade pasta. Try a hot and spicy linguine shrimp diavolo for $17 or perhaps linguine with salmon, bluefish, scallops, and shrimp for $14. (Knock

$2 off if you want it as an appetizer; everything on the menu is also available for take-out.) A low-key, casual atmosphere reigns here. Expect to wait if you arrive after 7pm; there's a terrific following among the locals—Louis' really packs 'em in here.

TISBURY INN CAFE, Main St. Tel. 693-3416.
   Cuisine: NEW AMERICAN. **Reservations:** Recommended.
$ Prices: Appetizers $2.25–$8; main courses $2.50–$9 at lunch, $30 at dinner. MC, V.
   Open: Mid-Mar to mid-Nov, lunch daily 11:30am–2:30pm; dinner daily 5:30–9:30pm.

The specialty here is New American cuisine with Cajun accents. The scrod jambalaya, for example, is a unique blending of New England and New Orleans. There is also a good selection of pasta dishes.

UP ISLAND

BEACH PLUM INN, North Rd., Menemsha. Tel. 645-9454.
   Cuisine: NEW ENGLAND. **Reservations:** Required.
$ Prices: Dinner $35–$50. AE, DISC, MC, V.
   Open: June-Sept, dinner daily 5–10pm.

It's hard to say what you'll like best about the Beach Plum Restaurant: the New England cuisine, the sunset views, or the pianist who plays Gershwin, Cole Porter, and Nat King Cole on a white grand piano. The menu—which changes nightly—has some lovely selections, including roasted boneless duck with a honey-curry sauce and salmon baked in a puffed pastry. For dessert, hope they'll be serving the crème brûlée; it's celestial.

HOME PORT, North Rd., Menemsha Harbor, Tel. 645-2679.
   Cuisine: SEAFOOD. **Reservations:** Recommended.
$ Prices: Main dinner courses $15–$25; dinner for two $45–$50. AE, MC, V.
   Open: May to Oct, dinner daily 5–10pm.

There's no better seafood platter (baked, broiled, or fried) on the island than at Homeport, on the harbor. It's not an intimate place, but the sunset from here will bring out the romantic in anyone. At first, the main course price of $25 for swordfish or $22 for Vineyard scallops may seem high, but the price includes an appetizer of your choice, salad, beverage, and dessert. Bring your own wine. There is an outdoor raw bar on the patio.

NANTUCKET

More difficult of access than Martha's Vineyard (at least in terms of time and price), Nantucket draws an elite crowd. But the crowd is no smaller for it; prepare for your visit in advance, by booking reservations.

   To its year-round inhabitants, Nantucket is not just another resort island off Cape Cod, but is a special seagoing world of its own. All the brochures and booklets handed out on the island seem to bear the legend THIRTY MILES AT SEA. With its history of whaling, its choppy Native American name, and its people's reputation for hardiness, you might expect to find clusters of peasant dwellings and strong-armed shipwrights making rough island boats, but in fact the opposite is true: Nantucket's Main Street is lined with gracious buildings and towering elms, and the rest of the town boasts street after street of charming and dignified houses from the 18th and 19th centuries. This is to be expected when you think of the money that whaling brought to Nantucket. Before the oil sheiks, there were the whale-oil magnates, for whale oil fired the lamps of all New England, whalebone provided the stays for the corsets then in style, and ambergris was the base for perfume, a luxury item.

In 1659 the first colonists came ashore to settle the island, already inhabited by four tribes of Native Americans. The Jethro Coffin House, the first fine house to be built, went up in 1686, almost 20 years after the first whale had been claimed off Nantucket's shores. By the time of the Revolution, Nantucket was already wealthy from the whale-oil trade and contributed greatly to the Revolutionary cause, losing more than 100 whaling ships and 2,000 Nantucketers in the war. Before the island could recover fully, the War of 1812 again interfered with its prosperity. In another 50 years, the age of the sail-rigged whaling ship was at an end, but the same device which put an end to that era—the steamship—brought the beginning of a new era for Nantucket as a vacation destination. In summer, the cobblestones of Main Street are worn down by visitors from Boston, New York, and even farther away, and in winter the islanders go about their business getting ready for the next summer season.

Nantucket is well organized and well governed, and local residents have various regulations that they want visitors to observe, such as not wearing bathing suits on Main Street, obeying all traffic rules when riding a bicycle, and not camping—whether in a vehicle or a tent or under the stars—anywhere on the island.

SEEING NANTUCKET

GETTING THERE   By Plane   Flights to Nantucket's Memorial Airport are operated by several national carriers and by various local air services. Except at the evening rush hour, or on weekends, you should be able to show up at Hyannis's Barnstable Municipal Airport or New Bedford Municipal Airport, buy a ticket, and be in the air, bound for Nantucket, within ½ hour, even without advance reservations.

By the way, parking at the New Bedford airport is free of charge.

Business Express, a Delta Connection carrier, operates flights to Nantucket from New York (La Guardia) and Boston (Logan), with connections from many cities in the region, including points as far away as Albany; Baltimore; Burlington, Vt.; Montréal; Philadelphia; Presque Isle, Me.; Toronto; and Washington, D.C. For reservations and information, call toll free 800/345-3400.

Cape Air flies between New Bedford, Martha's Vineyard, and Nantucket. For reservations and information, call toll free 800/999-1616.

Coastal Air Services, with offices at Groton–New London Airport, Groton, CT 06340 (tel. 203/448-1001), at Nantucket Memorial Airport (tel. 508/228-3350), and at Martha's Vineyard Airport (tel. 508/693-5942), provides air-charter and aircraft rentals. If you don't want to charter the entire plane, you can join an "Open Charter" with a few other people who want to fly to the same point at the same time.

Continental Express (tel. toll free 800/525-0280) has daily flights between Newark, N.J. and Nantucket, and twice-weekly flights between Martha's Vineyard and Nantucket.

Island Airlines (tel. 508/775-6606, or toll free 800/248-7779) has ten round-trip flights between Hyannis and Nantucket daily. It's a 20-minute flight.

Nantucket Airlines, at Nantucket Memorial Airport (tel. 508/790-0300 or 228-6234, or toll free 800/635-8787 in Mass.), flies daily shuttle service between Nantucket and Hyannis, departing about a dozen times a day from each place.

Northwest Airlink, a regional airline associated with Northwest Airlines (tel. toll free 800/225-2525) and operated by Northeast Express Regional Airlines, flies between Boston and Nantucket four times daily from mid-May to mid-September.

Charter service is available with **Westchester Air, Inc.,** from the Tri-State area (New York, New Jersey, and Connecticut). Flights carry six passengers at a time. For more details, call 914/761-3000, or toll free 800/SKY-AWAY.

By Ferry   In summer, ferryboats carrying both cars and passengers run to Nantucket from Hyannis (see Chapter 6) and Martha's Vineyard. When taking a ferry, note which island port—Oak Bluffs or Vineyard Haven—the ferry operates from or to.

The **Steamship Authority** makes six trips a day both ways, between Hyannis and Nantucket from mid-May through mid-September. The trip is 2¼ hours and costs $9.75 one-way for adults, $4.90 for children (ages 5 to 12). Bicycle fares are

NANTUCKET

Great Point

Nantucket Sound

Ferry to Hyannis Port (Summer Only)

Ferry to Martha's Vineyard (Summer Only)

Coskata Beach

Wauwinet

Nantucket Harbor

Quidnet

Coatue Point

Coatue Beach

Wauwinet Rd.

Eel Point Rd.

Nantucket Cliffs

Eel Point Rd.

Cliff Rd.

Nantucket Town

Sesachacha Pond

Polpis Rd.

Polpis Rd.

Madaket

Madaket Rd.

Massasoit Rd.

Hummock Pond

Hummock Pond Rd.

Milestone Rd.

Old South Rd.

Atlantic Ave.

Siasconset

Cisco

Miacomet Pond

Nantucket Memorial Airport

South Shore

Surfside

New South Rd.

Beach Rd.

Atlantic Ocean

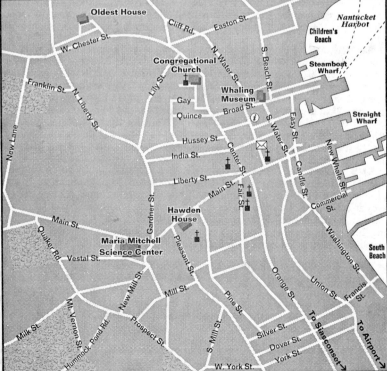

Oldest House

Cliff Rd.

Easton St.

Nantucket Harbor

Children's Beach

W. Chester St.

N. Water St.

S. Beach St.

Steamboat Wharf

Congregational Church

Franklin St.

N. Liberty St.

Lily St.

Whaling Museum

Straight Wharf

New Lane

Gay

Quince

Broad St.

S. Water St.

Easy St.

Hussey St.

India St.

Center St.

New Whale St.

Liberty St.

Candle St.

Commercial St.

Gardner St.

Main St.

Fair St.

Hawden House

Main St.

Quaker Rd.

Maria Mitchell Science Center

Washington St.

South Beach

Vestal St.

Pleasant St.

Mill St.

Orange St.

Union St.

Francis St.

New Mill St.

Pine St.

To Siasconset

Milk St.

Mt. Vernon St.

Prospect St.

S. Mill St.

Silver St.

Dover St.

To Airport

Hummock Pond Rd.

W. York St.

York St.

Information ⓘ   Post Office ⊠   Church ✝

$4.50 one-way. One-way auto rates are $83 (May 15 to October 14) or $65 (October 15 to November 30). Special reduced rates are available for those taking their cars over for short periods of time; from May 15 to October 14 for 1 to 5 days, the round-trip rate is $105 (includes 2 adults and 2 children); from October 15 to November 30, it's $85. For reservations (which are a must during summer months and should be made far in advance) and more information, call 508/540-2022. Be prepared to be put on hold for a while, especially if you're calling just before the summer months. You can also send away for a schedule by writing to the Martha's Vineyard and Nantucket Steamship Authority, P.O. Box 284, Woods Hole, MA 02543.

Hy-Line Cruises, Ocean Street Dock, Hyannis (tel. 508/778-2600), takes passengers only between Hyannis and Nantucket six times a day from June 12 to September 15) and at least once a day in the spring and fall. The one-way adult fare is $10.50; children (12 and under), $5.25. The round-trip fare for adults is $21; children, $10.50. The bicycle rate each way is $4.50. Children 4 and under ride for free. Buy tickets (for cash or traveler's checks only) in Oak Bluffs, Martha's Vineyard (tel. 508/693-0112) and on Straight Wharf, Nantucket (tel. 508/228-3949).

INFORMATION The **Nantucket Chamber of Commerce** (tel. 508/228-1700) and its Public Relations Committee have done a lot to organize the tourist industry on the island, and information about rooms, tours, and sights is surprisingly easy to get. The **Nantucket Information Bureau,** 25 Federal St. (tel. 508/228-0925), is the place to get daily information on room availability, activities, and island services and businesses. The bureau is not far from Main Street and the ferry docks, and it's open from 9am to 5pm Monday to Friday, 11am to 3pm Saturday.

Nantucket Cottage Hospital, at South Prospect Street and Vesper Lane (tel. 228-1200), is a modern, accredited facility. You can contact the Massachusetts State Police at their office on North Liberty Street (tel. 228-0706), and the Nantucket Town Police on East Chestnut Street (tel. 228-1212). The emergency number for police, firefighters, and ambulance service is 911. The **area code** for the entire island is 508.

By Rental Car Rental cars are available from several companies, including Ray Conlon's **Nantucket Windmill Auto Rental,** Nantucket Airport (P.O. Box 1057), Nantucket, MA 02554 (tel. 508/228-1227, or toll free 800/228-1227, which rents cars, vans, and four-wheel-drive vehicles at the airport. Also at the airport is **Hertz Rent-a-Car** (tel. 508/228-9421, or toll free 800/654-3131). Elsewhere on the island, you'll find **Nantucket Car Rental,** at 4 Broad St. and 15 North Beach St. (tel. 508/228-7474); **Nantucket Jeep Rental,** 3 Square Rigger Rd. (tel. 508/228-1618); **Preston's Rent-a-Car,** Somerset Road (tel. 508/228-0047); and **Young's Car Rental,** on Steamboat Wharf (tel. 508/228-1151).

By Bus **Barrett's Tours,** 20 Federal St. (tel. 228-0174), runs buses from their office in Nantucket Town to 'Sconset daily in summer at 10am, 11am, noon, 2:15pm, and 4pm; return trips leave 'Sconset a half hour after those times (except one that leaves at 2:30pm). Round-trip tickets cost $5 for adults, half-price for children.

Other Barrett's buses depart the office for Surfside Beach at 10am, 11am, noon, 1pm, 2pm, 3pm, 4pm, and 5pm; return trips depart Surfside 15 minutes after those times. Round-trip tickets cost $3 for adults, half-price for children.

By Taxi Taxis abound and their rates are $4 for one person within town limits, $1 for each additional person; between airport and town, $6 for one person, $1 for each additional person. Rates are higher at night. Other rates are established for trips to the beaches and sights, and are posted in the cab. Incidentally, almost any taxi driver will be glad to give you a tour of the island, with rates depending on how much ground you want to cover and time you want to spend.

By Bicycle and Moped Traveling around Nantucket by bicycle or moped is one of the best ways to see the island. However, keep the following in mind: If you're riding a bike, obey all traffic laws (especially one-way streets), use bike paths, and always lock up your bike. Bicycles are not permitted in the Old Historic District between 10pm and 7am. If you're renting a moped, you must wear a helmet and drive on the road only, following the rules of the road that cars must follow. Take care when driving on beach roads that are sandy; mopeds skid very easily.

Bikes generally rent for between $13 (3-speed) and $18 (mountain bike) a day; you can also rent bikes by the hour or by the week. Mopeds cost roughly $40 per day.

Both bicycles and mopeds can be rented at **Nantucket Bike Shop,** at 4 and 10 Broad St. and on Straight Wharf (tel. 508/228-1999), and **Young's Bicycle Shop,** on Steamboat Wharf (tel. 508/228-1151).

4. WHAT TO SEE & DO ON NANTUCKET

Once on Nantucket, you'll find that your activity schedule will take care of itself. In good weather everyone takes off to the beaches, by taxi, bus, or bike. For variety, the island offers tennis, golf, horseback riding, movies, antique stores, and art galleries. Sports fishers should wander down to Straight Wharf to talk to one of the charter-boat captains about a day's run for bluefish or striped bass. Those who just like being in a boat can rent a sailboat and take sailing lessons at one of the establishments on Washington Street Extension or Steamboat Wharf. There are also sea kayaks available for rent and for tours. The island's information office on Federal Street will be able to help you out with details.

TOURS

BIKE & MOPED TRIPS

Between the cobblestones and the summer crowds, riding bikes and mopeds in town can be quite annoying. Elsewhere on the island, however, you'll find it's easy and very enjoyable to travel via two wheels. Here are some destinations to head for:

SURFSIDE AREA   Located within easy riding distance of town (about 3 miles) on the island's south shore, Surfside is a popular spot for beachgoers. There's a lunch bar, lifeguards, and a changing facility. The surf here is substantial and the beach wide and white.

HUMMOCK AREA & CISCO BEACH   Also on the south shore is Cisco Beach, which is a popular swimming and surfing spot. The trip out takes you through some of the island's most scenic farmland.

MADAKET   A 6-mile ride on paved bike paths from town, Madaket is as far west as you can go on Nantucket. The big attractions here are the beaches and sunsets.

'SCONSET AREA   A bike path connects Nantucket with 'Sconset, the island's easternmost town, 7½ miles away. Back in the 18th century, this area was colonized by a group of fisherman who built little cottages. Today, it's a summer resort area with long sandy beaches and Atlantic waves. The tiny town is home to a handful of restaurants, a post office, and a collection of gray-shingled cottages. Bikers customarily stop at **Claudette's** (tel. 257-6622) for box lunches to take to the beach ($4.95 to $5.75). En route to 'Sconset, you can turn off (about 6 miles out of town) to the right and head for **Tom Nevers Head.** This is a bluff (about 65 feet high) overlooking the ocean.

WAUWINET   This small village is located on that skinny strip of land you see curving to the north on any map of Nantucket. About 9 miles from Nantucket town, it's wedged between the ocean and the harbor. You'll need a four-wheel vehicle to travel beyond the village—or strong legs and stamina. It's a protected area, home to many rare and endangered birds.

BUS TOURS

Tour buses meet some ferryboats at Steamboat Wharf or Straight Wharf, ready to take you on a 1½-hour tour of the island. There's no better way to get your bearings, and the short time spent will help you better organize the few precious days you'll have on the island.

Nantucket Island Tours (tel. 228-0334), with offices on Straight Wharf, offers five island tours daily in summer, charging $10 per adult, $5 per child.

Barrett's Tours, 20 Federal St. (tel. 228-0174) operates six daily tours between Nantucket Town and 'Sconset. The 1½-hour tour costs $9 for adults, half-price for children. Senior citizens get discounts on all tours departing from Barrett's office.

CRUISES

Nantucket Harbor Cruises, Straight Wharf (tel. 228-1444), operates the most original cruises: morning trips to pull up live lobsters from the company's own traps, afternoon "ice cream" voyages, evening and moonlight cruises. Fares range from $10 to $20 for adults, $7.50 to $15 for children. Call for reservations.

Friendship Sloop *Endeavor*, Slip 15, Charter Boat Dock, Straight Wharf (tel. 228-5585), makes four or five voyages daily in summer. Cruises last 1 or 1½ hours and cost $20 to $25 per person, depending upon the time and length of the cruise.

MUSEUMS

MARIA MITCHELL SCIENCE CENTER, 2 Vestal St. Tel. 228-0898 or 228-9198.

This is a group of buildings organized and maintained in honor of Nantucket's foremost astronomer, Maria Mitchell (1818–89). Born on Nantucket to an astronomer father and teacher-librarian mother, Mitchell became interested in the stars at an early age. Out here on Nantucket, away from the pollution and haze of cities, she studied the heavens, and in 1847 discovered a hitherto uncharted comet. Her scientific feat earned her a gold medal from the king of Denmark and membership in the American Academy of Arts and Sciences (the only woman so honored at the time), and led to a distinguished career as a professor at Vassar College. Founded in 1902, the Nantucket Maria Mitchell Association seeks to preserve a fitting memorial to the island's famous astronomer, and to make available science facilities to residents and visitors. The science center consists of astronomical observatories, with lectures on Monday at 8pm and stellar observations on Wednesday at 9pm if the sky is clear; the Hinchman House at 7 Milk St., with its Museum of Natural Science, Thursday evening (8pm) lectures, birdwatching, wildflower and nature walks, and children's nature classes; the Mitchell House at 1 Vestal St., birthplace of Maria Mitchell, with wildflower and herb gardens; the Science Library at 2 Vestal St.; and the aquarium at 28 Washington St. Check with the center for current activity schedules.

Admission: $3 adults, $1 children.

Open: Science center lecture Mon 8pm, observations Wed 9pm; Hinchman House lecture Thurs 8pm.

NANTUCKET HISTORICAL ASSOCIATION, 5 Washington St. Tel. 228-1894.

Nantucket's history can keep you occupied for days. To run the gamut, buy a special visitor's pass to the 12 buildings filled with the exhibits of the Nantucket Historical Association. These buildings include the famous Whaling Museum, the Thomas Macy Warehouse (Nantucket history museum), the oldest house on the island, and a windmill built in 1746 and still functioning. Individual admissions to all buildings would cost much more, and the pass gives you the advantage of being able to browse in a museum for a while, go to the beach, and return to another museum later in the afternoon. You can get your pass at the Whaling Museum on Broad Street, or at any of the other association buildings.

    Admission: Special museum pass for all sites $5 adult, $2.50 children aged 5–14. Admission to individual buildings are $2–$3 each and total $17 if purchased separately.

    Open: In season, Thomas Macy Warehouse daily 10am–5pm and 7–10pm; all other buildings daily 10am–5pm. Off-season, hours as posted. **Directions:** Tour begins on Straight Wharf, three wharves south of ferry landing.

CHAMBER MUSIC & THEATER

In the past few years, Nantucket has supported chamber music concerts and theater productions at various times, particularly in the weeks of high summer. Ask at the information bureau, or look for notices of upcoming events. A calendar of events is provided in *Nantucket Vacation Guide,* published monthly (available at the information bureau).

5. WHERE TO STAY ON NANTUCKET

Nantucket Island harbors nearly 100 places to stay, but the real character of the place is best captured in the old whaling merchants' and ship captains' houses converted to inns and guesthouses. Many of these are carefully restored, luxuriously appointed, and staffed with professionals; others are run by one person or a couple and are modest but warm and friendly.

    Rooms may be hard to find in July and August unless you reserve well in advance, and while you will have a chance of finding a room for a day or two during the week, on weekends it's sometimes impossible. If you plan to try to find a last-minute room in those 2 months, arrive on the island early in the day—fly over and beat the ferryboat crowds—and go straight to the town information booth and ask what's available in town.

    Although some lodging establishments on Nantucket stay open all year, many operate only between May and October. Any place will give you an off-season discount on room rates if you come in spring or autumn, although the dates vary from one place to the next. In high season (roughly mid-June to mid-September), you'll certainly have to send a substantial deposit to hold your room reservation. Minimum-stay requirements may be imposed during the high season as well. Some lodging and dining places may not accept credit cards.

EXPENSIVE

ANCHOR INN, 66 Center St., Nantucket, MA 02554. Tel. 508/228-0072. 10 rms (all with bath). **Directions:** From the dock, walk up the street and take a right onto Center St.

    $ Rates (including continental breakfast): Peak season, $94–$148 double. Off-season, rates at least 20% less. MC, V. **Parking:** Free. **Closed:** Jan–Mar.

The Anchor Inn is aptly named, considering that it was built (1806) by Archaelus Hammond, the first man to strike a whale in the Pacific Ocean. The location is good—close enough to the center to be convenient, far enough away to be quiet. Pass through the white picket fence and you'll find a shady garden and a sea captain's house, which has many of its original features, including old floorboards and working fireplaces. The guest rooms are done in Federal style, with some four-poster beds and Turkish carpets. Outside there is a shady garden.

CHESTNUT HOUSE, 3 Chestnut St., Nantucket, MA 02554. Tel. 508/228-0049. 7 rms (all with bath), 1 cottage.

$ Rates: Early June to mid-Oct, $93–$104 double; $153 suite; $202 cottage. Minimum stay 3 nights in summer. Off-season, rates available. AE, MC, V. **Parking:** Free.

Jeannette and Jerry Carl open their home to visitors. There's a common room with television available to all guests, and rooms are furnished in the style of Nantucket's heyday with original details—hooked rugs, stained glass, and handmade quilts. A connecting cottage sleeps four and has a private bath. Chestnut House is next to the Quaker House Inn, between Center and Federal Streets, in the middle of town.

CLIFF LODGE, 9 Cliff Rd., Nantucket, MA 02554. Tel. 508/228-9480. 12 rms (all with bath). TV TEL **Directions:** From ferry, take second right onto North Water St., cross over Easton and North Water becomes Cliff Rd. Cliff Lodge is third house on right.

$ Rates (including continental breakfast): High season, $65 single; $82 double; $190 apartment ($1,275 per week). Spring and fall, $55 single; $71 double; $150 apartment ($975 per week). Winter, $44 single; $55 double; $125 apartment ($650 per week). MC, V. **Parking:** Free.

Built in 1771, the house has been redecorated in English Country style, with lots of Laura Ashley wallpaper and spatter-painted floors. There are marvelous views from the guest rooms, the garden patio, and the widow's walk. Some rooms have king-size beds and fireplaces. Use of the pantry, refrigerator, kitchen utensils, and beach towels is included. Other apartments are available at Cliff Lodge's twin facility, called Still Dock.

FAIR GARDENS, 27 Fair St., Nantucket, MA 02554. Tel. 508/228-4258, or toll free 800/377-6609. 10 rms (all with bath). **Directions:** From Main St., go south on Fair St.

$ Rates (including continental breakfast): Summer, $104–$142 double. Spring and fall, $104–$131 double. Winter, $82–$93 double. Extra person $22. MC, V. **Closed:** Jan–Mar.

Fair Gardens is a lovely 18th-century house located in the historic district of Nantucket town. Behind the house is an English-style garden, complete with a Shakespearean herb plot (with plants mentioned in the Bard's plays), carefully tended flowers and lawns, and a patio for breakfast or an afternoon's cup of tea. Each room has a unique decor, and there are two deluxe rooms in the Garden House. Breakfast includes freshly baked bread or muffins and is served in the garden in good weather. Parking is on the street.

GREAT HARBOR INN, 31 India St., Nantucket, MA 02554. Tel. 508/228-6609, or toll free 800/377-6609. 9 rms (all with bath). TV **Directions:** From ferry dock, take Broad St., turn right onto Center St., then right again onto India St.; it's 3 blocks down.

$ Rates (including continental breakfast): Summer, $115–$186 double. Spring and fall, $93–$164 double. Winter, $82–$93 double. MC, V.

This is an 18th-century sea captain's home now restored and furnished in 19th-century style with handmade patchwork quilts and four-poster or canopy beds. All rooms have 20th-century facilities. The continental breakfast can be served in your room, in the parlor, or on the pretty terrace. The inn, about a 5-minute walk from the town center, is open all year. Parking is on the street.

HARBOR HOUSE, S. Beach St. (P.O. Box 359), Nantucket, MA 02554. Tel. 508/228-1500, for information, 228-5500 for reservations, or toll free 800/ISLANDS. 111 rms (all with bath). TV TEL **Directions:** From ferry wharf, take Broad St., turn right on S. Beach St.

$ Rates: Summer, $170–$230 double; $230–$263 town house. Spring and fall, $104–$159 double; $148–$186 town house. Extra person $27. AE, DC, MC, V. **Parking:** Free, on premises.

Set on a private street amid groves of shade trees, this modern hotel looks just like a small group of old Nantucket houses. The nine buildings of the Harbor House give you a choice of staying in the town house (which has six dwellings holding a total of 57 large and luxurious rooms), in the main hotel, in the neighboring Garden Cottage, or in the Springfield House. All rooms are modern and have every comfort, despite the Federal-inspired decor. The location is good—walking distance from the center of town, and not far from Children's Beach and Brant Point. The hotel's main dining room is named the Hearth, and there's a cocktail lounge as well.

JARED COFFIN HOUSE, 29 Broad St., Nantucket, MA 02554. Tel. 508/228-2405, or toll free 800/248-2405. Fax 508/228-8549. 60 rms (all with bath). TV TEL **Directions:** Walk straight up Broad St. from ferry dock.
$ Rates: Summer, $55–$110 single; $137–$192 double. Spring, $55–$82 single; $110–$165 double. Winter, $44–$66 single; $82–$110 double. AE, DC, DISC, MC, V. **Parking:** Free, on premises.

A wealthy shipowner built this impressive Federal-style brick house, the first three-story mansion to be built on the island, in 1845, just before deciding to move to Boston. He and his family lived in the house for a matter of months, after which it became, and still is, a hotel.

Since its conversion to a hotel in 1846, additions have been built, and neighboring houses bought and converted to lodgings, so that the hotel now has rooms in six different structures. The Jared Coffin House proper and its Eben Allen wing of the building have 25 rooms with single, twin, or double beds. The neighboring Swain House, dating from the 1700s, has three rooms, each with a queen-size canopy bed. Similar beds are in the rooms of the Federal-style Henry Coffin House (1821), and also in the rooms of the Greek Revival Harrison Gray House (1842). The Daniel Webster House (1964) is a recent building in a Federal-inspired style, with canopy-bedrooms and a conference room. No matter which building you choose, you will enjoy the elegant public rooms of the several buildings. Most rooms have televisions.

Jared's has two restaurants worthy of consideration; one of them, the Tap Room, is recommended below (see "Where to Dine on Nantucket").

NANTUCKET LANDFALL, 4 Harbor View Way, Nantucket, MA 02554. Tel. 508/228-0500. 7 rms (all with bath).
$ Rates: (including continental breakfast): Mid-June to Sept, $104–$164 double. Mid-May to mid-June and Oct, $82–$131 double. Nov–Dec and mid-Apr to mid-May, $71–$104 double. No credit cards. **Parking:** Free, on premises. **Closed:** Jan to mid-Apr.

Wander by this inn and you may see a flag of Kenya hanging out front. No, it's not owned by a Kenyan. Every year the owners fly the flag of the country of the winner of the Boston marathon. This is an inn full of conversation pieces. Each room is filled with antiques and centerpieced by beds festooned in beautiful lace and linens. Four rooms have views of the water. It's right near the center of town and on the water. There's a little lawn out front and a porch with white rocking chairs where you can sit and watch boats puttering around the harbor.

SEVEN SEA STREET, 7 Sea St., Nantucket, MA 02554. Tel. 508/228-3577. Fax 508/228-8700. 8 rms (all with bath). **Directions:** Sea St. is only 1 block long, running between N. Water St. and S. Beach St. From ferry landing, go up Broad St., right on N. Water, then left on Sea St. 2 blocks up.
$ Rates: (including continental breakfast): Summer, $137–$181 double; $181–$230 2-room suite. Extra person $16.50. MC, V.

Operated by Matthew and Mary Parker, the publishers of *Nantucket Journal* magazine, this is among Nantucket's best small lodging places. Though built fairly recently, it follows the canon of post-and-beam construction and is furnished in colonial style, so that you will feel Nantucket all around you. The guest rooms have queen-size canopy beds, exposed beams, and lots of colonial touches, but also cable color TV sets and small refrigerators. The theme of modern comforts in colonial atmosphere continues in the public spaces. You can relax in a full-size, heated whirlpool bath, and then sit by the fireplace or go up to the widow's walk to take in the view. The location, just a few blocks from Steamboat Wharf and the center of town, couldn't be better. The good continental breakfast is served in bed if you wish. Parking is available on the street.

THE WAUWINET, Wauwinet Rd. (P.O. Box 2580), Nantucket, MA 02584. Tel. 508/228-0145, or toll free 800/426-8718. Fax 508/228-6712. 35 rms (all with bath). A/C TV TEL.

$ Rates: (including full breakfast and use of sporting facilities): Spring and fall, $241–$493 double. Summer, $274–$680 double. Cottage suites also available. Inquire about special packages. AE, DC, MC, V. **Parking:** Free, on premises. **Closed:** Dec–Apr.

Off in a world of its own on the northeastern corner of the island, The Wauwinet offers the ultimate getaway vacation. Here you'll find all the luxuries of a grand resort (sports, fine dining, elegantly appointed guest rooms and common rooms) in a scenic setting (right on the bay, within view of the ocean). However, the inn is not a huge hotel, and it has a wonderful country club feel to it. Rooms are attractively decorated and full of handmade quilts, antiques, a selection of hard-cover books, his and her robes, and Crabtree & Evelyn toiletries. Some have bay views.

Dining/Entertainment: Topper's Restaurant is one of the island's finest restaurants. There's also a small bar with a bar menu served throughout the afternoon and into the evening.

Services: Concierge, daily bay cruises, jitney service to and from Nantucket town, natural history excursions (4-wheel drive safaris), guided island tours, evening housekeeping service, early risers' coffee service, afternoon cheese, sherry, and port in the library.

Facilities: Two beaches (private bay beach and access to ocean beach), two Har-tru tennis courts, sailboats, rowing sculls, electric motor boats, surf fishing, bicycles, beach chess, fitness center, indoor pool, croquet, library, video cassette library.

THE WHITE ELEPHANT, Easton St. (P.O. Box 359), Nantucket, MA 02554. Tel. 508/228-2500, for reservations, 508/228-5500 or toll free 800/ISLANDS. 80 rms (all with bath). A/C TV TEL

$ Rates: $181–$433 single or double; $213–$652 cottage. Extra person $27. 3-night minimum stay July 9–Labor Day. AE, DC, MC, V. **Closed:** Columbus Day–Memorial Day.

The White Elephant is under the same ownership as the Harbor House (see above), and is equally well run. This elegant old hotel near the center of town has fine views of the harbor, and recent renovations have made it a designer's showcase of white on white, bleached oak floors, and other up-to-date elements. The restaurant and bar have fine harbor views, as do some guest rooms (ask for one when you reserve). Rooms in the main building are simplest, those in the Breakers building the most luxurious; cottages (some with kitchens) with or without harbor views are also available.

Dining/Entertainment: The Regatta dining room serves New American and continental cuisine; the view of boat traffic from the bar is delightful.

Services: Concierge desk.

Facilities: Beautifully kept grounds, harborside pool, tennis courts, one nine-hole putting green.

MODERATE

BRASS LANTERN INN, 11 N. Water St., Nantucket, MA 02554. Tel. 508/228-4064, or toll free 800/377-6609. 18 rms (10 with bath). **Directions:** From ferry, walk up Broad St., turn right onto N. Water St. just after S. Beach St.

$ Rates: (including continental breakfast): Summer, $93–$164 double. Winter, $82–$93 double. MC, V. **Closed:** Jan–Mar.

This attractive old Nantucket house, only a few blocks from downtown, has not only the traditional rooms but also a more modern annex with larger, lighter rooms that still carry 19th-century touches in their decor. You can have breakfast in your room, on the patio, or in a small grassy yard. Afternoon hors d'oeuvres are served as well. Parking is on the street.

FAIR WINDS GUEST HOUSE, 29 Cliff Rd., Nantucket, MA 02554. Tel. 508/228-1998. 9 rms (all with bath). A/C **Directions:** From Main St., follow Center St. to Cliff Rd.
$ Rates: (including continental breakfast): $104–$170 double. MC, V. **Parking:** Free.

Cliff Road has many guesthouses, and Fair Winds is one of the most pleasant and comfortable of all. Built between 1830 and 1860, it stands on high land and commands some good views of the harbor. The guest rooms at the back of the house—the ones with water views—are the more expensive ones. Kathy and George Hughes restored the house nicely and now provide a warm welcome for their guests.

HOUSE OF ORANGE, 25 Orange St., Nantucket, MA 02554. Tel. 508/228-9287. 7 rms (3 with bath). **Directions:** Follow Orange St. south from Main St.
$ Rates: $45 single without bath; $77–$88 double without bath, $105–$121 double with bath. No credit cards. **Parking:** Free.

The inn is decorated with an artist's eye for color and harmony—one of the house's owners is a painter. The rooms are as lovingly furnished and as carefully kept as is the little garden. Some rooms have fireplaces, although, as is often the case, local regulations prohibit guests from using them.

HOUSE OF THE SEVEN GABLES, 32 Cliff Rd., Nantucket, MA 02554. Tel. 508/228-4706. 10 rms (8 with bath). **Directions:** From Main St. follow N. Water St. to Cliff Rd.
$ Rates: (including continental breakfast): Mid-June to mid-Sept, $98–$153 double. Off-season, discounts available. AE, MC, V. **Parking:** Free.

This was once the Victorian annex to an even larger old Victorian seaside hotel. Actually, "Seven Gables and a Tower" would be an even more accurate description. All rooms are bright and sunny; some have views of the water and rates vary according to whether rooms have a shared or private bath. The continental breakfast is served in your room. Mid-September to mid-June rates drop by about a third. The location is a 10-minute walk from Main Street, not as close to town as some other houses; but the area is a quiet residential one.

PERIWINKLE GUEST HOUSE, 7 & 9 N. Water St. (P.O. Box 1436), Nantucket, MA 02554. Tel. 508/228-9267, or toll free 800/992-2899. 18 rms (all with bath). **Directions:** From ferry landing, turn right onto N. Water St. from Broad St.
$ Rates: (including continental breakfast): Summer, $131–$142 double. Off-season, reduced rates available. No credit cards.

A tasteful old Nantucket house run by Sara Schlosser-O'Reilly, the Periwinkle has rooms of various shapes, sizes, sleeping capacities, and bath facilities. The location is excellent, on a charming street only a few short blocks from Main Street. The Periwinkle—which is the name of a spiral-shaped saltwater snail—is open all year, and rates are 25% to 50% lower off-season.

QUAKER HOUSE INN, 5 Chestnut St., Nantucket, MA 02554. Tel. 508/228-0400. 8 rms (all with bath). **Directions:** From Broad St., turn south onto S. Water, then take your first right onto Chestnut.
$ Rates: $87–$142 double. MC, V. **Closed:** Mid-Oct to Apr.

S This inn was built in 1847, and the huge tree out front may date from the same year, or even earlier. Located right in the heart of the Historic District, just a few steps from shops and restaurants, the Quaker House is something of an anomaly in Nantucket. Because Caroline and Bob Taylor and their family do much of the work at the inn, and because they own the building, their costs are kept down, and so are yours. Their restaurant (see "Where to Dine on Nantucket," below) is justly famous for providing excellent dinners in attractive surroundings at moderate prices, and a similar level of quality is found in the inn's guest rooms. Each room is different, but all have queen-size beds: in one a brass bed, in another a carved four-poster. Dressers and wardrobes also echo the era when the inn was built, and tab curtains are a reminder of even earlier colonial days. Rooms are simple, but comfy and attractive, as befits an inn with a Quaker name. Five rooms are air conditioned. Parking is available on the street.

INEXPENSIVE

BARTLETT HOUSE, 14 Gardner St. (P.O. Box 218), Nantucket, MA 02554. Tel. 508/228-1139. 5 rms (3 with bath). TV **Directions:** Follow Main St. to the intersection of Gardner and Milk Sts. Turn right onto Gardner.

$ Rates: High season, $82–$121 single or double. Off-season, $71–$110 single or double. Minimum stay of 3 nights required on weekends. No credit cards.

This establishment prides itself not merely on the attractiveness of the 170-year-old house and the coziness of its rooms, but also on the quietness of its clientele. Bartlett House has no living room for guests' use, but there is a garden. All rooms have refrigerators. Room prices are among the best in town, and the silence, as they say, is golden.

BEACHWAY GUESTS, 3 N. Beach St., Nantucket, MA 02554. Tel. 508/228-1324. 7 rms (5 with bath). **Directions:** From ferry, take your first right onto South Beach. Follow it around to North Beach. Beachway will be on your right.

$ Rates: (including continental breakfast): $71 double without bath, $98 double with bath; $110 cottage room. MC, V. **Parking:** Free.

Having served the traveling public for more than two decades, the Beachway has added some very comfortable rooms in the renovated cottage; these have TV and refrigerator as well as private bath. The shared-bath rooms offer the best bargains however.

HUNGRY WHALE, 8 Derrymore Rd., Nantucket, MA 02554. Tel. 508/228-0793. 2 rms (1 with bath). **Directions:** From Monument Sq. at the west end of Main St., go north on Gardner St., Liberty St., and N. Liberty St. to Derrymore Rd. on the left.

$ Rates: (including breakfast): $65 double without bath, $71 double with bath. No credit cards. **Parking:** Free.

The Hungry Whale is exceptional in several ways. Mrs. Johnson, the smiling and hospitable owner, charges several dollars less than most other houses, and includes a hearty breakfast to boot! The residential location is extremely quiet the 10-minute walk to town a pleasant tour through Nantucket's neighborhoods. There's a sunny deck for sitting and sipping.

IVY LODGE, 2 Chester St., Nantucket, MA 02554. Tel. 508/228-0305. 8 rms (all with bath). **Directions:** From Main St., follow Center St. northwest to Chester St.

$ Rates: (including continental breakfast): $106 double; $126 suite. No credit cards. **Parking:** Free.

Located at North Water Street, this is a homey, tidy 200-year-old house far enough from downtown to have reasonable prices, and close enough to be very handy. Wide pine-board floors, wood paneling, and some old Nantucket decorations set the mood.

NESBITT INN, 21 Broad St., Nantucket, MA 02554. Tel. 508/228-0156. 13 rms (none with bath).

$ Rates: (including continental breakfast): Mid-June to mid-Sept, $42 single without bath; $65.75 double without bath. Off-season, $32 single without bath; $55.75 double without bath. MC, V. **Parking:** Free.

Despite its appellation and downtown location, the Nesbitt Inn is one of the island's lodging bargains and is a nice big mansard-roofed Victorian house (1872) located 3 blocks from the wharf. All rooms have sinks; many rooms have original Victorian furnishings, including brass beds and marble-topped tables. Guests have use of a refrigerator, and of the common rooms with fireplace. The innkeepers, Dolly and Nobby Noblit, are the third generation of a Nantucket innkeeping family that has been welcoming guests here since 1914.

6. WHERE TO DINE ON NANTUCKET

All of Nantucket's dining places are surrounded by waters full of fish, lobsters, crabs, clams, scallops, and squid. But visitors do not live by seafood alone. Island restaurants offer many wonderful meat and fowl dishes as well as the occasional vegetarian platter. The range of cuisines includes French, Italian, New England, and New American, with the occasional Mexican main course. On weekends in July and August, dinner reservations are advisable at the restaurant of your choice; otherwise, you may end up dining somewhere else—just as good perhaps, but not the place you had in mind.

EXPENSIVE

COMPANY OF THE CAULDRON, 7 India St. Tel. 228-4016.
   Cuisine: NEW AMERICAN. **Reservations:** Required.
$ **Prices:** Fixed-price dinner for two including wine, tax, and tip $110–$120. MC. V.
   Open: Dinner daily 7pm and 9pm.
   The Company of the Cauldron, in the center of town, serves only dinner, at one or two sittings (usually 7 and 9pm)—and you must have a reservation. The menu is completely table d'hôte, and fixed price: You have no choice, so ask about the menu when you call for reservations. You might have homemade fettuccine tossed with eggplant, capers, and olives, followed by an apple-and-watercress salad, and then médaillons of veal rolled with spinach and mozzarella, served with a parfait of pimentos. The dining room is small, with kitchen and wine racks in the rear. A harpist plays at dinner. An antique-fancier's collection of old tubs, buckets, and cauldrons serves to show off a cascade of flowers. As you walk to the restaurant, look for the old copper tub (cauldron?) hanging above the entrance; that is the sign.

DE MARCO, 9 India St. Tel. 228-1836.
   Cuisine: NORTHERN ITALIAN. **Reservations:** Recommended. **Directions:** Turn off Center St. between Rose Lane and Hussey St.
$ **Prices:** Dinners $25–$35. AE, MC, V.
   Open: Dinner daily 6–10:30pm.
Near Center Street, the downstairs rooms of this old Nantucket house are furnished as simple but elegant dining rooms offering, among other treats, fresh lobster and tomato with angel hair pasta. All the pasta, baked goods, and desserts are made on the premises daily. Seafood is prominent on the menu, but so are the classics, such as veal médaillons and rack of lamb.

LE LANGUEDOC, 24 Broad St. Tel. 228-2552.
   Cuisine: NEW AMERICAN/CONTINENTAL. **Reservations:** Not required for bistro; required for dining rooms.
$ **Prices:** Appetizers $7.50–$10.50; main courses $18.50–$24; bistro dishes $9–$15.50. AE, MC, V.
   Open: May 15–Sept 15, dinner daily 6–10pm. Sept 15–Dec, lunch daily noon–2pm; dinner daily 6–10pm. **Closed:** Sun in early spring and late fall.

Right in the heart of Nantucket's Old Historic District, Le Languedoc offers two dining styles. Downstairs and on the terrace, bistro fare is served; upstairs fine dining is offered in five small dining rooms charmingly decorated in French Provençale style. Two of the most popular main dishes are the warm lobster salad and roast rack of lamb. A complete dinner with a moderately priced bottle of wine generally runs about $110 to $125 for two.

OBADIAH'S NATIVE SEAFOOD, 2 India St. Tel. 228-4430.
  Cuisine: SEAFOOD. **Reservations:** Recommended.
$ **Prices:** Appetizers $2–$5; main courses $9–$18; dinner $30–$40. AE, MC, V.
  Open: Early June to mid-Oct, lunch daily 11:30am–3pm; dinner daily, 5–10pm.
You can start your meal here with quahog pie (clams, salt pork, potatoes, and onions in a pastry shell) or scallop chowder, then go on to any of 20 main courses, including all the fresh seasonal fish and dishes like baked yellowtail sole stuffed with lobster scallops. You can eat lunch with appetizer, main course, and beverage for under $10. Dining areas include the cozy main room in the cellar of the building and the cool, shady porch and patio behind it. Obadiah's is between Center and Federal Streets.

TOPPER'S AT THE WAUWINET, Wauwinet Rd., Wauwinet. Tel. 228-0145.
  Cuisine: NEW AMERICAN. **Reservations:** Recommended.
  Transportation: Complimentary jitney service from Information Bureau on Federal St. It's a 25-minute trip. For exact times, call the number above.
$ **Prices:** Appetizers $10–$16; main courses $6.50–$13.50 at lunch, $27–$31 at dinner; 3-course Sun brunch $25. AE, DC, MC, V.
  Open: May–Nov, breakfast daily 8–10:30am; brunch daily 10:30am–2pm; lunch daily noon–2pm; dinner daily 6–9pm (last seating). Bar menu daily 2–8:30pm.
Expect perfection at Topper's; this highly acclaimed restaurant will not let you down. Everything seems to conspire to please you—the artwork in the dining rooms (take a look at the portrait of Topper, the owner's dog and restaurant's namesake), the view (at dinner you can watch the sun melt into the water), the service (attentive, but not fawning), and the food (main courses such as spring chive fettuccine with Nantucket lobster and truffle oil are deliriously good).

THE WOODBOX, 29 Fair St. Tel. 208-0587.
  Cuisine: CONTINENTAL/GOURMET. **Reservations:** Recommended.
  Directions: Turn onto Fair St. (at the Pacific National Bank on Main St.). It's 1½ blocks away.
$ **Prices:** Main courses $16.50–$24; breakfast $8–$9.
  Open: Breakfast Tues–Sun 8:30–10:30am; dinner Tues–Sun 6:45pm and 9pm.
  Closed: Nov–May.
This is the kind of restaurant you imagine people propose marriage in. There are three small dining rooms, each with a fireplace and candlelight. The building itself is an utterly romantic old sea captain's house that was built circa 1709. Specialties include roast duck and rack of lamb plus whatever kind of fresh seafood and fish the chef gets that day (clams, swordfish, scallops). Homemade popovers accompany each meal.

MODERATE

MORNING GLORY CAFE, 14 Old South Wharf. Tel. 228-2212.
  Cuisine: ITALIAN/AMERICAN. **Reservations:** Not accepted. **Directions:** Head down near the water end of the wharf.
$ **Prices:** Appetizers $3–$6; main courses $10–$18; lunch $10–$15; dinner $25–$30. MC, V.
  Open: Breakfast daily 7–11:30am; lunch daily noon–3pm; dinner daily 5:30–10pm.
Tables are set out on a brick patio beneath an awning. All three meals are served: omelets, french toast, and pancakes for breakfast; and seafood chowder, sandwiches,

salads, and pizzas for lunch. Dinner is fancier, but prices are still moderate and service is informal—all the utensils and plates, except for the wine glasses, are disposable (the location on the wharf doesn't permit the café to have a dishwasher). Cuisine is an eclectic mix of gourmet pizzas, California grill entrees, and Italian dishes.

TAP ROOM, 29 Broad St. Tel. 228-2400.

Cuisine: AMERICAN. **Reservations:** Not accepted. **Directions:** From ferry wharf, head straight up Broad St. away from water; it's in the Jared Coffin House inn.

$ Prices: Appetizers $2–$9; main courses $12–$17; dinner $30. AE, DC, DISC, MC, V.

Open: Daily 11:30am–9pm.

Informal counterpart to the main dining room at the Jared Coffin House (see "Where to Stay on Nantucket," above), this 19th-century tavern has a wonderful verdant terrace shaded by lofty elms. The food is hearty and traditional, from baked sole Florentine to sirloin steak. Prices are reasonable, and there is entertainment most evenings in summer. You can eat lunch with an appetizer, main course, and beverage for under $15.

INEXPENSIVE

ESPRESSO CAFE, 40 Main St. Tel. 228-6930.

Cuisine: CAFE/BAKERY. **Reservations:** Not accepted.

$ Prices: Menu items $1.95–$8. MC, V.

Open: Sun–Thurs 8am–5pm, Fri–Sat 8am–11pm.

Perhaps the best coffee in town can be found at Espresso Café on Main Street, in the center of town. Try the "Nantucket Blend" or the "Harvard Blend," two local favorites. The café is a pleasant spot for breakfast, lunch, mid-afternoon snack, or a light dinner. In addition to the marble-top tables inside, there's a sun-splashed garden patio out back.

QUAKER HOUSE RESTAURANT, 31 Center St. Tel. 228-9156.

Cuisine: AMERICAN. **Reservations:** Not accepted. **Directions:** From Broad St., turn left onto Center St., and walk to the corner with Chestnut St.

$ Prices: Fixed-price dinner $15–$24. MC, V.

Open: Breakfast daily 8–11:30am; dinner daily 6–9pm.

The simple but charming dining rooms in this inn have fireplaces, lace curtains, crisp tablecloths, antique accent pieces, and candlelight in the evening. At breakfast, try the baked apple pancakes, baked German pancakes, waffles or pancakes made with blueberries or pecans, fresh vegetable omelets, and fresh-squeezed orange juice. At dinnertime, order one of the seven main courses—such as filet of sole, shrimp scampi, Bombay chicken, or beef burgundy—and you get Nantucket clam chowder, Portuguese bread and butter, a tossed garden salad, and a choice of dessert all included in the price. Beer and wine by the glass, carafe, or bottle are available at moderate prices. Note that the Quaker House has room for only 40 diners at a time, so arrive early in order to be assured of finding a table.

WHITE DOG CAFE, 1 N. Union St. Tel. 228-4479.

Cuisine: AMERICAN/SEAFOOD. **Reservations:** Not accepted.

$ Prices: Lunch $8–$12; dinner $15–$25. AE, MC, V.

Open: Lunch daily 11:30am–4pm; dinner daily 5–10pm. **Closed:** Early Oct to mid-May.

Just off Main Street, this café is on the terrace of the Gaslight Theatre. The tiny patio is usually crowded with diners having lunch or dinner, perhaps before attending the show, or perhaps just because of the excellent people-watching possibilities. Burgers, seafood kebabs, and fancier items, such as grilled tuna steaks, are offered.

BUDGET

HENRY'S SANDWICHES, Steamboat Wharf. Tel. 228-0123.
   Cuisine: SANDWICHES. **Reservations:** Not accepted. **Directions:** On Steamboat Wharf at the foot of Broad St.
$ Prices: Sandwiches $3–$4.50. No credit cards.
   Open: Mid-May to mid-Oct, daily 10am–10pm.
Everyone should pick up a mammoth sandwich from Henry's before getting on the boat. Henry's huge sandwiches are made in the best Italian sub/grinder/hoagie/po'boy tradition. Soft drinks are available, and everything can be wrapped to go or consumed post-haste at small tables on the premises. Remember Henry's if you're planning a picnic, or are down to your last $3 plus your ticket home.

7. AN EASY EXCURSION

Almost everyone who gets to Nantucket for a few days has a chance to ride a bike to **'Sconset** on the other side of the island. The village of Siasconset is called nothing but 'Sconset by islanders—the contracted name is hallowed by tradition. The village consists of Post Office Square, a rotary (traffic circle) from which you can see the tennis courts, post office, 'Sconset Café, Claudette's, and various houses. To the right of Claudette's is the road to the beach, only 100 yards away.
   The rest of 'Sconset is residential, with many typical Nantucket houses, but also a few streets of small, low-roofed bungalows that sit squarely as though avoiding the violence of winter storms.
   Though there are several daily buses to 'Sconset, the best way to go is by bicycle along the bike path from Nantucket Town. The journey from the center of Nantucket Town to the center of 'Sconset is 7 miles. If you make the trip in late July or early August, watch for the carpet of low-bush blueberries. Maybe you'll be in luck and find the bushes full of tangy fruit, yours for the picking.
   Once in 'Sconset, have something to eat, go to the beach, take a walk or bike ride around, and in the evening drop in at the Siasconset Casino (on the opposite side of the tennis courts from Post Office Square) for a movie or a show. Just across the street from the casino is the Chanticleer Inn, founded in 1909, and still 'Sconset's prime spot for elegant dining (see below for details).

WHERE TO DINE

At the Siasconset Market, just around the corner from the post office, you can choose the makings of a sandwich or picnic lunch, and the clerk will put it all together for you so that all you have to do is the eating.

CHANTICLEER INN, 9 New St. Tel. 257-6231.
   Cuisine: FRENCH. **Reservations:** Required well in advance.
$ Prices: Appetizers $5–$15 at lunch; main courses $17–$20 at lunch; fixed-price dinner $55. AE, MC, V.
   Open: Late May to mid-Oct, lunch daily noon–2pm; dinner daily 6:30–9:30pm.
   The Chanticleer, owned by chef Jean-Charles Berruet, is noted for its elegant French cuisine and for the charm of its dining area, which at lunchtime in the summer is a courtyard surrounded by rose-covered trellises under which tables are set. At dinnertime, you can sit in one of three lovely indoor rooms. Order à la carte to get whole sea bass grilled with roasted peppers or Nantucket bay scallops in a Madeira sauce. There's a bar and lounge called the Grill Room. This is 'Sconset's—perhaps Nantucket's—most elegant spot, and a meal here becomes a nice memory. Dress is jacket-and-tie formal in the evening.

'SCONSET CAFE, Post Office Sq. Tel. 257-4008.
   Cuisine: ECLECTIC. **Reservations:** Not accepted.

$ Prices: Appetizers $6–$9 at dinner; main courses $4–$11 at lunch; dinner $16–$24. No credit cards.

Open: Daily 8:30am–10pm.

'Sconset's all-purpose eating place is light, pleasant, and has pastel walls hung with local artists' works and a tempting array of edibles, such as breakfast pancakes made with blueberries and cranberries ($4.25) and a soup-and-salad special at lunch ($7.50). The fare at dinnertime is fancier and includes homemade pastas, confit of duck, and fresh grilled seafood.

CHAPTER 8

CENTRAL & WESTERN MASSACHUSETTS

West of Boston spreads a landscape familiar to the early pioneers, a beautiful land of clear lakes and glacial ponds, cool forests and massive granite outcrops. Farming, forestry, and light industry occupy the people of central and western Massachusetts; there are also textile and paper mills dotted along the region's many rivers. Amid this bucolic scenery you'll also find several of America's finest colleges, posh 19th-century mountain resorts, and New England's premier summer music festival.

Wealthy vacationers of the 19th century who loved the sea would get away to Newport, Cape Cod, or Bar Harbor; those who loved the mountains would head for Saratoga Springs, N.Y., or for the storybook New England towns scattered through the low mountains known as the Berkshires in western Massachusetts. The grand residences and hotels of the wealthy remain in Stockbridge, Lenox, Williamstown, and other Berkshire communities, adding to the romance and interest of the area.

Today the lure of the Berkshires is enhanced by the Berkshire Music Festival at Tanglewood, near Lenox; Williamstown, in the northern Berkshires, the home of Williams College since 1785, continues to draw crowds attracted to its beauty and educational opportunities. Whatever your reason for going, you can't fail to enjoy the lush countryside, the picturesque towns with rows of fine houses, and the acres of manicured greenery.

SEEING CENTRAL & WESTERN MASSACHUSETTS

Thanks to the major east-west highways Mass. Route 2 and the Massachusetts Turnpike (I-90), traveling to central and eastern Massachusetts is easy. Worcester is about an hour's drive west of Boston, Sturbridge just over an hour, and Springfield less than 2 hours. In 3 hours you can be amid the cool Berkshire hills.

Coming from New York City, the Taconic State Parkway is the chosen route because of its beauty and directness.

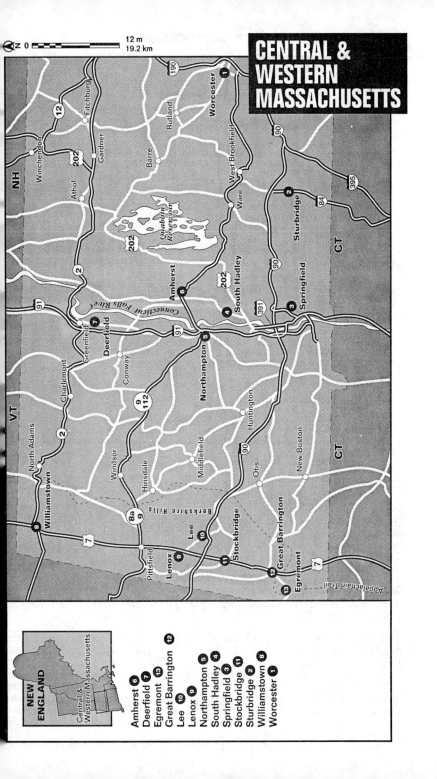

CENTRAL & WESTERN MASSACHUSETTS

N 0 ▭▭▭▭ 12 m
19.2 km

NH

90

395

12

190

Winchendon

Fitchburg

Gardner

202

Athol

2

Rutland

Barre

West Brookfield

Worcester ❶

Ware

Sturbridge ❷

84

2

CT

Quabbin Reservoir

202

202

South Hadley

90

Springfield ❸

Amherst ❻

2

391

❹

97

Connecticut Falls River

Deerfield ❼

91

Northampton ❺

VT

Charlemont

Conway

9 112

North Adams

2

Windsor

Hinsdale

Middlefield

Huntington

90

Otis

New Boston

CT

Williamstown ❽

7

8

Pittsfield

Lenox ❾

8a 9

Berkshire Hills

Lee ❿

Stockbridge ⓫

Great Barrington

7

⓬ Egremont

⓭

Appalachain Trail

☑ WHAT'S SPECIAL ABOUT CENTRAL & WESTERN MASSACHUSETTS

Museums

☐ Old Sturbridge Village, an authentic re-creation of a New England town in the early 1800s.

☐ Worcester Art Museum, home of Hicks's famous *Peaceable Kingdom* and Mary Cassatt's *Woman Bathing*.

☐ Springfield's Museum of Fine Arts, with its fine collection of impressionists, and the Smith Art Museum, with art objects from around the world.

☐ The Norman Rockwell Museum in Stockbridge, with an outstanding collection of works by this beloved illustrator/painter.

☐ Chesterwood, the Stockbridge estate of sculptor Daniel Chester French, who made the statue of Lincoln in the Lincoln Memorial.

☐ Clark Art Institute in Williamstown, with 18 significant collections of European and American artists, including Fragonard, Gainsborough, the impressionists, Cassatt, Homer, and Sargent.

Parks & Gardens

☐ Mount Greylock, highest mountain in Massachusetts, topped by a war memorial originally designed as a lighthouse.

Events/Festivals

☐ Tanglewood Music Festival in Lenox, with symphony and chamber music, solo recitals, and even jazz, from July through August.

☐ The "Big E," or Eastern States Exposition, in Springfield in mid-September, New England's largest state fair.

☐ Jacob's Pillow Dance Festival in Lee, from late June through August.

Cool for Kids

☐ Higgins Armory Museum in Worcester, with more than 100 suits of medieval armor, even for children and dogs.

☐ Basketball Hall of Fame in Springfield, with lots of video displays and hands-on exhibits.

GETTING THERE By Train Amtrak's *Lakeshore Limited* runs daily between New York/Boston and Chicago, one section leaving Boston (South Station) in mid-afternoon and another leaving New York City (Penn Station) in early evening. The two sections link up in Albany-Rensselaer and continue on to Chicago. The section from Boston passes through Worcester and Springfield, and then Pittsfield, Mass., in the evening. The *Adirondack,* traveling between Montréal and New York City (Grand Central Terminal), passes through Albany-Rensselaer as well. From that point, you'll have to get to your destination by bus.

In addition, Amtrak's Inland Route trains traveling between Boston and New York pass through Wellesley, Framingham, Worcester, and Springfield, Mass., as well as Hartford and New Haven, Conn. There are at least two trains daily on this route. Call Amtrak toll free at 800/USA-RAIL.

By Bus Greyhound (tel. 617/423-5810) provides direct service between Boston and Albany via Worcester, Sturbridge, Springfield, Lee, Lenox, and Pittsfield, Mass., with several buses a day. In addition, there is direct Toronto–New York service with a stop in Albany, where transfer can be made to a Lenox-bound bus.

Vermont Transit (tel. 617/423-5810 in Boston) operates buses between Montréal and New York City, stopping in Albany at the Greyhound terminal, where transfer can be made for the trip to Lenox. There are also direct buses between Montréal and Pittsfield, Mass., passing through Williamstown; in Pittsfield the transfer can be made for Lenox.

Englander Coach Lines (tel. 617/423-5810), operating from the Greyhound terminal in Boston, has several buses a day between Boston and Albany, stopping in Pittsfield; connecting services are also run between Boston and Providence.

Bonanza Bus Lines (tel. 212/564-8484 in New York City, 617/423-5810 in Boston, or toll free 800/556-3815) has direct Providence-Albany service, with stops in Pittsfield, Lenox, and Lee, and also direct buses between New York City and Great Barrington, Stockbridge, Lee, Lenox, and Pittsfield. There is direct service from Boston's Greyhound terminal to Springfield, Pittsfield, Greenfield, North Adams, and Williamstown.

Peter Pan Bus Lines (tel. 617/426-7838 in Boston or 413/781-3320 in Springfield), which operates from its terminal near Boston's South Station, provides service from Boston to Amherst, Northampton, Holyoke, South Hadley, Worcester, and Springfield, Mass., and thence to Pittsfield, Lee, and Lenox.

By taking a Greyhound bus from Hartford or New York City to Springfield, you can connect with the Bonanza or Peter Pan buses to reach just about anywhere in western Massachusetts.

Local buses connect Berkshire County towns and resorts with one another.

By Car   From New York City, the Taconic State Parkway provides a very pleasant route to the Berkshires; from other points I-90 (the Massachusetts Turnpike) and I-91 are the fastest routes to the area.

---

1. WORCESTER

43 miles (69km) W of Boston, 51 miles (82km) E of Springfield

GETTING THERE   See the beginning of this chapter.

ESSENTIALS   The **area code** is 508. **Worcester County Convention and Visitors Bureau,** 33 Waldo St., Worcester, MA 01608 (tel. 508/753-2920), can answer your questions.

Massachusetts's second-largest city has much to recommend it, and only one serious drawback (which is not its own fault): Worcester is only an hour's drive west of Boston. What this means is that people consider Boston the Massachusetts metropolis, and they simply forget about the neighboring city so close at hand.

Worcester's claims to fame are considerable: It is the home of the American Antiquarian Society (founded in 1812), the famed Worcester Art Museum, and the Higgins Armory Museum. If you're searching for documents dating from America's early years, Edward Hicks's famous painting *The Peaceable Kingdom,* or rare suits of medieval armor, you've come to the right place.

WHAT TO SEE & DO

Worcester is very pleasant; there are spacious parks and gardens, several academic institutions of note (Clark University, College of the Holy Cross, and Worcester Polytechnic Institute), and many attractive buildings—the evidence of Worcester's active manufacturing days during the mid-1800s. The city was the birthplace of ingenious machines that were the first to weave carpets, fold envelopes, and turn irregular shapes on a lathe. You can still see many of the old mill buildings in town. Some have been converted to office or retail centers, others lie abandoned, and many are still turning out products: men's and boys' clothing, raincoats, sportswear, winter coats, shoes, and dozens of other items. Worcester kept its spirit of Yankee ingenuity right into the 20th century. Dr. Robert Goddard, the father of modern rocketry, was a Worcester native.

Most of Worcester's products can be bought at a discount in the **factory outlets** sprinkled across the city—you'll see them. **Spag's,** at 193 Boston Turnpike (Route 9) in neighboring Shrewsbury, could be considered the L. L. Bean of discount houses. Vast quantities of discount merchandise are trucked in and sold out each day to a horde of loyal customers.

A SUGGESTED ITINERARY Get to Worcester, take a turn through the center of town, stopping at the fine Town Common and impressive City Hall, and perhaps at the modern shopping, dining, and entertainment complex called the Galleria; then admire the massive auditorium named Mechanics Hall, 321 Main St., as you make your way to the Worcester Art Museum. Spend the morning at the museum and nearby sights, perhaps have a bite of lunch in the museum's nice café (see below), go on to the Higgins Armory, then head for Sturbridge (18 miles) to spend the night. Don't plan this tour for a Monday, when all of Worcester's museums are closed.

WORCESTER ART MUSEUM, 55 Salisbury St. Tel. 799-4406.

Worcester's famous art museum, off Park Avenue and Main Street, will surprise you. It's one of those smaller museums with an amazingly comprehensive collection, studded with masterpieces. Besides Hicks's *Peaceable Kingdom,* you'll see Paul Gauguin's famous *Brooding Woman,* Rembrandt's *St. Bartholomew,* and Mary Cassatt's *Woman Bathing.* The collection ranges from ancient Chinese, Egyptian, and Sumerian objects through Roman statuary and mosaics, Pre-Columbian artifacts, Japanese *ukiyo-e* prints and European paintings by the great masters, to American primitives and works by the great American painters.

The museum has a pleasant café serving an interesting menu of soups, salads, and sandwiches (including its own oven-roasted beef). There are daily specials and a children's menu, as well as lots of desserts. Wine and beer are served. Lunch can cost as little as $4 or as much as $12 per person. The café is open Tuesday through Saturday from 11:30am to 2pm for luncheon, to 3pm for desserts and beverages, on Thursday for dinner from 5 to 8pm, and on Sunday for brunch from 1pm to 4pm.

Admission: $4 adults, $2.50 students and seniors, free for youths under 18. All admitted free Sat 10am–noon.

Open: Tues, Wed, and Fri 11am–4pm; Thurs 11am–8pm; Sat 10am–5pm; Sun 1–5pm. **Closed:** Jan 1, Easter, July 4, Thanksgiving Day, Dec 25.

WORCESTER HISTORICAL MUSEUM, 30 Elm St. Tel. 753-8278.

Chartered in 1877, the Worcester Historical Museum serves to record and interpret the city's industrial and societal achievement and community progress for those who visit Worcester every year. There are several permanent and changing exhibitions as well as special events, educational programs, and library services. The museum recently restored the Salisbury Mansion (located at 40 Highland St.) to its 1830s appearance as a part of this interpretive process. It is Worcester's first historic house museum.

Admission: $2 suggested donation.

Open: Tues–Sat 10am–4pm, Sun 1–4pm.

AMERICAN ANTIQUARIAN SOCIETY, 185 Salisbury St. Tel. 755-5221.

This research library has American printed materials dating from 1640 to 1877. The library preserves the largest single collection of printed source materials relating to the history, literature, and culture of the first 250 years of our country. Tours are given on Wednesday at 2pm.

Admission: Free.

Open: Mon–Fri 9am–5pm.

HIGGINS ARMORY MUSEUM, 100 Barber Ave. Tel. 853-6015.

That Worcester should have one of the world's great collections of medieval armor is not as odd as it may seem. The ingenious Yankees who lived here in the 1800s were fascinated by machinery, and thus deeply involved with metallurgy. John Woodman Higgins wanted to know how medieval armorers made such excellent steel, so he collected their work. Now more than 100 magnificent suits, true works of art, are arranged in the museum. You'll even see armor made for kids, and for dogs. Among the museum's most popular exhibits is the Quest Gallery, with hands-on exhibits, including replica armor and "castle clothing" you can try on for size.

Admission: $4.25 adults, $3.50 senior citizens, $3.25 children aged 6–16.
Open: Tues–Sat 10am–4pm, Sun noon–4pm; also Mon in July–Aug 10am–4pm.
Closed: Holidays.

---

2. STURBRIDGE

18 miles (29km) SW of Worcester, 32 miles (51.5km) E of Springfield

GETTING THERE   By Car   Take Exit 9 from the Massachusetts Turnpike, and Exit 2 from I-84, to U.S. Route 20 West.

ESSENTIALS   The **area code** is 508. For more information, contact the **Tri-Community Area Chamber of Commerce**, 380 Main St., Sturbridge (tel. 508/347-2761), open Monday to Friday 9am to 5pm.

The creators of Old Sturbridge Village couldn't have chosen a better spot for their "living museum." It's set in the beautiful hills of east-central Massachusetts right where the Massachusetts Turnpike (I-90) intersects with I-84, a major route to Hartford and New York City. Anyone who passes should certainly stop to see Old Sturbridge Village, and perhaps to spend the night.

WHAT TO SEE & DO

Besides the obvious headline attraction in Sturbridge, you might want to have a picnic in **Wells State Park,** a few miles north of Sturbridge (take U.S. 20 east, then Route 49 north and follow the signs). Swimming and camping are available here as well.

Don't miss the chance to pore over junk and treasures at the **Brimfield Antiques Fair,** in nearby Brimfield (7 miles west along U.S. Route 20). Up to 2,000 antique dealers fill several fields near town in mid-May, with similar fairs in early or mid-July and mid-September. If Brimfield is not in session, you can still do some browsing in the many shops on U.S. 20 between Brimfield and Sturbridge.

OLD STURBRIDGE VILLAGE, Rte. 20. Tel. 347-3362.

Old Sturbridge Village, off U.S. Route 20, is one of the first of America's outdoor museums. It's a re-creation of an early 1800s New England town actually formed with the artifacts: Buildings and tools, machines and methods of work were all collected and brought together in this beautiful part of the Massachusetts hinterland so that Americans could see whence their ancestors had come. Like Plimoth Plantation and Mystic Seaport, Old Sturbridge Village is peopled with authentically dressed "interpreters," folks who perform the tasks of the village's daily life, and explain to visitors how things are done. Plan at least a few hours, or perhaps a full day, to get into village life.

The admission fee entitles you to a map/guide to exhibits in the village, and readmission the following day at no extra charge. Within the village are several varied places to eat: a bake shop, the Pantry (serving soft drinks), a cafeteria, and the Tavern, which serves full meals, cocktails, and—from late May to late October—a luncheon buffet.

Admission: $15 adults, $7 youths aged 6–15, free for children under 6.
Open: May–Oct, daily 9am–5pm. Nov–Apr, Tues–Sun 10am–4pm.

ST. ANNE SHRINE, 16 Church St., Fiskdale, MA 01518. Tel. 347-7338.
Those interested in Russian icons will want to stop at the St. Anne Shrine. The

icons were collected by Msgr. Pie Neveu, an Assumptionist bishop who served in Russia from 1906 to 1936, and by other Assumptionist fathers who served as chaplains at the U.S. Embassy between 1934 and 1941. The collection of 60 treasured icons is rare.

Admission: Free, but donations accepted.

Open: Daily 9am–6pm. **Directions:** Go 1 mile west from Old Sturbridge Village along U.S. 20; drive through Fiskdale and watch for a sign on the right. Just before the junction with Rte. 148, turn right on Church St. up the steep hill.

WHERE TO STAY

Motels abound in Sturbridge and nearby. Trade is brisk in summer, autumn, and during the three annual Brimfield Flea Market weekends (in May, July, and September), when nearby Brimfield, a normally sleepy place 8 miles west of Sturbridge on U.S. 20, springs to life. As Brimfield has few hotels and motels itself, those in Sturbridge—and even in Springfield, 35 miles away—are packed with people, so if you come at flea-market time, have ironclad reservations. During the slow months of January through March, several Sturbridge inns and motels band together to offer attractive discount "Winter Weekend" package plans. For details, contact the Publick House (described below).

In summer, some visitors and music lovers actually stay as far east as Sturbridge, where rooms are plentiful. With Sturbridge as a base, a tour through the Berkshires, including a stop at Tanglewood, can be a day's outing.

You should note that the village of Sturbridge, a bona-fide Massachusetts colonial-era town, and Old Sturbridge Village, a "living museum," are actually two different places in the same general area. They're only about a mile apart, but the village of Sturbridge's Town Common, or center, is on Route 131, while the entrance to Old Sturbridge Village is on Route 20.

INNS & GUESTHOUSES

PUBLICK HOUSE ON THE COMMON, On the Common (P.O. Box 187), Sturbridge, MA 01566-0187. Tel. 508/347-3313. 118 rms, 12 suites
   Directions: Follow Rte. 131 to Sturbridge's town common.
   $ Rates (including continental breakfast): $69–$145 single or double, depending on season; $99–$150 suite. AE, CB, DC, MC, V. **Parking:** Free.
The Publick House is a local institution. Founded in 1771 by Col. Ebenezer Crafts, it occupies the original building plus several large but tasteful additions, mostly furnished for dining. In the adjoining Chamberlain House and motor lodge are suites with queen-size beds, color TV, and living-room area; each suite accommodates up to four people. At the summit of Fiske Hill, a mile from the Publick House, is the Colonel Ebenezer Crafts Inn. The fine old house was built by David Fiske in 1786, and later converted to an inn by the management of the Publick House. It's gracious, filled with antiques, and small, taking only about 20 people at one time.

There are three restaurants—the Public House (see "Where to Dine," below), Ebenezer's, and Crabapples. There are two bars. Facilities include an outdoor swimming pool, tennis court, shuffleboard courts, a children's playground, and running/walking trails.

MOTELS

DAYS INN AT STURBRIDGE, U.S. 20 (P.O. Box 206), Sturbridge, MA 01566. Tel. 508/347-9000. 79 rms (all with bath). A/C TV TEL
   $ Rates (including continental breakfast): Summer, $62 single; $67 double. Oct–Apr, rates slightly higher. AE, DC, DISC, MC, V. **Parking:** Free.
Right near the intersection of Routes 15, 20, and 131 is the modern and attractive Days Inn, a brick-and-wood motel with a swimming pool. It's comfortable and conveniently located.

OLD STURBRIDGE VILLAGE MOTOR LODGE, Rte. 20 West, Sturbridge, MA 01566. Tel. 508/347-3327. 60 rms. A/C TV TEL
$ Rates: $65 Village double; $90 Wight House and Dennison Cottage suite. Extra person $5. Children 12 and under stay free in parents' room. AE, MC, V. **Parking:** Free.

This motel is owned by Old Sturbridge Village, which is right next door. It has guest rooms clustered in a variety of buildings designed along colonial lines and positioned as though in an Early American village. The rooms in the Oliver Wight House (1789), a Revolutionary-era 10-room inn right next door, have a bit more character.

STURBRIDGE COACH MOTOR LODGE, 408 Main St., Sturbridge, MA 01566. Tel. 508/347-7327. 54 rms. A/C TV TEL
$ Rates: $38–$49 single; $40–$76 double. Extra person $5. AE, MC, V. **Parking:** Free.

Although it's obviously a modern two-floor luxury hotel, the Sturbridge Coach, on U.S. 20 almost opposite Old Sturbridge Village, is colonial in both its design and decor. There's nothing colonial about the swimming pool, though, or the rooms, each quite modern and equipped with a dressing room area separate from the bathroom. There's a seasonal outdoor pool.

STURBRIDGE HOST HOTEL, U.S. 20, Sturbridge, MA 01566. Tel. 508/ 347-7393. 241 rms. A/C TV TEL
$ Rates: $98–$148 single; $109–$148 double. AE, CB, DC, DISC, MC, V. Weekend packages available. **Parking:** Free.

Prime among Sturbridge's modern hostelries and right across from Old Sturbridge Village is the Host Hotel (formerly a Sheraton Inn). This lavish spread on the shores of Cedar Lake has its own tennis and racquetball courts, health clubs, indoor swimming pool, and miniature golf course. Decor in the plush guest rooms is, of course, colonial. A special group of VIP rooms, has its own private lounge and concierge services.

WHERE TO DINE

OXHEAD TAVERN, 366 Main St. Tel. 347-9994.
 Cuisine: AMERICAN. **Reservations:** Not accepted.
$ Prices: Appetizers $5–$9.75; main courses $7–$15.25. AE, DC, DISC, MC, V.
 Open: Mon–Sat 11am–11pm, Sun noon–11pm.

The fare here is designed with transients in mind. It's not an elegant restaurant, and doesn't try to be, but it succeeds beautifully in being a roadside tavern. Furnished in rustic colonial, it has an old-fashioned pub bar at one end, and a big stone fireplace at the other. The menu is well suited to what a roadhouse must provide: various meals at any time of day or evening. The fare includes New York sirloin for $14 and various meat and fish dishes for $9 to $12; lots of sandwiches are cheaper ($5 to $7) and equally filling. The Oxhead is off U.S. 20 near the Sturbridge Host Hotel.

PUBLICK HOUSE, On the Common, Rte. 131. Tel. 347-3313.
 Cuisine: AMERICAN. **Reservations:** Recommended. **Directions:** Follow Rte. 131 to Sturbridge's town common.
$ Prices: Appetizers $3.25–$7.25; main courses $12.50–$26.50. AE, CB, DC, DISC, MC, V.
 Open: Mon–Sat 7am–10:30pm, Sun 8am–10pm.

This is a Sturbridge favorite, located right on the Town Common on Route 131. It's big: The several dining rooms can handle a large number of diners at once, yet the feeling of an old New England inn has not been lost. The lunch menu lists a few sandwiches, but concentrates on hot main courses and cold meat or salad plates. Prices of main courses like omelets, chicken, and broiled fish include vegetable, potato, assorted relishes, and a bakery basket filled with freshly baked bread and rolls. Dinner is fancier, and more expensive, but you get almost a full meal, with all the extras that are given with a comparable luncheon plate plus salad. The Publick House's wine list is fairly short, diverse, and moderate-to-expensively priced.

ROM'S, Rte. 131. Tel. 347-3349.
   Cuisine: AMERICAN/ITALIAN. **Reservations:** Recommended.
   Directions: Follow Rte. 131 southeast from U.S. Rte. 20 and Sturbridge to the restaurant, across from a shopping center.
$ Prices: Appetizers $4–$8; main courses $4–$14.50; dinner $10–$15. AE, V.
   Open: Sun–Fri 11am–9pm, Sat 11am–10pm.

This Italian-American restaurant is an all-American success story. Started as a roadside sandwich-and-seafood stand, Rom's now seats up to 700 people in attractive, air-conditioned surroundings. What packs 'em in is Rom's unbeatable formula: good, plentiful food in pleasant dining rooms at low prices. A lunch of soup, broiled halibut steak, potato, vegetable, and coleslaw costs less than $10. The menu features Italian dishes, steaks, seafood, and traditional meals. The original dairy bar/lunchstand is still here, by the way. Food to go, including Italian dishes, is even lower in price.

---

3. SPRINGFIELD

89 miles (143.5km) W of Boston, 32 miles (51.5km) W of Sturbridge,
21 miles (34km) S of Northampton, 23 miles (37km) N of Hartford,
45 miles (72.5km) E of Lee

GETTING THERE   By Train   Amtrak's *Lakeshore Limited* runs daily between Boston and Chicago. It leaves Boston (South Station) in mid-afternoon and passes through Springfield.
   In addition, Amtrak's Inland Route trains traveling between Boston and New York City pass through Springfield. There are at least two trains daily on this route. Call Amtrak toll free at 800/USA-RAIL.

By Bus   Greyhound (tel. 617/423-5810 in Boston) provides direct service between Boston and Albany, N.Y., via Worcester, Sturbridge, Springfield, Lee, Lenox, and Pittsfield, with several buses a day.
   Bonanza Bus Lines (tel. 212/564-8484 in New York City, 617/423-5810 in Boston, or toll free 800/556-3815) has direct Providence–Albany buses, which stop in Springfield, Pittsfield, Lenox, and Lee. There is direct service from Boston's Greyhound terminal to Springfield, Pittsfield, Greenfield, North Adams, and Williamstown.
   Peter Pan Bus Lines (tel. 617/426-7838 in Boston or 413/781-3320 in Springfield), which operates from its terminal near Boston's South Station, provides service from Boston to Amherst, Northampton, Holyoke, South Hadley, Worcester, and Springfield, and thence to Pittsfield, Lee, and Lenox.
   By taking a Greyhound bus from Hartford or New York City to Springfield, you can connect with the Bonanza or Peter Pan buses to reach just about anywhere in western Massachusetts.

By Car   Located near the junction of the major east-west artery, the Massachusetts Turnpike (I-90), and the major north-south artery, I-91, Springfield is easily accessible.

ESSENTIALS   The **area code** is 413. The **Greater Springfield Convention and Visitors Bureau,** 34 Boland Way, Springfield, MA 01103 (tel. 413/787-1548, or toll free 800/723-1548), can provide visitor services.

SPECIAL EVENTS   Starting on the second or third Wednesday in September, for about 12 days, West Springfield hosts New England's great state fair, **The Big E,** located on the grounds of the Eastern States Exposition (tel. 737-2443). There's an admission fee to the grounds, but lots to do once you're inside. Call for exact dates and ticket information. The fairgrounds are on Route 147, near the Westfield River.

Springfield is Massachusetts's third-largest city, with a solid place in American history and life. The Springfield Armory produced weapons for American troops in the War of 1812, and Union soldiers in the Civil War used the famous Springfield rifle. The armory was a virtual cornucopia of small arms, many examples of which you can still see in its museum.

Yankee ingenuity and technical prowess were lavished on weapons, yes, but on other things as well. The monkey wrench was invented in Springfield, as were steel-bladed ice skates and the first American planetarium.

Elegant as these things may be, they were not Springfield's finest products. This honor is reserved for Duryea and Rolls-Royce automobiles. The Duryea brothers, Charles and Frank, built the first practical internal-combustion engine automobile (1894) on the top floor of the building at 41 Taylor St. And for a short time in the 1930s the world's most elegant auto, the Rolls-Royce, was assembled here in Springfield.

Among all its inventions, only one has brought real world fame to Springfield: basketball. Yes, this is the place where, in 1891, Dr. James Naismith, a physical education instructor at Springfield's YMCA college, originated the game. The city has a suitable memorial, the Naismith Memorial Basketball Hall of Fame, a place that's fascinating and fun even if you're not sports-minded.

WHAT TO SEE & DO

Located at the junction of I-90 (Mass. Turnpike) and I-91, Springfield is a city most people know only through the car window. Even if you're headed for somewhere else, spend a few hours here. Exit from I-91 at State Street, go to Main Street and you'll find Court Square, Springfield's heart, surrounded by fine buildings, including Symphony Hall, the First Congregational Church (1819), and the granite Hampden County Superior Courthouse, modeled somewhat on Venice's Palazzo Vecchio by H. H. Richardson. The statue in the square is of William Pynchon, who led the group of Puritans who settled here in 1636, and incorporated the town 5 years later.

Just northeast of Court Square is the Springfield Library (tel. 739-3871), at **museum Quadrangle,** corner of State and Chestnut Streets, open from noon to 5pm (closed Monday).

At the entrance to the quadrangle, in Merrick Park, is Augustus St. Gaudens's statue called *The Puritan.*

GEORGE WALTER VINCENT SMITH ART MUSEUM, Museum Quadrangle. Tel. 733-4214.

The oldest building on the Quadrangle, the George Walter Vincent Smith Art Museum, built in 1895 in the style of an Italian villa, houses the vast collections of its Victorian namesake and his wife, Belle Townsley Smith. Avid collectors, the couple acquired an exotic array of Japanese arms and armor, screens, lacquers, textiles, and ceramics; exquisite Islamic rugs; and the largest collection of Chinese cloisonné in the western world. A focal point of the collection is an elaborately carved Shinto shrine. An outstanding selection of 19th-century American paintings includes Frederic Church's early masterpiece, *New England Scenery,* and the largest number of paintings by J. G. Brown in a public museum.

Admission (to all four museums): $3 adults, $1 children 6–18, free for children under 6.

Open: Thurs–Sun noon–4pm.

MUSEUM OF FINE ARTS, Museum Quadrangle. Tel. 732-6092.

This museum has more than 20 galleries. Its collection is built on lesser masters, or lesser paintings of the great masters, but is a fine representation nonetheless. Pride of place—right above the main stairway—goes to Erastus Salisbury Field's *The Rise of the American Republic,* which can keep you busy for the better part of an hour. You'll see why. The impressionist and expressionist gallery includes a painting from Monet's *Haystacks* series, and works by Degas, Dufy, Gauguin, Pissarro, Renoir,

Rouault, and Vlaminck. In the contemporary gallery you'll find works by George Bellows, Lyonel Feininger, Georgia O'Keeffe, and Picasso, among others. Modern sculptors featured include Leonard Baskin and Richard Stankiewicz.

Admission (to all four museums): $3 adults, $1 children 6–18, free for children under 6.

Open: Thurs–Sun noon–4pm.

SPRINGFIELD SCIENCE MUSEUM, Museum Quadrangle. Tel. 733-1194.

At the Springfield Science Museum visitors step into a world filled with the wonders of natural and physical science. Dominated by a huge African elephant, the multilevel R. E. Phelon African Hall reveals the diversity of the continent's wildlife and peoples. In Dinosaur Hall, a full-sized replica of a Tyrannosaurus towers over visitors. In the Exploration Center, children and families are encouraged to participate in the hands-on exhibits. Habitat groupings of mounted animals, a 100-seat planetarium, an aquarium, rock and mineral displays, a 1937 Springfield-built Gee Bee airplane, Native American Indian artifacts, and interactive life science exhibits fascinate children and adults alike.

Admission (to all four museums): $3 adults, $1 children 6–18, free for children under 6.

Open: Thurs–Sun noon–4pm.

CONNECTICUT VALLEY HISTORICAL MUSEUM, Museum Quadrangle. Tel. 732-3080.

The history and traditions of the Connecticut River Valley are preserved at the Connecticut Valley Historical Museum. Built in 1927, the stone Colonial Revival building houses artifacts and documents that tell the story of the region from 1636 to the present. Three period rooms—a kitchen from a late 17th-century home, and a guest bedroom and public entertainment room from the late 18th century Chapin Tavern—re-create life in the Valley. Hand-crafted furniture, pewter, silver, and portraits by itinerant artists capture more than 300 years of Valley history. The museum also has a Genealogy and Local History Library, which holds, among many other things, the Ellis Island passenger records.

Admission (to all four museums): $3 adults, $1 children 6–18, free for children under 6.

Open: Thurs–Sun noon–4pm.

SPRINGFIELD ARMORY NATIONAL HISTORIC SITE, 1 Armory Sq. (Federal St. at State St.). Tel. 734-8551.

The Springfield Armory, just 10 minutes from Museum Quadrangle, was where, from 1795 to 1968, a good proportion of our national defense budget was spent. Springfield Technical Community College now occupies the gun factories and officers' quarters, except for the Small Arms Museum, which is what you've come to see. There's an awful lot of firepower here; not just the Springfields and Garands that were made in the armory, but even some weapons dating from the 1600s, and lots of Remingtons, Colts, and Lugers. It's thought to be the world's largest such collection of weaponry, and it is mighty impressive. Don't miss the Organ of Rifles.

Admission: Free.

Open: Daily 9am–5pm. **Closed:** Thanksgiving, Christmas, New Year's Day.

NAISMITH MEMORIAL BASKETBALL HALL OF FAME, W. Columbus Ave. at Union St. Tel. 781-6500.

The Hall of Fame is no stuffy museum, but a very active place; this is where you'll have some fun. The light, spacious structure is decorated with elements relating to the sport: One whole wall is made of those tiny strips of hardwood used on courts. Video displays abound, telling the history of the sport and recalling its most exciting games and players. In a stand-up cinema, you're surrounded by giant movie screens synchronized to make it seem as though you are right in the middle of the frenzied action on the court. In another exhibit, you step onto a conveyor belt from which you can shoot balls at baskets which vary in height and distance from you. At the end of the belt, try your skill at jumping to touch one of the tapes hanging from the ceiling, suspended at heights from 7 to 11 feet. You can see and do a lot here in less than an hour, but you could also spend an entire morning.

Admission: $6 adults, $3 children aged 7–15.

Open: July–Aug, daily 9am–6pm. Sept–June, daily 9am–5pm. **Directions:** Go west on Union St. (south of State St.); just after you pass under I-91, you'll see the Hall of Fame.

WHERE TO STAY

SUSSE CHALET INN, 1515 Northampton St., Holyoke, MA 01040. Tel. 413/536-1980, or toll free 800/258-1980, 800/572-1880 in New Hampshire. 52 rms (all with bath). A/C TV TEL **Directions:** Take I-91 to Exit 17 or 17A; the motel is 7 miles from downtown Springfield.

$ Rates: $39.70–$49.03 single; $48.84–$54.52 double. MC, V. **Parking:** Free.

Look for the Susse Chalet on the right-hand side, behind a Howard Johnson's restaurant, as you head south from Northampton on U.S. 5. Susse Chalet Inn rooms are comfortably furnished with all the usual services, yet they cost a lot less than "standard" motel rooms. Here you get an outdoor swimming pool, no-smoking rooms, and free HBO and ESPN channels on the TV. Several restaurants are nearby.

SUSSE CHALET MOTOR LODGE, Burnett Rd., Chicopee, MA 01020. Tel. 413/592-5141, or toll free 800/258-1980, 800/572-1880 in New Hampshire. 88 rms (all with bath). A/C TV TEL **Directions:** From I-90 (Mass. Tpk.) take Exit 6 (Rte. 291).

$ Rates: $42 single; $48.84 double. MC, V. **Parking:** Free.

Among the best bargain lodgings in the area is this modern motel. The conveniences include ice machine, coin-op laundry, outdoor swimming pool, and free HBO and ESPN channels on the TV. Continental breakfast is available, and there are several restaurants nearby.

4. SOUTH HADLEY

15 miles (24km) N of Springfield, 7 miles (11km) S of Amherst

GETTING THERE **By Train** See "Springfield," above.

By Bus See "Springfield," above.

By Car From the Mass. Turnpike, follow I-391 and Mass. Route 116 north.

ESSENTIALS The **area code** is 413. The **chamber of commerce** is at 362 North Main Street (tel. 413/532-6451).

South Hadley is a small town most famous as the home of one of New England's most highly respected women's colleges.

WHAT TO SEE & DO

Mount Holyoke College in South Hadley bears the distinction of being the country's oldest women's college, founded in 1837. The lovely campus was originally designed by Frederick Law Olmsted, who fashioned many beautiful parks and forests during the 19th century. The campus now boasts a $9-million sports complex, an equestrian center, a Japanese teahouse and meditation garden, and a unique handcrafted classical organ (one of the last designed by Charles B. Fisk) in the chapel. The College Art Museum is open year round to campus visitors, and the Summer Theater offers plays in a tent on the green Tuesday through Saturday nights. The enrollment at Mount Holyoke is about 1,900 women. For a campus tour, call 538-2222.

On the way from South Hadley to Northampton on Route 47 (a gorgeous drive especially in the spring and fall), take a detour to **Skinner State Park** at the top of Mt. Holyoke (the mountain, not the college). On a clear day from the Summit House you'll have a great view of the winding Connecticut River, the fertile valley's patchwork of farmland, church and college steeples, and distant mountain ranges.

5. NORTHAMPTON

21 miles (34km) N of Springfield, 16 miles (26km) S of Deerfield,
7 miles (11km) W of Amherst

GETTING THERE   By Train   See "Springfield," above.

By Bus   See "Springfield," above.

By Car   Go north on I-91; from South Hadley, go north on Route 116 to Route 47, then west on Route 9.

ESSENTIALS   The **area code** is 413. The **Greater Northampton Chamber of Commerce,** on State Street (tel. 413/584-1900), will answer your questions.

Another pretty New England college town, Northampton is the home of Smith College.

WHAT TO SEE & DO

The pretty campus of **Smith College,** founded in 1871, is worthy of a stroll. You can arrange for a tour of the campus by contacting the Office of Admission, Garrison Hall, Northampton, MA 01063 (tel. 585-2500). But the handy campus guide folder available at the college switchboard in College Hall, and from the Office of Admission, may well satisfy your needs. Smith's enrollment is about 2,700 women.

WHERE TO STAY

Accommodation in the area is very much geared to college life. Most visitors come on college business, and when big college events—such as homecomings and graduations—draw big crowds, rooms are scarce throughout the area. Try to reserve well in advance if you think you'll arrive at a busy time.

AUTUMN INN, 259 Elm St., Northampton, MA 01060. Tel. 413/584-7660. 34 rms (all with bath). A/C TV TEL
$ Rates: $62–$68 single; $80–$92 double. Extra person $12. Children under 6 $8. AE, CB, DC, MC, V.
This is the closest thing in Northampton to the traditional college inn. From the street you see an attractive brick house, but behind the house are comfortable motel units and a small, pretty swimming pool. Special attention is given to good-quality furnishings and equipment here; a lounge and dining room provide sustenance.

HOTEL NORTHAMPTON, 36 King St., Northampton, MA 01061. Tel. 413/584-3100. 72 rms (all with bath). A/C TV TEL
$ Rates: $79 single; $95–$116 double; $125–$132 suite. AE, CB, DC, DISC, MC, V.
Parking: Free.

At the corner of Main and King Streets, the grand Hotel Northampton is the most prominent place to stay in town, and has been so since 1916. After undergoing a substantial period of renovation (completed in 1987), the rooms and suites have been furnished with classic pieces (including some four-poster beds) and Laura Ashley fabrics. The various eateries within are popular meeting places for Northampton's young and old alike.

Wiggins Tavern is a dark, colonial restaurant serving traditional American fare. The Coolidge Park Cafe dishes up lighter items and drinks; customers spill out onto the patio for dining in warmer months.

WHERE TO DINE

CURTIS AND SCHWARTZ, 116 Main St. Tel. 586-3278.
Cuisine: INTERNATIONAL. **Reservations:** Not accepted.
$ **Prices:** Breakfast $2.25–$7; main courses $4.25–$8.95. DC, MC, V.
Open: Mon 7:30am–3pm, Tues–Sat 7:30am–10pm.
This is the place for breakfast and lunch (and I do mean breakfast *and* lunch—some devotees come with the newspaper at breakfast, do some shopping, and return for lunch). There's much to love here: pecan waffles with fresh fruit, crème fraîche, and real maple syrup, ravioli filled with broccoli, goat cheese, and sun dried tomatoes in a garlic herb butter, and a cheesy herb omelet served with a warm scone. In a town with many breakfast places, this one reigns. There's always a line, but the wait never seems too long. There is a short wine list.

LA CAZUELA, 7 Old South St. Tel. 586-0400.
Cuisine: SOUTHWEST/MEXICAN. **Reservations:** Recommended for 5 or more.
$ **Prices:** Appetizers $2.75–$4.50; main courses $7.75–$9.50. AE, DC, MC, V.
Open: Dinner Mon–Thurs 5–9pm, Fri 5–10pm, Sat–Sun 3–10pm; brunch Sat–Sun 11am–3pm.
Good Mexican and Southwestern cooking in Northampton? You bet, at La Cazuela (it means "earthen cooking pot"), off Main Street. The dining room accented with regional artwork is pleasant, but in the warmer months if the mosquitoes aren't too fierce, you might prefer eating outside on the terrace. A complimentary basket of corn chips and salsa was hastily dispatched before I settled into pollo verde, a breast of chicken sautéed with garlic and cilantro and covered with a sauce of mild green chiles, tomatillos, cheese, and cilantro. Portions of food and drink are generous; a frosty margarita costs $3.25. Buen provecho!

PAUL AND ELIZABETH'S, 150 Main St. Tel. 584-4832.
Cuisine: NATURAL FOODS. **Reservations:** Not accepted.
$ **Prices:** Appetizers $2.50–$4.75; main courses $7–$16 MC, V.
Open: Mon–Thurs 11:30am–9:15pm, Fri–Sat 11:30am–9:30pm, sometimes later.
On Northampton's main street is Paul and Elizabeth's, a natural-foods restaurant. There's a second entrance on Old South Street above Herrell's Ice Cream. In the pleasant dining room you'll see a cross section of Northampton society dining on fresh fish, salads, tempura, fresh-baked breads, and desserts. Prices are quite moderate. For the fish lunch of the day, with salad, rice, and tea, you can get away for under $10. Wine and beer are served.

SZE'S, 50 Main St. Tel. 586-5708.
Cuisine: CHINESE. **Reservations:** Recommended.
$ **Prices:** Appetizers $3–$5; main courses $6–$14. MC, V.
Open: Lunch Mon–Sat 11:30am–3pm; dinner Sun–Thurs 3–9:15pm, Fri–Sat 3–10:45pm; Sun brunch 11:30am–3pm.
Sze's, in the center of town, is not your average Chinese restaurant. It serves gourmet meals in a contemporary, stylish, and open (and thus rather noisy) dining room. All the old standbys are here—sweet-and-sour chicken, moo shu pork, beef with pea pods—but they're done with flair. More exotic dishes include sesame game hen with

a Szechuan sauce and General Tso's chicken, cooked in a spicy sauce with green and red peppers. Check the blackboard for daily specials; my favorite is the crispy orange chicken. The Sunday brunch is always a good value, and the lounge is a nice place for a before- or after-dinner drink.

6. AMHERST

7 miles (11km) E of Northampton, 16 miles (26km) SE of Deerfield

GETTING THERE By Train   See "Springfield," above.

By Bus   See "Springfield," above.

By Car   Follow Route 9 east from Northampton, or I-91 and Route 116 north from the Mass. Turnpike.

ESSENTIALS   The **area code** is 413. There's an **information booth** right on the Town Common across the street from the bus depot, or you can look to the **Amherst Chamber of Commerce,** 11 Spring St., Amherst, MA 01002 (tel. 413/253-0700).

Amherst is a college town, through and through. Though Amherst College is perhaps its best-known institution of higher learning, the University of Massachusetts has a larger presence here.

WHAT TO SEE & DO

You'll want to take a tour of **Amherst College,** founded in 1821. The information booth on the Town Common in Amherst can furnish you with a handy map and guide. The college is all around you. Want more information? Contact Amherst College, Converse Hall (tel. 542-2000).

The sprawling campus of the **University of Massachusetts** takes more time to see, but there is a free PVTA bus line you can use, and an excellent campus map. Ask at the information booth on the common, or at the information desk in the Campus Center (east end of second-floor concourse; tel. 545-0111). U. Mass., by the way, was founded in 1863 as Massachusetts Agricultural College. Present enrollment on the Amherst campus is about 24,000—compare that to Amherst College's 1,500.

The roads between Amherst, Northampton, and South Hadley form a triangle and are some of the prettiest in the area. Route 116 between Amherst and South Hadley passes **Hampshire College,** the newest and most unconventional of the area's colleges. Farther along the road you may want to stop at **Atkins Fruit Bowl** (tel. 253-9528). Cider, pumpkins, apple picking, maple sugar products, and locally grown produce are all here. Atkins has grown so large from its humble beginnings as a farm stand that it now stays open daily, year round. Continuing along, you'll climb into the tiny Holyoke Mountain Range, the only range of mountains that runs east to west. Well-marked hiking trails begin from the visitors center here. Once over "the notch," you'll coast down toward South Hadley.

WHERE TO STAY

Accommodation in the area is very much geared to college life. Most visitors come on college business, and when big college events such as homecomings, graduations, and major football matches draw big crowds, rooms are scarce throughout the area. Try to reserve well in advance if you think you'll arrive at a busy time.

CAMPUS CENTER HOTEL, Murray D. Lincoln Campus Center, U. Mass., Amherst, MA 01003. Tel. 413/549-6000. Fax 413/545-1210. 116 rms (all with bath). A/C TV TEL **Directions:** Head north on N. Pleasant St., enter the U. Mass. campus, and follow signs to Campus Center Parking, an underground lot right next to the hotel.

$ Rates (tax exempt): $60 single; $70 double; $81 triple. AE, MC, V. **Parking:** Underground garage, $2.50 a night.

U. Mass. has its own major lodging facility for out-of-towners. Within the Murray D. Lincoln Campus Center, a modern tower, is the Campus Center Hotel. Besides the standard luxuries, most rooms have wonderful, panoramic views of the campus, the town, and the surrounding farmland.

HOWARD JOHNSON LODGE, 401 Russell St., Hadley, MA 01035. Tel. 413/586-0114, or toll free 800/654-2000. 62 rms (all with bath). A/C TV TEL **Directions:** Northampton Rd. is the highway (Rte. 9) between Amherst and Northampton. The road starts at the southern end of the Town Common, and exactly 1 mile later, after crossing the Amherst town line, it enters a commercial zone. A little farther along Rte. 9 toward Northampton is the local Howard Johnson Lodge.

$ Rates: $43–$89 single or double. Extra person $10. Children under 18 stay free in parents' room. MC, V. **Parking:** Free.

Even though it's very close to Amherst—only a few miles from the Town Common—its mail address is Hadley. Rooms are of the high Hojo standard, some with cathedral ceilings and balconies, and in addition the lodge has a nice big outdoor pool and lots of deck chairs for sunning. All rooms are newly renovated and have two double beds. VIP, handicapped, no-smoking, and adjoining family rooms are also available.

LORD JEFFERY INN, 30 Boltwood Ave., Amherst, MA 01002. Tel. 413/253-2576. 49 rms (all with bath), 6 suites. A/C TV TEL

$ Rates: $80–$110 single; $110–$120 suite. AE, DC, MC, V. **Parking:** Free.

Every college town has its college inn, usually a gracious old place with a refined atmosphere and very comfortable—often plush—accommodations. Amherst is no exception, and the Lord Jeffery, named for Lord Jeffery Amherst, stands right on the Town Common. The Lord Jeff is cozy, colonial, and collegiate, but with all the conveniences in the comfortable guest rooms. Ask for a room overlooking the garden courtyard. A tavern, lounge, and dining room provide food and refreshment from morning to night.

WHERE TO DINE

JUDIE'S, 51 N. Pleasant St. Tel. 253-3491.
 Cuisine: AMERICAN. **Reservations:** Not accepted.
$ Prices: Appetizers $3.75–$7; main courses $5–$10 at lunch, $8–$15 at dinner. AE, DISC, MC, V.
 Open: Sun–Wed 11:30am–10pm, Thurs–Sat 11:30am–11pm.

Among the longtime favorites is Judie's, on the town's main street. The eclectic menu has something for everyone, from seafoods to salads, from beerbatter potato skins to gooey desserts. For lunch, you might try a cup of shrimp bisque and a hamburger with swiss cheese and mushrooms. Many people come just for a light meal of soup and a popover with apple butter (a specialty) for $5. At dinner you dine in one of several small, attractive rooms in this converted house or on the glassed-in streetside porch. Go early to get a porch table for lunch. Liquor is served.

LORD JEFFERY INN, 30 Boltwood Ave. Tel. 253-2576.
 Cuisine: CONTINENTAL. **Reservations:** Recommended.
$ Prices: Appetizers $4–$8; main courses $14–$22; dinner $30–$40. AE, DC, MC, V.
 Open: Breakfast daily 7:30–9:30am; lunch daily noon–2pm; dinner daily 6–9pm; Sun brunch 11:30am–2:30pm.

The Lord Jeffery, facing the Town Common, offers an interesting if mostly traditional menu (steaks, seafood, chicken) in elegant colonial-style formality. Chandeliers provide soft light; in winter a fireplace adds visual as well as thermal warmth.

7. DEERFIELD

16 miles (26km) N of Northampton, 16 miles (26km) NW of Amherst,
3 miles (5km) S of Greenfield

GETTING THERE **By Train** The closest you can get is Springfield; see above.

By Bus See "Springfield," above. The closest service is to Greenfield.

By Car From Boston, follow Mass. Route 2 west, then U.S. Route 5/Mass. Route 10 south. From Springfield and the Mass. Pike, follow I-91 north, then Mass. Route 116 east and U.S. Route 5/Mass. Route 10 north.

ESSENTIALS The **area code** is 413. The **information desk** at the museum across from the Deerfield Inn has maps, brochures, information, and a short audiovisual show which gives you an overview of the village. For information in advance, contact **Historic Deerfield,** P.O. Box 321, Deerfield, MA 01342 (tel. 413/774-5581). The **Greater Springfield Convention and Visitors Bureau,** 34 Boland Way, Springfield, MA 01103 (tel. 413/787-1548), also has information on the area.

About 15 miles north of Northampton and Amherst on Routes 5 and 10 is **Historic Deerfield,** a wide street lined with well-preserved 18th-century houses. Unlike Old Sturbridge Village or Mystic Seaport, Deerfield lets you walk its streets for free and admire the nice old buildings and the setting, though you pay to tour inside the old buildings. Each of the houses has a guide or two who will give a 30-minute tour. For an admission ticket valid for all buildings for 2 days, adults pay $10, children 6 to 17 pay $5. You can visit every day of the year (except Thanksgiving, Christmas Eve, and Christmas Day) from 9:30am to 4:30pm.

The **Wright House** (1824), beautiful in itself, holds collections of Chippendale and Federal furniture, American paintings, and Chinese export porcelain. The **Flynt Textile Museum** (1872) houses a large collection of textiles, costumes, and needlework from America, England, and continental Europe. The **Henry N. Flynt Silver and Metalwork Collection** (1814) holds the museum's collection of silver, pewter, and other base metals. **Allen House** (1720) is furnished with items made in Boston and the Connecticut River Valley. **Stebbins House** (1799–1810) is a wealthy landowner's residence, with rich period furnishings. **Barnard Tavern** (1740–95) is a favorite with children because some of its rooms have exhibits that are okay to touch. **Wells-Thorn House** (1717–51) has a series of period rooms extending from the frontier to the Federal periods. **Dwight House** (1725) was actually built in Springfield, and moved to Deerfield in 1950. Local furniture and a period doctor's office are the attractions. The **Sheldon-Hawks House** (1743) was home to the same family during two centuries. The Sheldons, rich Deerfield farmers, were able to buy the best available land at the time. **Ashley House** (1730) was the minister's residence in old times, and by the look of it, this wasn't such a bad life.

One of the most fascinating exhibits is the **Ebenezer Hinsdale Williams House** (1816), which is open to view as a restoration-in-progress. The tour fills you in on the technical and historical work being done to re-create the house as it may have been between 1816 and 1838.

Besides the exhibits of Historic Deerfield, you should see the **Memorial Hall Museum,** at the corner of Memorial Street and U.S. 5 and 10 (tel. 774-7476), open every day May through October from 10am to 4:30pm (from 12:30 to 4:30pm on weekends). Admission (separate from the other buildings of Historic Deerfield) costs $5 for adults, $3 for students, $1 for children ages 6 to 12.

Memorial Hall (1798) was the original home of famed Deerfield Academy, still one of New England's most prestigious private schools. Less than a century after its construction, the building became a historical museum of Pocumtuck Valley life, both Native American and Puritan. Local furniture, pewter, tools, textiles, decoration, and tribal artifacts, arranged in period rooms, make up the collection. There are special collections for carved and painted chests, local embroidery, musical instruments, and glass-plate photographs (1880–1920) by the Allen sisters, Deerfield's talented early photographers.

But no exhibit brings life in Old Deerfield closer than the **Indian House Door.** Deerfield survived two Native American massacres and numerous other battles in its early days. On February 29, 1704, during the French and Indian War, the Sheldon House (now gone) was attacked, its door suffering chops and bashes. The attackers finally hacked a hole in the center, through which they got at the inhabitants. The door is pretty dramatic.

For a closer look at the Connecticut River, climb aboard the *Quinnetukut II* riverboat, Route 63 North (tel. 659-3714) for a 12-mile, 1½-hour interpretive **boat cruise.** Geology, ecology, and history of the river are the featured subjects, but the scenery alone is worth the fee: $7 per adult ($6 for seniors), $3 per child 14 and under. Call to check prices and schedules. Call to make reservations so that you're sure to get the cruise you want. Buy your tickets at the Northfield Mountain Recreation and Environmental Center, on Route 63 to the north of Route 2, due east of Greenfield (take I-91 north to Exit 27, then Route 2 east, then Route 63 north). It's open Wednesday through Sunday 9am to 5pm.

WHERE TO STAY
IN DEERFIELD

DEERFIELD INN, The Street, Deerfield, MA 01342. Tel. 413/774-5587, or toll free 800/926-3865. Fax 413/773-8712. 23 rms (all with bath). A/C TEL

$ Rates (including breakfast and service): $106 single; $122 double. Extra person $37. AE, DC, MC, V. **Parking:** Free. **Closed:** Christmas.

Built in 1884, and modernized in 1981 after a fire, the Deerfield Inn, in the center of town, has rooms inspired by the 18th century, shall we say, but constructed with 20th-century materials and comforts. They're decorated with period pieces and good replicas to put you in the mood of two centuries ago. There's a good restaurant, coffee shop, bar, and lounge; on the very fine front porch rocking chairs are all set to take in the view of Historic Deerfield, with its 12 museum houses. The inn is open all year (except for several days at Christmas). Jane and Karl Sabo are your innkeepers here.

NEARBY

1797 HOUSE, Charlemont Rd., Buckland, MA 01338. Tel. 413/625-2975. 3 rms (all with bath).

$ Rates (including breakfast): $55–$66 single; $77–$85 double. No credit cards. **Parking:** Free.

In Buckland, on the green, stands the 1797 House, run by a very hospitable lady named Janet Turley. The house (built guess when?) has immaculate guest rooms with down quilts; there are numerous fireplaces, a screened porch for warm-weather breakfast or relaxation, and interesting nooks and corners. The full country breakfast is juice, fruit, eggs, breakfast meats, french toast (or other main dish), and a hot beverage. Buckland is a few miles southwest of Shelburne Falls, just off Route 112.

8. LEE

45 miles (72.5km) W of Springfield, 134 miles (216km) W of Boston, 5 miles (8km) SE of Lenox, 11 miles (18km) NE of Great Barrington

GETTING THERE **By Train** Coming from Boston, trains stop in Pittsfield, 11

miles (18km) to the north. From New York City and Montréal, nearest station is Albany-Rensselaer.

By Bus   See "Getting There," at the beginning of this chapter.

By Car   Take the Mass. Turnpike to the Lee exit.

ESSENTIALS   The **area code** is 413. The local chamber of commerce maintains an **information booth** (tel. 413/243-0852) right on U.S. 20 (Main Street) in the center of town by the park (officially 10 Park Place, Lee, MA 01238). The **Berkshire Visitors Bureau,** Berkshire Common, Pittsfield, MA 01201 (tel. 413/443-9186, or toll free 800/237-5747 in the U.S. and Canada), can provide you with information on all of Berkshire County, covering the entire western end of Massachusetts.

Lee is famous for its summer dance festival, and many people pass through the town on their way to the Tanglewood Music Festival in Lenox. By the way, the hamlet named South Lee is on Route 102, south of the Massachusetts Turnpike (I-90) and Lee proper.

WHAT TO SEE & DO

In 1932, a dilapidated barn served as the birthplace of a major American dance festival in Lee. Bought by Ted Shawn and renovated for performances, the barn and the festival grew larger and more important over the years, enlisting the talents of Alvin Ailey, Merce Cunningham, and similar lights.

The 10-week **Jacob's Pillow Dance Festival** season begins in late June and runs through August. For a season brochure, contact Jacob's Pillow Dance Festival, P.O. Box 287, Lee, MA 01238 (tel. 243-0745). The performance center is 8 miles east of downtown Lee, off U.S. 20. Performing groups change weekly and ticket prices range from $24 to $28 in the Ted Shawn Theatre and cost $10 in the Studio/Theatre.

Besides the dance festival, the most notable sight in Lee is not in Lee at all, but in the tiny neighboring village of Tyringham, 5 miles south of Lee along the Tyringham Road. It's the **Tyringham Art Galleries** (known by many as the Gingerbread House), a curious thatched cottage built as a studio by sculptor Henry Hudson Kitson at the turn of the century. Kitson's most famous statue is the one of Captain Parker (*The Minute Man*) on Lexington Green. The art galleries are open 10am to 5pm daily from Memorial Day to Labor Day. Admission is $1 for adults, children under 12 free.

WHERE TO STAY

EXPENSIVE

APPLEGATE, 279 West Park St., Lee, MA 01238. Tel. 413/243-4451. 6 rms (all with bath). A/C **Directions:** Take I-90 to Exit 2. Follow Rte. 20 to W. Park Street. Applegate is on the left.

$ Rates: Nov–May, $90–$115 weekday double, $100–$160 weekend double. June–Oct, $100–$175 weekday double, $100–$195 weekend double. MC, V **Parking:** Free.

Built in the 1920s by a New York surgeon as a summer home, Applegate is a Georgian colonial home built on six acres of land and surrounded by apple and pine trees. Nancy and Rick Cannata, the innkeepers, will escort you to one of six individually decorated rooms. Several of the rooms have fireplaces, and Room 1 has a sauna shower. Room 6 has grandma's evening cape and topper on the nightstand. Most of the beds are antiques or reproductions, and all have down comforters. Room colors vary from white to peach to forest green, and brandy and chocolates await your arrival.

Breakfast, served in the dining room, might consist of orange scones and sour cream loaf, cereal, yogurt, coffee, and tea. Wine and cheese are served every evening at 5pm. Be on the lookout for Ray, the resident cockatoo.

**CHAMBERY INN, P.O. Box 319 (corner of Main and Elm Sts.), Lee, MA
01238. Tel. 413/243-2221,** or toll free 800/537-4321. 6 suites (all with bath).
A/C TV TEL **Directions:** From Rte. 90 take Exit 2 to Rte 20. The inn is 1 mile from
Rte. 90.

$ Rates: $155 weekday single or double, $195 weekend single or double. AE, MC,
V. **Parking:** Free.

Constructed in 1885, the Chambéry Inn was once Saint Mary's School, a parochial
school run by the teaching order Sisters of Saint Joseph, who came to the United States
from Chambéry, France (hence the name). Originally located only a block away, the
building was scheduled to be demolished in 1988, but was saved by the current
owners, Joe and Lynn Toole, and moved to its present location. The inn is a luxury
hostelry with a unique twist—the schoolhouse chalkboards still remain in the rooms.
You are, of course, supplied with chalk and erasers, and you can read all of the
wonderful things people have written on the boards about their stay at the inn. Also,
because it was a schoolhouse, the rooms are extraordinarily large and have 12-foot
ceilings. Each suite has a queen- or king-size bed, a sitting area, a fireplace, and a
whirlpool tub. Guests are allowed kitchen privileges, and a continental breakfast of
granola or breakfast pastries with coffee, tea, or juice, will be delivered to your door at
the time you specify on the card you hang on your door at night.

FEDERAL HOUSE, Main St., South Lee, MA 01260. Tel. 413/243-1824.
7 rms (all with bath). A/C **Directions:** Follow Mass. Rte. 102 south to South Lee;
Federal House is on the right-hand side in the center of town.

$ Rates (including breakfast): July–Aug, $159 double. 3-night minimum. No credit
cards. **Parking:** Free.

Thomas O. Hurlbut had the brick Greek Revival mansion built in 1824 when he was
head of the Owen and Hurlbut Paper Company here. Owned by the original family
for 124 years, it was just recently converted to an inn. The guest rooms have many
original Hurlbut touches and furnishings. The Federal House is famous for its cuisine
as well as its rooms (see below).

**MERRELL TAVERN INN, Main St., South Lee, MA 01260. Tel. 413/243-
1794.** 9 rms (all with bath). A/C TEL **Directions:** Follow Mass. Rte. 102 south to
South Lee; the inn is on the left-hand side in the center of town.

$ Rates (including breakfast): $65–$125 single; $85–$145 double. Extra person
$15. MC, V. **Parking:** Free.

Right on Main Street and along a riverbank is Charles and Faith Reynolds's elegant
and authentic inn. Authentic describes it well, for this house, built in 1800, has been
an inn since 1817. From 1947 to 1981 it belonged to the Society for the Preservation
of New England Antiquities. Preservation of the inn's character, including a
nonfunctioning but historic cagelike bar and authentic period furnishings, has
obviously been of paramount importance. Higher-priced rooms have fireplaces.
During the week, prices are lower.

INEXPENSIVE

Lee has numerous guesthouses. They're not furnished in antiques like Lenox's inns
and many don't have dining rooms, but they offer good lodging value in the
Berkshires. Exactly what you pay depends on the particular room in the particular
private home, but the price will easily be less than half that for a room in Lenox. As
the rooms are scattered around town, the **Lee Chamber of Commerce,** 10 Park
Place, Lee, MA 01238 (tel. 413/243-0852), handles reservations. An after-hours
phone number is placed in the window of the information booth when it's closed.

WHERE TO DINE

FEDERAL HOUSE, Rte. 102. Tel. 243-1824.
Cuisine: CONTINENTAL. **Reservations:** Required, especially on weekends.
Directions: Follow Mass. Rte. 102 south to South Lee; Federal House is on the
right-hand side in the center of town.

$ Prices: Appetizers $5–$11; main courses $16–$24; dinner $40. No credit cards.
Open: Dinner daily 6:30 or 8:30pm; Sun brunch 11:30am–2:30pm.

The aforementioned Federal House is among the Berkshires' more acclaimed restaurants. Elegantly set tables are arranged in the mansion's original dining room, front parlor, and billiards room. To get a table on Friday or Saturday evening you must reserve well in advance for one of the two seatings. The fare is continental and classic, with innovative touches: flounder stuffed with scallops, roast duckling with brandied plums, or perhaps thinly sliced veal sautéed in Grand Marnier. No lunch is served, but there's brunch on Sunday.

9. LENOX

5 miles (8km) NW of Lee, 7 miles (11km) S of Pittsfield,
23 miles (37km) S of Williamstown

GETTING THERE   By Train   Coming from Boston, trains stop in Pittsfield, 7 miles (11km) to the north. From New York City and Montréal, nearest station is Albany-Rensselaer.

By Bus   See "Getting There" at the beginning of this chapter.

By Car   Take the Mass. Turnpike to the Lee exit, then follow U.S. Route 20 west. From Williamstown, follow U.S. Route 7 south. Mass. Route 183 goes right to Tanglewood. See also "Getting There," at the beginning of this chapter.

ESSENTIALS   The **area code** is 413. For information, apply to the **Lenox Chamber of Commerce,** Lenox Academy Building, Main Street (P.O. Box 646), Lenox, MA 01240 (tel. 413/637-3646). The **Berkshire Visitors Bureau,** Berkshire Common, Pittsfield, MA 01201 (tel. 413/443-9186, or toll free 800/237-5747 in the U.S. and Canada), can provide you with information on all of Berkshire County, covering the entire western end of Massachusetts.

SPECIAL EVENTS   For information on **Tanglewood,** see below. In nearby Pittsfield **South Mountain Concerts** (tel. 442-2106), specializes in chamber music, and concerts begin in August and last into October. South Mountain Concerts was started in 1918 in a lovely old hall located a mile south of Pittsfield on U.S. 7 and 20. For a printed schedule of concerts, drop a line to the South Mountain Association, P.O. Box 23, Pittsfield, MA 01202.

In the 1700s, pioneers spreading through the lands west of Boston came to settle among the fertile fields of the Berkshires. At first the settlement at Lenox was called Yokuntown, after a Native American chief, but the name was later changed to honor an English lord—Charles Lenox, duke of Richmond—who was sympathetic to the American Revolutionary cause. Although small industries have at times appeared in the town, it has been predominantly rural and agricultural, and has remained unspoiled. In the 19th century business tycoons (including Andrew Carnegie) came to admire the tidy farms and streets of Lenox as the perfect place for a summer's retreat, and many of them bought up farms for this purpose. The houses are still standing for visitors to admire.

WHAT TO SEE & DO
TANGLEWOOD

The number-one activity in Lenox is, of course, the **Tanglewood Music Festival,** the summer home of the Boston Symphony Orchestra. Since 1934 concerts have been held in July and August on the grounds of Tanglewood, a fine estate about a mile from the center of Lenox out in the Berkshire Hills. More than 50 concerts—by full orchestra, chamber groups, and soloists in recital—take place during the Tanglewood season, including the famous weekend BSO concerts. In addition to the seasoned musicians from the Boston Symphony, there are performances by the young and extremely promising musicians who attend the Tanglewood Music Center for study and advanced training. Maestro Seiji Ozawa, now music director of the BSO, was once among this young up-and-coming elite.

Programs of the concert series are available from the information booth in Lenox, or by mail from Symphony Hall, 301 Massachusetts Avenue, Boston, MA 02115. For concert information, call the Tanglewood Concert Line (tel. 637-1666), July and August. For other information, call Symphony Hall (tel. 617/266-1492) until early June; from early June until the end of the season, call Tanglewood (tel. 637-1940).

Seats in the Music Shed ($12 to $60) are bought up early, but lawn tickets ($8 or $9.50, depending upon the concert) are easy to find at Tanglewood. All tickets can be bought by phone through **TicketMaster** (tel. 617/931-2000 in Boston, 212/307-7171 in New York City, toll free 800/877-1414 elsewhere); you'll pay a small service charge for this convenience.

Tanglewood has also begun to sponsor a series of popular, folk, and rock concerts in addition to the more lofty Tanglewood Music Festival series. When you call 637-1600, ask about what's coming up in the **Popular Artists' Series.**

Special excursions to Tanglewood concerts are offered by various tour companies, including, in New York City, **Biss Tours** (tel. 718/426-4000), and **Parker Tours** (tel. 718/428-7800). From Boston, **K & L Tours** (tel. 617/267-1905) will take you there, or you can catch a bus run by Peter Pan Bus Lines (tel. 617/426-7838).

Tips If you drive to Tanglewood, here are some tips to make things easier. First, expect heavy highway traffic. Plan to get to Tanglewood proper at least 2 hours before the concert begins. Bring your picnic—everyone does, and that's why the parking lots fill up early. Expect a tremendous jam of traffic when you leave at the end of the concert. The flood is ably directed by Tanglewood staff, but the exodus takes time nonetheless.

OTHER ATTRACTIONS

What do Shakespeare and Edith Wharton have in common? **The Mount** (tel. 637-1899) is a house and gardens planned by Wharton, a Pulitzer Prize–winning author. You can tour the house, and watch a salon drama based on Ms. Wharton's life and works, June through October, Tuesday through Friday from noon to 4pm, on weekends from 10am to 4pm.

You can see Shakespeare under the stars or under the sun at The Mount, the regal home in a pastoral setting of Shakespeare & Company, Lenox, MA 01240 (tel. 637-1197; box office 637-3353). An average of five performances daily of both Shakespearean and modern plays are presented May 22 through September 6 in two outdoor and two indoor theaters (closed Monday). Performances begin at 1pm (10:30am Saturday and Sunday) and continue through the evening. Shakespeare in the open air on a warm summer evening is definitely among the finer things in life!

The Mount is located just south of Lenox, at the junction of Routes 7 and 7A.

Lenox is also home to the **Berkshire Scenic Railway Museum,** Willow Creek Road (tel. 637-2210), where you can find out about local railroad lore, poke around in a New Haven Railroad caboose, watch a complex model railroad run, and see railroading videos; there's a gift shop, too. Nostalgic excursion trains should be running (by now) from the museum on a 15-mile route connecting Lenox, Lee,

IMPRESSIONS

I went a hundred miles north into the Berkshires. It was April . . . Was I in England? Almost, but not quite.
—E. M. FORSTER, "THE UNITED STATES," 1947,
IN *TWO CHEERS FOR DEMOCRACY,* 1951

Stockbridge, and Great Barrington. Service was temporarily suspended in 1991 in order to rehabilitate the tracks. Drop by, or call, for latest information on the trains.

In Lenox proper, be sure to walk to the top of the hill on Main Street (U.S. 7), north of the center of town, to see the **Church on the Hill,** a very fine New England Congregational church building erected in 1805.

Otherwise, long walks or a drive around the "back streets" and lanes of Lenox can turn up unexpected sights: tremendous mansions, even small castles, nestled in fine parks and copses of trees, once occupied for a few months in summer by commercial and industrial magnates and their immediate families. Many of the mansions are still in private hands, enjoyed by an ever-widening circle of the descendants of the original builders. Most are not open to the public, so you must settle for tantalizing looks from the sidewalk.

For a beautiful hike through 1,000 acres of the Berkshire countryside, find your way to the **Pleasant Valley Sanctuary,** northwest of Lenox. Follow the signs, or take Route 7A north to West Dugway Road, then West Mountain Road. Pay the admission fee ($3 adults, $1 children 6 to 12), and set out on the 7 miles of nature trails to explore native Berkshire flora and fauna. It's open Tuesday through Sunday from dawn to dusk.

WHERE TO STAY

The overnight lodging situation in Lenox is not the best. Proprietors of inns and motels bemoan the short season and the incredible press of traffic on Tanglewood weekends, which thins out to less-than-capacity during the week. For most lodging places, rooms are in great demand. Some Tanglewood travelers stay as far east as Springfield, and drive to the concert, then back to Springfield. In any case, have reservations for weekends.

During the off-season, though, all that's missing from Lenox is Tanglewood and the crowds. The same gorgeous rooms are still here, but at a fraction of the price. More and more travelers are realizing this value and making the Berkshires a year-round destination.

If you'd like to stay in a bed-and-breakfast, contact **Berkshire Bed and Breakfast,** P.O. Box 211, Williamsburg, MA 01096 (tel. 413/268-7244). They publish a directory of homes scattered throughout the Berkshires, Eastern New York State, southern Vermont, northern Connecticut, Greater Springfield, the Pioneer Valley, and Sturbridge. Write for a copy or call between 9am and 6pm weekdays.

VERY EXPENSIVE

GATEWAYS INN, 71 Walker St., Lenox, MA 01240. Tel. 413/637-2532.
7 rms (all with bath). TEL
$ Rates (including continental breakfast): $85–$135 single or double. 3-night minimum stay required July–Aug Thurs–Sun. AE, DC, DISC, MC, V. **Parking:** Free.

★ The rather formal Gateways Inn is a fine place to stay and an even finer place to dine. Quite near the center of Lenox, the Gateways is a grand old white mansion built by Harley Proctor of Proctor & Gamble in 1912. With accommodations as large as these, including the cavernous Fiedler suite, it's no wonder the huge house boasts only eight rooms. The main courses at dinner cost between $19.50 and $27.50 and may include médaillons of beef or rack of lamb. Lunch is offered July through October.

WHEATLEIGH, W. Hawthorne Rd. (P.O. Box 824), Lenox, MA 01240. Tel. 413/637-0610, or toll free 800/321-0610. Fax 413/637-4507 17 rms (all with bath). A/C TEL **Directions:** From the monument intersection in Lenox, go down the hill on Old Stockbridge Rd., turn right onto Hawthorne. At W. Hawthorne Rd., turn left.
$ Rates: July–Oct, $165–$425 double. Nov–June, $110–$275 double. AE, DC, MC, V. **Parking:** Free.

Of the Berkshire inns, none is more dignified or luxurious than Wheatleigh. Center of the vast estate is the tawny brick mansion in the style of a 16th-century Florentine villa which once belonged to the American-born Contessa de Heredia. The gracious turn-of-the-century, top-of-the-heap life-style has been preserved in the airy public rooms, the porticoed and balconied guest rooms and suites, and the sweeping lawns. There are Tiffany windows and beautiful views. Full payment is required for a confirmed reservation. Don't miss the unrestored clock tower-water tower-lookout down by the parking area. The contessa's poodles, all 20 of them, are buried nearby. The restaurant is comparable to New York's finest; dinner is served Tuesday to Sunday. The inn also has tennis courts.

EXPENSIVE

APPLE TREE INN AND RESTAURANT, 224 West St., Lenox, MA 01240. Tel. 413/637-1477. 33 rms (most with bath). A/C **Directions:** Just past Tanglewood's main gate, bear right at fork and look for inn's sign.
$ Rates (including continental breakfast): High season, $135–$240 double; $275–$290 suite. Off-season, $60–$90 double; $150–$225 suite. AE, DC, MC, V. **Parking:** Free.
"Across the road from Tanglewood" is how the owners describe the Apple Tree Inn and Restaurant. The name suits, for the century-old mansion is indeed in the midst of an apple orchard. Perched high on the hill directly opposite Tanglewood's West Street entrance, the gracious restaurant and public rooms, and many of the guest rooms, look out on a gorgeous panorama. Some rooms in the main house have a fireplace, most have private bath, and some have televisions. There are also 20 modern rooms in the nearby guest lodge. The inn has a heated swimming pool and a clay tennis court.

CLIFFWOOD INN, 25 Cliffwood St., Lenox, MA 01240. Tel. 413/637-3330. 7 rms (6 with bath). A/C
$ Rates (including continental breakfast): High season, $105–$190 double. Off-season, $85–$145 double. No credit cards. **Parking:** Free.
The Cliffwood is a vast 1889 mansion set back from the street on its own crescent-shaped drive. As you pass through the curious split Dutch front door into the spacious foyer, you'll be surprised to learn there are only seven bedrooms (six with private bath, fireplace, and king-size bed) for rent—the huge place looks like it should hold many more. In 5 minutes you can walk to town. Evening wine and hors d'oeuvres are included in the room price, and there's a pool.

ROOKWOOD INN, 19 Stockbridge Rd. (P.O. Box 1717), Lenox, MA 01240. Tel. 413/637-9750. 19 rms (all with bath). **Directions:** From statue at town center, take a left onto Stockbridge Rd. Rookwood is first building on left.
$ Rates (including breakfast): $80–$190 double. AE. **Parking:** Free.
Just a short walk down the hill from the monument intersection in Lenox is Rookwood Inn, a charming Victorian place with a nice lawn and formal gardens. It can accommodate up to 35 guests. A few rooms have a small screened-in porch, one has a multiwindowed turret. Spaces in this gracious turn-of-the-century "cottage" are larger than normal. The welcome from innkeepers Betsy and Tom Sherman is warm and friendly.

WALKER HOUSE, 74 Walker St., Lenox, MA 01240. Tel. 413/637-1271, or toll free 800/235-3098. 8 rms (all with bath). A/C **Directions:** After stop sign in Lenox Village, turn left and Walker House is right on left.
$ Rates (including breakfast): $50–$150 double. Extra person $15. No credit cards. **Parking:** Free, on premises.
This spacious house, right in the heart of town, was built in 1804. Each room is named after a composer, some have fireplaces, and many look onto the 3 acres of lawn, gardens, and woods. Common rooms are decorated with modern art and attractive antiques, creating gracious eclectic spaces. Room prices include afternoon

tea and a small bottle of wine in your room. There's also a 100-inch television for screening movies or general television.

MODERATE

BROOK FARM INN, 15 Hawthorne St., Lenox, MA 01240. Tel. 413/637-3013. 12 rms (all with bath). **Directions:** Go down hill from monument intersection on Old Stockbridge Rd., turn right onto Hawthorne St.

$ Rates (including breakfast): July–Sept 7, $105–$170 weekend double, $95–$115 weekday double. Sept 8–Sept 30, $95–$110 weekend double, $65–$90 weekday double. Oct, $95–$135 weekend double, $75–$110 weekday double. Nov–June, $75–$110 weekend double, $65–$100 weekday double. MC, V. **Parking:** Free.

About 2 blocks from the center of town is the Brook Farm Inn, run by Joe and Anne Miller, with a cozy, authentic Victorian atmosphere and a swimming pool. The brochure claims "there's poetry here," and there is: Hundreds of volumes are carefully organized on shelves, and there are poetry readings on Saturday afternoon. In the library, an unfinished jigsaw puzzle tempts you to add a piece, or you can just read a book and sit by the fire.

You might like Room 5, a bright room with butterfly-and-flower wallpaper and a pastel-colored quilt, a wicker rocker, and a white dresser. Room 8, which is under the eaves, has deep purple wallpaper, rose carpeting, oak furnishings, and a skylight. Five of the rooms have fireplaces.

Breakfast is served buffet style at a formal dining table and includes granola, fresh fruit and juices, bread pudding, and an egg dish. In the afternoon, tea and scones are served, and each room comes equipped with a decanter of sherry.

CANDLELIGHT INN, 53 Walker St., Lenox, MA 01240. Tel. 413/637-1555. 8 rms (all with bath). A/C

$ Rates: July–Aug and Oct, $120–$155 double. Nov–June and Sept, $90–$135 double. AE, MC, V. **Parking:** Free, on premises.

The Candlelight Inn, at the corner of Church Street in the center of town, is best known for its restaurant, but there are rooms for rent in the big and graceful old house. The location is excellent. Call early for July, August, or October reservations.

THE GABLES INN, 103 Walker St., Lenox, MA 01240. Tel. 413/637-3416. 19 rms (all with bath). A/C

$ Rates (including breakfast): $60–$195 single or double. DISC, MC, V. **Parking:** Free.

Built in 1885, the Gables, in the center of town, is a Queen Anne–style Berkshire "cottage." Once owned by the family of Edith Wharton's husband, this was her home for 2 years while she waited for her own cottage, the Mount, to be built. The present innkeepers have re-created the famous eight-sided library where Mrs. Wharton wrote many short stories. Stay at the Gables to surround yourself with all this grace and history (as well as a swimming pool and tennis court).

GARDEN GABLES INN, 141 Main St., Lenox, MA 01240. Tel. 413/637-0193. 14 rms (all with bath).

$ Rates (including full breakfast): June–Oct, $65–$170 single or double. Nov–May, rates dramatically lower. 3-night minimum stay required on weekends July–Aug. MC, V. **Parking:** Free.

The Garden Gables Inn, at the bottom of Church Hill down its own private road, is very near the center of town. The inn's name is appropriate, as you'll see when you drive or walk down the road through the gardens to the large white house with three sharply triangular gables set in its roof. The shape of the house gives you a clue that all the rooms are of different shapes and sizes, with lots of interesting nooks, crannies, and angles. All are furnished differently. Downstairs there are two cozy low-ceilinged living rooms with rows of books and fireplaces. The lowest price is for a midweek small room, and the highest price for a large room with private bath on a weekend. The inn has its own 72-foot swimming pool out back.

VILLAGE INN, 16 Church St. (P.O. Box 1810), Lenox, MA 01240. Tel. 413/637-0200, or toll free 800/253-0917. Fax 413/637-9756. 30 rms (all with bath). A/C TEL
$ Rates: Summer, $85–$155 double. Fall, $75–$145 double. Winter, $60–$135 double. Spring, $50–$110 double. AE, DC, MC, V. **Parking:** Free.

Right downtown is the Village Inn, a charming old landmark built in 1771. All rooms are individually furnished with country antiques. Six of the rooms have fireplaces, and many have four-poster beds. The Albion Restaurant is good for breakfast, English tea, and dinner, and the Tavern features English ales and a light menu.

WHERE TO DINE

Most of the inns mentioned above have excellent dining rooms. For a change of pace, try this place.

CHURCH STREET CAFE, 69 Church St. Tel. 637-2745.
Cuisine: AMERICAN/ECLECTIC. **Reservations:** Required.
$ Prices: Appetizers $3.50–$5.50; main courses $13–$18; dinner $34. MC, V.
Open: Lunch daily 11:30am–2:15pm; dinner daily 5:30–9pm. **Closed:** Sun–Mon in winter.

This very successful "American bistro" serves lunch, dinner, and Sunday brunch daily in small, cozy dining rooms or out on pleasant covered decks. Service is personal and informal, and prices are quite moderate for Lenox. Try the native goat cheese with minced greens to start, then charcoal-grilled Jamaican chicken, and lemon-almond tart and espresso to finish up; your bill—including tax, tip, and a half bottle of the California house wine—will be $34. The pasta is homemade here, and the country pâté, too. Luncheon prices include $7 sandwiches and a few good Southwestern items.

10. STOCKBRIDGE

6 miles (10km) S of Lenox, 4 miles (6.5km) SW of Lee,
7 miles (11km) N of Great Barrington

GETTING THERE See "Getting There" in "Lee," above, and at the beginning of this chapter.

ESSENTIALS The **area code** is 413. The Stockbridge Kiwanis Club maintains and **information booth** open 24 hours on Main Street right in the center of town. Guides will provide you with pamphlets and brochures, answer your questions, and even help you find an inexpensive room in a private home—but only if lodging conditions are tight. If the local motels are not full, they'll direct you to one of those, as the private-home rooms are more of an emergency measure.

The **Berkshire Visitors Bureau,** Berkshire Common, Pittsfield, MA 01201 (tel. 413/443-9186, or toll free 800/237-5747 in the U.S. and Canada), can provide you with information on all of Berkshire County, covering the entire western end of Massachusetts.

SPECIAL EVENTS In the **Berkshire Playhouse** (tel. 298-5536) and in a big red barn close by, the Berkshire Theater Festival hosts a series of performances now in its second half century. From late June through August, plays are staged Monday through Saturday evenings, and on Thursday and Saturday afternoons. The classic plays with name performers are in the playhouse proper. The Unicorn Theater Company puts on experimental and new plays in the barn, and throughout July and August special children's theater performances are held outside, under a tent, Thursday through Saturday at 11am.

Any way you look at it, Stockbridge is a very beautiful town. Its wide Main Street is lined with grand houses and other buildings each set apart in its own lawns and gardens. Stately trees fill the skyline. Stockbridge is the center of many Berkshire activities, including the Berkshire Playhouse (details below); it was also once the home of famed painter Norman Rockwell. It is rich in historical and cultural attractions.

In addition to the sights listed below, it's also worth taking a look at a sumptuous estate atop Eden Hill in Stockbridge. From its beginning as a Native American mission in 1734, the estate has seen many additions over the years. Having served as a mansion for the wealthy and as a private school, it is now a monastery for the **Marian Fathers,** and visitors are welcome to stroll the grounds and take in the impressive buildings and the views of the Berkshire Hills.

The town of **West Stockbridge** is a different municipality altogether, 4 miles west of Stockbridge and Lenox. The dilapidated town was bought up by developers some years ago and reconstructed, expanded, and spruced up as a real-life Disneyland for shoppers, browsers, and sightseers. Purists may say the town is now like a movie set, but most visitors enjoy their time here, meandering along the short streets, peering in windows and shops, having a meal or a cool refresher. It's all pretty commercial, it's true, but that's the attraction.

WHAT TO SEE & DO
SIGHTS

NORMAN ROCKWELL MUSEUM, in the Old Corner House, Main St. Tel. 298-3822.

In the Old Corner House in the center of Stockbridge is a large permanent collection of Norman Rockwell paintings. Rockwell, the famed American illustrator who did many pictures for magazine covers and posters, lived in Stockbridge for 25 years, up to his death in 1978. In fact, the museum has the world's largest collection of his work, and is building a large new museum on the outskirts of town to house it. The new museum is scheduled to open in April of 1993; call for details.

Admission: $6 adults, $1 children aged 5–16.
Open: Daily 10am–5pm. **Closed:** Last 2 weeks of Jan.

MISSION HOUSE, Main St. Tel. 298-3239.

Owned by the Trustees of Reservations, Mission House (1739), in the center of town, is worth a visit. It was built by the Rev. John Sergeant to carry out his Christian mission to the Stockbridge Native Americans. The house is a National Historic Landmark, and is furnished in American pieces all dating from 1740 or earlier. Guided tours are offered.

Admission: $4 adults, $1 children aged 6–12.
Open: Memorial Day–Columbus Day, Tues–Sun 11am–4pm. **Closed:** Tues after Mon holidays.

NAUMKEAG, Prospect Hill, Prospect St. Tel. 298-3239.

The palatial Naumkeag was built by Stanford White for Joseph Choate, a New York City attorney, in 1886. Many of the sumptuous furnishings are still in place, and there are extensive formal gardens.

Admission: House and garden $6 adults, garden only $4 adults; $1.50 children aged 6–12.
Open: Late May–early Sept, Tues–Sun 10am–4:15pm. Early Sept to mid-Oct, Sat–Sun 10am–4:15pm. **Closed:** Tues after Mon holidays. **Directions:** Take Pine St. from the Red Lion Inn, then turn onto Prospect St. to reach Naumkeag.

CHESTERWOOD, Williamsville Rd. Tel. 298-3579.

Just a few miles from Stockbridge is Chesterwood, the former summer estate of Daniel Chester French, sculptor of the statue of Lincoln that graces the Lincoln Memorial, and also of *The Minute Man* at Concord North Bridge. French (1850–1931) summered here from 1897 until 1931 and used the studio (built in 1898) near the house for his work. You can visit both the mansion and studio as well as an 1800s barn which has been converted to a gallery featuring exhibits on French's life and work. A lovely country garden, a woodland walk laid out by French himself, a panoramic view of Monument Mountain, and a museum store are unexpected extras to a Chesterwood visit. Admission fees go toward the upkeep of the property, which is maintained by the National Trust for Historic Preservation.

Admission: $5.50 adults, $3 children 13–18, $1 children 6–12, free for children under 6.

Open: May–Oct, daily 10am–5pm. **Directions:** Drive west on Rte. 102 and follow the signs.

HANCOCK SHAKER VILLAGE, Rte. 20 (P.O. Box 898), Pittsfield, MA 01202. Tel. 443-0188.

Hancock Shaker Village is one of the most fascinating sights in the Berkshires. Up until 1960, the village was home to members of a religious sect noted for their quiet, simple lives, hard work, and quality handcrafts.

"The United Society of Believers in Christ's Second Appearing" or "The Millennial Church," more readily known as the Shakers, was a movement begun in 1747 in England as an offshoot of Quakerism. It gained momentum when Ann Lee, "Mother Ann," proclaimed that she had received the "mother element" of the spirit of Christ. After being imprisoned for her zeal, Mother Ann and eight followers immigrated to the American colony of New York and founded a settlement near Albany in 1774. After Mother Ann died in 1784, her followers founded other Shaker communities based on the principles of communal possessions, celibacy, pacifism, open confession of sins, and equality of the sexes. The communities were organized into "families" of 30 to 90 people. Work was a consecrated act, reflected in the high quality of workmanship and design in Shaker furniture and crafts: In effect, every product was a prayer.

Shakers, named for the trembling that came upon them from their religious zeal, believed that God had both a male and female nature. The male was embodied in Jesus, the female in Mother Ann. Though converts devoted themselves and all their possessions to the community, they were free to leave at anytime. Celibacy and the onslaught of the 20th century's complex life-style almost put an end to Shakerism after more than two centuries; there are only a handful of the faithful left now, living in small communities in Maine and New Hampshire.

One cannot help but admire a life-style based on kindliness and hard work. Shaker products are still copied and admired, because these good people treated even daily tasks as an art. Twenty of the original Shaker buildings at Hancock have been restored, furnished with artifacts of Shaker life, and staffed with men and women who can explain and demonstrate the customs of the Shaker life to you. Don't miss it.

Admission: $9 adults, $4.50 children aged 6–12, $8 seniors and students, $25 family of two adults and children under 18.

Open: Apr and Nov, daily 10am–3pm (guided tours only). May–Oct, daily 9:30am–5pm. **Directions:** Drive north of West Stockbridge 9 miles along Rte. 41, then west on U.S. 20, to the outskirts of Pittsfield and Hancock Shaker Village.

SKIING

There are at least six well-known downhill ski areas in the Berkshires. Call to get information on ski conditions and year-round activities: **Butternut** (tel. 528-2000), **Bosquet** (tel. 442-8316), **Catamount** (tel. 582-1262), **Brodie** (tel. 443-4752), **Berkshire East** (tel. 339-6617), **Jiminy Peak** (tel. 738-5500), and **Otis Ridge** (tel. 269-4444).

WHERE TO STAY

IN STOCKBRIDGE

RED LION INN, Main St., Stockbridge, MA 01262. Tel. 413/298-5545.

108 rms (75 with bath).

$ Rates: Weekends $85 double without bath, $125–$155 double with bath; weekdays $70 double without bath, $95–$130 double with bath. AE, CB, DC, DISC, MC, V. **Parking:** Free.

The Red Lion Inn in the center of town is a town institution. The huge white frame hotel with a wide front porch was established as an inn in 1773. Always bustling with guests and diners in summer, the Red Lion charges its high-season rates on weekends from late May through October. Minimum weekend stay is 2 nights. By the way, the building dates from 1897, when it was constructed on the site of an earlier inn which was completely destroyed by fire.

Dining/Entertainment: The Red Lion is also Stockbridge's premier place for dining. Besides the formal dining room, there's the Widow Bingham Tavern, a rough-hewn and woody place of colonial flavor. The Lion's Den, downstairs, is the cocktail lounge with a sandwich-and-salad menu. Plan to spend about $35 to $45 per person for a luxurious beef dinner in the dinning room, about the same in the Widow Bingham Tavern. In summer there's dining in the pretty courtyard in back.

IN WEST STOCKBRIDGE

West Stockbridge harbors several establishments offering lodging and meals at lower rates than in Stockbridge proper. These are well worth a look.

WILLIAMSVILLE INN, Rte. 41, West Stockbridge, MA 01266. Tel. 413/274-6118. 15 rms (all with bath). **Directions:** From West Stockbridge, follow Rte. 41 south 4 miles.

$ Rates (including full breakfast): $100–$170 single or double. MC, V. **Parking:** Free.

Many places call themselves country inns these days, even though they have downtown locations, Muzak, and cable color TV, bus tours, and whirlpools. The Williamsville is a true country inn, however. It's out in the country. Some of the guest rooms have fireplaces, some have four-poster beds; all have fine old furnishings. Some are in the main house, some out back in a renovated barn and a cottage. The inn, built in 1797, has 10 acres of grounds, a swimming pool, clay tennis court, and woodland trails. The dining room is well known and well regarded. A 3-day minimum stay is applied on summer and holiday weekends.

WHERE TO DINE

TRUC ORIENT EXPRESS, Harris St. Tel. 232-4204.
Cuisine: VIETNAMESE. **Reservations:** Required in summer.
$ Prices: Appetizers $2–$7; main courses $7–$11 at lunch, $16–$25 at dinner. AE, MC, V.
Open: Daily 11:30am–10pm. **Closed:** Mon in winter.

Over in West Stockbridge for the day, one of the very best things you can do is have a meal at the Truc Orient Express. Light and airy, with wicker furniture, it is an exceptionally attractive place, and a welcome change from the antique-packed dining rooms hereabouts. The cuisine is Vietnamese: appetizers such as *mien cua* (crab and bean-thread soup) or *ga nuong chanh* (skewered lemon chicken) with a main course of sautéed squid with bamboo shoots or fresh flounder in a spicy sweet-and-sour sauce. For dessert, the customary lychee or not-so-customary flan finish up nicely. Such a dinner costs $16 to $25, and if you choose carefully you might even be able to squeeze a glass of saké or plum wine into the price. There are lots of vegetarian dishes, too. Open for lunch and dinner. Don't miss it.

11. GREAT BARRINGTON

7 miles (11km) S of Stockbridge, 11 miles (18km) SW of Lee, 4 miles (6.5km) NE of South Egremont

GETTING THERE See "Getting There" in "Lee," above, and at the beginning of this chapter.

ESSENTIALS The **area code** is 413. There's a little **information kiosk** in the center of town, by the Berkshire Motor Inn and Searles' Castle, on Main Street. It's operated by the **Southern Berkshire Chamber of Commerce,** 362 Main Street, Great Barrington, MA 01230 (tel. 413/528-1510). You'll get help finding a room if you need one. Donations are accepted to defray expenses. The **Berkshire Visitors Bureau,** Berkshire Common, Pittsfield, MA 01201 (tel. 413/443-9186, or toll free 800/237-5747 in the U.S. and Canada), can provide you with information on all of Berkshire County, covering the entire western end of Massachusetts.

Although it is certainly not a city, Great Barrington is the largest town in the southern Berkshires, a major crossroads and commercial center. Supplies and services that you might not find in Stockbridge or Lenox will be available here.

Great Barrington was an important town even before the Revolution. The citizenry, angered at Britain's denial of the colonials' rights, prevented the king's judges from convening in the courthouse here in 1774. In the 19th century Mr. and Mrs. Edward Searles became the town's benefactors, establishing many public buildings and constructing for themselves an immense mansion in a 100-acre park which nudges right into the center of town.

WHAT TO SEE & DO

Great Barrington and South Egremont are the antique collector's towns *par excellence.* Everyone here, it seems, deals in **antiques** and old stuff. Browsing the shops is the daily passion, but several excursions out of town to nature spots provide an antidote to buying-and-selling.

Take U.S. 7 south from Great Barrington for about 10 miles, and turn onto Route 7A for Ashley Falls. Your destination, a mile from Ashley Falls along Rannpo and Weatogue roads, is **Bartholomew's Cobble,** bordering the Housatonic River. A "cobble" in this case is a high knoll of limestone, marble, or quartzite, 500 million years old, and covered with a rich and varied collection of native flora: trees, ferns, mosses, wildflowers. The nature reservation, open year round, is owned by the Trustees of Reservations (tel. 229-8600), and has 6 miles of hiking trails. A naturalist is on duty from mid-April to mid-October, Wednesday through Sunday from 9am to 5pm, to answer your questions and point out highlights.

Another pretty nature nook, good for a picnic, is **Bash Bish Falls,** 12 miles southwest of South Egremont, right on the New York state line. Take Route 41 south out of town, and turn right onto Mount Washington Road (signs for Catamount ski area). Follow signs to the falls, taking East Street, then West Street, and finally Bash Bish Falls Road, deep in the Mount Washington State Forest. You'll plunge into the valley carved by the Bash Bish Creek, and finally come to a parking area from which a steep trail leads to the falls. Stay on the road a bit farther and you'll come to another parking place, and an easier—but longer—trail. Stay on the road any longer and you'll end up in New York.

At the end of the trails, deep in the forest, is the 50-foot Bash Bish Falls, cascading into a chilly pool. A ½ hour's relaxation here on a hot summer's day is pretty close to nirvana.

If mountain hiking is more to your taste, head north out of Great Barrington on U.S. 7, and after 4½ miles you'll see signs for **Monument Mountain.** There are two trails to the summit, one easier but slightly longer than the other. The hike to the top, a rest, and back down will take between 2 and 3 hours. The view at the summit is very fine.

WHERE TO STAY

IN GREAT BARRINGTON

ELLING'S GUEST HOUSE, R.D. 3, Box 6, Great Barrington, MA 01230. Tel. 413/528-4103. 6 rms (3 with bath). A/C **Directions:** Take Rte. 102 south off the Mass. Tpk. to Rte. 7 south to Great Barrington, then follow Rte. 23 southwest for 1 mile.

$ **Rates** (including continental breakfast): $72 single or double without bath, $85 single or double with bath. Extra person $15. No children under 12. 2-night minimum stay during July–Aug and foliage season. Discounts of $10 to $15 per room in winter. No credit cards. **Parking:** Free.

Jo and Ray Elling run Elling's Guest House, which is actually more like an inn. The rooms in the nice old house (which dates from 1746) are all pretty and quaint, the hospitality first-rate. Quiet, friendly, reasonably priced, this is among the best in the Berkshires.

SEEKONK PINES INN, 142 Seekonk Cross Rd., Great Barrington, MA 01230. Tel. 413/528-4192, or toll free 800/292-4192 (for reservations only). 6 rms (4 with bath). **Directions:** From the center of Great Barrington, follow Mass. Rte. 41 southwest 2½ miles to the inn.

$ **Rates** (including full breakfast): High season $55 single; $75–$95 double; extra person $20. Off-season, $44–$55 single; $65–$85 double; extra person $15. MC, V. **Parking:** Free, off-street.

Linda and Chris Best are your hosts at the Seekonk Pines, and their inn features a nice swimming pool, a garden from which they will sell you fresh produce, bicycles for rent, and a full breakfast; and in winter, a fireplace in the large living room, besides the cozy rooms. Its clean, neat rooms are decorated with antiques, old quilts, and Linda's watercolors. There's also a suite with sitting area which sleeps four (perfect for a family or couple on a longer visit), with private bath. Discounts are given on stays of 5 days or more.

NEARBY

NEW BOSTON INN, Rte. 8, Box 166D, Sandisfield, MA 01255. Tel 413/258-4477, or toll free 800/245-2938. 8 rms (all with bath). **Directions:** Take Rte. 90 East to Rte. 8 South to the inn which is at the junction of Rtes. 8 and 57.

$ **Rates:** May 24–Oct 31, $65–$135 double. Nov 1-May 23, $55–$125 double. Extra person $35. AE, MC, V. **Parking:** Free.

The New Boston Inn is "Berkshire County's oldest Publick House, faithfully serving travelers since 1737." The inn, which has uniquely decorated rooms and a restaurant is a good deal for the price. Some of the rooms are located in the Main House, which is more formal, and therefore a bit more pricey, while the others (in the Carriage House) are less formal and might fit a tighter budget. The inn is entirely no-smoking and has some handicapped accessible rooms.

THE OLD INN ON THE GREEN & GEDNEY FARM, Star Rte. 70, New Marlborough, MA 01230. Tel. 413/229-3131. 16 rms (12 with bath).

$ **Rates:** Inn on the Green $85–$130 double; Gedney Farm $155–$235 double. MC, V. **Parking:** Free.

You'll get your money's worth at the Old Inn on the Green & Gedney Farm. The Old Inn houses several rooms with private or shared bath that are decorated with antique or country furnishings—they are lovely rooms, but they're similar to those you'd find in any other country inn. However, the rooms in the Gedney Farm building (which is a converted dairy barn) are extraordinary and quite special. In the barn you will find two-level suites with a bedroom and bathroom upstairs and a sitting area downstairs. You'll be charmed by the rich colors (which lend almost a southwestern touch to the country inn), exposed beams, Turkish kilim rugs, French tapestry, down sofas, whirlpool tubs, and indoor balconies. Some of these rooms even have fireplace. Everything here is meant to please the eye and ease the spirit—all the way down to the 80 acres of land on which the inn is situated.

ORCHARD SHADE, Maple Avenue (P.O. Box 669) Sheffield, MA 01257

Tel. 413/229-8463. 7 rms (none with bath). **Directions:** Take Rte. 7 to Maple Ave. Orchard Shade is about 200 yards down the road.
$ Rates: (including breakfast): $55–$70 single or double. No credit cards. **Parking:** Free.

Orchard Shade, a white clapboard house built in 1840, has been operating as a guesthouse since 1888. As you enter, you'll see the living room on your right, which is filled with interesting little knick-knacks, a grand piano, family portraits, a lacquer desk, books, sculpture, and a comfortable sitting area. To the left is the dining room, where each morning you'll dine at a Georgian table in front of a brick fireplace on a breakfast of bread, muffins, sticky buns, fruit, and cereal. The rooms share bathrooms and are brightly decorated with floral wallpapers, wicker, and painted cottage furnishings, and some antiques.

WHERE TO DINE

CASTLE STREET CAFE, 10 Castle St. Tel. 528-5244.
   Cuisine: NEW AMERICAN. **Reservations:** Recommended.
$ Prices: Appetizers $2.50–$5; main courses $8–$19. DISC, MC, V.
   Open: Lunch daily noon–4pm; dinner daily 5–10pm.

The Castle Street Café is one of Great Barrington's hottest new restaurants, and it offers good food in a casual yet cosmopolitan atmosphere. The restaurant consists of a large room with exposed brick on one side, and a white wall decorated with paintings and food ads. While relaxing with a drink and listening to the soft jazz playing in the background, you might consider ordering the grilled shiitake mushrooms to start (they're wonderful!), and then move on to sautéed shrimp with broccoli and sundried tomatoes and garlic sauce; or steak chasseur with a shallot, tarragon, and mushroom sauce. As a side dish, try the grilled peasant bread with garlic, olive oil, and tomato. Dessert is a must—they're famous for their chocolate mousse cake. There's a small bar at the back of the restaurant. This is a great place for a romantic dinner.

12. EGREMONT

4 miles (6.5km) SW of Great Barrington

GETTING THERE   See "Getting There" in "Lee," above, and at the beginning of this chapter.

ESSENTIALS   The **area code** is 413. The **Berkshire Visitors Bureau,** Berkshire Common, Pittsfield, MA 01201 (tel. 413/443-9186, or toll free 800/237-5747 in the U.S. and Canada), can provide you with information on all of Berkshire County, covering the entire western end of Massachusetts.

The first thing you must know is that Egremont actually consists of two towns. North Egremont is a tiny place on Route 71, due west of Great Barrington. It has a country store, an inn-restaurant, and a few houses. South Egremont is a much bigger place, with several inns and restaurants, shops, and churches, and more antique dealers than you've ever seen in one place before. South Egremont, on Routes 23 and 41, is 4 miles southwest of Great Barrington.

WHERE TO STAY

IN SOUTH EGREMONT

EGREMONT INN, Old Sheffield Rd., South Egremont, MA 01258. Tel. 413/528-2111. Fax 413/528-6133. 22 rms (all with bath). A/C TEL

$ Rates: $90–$110 single; $100–$120 double. Extra person $15. AE, MC, V. **Parking:** Free, on premises.

A block off the highway in South Egremont (follow the signs) is the Egremont Inn, sometimes called the 1780 Egremont Inn. A stagecoach inn since the early days of the Republic, the inn's guest rooms now are fitted out with period furnishings. A swimming pool and tennis courts provide entertainment the stagecoach never had. All of the village is within walking distance. Weekends in July and August there is a 2-night minimum stay.

IN SHEFFIELD

STAVELEIGH HOUSE, S. Main St. (P.O. Box 608), Sheffield, MA 01257. Tel. 413/229-2129. 6 rms (1 with bath). **Directions:** Located on Rte. 7 in Sheffield.
$ Rates: (including breakfast): $61–$88 single; $66–$93 double. No credit cards. **Parking:** Free.

Five miles south of Great Barrington is the Staveleigh House, a homey bed-and-breakfast run by two women who enjoy the slower pace of life in this quiet corner of the state. The mood is reflected in their comfortable living room and simple but lovely guest rooms. Antiques are used here, not doted over. The innkeepers enjoy chatting with the guests, suggesting outings, and making sure repeat guests aren't served the same breakfast twice.

13. WILLIAMSTOWN

145 miles (232km) W of Boston, 165 miles (264km) NE of New York City, 23 miles (37km) N of Lenox, 14 miles (22.5km) S of Bennington

GETTING THERE   By Bus   If you are coming directly from Boston or New York City, contact **Bonanza Bus Lines** (tel. toll free 800/556-3815 or 617/423-5810 in Boston). You may have to change buses in Springfield or Pittsfield. From Montréal, take Vermont Transit (see "Getting There" at the beginning of this chapter). Local buses connect Berkshire County towns and resorts with one another.

By Car   Take U.S. 7 or Route 2 in Massachusetts or New York.

ESSENTIALS   The **area code** is 413. During the summer months, the town operates an **information booth** in the middle of town at the intersection of Routes 2 and 7, a short distance from the Williams Inn. The **Northern Berkshire Chamber of Commerce** is at 69 Main Street, North Adams, MA 01247 (tel. 413/663-3735). The **Berkshire Visitors Bureau,** Berkshire Common, Pittsfield, MA 01201 (tel. 413/443-9186, or toll free 800/237-5747 in the U.S. and Canada), can provide you with information on all of Berkshire County, covering the entire western end of Massachusetts.

SPECIAL EVENTS   The big draw from late June through the end of August is the **Williamstown Theatre Festival,** Box 517, Williamstown, MA 01267 (tel. 597-3399 for information, 597-3400 for the box office). The **Main Stage** company puts on five principal productions in the 500-seat Adams Memorial Theatre on Main Street, and the smaller (96-seat) **Other Stage** next door is the scene for new works by both young and established playwrights. The festival's **Cabaret** performances take place at area restaurants. There are special Sunday dramatic events at the **Clark Art Institute,** and even an open-air Free Theatre literary adaptation staged at twilight in a meadow near the town (bring a picnic dinner). After June 5, call the box office to charge tickets on your credit card.

The **Williams College Department of Music** arranges numerous concerts when college is in session. Call the Concertline at 413/597-3146 for information. In the summer, **Williamstown Chamber Concerts** (tel. 458-8273) organizes several chamber music performances at the Clark Art Institute.

The town was founded in 1753 as West Hoosuck, but its life and its name were soon affected by the career of Ephraim Williams, Jr., a soldier in the British colonial army. Born in 1714, Williams surveyed several townships in these parts, then took command of fortifications which demarcated the frontier between the British and French North American empires. Among these defenses was Fort Massachusetts, which stood in North Adams.

Williams led a column of troops from Massachusetts toward the French positions on Lake George, and died in the fighting (1755). His will provided for the founding of a school in West Hoosuck, but only if the town took his name. It did, and Williams College enrolled its first students in 1793. The college now looks forward to celebrating its 200th anniversary in 1993.

Williams College, with an annual freshman class of 2,000, is the reason the town of 8,500 exists. It's a beautiful, delightful example of the New England rural college town.

WHAT TO SEE & DO

Stop by the information booth and pick up the brochure entitled "Williamstown: A Walk Along Main Street," which gives details on the interesting buildings lining Main Street (Route 2 East), many of them now part of Williams College.

IN TOWN

STERLING AND FRANCINE CLARK ART INSTITUTE, 225 South St. Tel. 458-9545.

This is perhaps the most famous of Williamstown's cultural attractions. The institute's marvelous collections are the achievement of Robert Sterling Clark (1877–1956), a Yale engineer whose forebears had been successful in the sewing-machine industry. Clark began collecting works of art in Paris in 1912, married a French woman named Francine, and eventually housed his masterpieces in a classic white marble temple here in Williamstown.

The pristine original museum was greatly expanded in 1973, and now has strong collections of paintings by the impressionists, their academic contemporaries in France, and the mid-century Barbizon artists, including Millet, Troyon, and Corot. Of the Americans, there are significant works by Cassatt, Homer, Remington, and Sargent. Earlier centuries are represented by well-chosen pieces of Piero della Francesca, Memling, Gossaert, Jacob van Ruisdael, Fragonard, Gainsborough, Turner, and Goya. There are some sculptures, including Degas's famous *Little Dancer of Fourteen Years,* as well as prints, drawings, and noteworthy collections of silver and porcelain.

Admission: Free.

Open: Tues–Sun (also Memorial Day, Labor Day, and Columbus Day) 10am–5pm. **Closed:** Jan 1, Thanksgiving Day, Dec 25. **Directions:** From the information booth, follow South St. for less than a mile to the museum.

WILLIAMS COLLEGE MUSEUM OF ART, Main St. Tel. 597-2429.

The museum is in Lawrence Hall, the Greek Revival building with the rotunda, on Main St. Call to ask about current exhibits, which are lively, timely, and well displayed in the museum's galleries and dramatic open spaces.

Admission: Free.

Open: Mon–Sat 10am–5pm, Sun 1–5pm.

NEARBY

Five miles east of Williamstown along Route 2, in North Adams, a road goes off to the right, climbing the slopes of **Mount Greylock** (3,491 ft.), the highest point in Massachusetts. If the weather is clear, drive the several miles to the top, where you'll find marvelous views, the AMC Bascom Lodge (see below under "Where to Stay"), and a curious, imposing 92-foot-high war memorial that was originally designed as a lighthouse. The memorial is open to the public.

Other roads approach the summit from the south, starting from U.S. 7 at New Ashford or Lanesboro.

While you're up here, explore some of the 40 miles of **hiking trails** (including part of the Appalachian Trail) which thread through the forest of the Mount Greylock State Reservation's 11,000 acres. Bascom Lodge will sell you a simple but satisfying and portable trail lunch for less than $3.

WHERE TO STAY

Far enough from Tanglewood to avoid the crush of its summer crowds, Williamstown is favored with a fine selection of small guesthouses and inns, two full-service hotels, and several moderately priced motels. You should have little trouble finding the sort of room you want in this charming Berkshire town, except when college events are in progress. Reserve early for dates in September (classes begin), October (foliage season), and early June (graduation).

SMALL INNS & GUESTHOUSES

FIELD FARM GUEST HOUSE, 554 Sloan Rd., Williamstown, MA 01267.
   Tel. 413/458-3135. 5 rms (all with bath). **Directions:** Follow U.S. Rte. 7 south 4 miles to junction of Rte. 43. Turn right onto 43, then immediately right onto Sloan Rd. Field Farm is 1 mile up Sloan Rd.
$ Rates: (including breakfast): $83 double. No credit cards. **Parking:** Free.

A guesthouse in the country near historic Williamstown conjures images of a quaint Berkshire farmhouse or exuberant Victorian inn, so Field Farm comes as a surprise, almost as a shock. Set on 254 acres, the house was the country villa of Lawrence H. and Eleanore Bloedel, noted art collectors, who built it in 1948 in the clean, spare, understated style that came to dominate in the 1950s. Field Farm was bequeathed to The Trustees of Reservations in 1984. Dave and Judy Loomis of River Bend Farm administer the Field Farm Guest House. The guest rooms share baths; four face the sunny lawns (three have their own decks), one faces the back. The huge, airy living room and dining room, tennis court, swimming pool, and hiking trails are yours to enjoy. Field Farm is open all year.

HOUSE ON MAIN STREET, 1120 Main St., Williamstown, MA 01267.
   Tel. 413/458-3031. 6 rms (3 with bath).
$ Rates: (including breakfast): $66 single without bath; $82 double without bath; $93 double with bath. MC, V. **Parking:** Free.
This nice old Victorian house renovated by Henny Poses is open as a bed-and-breakfast in the warm months. Call for advance reservations if you can.

RIVER BEND FARM, 643 Simonds Rd. (U.S. 7 North), Williamstown, MA 01267. Tel. 413/458-5504 or 458-3121. 5 rms (none with bath). **Directions:** Go north on U.S. 7 a mile from Williamstown's information booth in the center of town; turn left onto the private drive immediately after crossing a bridge over the river.
$ Rates: (including breakfast): $60 double without bath. No credit cards. **Parking:** Free.

Our favorite place in Williamstown is the River Bend Farm, open April through November. This 1770 roadside inn and tavern-turned-farmhouse has been lovingly restored by Dave and Judy Loomis, who run it with an engaging, low-key, unpretentious style that makes guests immediately feel at home. Tru-country-inn feeling is provided by the hosts' warm welcome, the variety of interesting old furnishings at the inn, and the bounteous, delicious breakfast included in the price.

FULL-SERVICE HOTELS

THE ORCHARDS, 222 Adams Rd., Williamstown, MA 01267. Tel. 413/ 458-9611, or toll free 800/225-1517. Fax 413/458-3273. 49 rms (all with bath). A/C TV TEL **Directions:** Head 1 mile east of the center of campus on Rte. 2.
$ Rates: Late May–Oct, $135–$215 single or double. Nov–late May, $115–$195 single or double. AE, CB, DC, MC, V. **Parking:** Free.

The Orchards is the top-of-the-line hostelry in Williamstown. Thought it's a fairly simple modern stucco building on the outside, the inn's interior is an eclectic gallery of English antiques, Oriental carpets, and furnishings of classic design. The owners are especially proud of the 18th-century carved oak mantelpiece in the lounge, a nice little army of Victorian tin soldiers, and a fine collection of silver teapots. The courtyard has a quiet garden; there's also a swimming pool and exercise room. Standard guest rooms are nicely furnished in subdued colors, with thick carpets, his-and-hers washbasins, tub and shower trimmed in marble, and all the expected luxury-hotel touches. Superior rooms are larger, and some have a four-poster bed, fireplace, and little refrigerator. All rooms have one or two antique accent pieces (perhaps an armoire, desk, or dresser). The dining room is the fanciest in town (see "Where to Dine," below). There is live music on Friday and Saturday nights from 8:30pm to 12:30am.

WILLIAMS INN, On the Green, Williamstown, MA 01267. Tel. 413/458- 9371. Fax 413/458-2767. 100 rms (all with bath). A/C TV TEL **Directions:** At the junction of Rtes. 2 and 7 on the Williams College campus.
$ Rates: Apr–Oct, $88–$110 single; $121–$148 double. Nov–Mar, $5–$20 less. Package plans available. Children under 14 stay free in parents' room. AE, DC, DISC, MC, V. **Parking:** Free.

The Williams Inn is the town's largest hostelry, with rooms equipped with colonial-style furniture and the amenities expected in a comfortable full-service hotel. This is the "college hotel," a very comfortable place with a good dining room, a less formal tavern lounge, a heated indoor pool, men's and women's saunas, and a spa. You can walk to any point on campus from here. Pets are welcome in first-floor rooms. November through March, prices are lower.

A HIKERS' LODGE

The Appalachian Mountain Club operates **AMC Bascom Lodge,** P.O. Box 1652, Lanesboro, MA 01237 (tel. 413/743-1591; off-season, call 603/466-2727) in the Mount Greylock State Reservation atop Massachusetts's highest peak. Bascom Lodge is one of those substantial, well-designed rustic hostelries built by the Civilian Conservation Corps in the 1930s; it's open from mid-May through late October. The simple accommodations here benefit from the mountain air and the closeness of the park's hiking trails, not to mention the panoramic views. The 28 beds in the bunkroom, covered in snowy sheets and red wool blankets, cost $20 per adult, $11 per child under 12, excluding tax; the four private rooms go for $45 double. These nonmember rates are for Friday and Saturday from July on; prices are a few dollars lower on other days, and for AMC members. Simple but hearty, wholesome meals are served from an open kitchen in the spacious dining room overlooking the mountains; dinner costs less than $10 and an all-you-can-eat breakfast $5 for adults, $3 for children. Call first, then write for reservations.

WHERE TO DINE

You can easily find a good meal in town, and you may get entertainment as well. During the summer months when the Williamstown Theater Festival is in progress, cabaret troupes offer song-and-dance revues in some local restaurants after the curtain has fallen on the festival's main evening performance. When you've exhausted all the dining possibilities in Williamstown, try one of the places in Bennington, Vt., a mere 13 miles to the north along U.S. 7.

EXPENSIVE

LE COUNTRY, 101 North St. Tel. 458-4000.
Cuisine: AMERICAN. **Reservations:** Recommended.
$ Prices: Appetizers $3–$9; dinner $30–$40. AE, MC, V.
Open: Lunch Tues–Fri 11:30am–1:30pm; dinner Tues–Sun 5–9pm.
Le Country, located 100 yards down the hill from the information booth, has a long-standing reputation for good, standard fare in pleasant surroundings. Rough boards accent the dining room's white walls, and hunting prints add a note of country gentry life. The menu is short and to the point, listing longtime favorites such as coquilles St-Jacques, chicken divan, filet mignon, coq au vin, and veal curry. Start with marinated herring or shrimp cocktail, and end with cheesecake, pecan pie, or baba au rhum. The wine list, too, is short and to the point, with bottles well chosen and prices surprisingly moderate, about $10 to $20, with a few up to $35. Service is slow (you are warned on the menu) but competent and friendly.

LE JARDIN, 777 Cold Spring Rd. Tel. 458-8032.
Cuisine: FRENCH/AMERICAN. **Reservations:** Recommended. **Directions:** Go 2 miles south of town along U.S. Rte. 7.
$ Prices: Appetizers $3–$8; main courses $13–$20; dinner $40. AE, MC, V.
Open: Dinner Mon–Sat 5–10pm, Sun 5–9pm.
The inn named Le Jardin is noted for excellent dinners graciously served in semiformal old-fashioned country-inn dining rooms.

THE ORCHARDS, 222 Adams Rd. Tel. 458-9611.
Cuisine: CONTINENTAL. **Reservations:** Required. **Directions:** From the information booth, go 2 miles east along Rte. 2 to the hotel, on the right.
$ Prices: Appetizers $2.75–$8; main courses $5.50–$10.50 at lunch, $35–$45 at dinner. AE, DC, MC, V.
Open: Breakfast Mon–Sat 7:30–10am, Sun 8–9am; lunch Mon–Sat noon–2pm; dinner daily 5:30–9pm; Sun brunch 9am–2pm.
Williamstown's fanciest is the dining room of The Orchards, open for all three meals every day. The inn's several small dining rooms, though of modern construction, gleam with dark-wood accents, mirrors, and brass candle lamp sconces. Potted plants and antiques lend an old-fashioned air. Chef Kevin Cook's interesting menu of comestibles combines traditional favorites with original creations. It changes daily, but recently he offered appetizers of smoked trout with Gribiche sauce, sautéed escargots with roasted red peppers, and grilled quail with wild mushrooms alongside shrimp cocktail, clam chowder, and lobster bisque. Main courses included grilled sirloin, poached salmon, and such intriguing dishes as braised pheasant and polenta with shiitake-rosemary demiglace, or sautéed sweetbreads with crawfish Madeira demiglace. The pastry cart is bounteous, as you might imagine. On Sunday, come for brunch; any afternoon, come for tea in the parlor.

MODERATE

For moderately priced meals in Williamstown you must seek out Water Street (Route 43), the town's small commercial district; turn south off Route 2 by the Methodist church in the midst of the campus.

RIVER HOUSE, 123 Water St. Tel. 458-4820.
Cuisine: REGIONAL. **Reservations:** Recommended.
$ Prices: Appetizers $2–$6; main courses $9–$16; dinner $10–$16. AE, MC, V
Open: Dinner Tues–Sun 4–10pm.
The River House, on Route 43 in the center of town, is Williamstown's most popular downtown restaurant. The homey, rustic dining room is pleasant and informal, with a

fireplace, soft candlelight, a long wine-and-spirits list, and a menu that pleases everyone. Have roast turkey, steak, an Italian specialty, or baked scrod for dinner, and you'll get a salad, fresh bread, and rice pilaf with it. The Tavern Room opens at 4pm.

SPECIALTY DINING

For a quick breakfast, sandwich, pizza, snack, or ice-cream cone the place to go is **Spring Street,** 1 long block west of Water Street in the midst of the campus. This short commerical street is crowded with good places to find quick pick-me-ups, like the **Slippery Banana Deli** (tel. 458-4788), **Colonial Pizza** (tel. 458-8014), a bakery called the **Clarksburg Bread Co.,** 37 Spring St. (tel. 458-2251), and **Goodies Cafe** (tel. 458-3916).

CHAPTER 9

RHODE ISLAND

- **WHAT'S SPECIAL ABOUT RHODE ISLAND**
1. **PROVIDENCE**
- **WALKING TOUR—PROVIDENCE OLD & NEW**
2. **NEWPORT**
3. **FROM SAUNDERSTOWN TO POINT JUDITH**
4. **BLOCK ISLAND**
5. **WATCH HILL**

Just because Rhode Island is the smallest state in the Union, many people assume that the variety of things to see and do in this corner of New England is limited. Not so. The state's beaches are famed throughout the region, sites and structures of historical importance abound, the cities are pleasant and of manageable size, and then there's Newport —a world apart. In fact, the only real effect the state's small size seems to have is to make the residents feel that they are a part of a very special place—which they are—and to make everything easily accessible to the visitor.

In the 1600s, when New England was being colonized by Europeans, the best solution to a community conflict was for the weaker of the conflicting parties to shove off into the wilderness and found and develop their own community. To save his skin and freely express his beliefs, Roger Williams left Puritan Salem in 1636 and came to Narragansett Bay, followed soon afterward by others who shared his views, or at least knew they would be allowed to disagree. Williams was ahead of the times in his political, religious, and ethical thinking, and his contribution to the American democratic tradition is very important: In his new community of Providence, citizens could think and say what they liked. In the years that followed the founding of Providence, Williams persuaded Parliament to include the settlements of Portsmouth and Newport on Rhode Island with his own Providence Plantation under the same charter—these towns had also been founded by dissenters who desired freedom of thought and speech—thus securing for the colony as a whole the right of absolute liberty in matters of belief. The official name of the state to this day remains "Rhode Island and Providence Plantations."

Today Rhode Island is a manufacturing center, a maritime state, with a lot of rich agricultural land and several important industries. But the summer vacationers who come to Rhode Island—beginning with the very wealthy socialites who started the custom in the 19th century—are also an important part of the economy, and the state government does a lot to see that "Little Rhodie" retains the lure it had for those discriminating types who built palatial mansions in Newport, Watch Hill, and other coastal towns.

One event not to miss, if you take your vacation at the right time, is **May Breakfasts.** May is officially celebrated as Heritage Month in Rhode Island, commemorating that "Little Rhodie" was the first colony to declare independence from British rule (May 4, 1776). On May 1, or thereabouts, May Day Breakfasts are held by all sorts of church, civic, and fraternal organizations across the state, and the public is invited to most of them. These can be pretty lavish affairs, and you're sure to get your money's worth.

Rhode Island is known for its beaches, and some of the finest are along the state's southwestern shore: wonderful names such as Misquamicut, Weekapaug, an

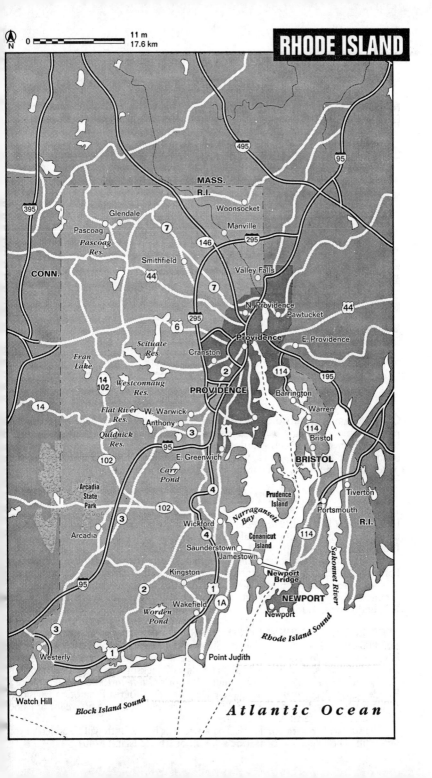

RHODE ISLAND

0 ⟶ 11 m
17.6 km

MASS.
R.I.

CONN.

Glendale
Pascoag
Pascoag Res.
Woonsocket
Manville
Smithfield
Valley Falls
N. Providence
Pawtucket
Providence
Cranston
E. Providence
Scituate Res.
Fran Lake
Westconnaug Res.
PROVIDENCE
Barrington
Warren
Flat River Res.
W. Warwick
Anthony
Bristol
BRISTOL
Quidnick Res.
E. Greenwich
Arcadia State Park
Carr Pond
Prudence Island
Tiverton
Portsmouth
R.I.
Arcadia
Wickford
Narragansett Bay
Conanicut Island
Saunderstown
Jamestown
Newport Bridge
Sakonnet River
Kingston
NEWPORT
Wakefield
Newport
Worden Pond
Westerly
Point Judith
Watch Hill
Block Island Sound
Rhode Island Sound
Atlantic Ocean

WHAT'S SPECIAL ABOUT RHODE ISLAND

Museums
- ☐ The Rhode Island School of Design's Museum of Art, in Providence.
- ☐ Newport, the home of the International Tennis Hall of Fame and Tennis Museum.

Houses & Gardens
- ☐ The palatial mansions of Newport, bringing to life the resort's turn-of-the-century opulence.

Architectural Highlights
- ☐ Rhode Island's harmonious white-marble Capitol in Providence.
- ☐ Touro Synagogue, in Newport, designed by Peter Harrison and built in 1763.

Events/Festivals
- ☐ "May Breakfasts" celebrating Rhode Island's patriotic heritage.

- ☐ The Newport Music Festival, bringing together well-known artists each July to perform in the great mansions.
- ☐ Block Island Race Week, in late June, featuring boat races and parties.
- ☐ Newport Folk Festival & JVC Jazz Festival in August.

Cool for Kids
- ☐ The 1883 Carousel in Watch Hill, one of the oldest merry-go-rounds in the nation.

Beaches
- ☐ Narragansett Bay and Rhode Island's southern shore, known for their broad swaths of sand.

Quonochontaug identify the built-up areas along the strand. The buildings are usually private homes, or snack bars and restaurants, and much of the waterfront land is privately owned and fiercely guarded. But the state beaches dotted along the shore are open to all at a fee of $2 per car with Rhode Island plates, $4 per car with out-of-state plates during the week, a dollar more on weekends and holidays.

SEEING RHODE ISLAND

I-95 connects Rhode Island to the Connecticut coast and Boston. From Cape Cod, take I-195 via New Bedford to Fall River (where you turn south for Providence), or to Providence.

For orientation purposes, remember that Rhode Island has three main towns: Portsmouth in the north, Newport at the southern end, and Middletown in between.

Car-ferries connect Block Island with the mainland at Galilee year round. In summer, passenger ferries operate to Block Island from Providence and Newport, R.I., and New London, Conn.

INFORMATION/ORIENTATION For Rhode Island tourist information, call toll free 800/556-2484 from the United States and Canada. You can also write to the **Rhode Island Tourism Division,** which issues brochures, maps, lists of festivals and special events, and other useful materials, at 7 Jackson Walkway, Providence, R 02903 (tel. 401/277-2601). For the state's *Visitor's Guide to Rhode Island,* write to Rhode Island Department of Economic Development, Tourist Promotion Division, 7 Jackson Walkway, Providence, RI 02903. This pamphlet has a complete list of Rhode Island events and festivals for the current year.

The statewide **room tax** is 5%. The **sales tax** is 7%. Both will be added to your hotel bill. The telephone **area code** for all of Rhode Island is 401.

1. PROVIDENCE

32 miles (51.5km) NW of New Bedford, 45 miles (73km) SW of Boston,
55 miles (89km) NE of New London, 30 miles (48km) N of Newport

GETTING THERE By Plane Rhode Island is so compact that one airport handles all the important national flights. **T. F. Green State Airport** in Warwick, is just a few miles south of Providence. From the airport, you'll have to take a taxi to the center of Providence.

By Train Ten trains a day each from New York (trip time: 4 hr.) and Boston (trip time: 1 hr.) arrive in Providence's modern, white marble **Amtrak** railroad station (tel. 800/USA-RAIL).

By Bus The terminals for **Bonanza** (tel. 401/751-8800) and **Greyhound** are a block from Kennedy Plaza. Both run several buses daily to Providence from New York City, Boston, Newport, Hartford, Cape Cod, Springfield (Mass.), and Albany. Travel time from New York is about 4 hours; from Boston or Newport about 1 hour, from Cape Cod (Hyannis) about 1½ hours.

By Car I-95 goes right through the center of Providence on its way between New York and Boston; right downtown I-195 branches off to go through Fall River (the turnoff for Newport), New Bedford, and then on to Cape Cod.
   Note: Street **parking** in Providence is scarce, and meters are checked frequently. The center of town has lots of private pay lots, which is best to use if you need to be downtown. Otherwise, park on a side street on College Hill, where there's plenty of shade and no time limit.

ESSENTIALS The **area code** is 401. The information office is at the **Greater Providence Convention and Visitors Bureau,** 30 Exchange Terrace, Providence, RI 02903 (tel. 401/274-1636). Drop by, or telephone them, with any of your questions about the city.

Providence is a pretty city. The downtown area is compact enough that a visitor can get off the train, or park the car, and walk to just about everything there is to see and do. The State Capitol, a pleasant and harmonious building of white Georgia marble, crowns a hilltop on the edge of the downtown section. College Hill rises from the east bank of the Providence River, which runs through downtown; Brown University, the Rhode Island School of Design, and a collection of exceptionally beautiful and interesting houses from the 17th, 18th, and 19th centuries give College Hill its character.
   The city was founded in 1636 by Roger Williams (1603–83), who had been minister of the church at Salem, Mass., but whose freethinking religious ideas had made the General Court banish him from Massachusetts Bay. (He held that the Massachusetts Bay charter was not legal; that the Puritans should face the fact that they had really separated from the Church of England, whether they chose to admit it or not; and that in matters of conscience no civil authority had any power—no wonder the powers-that-be thought him a dangerous man!) He dedicated his new settlement of Providence to the proposition that all people should have freedom of conscience. A good number came from Massachusetts, and others came directly from England, to the new colony. Williams had bought the land for the town from the Narragansett tribe, and he remained on very good terms with them, even writing a book on their language that was published and sold in England.
   Providence became the first colony to declare independence from England, in May 1776. After the revolutionary war, it took over from Newport the position as the state's most important seaport. It's still an important port, and its industries of

textiles, machine tools, rubber, jewelry, and boatbuilding also contribute to its prosperity.

WHAT TO SEE & DO

Preservation and urban redevelopment have done much to make Providence a delightful place to walk in today. The most interesting districts are small enough that you can make your way around on foot. For an expert look at Providence's historical treasures, consider the following.

WALKING TOURS

The **Providence Preservation Society,** 21 Meeting St. (tel. 401/831-7440), offers two audiocassettes and seven self-guided walking-tour booklets of historical areas in the city. Areas include Benefit Street, with its restored 18th- and 19th-century houses, the downtown section with its 19th- and 20th-century architecture, the waterfront, Brown University, and three Victorian neighborhoods, named Armory District, Elmwood, and Broadway. Rent a cassette for $5 or buy the booklets for 80¢ each at the society's headquarters Monday through Friday from 9am to 5pm.

WALKING TOUR — Providence Old & New

Start: Kennedy Plaza.
Finish: Prospect Terrace.
Time: About 2 hours, not including stops.
Best Times: Weekends, when there is less traffic.
Worst Times: Morning or evening rush hour.

Start your tour in:

1. **Kennedy Plaza,** in the center of town. Shady trees and benches make the plaza an oasis in the middle of the city, and an equestrian statue of Gen. Ambrose Burnside, the Civil War officer whose long side whiskers were the first "side burns," watches over the eastern end of the plaza. At the western end is:
2. **City Hall,** an agreeable Second Empire building completed in 1878 (go inside to see a wall display of other entries in the competition for the city hall design).
    Go 1 block southeast from Kennedy Plaza to reach the **Westminster Mall,** a 6-block section of Westminster Street closed to vehicles. The mall is a pleasant place to stroll or to sit and people-watch. Just past its eastern end, at 130 Westminster Street, is:
3. **The Arcade,** which looks like an imaginative bit of urban renewal, but is in fact the creation of Russell Warren and James Bucklin, who designed the building in 1827. For a century and a half some of Providence's better shops have operated in the Arcade. There are three levels of shops topped by a roof of glass panes; one modern addition to the Arcade is an elevator to take shoppers to the upper floors. Besides restaurants, the Arcade has stores selling antiques, jewelry, rare books, fine tobaccos, cosmetics, and other luxury items. Decorative cast-iron balustrades and stairways recall the Arcade's early 19th-century construction. Look at both facades—on Westminster Street and on Weybosset—which clearly show that each architect had his own idea of how the exterior should look. With two facades, each got his chance to do what he wanted.
    Walk through the Arcade from Westminster Street to Weybosset Street, and turn right. Look for the golden dome, which marks Providence's historic:
4. **Round Top Church,** officially known as the Beneficent Congregational Meetinghouse. It got its popular name because of its dome, which is a departure from the usual New England church spire. Finished in 1810, it was influenced by

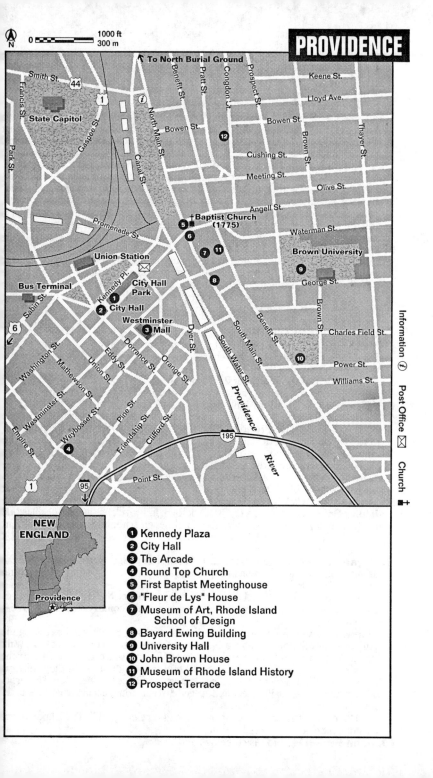

PROVIDENCE

0 ___ 1000 ft
___ 300 m

N

To North Burial Ground

Smith St.
44
Francis St.
Park St.
State Capitol
Gaspee St.
Benefit St.
Pratt St.
Congdon St.
Prospect St.
Keene St.
Lloyd Ave.
Bowen St.
Bowen St.
Brown St.
Thayer St.
North Main St.
Canal St.
Cushing St.
Meeting St.
Olive St.
Angell St.
Promenade St.
Baptist Church (1775)
Waterman St.
Brown University
Union Station
City Hall Park
Bus Terminal
Sabin St.
Kennedy Pl.
City Hall
Westminster Mall
George St.
Washington St.
Mathewson St.
Union St.
Dorrance St.
Eddy St.
Orange St.
Dyer St.
South Main St.
South Water St.
Benefit St.
Brown St.
Charles Field St.
Power St.
Williams St.
Westminster St.
Empire St.
Weybosset St.
Pine St.
Friendship St.
Clifford St.
Providence River
195
Point St.
1
95

Information ⓘ   Post Office ⊠   Church ∎✝

NEW ENGLAND

Providence

1 Kennedy Plaza
2 City Hall
3 The Arcade
4 Round Top Church
5 First Baptist Meetinghouse
6 "Fleur de Lys" House
7 Museum of Art, Rhode Island
   School of Design
8 Bayard Ewing Building
9 University Hall
10 John Brown House
11 Museum of Rhode Island History
12 Prospect Terrace

the classical revival then going on in Europe. The interior is as pleasant to look at as the exterior: Besides the gracious New England meetinghouse furnishings, the Round Top Church has a crystal chandelier consisting of almost 6,000 pieces. (Enter by the door on the side, around to the right.)

Now head northeast down Weybosset, past the Arcade, to the intersection of this street with Westminster and Exchange. Here in front of the Hospital Trust Bank, activities and shows are held during the warm months—perhaps a Boy Scouts' display of fancy marching or a small (but highly amplified) jazz combo giving a lunch-hour concert.

Walk 2 more blocks east and you will cross the Providence River to the foot of College Hill. The hill is the prettiest section of the city, its streets lined with 18th- and 19th-century houses, most of which have been well preserved or restored and many of which bear plaques, put up by the Providence Preservation Society, giving the builder's name and the date of construction. At the bottom of College Hill, on South Main Street between Thomas and Waterman Streets, take a stroll past the:

5. First Baptist Meetinghouse. Roger Williams founded the first Baptist congregation in the New World in 1638, but this building dates from 1775. The architect was Joseph Brown, and the steeple—designed from a plate in James Gibbs's *Book of Architecture* representing suggested steeples for St. Martin-in-the-Fields in London—rises to a height of 185 feet. It's one of the outstanding churches in New England, and a guide will take you through for free between the hours of 10am and 3pm Monday through Friday, 10am to noon on Saturday, and at noon on Sunday following the weekly church service. Between November and March the church is open daily, but guides are available only by appointment (tel. 751-2266). The front door of the church will probably be locked, so go around to the right to the side (office) door.

To the left of the church, at 7 Thomas Street, is a fantastic old building with half-timbering and stucco bas-reliefs on its facade. This is Sidney Burleigh's:

6. "Fleur de Lys" House, built by this Providence artist in 1885 (the date is in the stucco). Thomas Street might be called "Artists' Row," because very near Burleigh's house is the Providence Art Club, at no. 11. Open from 10am to 4pm (3 to 5pm on Sunday), the club has changing shows exhibited in its galleries. The club also runs the Dodge House at 10 Thomas Street, which has contemporary shows from September through May.

At the intersection of Waterman and Benefit Streets, turn right and go south on Benefit for a block to the:

7. Museum of Art, Rhode Island School of Design (see below). The **Rhode Island School of Design** or **RISD** (known in Providence as "*riz*-dee") is one of the country's best art, architecture, and design schools. Founded in 1877, it shares College Hill with Brown University.

You can also visit the:

8. Bayard Ewing Building, at 231 South Main St., which houses RISD's architectural division. Exhibits here change frequently, and feature architectural and industrial design.

Also up here on College Hill is Brown University (tel. 863-1000), a member of the Ivy League and the seventh-oldest university in the country. Founded in 1764, Brown's first building was:

9. University Hall, used as a barracks for colonial and French soldiers during the American Revolution. It's now a National Historic Landmark. To get to it, walk up the hill (east) on Waterman Street, cross Prospect Street, and turn into the gates on your right. If you want a full, free tour of the beautiful and historic campus, find your way to the College Admission Office, 1 block from University Hall at the corner of Prospect and Angell Streets. Tours depart from here at 10 and 11am, and 1, 3, and 4pm.

There are several other historical buildings on College Hill. The Rhode Island Historical Society operates both the:

10. John Brown House (listed below) and the:

11. Museum of Rhode Island History (tel. 331-8575), in the Aldrich House, a Federal-style mansion (1822) at 110 Benevolent Street. Changing exhibitions highlight various aspects of Rhode Island's history and citizens. Hours are Tuesday through Friday 9am to 5pm; closed holidays. Adults pay $2 for admission; seniors pay $1.50, and children under 17 pay $1; families pay a maximum of $6.

Prospect Street is so named because it passes near:

12. Prospect Terrace (go to Cushing Street and turn left). From the Terrace, a small park, you can see downtown Providence and the State Capitol, along with a famous but—rather wooden statue of the founder, Roger Williams. His grave is here as well. Trees have grown up below and block a bit of the perspective, but the view is still panoramic and impressive.

SIGHTS

MUSEUM OF ART, RHODE ISLAND SCHOOL OF DESIGN, 224 Benefit St. Tel. 454-6500.

The museum is Providence's finest, and one of the best small museums in the country, with collections from Greece and Rome, China and Japan; paintings by Manet, Monet, Degas, Cézanne, and Matisse, as well as other masters; and a good collection of American painting, furniture, costumes, and modern works of art. Of the choicest pieces in this impressive collection, Rodin's famous statue of Balzac ranks high, as does Monet's *Bassin d' Argenteuil* and the collection of Townsend/Goddard furniture in Pendleton House, the museum's "American wing."

Admission: Sun–Fri $2 adults, 50¢ senior citizens and children aged 5–18, free for children under 5; Sat free.

Open: Mid-June to Aug, Tues–Sat noon–5pm. Sept to mid-June, Tues–Wed and Fri–Sat 10:30am–5pm, Thurs noon–8pm, Sun 2–5pm.

JOHN BROWN HOUSE, 52 Power St. Tel. 331-8593.

One of the fanciest historic houses on College Hill, the late-Georgian mansion constructed in 1786 is now owned and operated by the Rhode Island Historical Society. Proclaimed by John Quincy Adams to be "the most magnificent and elegant private mansion that I have seen on this continent," this restored house-museum reveals the prosperity of post-Revolutionary Providence and houses an outstanding collection of furnishings and decorative arts. John Brown was a merchant whose ships plied the seas both east and west out of Narragansett Bay and ultimately made him a wealthy man. The Brown family, by the way, had been prominent in Providence commerce and industry since the early 1700s. John's brother, Moses, joined with Samuel Slater to set up the first water-powered cotton-spinning mill in America in 1790, now known as Slater Mill (see below). One of his nephews, Nicholas Brown, was a graduate of Rhode Island College, which was later renamed Brown College (and later, University) in his honor.

Admission (including guided tour): $5 adults, $3 seniors and college students, $2 children. Combination tickets for John Brown and Aldrich House available.

Open: Mar–Dec, Tues–Sat 11am–4pm. Jan–Feb, Sat 11am–4pm, Sun 1–4pm. **Closed:** Holidays.

THE STATE HOUSE, 82 Smith St. Tel. 277-2311 or 277-2357.

Rhode Island government was conducted in the Old State House (1762), on North Main Street between North and South Court streets, from 1762 to 1895, when the cornerstone of the new State House building was laid. The State House is a pleasant sight, its tall dome of white Georgia marble floating over the Providence skyline. Modeled on the dome of St. Peter's basilica at the Vatican, it is the world's second-largest unsupported dome (St. Peter's is first). Whether it is "the most beautiful state capitol in the country," as the state's tourist brochures claim, might be disputed by admirers of 49 other such capitols, but certainly it is one of the more beautiful.

Enter by the portal on Smith Street (Route 44) to see display cases filled with battle flags from the state's proud military units which served in the Civil War, the

Spanish-American War, and the world wars. Here also is a Civil War cannon that was hit right in the muzzle by another cannon's ball. When the crew tried to charge the cannon again, they put the powder and wad in but couldn't get the ball in; then they couldn't get the ball out. The gun was retired, but it was only in the 1960s, after the cannon had been in the Capitol for decades, that someone remembered the gunpowder charge! So after 100 years of being loaded and ready, the Civil War cannon was finally decharged. Beyond the cannon is the rich, gleaming marble interior and hallways decorated with paintings of the founding fathers of Rhode Island and Providence Plantation.

Admission: Free.

Open: Mon–Fri 8:30am–4:30pm. Last tour at 3:30pm. **Directions:** From I-95 take Smith St. (U.S. Rte. 44) west; from I-195 take S. Main St. (U.S. Rte. 44) north.

NEARBY ATTRACTIONS

Two more places to visit lie a few miles outside the center of town. **Roger Williams Park** is south of the city on Elmwood Avenue (Exit 17 from I-95) and boasts magnificently restored 19th-century Victorian buildings, the **Charles E. Smith Greenhouses,** a museum of natural history, zoo, and amusement area besides its 430 acres of beautifully kept lawns, copses, lakes, and paths. The park is open to the public for free, and special concerts and programs are scheduled throughout the summer—call 785-9450 for the latest information. The zoo is open daily from 10am to 4pm.

Water-powered cotton and textile mills changed all of New England in the 19th century, and it all started in Pawtucket, a few miles from downtown Providence. In 1793 three enterprising men named Slater, Almy, and Brown set up the first water-powered cotton-spinning factory in America, on the Blackstone River. Today the early mills and the **Sylvanus Brown House** (1758), home of the skilled artisan, make up the **Slater Mill Historic Site.** The mills have many of their old machines in working order, such as the water wheel, shafts, and pulleys in **Wilkinson Mill** (1810), and you can see them in action. Earlier handcraft devices for doing the same jobs are also on display to show you what a breakthrough the machine-filled **Slater Mill** (1793) was. Besides the permanent exhibits, traveling and temporary displays are set up from time to time, and guided tours interpret the history of the textile industry and the impact of factories on working conditions. Admission is $4 for adults, $3 for seniors, and $2 for children 6 through 14. Group rates are available. The site is open in summer, June to Labor Day, Tuesday through Saturday from 10am to 5pm, on Sunday from 1 to 5pm; in spring and fall it's open on weekends from 1 to 5pm, but closed in January and February. Call 725-8638 or write P.O. Box 727, Pawtucket, RI 02862-0727, for information. To get there, take I-95 north from Providence, get off at Exit 28, and turn left (under the highway) onto School Street. Cross the Blackstone River and turn right into Roosevelt Avenue; the site is on your right. From I-95 south take Exit 27 and follow signs to the mills.

WHERE TO STAY

Most people who visit Providence stay in motels on the outskirts of town; these offer the best value and the greatest selection, although staying out of the center entails driving and parking problems. Providence does have a choice place to stay right downtown, plus a few of the familiar and comfortable chain hotels. You could also opt for **Bed & Breakfast of Rhode Island,** 38 Bellevue Ave. (P.O. Box 3291) Newport, RI 02840 (tel. 401/849-1298, or toll free 800/828-0000; fax 401/849-1306), which will find a room for you near Providence or any other Rhode Island town. Rates depend on the room, of course, but range from $45 to $90 single, $50 to $125 double. You can call weekdays from 9am to 8pm in summer and 9am to 5pm off season, Saturdays from 9am to noon.

A tax of 11% will be added to your hotel bill.

IN PROVIDENCE

HOLIDAY INN–PROVIDENCE, 21 Atwells Ave. (at I-95), Providence, RI 02903. Tel. 401/831-3900. Fax 401/751-0007. 274 rms (all with bath). A/C TV TEL

$ Rates: $80 single; $90 double. Children 16 and under stay free parents' room. AE, DC, DISC, MC, V.
Parking: Covered, free.

Right next to the Civic Center, the 13-story, handicapped-accessible hotel has a good restaurant called the Black Swan, a lounge with live entertainment, an indoor pool, a Jacuzzi, and an exercise room. The bus and train stations are less than ½ mile away—the hotel offers free shuttle service to and from both stations. It's a good value for quality, price, location, and services.

THE OLD COURT, 144 Benefit St., Providence, RI 02903. Tel. 401/751-2002 or 351-0747. 11 rms (all with bath). A/C TEL

$ Rates (including breakfast): $75–$120 single or double. AE, MC, V. **Parking:** Free.

This handsome old three-story brick mansion is only a short walk from downtown, at the corner of North Street, on the slopes of College Hill. The house was built in 1863 as a rectory, but takes its name from the old Rhode Island Courthouse next door, which now houses the Rhode Island Historical Preservation Commission. The inn itself is a fine example of historic preservation: All of its Italianate features—12-foot ceilings, plaster moldings, crystal chandeliers, brass sconces, and ornately carved marble mantelpieces—are in place. Furnishings in the spacious, airy guest rooms are true to the period, with wallpapers sporting large flowered patterns and old-fashioned alarm clocks. But the full tiled bath attached to each room is thoroughly modern in plumbing and fixtures. This place is very nicely done, and quite charming.

OMNI BILTMORE HOTEL, 11 Dorrance St., Kennedy Plaza, Providence, RI 02903. Tel. 401/421-0700, or toll free 800/843-6664. 289 rms (all with bath). A/C MINIBAR TV TEL

$ Rates: $134–$174 single; $154–$174 double. Reduced weekend rates available. AE, CB, DC, MC, V. **Parking:** $14.

Right on Kennedy Plaza in the center of Providence, the Biltmore was the most elegant hotel in Providence when it was built in 1922, and after a $14-million renovation, it's Providence's poshest place to stay once again. More than 100 rooms have their own lounge areas; 14 are designed especially for the disabled. If you knew the Biltmore before, you'll hardly recognize it now, as much has been changed. The outstanding features of 1920s elegance have been carefully preserved, but even the facade has been redone. Now a glass-enclosed elevator starts from the hotel lobby, penetrates the three-story-high lobby ceiling, and glides up the side of the 18-floor hotel to the top.

NEARBY

Most of Providence's hotel capacity is on the outskirts of greater Providence, in the neighboring cities of Warwick near the airport to the south, Pawtucket to the north toward Boston on I-95, and Seekonk, Mass., on I-195, the road to Cape Cod. As most of these hotels and motels are right off the highway, it's a good idea to pick them according to your plans for tomorrow: If it's evening as you approach Providence, stay in Warwick and then see Providence the next day; if it's early in the day, tour through Providence and then head out I-95 to Pawtucket if your next stop is Boston, or I-195 to Seekonk if you're headed for Cape Cod. You can call for a reservation while you're seeing the sights in Providence.

COMFORT INN, 2 George St., Pawtucket, RI 02860. Tel. 401/723-6700, or toll free 800/654-2000. Fax 401/467-6780. 124 rms (all with bath). A/C TV TEL
$ Rates: $55–$98 single or double. Extra person $10. Children under 18 stay free in parents' room. AE, DC, DISC, MC, V. **Parking:** Free.
In Pawtucket, a few miles north of Providence off I-95, this is your best bet. The lodge has an indoor heated pool, a sauna, and an adjacent Hojo's restaurant open 24 hours a day. The hotel offers free shuttle service to Green State Airport.

RAMADA INN, 940 Fall River Ave. (Rte. 114A), Seekonk, MA 02771. Tel. 508/336-7300, or toll free 800/228-2828. Fax 508/336-2107. 128 rms (all with bath). A/C TV TEL **Directions:** From I-195, take the Seekonk exit to Rte. 114A.
$ Rates: $75 single; $90 double. Extra person $5. AE, DC, DISC, MC, V. **Parking:** Free, on premises.
The Ramada is structured and priced very competitively, with an indoor pool, sauna, tennis courts, lounge with live entertainment, and a children's playground.

WHERE TO DINE

Providence's sophisticated university crowd generates a need for good restaurants, and Providence has plenty. Not all of them are up on College Hill, however.

BLUEPOINT, 99 N. Main St. Tel. 272-6145.
 Cuisine: SEAFOOD. **Reservations:** Recommended.
$ Prices: Appetizers $6.50–$12.75; main courses $13.75–$24.75. AE, CB, DC, MC, V.
 Open: Dinner daily 5:30–10:30pm; bar daily 5pm–midnight.
Providence consumes almost as much succulent seafood as Newport, and a lot of the best seafood in Providence disappears at this one-room restaurant, with the oyster-and-spirits bar on the right as you enter. Bluepoint is usually filled with a classy young clientele busy talking but mostly eating. The clam chowder comes Provença (with tomatoes) or New England (with cream and potatoes). Oysters of many varieties are available on the half shell, as are littleneck and cherrystone clams. The entire menu, which changes daily, is printed on the blackboard. The specials, whether they be squid, grilled prawns, swordfish, bluefish, or scallops, constitute the best and freshest seafood at the lowest price. It's an easy walk from downtown. Smoking is only permitted in the bar.

RUE DE L'ESPOIR, 99 Hope St. Tel. 751-8890.
 Cuisine: INTERNATIONAL. **Reservations:** Recommended.
$ Prices: Appetizers $5.50–$17.50; main courses $8.95–$17.95. AE, DC, MC, V
 Open: Breakfast Tues–Fri 7:30–11am, Sat–Sun 8:30am–noon; lunch Tues–Fri 11:30am–2:30pm; dinner Sun–Thurs 5–9pm, Fri–Sat 5–10pm; brunch Sat–Sun noon–2:30pm.
About 10 blocks from Brown University, on College Hill, this restaurant takes it name from a French translation of the street it's on. Its menu is an international collection of fare, light and hearty, minceur and gourmande. There are soups, salads pastas, whole-wheat pizza, and main courses such as rack of lamb, filet mignon, and veal médaillons. Note especially the menu of "small plates"—chicken and cashew spring rolls or petite ravioli is just the thing to order with a glass of wine for a light lunch or supper. Your bill can be anything from $7 to $40, depending on how hungry and thirsty you are.

STANFORD'S, in the Omni Biltmore Hotel, Kennedy Plaza. Tel. 421-0700.
 Cuisine: AMERICAN. **Reservations:** Recommended.

$ Prices: Appetizers $2.25–$7; main courses $11–$23; meals $20–$45. AE, DC, DISC, MC, V.
Open: Daily 6:30am–1am.

On the ground floor of the Omni Biltmore Hotel is Stanford's, named for Stanford White, the famed architect who designed the Rhode Island State Capitol, the Newport and Narragansett casinos, and the original Madison Square Garden. Stanford's is "an American Bar and Grille," but both its food and decor are quite eclectic. This is a place where you can truly take your choice: Dine in the brightly colored modern café section with its angles and split levels, openness and coziness; in the more formal salon; or even in the bistrolike lounge which features live jazz Tuesday through Saturday. The long menu includes prime rib, many steaks, and jumbo shrimp.

SPECIALTY DINING

The place to go if you're just interested in an informal bite is the **Arcade,** 65 Weybosset St. (tel. 272-2340). This National Historic Landmark was built in 1828—a Greek Revival shopping arcade running between Weybosset and Westminster Streets, with three stories of shops surmounted by a glass canopy. The Arcade's ground floor is nothing but food shops, including the following: the China Inn, specializing in Chinese food; the Grand Central Cafe, serving hot and cold beverages and pastries; Hot Dogs & More; the Providence Cookie Co.; Periwinkles, which has a very full sandwich menu; Villa Pizza; the Grog Boy Bar for stronger stuff; Natural Sweetness, a vegetarian restaurant; Great Soups, which serves just that; the Ritz, serving Middle Eastern pita-bread sandwiches; Le Greque, with a full menu of Greek dishes; Baby Watson, nationally famous for its cheesecake and other desserts; and Creme de la Creme, which may not have the right French accents, but has wonderful ice cream and candy nonetheless.

---

2. NEWPORT

30 miles (48km) S of Providence, 17 miles (27km) SW of Fall River

GETTING THERE By Plane Several national and regional airlines fly into T. F. Green State Airport in Warwick, south of Providence, 30 miles (48km) northwest of Newport.

By Train Amtrak trains between Boston and New York stop in Providence, and buses run from Providence to Newport.

By Bus Bonanza Bus Lines serves Newport with a stop downtown at Newport Gateway Center, 23 America's Cup Ave. (tel. 401/846-1820). Bonanza works in conjunction with Greyhound and the Rhode Island Public Transit Authority, and has frequent daily buses from Boston (2 hr.), from Providence (1 hr.), and from New York City (5½ hr.).

By Car From I-195 in Fall River, take Route 24 south to Route 114. From western Rhode Island, follow U.S. Route 1 to Route 138 east, which crosses the Jamestown and Newport bridges to reach Newport.

By Boat There are daily boats in summer between Providence, Newport, and Block Island. (See "Block Island," below for details.)

ESSENTIALS The two most important streets in Newport are **Thames Street** (pronounced *thaymz,* not *temz*), center of the colonial section, the wharves, and modern downtown; and **Bellevue Avenue,** southeast of and parallel to Thames. Bellevue is the street with many of the old mansions on it. America's Cup Avenue is parallel to Thames and runs right along the water downtown.

The information office is the **Newport County Chamber of Commerce** office, 10 America's Cup Ave. (P.O. Box 237), Newport, RI 02840 (tel. 401/847-1600), open from 9am to 5pm daily in summer; weekends in winter from 9am to 4pm. Get help here if you're stuck without a reservation and can't find a room. They also have maps.

SPECIAL EVENTS   Newport seems to have one festival or another all summer long. For current information on exact dates and offerings, contact the **Newport County Chamber of Commerce** (see above).

Music Festivals: Perhaps the biggest annual event in the town, the **Newport Music Festival** attracts great crowds to the grand mansions for the many different concerts. There are performances morning, afternoon, and evening for 2 consecutive weeks in mid-July. Because the capacity of all the mansions and halls is limited, it's best to order tickets—and to make reservations for a hotel room—in advance. Write to the Newport Music Festival, P.O. Box 3300, Newport, RI 02840 (tel. 401/846-1133), for a list of all the concerts and performers, and the prices of tickets (usually $20 to $25). You can order tickets by phone (tel. 401/849-0700) starting in June.

The **Newport Folk Festival & JVC Jazz Festival** draw thousands of music lovers to Fort Adams State Park on alternate weekends in August. Performers include such big names as Suzanne Vega, Judy Collins, Randy Newman, B. B. King, Ray Charles, and Tony Bennett. For information on schedules and tickets ($24 to $40) call 401/847-3700. For lodging and general help contact the Newport County Chamber of Commerce (see above).

Outdoor Art Festival: The end of July sees Newport's Outdoor Art Festival, when painters, sculptors, and craftspeople display their works downtown and in several parks throughout the city.

Fishing Tournaments: From June to October, tournaments are organized periodically to see who can make a record catch of one of the familiar fish in the waters off Newport. The chamber of commerce can tell you more.

Tennis: Championships are held in July at the Newport Casino (Tennis Hall of Fame), hosting the top professional male stars. For tickets and information, contact the Hall of Fame, 194 Bellevue Ave., Newport, RI 02840 (tel. 401/849-3990).

Whatever glittering reports you've had of Newport, they're probably correct, because Newport is a fascinating, diverse place. Palatial mansions, the wealthy yachting set, major naval and Coast Guard installations, tennis tournaments, cocktails on marble terraces in the soft air of a summer's evening, or succulent seafood served in a waterfront restaurant—Newport is all of these.

Newport has enjoyed prominence during two periods in American history. In colonial times it was an important trade center, and so, like Salem, Mass., it has a lovely colonial section right downtown, much of which has been restored authentically in the styles of centuries ago. In the mid-19th century it became a resort for the very wealthy, who built what are indeed palaces in another part of town. Newport preserves remembrances of this past while pursuing its future as one of New England's prime vacation destinations: people who own yachts and people who can only afford to look at yachts, people who play tennis and those who watch it, people who live in mansions and people who take guided tours through mansions—they all flock to Newport. Besides the visitors, Newport is home to tens of thousands of Rhode Islanders who take all the glamour and glitter for granted, and who live here year round.

Several things are important to remember when you're planning a visit to Newport. First, it's crowded in summer, particularly on weekends, and when the important tennis tournaments and yacht races are being held. Second, prices tend to go up on weekends and when the yachters are around. Third, Newport prides itself or

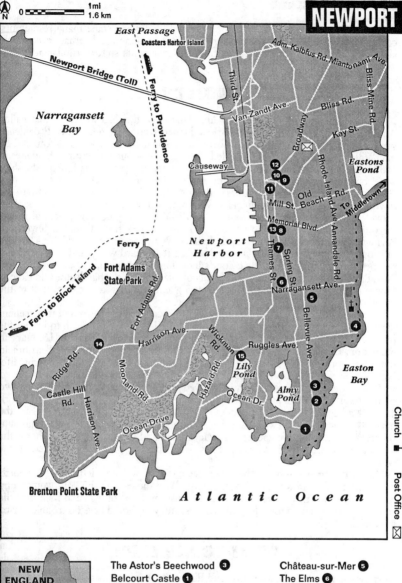

0 | 1mi
N | 1.6 km

East Passage
Coasters Harbor Island
Newport Bridge (Toll)
Ferry to Providence

Narragansett
Bay

Adm. Kalbfus Rd. Miantonami Ave.
Van Zandt Ave.
Third St.
Broadway
Bliss Rd.
Bliss Mine Rd.
Kay St.
Causeway

Eastons
Pond

Mill St.
Old
Beach Rd.
Rhode Island Ave.
Annandale Rd.
To Middletown

Newport
Harbor

Memorial Blvd.
Spring St.
Thames St.
Narragansett Ave.
Bellevue Ave.

Ferry
Ferry to Block Island
Fort Adams
State Park

Fort Adams Rd.
Harrison Ave.
Wickman Rd.
Ruggles Ave.
Hazard Rd.
Lily Pond
Ridge Rd.
Mooreland Rd.
Castle Hill Rd.
Harrison Ave.
Ocean Dr.
Ocean Drive
Almy Pond

Easton Bay

Brenton Point State Park

Atlantic Ocean

Church ✝

Post Office ⊠

NEW
ENGLAND

Newport

The Astor's Beechwood ❸
Belcourt Castle ❶
Hammersmith Farm ⑭
International Tennis Hall
of Fame and Tennis
Museum ❽
Newport Art Museum ⑬
Old Colony House ⑩
Preservation Society of Newport
County's Mansions
The Breakers ❹

Château-sur-Mer ❺
The Elms ❻
Kingscote ❼
Marble House ❷
Rosecliff ⑮
Quaker Meeting House ⑫
Touro Synagogue ❾
Trinity Church ⑪

having style, and many visitors will be dressed like movie stars; many restaurants, cocktail lounges, and hotels require "proper" dress at dinner, and perhaps even lunch: jacket, or jacket and tie for men, skirt and top or pants suit, or similar attire, for women.

HISTORY

Newport is at the southern tip of an island that the Native Americans called Aquidneck, and that the colonial settlers dubbed Rhode Island. Just as Providence was settled by Roger Williams, dissident from Salem, so Newport was founded by one William Coddington, who decided to strike out on his own from Providence in 1639. The new town soon became famous for shipbuilding, and as soon as the ships were built in sufficient numbers, for trade. The famous "triangle trade," from Newport to ports in the West Indies and Africa, would later bring great wealth to the town from the buying and selling of slaves, rum, molasses, and other goods. Because Providence and Newport were founded by dissidents, they became places of refuge for others wishing to worship as they pleased: Quakers from England, Jews from Portugal and Spain, and Baptists all came to Newport in the mid-1600s to find religious freedom. They brought talent and a gift for hard work, and the settlement prospered so that it became the colony's most important town, and one of the New World's busiest ports. The many beautiful colonial homes, the handsome Old Colony House (center of government), Touro Synagogue, and other landmarks attest to the wealth and prosperity of Newport at the time.

During the American Revolution the British occupied the town and its excellent harbor, and held it for 3 years. A British frigate, HMS *Rose*, did much to hinder the transport of supplies to the Americans, and spurred them to found the U.S. Navy in retaliation. Despite a French naval blockade and an American siege, the British held onto Newport until 1779, and after this interruption in its social and economic life, Newport never regained its status as Rhode Island's prime trade center.

Several decades later, however, it achieved prominence in another fashion. Drawn by the beautiful woods and dramatic coastline, wealthy merchants from New York and Philadelphia began to come to Newport to spend their summers. In the mid-1800s the first of Newport's famous mansions, Château-sur-Mer, was built, and others followed until Newport's Bellevue Avenue and Ocean Drive could boast the highest concentration of summer palaces—and they are *palaces*—anywhere in the world.

Today the city's symbol is the pineapple, a sign of welcome left from Newport's great commercial era when traders back from West Indies with this fruit would put a pineapple outside their warehouses to invite customers to come in and look over the stock. Newport is used to welcoming visitors, and you should have no trouble having a good time.

WHAT TO SEE & DO

There is plenty to see in Newport, and during the summer there are also plenty of people here to see it. Parking places are at a premium, although the situation is certainly not hopeless. But why bother? If you are among the readers of this book who live close enough to Newport to make it practicable, why not bring a bicycle, or rent one when you get here? You can't really see the mansions by car—you always have to keep moving (the car behind you will make sure you do)—and Newport is small enough so that even an out-of-shape biker can see the town without much of a strain.

The **Newport Historical Society** sponsors **walking tours** of historic Newport on Friday and Saturday from mid-June through September, departing at 10am from the society's headquarters at 82 Touro St. (tel. 846-0813). The cost for an adult is $5; children under 12 can come along for free.

Should you want to get the "lay of the land" before heading out to see individual sights, take a bus tour of the town, Ocean Drive, Bellevue Avenue, and other districts. You don't necessarily have to take a tour that stops and goes through a mansion, although those are offered as well. **Viking Tours,** in the Gateway Visitor's Center (tel. 847-6921), will take you on a 22-mile Newport tour for $11 (kids, $4.50); throw in another few bucks to go through one mansion. Viking also has hour-long harbor tours from Goat Island for $6 (kids, $3) that include a visit to Hammersmith Farm.

THE MANSIONS

Newport boasts mansions of two types these days: those that are museums open to the public, and those that are still private summer residences and are emphatically *not* open to the public. Believe it or not, many of these palatial houses are indeed still privately owned, maintained, and lived in. Interestingly, the wealthy people who live in private Newport mansions are often also responsible for opening others to the public. Through the efforts of The Preservation Society of Newport County, to which many of the mansion-owners belong, the marvelous houses we can tour today were preserved. To think that The Elms, perhaps the most graceful and charming of all the mansions, was to be torn down to make way for a housing development before The Preservation Society bought it is astounding.

Not all the mansions that are open to the public are owned by The Preservation Society, however. Several notable houses are privately maintained and open to visitors on terms similar to those of the society houses. When visiting the mansions, remember these two rules of thumb: First, figure on at least an hour per house to take it all in; second, don't try to see more than three or four houses in 1 day unless you have a tremendous capacity for absorbing glitter and magnificence. More than that in 1 day will leave you dizzy and exhausted. Also, try to visit the mansions on a weekday, when the crowds are smaller, saving Saturday and Sunday for Newport's other attractions. If you must go on Saturday, get there early.

PRESERVATION SOCIETY OF NEWPORT COUNTY'S MANSIONS, 118 Mill St. Tel. 847-1000.

The Preservation Society of Newport County maintains six Newport mansions, plus **Hunter House** (a colonial house built in 1748), and **Green Animals** (a topiary garden with 80 sculptured trees and shrubs, many in the shapes of animals, in Portsmouth to the north of Newport). Marble House, The Elms, Château-sur-Mer, and Green Animals are decorated for the holiday season in December.

The Breakers: Certainly the most grandiose of the mansions and most popular with visitors is The Breakers, an Italian Renaissance palace built for Cornelius Vanderbilt. It is nothing short of sumptuous, with lavish use of the finest marble. The marble columns in the two-story-high Great Hall have capitals carved of alabaster. Priceless tapestries, fine mosaic work, irreplaceable paintings, and ornate furniture testify to the wealth of The Breakers' owners. Designed by Richard Morris Hunt, who did a great many buildings in New England and particularly in Newport, The Breakers was built in only 2 years—hard to believe.

Besides the mansion, there is a children's cottage on the grounds (included in the price of admission to the mansion.).

The Elms: E. J. Berwind, son of a Philadelphia tradesman, got an appointment to the U.S. Naval Academy, and served in the Navy until mustered out with high rank because of an injury. He soon made it big in the coal business, and secured the contract to supply all U.S. Navy ships with coal. With the profits he built The Elms, perhaps the most gracious and pleasant of the Newport mansions. Although it is grand, it is also supremely harmonious, having been modeled on a château in France. The sunken formal garden at the far end of the spacious lawn was designed by a French landscape artist. The Elms is the masterpiece of Philadelphia architect Horace Trumbauer. It was threatened with destruction when a land development firm bought it and planned to build a housing project on the site, but was saved by the zoning laws and The Preservation Society. Few of the original furnishings are left, but the mansion has been furnished with pieces from museum collections and private lenders.

Château-sur-Mer: The first stone mansion to go up on Bellevue Avenue was Château-sur-Mer (1852), built as a home for William S. Wetmore of New York. Wetmore's son, who met Richard Morris Hunt while on a tour of Europe, was responsible for bringing the American-born architect to Newport to rebuild his mansion, and later the mansions of others. (The senior Wetmore had lived in the mansion 10 years before he died, and upon his death his son took it over.) The Château is very rich Victorian Gothic, and to modern tastes it seems luxurious, but dark and heavy. Château-sur-Mer has the feeling of being lived in and enjoyed— something that can't be said of some of the other mansions.

Marble House: Richard Morris Hunt threw himself into building this mansion for William K. Vanderbilt and finished it in 1892. It was modeled on the palace at Versailles, and is therefore decorated pretty much in the style of Louis XIV, which was, well, pretty grandiose—you'll see! As in The Breakers, the furnishings in Marble House are all original to the building. You'll see the Gold Room, a ballroom decorated with a king's ransom in gold, the kitchen, and the fascinating Chinese teahouse.

Kingscote: Built in 1839, Kingscote is the type of "summer cottage" lived in by wealthy visitors to Newport before the great stone mansions were built. First built for G. N. Jones of Georgia by Richard Upjohn, it was later acquired by a merchant in the China trade called William H. King, who gave the house its name. A cottage it isn't, for no peasant lived here; but rather a man who appreciated Tiffany glass and a gorgeous dining room.

Rosecliff: Another famous New England architect, Stanford White, built Rosecliff in 1902 for Mrs. Hermann Oelrichs, whose father had made a fortune in the Comstock Lode of the California Gold Rush. The building is modeled on the Grand Trianon, the larger of the two châteaux in the park at Versailles, but was meant to be even more lavish in layout and decor. Its ballroom is the largest one in Newport, and the mansion is still used for summer entertainment.

Admission: A combination ticket for all attractions costs $32.50 for adults, $10 for children aged 6–11. Tickets for individual mansions cost $6–$7.50 adults, $3–$3.50 children, but since you'll probably be seeing more than one mansion, buy a "strip ticket" good for two mansions ($11), three ($16), four ($19), five ($22), six ($25.50), or seven mansions ($29.50). (All eight houses will cost you $32.50. Children's prices are less than half of these. Tickets are on sale at any of the society' mansions.

Admission to any mansion includes an informative tour through the rooms, and the right to stroll about the grounds at your leisure. Tours are frequent, and the guides are usually well informed.

Open: May–Oct, daily 10am–5pm (July–Sept, The Breakers is open Sa 10am–8pm). In Apr, the three fanciest mansions (The Breakers, Marble House, and Rosecliff) open daily 10am–5pm; the rest open Sat–Sun 10am–5pm. Nov–Mar Marble House and Château-sur-Mer open Sat–Sun 10am–4pm.

BELCOURT CASTLE, Bellevue Ave. Tel. 846-0669.

Of the rest of the mansions in Newport, Belcourt Castle is the grandest. Another creation of Richard Morris Hunt, it was built in 1891. Oliver Belmont and his wife formerly Mrs. William Vanderbilt, had Hunt make them a castle in the style of Louis XIII (1610–43). Today the castle is filled with appropriate memorabilia: stained glass armor, silver, and carpets. It even boasts a golden coronation coach. Well-informed guides escort the visitor through the beautiful period rooms and explain the collection. Tea or coffee is then served. Special parties can be arranged by calling the number above.

Admission: $6 adults, $5 senior citizens, $2 children aged 6–12.
Open: Mid-June to Oct 29, daily 9am–5pm.

THE ASTOR'S BEECHWOOD, 580 Bellevue Ave. Tel. 846-7288.

The house of William B. Astor was built in 1856. The "tour" here is quite different from what you'll find at any other Newport mansion. Here, Beechwood Theater Company actors and actresses play characters (tongue-in-cheek) who might have lived in such a summer cottage during Newport's gilded age. It's all done in fun and with spirit, and it gives you quite another view of Newport life.

Admission (including the show/tour): $7.50 adults, $6 for seniors.
Open: Daily 10am–5pm.

OCHRE COURT, 100 Ochre Point Ave. Tel. 847-6650.

This mansion, designed by Richard Morris Hunt and built for Ogden Goelet, is styled after a French château, yet another example of Newport's architectural extravagance.

Admission: Free.
Open: Mon–Fri 9am–4pm.

HAMMERSMITH FARM, Ocean Dr. Tel. 846-0420.

Want to visit a summer White House? Hammersmith Farm was built by John W. Auchincloss in 1887 as his family's 28-room summer "cottage." After Jacqueline Bouvier, daughter of Mrs. Hugh Auchincloss, became Mrs. John F. Kennedy, the wedding reception was held at Hammersmith Farm. President Kennedy and his wife enjoyed visiting the farm when they could find the time, and no wonder. Beautiful rolling lawns and gardens, nature paths and copses of trees—not to mention the lovely old house itself—make the farm a seaside paradise. Mrs. Auchincloss sold Hammersmith Farm mansion in 1977, and it is now open to the public with many of the original furnishings.

Admission: $6 adults, $3 children.
Open: Apr to mid-Nov and "Christmas in Newport," daily 10am–5pm (to 7pm in summer). Guided tours given daily.

A WALK IN WASHINGTON SQUARE

Right downtown between Thames and Spring Streets, next to the new Brick Marketplace shopping mall, is Washington Square, the center of colonial Newport. At the western tip of the square is the Brick Market, a Newport landmark, built in 1762 and designed by Peter Harrison. (The name derives from its use as a market and its brick construction, even though no bricks were sold!) Having served variously as a town hall, theater, and crafts center, it is now occupied by shops.

At the other end of the square stands the **Old Colony House,** center of Newport governmental affairs from its construction in 1739 until the Rhode Island General Assembly (which met in Newport in the summer) last used it in 1900. It was from the Colony (later State) House's balcony that the Declaration of Independence was read to Rhode Islanders. In the assembly room is Gilbert Stuart's famous portrait of George Washington. You can get a free tour of the building July through Labor Day from 9:30am to noon and 1 to 4pm on weekdays, 9:30am to noon on Saturday and Sunday.

OTHER ATTRACTIONS

TOURO SYNAGOGUE, 82 Touro St. Tel. 847-4794.

The Touro Synagogue (the name may come from a 19th-century benefactor, Abraham Touro, son of the rabbi who presided at the synagogue's dedication) is the most famous early house of worship. Designed by Peter Harrison (it resembles his King's Chapel in Boston) and built in 1763, the temple was the spiritual center of Congregation Jeshuat Israel, an Orthodox Sephardic congregation. The synagogue and congregation prospered along with Newport, but after the British occupation of the town during the revolutionary war, prosperity fled Newport and few of its erstwhile citizens returned. In the late 19th century Newport came to life again. The temple reopened in 1883, and has been used for services ever since. During the summer, short tours are conducted. You can see a copy of George Washington's historic letter on religious freedom to the congregation, written while he was president in 1790.

Admission: Free, but donations accepted.

Open: May–late June, Sun–Fri 1–3pm. June–early Sept, Sun–Thurs 10am–5pm, Fri 10am–3pm. Early Sept–Apr, Sun 1–3pm, and by special arrangement. On Fri night and Sat morning, you may attend services.

QUAKER MEETINGHOUSE, corner of Marlborough and Farewell Sts. Tel. 846-0813.

This was built in 1699, but was greatly modified in the early 1700s and again in the early 1800s. The congregation, founded in 1657, is the oldest of the Society of Friends in this country. The meetinghouse has been restored to look as it did in the early 1800s.

Admission: Free.
Open: Call for an appointment.

TRINITY CHURCH [1726], corner of Spring and Church Sts. Tel. 846-0660.

Newport, of course, has a beautiful old pre-Revolutionary church, and this one, just restored, is a real gem. It was built from plans by Sir Christopher Wren, and still has the "bishop's miter" weathervane, as it did before the Revolution. The church is full of history: Bishop George Berkeley gave the organ (1733), Washington was known to have worshiped here (pew no. 81), and its famous three-decker "wineglass" pulpit is widely admired. Handicapped accessible.

Admission: Free, but donations accepted.
Open: Late June–Labor Day, Mon–Sat 10am–4pm. Labor Day–late June, Sat–Sun 10am–1pm. Sun services at 8 and 11am.

INTERNATIONAL TENNIS HALL OF FAME AND TENNIS MUSEUM, 194 Bellevue Ave. Tel. 849-3990.

This is sure to be of interest to anyone obsessed with the game. It's in the Newport Casino building across from the shopping center. The casino (1880) is the perfect location for a tennis museum, as it was here that the first national tennis tournaments were held. Major professional tournaments are played here during June, July, and August. The museum has trophies, tennis fashions, and displays explaining the evolution of tennis equipment. The 13 grass courts (and 3 indoor courts) are open to the public for play, so bring your racket and call to make arrangements.

Admission: $5 adults, $2.50 seniors, 3 children aged 5–16.
Open: Daily 10am–5pm.

MUSEUM OF YACHTING, in Fort Adams State Park, Ocean Dr. Tel. 847-1018.

As you might imagine, Newport has a Museum of Yachting; it's a short drive along Ocean Drive from the center of town. If you're at all interested in small wooden craft, boatbuilding, or yachting, you should make a visit. A new exhibit highlighting the single-handed sailor is on the second floor.

Admission: $3 adults, $2 seniors, free for children under 12.
Open: Mid-May to Oct, daily 10am–5pm.

NEWPORT ART MUSEUM, 76 Bellevue Ave. Tel. 848-8200.

Here you'll find changing exhibits in a house (1862) designed by Richard Morris Hunt. Call for information on current shows.

Admission: $3 adults, $2 seniors, free for those 18 and under (prices may be higher in summer).
Open: July–Sept 7, Mon–Sat 10am–5pm, Sun 1–5pm. Sept 8–June, Wed–Sat 10am–4pm, Sun 1–4pm.

SPORTS/RECREATION

OCEAN DRIVE & CLIFF WALK Take a drive (or ride your bike, if you're in shape) along Newport's 10-mile Ocean Drive. The scenery is very beautiful, with low heath, evergreens, stretches of rugged coast, and several smooth, grassy lawns maintained as state parks. **Brenton Point State Park** has parking, walking, and picnic areas, and there's a public Fishing Area with parking nearby. Ocean Drive also gives you a look at some of the yachts sailing on Rhode Island Sound, and at the mansions around the end of the island.

For walkers, the pedestrian equivalent of Ocean Drive is Cliff Walk, a path that runs along the shore and along the edge of the "front yards" of the mansions on Bellevue Avenue. The official start of the hour-long walk is off Memorial Boulevard just before Newport Beach beneath the Cliff Walk Manor, but you can also get to the path by going east on one of the side streets off Bellevue Avenue. You needn't take the entire walk, but can head back to Bellevue Avenue at various points along the way.

FORT ADAMS STATE PARK   On a peninsula jutting into Newport Harbor, Fort Adams State Park (tel. 847-2400) offers several attractions. The park is open daily from 6am to 11pm all year, and picnic and fishing sites are open to all. The fort itself, named after Pres. John Adams, is open for guided tours from 11:30am to 4:30pm Wednesday through Sunday in the summer (for a fee). Boat-launching ramps, beach with lifeguard, picnic area, the Museum of Yachting (see above), and soccer fields are among the services. The fort's defenses are some of the most impressive in the country—so impressive, in fact, that it rarely came under fire. Views of the town and the harbor from hills in the park are well worth the short climb.

BEACHES   Newport's beaches are of two types, public (open to everyone for a fee), and private (open to members only). Bailey's Beach, at the southern end of Bellevue Avenue, is definitely private, but **Newport Beach,** also called First Beach, is public and quite large. It's on the isthmus at the eastern reach of Memorial Boulevard. Second Beach is in Middletown, a bit farther along the same route where the street changes names to become Purgatory Road. Just around the corner from Second Beach is Third Beach, at the mouth of the Sakonnet River, facing east. It may be a bit chilly at any time except July and August.

Gooseberry Beach, on Ocean Drive, is an especially attractive beach, open to the public for a car-parking fee of $5 on weekdays, $1 for pedestrians and cyclists. It's framed by nice mansions on either side, and has interesting rock formations.

JAI ALAI   An unusual spectator sport and game of chance in Newport is the fast-moving game of jai alai ("high-lie"), familiar to those who have traveled to Latin America and Florida. The Newport Fronton is at 150 Admiral Kalbfus Rd., near the Newport end of the Newport Bridge. Seats cost $2 to $5, general admission (standing room) is $2 and $2 for the lounge and restaurant. Betting is on which player or team will win, and is pari-mutuel as it is at horse and dog tracks. The game is fast and exciting, and the ball (harder than a golf ball) moves at murderous speeds approaching 188 miles an hour. If you've never seen it before (or bet before), you can get a brochure at the door explaining it all. For seat reservations, call 849-5000 in Rhode Island, or toll free 800/556-6900 out-of-state. Seniors are admitted free for the matinees on Sunday, Monday, and Saturday; women are admitted free on Wednesday; closed Sunday. There's a moderately priced restaurant and a lounge that overlooks court action.

WHERE TO STAY

Newport has several large, comfortable hotels, a good number of charming small inns, and numerous bed-and-breakfast houses. Neighboring Middletown, which has many inexpensive motels and more guesthouses, is so close that many visitors to Newport stay in motels in Middletown and then drive the mile or two into Newport to see the sights. No matter what sort of accommodation you choose, it's a good idea to have reservations in advance, particularly in summer and especially on weekends. If you arrive in Newport on Friday from mid-July through Labor Day, you may well have to spend hours searching for that last hotel or inn room. On summer weekdays there may be more rooms, but you may not be able to find your preferred facilities and price unless you reserve in advance. The listings begin with some of Newport's fine inns, which are moderate in price but high in comfort and good looks, then go on to guesthouses (almost as charming, but cheaper), and hotels and motels.

The **Newport County Chamber of Commerce** (tel. 401/847-1600) has a nice long list of bed-and-breakfast guesthouses and small inns. Send for it if you have the time; pick one up when you arrive if you don't; or call and ask for help in locating a room.

The **Newport Historic Inns,** P.O. Box 981, Newport, RI 02840 (tel. 401/846-7666), will send you a list of its member establishments. You can call to find out where there are vacancies—but you'll have to contact the guesthouse directly to make reservations. Members of the association tend to be the larger establishments with about 6 to 16 rooms.

Remember that Rhode Island has a 7% sales tax, and a 5% room tax is also applied to prices in establishments with 3 or more rooms.

INNS

Expensive

FRANCIS MALBONE HOUSE, 392 Thames St., Newport, RI 02840. Tel. 401/846-0392. Fax 401/848-5956. 9 rms (all with bath). A/C **Directions:** Coming from the Newport Bridge, take a right onto America's Cup Ave. at the second set of lights. At the sixth set of lights, turn right onto lower Thames St. at the Perry Mill Market/Newport Bay Club. The Francis Malbone House is 3 blocks down on the left. To reach the parking area, turn left onto Brewer St. (the third left off Thames St.) into the first driveway on the right.

$ Rates: May–Oct, $125–$225 double. Nov–Apr, $80–$125 double. AE, MC, V. **Parking:** Free.

The Francis Malbone house was built in 1760 for shipping merchant Col. Francis Malbone by the same architect who designed Touro Synagogue and the Redwood Library. An elegant staircase with individually turned spindles graces the foyer, to the left of which is a formal gray, wood-paneled sitting room with a striped camelback couch, wingback chairs, and a gray marble fireplace. To the right you'll find a small library and, a bit farther back, a casual sitting room that houses the television, telephone, books, and a comfortable couch.

The guest rooms are comfortable and meticulously clean with lovely fabrics and reproduction antiques throughout. For instance, the front room on the second floor is done in Wedgwood blue with white trim and holds a rice four-poster bed with a white eyelet, lace-trimmed quilt, a highboy, pier mirror, window seats, an Oriental carpet, and two Martha Washington Queen Anne chairs in front of a marble fireplace with a wood mantel.

Jim, Stephanie, and Will tend to your every need and serve you breakfast every morning at the lace-covered dining room table in front of the hearth. Breakfast consists of juices, cereals, fresh fruit, muffins, and a hot dish, as well as coffee and tea. You might like to take your final cup of coffee out to the beautifully maintained garden and sit in one of the Adirondack chairs on the flagstone patio. The Francis Malbone House is definitely one of the best places to stay in Newport.

INN AT CASTLE HILL, Ocean Ave., Newport, RI 02840. Tel. 401/849-3800. 10 rms (7 with bath). **Directions:** Follow Ocean Ave. to the inn.

$ Rates (including continental breakfast): Peak season, $89 double without bath, $128 double with shower in Harbor House, $200 double with bath. Off-season rates available. AE, MC, V. **Parking:** Free.

This marvelous Victorian summer mansion, perched on a hill at the southwestern tip of Rhode Island, overlooking Narragansett Bay, is a Newport favorite. The house was built in 1874 for Alexander Agassiz (1835–1910), naturalist, industrialist, and great benefactor of Harvard. It has been authentically maintained and restored, and is a fine example of a wealthy family's Victorian summer cottage extravaganza: dark wood, ornate fireplaces, large-flower-pattern wallpaper (different in each room, of course), Oriental carpets, a sunny solarium—it's all here. The Harbor House, an unobtrusive motel-style structure, is next to the inn and just above the pebble beach. The inn also has a number of beach cottages capable of lodging two to four people. The cottages are rented by the week in summer, and are booked very far in advance. There's a good dining room.

INN OF JONATHAN BOWEN, 29 Pelham St., Newport, RI 02840. Tel. 401/846-3324. Fax 401/847-7450. 11 rms (9 with bath). TV
$ Rates (including buffet breakfast): $110–$175 double. MC, V. **Parking:** Free.
This nice old gambrel-roofed house is only ½ block off America's Cup Avenue up Historic Hill. The interior of the house has been beautifully redone and is as neat as a pin, with wall-to-wall carpeting and large modern tile bathrooms. But true to its historical heritage, the inn's guest rooms are furnished with brass beds and old oak wardrobes and dressers. Room 7, which shares a bath, is particularly bright and sunny. You'll enjoy relaxing in the parlor amid the antiques and Oriental carpets. If you like antique charm, but can do without squeaky floorboards and ancient woodwork, this is the place for you.

WAYSIDE, Bellevue Ave., Newport, RI 02840. Tel. 401/847-0302. 6 rms (all with bath). TV **Directions:** Drive from Newport Casino (International Tennis Hall of Fame) down Bellevue Ave. Pass The Elms on right, then Oakwood Healthcare Center on left; next building on left is the Wayside, marked by a small marble plaque by the driveway.
$ Rates (including continental breakfast): $95–$125 double. No credit cards. **Parking:** Free.
For the full Newport experience, stay in the Wayside, a mansion right on Bellevue Avenue. This fine 1890s house of tawny brick is set back from the avenue with its own little driveway and porte cochere. The interior spaces are rich and elegant, but austere rather than fussy. The many parlors and bedrooms have been redone into comfortable accommodations with private baths.

Moderate

CLIFFSIDE INN, 2 Seaview Ave., Newport, RI 02840. Tel. 401/847-1811, or toll free 800/845-1811. 11 rms. **Directions:** Take America's Cup Ave. to Memorial Blvd. (Rte. 138A), follow Memorial east to Cliff Ave.; turn right and go 2 blocks to Seaview Ave. Turn left onto Seaview; Cliffside is on left.
$ Rates (including breakfast): May–Oct, $125 single; $155 double; $205 suite. Nov–Apr, rates are 25% less. Extra person $30. AE, DC, MC, V. **Parking:** Free.
Very near Cliff Walk and the beach is the Cliffside Inn, owned at one time by a painter named Beatrice Pasatorius Turner. Many of the antique furnishings date from 1880, when the house was built as a summer cottage for Governor Swann of Maryland, and the inn exudes Victorian charm.

MELVILLE HOUSE, 39 Clarke St., Newport, RI 02840. Tel. 401/847-0640. 7 rms (5 with bath).
$ Rates (including breakfast): Late May–early Sept, $75–$85 double without bath, $85–$100 double with bath. Early Sept–late May, rates are 20%–40% less. AE, MC, V. **Parking:** Free.
"Where the past is present" is how innkeepers Rita and Sam Rogers describe their inn, on a quiet street only a few blocks up Historic Hill from America's Cup Avenue and the Brick Marketplace. The inn couldn't be situated better. It is not one of Newport's Victorian palaces, but rather a beautiful old colonial house dating from about 1750. The owners have been true to the period in their decorations, which recall colonial and Early American times, yet they've also catered to guests' desires for modern facilities by installing up-to-date, if small, private bathrooms. The mood here is one of antiques, good taste, quiet, and friendliness. Breakfast includes granola, fresh–baked muffins, and orange juice. You'll love it.

GUESTHOUSES

Many of the lodging establishments listed below are similar in ambience and facilities to the inns listed above. The distinction between inn and guesthouse is somewhat arbitrary. Our feeling is that guesthouses have just a little more of the feeling you get when you stay in someone's home.

THE COVELL HOUSE, 43 Farewell St., Newport, RI 02840. Tel. 401/ 847-8872. 6 rms (3 with bath).

$ Rates (including continental breakfast): Mid-May to mid-Oct, $70–$95 single or double. Mid-Oct to mid-May, rates are lower. MC, V. **Parking:** Free.

Built in 1805, this was completely renovated in 1982, with antique-decorated guest rooms. The neighborhood is a quiet, residential one, but you're still only a short walk from the bustling waterfront.

ELM TREE COTTAGE, 336 Gibbs Ave., Newport, RI 02840. Tel. 401/ 849-1610, or toll free 800/882-3ELM. 6 rms (all with bath). A/C **Directions:** Via Newport Bridge, exit at "Scenic Newport" and turn right off exit ramp. At second set of lights, turn right onto America's Cup Ave. Follow to seventh set of lights, stay to left, proceed up hill onto Memorial Blvd. toward First Beach. Cross over Bellevue Ave. Make a left onto Gibbs Ave. Proceed to first stop sign. Elm Tree Cottage is third house on right.

$ Rates: (including full breakfast): $150–$250 weekend double, $125–$185 weekday double. MC, V. **Parking:** Free.

"Casual elegance," is the way Pricilla and Tom Malone describe their two-year-old bed-and-breakfast inn, and it is a description that couldn't be more fitting. Once owned by the heiress to the Pennsylvania Railroad, the house is full of interesting stories—in particular the one about the bar—ask Pricilla to tell you. The bar (not stocked, but available for use) is built like the interior of a ship and originally had 45 1921 silver dollars imbedded in the top (some have since been stolen). Around the corner from the bar is a sunroom with wicker furnishings and floral draperies. The living room holds a grand piano, a stand-up piano, clawfoot wingback chairs, and camelback couches. There's a fireplace, and an enormous mirror that took four men to hang. There's stained glass all over the house—that's because Tom and Pricilla make stained-glass windows (they're definitely not your average innkeepers). They'll gladly take you down into the basement to show you how it's done.

The rooms are elegantly furnished with Louis XV beds, antique complementary pieces, and English and French Country bed linens and fabrics. Most of the rooms have functional fireplaces. The light fixtures and Austrian crystal vanity in what is known to many as the Honeymoon Suite are original to the house. Every morning (as early as 7:30 if you wish), Pricilla has coffee and tea ready and then whips up a gourmet breakfast that might include crêpes, French toast, orange waffles, or some other wonderful creation (never scrambled eggs). In the afternoon, you'll find hors d'oeuvres waiting with, perhaps, a raspberry iced tea.

HYDRANGEA HOUSE INN, 16 Bellevue Ave., Newport, RI 02840. Tel. 401/846-4435, or toll free 800/945-4667. 6 rms (all with bath). A/C

$ Rates: (including full breakfast): May–Oct, $120–$165 double. Nov–Apr, $80–$120 double. **Parking:** Free.

The Hydrangea House Inn, built in 1876, has been beautifully but modestly restored. The Rose Dutches Room overlooks Bellevue Avenue and is done in rose with floral chintz draperies. There's a queen-size bed, a Queen Anne flat-top desk, two camelback chairs and a wingback chair. La Petite Rouge Chambre, located across the hall from the tiny sitting room, is the smallest of the rooms. The plum-red painted walls, hand-painted Edwardian chest of drawers, French cartoon prints, and fireplace (non-working) make it one of the coziest spaces in the inn. The largest of the rooms is the Hydrangea Garden room, which is located on the ground floor and faces the back garden. It can accommodate up to four people.

A breakfast of coffee, tea, juice, fruit, granola, and a hot main dish is available in the morning downstairs in the art gallery—yes, in the gallery. You can eat breakfast while admiring the original works by Rhode Island and New England artists. Much of the art in the inn is for sale.

IVY LODGE, 12 Clay St., Newport, RI 02840. Tel. 401/849-6865. 9 rms (7 with bath). A/C **Directions:** Drive along Bellevue Ave. and watch for the Oakwood Healthcare Center on left; turn left onto Parker Ave. Just before Center, then right onto Clay St. Ivy Lodge is on left.
$ Rates (including continental breakfast): May to mid-Oct, $110–$165 single or double. Mid-Oct to Apr, $105 single or double. MC, V. **Parking:** Free.

This huge, shingled summer cottage, with its gables and chimneys, its curving veranda with wicker furniture, and its tidy carriage house, stands proudly even in the midst of the mansions. Its lofty entrance hall, done completely in glowing, artfully carved woodwork which rises all the way up to the third-floor roof, further proves the house's elegance. Staircases cascade in front of you, and stained glass glows above. There's a fireplace, and to the right a reading room with etched-glass windows. To the left is the formal dining room, where a full buffet-style breakfast is served. Guest rooms are similarly ornate and authentic. The hosts, Ed and Mariann Moy, will welcome you and then leave you pretty much to enjoy yourself as you please. Little extras include bicycles, coolers, and beach chairs, and transportation to the airport.

QUEEN ANNE INN, 16 Clarke St., Newport, RI 02840. Tel. 401/846-5676. 10 rms (4 with bath).
$ Rates: (including continental breakfast): Late May–Sept, $77–$99 single or double. Oct–late May, $60–$82 single or double. MC, V. **Parking:** Free.

Of the several guesthouses downtown in Newport, this one is perhaps the most conveniently located—½ block off Touro Street at Washington Square, 2 blocks from the harbor, in the Historic District. Peg McCabe, the affable owner of the Queen Anne, advertises that you can "park your car in our lot and walk to everything," which is true of everything downtown, and even of the mansions if you're a good walker. One of the old Victorian town houses (rather than a wooden summer mansion), the Queen Anne has a dozen rooms furnished in a cheerful way with lots of nice little antique touches. The Queen Anne has its own patio and garden. You can't miss the place: Headquarters of the Newport Artillery Company is right across the street. Open year round.

SANFORD-COVELL VILLA MARINA, 72 Washington St., Newport, RI 02840. Tel. 401/847-0206. 8 rms (all with bath). **Directions:** Follow Thames St. to America's Cup Ave. (on left). Continue to Long Wharf on left which turns right into Washington St. Sanford-Covell Villa Marina will be on left.
$ Rates: (including continental breakfast): $65–$250 double. No credit cards. **Parking:** Free.

Walking into the Sanford-Covell Villa Marina is like walking into a different era. In 1869 Milton Sanford, a New York industrialist commissioned William Ralph Emerson, the cousin of Ralph Waldo Emerson, to build this stick-style Victorian building as a summer home. This commission is said to have been a catalyst of the famous Newport mansion wars. Today the rooms and hallways are filled with Victorian knick-knacks, as well as toys, quilts, and antiques. Each room is unique. The Play Room, not the biggest or most elegant of the rooms, but still very nice, was originally the Smoking Room. If you go into the Play Room and step out onto the balcony that overlooks the foyer, you'll be awed by the 35-foot drop to the ground floor, and you'll also be able to get a better view of the original lamp fixtures (which were converted to electricity in 1920) and the painting around the tops of the walls. It's not paper, and it's not stenciled—the technique used to apply the paint is called "pouncing." It's not just painted on, it's actually pounded into the wall at the end of a lead weight. The most fascinating thing about the Play Room is the diaries of William King Covell (the second owner of the home) displayed on the bookshelf.

The house has a wraparound porch with porch swings and the most incredible view (since it's practically at water's edge) at the back. Here's where you'll head if you want to swim in the black-bottom saltwater pool or lounge in the saltwater Jacuzzi. You can't beat the Sanford-Covell Villa Marina for luxury, history, and a bit of adventure.

HOTELS & MOTELS

Besides these downtown hotels, there are many motels on the outskirts, in Middletown, particularly along West Main Road (Route 114). Prices are lower, but so are quality, convenience, and ambience. All of the rooms in the following hotels have private baths.

NEWPORT ISLANDER DOUBLETREE HOTEL, Goat Island, Newport, RI 02840. Tel. 401/849-2600, or toll free 800/528-0444. 250 rms (all with bath). A/C TV TEL

$ Rates: $129–$209 single; $139–$219 double. Extra person $15. Children under 18 stay free in parents' room. AE, DC, MC, V. **Parking:** Free.

Perched on an island in the midst of the yachts, the Islander has good views all around, comfortable modern rooms, lots of nautical decor, and many big-hotel services including separate indoor and outdoor pools, a health center and sauna, a beauty salon, two racquetball courts, and two restaurants. Goat Island is due west of Washington Square, connected to the mainland by a causeway.

NEWPORT MARRIOTT, 25 America's Cup Ave., at Long Wharf, Newport, RI 02840. Tel. 401/849-1000, or toll free 800/228-9290. 317 rms (all with bath). A/C MINIBAR TV TEL

$ Rates: $125–$219 double. AE, DC, MC, V. **Parking:** Free.

The Marriott, one of Newport's newest hotels, is the prime place to stay if you like modern elegance and comfort. The many services include an indoor-outdoor swimming pool, racquetball courts, health club, sauna, and four dining and drinking places. Many of the very comfortable rooms have water views.

WHERE TO DINE

Dining in Newport is anything you want to make it, from a seaside clambake on paper plates to an elegant dinner with candlelight, soft music, and polished service. **Bannister's Wharf/Bowen's Wharf** is the most charming of the waterfront redevelopment projects, and it has a selection of good restaurants. Bannister's Wharf is right next to the Treadway Inn, downtown on the waterfront, and would be West Pelham Street's extension if the wharf were still a street. On upper Thames Street, across from Memorial Boulevard, there are lots of places where you can get delicious seafood at very reasonable prices. Some restaurants allow you to bring your own wine or beer, which also helps to keep the price of a good seafood dinner in the reasonable range. You can pick up your favorite vintage or brew at **Thames Street Liquors,** 520 Thames St., or at one of several other stores in the area. The BYO restaurants can tell you how to find the nearest liquor store.

There are two things you should know about much of Newport dining. First, if you plan to dine in one of the better restaurants, you may have to meet the requirements of a dress code. Many restaurants ask that their patrons meet jacket-and-tie/skirt-and-sleeved-blouse formality. Second, call for reservations. Some restaurants are booked solid a week in advance for dinner on Saturday evenings in July and August.

EXPENSIVE

BLACK PEARL, Bannister's Wharf. Tel. 846-5264.
   Cuisine: FRENCH/AMERICAN. **Reservations:** Required in summer.

$ Prices: Appetizers $4.50–$9; main courses $9–$18; meals in Commodore's Room $50. AE, MC, V.
Open: Commodore's Room dinner daily 6–10pm. Tavern daily 11am–11pm.
Closed: Mid-Jan to mid-Feb.

The Black Pearl, Newport's well-established restaurant, is crowded for lunch and dinner, weekdays and weekends with the blonde and beautiful, the tanned and handsome. There are actually four places to dine here. In the Commodore's Room, a jacket is required for men and similarly suitable dress for women. This is not the busiest of the Pearl's eating areas; rather, it's a refuge from the busy places. Table settings are quietly elegant and include a candle lantern. The decor is subdued, quite unlike the overdone or garish atmosphere characteristic of many waterfront restaurants. Next to the Commodore's Room is the Tavern, where a jacket is not required, and happy, hungry yachting types press in for a drink, a "Pearlburger," an omelet, or perhaps a daily special, such as fresh bluefish with lemon-caper butter. Outdoors, next to the Black Pearl, is the outdoor bar, a sort of waterfront café, with white metal tables and chairs set out on a patch of white gravel, shaded by brightly colored umbrellas. The Black Pearl is next to the Clarke Cooke House.

CLARKE COOKE HOUSE, Bannister's Wharf. Tel. 849-2900.
Cuisine: FRENCH. **Reservations:** Required.
$ Prices: Appetizers $4.50–$11.50; main courses $21.75–$25.50; light supper in Bistro $20. AE, MC, V.
Open: Daily 11:30am–10pm.

This is the poshest place on this very posh wharf, with one of the most interesting French menus in Newport (not all frogs' legs and escargots) and two very different dining rooms. To your left at the top of the short flight of steps is the Dining Room, a very authentic-looking colonial room with rugged ceiling beams (original to the house, which is colonial), wood chairs and tables, gleaming crystal stemware, and tuxedoed waiters. Note that a jacket-and-tie dress code is enforced here.

To the right as you enter the Bistro, a less formal room overlooks the wharf and the water.

DRY DOCK SEAFOOD, 448 Thames St. Tel. 847-3974.
Cuisine: SEAFOOD/SANDWICHES. **Reservations:** Not accepted. **Directions:** From Memorial Blvd., go 7 short blocks south on Thames St.
$ Prices: Appetizers $1.95–$5.25; main courses $4.25–$9.95; lunch $6–$8; dinner $20–$25. No credit cards.
Open: Daily 11am–10pm.

This attractive, clean, and modern eatery has lots of bright, cheerful wood and tile, a lunch counter, and tables with bentwood chairs. Ceiling fans keep you cool, and hanging plants add a touch of greenery. Order New England clam chowder for starters, and then a sandwich of fish, meatballs, or chouriço (spicy Portuguese sausage) and peppers. Or you can order a main-course dinner, such as fish-and-chips, a fisherman's platter, swordfish steak, or broiled scallops. You get about a pound of succulent sea scallops perfectly broiled in a light coating of crumbs, with an immense mound of french fries and a paper thimble of coleslaw, for a mere $9.95. One of the things that keeps prices reasonable here is that you bring your own wine or beer. Try a cup of soup and a sandwich, or a bowl of soup and a swordfish steak. This place is great!

WHITE HORSE TAVERN, corner of Marlborough and Farewell Sts. Tel. 849-3600.
Cuisine: AMERICAN/CONTINENTAL. **Reservations:** Required.
$ Prices: Appetizers $6–$9; main courses $21–$33; meals $50–$70. AE, DC, MC, V.
Open: Lunch Mon and Wed–Sun noon–3pm; dinner daily 6–10pm.

Boasting that it is America's oldest tavern building, the White Horse, 2 blocks north of Washington Square, is certainly a Newport institution, having served the hungry and thirsty since about 1687. One family, the Nichols, ran the tavern for almost two centuries. Rescued from a period of neglect by the Newport Preservation Society in the 1950s, it is again in private hands and in excellent condition.

The old tavern is authentic and totally charming, with large fireplaces, huge exposed beams, and old oil paintings. Staff are formal in black and white, soft classical music wafts through the air, and the menu lists dishes which are a fascinating blend of the old and new: Duck is served with a spicy oriental orange glaze, beef Wellington with sauce périgourdine (Périgord is a region of France where geese are force-fed to produce foie gras), and sautéed lobster. Appetizers include gravlax brushed with dilled olive oil, and escargots en croûte with garlic butter and Roquefort. Lunch includes a duck-salad sandwich ($8) or grilled sea scallop on angelhair pasta ($11). Desserts are rich and delicious. Arrive well dressed.

YESTERDAY'S WINE BAR AND GRILLE, 28 Washington Sq. Tel. 847-0116.

Cuisine: INTERNATIONAL. **Reservations:** Recommended.
$ Prices: Appetizers $5.95–$7.95; main courses $14.95–$20.95. AE, MC, V.
Open: Mon–Wed 11:30am–10pm, Thurs–Sun 11am–11pm.

The food at Yesterday's Wine Bar and Grille is terrific. Here you'll find a place that cares equally as much about ingredients as it does about presentation. Don't be confused when you walk in—there are two restaurants in one here—Yesterday's is straight ahead past the brass-trimmed mahogany bar. You'll have your choice of a booth or a table and you'll be attended to by several members of the staff. Being a wine bar, Yesterday's has an extensive wine list (by the glass as well as by the bottle). In addition, you are given a menu of the "flights" of wine available. A flight consists of four 3-ounce glasses of different wines, so you can conduct your own individual wine tasting.

Begin your meal with the gratin of wild mushrooms (a combination of shiitake, oyster, and other seasonal mushrooms cooked in a sauce of rosemary, thyme, shallots, sherry, and a bit of cream). Or perhaps you'd rather try the smoked pheasant salad with poached pears and hazelnuts. By the time you finish your appetizer you'll be begging for more, wondering if the main course could be as good. I can assure you, it's better. The grilled chicken with Bel Paese and smoked bacon, stuffed with kale and served in a sauce of fresh tomatoes, roasted peppers, and fresh herbs, is a work of art. If you're more interested in seafood, give the pan seared red snapper with lobster and guava sauce a try. Each dish comes with an assortment of vegetables cooked to perfection, such as miniature string beans, miniature carrots, potatoes, and bell peppers. By the time you get through this you'll want to have dessert (even if you don't have room). Give the light and delicious chocolate strawberry shortcake a try—it's not your average strawberry shortcake.

MODERATE

ANTHONY'S SEAFOOD & SHORE DINNER HALL, Newport Harbor Marketplace, Waites Wharf, off upper Thames St. Tel. 848-5058.

Cuisine: SEAFOOD. **Reservations:** Not accepted. **Directions:** Turn right off lower Thames St. when you reach the upper 400 block; there's a small sign for Shore Dinner Hall.
$ Prices: Main courses $6–$15. MC, V.
Open: Mid-Apr to Nov, daily 11am–10pm. **Closed:** Dec to mid-Apr.

⑤ A shore dinner, an old New England custom, is a no-frills clambake, with clam chowder, steamed clams, boiled corn on the cob, steamed lobsters, and other simple but delicious dishes served on paper plates to diners seated at wooden picnic tables. Newport's most authentic shore dinner is served here, in a large, open warehouse-type building that has been nicely spruced up, painted, and hung with colorful flags. Pick up wine or beer on your way here, or decide on soft drinks with your dinner, then order any of the aforementioned items, or lobster rolls, clam rolls mussels, hot dogs, french fries, or clam cakes. Try fish-and-chips, a large steaming plate of clams, or a steamed lobster weighing over a pound (price depending on the season). The view, through large, open doorways overlooking the bay, is among the best in Newport. The Shore Dinner Hall is operated by the SS *Newport* restaurant next door. There's plenty of free parking here.

BRICK ALLEY PUB AND RESTAURANT, 140 Thames St. Tel. 849-6334 or 849-8291.
   Cuisine: AMERICAN. **Reservations:** Recommended.
$ Prices: Appetizers $1.95–$7.95; main courses $5.45–$16.95. AE, CB, DC, MC, V.
   Open: Daily 11am–1am
After a hot morning's sightseeing in Newport, this is just what you want: a cool, quiet place to sit down and have some refreshment. It's right across the street from Brick Marketplace and right behind the block of shops housing the Newport Chamber of Commerce's information office. Walk up the passage beside the restaurant and you'll come to a shady courtyard with tables set out. The selection of sandwiches, burgers, salads, and omelets is enormous, all costing about $5 to $8, and for $3 more you can have soup and a trip to the salad bar. The pub also has a wide choice of fresh seafood dishes. The Brick Alley has indoor dining rooms as well as an outdoor bar in the courtyard.

MURIEL'S, 58 Spring St. Tel. 849-7780.
   Cuisine: INTERNATIONAL. **Reservations:** Recommended.
$ Prices: Appetizers $3.95–$6.95; main courses $6.50–$15.95. MC, V.
   Open: Breakfast Mon–Sat 8–11:30am; lunch Mon–Sat 11:30am–2pm; dinner Wed 5–9pm, Tues and Thurs–Sat 5–10pm; brunch Sun 9am–2pm.
Muriel's is wacky and fun. Inside you'll find Maxfield Parrish posters on the wall, banquettes, glass-topped tables with floral-and-lace-confetti covered cloths (under the glass), globe lights, jade-colored walls, fica trees, and (if you go on Thursday or a summer weekend) a guitarist and/or pianist playing classical or jazz music. One of the busiest times at Muriel's is breakfast, when you can get huevos rancheros, eggs benedict, French toast in spiced butter with walnuts and syrup, and waffles of all kinds. At lunch and dinner you'll find fresh fish, such as blackfish and salmon, salads, burgers, and Muriel's own famous crêpes. Muriel's is BYOB and is located on the corner of Spring and Touro Streets.

MUSIC HALL CAFE, 250 Thames St. Tel. 848-2330.
   Cuisine: MEXICAN. **Reservations:** Recommended for dinner.
$ Prices: Appetizers $4.50–$7.50; main courses $3.75–$11.50 at lunch, $8–$16.75 at dinner. AE, MC, V.
   Open: Lunch daily 11:30am–2:30pm; dinner daily 5:30–10pm.
The Music Hall Café is identifiable by the green, yellow, and maroon awning and the wrought iron tables and chairs out front. Inside you'll find exposed brick walls, a spanish-style iron chandelier, southwest colors, a kiva ladder hanging on the wall, buffalo skulls, and wood tables (on each of which is a small cactus). Country music plays softly in the background, and you can order a drink from the full bar—perhaps a cactus colada. On the menu you'll find the usual Mexican dishes, such as nachos, tacos, fajitas, burritos, and enchiladas, as well as burgers and sandwiches at lunch, and barbecue or chicken at dinner. The menu doesn't show many vegetarian dishes, but the chef is very accommodating if that is what you want. The Music Hall Café is new and popular, so either call for a reservation or be prepared to wait.

PUERINI'S, 24 Memorial Blvd. West. Tel. 847-5506.
   Cuisine: ITALIAN. **Reservations:** Not accepted.
$ Prices: Main courses $6.75–$12.95. No credit cards.
   Open: Dinner daily 5–11pm.
Puerini's is a wonderful little Italian restaurant, located just a few blocks from the waterfront. Instead of chianti bottles hanging from the ceiling and red-and-white checked cloths on the tables, you'll find an interesting collection of black-and-white

photographs of Italy hanging on the walls and black vinyl tablecloths with butcher paper and mismatched (even chipped—in a charming way) dishes on the tables. The bi-level restaurant is small but constantly bustling with a busy staff racing to and from the kitchen and patrons coming and going. The food is great and the portions are large. To start, you might have garlic bread smothered with cheese and red sauce, or sweet roasted peppers in oil and garlic served with provolone cheese. If you like ravioli, try the spinach pasta ravioli stuffed with ricotta and parmesean cheese (with just the right amount of cheese) and covered in a delicious pesto sauce. Also good are the vegetable lasagne and the pollo al marsala. You probably won't make it to dessert, but Puerini's does have a good selection. Puerini's is BYOB.

SALAS', 341 Thames St. Tel. 846-8772.
   Cuisine: SEAFOOD. **Reservations:** Not accepted.
$ **Prices:** Appetizers $1.85–$9.95; main courses $3–$23. AE, DC, DISC, MC, V
   Open: Dining room daily 4–10pm; brasserie daily 6–11pm; fish market and raw
   bar daily (in summer) 11am–1am.

Salas' on lower Thames, ½ block past the post office, actually consists of three establishments in one: a fish market and raw bar, a brasserie, and the dining room. For dinner you might try a stuffed quahog to start, followed by baked stuffed sole or surf and turf. The "No. 1 Clambake" includes a 1-pound lobster, clams, corn on the cob, sausage, clam broth, and so forth. There are also several pasta dishes, as well as sandwiches for those who don't enjoy seafood. For dessert, try the carrot cake.

---

3. FROM SAUNDERSTOWN TO POINT JUDITH

Narragansett Pier: 17 miles (27km) W of Newport Galilee:
5 miles (3km) S of Narragansett Pier

GETTING THERE By Car To get across Narragansett Bay from Newport, you will have to cross two bridges on Route 138: first, the Newport Bridge from Newport to Jamestown Island ($2, payable in both directions), and then the Jamestown Bridge from Jamestown Island to Saunderstown (free). The total fee, therefore, to cross from Newport to Saunderstown or vice versa is $2. From Saunderstown, head south on Route 1A (Alternate U.S. 1).

ESSENTIALS The **area code** is 401. The **Narragansett Chamber of Commerce** maintains a Tourist Information Office (tel. 401/783-7121) in the base of the prominent stone Towers in Narragansett Pier (see below). The **South County Tourism Council,** 4808 Tower Hill Rd., Wakefield, RI, 02879 (tel. 401/789-4422 or toll free 800/548-4662), may be able to answer your questions as well. If you're approaching from the west along I-95, there is a State of Rhode Island **Visitor Information Center** at the state line.

Coming from Newport or Providence, take Route 1A south from Route 138. As you drive south along U.S. 1A to Saunderstown, look for signs off to the right (west) that point the way to the **Gilbert Stuart birthplace.** Stuart (1755–1828), America's most famous portrait painter after the Revolutionary era, did no fewer than three portraits of George Washington from life, perhaps the most famous of which is the so-called *Athenaeum Head,* model for the portrait of Washington on the dollar bill. (Look for the original of this in the Museum of Fine Arts in Boston.) Stuart was the son of a snuff-maker. Judging from the house, his father had a comfortable living, and the son was able to go to London to study painting with Benjamin West. Period furnishings, a water wheel–powered snuff mill, and copies of Stuart's portraits adorn the house. Open Saturday to Thursday from 11am to 4:30pm; closed from November through March. Admission is $1.50 for adults, 50¢ for children.

Route 1A skirts the southwestern shore of Narragansett Bay passing through **Narragansett Pier,** a famous Victorian resort town, which is also the main town on the peninsula here. Although not quite so famous now, the town is still popular for the same reasons as in an earlier age: beautiful sea views, a fine waterfront promenade, and gracious old Victorian houses.

Passing through Narragansett on Ocean Road, you'll drive right under the last standing remnant of Stanford White's mammoth Narragansett casino, the **Towers,** built in 1882. The town's chamber of commerce maintains a Tourist Information Office in the base of the seaward tower—park on either side of the underpass arch and walk to the door.

The main beach in Narragansett Pier is north of the Towers, about ½ mile distant.

South of Narragansett Pier, Route 1A passes by the **Scarborough State Beach** facilities, very popular on hot summer days although never filled to capacity. Scarborough Beach, like all Rhode Island beaches, works on a system of parking/admission fees, charged *per car.*

Continuing along U.S. 1A south will bring you to the village of Galilee and the departure dock for ferryboats to Block Island.

POINT JUDITH/PORT GALILEE

Jutting southeast into the Atlantic Ocean and dividing Block Island Sound from Rhode Island Sound is Point Judith. The peninsula of Narragansett's southern extremity offers several things to travelers: The car and passenger ferry docks for boats to Block Island, located at Port Galilee; camping and picnic facilities at Fishermen's Memorial State Park, only 2 miles from Port Galilee; and good sand beaches along the southern and eastern shores of the peninsula. Port Galilee exists for the ferries to Block Island, the Wheeler Memorial Beach, several small fisheries, and a Coast Guard station.

THE BEACH & THE FERRY   First of all, be warned that Port Galilee has very few parking places on the street, and that these are usually taken up quickly by the people who work for the fishing companies. Parking for the beach is $2 a day ($3 on weekends and holidays) for Rhode Island residents, $4 a day ($6 on weekends and holidays) for out-of-state cars, but this includes the entry fee to the beach for everyone in your party, and is standard practice at all state beaches in Rhode Island. Whether you park next to George's of Galilee or at the large lots of the Wheeler Memorial Beach several hundred yards east, the rate and arrangement are the same.

For the ferry, parking fees are of the same order, and the lot is across the street and down a few yards from the ferry dock. Note that the restaurants and motel in Galilee have parking lots, but they also put out fierce signs that threaten to have your car towed if your intention is other than patronizing their establishments. It's best to take them at their word, especially if you're going to Block Island for the day.

4. BLOCK ISLAND

Sailing time to Block Island from Point Judith (Galilee) is 1¼ hours,
from New London 2 hours

GETTING THERE   By Plane   New England Airlines, Block Island's own airline, will fly you over from the State Airport in Westerly, RI., on any of 14 daily flights year round. The $28 flight one-way ($51 round-trip) takes 15 minutes. You must have reservations, so call 401/596-2460, or toll free 800/243-2460 outside Rhode Island. If you're on Block Island, dial 466-5881. The airport is on Airport Road, Westerly, off Route 78.

By Boat   From Port Galilee: This is the port with the most frequent service, and there are six to nine daily sailings in each direction from mid-June to early September. The trip takes less than 1¼ hours and costs $6.60 per adult, one-way, or $10.50 for a same-day round-trip; children pay half price. It costs $40.50 round-trip for a car (driver not included), and you must have reservations in advance. The Port Galilee agent is the **Interstate Navigation Co.,** Galilee State Pier, Point Judith, RI 02882 (tel. 401/783-4613). Motorcycles and bikes are also carried. During spring, fall, and winter there are fewer trips: two daily in each direction in May and early June, and late September through October; in winter, there's one trip daily.

From New London: Mid-June to early September there's one trip daily (plus an additional Friday evening boat) in each direction between New London and Block Island, leaving New London mid-morning, returning from Block Island mid-afternoon. The trip takes about 2 hours and costs $12 for adults ($16 for same-day round-trip), and $8 for children over 5 ($10 for same-day round-trip). A car costs $44 round-trip. The fee for bikes is $6 round-trip. The boat leaves from Ferry Street, about ⅛ mile from the railroad station. Advance reservations for cars is a must. For more information, contact the **Nelseco Navigation Co.,** P.O. Box 482, New London, CT 06320 (tel. 203/442-7891 or 442-9553 during business hours). By the way, ferries from New London arrive at Old Harbor on Block Island, and you may have to take a taxi to reach hotel and restaurant choices.

From Providence: The **Interstate Navigation Co.** (see above), also runs a daily passenger boat from Providence via Newport to Block Island. Departure from Providence's India Street dock is at 8:30am, from Newport's Fort Adams dock at 10:30am, arriving at Block Island around 12:30pm. The return trip leaves Block Island at 3:45pm, leaves Newport at 5:30pm, and arrives in Providence at 7:45pm.

One-way fares between Providence and Block Island are $7 for an adult, $3.60 for a child. Bicycles and motorcycles can be transported, but no cars. Ask about special same-day round-trip fares.

ESSENTIALS The **area code** is 401 and the ZIP Code is 02807. Block Island ordinances prohibit camping (except Scout groups and the like), sleeping overnight in cars or on beaches, riding motorcycles on the beaches, and shellfishing without a license.

The **Block Island Chamber of Commerce,** P.O. Drawer D, Block Island, RI 02807 (tel. 401/466-2982), can answer many of your questions about local services.

In 1614 a man named Adriaen Block visited a small island off the coast of Rhode Island, but his visit did little more than give the island its name. Slightly over 20 years later a colonist was found in a boat near the island, presumed murdered by the local Pequots, and this unhappy event precipitated a battle between Pequots and colonists that turned out to be very bloody.

A generation later, these events forgotten, settlers from the colony moved onto the island and the town of New Shoreham (incorporated in 1672) was built. For almost 200 years the people of Block Island lived their quiet lives, fishing in boats from the island's two natural harbors, growing what they could in the sandy and windswept soil. But in the mid-1800s the Age of Steam changed Block Island from a fishing outpost in the Atlantic to a summer excursion paradise, with regularly scheduled steamboats bringing residents of the sooty factory cities out for fresh air and bright sunshine. Late 19th-century frame hotels, huge and sprawling, went up to accommodate them, and the island's economy came to depend on tourism rather than fishing, and so it has remained. Most of the island's buildings—houses as well as hotels—date from the late 1800s or the turn of the century. The roads are rough and sandy (nobody has to be in a hurry to get quickly from one end of the island to the other—it's only 7 miles); the pace is very relaxed; and the citizens of New Shoreham, which takes up all of the island, have a strong sense of community.

The boat trip is pleasant enough, with plenty of room to sun on the top-deck benches, and a small bar and snack counter on board. As you approach Block Island, the character of the place becomes clear: dunes and white cliffs, low shrubs and grass with a few trees, ponds, and hillocks (highest point on the island is 211 feet above sea level). The big old hotels come right down to the harbor, most looking pretty weathered from the stiff breezes and salt air, not to mention the winter storms, that are the norm here. Several of the hotels have vans which will be waiting at the dock to pick up passengers who have reservations, or those who want a room but have not reserved.

WHAT TO SEE & DO

Most people coming to Block Island are looking for an easy schedule, quiet relaxation, time at the beach, bicycle trips, and seafood dinners. The island has a movie theater and a number of cocktail lounges, mostly in the hotels. A few small art galleries and craft shops are good for a browse. But beaching and bicycling are the two main activities.

You can't miss **Crescent Beach,** to your right as you approach Old Harbor on the ferry. It stretches from the ferry dock for several miles north to the cliffs of Clay Head. It's simply beautiful, although the water is a bit brisk this far out in the Atlantic (it's warmest in late July and August, of course). Crescent Beach is divided into the State Beach, with a bathhouse, which is the section nearest the ferry dock, and Scotch Beach, which is the section farther north. Other beaches are over in the New Harbor area, several small ones on Great Salt Pond, and Charleston Beach facing west on the Atlantic.

BICYCLE TOURING Block Island is too small to handle many cars, so most visitors get around by bicycle. Rental places abound and rates are about $6 per day for a three-speed, $12 for a 10-speed. The rental shop at the **Seacrest Inn,** High Street (tel. 466-2882), has good equipment and helpful personnel.

Mopeds are available for rent as well, but many local residents—especially those who belong to the medical rescue squad—advise visitors to rent a bike rather than a moped. If you are not an experienced motorcyclist, it's best to heed their advice. The medics respond to some six dozen moped accidents annually, some of them serious injuries. You'll get along better with the Block Islanders if you rent a bicycle.

A suitable Block Islandish goal for your bicycle outing is **Mohegan Bluffs,** and the nearby **Southeast Lighthouse,** about 1½ miles due south of town. Head out of town on Spring Street, until it becomes Southeast Light Road, which traces the heights of the bluffs.

About 2½ miles farther along, on Cherry Hill Road, lies **Rodman's Hollow,** a glacial ravine that's now protected as a wildlife refuge. Bring your binoculars if you plan to explore it.

Three miles north of town, on the eastern shore off Corn Neck Road, is the **Clayhead Nature Trail,** as well as a network of other trails on private land once known as the Maze. Take the nature trail east to the shore (less than a mile), then north all the way to Sandy Point, where you'll see the **North Lighthouse** and also **Settler's Rock.** The granite lighthouse, now being considered for restoration, dates from 1867 and is no longer in use. Settler's Rock monument, erected in 1911, marks the spot where the island's first English settlers landed in 1661.

Only about a mile northwest of town along Ocean Road and West Side Road is the island's **cemetery,** with headstones dating from the 1600s and 1700s. It's a pretty spot, and interesting to anyone intrigued with Block Island's history.

FISHING Several marinas on the island have fishing boats for hire, and surfcasting for striped bass and other delicacies is popular. Even if you're alone, the marina hands may be able to get together a party to go out, thereby reducing your costs greatly. For details, drop by any one of the marinas. All the boat-rental and sport-fishing businesses operate out of the New Harbor.

WHERE TO STAY

Block Island is currently enjoying a tourist boom. Most of the large old Victorian hotels have been renovated and modernized, many small family guesthouses have been opened, and in general the lodging picture is good but pricey. Because demand for rooms is high, you should be sure to have reservations in advance during high season (from mid-July through Labor Day). You can save 10% to 20% on many lodging establishments by staying during the week (Monday through Thursday) instead of the weekend if your schedule allows it.

Most hotels on Block Island serve breakfast to their guests at no additional charge. Breakfast may be anything from pastries and coffee to a full all-you-can-eat buffet. Also, all hotel prices are subject to the Rhode Island 12% sales plus room tax, and some hotels levy a service charge (usually 4% to 6%) in place of your tips to the staff. These extra costs have been included in the prices given below, unless otherwise noted.

If you plan to fly, be aware that fog may cause cancellation of your flight, and you should plan your schedule so that in the event of bad weather you will still be able to catch a ferry and get to your hotel in time to claim your reserved room. If you don't make it, you will forfeit your deposit and your reservation.

VERY EXPENSIVE

HOTEL MANISSES, Spring St., Block Island, RI 02807. Tel. 401/466-2421 or 466-2063. Fax 401/466-2858. 17 rms (all with bath). MINIBAR TV TEL **Directions:** Walk up the hill from the ferry dock, following the signs.
$ Rates: (including buffet breakfast and service): $65–$295 single or double (lower rates are for the winter season); third person in room is $25. AE, MC, V. **Parking:** Free.

Operated by Block Island's premier hoteliers, the Abrams family, this is without a doubt Block Island's loveliest place to stay. The Manisses was built in 1870 as a small Victorian resort hotel. Restored by the Abramses in 1972, it is at least as fine a hotel as it was 100 years ago—probably better. The large-pattern floral wallpaper, white wicker and wrought-iron furniture, beveled mirrors, heavily carved and marble-trimmed parlor pieces, even the bubbling garden fountain, recall the best of a more gracious time. The guest rooms have double, queen-size, or king-size beds; some have whirlpool bath and little refrigerator, and all have period furnishings. In the afternoon, wine and "nibbles" are served. The hotel's dining room (see "Where to Dine," below) is the best on the island. You'll love the Manisses.

1661 INN AND GUEST HOUSE, Spring St., Block Island, RI 02807. Tel. 401/466-2421 or 466-2063. 28 rms (26 with bath). **Directions:** Walk up the hill from the ferry dock, following the signs.
$ Rates: (including buffet breakfast and service): $88–$100 single or double without bath, $145–$290 single or double with bath. AE, MC, V. **Parking:** Free.

✪ Just up the hill from the Manisses is the Abramses' original establishment. A large white island house, the inn has been nicely adapted to hospitality, with many good-sized guest rooms, pleasant public spaces, and decks with sweeping views of the Atlantic. As at the Manisses, guests at the 1661 Inn and its neighboring guesthouse find all the little touches for which the Abramses are famous: a full buffet breakfast, beach towels, and a decanter of brandy and dish of hard candy in each room. Some rooms have private bath, refrigerator, and private deck with ocean view. The 1661 Inn closes from mid-November through March, but the guesthouse stays open year round. The buffet breakfast is the only meal served in the 1661 Inn's dining room. For other meals, by reservation, you can stroll down the hill to the Manisses.

EXPENSIVE

BLUE DORY INN, 488 Dodge St. (P.O. Box 488), Block Island, RI 02807. Tel. 401/466-2254. 10 rms (all with bath). **Directions:** From the ferry dock, turn right and follow Dodge St.

$ Rates: (including continental breakfast and service): Mid-June to early Sept, $139–$183 inn double with bath; $281 Cottage; $195 Tea House; $155 double in Doll House. Low-season and off-season, rates available. AE, MC, V. **Parking:** Free.

The Blue Dory, right next to the Surf Hotel and the National Hotel, is actually a guesthouse and several cottages perched right at the tip of Crescent Beach. The main building has guest rooms with Victorian furnishings, a living room, and a kitchen, which serves as the breakfast room. The Cottage can sleep up to six, has kitchen facilities, and is perfect for a family or for two couples traveling together. The Doll House is a one-room house good for couples who get along very well (it's tiny), and the Tea House sleeps two, and has its own kitchen, plus a porch overlooking the beach and the sea.

INN AT OLD HARBOUR, Water St. (P.O. Box 994), Block Island, RI 02807. Tel. 401/466-2212; off-season 914/967-4670. Fax 401/466-2951. 10 rms (5 with bath). **Directions:** Walk from the ferry to Water St., turn left, and walk ½ block.

$ Rates: (including continental breakfast): Summer, weekend $125 single or double without bath, $145 single or double with bath; weekday $95 single or double without bath, $115 single or double with bath. AE, MC, V. **Parking:** Free, on premises. **Closed:** Columbus Day–Memorial Day.

On a rise overlooking the ferry docks, facing the statue of *Rebecca at the Well,* is this three-story gambrel-roofed Victorian inn dating from 1882. What was once the lobby is now occupied by shops, but the guest rooms upstairs have all been totally renovated and fitted with modern fixtures and carpeting. Each room is different, the decor blending Victorian period pieces and a modern style. The inn has its own eating establishment, the Water Street Café, and a Ben & Jerry's Ice Cream Parlour.

THE ROSE FARM INN, Box E, Block Island, RI 02807. Tel. 401/466-2021. 10 rms (8 with bath).

$ Rates: (including continental breakfast): June 11–Sept 15, $95–$160 double. May 22–June 10 and Sept 16–Oct 11, $95–$160 weekend double, $80–$140 weekday double, May 1–May 21 and Oct 12–Oct 31, $80–$140 weekend double, $70–$130 weekday double. Extra person $25. AE, MC, V. **Parking:** Free. **Closed:** Nov–Apr.

The Rose Farm Inn, a turn-of-the-century farmhouse, is inconspicuously tucked away behind the Atlantic Inn. The rooms here are exceptionally clean and tastefully furnished with Victorian antiques. Some of the most sought after rooms feature king-size canopy or four-poster beds and ocean views. You can relax with a drink from the wet bar in the parlor, read on the stone porch, or sun yourself on the deck. In the morning, head for the sun-warmed breakfast room where you will find coffee, fresh fruit, cereals, and muffins or bread waiting for you at the buffet.

MODERATE

SEACREST INN, 207 High St., Block Island, RI 02807. Tel. 401/466-2882. 17 rms (all with bath). **Directions:** From the ferry docks, turn left and walk 100 yards.

$ Rates: (including continental breakfast): High season, $55 single; $105 double. AE, MC, V. **Parking:** Free.

Just a few steps from the statue of *Rebecca at the Well* is the Seacrest, renovated in 1982 and now offering very comfy, modern guest rooms. The inn also has rooms which sleep up to four people. If I were you, I'd take some of my continental breakfast outside and sit in the cute little Victorian gazebo. The Seacrest is family-owned and -operated, providing pleasant, comfortable lodging at moderate prices, with a smile and an honest welcome. It also has its own bicycle-rental shop ($5 to $12 a day) including mountain bikes, so you can be easily equipped for touring the island.

WHERE TO DINE

There is good food on Block Island even though there are not very many restaurants. You probably will have had breakfast at your hotel, so here are recommendations on where to have lunch and dinner.

HARBORSIDE INN, Water St. Tel. 466-5504.

Cuisine: SEAFOOD. **Reservations:** Recommended.

$ **Prices:** Appetizers $2.75–$6.50; main courses $8–$18; lunch $10–$20. AE, MC, V.

Open: Daily 8am–10pm. **Closed:** Nov–Apr.

Block Island's most popular luncheon spot is definitely the front terrace café of the Harborside. Take in the sun, or duck beneath one of the shady café-table umbrellas, and order something simple like a hamburger or club sandwich, or something fancier, like baked stuffed clams, broiled scallops, or sirloin steak. Wine, beer, and cocktails are served. At dinnertime, the fare is somewhat fancier but similar; and prices are still reasonable.

HOTEL MANISSES, Spring St. Tel. 466-2836.

Cuisine: AMERICAN. **Reservations:** Recommended, especially on weekends in high season. **Directions:** Walk up the hill from the ferry dock, following the signs.

$ **Prices:** Appetizers $4–$9; main courses $13–$25; dinner $40–$50. AE, MC, V.

Open: Light fare daily 3–6pm; dinner daily 6–10:30pm. **Closed:** Nov to mid-Apr.

As with lodging, this is the best place for dining. You can have dinner in the hotel's cozy dining room, or out in the glassed-in room that overlooks the fountain. Dinner might be a black bean and feta cheese tostada, followed by two tournedos of beef with a sauce of two mustards, or quail, or bouillabaisse. Of course, you can always have lobster (if it's in) or the fresh fish of the day. The chef does not probe the exotic too deeply here, but neither does he ever bore your palate. The Manisses has the best situation and cuisine on the island.

---

5. WATCH HILL

6 miles (10km) S of Westerly; 10 miles (16km) SE of Stonington, Conn.; 17 miles (27km) SE of Mystic, Conn.

GETTING THERE By Train Most Amtrak trains on the run between New York City and Boston stop at Westerly.

By Car From Westerly, go south on Route 1A to Avondale, then follow signs to Watch Hill.

ESSENTIALS The **area code** is 401. The **Watch Hill/Misquamicut Chamber of Commerce,** 55 Beach St. in Westerly (tel. 401/596-7761, or toll free 800/SEA-7636) is open Monday to Friday from 9am to 5pm (daily June through August).

As a base for a day at the beach, you could choose no better place than Watch Hill, an old and genteel town at the end of a peninsula between the Atlantic Ocean and the Pawcatuck River. Watch Hill is a sort of Newport-in-miniature, with stately old homes (grand, but not palatial), yachts in the harbor (expensive, but not priceless), and a gentility still strongly felt if slightly faded. It's a quiet town, with fewer than a half dozen places to put up for a night or a week, unless, of course, you own a summer home.

WHAT TO SEE & DO

In Watch Hill, you spend time at the beach, you stroll along Bay Street and go window-shopping, you buy ice-cream cones early and often.

Children will jump at the chance to ride (50¢) on the **1883 Carousel** at the end of Bay Street, one of the oldest merry-go-rounds in the nation.

In the little park across Bay Street from the Olympia Tea Room is a **statue of Ninigret**, Great Sachem of the Narragansetts, a noble man and friend of the local English colonists. The statue was erected in 1914.

Watch Hill is a place to start a romance, or to pursue one; to read and relax, or swim strenuously all day—to do as you please. There are no crowds, no neon signs, no plastic "lifestyles." Watch Hill is a bit of fading glory, which, luckily for those who go there, the rest of the world has already passed by.

WHERE TO STAY

HARTLEY'S GUEST HOUSE, 7 Larkin Rd., Watch Hill, RI 02891. Tel. 401/348-8253. 10 rms (1 with bath).
$ Rates: $56–$78 single or double. Extra person $25. No credit cards. **Parking:** Free. **Closed:** Mid-Oct to mid-June.

Up behind the Inn at Watch Hill in the center of the village, with simple, homey rooms that can accommodate up to four people, is Hartley's. The house is spacious and there's a nice porch overlooking Narragansett Bay.

INN AT WATCH HILL, 118 Bay St., Watch Hill, RI 02891. Tel. 401/596-0665. 22 rms (all with bath). AC TV
$ Rates: $148–$175 double. Extra person $26. Weekly rates available. Children stay free in parents' room. MC, V. **Parking:** Free. **Closed:** Nov–Apr.

Of Watch Hill's lodging places, the most comfortable and pleasant by far is this inn, in the commercial center of the village. Don't expect a great old Victorian palace, for the inn here is actually a suite of motel-style rooms perched above a block of shops on the main street. You enter by going around to the rear and up the hill, where there is a large parking lot and a little office cabin. After check-in, you proceed along a wooden walkway to your room. Rooms 1 through 12 have the best harbor views; Rooms 14 and 15 have some water views; Rooms 16 and 17 see a bit of the harbor, but mostly shops. The view from all is interesting and attractive. The rooms themselves are very good, new, neat, and tidy, each with a microwave oven and small table for breakfast or snacks; all rooms have separate kitchen sink. White brick walls, natural-wood floors, and sliding glass doors opening onto little balconies overlooking the town make the rooms quite charming. Rates vary depending on the size and comforts of the room, and whether you rent on a weekday or on the more expensive weekend. Call for reservations early, as this is the village's prime hostelry and it fills up early.

WHERE TO DINE

OLYMPIA TEA ROOM, Bay St. Tel. 348-8211.
Cuisine: AMERICAN. **Reservations:** Not accepted.
$ Prices: Appetizers $2–$5; main courses $3.25–$8; lunch $7–$15; dinner $16–$25. No credit cards.
Open: Breakfast daily 8am–11am; lunch daily noon–5pm; dinner daily 6–9pm.

In a row of shops at the center of town, across from the little park and the police kiosk, is the most amusing place to dine in this pretty village. The Olympia is an authentic early 20th-century seaside-resort soda-fountain café, with black-and-white checkerboard floor tiles, well-used wooden booths, a few sidewalk tables, and waitresses in black dresses with white aprons. The atmosphere is refreshingly real, not "re-created." As for the food, there's plenty of it, and it's more up-to-date: sautéed shrimp with feta cheese, clam stew, chicken fajitas with hot tortillas and guacamole, bouillabaisse, and of course, lots of seafood, from clams and sausages on linguine to boiled lobster. The Olympia is a wonderful bit of old New England, lovingly preserved for us all to enjoy.

CONNECTICUT

Connecticut's landscape is sprinkled liberally with lakes, rivers, and streams. But the state's namesake is the mighty Connecticut River, which springs from the Connecticut Lakes in northern New Hampshire, flows southward forming the boundary between New Hampshire and Vermont, cuts through Massachusetts and Connecticut, finally to empty into Long Island Sound. The great river is navigable as far north as Hartford, a significant fact that was not lost on the region's Native American inhabitants. They were the ones who gave it the name *Quinnehtukqut*, "the long tidal river."

Later inhabitants pasted different labels on the land. "The Nutmeg State" used to be a popular nickname, coming from the time when itinerant peddlers sold nutmeg from door to door. As often as not, the "nutmegs" were cleverly carved balls of wood. By the time a customer discovered the fakery, the peddler was gone.

For obvious reasons, the people of Connecticut prefer the moniker "Constitution State," which reminds one and all that Connecticut was the first American colony to have a written constitution.

Almost three-quarters of the territory in Connecticut is woodland, and drives along the back roads through these forests reveal rich fields of corn, grain, vegetables, and tobacco. But the state's wealth comes not from agriculture, or from tourism, but rather from insurance and manufacturing. The capital city of Hartford is laden with tremendous buildings which are headquarters for dozens of insurance companies. As for manufacturing, Charles Goodyear, Eli Whitney, Seth Thomas, and Mr. Fuller (of Fuller Brush fame) were all Connecticut Yankees. In the old days the state's production of buttons, pins, doodads, and kitchenwares gave rise to the breed of men known as Yankee peddlers, who traveled from town to town in horse and buggy, spreading the products of Connecticut's industry far and wide. Today the state's industries are a bit different: Sikorsky makes helicopters, General Dynamics makes atomic submarines, and the rubber companies turn out tires and products such as Naugahyde, the synthetic leather named after the Connecticut town of Naugatuck where it's made.

The telephone **area code** for all of Connecticut is 203.

The **state tax** on rooms and meals is 8%.

SEEING CONNECTICUT

Although Connecticut has many historic houses and lovely New England villages, the places that are popular with tourists are mostly along the coast: New Haven, home of Yale University; Essex, a fine old town at the mouth of the Connecticut River; Groton and New London, submarine capital of the world; and of course Mystic Seaport, the

WHAT'S SPECIAL ABOUT CONNECTICUT

Museums
☐ Mystic Seaport, Connecticut's outstanding "living" museum of 19th-century New England maritime life.
☐ Yale University's outstanding museums, including the Center for British Art, the University Art Gallery, and the Peabody Museum of Natural History.
☐ Hartford's Wadsworth Atheneum's fine collection of more than 60,000 works of art.

Theater
☐ New Haven's several good theaters, including the Long Wharf and Yale Rep, the Shubert, and the Palace.

☐ Goodspeed Opera House in East Haddam, a Victorian gem mounting performances of American musical theater.

Literary Shrines
☐ Nook Farm, in Hartford, home to Mark Twain, who wrote *Tom Sawyer* here, and also Harriet Beecher Stowe.
☐ In West Hartford, the home of Noah Webster, America's first great lexicographer.

exciting and attractive re-creation of an old Connecticut maritime village. Hartford, although not what one would think of as a tourist mecca, is a pretty and interesting city well worth a short visit. Besides the attractions of the city itself, it can be used as a base for excursions into the lush farm and woodlands of Litchfield County, in the northwest corner of the state among the Litchfield Hills, Connecticut's "Berkshires."

GETTING THERE   By Plane   The state is served by **Bradley International Airport** in Windsor Locks, 12 miles north of Hartford. There's direct one-plane service between Bradley and more than 60 other North American airports, operated by United, TWA, Delta, American, and USAir. Buses leave the terminal for downtown Hartford and for Springfield, Mass., periodically, and limousines shuttle from Bradley to most cities in Connecticut.

By Train   Amtrak runs trains daily from New York City to Boston along both the coastal route (via New Haven, Old Saybrook, New London, Mystic, and Providence) and the inland route (via Hartford, Windsor Locks, and Springfield). Stopovers are allowed at no extra charge on most trains, so if you buy a ticket from New York to Boston, the stops in New Haven, New London, and Mystic, or New Haven and Hartford, need cost no more. It is usually possible to catch a train from New York in the morning, be in Mystic by noon, tour the Seaport thoroughly, catch another train around 5pm, arrive in Providence by about 6pm and Boston by 8pm. The trip from New York to Hartford takes less than 3 hours; to New Haven, about 1½ hours; to New London, about 2¾ hours; to Mystic, about 3 hours.

Besides the Amtrak trains, there are frequent and cheaper commuter runs operated on the Connecticut Department of Transportation's New Haven Line by **Metro North.** These trains depart New York City's Grand Central Terminal hourly from about 7am until after midnight on weekdays, with even more frequent runs during rush hours. Service on Saturday, Sunday, and holidays is almost as frequent, with trains at least every 2 hours. The trip by Metro North to New Haven takes 1 hour and 40 minutes. For exact schedule information, call toll free in Connecticut 800/223-6052 or in New York City 212/532-4900.

By Bus   Greyhound, Bonanza, and **Vermont Transit** all operate daily buses between New York City, New Haven, and Hartford. The trip to Hartford takes about

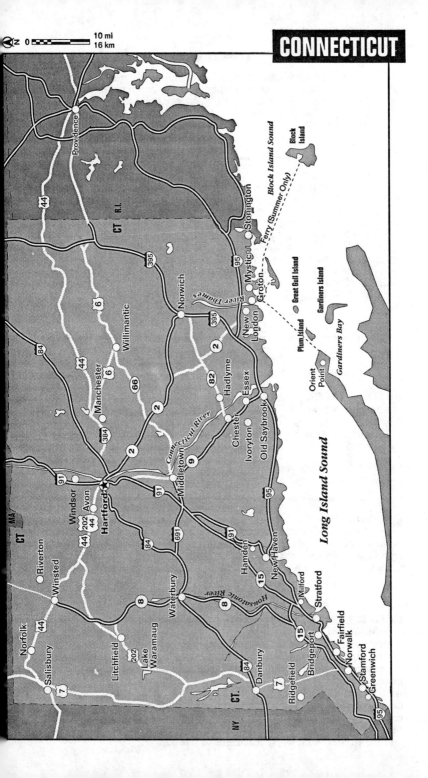

CONNECTICUT

IMPRESSIONS

The warm, the very warm, heart of "New England at its best," such a vast abounding Arcadia of mountains and broad vales and great rivers and large lakes and white villages embowered in prodigious elms and maples. It is extraordinarily beautiful and graceful and idyllic—for America.
HENRY JAMES, LETTER TO SIR T. H. WARREN, MAY 29, 1911, DESCRIBING CONNECTICUT

---

3 to 4¾ hours, depending on the line and the number of stops en route. Greyhound and Bonanza have services between New York and New London, and on to Providence and Cape Cod. The trip from New York City to New London takes about 3 or 3½ hours, depending on stops. It's difficult to take a bus to Mystic Seaport—the train's best way to get there.

From Hartford, Bonanza has buses to Providence and Hyannis; Vermont Transit operates buses to Vermont, New Hampshire, Montréal, and Québec City. All the large lines have buses between Hartford and Boston. In Hartford, the bus stations and the railroad station are all within a block of one another close to downtown. The terminal for Greyhound, Vermont Transit, and Bonanza is at 409 Church St. (tel. 203/547-1500).

---

1. RIDGEFIELD

58 miles (94km) NE of New York City, 8 miles (13km) S of Danbury

GETTING THERE   By Car   From the north, take I-84 to Exit 3 near Danbury, and head south on U.S. 7. From the south, take I-95 or the Merritt Parkway to Norwalk, exiting to U.S. 7 North. From the west, take I-684 (the New York Thruway) to Katonah and head east on N.Y. 35, which becomes Conn. 35 at the state line, then leads straight into Ridgefield.

Essentials   The **area code** is 203. The Ridgefield **chamber of commerce,** 7 Bailey Ave. (tel. 203/438-5992) is open Monday to Friday 9am to 5pm.

Connecticut's extreme southwest corner is a busy maze of light industry, highways, and bedroom communities serving New York. But only a short drive to the north of the bustle along U.S. 7 lies Ridgefield, as tranquil and beautiful a town as one can find. Stately old trees shade the grassy lawns along its quiet streets, and huge old houses are well sited among the gentle rises and hollows of its topography.

WHAT TO SEE & DO

KEELER TAVERN, 132 Main St., at the junction of Rtes. 33 and 35. Tel. 438-5485.
Ridgefield's history dates from colonial times, when the town was a way station on the carriage road from New York to Boston. Carriage passengers need inns for sustenance and lodging, and Ridgefield provided them. In the Keeler Tavern, now a museum, guides in colonial garb will take you through the historic (1715) building with its late 18th-century furnishings, pointing out the tap room, guest quarters, dining room, kitchen, and parlor. Despite the careful preservation and reconstruction of the tavern's early life, its most famous feature was added by accident. During the Battle of Ridgefield (1777) in the revolutionary war, a British cannon sent a ball right into the Keelers' wall, where it remains to this day.

Admission: $3 adults, $2 senior citizens, $1 children.
Open: Wed and Sat–Sun 1–4pm (last tour leaves 3:30pm). **Closed:** Jan.

ALDRICH MUSEUM OF CONTEMPORARY ART, 258 Main St. Tel. 438-4519.

Here you can see changing exhibits of work by contemporary artists. Even though the museum building itself is classic Ridgefield, having been built in 1783, a new wing and complete modernization make this an architectural gem. The museum's sculpture garden is a fine place for a stroll or a few precious moments of peace, quiet, and beauty. Concerts, films, and lectures are offered from time to time.
Admission: $3 adults, $2 seniors and children.
Open: Tues–Sun 1–5pm.

WHERE TO STAY

WEST LANE INN, 22 West Lane, Ridgefield, CT 06877. Tel. 203/438-7323. 20 rms (all with bath). A/C TV TEL **Directions:** Off Main St. in the center of town; look for the signs.
$ Rates: (including breakfast): $97 single; $140 double. Extra person $10. AE, DC, MC, V. **Parking:** Free, in rear.

Set back from the street on a large lawn, this is the grandest of Ridgefield's gracious old inns. Although the management advertises "colonial elegance," the building dates not from colonial times but from the early 1800s, and was completely renovated in 1978. You enter the fine old house to find a world of gleaming wood paneling, thick carpeting, wingback chairs, fine old fireplaces, and a hushed quiet. In the guest rooms, furnishings are classic and comfortable, and facilities are up-to-date. Among other amenities, you'll find a radio in each room. Rooms come with either one or two queen-size beds, and several have working fireplaces. The continental breakfast includes fresh-squeezed orange juice, muffins, and pastries. Other services provided by the inn include baby-sitting, bicycle rental, laundry, and dry cleaning.

As for meals, the West Lane Inn serves light fare "from the pantry," such as sandwiches, desserts, and cold platters, from noon until evening in the breakfast room or on the long, spacious front veranda furnished in wicker.

---

2. NEW HAVEN

75 miles (121km) NE of New York City, 36 miles (58km) S of Hartford, 46 miles (74km) W of New London

GETTING THERE Frequent and cheap commuter runs operated on the Connecticut Department of Transportation's New Haven Line by **Metro North** depart New York City's Grand Central Terminal hourly from about 7am until after midnight on weekdays, with even more frequent runs during rush hours. Service on Saturday, Sunday, and holidays is almost as frequent, with trains at least every 2 hours. The trip by Metro North to New Haven takes 1 hour and 40 minutes. For exact schedule information, call toll free in Connecticut 800/223-6052 or in New York City 212/532-4900.

Amtrak runs trains daily between New York City's Penn Station and Boston's South Station along the coastal route via New Haven. The trip from New York to New Haven takes about 1½ hours; from New Haven to New London, about 1¼ hours; from New Haven to Mystic, about 1½ hours; from Boston to New Haven, about 3 hours. An Amtrak ticket costs significantly more than a Metro North ticket.

By Bus **Greyhound, Bonanza,** and **Vermont Transit** all operate daily buses between New York City, New Haven, and Hartford. Greyhound and Bonanza have services between New York and New London, and on to Providence and Cape Cod.

The trip from New York City to New Haven takes about 1 or 1½ hours, depending on stops.

Connecticut Transit (tel. 203/327-7433) also operates intercity buses in southwestern Connecticut.

By Car   New Haven is easily reached from New York City via I-95, but this road carries heavy truck traffic. A more pleasant alternative is to take the Hutchinson River Parkway to the Merritt Parkway and the Wilbur Cross Parkway (both toll roads). From Hartford, take I-91 south to Meriden, then the Wilbur Cross Parkway. From the east, I-95 is the only fast road.

ESSENTIALS   The **area code** is 203. The **New Haven Convention & Visitors Bureau** has a year-round information center at 195 Church St. (15th floor) at the northeast corner of the green (tel. 203/777-8550, or toll-free 800/937-6428), open Monday through Friday from 8:30am to 5:30pm. There's another information center off I-95 at Long Wharf Exit 4B, open from mid-April to mid-October. At no cost guides will answer questions and give maps of the bus routes and streets, suggested walking tours, the city's attractions, and current material on recreational, educational, cultural, and special events in the area.

This is a town of spires and steeples, of Gothic towers and steel-and-glass towers, very much of the present and very much of the past. Although New Haven was founded in 1638, the crucial year in its history was 1718, when Connecticut's "Collegiate School" for the training of young men for the ministry decided to make its permanent and perpetual home in New Haven, ignoring the suits and blandishments of the other notable towns of Hartford and Saybrook. Perhaps the college came to New Haven because a local man offered a good deal of financial assistance, and in fact it was for this assistance that the school's name was changed to honor Elihu Yale.

New Haven has never been the same. Although today it is a town of business and industry—small arms, the telephone company, the county government—it is still more than anything the town where Yale is, and the presence of the great university dominates New Haven's social and cultural life.

WHAT TO SEE & DO

YALE UNIVERSITY

⭐ New Haven's prime attraction is Yale, almost three centuries old, founded in 1701 and moved to New Haven in 1716. Daily, Yale sponsors **free guided tours** of the campus (tel. 432-2300) weekdays at 10:30am and 2pm, weekends at 1:30pm. Tours start at 344 College Street across from the green, at Phelps Gateway (look for the inscription LUX ET VERITAS), where the university has its information office.

Yale's campus recalls England's Oxford, for it's much more American Collegiate Gothic than, say, Harvard, which is mostly Georgian and colonial in style. Yale's got lots of open, grassy courts, and flèched towers. Centerpiece of this English Gothic world is Harkness Tower, inscribed with the famous motto that has for generations admonished Yale students to move every upward: FOR GOD, FOR COUNTRY, AND FOR YALE. Harkness Tower has a carillon, which is played daily throughout the academic year. You can also see the art galleries, the Beinecke Rare Book Library, the Georgian-style Connecticut Hall, and the Gothic-style Sterling Memorial Library.

Churches

The churches on the green have illustrious heritages of design, for Gothic-style **Trinity Church** is said to have been modeled somewhat on England's York Minister; **Center**

Church and **United Church** are both said to have sprung from early plans for London's famous St. Martin's-in-the-Fields. Center Church, in Georgian style, is particularly interesting. It was built on an old burying ground, and today has a crypt underneath where you can see more than 100 of the early gravestones. Guided tours of the church are offered Tuesday through Sunday.

Three blocks northeast of the green is **Grove Street Cemetery,** a beautiful final resting place for such eminent New Haven citizens as Eli Whitney, Noah Webster, and Charles Goodyear.

Museums and Galleries

PEABODY MUSEUM OF NATURAL HISTORY, 170 Whitney Ave. Tel. 432-5050 or 432-5799.

The Peabody has one of those fine, turn-of-the-century collections assembled when American scientists were venturing into all the corners of the world to bring back specimens of terra, flora, and fauna for study and observation by university students. Dinosaur fossils, dioramas featuring North American animals in their habitats, exhibits on human origins and cultures, invertebrate life, meteorites, and minerals are all on display, although what the museum can show is only a fraction of its vast holdings. Besides the permanent exhibits, the museum sponsors special events, lectures, and films.

Admission: $3 adults, $2 seniors and children aged 3–15, free for children under 3; Mon–Fri 3–5pm free.

Open: Mon–Sat 10am–5pm, Sun noon–5pm, holidays 10am–3pm.

YALE UNIVERSITY ART GALLERY, 1111 Chapel St. Tel. 432-0600.

Yale's major art collection is housed in the oldest university art museum in North America. The Yale Gallery, located between High and York Streets, is justifiably proud of its Garvan Collection of American furniture and silver. Anyone interested in 18th-century American silver has got to see the Garvan—it's the best in the world. Along with van Gogh's masterpiece *The Night Café,* there are paintings by Rubens, Hals, Manet, Picasso, and others. The university's collections form a substantial holding of European, African, Pre-Columbian, American, Ancient, and Asian art. Lectures, concerts, films, and special exhibits are always on when the university is in session; see the listings for current events.

Admission: Free.

Open: Tues–Sat 10am–5pm, Sun 2–5pm. **Closed:** Aug.

YALE CENTER FOR BRITISH ART, 1080 Chapel St. Tel. 432-2800.

The center, located on the corner of High Street, opened to the public in April 1977. It has a fine collection of works by British artists from Elizabethan times to the present, and also features special exhibitions, lectures, films, and concerts. Check *New Haven Info* or the *New Haven Register* listings for current exhibits.

Admission: Free.

Open: Tues–Sat 10am–5pm, Sun noon–5pm.

PERFORMING ARTS

Because of Yale, New Haven has a rich cultural life in music, dance, and drama. Each academic year sees concerts and performances by more than a dozen excellent groups, including the New Haven Symphony Orchestra, the Yale Concert Band, Yale Glee Club, Yale Jazz Ensemble, the Bach Society, the New Haven Civic Orchestra, and the Community Choir. The Yale Repertory Theater and the Long Wharf Theater (a proving ground for New York–bound plays) get very good reviews each season, as does the Connecticut Ballet Company. New Haven also plays host to visits from the Boston Symphony Orchestra, major concert and popular performers, and groups.

Several buildings in and around the campus are foci for these events. The listings recommended above have full information on the current season's performances. Most will be within a few blocks of the green. **Long Wharf** is a bit farther out, next to Howard Johnson's, in the wholesale market at 222 Sargent Dr. (Connecticut Turnpike Exit 46; tel. 787-4282).

Downtown theaters include the **Shubert** (tel. 624-1825) and the **Palace** (tel. 789-2120), across from one another on College Street between Chapel and Crown, ½ block south of the green behind the Taft Apartments. The **Yale Rep** (tel. 432-1234) is in a former church building on Chapel Street, corner of York, 2 blocks west of the green.

EVENING ENTERTAINMENT

New Haven must retain its dignity as the seat of Yale University. But that doesn't mean things are dead at night. Try the **Foundry Cafe,** mentioned below, for live music.

Boppers, at the corner of College and Crown Streets (tel. 562-1957), is a re-created 1950s diner, complete with half the body of a '56 Buick Special. Though you can dine here on burgers and pizza, the attraction is the fifties music (recorded) for dancing.

WHERE TO STAY

New Haven is short on those cozy, charming lodging places (inns and bed-and-breakfasts) which are so densely scattered throughout the rest of New England. Most of the city's lodgings are to be found in modern hotels downtown, and motels on the outskirts.

DOWNTOWN HOTELS

THE COLONY INN, 1157 Chapel St., New Haven, CT 06511. Tel. 203/776-1234, or toll free 800/458-8810. Fax 203/772-3929. 80 rms, 6 suites (all with bath). A/C TV TEL
$ Rates: $86 single; $96 double; $125–$350 suite. Extra person $10. AE, DC, MC, V. **Parking:** $3.
The Colony Inn is known to Yalies and their parents as a comfortable and convenient place to stay during campus visits. It's located just a block from the Yale Rep Theater and the Yale Art Gallery between Park and York. The spacious rooms in this modern five-story building are done in contemporary style with colonial accents and reproduction pieces. All the comforts are here, including free cable TV in your room and turndown service. Other hotel services include indoor parking, a restaurant, and a lounge with live entertainment.

HOLIDAY INN–DOWNTOWN, 30 Whalley Ave., New Haven, CT 06511. Tel. 203/777-6221, or toll free 800/465-4329. Fax 203/772-1089. 160 rms (all with bath). A/C TV TEL
$ Rates: $82 single or double. Children stay free in parents' room. AE, CB, DC, MC, V. **Parking:** Free.
The modern, comfortable Holiday Inn, just west of the Yale campus, is only a 5-minute walk from the center of town. Rooms higher up in the hotel have better views and less traffic noise. The hotel has its own Cafe Sandalwood restaurant and lounge, serving dishes from all over the world.

HOTEL DUNCAN, 1151 Chapel St., New Haven, CT 06511. Tel. 203/787-1273. 90 rms (65 with bath). TV TEL
$ Rates: $40 single; $55 double. Extra person $15. Weekly rates available. AE, DC, MC, V. **Parking:** $3 per day, next door.

S This marvelous old hotel boasts that it is "New Haven's oldest established hotel," and it is certainly well established, having stood solidly on Chapel Street between Park and York for almost a century. To enter its Romanesque portal is to step back in time, right into a set for a black-and-white movie from the 1940s or 1950s. The Duncan's advantages are its location, just 4 blocks west of the green, and even fewer blocks from the Yale campus; its prices, and the friendly, unpretentious, low-key staff and management. Except for cable TV, don't expect up-to-the-minute comforts in these 90 rooms, for the Duncan is a true period piece. Expect basic, even worn, accommodations, but also basic cleanliness. The Duncan is a favorite with the young and the artistic, who love the fact that it is an honest, authentic echo of another time. A new Thai restaurant opened on the premises in April 1991.

PARK PLAZA HOTEL, 155 Temple St., New Haven, CT 06511. Tel. 203/772-1700, or toll free 800/243-4211. Fax 203/624-2683. 300 rms. A/C TV TEL
$ Rates: $97 single; $112 double. AE, DC, MC, V. **Parking:** $10, covered lot adjacent to hotel.
This is the prime downtown location, in the shopping and office complex facing the green. The Park Plaza has many big-hotel services, such as an outdoor swimming pool, rooftop restaurant, lounge with entertainment, and comfortable guest rooms. Yale, and most of New Haven's downtown sights, are within easy walking distance.

A DOWNTOWN INN

INN AT CHAPEL WEST, 1201 Chapel St., New Haven, CT 06511. Tel. 203/777-1201. 10 rms (all with bath).
$ Rates: (including breakfast): $175 double. AE, CB, DC, MC, V. **Parking:** Free.
☆ This well-located Victorian clapboard house fills a gap in New Haven's lodging market with its B&B service. The elegantly furnished rooms have mahogany period furniture, brass fixtures, four-poster beds, touches of lace, and down pillows. Some rooms have fireplaces. The innkeeper has breakfast catered from a local restaurant.

A NEARBY MOTEL

Your best bet for a good, moderately priced motel room is at the cluster of hostelries near New Haven on the Wilbur Cross Parkway. The parkway is the scenic alternative to I-95. Passing several miles northeast of New Haven, the parkway provides access to the city at its Exits 57 (Conn. 34, Derby Avenue), 59 (Conn. 63, Whalley Avenue), and 60 (Conn. 10, Dixwell Avenue). Motels are grouped at each exit, but the best selection is at Exit 59, Whalley Avenue.

Staying at Exit 59, you'll be exactly 3½ miles from the greensward of Yale's Old Campus, the very center of the city. Bus B-1 ("Amity Road") will shuttle you between the motels and the center of town. A small shopping center and several restaurants are within walking distance of each motel.

If you can't find what you want here, consider driving east to Branford.

BRANFORD MOTOR INN AND CONFERENCE FACILITIES, 375 Main St., Branford, CT 06405. Tel. 203/488-8314, or toll free 800/255-9296. Fax 203/488-8314. 76 rms (all with bath). A/C TV TEL **Directions:** Go 5 miles east of New Haven along I-95, take Exit 55, and turn right at stop sign to pass underneath highway.
$ Rates: $50–$66 single; $68–$74 double; $100–$165 suite. Extra person $8. Children under 16 stay free in parents' room. AE, DC, DISC, MC, V. **Parking:** Free.
This large U-shaped group of buildings faces U.S. 1 across a wide swath of lawn

complete with swimming pool. Scores of guest rooms fill the two-story buildings, and each room has, among other amenities, a coffee pot and Home Box Office movies on the television. Rooms in the newer annex are several dollars more expensive than those in the older main buildings. You'll find a coffee shop, restaurant, and guest laundry right on the premises.

WHERE TO DINE

New Haven's restaurants are spread throughout the metropolitan area, with no particularly rich concentration downtown, such as one finds in Hartford or Boston. But if you are selective, it is not difficult to find the meal you're looking for, at the price you want to pay, within walking distance of the green. Some New Havenites who enjoy dining out belong to private clubs (the famed Mory's is one of these), and thus tend not to patronize restaurants that are open to the general public.

RESTAURANTS NEAR THE GREEN

ATTICUS BOOKSTORE-CAFE, 1082 Chapel St. Tel. 776-4040.
   Cuisine: CAFE. **Reservations:** Not accepted.
$ **Prices:** Pastries $1.50–$3; sandwiches $4–$7.50. MC, V.
   Open: Mon–Fri 8am–midnight, Sat 9am–midnight, Sun 9am–9pm.
Book lovers (and there are plenty of them in New Haven) congregate at Atticus, next to the entrance to the Yale Center for British Art. Sip tea and consume pastry while scanning the shelves from the comfort of your table, or browse through the store accompanied by the heavenly smell of coffee brewing. Come in the morning for croissants and coffee, at lunchtime for a substantial sandwich, or in the afternoon for cakes and tea. To your café bill, add in the price of the book you'll discover, and buy

BRUXELLES, 220 College St. Tel. 777-7752.
   Cuisine: NEW AMERICAN. **Reservations:** Not accepted.
$ **Prices:** Appetizers $4–$9; main courses $11–$22; dinner $25–$40. AE, MC, V
   Open: Sun–Thurs 11:30am–11:30pm, Fri–Sat 11:30am–1:30am.
This chic brasserie and bar is at the corner of Crown Street, a block west of the green. Black bentwood chairs and tables are the main feature of the simple but elegant decor here. To the left as you enter is the well-stocked bar; to the right the dining rooms, and huge vertical grills with spits loaded with chickens, ducks, and whole roasts of pork and beef. At dinner you can start with something like goat cheese on an herbed tomato, then order Texas barbecue chicken, or roast tuna steak au poivre, or roast duck with peach-raspberry sauce. There is good luncheon fare as well. Add a glass or two of some premium vintage or brew from the well-selected wine and beer lists. The late hours also make this a good place for an after-theater drink and snack.

FOUNDRY CAFE, 104 Audubon St. Tel. 776-5144.
   Cuisine: AMERICAN. **Reservations:** Not accepted.
$ **Prices:** Appetizers $2–$4; main courses $4–$11. No credit cards.
   Open: Mon–Sat 11:30am–midnight.
Near the corner of Whitney Avenue and Audubon is this old standby for lunch or supper. The Foundry was just that, a machine foundry building, until it was recycled into a bookstore, shops, and the café. The one small café room has a bar/lunch counter, a blackboard menu, and some beautiful old inlaid-wood chess tables as dining tables. Fare is simple but tasty: a selection of sandwiches, seafood salad platters, and cheesecake. In the evening, the Foundry Cafe is a bar and nightclub. Happy hour, when the snacks are free, is every weekday evening from 4 to 7pm, and there's entertainment (usually jazz) on Wednesday through Sunday evenings.

LOUIS' LUNCH, 261–3 Crown St. Tel. 562-5507.
   Cuisine: AMERICAN. **Reservations:** Not accepted. **Directions:** On Crown St. 1 block west of the green.
$ **Prices:** Hamburgers $2.30–$3.10. No credit cards.

Open: Mon–Fri 9–11am and 11:30am–4pm.

⭐ It may seem an audacious claim to say that Louis' Lunch was the "purveyor of the first hamburger in the U.S.A.," but so it is. Louis' started in 1900, serving the first thinly sliced steak sandwich, and then developed the vertically grilled ground-beef sandwich. The beef is still ground fresh daily and grilled in the original antique vertical grills. Served on toast with tomato and onion, the hamburger ($2.30) is also available as a cheeseburger (introduced in 1931) for no extra charge. Threatened by downtown redevelopment some years ago, Louis' was rescued by faithful fans who saw to it that the brick structure was picked up and moved safely to its present location. Many—from all over the world—donated bricks for use in resettlement. Today Louis' continues to cater faithfully to New Haven's weekday lunch crowd.

SCOOZZI TRATTORIA AND WINE BAR, 1104 Chapel St. Tel. 776-8268.
   Cuisine: CONTEMPORARY ITALIAN. **Reservations:** Required.
$ **Prices:** Appetizers $2.50–$5.95; main courses $6.95–$15.95. AE, DISC, MC, V.
   Open: Lunch Tues–Sat 11:30am–5pm; dinner Tues–Sat 5–11:30pm, Sun 4–11:30pm; Sun brunch 11:30am–3pm.

Scoozzi Trattoria and Wine Bar has got to be New Haven's most popular restaurant this year. It's absolutely impossible to get a table if you haven't made a reservation, so if you're planning a pre-theater dinner, call well in advance for a reservation—perhaps even a night or two ahead.

Very popular items on the menu are the Pizzettes—small pizzas for one (aptly named). The spinach and goat cheese pizzette with fresh basil, garlic, red peppers, black olives, sundried tomatoes, and fontina is terrific. If you'd rather have pasta, "pasta Scoozzi" is a good choice—it's squid-ink pasta with tomato, Italian peppers, mushrooms, garlic, zucchini, pignoli nuts, fresh fennel, and olive oil. Of course, there are a few token chicken, veal, lamb, and pork dishes on the menu, and wine suggestions are listed for each type of dish. There is a good wine list and a full bar. Feel free to go just for appetizers (rather than a full meal) before a show.

RESTAURANTS NEAR WOOSTER SQUARE

About 6 blocks east of the green along Chapel Street lies Wooster Square, a lovely green park surrounded by some of this city's most interesting old houses. In this area, Chapel Street and Wooster Street (parallel, 1 block south) hold many restaurant choices, many of them featuring Italian cuisine.

FRANK PEPE'S, 157 Wooster St. Tel. 865-5762.
   Cuisine: PIZZA. **Reservations:** Not accepted.
$ **Prices:** Pizza $5–$18. No credit cards.
   Open: Mon and Wed–Thurs 4–10:30pm, Fri–Sat 11:30am–midnight, Sun 2:30–10:30pm.

For pizza, this is New Haven's favorite, two storefronts in which you will find bare wooden booths, brick walls, little in the way of atmosphere, but fantastic pizza. People line up in front of the restaurant to receive the hot pizzas that issue from the huge ovens in the back. The assortment is bewildering, ranging from a small grated-cheese pizza to large pies; large ones with chicken or fresh clams cost more.

3. CONNECTICUT RIVER VALLEY

Strictly speaking, the Connecticut River Valley extends all the way from Long Island South to northern New Hampshire. It's the lower valley that we're interested in, though. Besides being particularly beautiful, the last 100 or so miles of the river's course have figured prominently in Connecticut history. The small towns retain the charm of a bygone era, and the river's banks are scattered with state parks and forests.

From New Haven, it's about 30 miles along I-95 to the mouth of the river. About midway you pass **Hammonassett Beach State Park,** which has facilities for camping and picnicking, hiking trails, and a fine beach for boating, swimming, and scuba diving.

Before reaching the river's edge, the highway passes Westbrook, where there's a nice inn, and then Old Saybrook, a town with picturesque views. On the east bank of the river is Old Lyme, with several fine inns. Heading northwest up the river on Route 9 brings you to Essex, perhaps the busiest and most charming river town, with one of Connecticut's most acclaimed inns. Ivoryton, to the west, also has several fine inns, and an old steam railroad. Due north of Ivoryton lies Chester, a charming village with good possibilities for dining and lodging, and just across the river from it, by an antique car-ferry, is Hadlyme, with its own hilltop castle. North of Hadlyme, on the same (east) bank of the river is East Haddam, home of the famous Goodspeed Opera House, and several good inns. All of this is yours in a distance of 20 miles, from Westbrook to East Haddam.

OLD SAYBROOK

Old Saybrook is the gateway to scenic Saybrook Point, with its two lighthouses. If you have time for a pretty drive, come up from Westbrook on U.S. 1 East, then follow Route 154 through Knollwood, Fenwick (where Katharine Hepburn lives), and Saybrook Point to Old Saybrook. To cross the river to Old Lyme, you will have to leave all this tranquillity and climb back onto I-95 eastbound.

WHERE TO STAY & DINE

In Saybrook

SAYBROOK POINT INN, 2 Bridge St., Saybrook, CT 06475. Tel. 203/ 395-2000. 62 rms (all with bath), 7 suites. A/C MINIBAR TV TEL
$ Rates: $145 superior double, $175 deluxe double, $210 luxury double; $255– $495 suite. AE, DC, DISC, V. **Parking:** Free.
If you're interested in a luxury hotel right on the water, the Saybrook Point Inn is probably your best choice—there are even slips available if you're coming by boat. The rooms hold reproduction Chippendale and Queen Anne furnishings and king-sized beds with floral comforters. Many rooms have balconies and 42 of them have fireplaces. The rooms on the third floor have cathedral ceilings and paddle fans. All junior suites have jacuzzi tubs, and the one- and two-bedroom suites with separate sitting and dining areas are ideal for families.

Dining/Entertainment: The hotel's dining room offers continental cuisine as well as seafood, and it overlooks the marina. There is a more casual patio area available for dining as well. The 18th-century mahogany bar is open daily and provides live entertainment on weekends.

Facilities: Exercise room, indoor and outdoor pools, hot tub, sauna, and spa (massage, facials, aromatherapy, and accupressure are all available).

Near Old Saybrook

CAPTAIN DIBBELL HOUSE, 21 Commerce St., Clinton, CT 06413. Tel. 203/669-1646. 4 rms (all with bath). A/C
$ Rates: $70–$80 single; $80–$90 double. AE, MC, V. **Parking:** Free.
The Captain Dibbell house was built in 1866 for Capt. Edwin A. Dibbell and his wife Mary. Captain Dibbell remained in residence until he died in 1907. His wife continued to occupy the house until her death in 1917, after which the house remained a private residence until it was taken over by the present owners who have done their best to keep the house the way it was over a hundred years ago.

You'll cross an old footbridge to get to the inn, and once inside, you'll feel at home in the comfortable sitting room with its upright piano and puzzle-in-progress on the table. It will be no surprise that the rooms are equally comfortable. The Captain's Room, for instance, is Victorian in style and houses a queen-size brass bed, antique furnishings, and a blanket chest. In contrast, Elizabeth's Room is bright and airy with its king-size white iron bed, green-and-white quilts, and sitting area with a wingback chair and oak furnishings.

Breakfast is served buffet-style in the dining room. You might have fresh fruit muffins, scrambled eggs or an omelet, and freshly ground coffee. If the weather is nice and you'd prefer to eat outside, you can arrange to have breakfast in the gazebo.

OLD LYME

This village is a painter's paradise, and has been so for quite a while. During the early years of this century, Miss Florence Griswold opened the doors of her mansion on Lyme Street to painters, mostly American impressionists, whom she admired, including Charles Ebert, Childe Hassam, Willard Metcalfe, Henry Ward Ranger, and Guy and Carleston Wiggins. Painters being painters, no matter how talented, they were sometimes unable to scrape together the month's rent for a room in the mansion, so instead they did what they could: They painted the door panels of the house with scenes from around Old Lyme. The house is now a museum, and one of your prime reasons for stopping here. The other reason is that Old Lyme has several fine inns, good for lodging and for dining.

WHAT TO SEE & DO

FLORENCE GRISWOLD MUSEUM, 96 Lyme St. Tel. 434-5542.
This late-Georgian mansion, built in 1817, is home to the Lyme Historical Society. Visit the first-floor rooms where Miss Florence's artist guests used to paint. Upstairs are galleries concentrating on the works of this "Lyme School" of American impressionism, and on changing exhibits, including New England furnishings and decorative arts.
Admission: $3 adults, free for children under 12.
Open: June–Oct, Tues–Sat 10am–5pm, Sun 1–5pm. Nov–May, Wed–Sun 1–5pm.

LYME ACADEMY OF FINE ARTS, 84 Lyme St. Tel. 434-5232.
Primarily a school in a gracious house dating from 1817, the Lyme Academy of Fine Arts has a gallery of changing exhibits of traditional painters and sculptors.
Admission: Free.
Open: Mon–Fri 9am–5pm, Sat 9am–4pm, Sun 1–4pm.

WHERE TO STAY

BEE AND THISTLE INN, 100 Lyme St., Old Lyme, CT 06371. Tel. 203/434-1667. 12 rms (10 with bath). A/C **Directions:** From Exit 70 (off I-95), turn left off ramp. Take first right onto Halls Rd. (Rte. 1 East). Go to T in the road and turn left. Inn is third house on left.
$ Rates: (including continental breakfast): $64–$115 single or double. AE, DC, MC, V. **Parking:** Free, on premises.
Bob and Penny Nelson's inn dates from colonial times (1756), with many later additions. Its situation, on its own estate of more than 5 shady acres bordering the Lieutenant River, is superb. The guest rooms have furnishings reflecting the inn's long history—canopy, four-poster, or spool beds with handmade quilts and afghans, washstands, wing chairs—but also private baths in most cases. One room has a TV. The dining room is open for lunch and dinner as well (closed Tuesday). Fare at lunch can be as simple as a sandwich, but there are always daily-special plates which are

more elaborate. Dinner is full course, emphasizing seafood and game in elegant and ingenious preparations. The menu changes completely three times a year.

OLD LYME INN, 85 Lyme St. (P.O. Box 787), Old Lyme, CT 06371. Tel. 203/434-2600. Fax 203/434-5352. 13 rms (all with bath). A/C TEL **Directions:** Go north on I-95, take Exit 70, and turn right off the ramp. Turn right at the first light and follow this until the second light; the inn will be on your left.

$ Rates: (including continental breakfast): $85–$130 single; $95–$140 double. Extra person $30. AE, DC, DISC, MC, V. **Parking:** Free. **Closed:** First 2 weeks in Jan.

This gracious and elegant mansion, dating from the 1850s, is the village's prime hostelry. Innkeeper Diana Field Atwood has found period furnishings from many New England locales for the rooms, so you'll find canopy beds, marble-topped dressers and vanities, and antique mirrors. Eight of the guest rooms are in the new (1985) North Wing, which is designed to harmonize with the original mansion and other structures on historic Lyme Street. North Wing rooms are preferable because of their better size and quiet, though the five rooms in the original mansion are certainly charming. Each room has a clock radio.

The Old Lyme Inn's dining room is open Tuesday to Saturday for lunch from noon to 2pm and for dinner from 6 to 9pm; Sunday brunch is from 11am to 3pm, dinner from 4 to 9pm. Tapestries, gleaming silver, and a formal atmosphere greet you in the high-ceilinged dining room, renowned for its fine cuisine, especially local seafood and veal. There is also a less formal grill room, open Tuesday through Sunday.

ESSEX

This was a shipbuilding and sea captain's town, founded in 1648. At first life in Essex was centered on farming, but within 100 years the shipbuilding industry grew and brought Essex much greater prosperity. The early name, by the way, was the Native American one of Potapaug, which served to identify the town until well into the 19th century.

Today Essex is one of the most picturesque towns in Connecticut, its old houses well kept, its boatyards and marina bobbing with sleek yachts and powerboats. Walk up Pratt Street for a look at the old houses, and then from Essex Square, take a drive out North Main Street to view the fine old mansions. This quick tour leaves out lots of interesting side streets, corners, and crannies of Essex, and if you have the time, you could do worse than to poke around town, turning up quaint vignettes and fine river views.

WHAT TO SEE & DO

CONNECTICUT RIVER MUSEUM, Main St. Tel. 767-8269.

From Essex Square (the intersection of Main, North Main, South Main, and Pratt Streets), walk down Main Street past the Griswold Inn to the riverside end, known as the Foot of Main, where you'll come across this dockhouse for steamboats built in 1878 and recently restored. Ship's models, paintings, photographs, and other exhibits recall life on the Connecticut River in years gone by. Kids will love the replica of the first submarine, the *Turtle*. The museum is open year round.

Admission: $3 adults, $2 seniors, free for children 12 and under.
Open: Tues–Sat 10am–5pm.

WHERE TO STAY & DINE

GRISWOLD INN, 36 Main St., Essex, CT 06426. Tel. 203/767-1776. Fax 203/767-0481. 25 rms (all with bath). A/C TEL

$ Rates: (including continental breakfast): $80–$165 single or double; $80–$165 suite. AE, MC, V.

This fine old inn in the center of town is famous throughout Connecticut for its location, food, and lodging. The rooms are quaint and old-fashioned, with low ceilings and exposed rough-hewn rafters, hooked rugs on the floors, perhaps a marble-topped vanity or a similar piece in one corner. Both double beds and twin beds are available. Note that in summer it may be necessary to reserve a weekend date 2 months in advance, so call or write to the inn. On-street parking is available.

The Griswold's several dining rooms are well done and interesting. At lunch, have the Griswold's own brand of sausages for $7.25, or a sandwich for about the same. Luncheon plates are only $1 more. Dinner specialties are hearty, with seafood and steaks for $16.95 to $21.95. The wine list is quite good, the beer both domestic and imported, and one of the drafts is the English lager named Courage.

The Griswold is known for its Sunday "Hunt Breakfasts," when for $12 (11am to 2:30pm) you can help yourself to unlimited amounts of eggs, bacon, and ham, sausage, grits, fried potatoes, kippers, chicken, lamb kidneys, creamed chipped beef, smelts, or whatever else is offered for the day. For children 6 and under, breakfast is on the house, and sodas come in a "bottomless carafe."

EN ROUTE TO IVORYTON

On the way from Essex to Ivoryton, the road (Railroad Avenue) passes the station of the **Valley Railroad** (tel. 767-0103). You can ride the old steam train 5 miles upriver to Chester and back. At Deep River Station, if you wish, you can get off the train and onto the riverboat *Becky Thatcher* to motor farther upriver past Gillette Castle (see below). Trains leave four times a day in fall, two times a day during spring, and several times every day beginning at 10:30am in summer; they connect with the boat for a 2½ hour combination trip. The combination trip costs $14 for adults and $7 for children under 11. Call for the latest information on schedules and fares.

IVORYTON

Ivoryton is a part of Essex for municipal government purposes, but it has a character and history of its own. The name came from the ivory industry set up here by the Comstock family, and many of the ivory keys for America's pianos and organs were made here. The ivory industry is gone, but the company that makes Witch Hazel, that soothing and astringent distillate, is still going strong on the Essex/Ivoryton boundary.

WHERE TO STAY

The Copper Beech Inn, listed under "Where to Dine," below, also rents comfortable rooms.

IVORYTON INN, 115 Main St., Ivoryton, CT 06442. Tel. 203/767-0422. Fax 203/767-0318. 30 rms (all with bath). A/C TEL
$ Rates: (including continental breakfast): $89–$105 double. AE, DC, MC, V.
Parking: Free.
Once the favorite of ivory traders visiting the town, the Ivoryton is now a favorite with vacationers. You'll recognize the gray clapboard building with yellow awnings ½ mile west of the Copper Beech Inn, and just a few minutes' walk from the Ivoryton Playhouse. The rooms here are quite simple and homey, but comfortable and sufficient. On the ground floor of the inn is the tavern, a world of mellow wood and Windsor chairs, and the fairly formal restaurant.

WHERE TO DINE

COPPER BEECH INN, 46 Main St., Ivoryton, CT 06442. Tel. 203/767-0330.
Cuisine: COUNTRY FRENCH. **Reservations:** Recommended, especially on weekends **Directions:** Inn is 1¾ miles west of Exit 3 from Route 9 North.

$ Prices: Appetizers $5.95–$29.50; main courses $22.50–$25.75. AE, DC, MC, V.

Open: Tues–Thurs 6–8:30pm, Fri–Sat 6–9pm, Sun 1–8pm.

★ The reason to go to Ivoryton is to eat in the inn, built as the home of a prosperous ivory merchant, and now one of New England's most gracious places to dine: Tables have fresh flowers and a full French service in silver. The Comstock Room has fine dark-wood paneling; the garden porch is mostly windows and plants, with a floor of quarry tiles and a unique pineapple chandelier. Behind the inn is the Greenhouse, a real one set with wicker chairs and small tables, and it's here that cocktails are served. The menu for dinner is among the best in New England: boned breast of pheasant, filet of salmon sautéed in a crisp coat of potato served with sun-dried tomatoes, filet of beef Wellington with sauce périgourdine—it goes on to 14 items, none common, all interesting. Appetizers, such as duck sausage sliced and served warm with duck stock sauce, are offered. Desserts (about $6) include the Copper Beech Inn's famed charlotte aux framboises—raspberry mousse, lady fingers, and fresh raspberries.

The Copper Beech also has 13 fine guest rooms with air conditioning and private bath for $118 to $185 double, continental breakfast included.

CHESTER

The picture-perfect little Connecticut riverside village of Chester is nestled in the valley of the Pattaconk Brook. Its buildings are of white clapboard, yellow brick, or somber granite, its fences of fieldstone. Little shops line the short main street, along with the general store, the post office, and the library. It is charming, scenic, small, and wealthy.

Native American deeds to the land once known as the district of Pattaconk date from the 1660s. Colonial settlers moved to the district from Saybrook in the early 1700s, and by 1836 the town was incorporated as Chester. During the colonial period Chester was an industrial town, with a gristmill, a sawmill, and shipyards. The ferry service across the Connecticut River to Hadlyme was inaugurated in 1769, and continues to this day.

There is little to do in Chester except to enjoy the place itself, to stroll its main street, and to ride or walk through the surrounding countryside.

EN ROUTE TO HADLYME   If you're driving, the most enjoyable way to get from Chester to Hadlyme is to take the old **Chester-Hadlyme ferry.** Cars and pedestrians travel at prices more antique than the fairly modern boat which makes the run—$1 for car and driver, 25¢ for pedestrians. Although the boat is new, the history of the ferry run goes back to 1769, when one Jonathan Warner would drag you across the river for a small fee. Today the ferry is run by the State of Connecticut, and it operates April through November daily from 7am to 6:45pm. The trip across the river is made right in the shadow of Gillette Castle, and takes about 5 minutes, not counting the short waiting time.

HADLYME

Shortly after the turn of the century, an actor named William Gillette realized a lifelong dream by building himself a castle to live in. His stage career, including a very successful period in the role of Sherlock Holmes, had brought him the wealth he needed, and in 1914 he began. Over 5 years and a million dollars later, the result was a strange-looking mansion of fieldstone named "The Seventh Sister," complete with a commanding view of the Connecticut River and its own 3-mile-long excursion railroad. Inside the castle, on River Road in East Haddam, Gillette gave vent to his passion for detail and exotica, bringing furnishings from around the world and specifying in great detail the form that was to be given to the intricately carved oak trim and the ingenious wooden door latches. Today William Gillette's fantasy house is known as **Gillette Castle** (tel. 526-2336), and it's a state park open to all and sundry. The narrow-gauge railroad is gone, but forest paths, picnic tables, and river-vista spots have replaced it. Tours of the house itself are given daily Memorial Day to Columbus Day from 10am to 5pm, and weekends through mid-December, from 10am to 4pm, at a charge of $4 for adults, $2 for children under 12. Gillette Castle is either Connecticut's most distinguished medieval castle or the largest backyard barbecue ever constructed—you decide.

EAST HADDAM

From Hadlyme, drive northwest a few miles to East Haddam, where you'll find the wonderful old **Goodspeed Opera House** (tel. 873-8668). This riverside Victorian gem, built in 1876, has now been carefully restored to serve as a venue for American musical theater. The setting by the river and bridge is so picturesque that it's worth the ride just to see the exterior, but if you have the time, take a tour of the interior. It's on view Monday and Saturday, June through August; $1 for adults, 50¢ for children. Best of all, see a play; the specialty is the revival of early musicals and the production of new works. Thirteen Goodspeed shows have moved to Broadway. Three musicals are offered each season beginning in mid-April and continuing through mid-December with performances Wednesday through Sunday, and matinees on Wednesday, Saturday, and Sunday. Tickets cost $28.50 Friday through Sunday, $1 less on other days. Call for the latest information and ticket reservations.

RIVER CRUISES

Across the river from East Haddam in the village of Haddam is the office of **Camelot Cruises, Inc.,** 1 Marine Park, Haddam, CT 06438 (tel. 203/345-8591). From March through December, you can board the MV *Camelot* for a lunch, Sunday brunch, or Murder Mystery dinner cruise along the placid river. There's no better way to enjoy the scenery, and you get a meal and live entertainment to boot. This is fairly formal dining, and you are expected to dress "appropriately"—suit or sport jacket for men; a dress, skirt and blouse, or a nice slacks outfit for women.

Cruises depart rain or shine. The evening Murder Mystery dinner cruises board at 6:30pm and depart Thursday through Saturday at 7pm, returning at 10pm. The price, meal (but not tax and tips) included, is $24.75 per person for the luncheon cruise, $29 for the Sunday Brunch Cruise. Children under 12 pay half price on $47.75 for the mystery dinner cruise, luncheon and brunch cruises.

WHERE TO STAY

BISHOPSGATE INN, Goodspeed Landing, East Haddam, CT 06423. Tel. 203/873-1667. 6 rms (all with bath). **Directions:** Take Exit 69 off I-95 to Rte. 9. From Rte. 9 take Exit 7 to East Haddam. From the Goodspeed Opera House follow Rte. 82 ²/₁₀ mile to Bishopsgate on the left.

$ Rates: $80–$130 single or double. MC, V. **Parking:** Free.

This Colonial home was built in 1818 by East Haddam merchant and shipbuilder, Horace Hayden. Today the inn is run by gracious innkeepers Molly and Dan Swartz. Of the six rooms, four have fireplaces, and each floor has a comfortable sitting area with inviting couches and chairs, so you'll have somewhere to go to read or socialize with the other guests.

The rooms are furnished with period pieces or family antiques. The Jenny Lind Room has a wooden pine canopy bed with netting, an Oriental carpet, a wingback and a Windsor chair, pine side tables, and a fireplace. The room on the ground floor (also with a fireplace), has a cannonball bed with a pink quilt, a pine hutch, a wingback chair, and lace-edged curtains. The bathroom for this room is located across the hall, but don't worry about privacy, the walk to the bathroom is hidden by a well-placed screen.

Breakfast here is served in the country kitchen and might include stuffed French toast, fresh fruits, homemade breads and coffee cake, a breakfast meat, and some kind of eggs. Dinner can also be provided at the guests' request.

4. NEW LONDON & GROTON

46 miles (74km) E of New Haven, 45 miles (73km) SE of Hartford,
9 miles (15km) W of Mystic

GETTING THERE **By Train** **Amtrak** runs trains daily from New York City to Boston along the coastal route via New Haven, Old Saybrook, New London, Mystic, and Providence. The trip from New York City to New London takes about 2¾ hours; to Mystic, about 3 hours.

By Bus Bus transportation in the region is provided by **Southeastern Area Rapid Transit** (tel. 203/886-2631).

By Car Speedy access to New London is provided by I-95 and Conn. Route 52. A warning is in order: Rush-hour traffic (8 to 9am and 5 to 6pm) in the Groton/New London area is extremely heavy, especially along I-95 and its feeder roads. Make your getaway before 5pm, or stay and have dinner until the roads empty out.

ESSENTIALS The **area code** is 203. For information, contact the **Southeastern Connecticut Tourism District,** 27 Masonic St. (P.O. Box 89), New London, CT 06320 (tel. 203/444-2206, or toll free 800/222-6783).

Most visitors to these navy towns are here to see the U.S. Coast Guard Academy, or the navy submarine base at Groton. But there are other things to see and do as well. New London has a state park and a beachfront amusement park, as well as car-ferry services to Block Island, R.I., Fishers Island, N.Y., and Orient Point, Long Island, N.Y. Groton has Fort Griswold State Park.

The big draw in this region is, of course, Mystic Seaport (see "Mystic," below). Many visitors choose to stay near Mystic, and tour New London and Groton on a day-trip. There are some lodging possibilities, however, in New London, Groton, and the nearby towns of Niantic and East Lyme, to the west. Lodging establishments in this area consist almost exclusively of highway motels. Many are geared to the tourist trade rather than to the business or armed-forces traveler.

NEW LONDON

The major tourist attraction in New London is the **U.S. Coast Guard Academy,** 15 Mogehan Ave., New London, CT 06320 (tel. 203/444-8270). Start your tour of the grounds at the Visitors Pavilion (open daily 9am to 5pm). A special treat here is a visit to the Coast Guard's training barque, *Eagle,* generally in port at the academy in April and May (open to visitors on Friday, Saturday, and Sunday from noon to 5pm when in port). If you miss the *Eagle,* perhaps you can catch the colorful dress review of the Corps of Cadets, usually held (weather permitting) in April, May, September and October. For times and dates, contact the Public Affairs Office at the above number.

New London's major beach-and-amusement complex is at **Ocean Beach Park** near Harkness Memorial State Park south of the city (Exit 75-76 from I-95; tel 447-3031). Besides the beach, a boardwalk allows strolling to check out other members of the swimsuit set, miniature golf will test your reflexes, amusement rides provide a cheap thrill, and an Olympic-size pool is provided for diving and freshwater swimming. If amusement parks and commercial beaches are your thing, this is one of the best on the coast.

FERRY TO THE ISLANDS

New London is a major ferryboat port, with frequent summer sailings to Block Island, R.I., and Fishers Island and Orient Point, N.Y., on the tip of Long Island.

BLOCK ISLAND See "Block Island" in Chapter 9 for details. The pier in New London is north of the railroad station (tel. 203/442-7891 or 442-9553). Follow the red-and-white signs to the dock.

FISHERS ISLAND Daily ferries go to this New York island a few miles off the Connecticut coast, departing from the dock on State Street. For fares and schedules, call 203/443-6851.

ORIENT POINT, LONG ISLAND The dock is on Ferry Street; details from the Cross Sound Ferry Service are available by calling 203/443-5281; for reservations from Orient Point, call 516/323-2525. Cars are carried ($27, several dollars less Tuesday through Thursday), and reservations for the 1½-hour cruise (adults, $8 one-way, $12 round-trip; kids, half price) are a must in high summer.

GROTON

Groton, "The Submarine Capital of the World," makes its living from General Dynamics' Electric Boat Division and from Pfizer pharmaceuticals, besides the naval facilities at the submarine base.

No one comes to Groton to see anything but submarines, and there are plenty to see. Your tour here should be an auto cruise along **Submarine Drive,** the waterfront road along the eastern bank of the Thames River (named Thames Street) south of I-95 and Military Highway to the north. Take Exit 85 from I-95, and follow Bridge Street to Thames Street.

Near the point where Bridge Street runs into Thames, just south of the Gold Star (I-95) Bridge, is the **USS *Flasher* National Submarine Monument.** The conning tower of this World War II Angler-class sub has been established here as a memorial to the American submarine sailors who lost their lives during that war. The *Flasher* sank more than 100,000 tons of enemy shipping during the war, and its crew members were repeatedly cited by the president for their services.

While you're down in Groton, see the **Fort Griswold State Park** (tel. 445-1729), at Monument and Park Streets (Monument runs parallel to Thames Street). The heroic, tragic story of the American force which defended the fort in 1781 against the British is told in the museum, open from Memorial Day to Columbus Day. The Memorial Tower (view from the top) was erected for the courageous defenders who fought until overpowered and then perished in the massacre by the victorious British. The state park is open all year, and both the park and the museum are free of charge.

North of the Gold Star (I-95) Bridge, Submarine Drive continues along the Military Highway. Near the entrance to the U.S. Navy's Groton Submarine Base (Exit 86 from I-95) is the **USS *Nautilus* National Memorial** (tel. 449-3174, or toll free 800/343-0079), and the Submarine Force Library and Museum, featuring the world's first nuclear-powered submarine. Launched in Groton in January 1954, the *Nautilus* saw its finest hour when it passed beneath the ice cap at the geographic North Pole in 1958, the first ship ever to reach that geographically significant spot. Decommissioned after 25 years of service in 1980, the sub is now open for free to visitors Monday and Wednesday to Sunday from 9am to 5pm, from 1 to 5pm on Tuesday, and to 3:30pm in winter (mid-October to mid-April). Note that the sub is closed for a week in March, June, September, and December, and on Thanksgiving, Christmas, and New Year's Day. Displays in the library and museum chronicle the history of the U.S. submarine force since the revolutionary war. You can peer into working periscopes, inspect miniature submarines, wonder at the revolutionary war–era *Turtle,* all at no charge.

WHERE TO STAY

RADISSON HOTEL, 35 Governor Winthrop Blvd., New London, CT 06320. Tel. 203/443-7000, or toll free 800/333-3333. Fax 203/443-1239. 114 rms, 6 suites (all with bath). A/C TV TEL **Directions:** Take Exit 83 or 86S from I-95 to Governor Winthrop Blvd. and the hotel.

$ Rates: $96–$124 single; $116–$144 double. AE, CB, DC, MC, V. **Parking:** Free.

If you want to stay downtown in New London, this is perhaps the best and most comfortable place. Well located near the railroad station and just a short distance off I-95, the Radisson has many services, including an indoor swimming pool, restaurant, lounge with live entertainment, and an exercise room with whirlpool bath.

WINDSOR MOTEL, 345 Gold Star Hwy., Groton, CT 06340. Tel. 203/ 445-7474. 58 rms (all with bath). A/C MINIBAR TV **Directions:** Take Rte. 184 exit from I-95.

$ Rates: $48–$70 double. Children stay free in parents' room. Discounts available during off-season and for stays of a week or more. AE, MC, V. **Parking:** Free.

This is a good choice of accommodations—some especially good for families—at reasonable prices. Thirty-three of the motel rooms come with complete kitchens. Use only one double bed and you pay only $48 to $58; use both double beds and the price is $60 to $70. Since children of any age stay free with their parents, the two-bed price could cover a family of four.

---

5. MYSTIC & STONINGTON

Mystic: 9 miles (15km) E of New London, 5 miles (8km) NW of Stonington

GETTING THERE By Train Amtrak runs trains daily from New York City to Boston along the coastal route via New Haven, Old Saybrook, New London, Mystic, and Providence. The trip from New York City to Mystic takes about 3 hours, from Boston about 1½ hours.

By Bus Bus transportation in the region is provided by **Southeastern Area Rapid Transit** (tel. 203/886-2631).

By Car Speedy access to Mystic is provided by I-95 and Conn. Route 52. Take Exit 90 from I-95 for Mystic Seaport. A warning is in order: Rush-hour traffic (8 to 9am and 5 to 6pm) in the Groton/New London area is extremely heavy, especially along I-95 and its feeder roads. Make your getaway before 5pm, or stay and have dinner until the roads empty out.

ESSENTIALS The **area code** is 203. Each of the towns listed below has its own information booths and offices. For general inquiries your best bet is the **Mystic and Shoreline Visitors Information Center,** Olde Mistick Village, Mystic, CT 06355 (tel. 203/536-1641). Olde Mistick Village is the new colonial-style shopping complex just south of I-95 on Route 27, very near Mystic Seaport. The information center is in Building 1, and is open Monday through Friday from 9:30am to 5:30pm, to 6pm on Saturday, and on Sunday from 10am to 5pm.

Connecticut's maritime life, past and present, is all on view in the area comprising the open-air museum called Mystic Seaport, and the pretty old seaside town of Stonington. Mystic Seaport is one of the top tourist attractions in New England, drawing very large crowds every day of the summer. The huge open-air "museum" is big enough to handle the crowds, but the capacity of nearby motels is not—the motels are packed in July and August, and guests must prepay their entire stay.

You can avoid the hotel crush altogether by taking an Amtrak train through this area and getting off for the day at Mystic, where a bus will take you from the station to Mystic Seaport. After your day roaming around the ships, old buildings, and exhibits board an afternoon train to Providence or Boston (or New Haven, or New York). There's no extra charge for the stopover if you buy a through ticket, and you obviate the need for a room.

MYSTIC

WHAT TO SEE & DO

MYSTIC SEAPORT MUSEUM, Mystic. Tel. 572-5315.

One could return again and again to this impressive museum to see the various indoor exhibits, walk through the preserved 19th-century town, or climb aboard one of the venerable sailing ships moored and preserved here. (Foremost among these is the *Charles W. Morgan,* the last wooden whaling ship in the United States.) Although it is a nonprofit museum, there is much more life to it than just rows of glass cases housing exhibits. You will see scrimshaw, old tools, watches, clocks, chronometers, navigational instruments, and so on, but most of your time will be taken walking through the village and watching the interpreters (staff) do their jobs and explain what they're doing. You'll see a half dozen crew members high in the rigging of the square-rigged ship *Joseph Conrad,* furling a sail in time to a chantey they sing, with one rope supporting all of them high above the deck—among other demonstrations.

Mystic Seaport Museum began in 1929 as the Marine Historical Association, founded by three citizens of Mystic who were interested in preserving aspects and objects from the town's maritime past. The site of the museum is the former shipyard of George Greenman and Company, which built wooden clipper ships in the 19th century.

To get the feel of the place, stay at least 3 or 4 hours; if you've arrived late in the day, you can buy a ticket and have it validated for the next day as well. With your ticket you'll be given a very handsome map of the village and its exhibits, plus a list of the daily events, from special lectures to sea-chantey sings. In winter, interpreted exhibits and craft demonstrations don't begin until 10am. Look at the list to get an idea of what'll be in action for the hours you're in the village. The museum can be divided basically into four areas: the indoor exhibits of small boats, models, figureheads, and the like, mostly near the Seamen's Inne entrance gate; changing exhibits; the restored village and waterfront area; and the shipyard at the southern end of the grounds where the seaport cares for its ships (and where museum-goers can board ships).

The **Coastal Life Area** is the official name of Mystic's old-time seaside village at the northern reaches of the museum, near the Seamen's Inne. The village includes the shops of a shipsmith, ship-carver, and printer, a cooperage, bank, shipping office, grocery, chapel, schoolhouse, pharmacy, rope walk, clock and nautical instrument shop, mast-hoop shop, ship's chandlery, and tavern.

Indoor exhibits are housed in several buildings. In the three-story Stillman Building are ship's models, paintings, scrimshaw. The Mallory Building is devoted to exhibits explaining the Victorian-era shipping business of the Mallory family, and also shipbuilding in Mystic. In the Wendell Building are collections of figureheads and other nautical wood carvings. Changing exhibits of paintings, prints, and other artifacts are the specialty of the R. J. Schaefer Building.

Children are fascinated by the **Children's Museum,** where they can dress up in 19th-century clothing and play with 19th-century toys. Special events are planned for kids throughout the year.

Today, the museum's **collection of old ships** includes the *Charles W. Morgan* (1841), the full-rigged training ship *Joseph Conrad* (1882), and the fishing schooner *L. A. Dunton* (1921). It also owns a steamboat called the *Sabino* (1908), which once plied the waters off Casco Bay in Maine, but which now takes museum visitors on ½-hour cruises on the Mystic River from mid-May to mid-October, for a small fee. In addition, the museum has a collection of 300 small craft, many of which can be seen in the Small Boat Exhibit and the North Boat Shed.

Besides these exhibits, the museum boasts the **Henry B. duPont Preservation**

Shipyard (in the southern section), fully equipped and staffed to perform repairs and to preserve wooden vessels; and the **Seaport Planetarium,** where shows explain the significance of stars in the night sky, and the importance of celestial navigation.

Remember that the crowds are heavy in summer—although the museum seems large enough to absorb them all without too much crowding—and that traffic on the mile-long road from I-95 to Mystic Seaport may be pokey. At Mystic Seaport there's a lot of free parking.

Admission: $14.50 adults, $8.75 children aged 6–15, free for children under 6.

Open: June–Aug daily 9am–8pm. Apr–May and Sept–Oct, daily 9am–5pm Nov–Dec, daily 9am–4pm. Jan–Mar, daily 10am–4pm. **Closed:** Dec 25. **Directions:** Take Exit 90 from I-95, and follow the signs.

MYSTIC MARINELIFE AQUARIUM, 55 Coogan Blvd. Tel. 536-3323.

The Mystic Marinelife Aquarium has 50 living marine life exhibits and more than 6,000 sea creatures in the main aquarium. Marine mammal demonstrations, held every hour on the half hour, feature Atlantic bottle-nosed dolphins, California sea lions, and beluga whales in the marine theater. An outdoor exhibit area called Seal Island lets you watch five species of seals and sea lions sport and play in re-creations of their natural habitat. There's a penguin exhibit as well. You can stay 90 minutes after the last admission time.

Admission: $8.50 adults, $5 children aged 5–12, $7.50 seniors, free for children under 5.

Open: July–Aug, daily 9am–5:30pm. Sept–June, daily 9am–4:30pm. **Directions:** Take Exit 90 from I-95, and follow the signs.

WHERE TO STAY

During much of the year, and especially in high summer, Mystic is crowded with visitors who've come to tour famous Mystic Seaport. Though there are lots of lodging places, most will be full in July and August, so advance reservations are good to have

Lodgings in Mystic proper are mostly hotels and motels, with a few guesthouses In the nearby quiet village of Noank, a few miles south and east along Route 215 there are some quiet inns.

Hotels & Motels

In addition to the hostelries listed below, remember that the cluster of motels at Exit 90, the Route 27 interchange on I-95, includes several branches of big chains, and several local establishments.

COMFORT INN, 132 Greenmanville Ave., Mystic, CT 06355. Tel. 203/ 572-8531, or toll free 800/228-5150. 120 rms (all with bath). A/C TV TEL **Directions:** Take I-95 to Exit 90.

$ Rates: $98–$180 single or double. AE, DC, MC, V. **Parking:** Free.

The Comfort Inn at Mystic is clean, well located, and comfortable. It offers all the amenities you might expect of the major hotel chain, such as an outdoor pool and an exercise facility, direct-dial telephones, individual climate control, and some room even have whirlpool baths or jacuzzis. The continental breakfast is complimentary and is served between 6 and 10am. The Eatery is the Hotel's neighboring restaurant and it serves breakfast, lunch, and dinner.

INN AT MYSTIC, junction of Rtes. 1 and 27, (P.O. Box 216), Mystic, CT 06355. Tel. 203/536-9604, or toll free 800/237-2415. Fax 203/572-1635. 68 rms (all with bath). A/C TV TEL **Directions:** Follow Rte. 1 to the intersection with Rte. 27.

$ Rates: $65–$135 single; $65–$185 double; $110–$155 suite. Children stay free in parents' room. AE, DC, DISC, MC, V. **Parking:** Free.

One of Mystic's longtime favorites is this expansive inn. The large complex has several different classes of accommodation in separate buildings, all set atop a hill overlooking the water. As you drive up, you first approach the tidy motel units in several large buildings. The office is here, and also the Flood-Tide Restaurant. Motel rooms are modern, clean, and attractive, with some colonial reproductions to put you in the proper mood for visiting old Mystic. All have television, air conditioning, and private bath. Above the motel along a drive shaded by large trees is the inn, a fine old mansion at the summit of the hill. Green lawns complete with miniature waterfall surround the house, which has a number of fine guest rooms decorated with period furniture and replicas. The inn's wide veranda is a favored place to sit and take in the view. Beyond the inn is the Gatehouse, a smaller building, also very pretty. The inn has its own boat dock, tennis court, swimming pool and hot spa, and walking trail. This is a dependable favorite, and worthy of your consideration.

MYSTIC HILTON, 20 Coogan Blvd., Mystic, CT 06355. Tel. 203/572-0731, or toll free 800/445-8667. Fax 203/572-0328. 184 rms (all with bath). A/C TV TEL

$ Rates: $100–$130 single; $115–$150 double. Extra person $20. Children stay free in parents' room. Package rates available. AE, DC, DISC, MC, V. **Parking:** Free.

Across from the Mystic Marinelife Aquarium and Olde Mistick Village is the Mystic Hilton. All the modern conveniences, comforts, and luxuries are here, in the guest rooms, in the indoor swimming pool, and in the Moorings (the hotel restaurant) and Soundings (its lounge). It's just off Exit 90 of I-95.

RAMADA INN, 183 Greenmanville Ave., Mystic, CT 06355. Tel. 203/536-4281, or toll free 800/228-2828. Fax 203/572-1300. 150 rms (all with bath). A/C TV TEL

$ Rates: $81 single; $92 double. AE, DC, DISC, MC, V. **Parking:** Free, on premises.

Facilities in this large, comfortable motel at Route 27 on I-95 include a restaurant, sauna, indoor pool, live entertainment, and a playground, too.

TABER INN AND GUEST HOUSE, 29 Williams Ave., Mystic, CT 06355. Tel. 203/536-4904. 28 rms. A/C MINIBAR TV TEL **Directions:** Go east on U.S. 1 a short distance to the motel, on the right-hand side.

$ Rates: (including coffee): $55–$95 single; $65–$135 double; $180–$240 suite. Extra person $10. MC, V. **Parking:** Free.

This is more than a motel: Besides its very tidy motel rooms, it can rent you a room in a restored inn (1829), a restored farmhouse, a two-bedroom cottage, two-bedroom town houses, or an efficiency apartment. In high summer, rooms go for $100 double in the motel, about $15 less in the inn and farmhouse, about double that in the town houses.

Guesthouses

HARBOUR INNE & COTTAGE, Edgemont St. (Rte. 1, Box 398), Mystic, CT 06355. Tel. 203/572-9253. 4 rms and 1 cottage (all with bath). A/C TV **Directions:** From the Amtrak station, take dead-end street to right of station, then turn right on to Edgemont St.; guesthouse is on left.

$ Rates: $28–$115 single; $38–$193 double. Extra person $10. No credit cards. **Parking:** Free.

The Harbour Inne & Cottage is right next to the water in a part of town that is part residential and part industrial, but clean and quiet. The two small buildings of bright natural cedar, once a fisherman's house, are neat as a pin. In the guesthouse, the rooms are cozy and cheerful with that same honey-colored wood, private bath with shower stall, TV set, and air conditioning. In the cottage next door are one bedroom (with a fireplace), a kitchen and bath, and sofas that convert to beds so that the place can sleep up to six people. Charley Lecouras, Jr., the smiling owner, will rent you a canoe or rowboat, and you can set out for a cruise right from the inn's own dock.

RANDALL'S ORDINARY, Rte. 2, P.O. Box 243, North Stonington, CT 06359. Tel. 203/599-4540. 12 rms (all with bath). A/C **Directions:** Off I-95 drive ⅓ mile north of exit 92 on Rte. 2.

$ Rates: $90–$150 double in Jacob Terpenning Barn; $125–$155 double in John Randall House. AE, MC, V. **Parking:** Free.

Bill and Cindy Clark have created something very special with Randall's Ordinary. Situated on 27 acres, the inn and restaurant include the John Randall House (1685) and the Jacob Terpenning Barn, which was moved from New York and attached to a silo.

The three rooms in the John Randall House don't have televisions or telephones, but they do have fireplaces and queen-size canopy or four-poster beds. One of the rooms has teal-green paneling, a large bathroom, a blanket chest, a table, and a Windsor chair. The rest of the rooms, located in the barn, have canopy or four-poster beds (either double or queen-size and some with trundles)—Room 4 has a brass bed—and three of the rooms have sitting room lofts. A continental breakfast is included in the room rates.

Randall's Ordinary also features hearth cooking (the Colonial way) in its huge fireplace for breakfast, lunch, and dinner. Lunch is served daily from noon to 3pm and features a daily special such as roast pork loin or grilled venison sausage, a daily soup, and brick oven baked breads. A full meal will cost somewhere around $15 per person. If you'd like to try dinner here instead, arrive at 7pm for the one seating of the evening. Ready yourself to embark on a food odyssey from start to finish. You'll begin with hearth-roasted popcorn and Vermont cheddar crackers while you decide on your main course and a beverage. Soup is your first course, and it's served at around 7:30pm. The menu changes daily as well as seasonally, and on any evening you'll have your choice of meat or poultry or seafood. Desserts also change daily and are served with fresh whipped cream and coffee or tea. This will all cost around $30 per person (plus tax and tip). A reservation is a must.

THE WHALER'S INN, 20 East Main St., Mystic, CT 06355. Tel. 203/ 536-1506, or toll free 800/234-2588. Fax 203/572-7697. 41 rms (all with bath). **Directions:** From I-95 North, take exit 89, then turn right onto Allyn St. Go left at the second light onto Rte. 1. Look for the sign just over the drawbridge. From I-95 South, take exit 90 go left onto Rte. 27 to Rte. 1. Go right on Rte. 1 and look for the sign.

$ Rates: Apr–Nov 11, $77.50–$97.50 double; $90–$115 queen; $130 king. Nov 12–Mar, $67.50–$77.50 double; $80–$92 queen; $94 king. AE, MC, V. **Parking:** Free.

In the main building of the Whaler's Inn there are traditionally decorated and furnished rooms with canopy beds, wingback chairs, humpback couches, and rich color schemes, such as Chinese Red and forest green. The 1865 house has eight rooms decorated with dusty rose carpets and floral bed coverings with green accents. The furnishings in these rooms include king, queen, or double beds, two arm chairs, a coffee table, and a couch. Ask about special packages—they offer some good ones.

WHERE TO DINE

The great number of Mystic's restaurants—and there are many of them—are part of the many hotels and motels. There are exceptions, however. One quite good restaurant is on the grounds of Mystic Seaport, just outside the admission ticket office. Other good places to dine are in the town of Mystic, south of Mystic Seaport; head south on Route 27, then right onto Main Street, to reach the center of town. The restaurants are located in the commercial district, on the far side of the quaint old bascule bridge.

At Mystic Seaport

GIACO'S SHIPS LANTERN RESTAURANT, 21 W. Main St. Tel. 536-9821.
   Cuisine: AMERICAN/ITALIAN. **Reservations:** Not accepted.
$ Prices: Appetizers $3–$6; main courses $10–$18. AE, DC, MC, V.
   Open: Daily 10am–2am.

Giaco's, in the center of Mystic, always has an interesting blackboard menu out on the sidewalk. Last time I was there it listed fresh mako shark, fresh tuna steak, and a shore dinner featuring a 1-pound lobster with a pound of steamed clams. Nautical flotsam, jetsam, and memorabilia decorate the dining room, and seafood fills the menu (along with prime rib and Italian specialties).

SEAMEN'S INNE, 65 Greenmanville Ave. Tel. 536-9649.
   Cuisine: SOUTHERN AMERICAN/SEAFOOD. **Reservations:** Recommended.
$ **Prices:** Appetizers $3–$7; main courses $10–$18. AE, MC, V.
   Open: Mon–Thurs 11:30am–9pm, Fri–Sat 11am–10pm, Sun 11am–9pm.
The Seamen's Inne, a beautiful colonial restaurant located at Mystic Seaport, features Yankee fare and seafood. At lunch, try the oyster stew or grilled mussels with garlic butter and lemon honey mustard dip to start. There are light lunches, sandwiches, and salads available, as well as more substantial fare, such as the Yankee pot roast, which comes with a vegetable and potato. Fish and chips is on both the lunch and dinner menus, and of course, dinner also offers fresh fish. You might also consider trying the red beans and rice with smoked ham hocks and corn bread or the Inne's carpetbagger (butterflied filet mignon with fried oysters and Bearnaise sauce). There's a special Dixieland Country breakfast buffet served from 11am to 2pm every Sunday ($9.95 per person), which consists of southern fried chicken, bacon, sausages, scrambled eggs, cheddar cheese grits, creamed chipped beef, waffles, chicken fried steak, fresh baked muffins, candied sweet potatoes, mashed potatoes, home fries, fried fish, biscuits and honey, plus a lot more (including the grand finale, chocolate bread pudding with whiskey sauce). There is also a children's menu.

2 SISTERS DELI, 4 Pearl St. Tel. 536-1244.
   Cuisine: AMERICAN. **Reservations:** Not accepted.
$ **Prices:** Main courses $2–$6. No credit cards.
   Open: Daily 8:30am–7pm.
   Looking for just a sandwich, a salad, or dessert? Head here, just off Main Street, where the sandwiches are fresh and the menu is long. There are 42 sandwiches, plus various soups, bagels, salads, salad plates, cakes, pies, brownies, and cookies. Come for breakfast, lunch, picnic, or an early supper, any day.

In Noank

ABBOTT'S LOBSTER IN THE ROUGH, 117 Pearl St. Tel. 536-7719.
   Cuisine: SEAFOOD. **Reservations:** Not accepted. **Directions:** Follow Rte. 215 South to Noank, go left on Main St., then right on Pearl St.
$ **Prices:** Appetizers $2–$6; main lunch courses $4–$14; dinner $14–$25. MC, V.
   Open: May–Labor Day, daily noon–9pm. Labor Day to mid-Oct, Fri–Sun noon–7pm.
   If you love seafood, if you love shore dinners, if you love the real New England, Abbott's is a must. Here you will find a parking lot, a large restaurant, and numerous seaside picnic tables. Approach the cashier's window and order what you like: clam chowder, steamed clams or mussels, oysters, shrimp in the shell, steamed lobster, a lobster or crab roll, cheesecake, and carrot cake. Pay the tab and then take a table and wait for your number to be called. When your order is ready, you get to enjoy some of the finest seafood in the region. It's not fancy, but it's fantastically delicious. The lobsters at Abbott's are steamed (the way I do them), not boiled, and I can personally attest to the difference. A steamed lobster is sweeter and more tender. Abbott's handy tabloid newspaper–style menu bears full directions on how to eat a lobster. But when lobster is this good, you learn fast anyway. Stop at the Universal Package Store (open Monday through Saturday until 8pm) to pick up wine or beer if you like to accompany your feast.

STONINGTON

As you drive into the delightful village of Stonington, 5 miles east of Mystic along U.S. 1 and U.S. 1A, you'll cross a bridge over the railroad tracks, turn left, and proceed down Water Street, the town's main street. Water Street holds many boutiques, antiques shops, restaurants, and real estate offices. Beyond this commercial area is a residential one, ending in **Cannon Square.** The square is small, with two 18-pound cannons used in repelling a naval attack mounted by five English ships on August 10, 1814, during the War of 1812. The pretty square is surrounded by a neoclassical bank building, a fine old granite house, and several houses in Federal style.

Beyond Cannon Square, continue south along Water Street to visit the **Old Lighthouse Museum,** at 7 Water St. (tel. 535-1440), a fine old granite structure that was the first government lighthouse in Connecticut. Inside are displays of maritime gear from the days of wooden whaling and fishing craft, swords, firearms (some made right here in Stonington), local stoneware, toys, decoys, and 19th-century portraits. There's a special room for children's exhibits. The museum is open from May through October, Tuesday to Sunday from 11am to 4:30pm. Adults pay $2 admission; children 6 to 12 pay half price.

WHERE TO STAY

The village of Stonington is a traditional New England seacoast village, just the place to stay if you want to escape the crowded highways and modern motels. Stonington's bed-and-breakfast guesthouse list is beginning to grow. If you can't get a room at the following places, drop by the **State of Connecticut Tourism Division Information Center** off I-95 southbound at North Stonington for help.

ANTIQUES & ACCOMMODATIONS, 32 Main St., North Stonington, CT 06359. Tel. 203/535-1736. 3 rms (all with bath), 1 cottage. **Directions:** Take Exit 92 off I-95 head west on Rte. 2 for 2½ miles. Turn right on Main St. The inn is located ⁷⁄₁₀-mile down, on the right.
$ Rates: $90–$130 weekday double, $130–$190 weekend double. No credit cards. **Parking:** Free.
The furnishings in the sitting room of this Victorian bed-and-breakfast inn change all the time because they're for sale. If you're an antique lover, you'll like Antiques & Accommodations with its antique four-poster beds, blanket chests, Queen Anne and empire chairs, Federal mirrors, and Oriental rugs. The cottage has two units that are perfect for families, with brass beds, wicker pieces, wingback chairs (including a kid-size version), stenciling, and kitchens with electric stoves. The gardens are lovely, and outside on the stone patio you can sit and relax on the wooden garden furniture. The innkeepers use the herbs, berries, and vegetables that are grown in the garden to make the complimentary English breakfast that is served every morning by candle-light. At the formal dining table you might find walnut and banana waffles and ham steak with pumpkin bread.

FARNAN HOUSE, 10 McGrath Court, Stonington, CT 06378. Tel. 203-535-0634. 4 rms (1 with bath).
$ Rates: (including continental breakfast): $68–$70 single or double. No credit cards. **Parking:** Free.
This large, nice old Stonington house takes in travelers for the night. Originally a colonial homestead, it is now a guesthouse hosted by a nice lady, Ann Farnan. Breakfast is served in the big country kitchen.

LASBURY'S, 24 Orchard St., Stonington, CT 06378. Tel. 203/535-2681. 3 rms (1 with bath). TV **Directions:** Head into village on Water St., turn left on to Church St., then left on to Orchard.
$ Rates: (including continental breakfast): $87 single or double. No credit cards. **Parking:** Free.
Lasbury's bills itself as "a quiet guesthouse" in the village of Stonington.

WHERE TO DINE

HARBORVIEW RESTAURANT, 66 Water St., Cannon Sq. Tel. 535-2720.
Cuisine: FRENCH. **Reservations:** Recommended.

$ Prices: Appetizers $2.50–$8.50; main courses $7.95–$22; lunch $17; dinner $30–$45. AE, CB, DC, MC, V.
Open: Lunch daily 11:30am–4pm; dinner daily 5–10pm; Sun brunch 11am–4pm.
As you enter from Water Street, the darkish, cozy bar is to your right, and it features a special menu of lighter fare for lunches, snacks, and suppers. In the dining rooms, the atmosphere is nautical, with lots of ocean views, bentwood, and low lamps, but the service is polished and professional as well as friendly. The menu here is fairly classical, with appetizers such as Brie en croûte (baked in puff pastry), French onion soup, and smoked salmon. Your main course might be peppered tenderloin of beef with brandy, mushrooms, and heavy cream; or shrimp sautéed with Thai peanut sauce, and served over curried angel hair pasta. There's a wide variety of seafood featured, of course.

NOAH'S, 113–115 Water St. Tel. 535-3925.
Cuisine: AMERICAN. **Reservations:** Recommended.
$ Prices: Appetizers $2.75–$7.50; main courses $8–$16; breakfast $5; dinner $14–$22. No credit cards.
Open: Breakfast Tues–Sat 7–11am, Sun 7am–noon; lunch Tues–Sat 11:15am–2:30pm, Sun 12:30–2:30pm; dinner Tues–Thurs and Sun 6–9pm, Fri–Sat 6–9:30pm.

Right in the center of Stonington's commercial district is this informal restaurant of two rooms with tin ceilings, booths sporting nice etched glass, and wood tables draped with cloths. Prints and paintings ornament the walls, and Noah's has a feeling of the authentically old-fashioned. You can come for breakfast, when a tuck-in of the standard fare of eggs, pancakes, and muffins can be yours; or come for lunch, with a varied menu of light meals; or for dinner, you can order seafood, filet mignon, or pork chops, and get vegetable, potato, salad, bread, and butter with your main course.

SKIPPER'S DOCK, 66 Water St. Tel. 535-2000.
Cuisine: SEAFOOD. **Reservations:** Recommended.
$ Prices: Appetizers $2.75–$7; main courses $7–$17; lunch $15; dinner $18–$34. AE, CB, DC, MC, V.
Open: Lunch daily 11:30am–4pm; dinner daily 6–10pm. **Closed:** Nov–Feb Mon–Tues.
Behind the Harborview is another restaurant under the same management, right by the docks and meant to be convenient to the yacht crews who tie up nearby. The restaurant has nice waterside decks set with dining tables, as well as two indoor dining rooms with bentwood furniture. The air smells of the sea, the landward wall of the restaurant is hung with hundreds of salvaged lobster buoys, and the sound of bell buoys wafts easily on the air. The menu here is simple: seafood, with the requisite token offerings of chicken and steak. Have a big bowl of steamed clams, or linguine with shrimp and clams, or broiled scallops, or an entire clambake with steamed lobster.

---

6. HARTFORD

102 miles (165km) SW of Boston, 113 miles (182km) NE of New York City, 74 miles (119km) from Providence, 34 miles (55km) E of Litchfield

GETTING THERE   By Plane   Hartford is served by **Bradley International Airport** in Windsor Locks, 12 miles north of Hartford. There's direct one-plane service between Bradley and more than 60 other North American airports, operated by United, TWA, Delta, American, and USAir. Buses leave the terminal for downtown Hartford and for Springfield, Mass., periodically, and limousines shuttle from Bradley to most cities in Connecticut. By the way, the Connecticut Aeronautical Historical Association operates the **New England Air Museum** (tel. 623-3305) at the airport, with more than 70 aircraft, plus engines, accessories, and memorabilia, on display.

The collection is open to visitors all year from 10am to 5pm every day. Admission for adults is $5.50; children 6 to 11, $2; children under 6, free.

By Train **Amtrak** runs trains daily from New York City to Boston along the inland route via Hartford, Windsor Locks, and Springfield. The trip from New York to Hartford takes less than 3 hours; from Boston to Hartford, about 2½ hours.

By Bus **Greyhound, Bonanza,** and **Vermont Transit** all operate daily buses between New York City, New Haven, Hartford, and Boston. The trip from New York to Hartford takes about 3 to 4¾ hours, depending on the line and the number of stops en route.

Bonanza also runs buses between Hartford and Providence and Hyannis; Vermont Transit operates buses to Vermont, New Hampshire, Montréal, and Québec City. All the large lines have buses between Hartford and Boston. In Hartford, the bus station and railroad station are within 2 blocks of one another, close to downtown. The terminal for Greyhound, Vermont Transit, and Bonanza is at 409 Church St. (tel. 203/547-1500).

By Car Hartford is easily accessible by Interstate highways, being at the junction of I-91 and I-84. Hartford is very much a commuters' town, and traffic is very heavy at rush hours. The best day to visit the city is Saturday, when most everything is open and parking is easily available. On Sunday many places are closed.

ESSENTIALS The **area code** is 203. The **visitors' information desk** is in the Old State House, 800 Main St., Hartford, CT 06103 (tel. 203/522-6766), in Old State House Square, right in the center of town. The desk is open Monday through Saturday from 10am to 5pm, on Sunday from noon to 5pm. There is no short-term parking convenient to the Old State House, so plan to park for the length of your visit in a downtown lot, and then walk to the Old State House to ask questions and pick up maps and brochures.

―――――――――――――――――――――――――――――――――

Hartford is Connecticut's capital, a fairly small (pop. 150,000) and manageable city with an admirable range of attractive architectural styles and a businesslike spirit. It is and has been a city with a good amount of wealth, much of it generated by the tens of thousands of workers who sit in the thousands of offices of Hartford's great insurance companies and banks. Insurance companies seem to have a penchant for expressing their wealth and prestige through skyscrapers like the Prudential Tower in Chicago, and the John Hancock Tower in Boston, among others. Hartford has four dozen insurance companies, and therefore lots of skyscrapers. The downtown area has been given a new attractiveness by redevelopment, which has left most of the buildings of great historical value intact.

The city was founded by the Rev. Thomas Hooker, who left Newtown (Cambridge, Mass.) on foot with a band of followers in 1636 after a dispute with another clergyman over the strict rules that governed the colony of Massachusetts Bay. In 1639 Hooker and others drafted the Fundamental Orders as the legal constitution of their settlement, and it is upon this early document that Connecticut bases its claims as the first *place in the world* to have a written constitution. Every Connecticut auto license plate remembers Hooker when it proclaims Connecticut "The Constitution State."

WHAT TO SEE & DO
THE WALK

The **Greater Hartford Convention and Visitors Bureau** (tel. 203/728-6789) has organized all the sights in Hartford's downtown into what is called **the Walk**, and has published this walking tour and scenic guide in its annual "Hartford and Southern New England Guide," available through the mail (1 Civic Center Plaza), or from the visitors information desk in the Civic Center Plaza. The following are the highlights of the Walk.

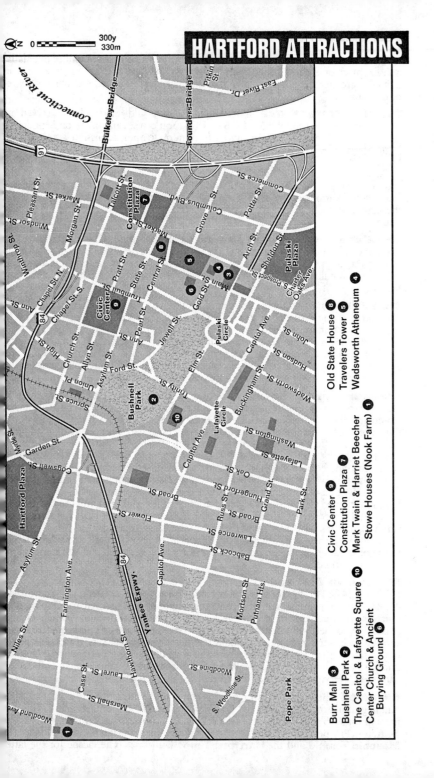

HARTFORD ATTRACTIONS

0 — 300y / 330m

Connecticut River

Burr Mall ③
Bushnell Park ②
The Capitol & Lafayette Square ⑩
Center Church & Ancient
Burying Ground ⑥

Civic Center ⑨
Constitution Plaza ⑦
Mark Twain & Harriet Beecher
Stowe Houses (Nook Farm) ①

Old State House ⑧
Travelers Tower ⑤
Wadsworth Atheneum ④

(*Note:* In addition to its other sights, Hartford has a surprising number of palatial houses, most of them still occupied by wealthy families, and anyone interested in domestic architecture should take a drive through the residential sections northwest of downtown.)

The Old State House   Pure Bulfinch, the Old State House served as Connecticut's state capitol from 1796 to 1878. You can see the inside on Monday to Saturday from 10am to 5pm, on Sunday from noon to 5pm; admission is free. On the Main Street side, have a look at the statue of Hartford's founder, the Rev. Thomas Hooker (1586–1647). Compare this state house with the one in Boston or the Capitol in Washington, both Bulfinch achievements. Outdoor concerts are often held in the precincts of the Old State House, and three galleries inside hold exhibits which change frequently. Warm weather finds farm markets, festivals, and concerts outside on the large lawn. The information center and museum shop are open during regular hours.

The Richardson   North on Main Street a block from the Old State House is the mass of Connecticut brownstone built in 1877 by Henry Hobson Richardson for the Cheneys, a Connecticut family of silk manufacturers (for many years it was known as the Cheney Building). It now houses the Brown, Thomson & Company restaurant (see below).

Constitution Plaza   Just east of the Old State House is Constitution Plaza, Hartford's triumph of urban renewal. The plaza has nice copses of trees (one of willows), a fountain designed not to splash or spray passersby in the wind, and the elliptical Phoenix Mutual Life headquarters, perhaps Hartford's most striking building. Hartford is particularly rich in works by Alexander Calder (who lived and worked in the state), and one of his mobiles is suspended from the ceiling of the commercial banking room in the Connecticut Bank and Trust Company.

Travelers Tower   Between Main and Prospect Streets, right next to the Old State House, rises Hartford's tallest observation point, the Travelers Insurance Company Tower (tel. 277-2431). On weekdays in summer from 10:30am to 3:30pm there are tours to the top of the building, leaving every half hour on the hour and half hour. In the 15 minutes spent at the top, you'll get the best possible view of the entire city, the suburbs, and the surrounding tobacco country. The Travelers Tower stands on a spot where there was once a tavern. In this tavern, during a dispute between colonials and royal officials, Connecticut's royal charter disappeared and was hidden in the cavity of a nearby oak tree. This was the famous "Charter Oak" incident. The king's men ruled Connecticut illegally for a time (they could not find the charter and thus could not destroy the legal instrument of Connecticut's self-rule), but the charter survived, and it's now on view at the State Library (see below).

By the way, there are 70 steps at the top of the tower which you must climb to get to the observation area. Also note that tours are run off-season, but you must call to make reservations.

Wadsworth Atheneum   Hartford's art museum, at 600 Main St. (tel. 278-2670, or 247-9111 for recorded information), has a fine collection of more than 45,000 items of painting, sculpture, and contemporary and modern art. Don't miss a visit. As you enter, ask for a guide leaflet to the collections. Major exhibits change seasonally, so there's always something new to see. The museum's pleasant café serves soups, salads, sandwiches, pasta, and a few heartier dishes at very reasonable prices ranging from $5 to $9. Admission costs $3 for adults, $1.50 for seniors, and children under 13 are admitted free; however, on Saturday from 11am to 1pm and all day on Thursday, everyone is admitted for free.

Burr Mall   Between Wadsworth Atheneum and the attractive city executive office building, Burr Mall is a shady, fragrant spot with a fountain and a fine—if incongruously placed—stabile of Calder's called *Stegosaurus* (1971).

Across Prospect Street from Burr Mall, take a look at the interesting buildings: the **Masonic Temple** and the **Hartford Times Building.** The facade for the latter was once the front of a church in New York, which explains its architecture, odd for a newspaper building!

Center Church and Ancient Burying Ground   Across Main Street from the Travelers Tower is the site of the first church in Hartford, whose pastor was Thomas Hooker (he's thought to be buried under the church). The present church dates from 1807. The gravestones in the cemetery date as far back as 1640.

Bushnell Park   With 500 trees of 150 varieties, Bushnell Park is an oasis in the middle of the busy city. It was laid out by the famous landscape architect Frederick Law Olmsted, the Hartford resident who also landscaped Central Park in New York, the Fenway parks in Boston, and Montréal's Mount Royal Park. The twin-towered Gothic gateway on Trinity Street is Hartford's memorial to its Civil War dead. Be sure to visit the park's carousel, one of the finest restored merry-go-rounds you'll ever see, complete with calliope and automatic drums and cymbals. Rides cost 10¢, and it is by no means only children who take advantage of this low price. The carousel has three types of seating accommodation: "lovers' chariots" for the unadventurous, stationary wooden horses, and horses that move up and down. Remember to grab at the brass ring. Note that the carousel doesn't operate on Sunday, and you must see it with all the lights on and the music trilling to really get the feeling.

The Capitol & Lafayette Square   Richard M. Upjohn is the architect responsible for Hartford State Capitol, a great potpourri of architectural styles and periods, including Gothic niches housing soldiers in Civil War uniforms. For all its eclecticism, the Capitol is fine to look at. At one time it was topped by a statue of *The Genius of Connecticut,* a woman. You can see that statue inside the building, and also the battle flags and memorabilia preserved here. Across Capitol Avenue is the **State Library** and **Supreme Court,** a pretty building housing the paper treasures of Connecticut history, including the famous royal charter once hidden in an oak tree. Besides preserving the documents, the library is now the repository of the Samuel Colt collection of more than 1,000 firearms. All together, the collections here make up the **Museum of Connecticut History,** and you can visit it Monday through Friday from 9am to 4:45pm, on Saturday to 12:45pm; no charge for admission.

The Bushnell   Near the Capitol and State Library, in Lafayette Square, is The Bushnell, where many of the city's concerts, plays, and recitals are held. The interior is of the purest 1930s art deco, a style which has seen a resurgence in recent years. The Vienna Boys Choir or the Boston Symphony—you may find either on the playbill here depending on current schedules. For current information, call the Bushnell Memorial at 246-6807.

The Civic Center   A complex of several city blocks, the Civic Center follows some of the best modernistic architecture, with fine shopping arcades, lots of open spaces, and mezzanines with hanging plants, small potted trees growing up a story or two, and meeting rooms, restaurants, and clubs. The thing to do, especially on a hot summer day, is to enter the air-conditioned spaces and wander around enjoying the sights, perhaps stopping for a snack or a meal.

✪ The Mark Twain & Harriet Beecher Stowe Houses [Nook Farm]   The famous American author from Hannibal, Mo., settled in Hartford in the early 1870s. One of the wealthiest young men in town, Samuel Clemens (1835–1910) had a house designed by Edward Tuckerman Potter. It was finished in 1874 at a cost of $131,000, and is extremely rich in the sort of detail that makes Victorian architecture so much fun to inspect. Twain lived here for 17 years, moving out only after bad investments forced him to take a lecture tour of Europe for some quick money. He loved this place for the best years of his life, and *Tom Sawyer, Huckleberry Finn, Life on the Mississippi, The Prince and the Pauper,* and *A Connecticut Yankee in King Arthur's Court* were all written while he lived here. To see the Mark Twain House, 77 Forest St. (tel. 525-9317), you must take the tour, which is just as well, for the guides have an encyclopedic knowledge of the house and its occupants.

In the same complex of buildings, known as Nook Farm, is a house once lived in by Harriet Beecher Stowe. Although Mrs. Stowe wrote *Uncle Tom's Cabin* while living in Brunswick, Me., she lived and wrote in Nook Farm from 1873 until she died in 1896. Lots of the original furnishings of the author's remain in this Victorian "cottage."

Both houses are open year round, Monday to Saturday from 9:30am to 4pm, Sunday from noon to 4pm. They are open on Monday from June to the Columbus Day weekend, and in December 9:30am to 4pm; the houses are closed on Monday at other times and on major holidays. A tour of both houses takes slightly over an hour and costs $12.50 for adults, $4.50 for children under 16. To get there, drive out Asylum Street and Farmington Avenue about 15 blocks. Look for the art deco steeple of Trinity Church, and 4 blocks later, turn left. If you want to take the bus, wait at the Old State House or along Asylum Street and take the E1 ("Westgate—Health Center"), E-2 ("Unionville"), E-3 ("Bishops Corner"), or E-4 ("Corbins Corner").

NEARBY ATTRACTIONS

The region around Hartford has numerous other sights to see. In West Hartford is the birthplace of America's first great lexicographer, Noah Webster. And the colonial town of Old Wethersfield, about 10 miles south of Hartford, has a treasure trove of old houses.

West Hartford

Noah Webster (1758–1843) was born in a farmhouse on the outskirts of Hartford. He lived there with his strict Calvinist parents and four siblings, helping to work the land until he was 16. Webster left home to attend Yale on the eve of the American Revolution, and was caught up in the intellectual ferment of the time. He served with the American forces and later returned to Hartford to practice law. Webster saw it as his purpose in life to give Americans a new "national language" to go along with their new order of government and society. By 1828, working alone with pen and paper, he had completed a 70,000-word dictionary, which included 12,000 words never previously included in a dictionary. The dictionary sold more than 300,000 copies in some years. Along with his *Elementary Spelling Book* and grammer, the dictionary standardized Americans' distinctive spelling, pronunciation, and usage. His spelling book alone sold more than one million copies annually after 1850, and that was in a nation of only 23 million people! After Webster, Americans no longer had to use schoolbooks and dictionaries written and published in England; thus, we are indebted to him for such simplified spellings as "honor" instead of the English "honour," and "neighborhood" instead of "neighbourhood."

West of central Hartford is Webster's boyhood home and a modern museum, the **Noah Webster House and Museum,** 227 South Main Street, West Hartford (tel 521-5362). The house, a simple center-chimney colonial dwelling, is furnished authentically in period style, and costumed guides give you a tour and explain what life was like in the America of two centuries ago. There is a garden typical of the period with herbs and dye plants. Admission costs $3 for adults, $2 for seniors, and $1 for children aged 6 to 15. The museum is open from mid-June to September on Monday, Tuesday, Thursday, and Friday from 10am to 4pm; and on Saturday and Sunday from 1 to 4pm. From October to mid-June, it's open Monday and Tuesday and Thursday to Sunday from 1 to 4pm. To get there, take I-84 to Exit 41.

Old Wethersfield

Take I-91 south for about 10 miles to Exit 26 and follow the signs to the town.

BUTTOLPH-WILLIAMS HOUSE, Broad St. Tel. 529-0460, or 247-8996.
This mansion from the 1600s has excellent authentic period furnishings. Th

kitchen is especially good, and may be the most real-to-life of any extant in New England.

Admission: $2 adults, 75¢ children.

Open: Mid-May to mid-Oct, Tues–Sun noon–4pm.

ISAAC STEVENS HOUSE, 215 Main St. Tel. 529-0612.

This was a craftsman's home built in 1788, and it still has many of the family's original furnishings. Of particular interest are the collections of toys and women's bonnets.

Admission: $5 adults, $1 children. With Joseph Webb House and Silas Deane House, $5 adults, $2.25 children.

Open: Tues–Sat 10am–4pm, plus mid-May to mid-Oct Sun 1–4pm.

JOSEPH WEBB HOUSE, 211 Main St. Tel. 529-0612.

This was the site of a strategy conference (1781) between the American commander-in-chief, Gen. George Washington, and his French ally, the Comte de Rochambeau. At the conference, Rochambeau outlined his plan to engage the British at Yorktown. It worked, and the battle ended the revolutionary war. The house was built in 1752, and now contains period furniture, fabrics, porcelain, and silver.

Admission: $2 adults, 75¢ children. With Isaac Stevens House and Silas Deane House, $5 adults, $2.25 children.

Open: Tues–Sat 10am–4pm, plus mid-May to mid-Oct Sun 1–4pm.

SILAS DEANE HOUSE, 203 Main St. Tel. 529-0612.

Built in 1766 by a member of the First Continental Congress (1774–76) and commissioner (ambassador) to France (1776), the Silas Deane House is an elegant place for an elegant gentleman, with interesting architectural details. Although he was a patriot, Deane was ill-used by some of his American diplomatic colleagues, and he found himself condemned for profiteering by Congress. He lived the rest of his life in exile, but in 1842 Congress made amends to his family and restored his good name and fortune.

Admission: $2 adults, 75¢ children. With Isaac Stevens House and Joseph Webb House, $5 adults, $2.25 children.

Open: Tues–Sat 10am–4pm, plus mid-May to mid-Oct Sun 1–4pm.

WETHERSFIELD HISTORICAL SOCIETY, 150 Main St. Tel. 529-7656.

If you've now become intrigued by Wethersfield's deep history, drop in at the Historical Society, located in the Old Academy, a fine Federal-style brick building dating from 1804.

The society is in charge of the nearby Keeney Memorial Cultural Center at 200 Main Street, with visitor orientation, a museum shop, and exhibits on Wethersfield, and also the Capt. James Francis House, 120 Hartford Ave. This house, dating from 1793, has exhibits which trace a single Wethersfield family through a history of 170 years.

Admission: Free.

Open: Old Academy, Tues–Thurs and Sat 1–4pm. Keeney, Tues–Sat 10am–4pm, Sun (Apr–Sept) 1–4pm. Francis House, mid-May to mid-Oct, Sat 1–4pm.

WHERE TO STAY

As of this writing, Hartford has no wonderful little hotels and inns made from converted Victorian town houses or renovated farmhouses on the city's outskirts. The lodging stock here is large, business-oriented downtown hotels and highway motels. Generally speaking, the hotels offer more convenient locations. Many of them are within a few minutes' walk of all the downtown sights. The motels, on the other hand, are not really very far out of the city, and they offer clean and comfortable accommodations at moderate, and even budget, prices.

Note: If you're coming to Hartford for a weekend, you'd do well to make arrangements to stay in a downtown hotel. Most of the hotels feature weekend package plans which can save you substantial amounts of money from regular rates. In any case, regular weekend rates are significantly lower than the rates charged on business days. In many cases, this rule holds for the highway motels also.

There are some bed-and-breakfast services which will find you a room in a private home. For a room priced from $32 to $58 single, $47 to $89 double, contact **Four Seasons International Bed & Breakfast,** 11 Bridlepath Rd., West Simsbury CT 06092 (tel. 203/651-3045). Rates include full breakfast and tax. Many of these B&Bs will be out in the country or in small towns near Hartford.

Finally, if you're willing to stay some distance out of the city and just drive in for the day, the surrounding countryside has some lovely old inns in quiet small towns.

DOWNTOWN

HARTFORD HOLIDAY INN—DOWNTOWN, 50 Morgan St., Hartford CT 06120. Tel. 203/549-2400, or toll free 800/465-4329. 359 rms (all with bath). A/C TV TEL **Directions:** Call for instructions (which depend upon ongoing construction).

$ Rates: $65–$114 single; $65–$124 double. Extra person $10. Children stay free in parents' room. AE, DC, DISC, MC, V. **Parking:** $5 per night in hotel garage.

On the northern side of I-84, with access to Main Street's shopping, the Old State House, and the Civic Center, is the Holiday Inn. The hotel boasts comfortable guest rooms, some with views of the river, all with free movies. Other services include baby-sitting, a games room, an outdoor swimming pool, restaurants, and a kennel for your pet. A shuttle service runs to and from the hotel and Bradley International Airport for a small charge. There are two double beds in the double rooms.

RAMADA INN—CAPITOL HILL, 440 Asylum St., Hartford, CT 06103. Tel. 203/246-6591, or toll free 800/228-2828. 96 rms (all with bath). A/C TV TEL

$ Rates: $50 single or double. AE, CB, DC, MC, V. **Parking:** $8, adjacent.

The Ramada, near the Amtrak train station and the Greyhound bus station, has a very convenient location. The hotel has the advantage of being small, which allows for more personal service, and is also quite moderately priced, considering its excellent location. The restaurant, Honiss' Oyster House, is one of the city's better seafood dining places (call ahead as it was temporarily closed at printing).

SHERATON-HARTFORD, 315 Trumbull St., Hartford, CT 06103. Tel. 203/728-5151, or toll free 800/325-3535. 400 rms (all with bath). A/C TV TEL

$ Rates: $118–$173 single; $118–$184 double. AE, CB, DC, DISC, MC, V. **Parking:** $10 per day.

This modern 15-story tower is without a doubt the most convenient hotel to the Hartford Civic Center, and is also well located for seeing the sights in the center of the city. Being the city's largest hotel and the favorite with convention and meeting groups, it features a full list of services, including a swimming pool and health club with sauna and conditioning equipment, a cocktail lounge with live entertainment, parking garage, 55 shops, and bright, modern rooms. If you plan to be in Hartford over a weekend, take advantage of the weekend special rate.

The Stage Cafe restaurant specializes in New England and continental favorites that range in price from $15 to $25 at dinner; an extensive breakfast buffet and full lunch are also served.

NEARBY

SUPER 8 MOTEL, 57 W. Service Rd., Hartford, CT 06120. Tel. 203/246-8888, or toll free 800/800-8000. Fax 203/549-2972. 104 rms (all with bath). A/C TV TEL **Directions:** Take Exit 33 off I-91, north of the intersection with I-84.

$ Rates: (including continental breakfast): $39.88 single; $43.88 double. Extra

HARTFORD ACCOMMODATIONS & DINING

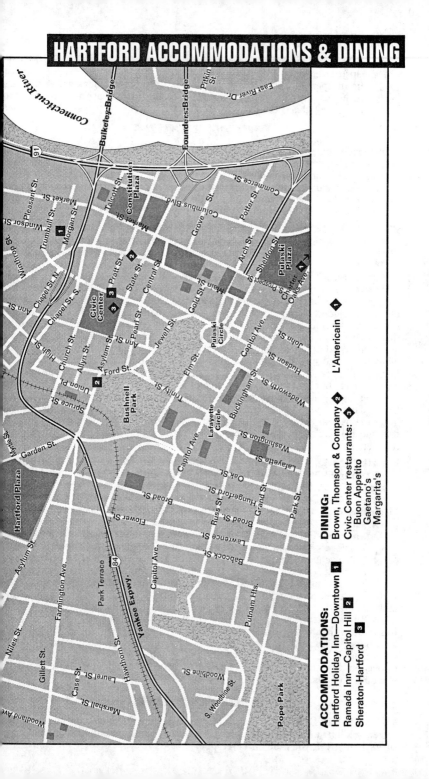

ACCOMMODATIONS:
Hartford Holiday Inn—Downtown 1
Ramada Inn—Capitol Hill 2
Sheraton-Hartford 3

DINING:
Brown, Thomson & Company 2
Civic Center restaurants: 3
  Buon Appetito
  Gaetano's
  Margarita's

L'Americain 1

person $4. Children under 12 stay free in parents' room. AE, DC, DISC, MC, V.
Parking: Free.

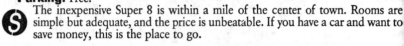

The inexpensive Super 8 is within a mile of the center of town. Rooms are simple but adequate, and the price is unbeatable. If you have a car and want to save money, this is the place to go.

WHERE TO DINE

Although it's not a particularly large or cosmopolitan city, Hartford has an interesting selection of restaurants. You should find it easy to please your appetite, your taste buds, and your budget, whatever they may be.

To satisfy a pang of hunger at any time of the day or night, Hartford's citizens head for the Hartford Civic Center, which has its own collection of restaurants and fast-food shops, some operating 24 hours a day. See "Specialty Dining," below.

BROWN, THOMSON & COMPANY, 942 Main St. Tel. 525-1600.

Cuisine: AMERICAN. **Reservations:** Required for six or more.

$ Prices: Appetizers $3.50–$7; main courses $7–$19; meals $15–$40. AE, DISC, MC, V.

Open: Sun–Thurs 11:30am–12:30am, Fri–Sat 11:30am–1:30am.

At least once, drop in here, just 1 block's stroll north of the Old State House. The dark stone building (1877), a wonder of American Romanesque architecture with lots of arched windows, columns, and turrets, was designed by Henry Hobson Richardson. The restaurant preserves the feeling of a century ago: matchboard walls, glass that is beveled or etched or stained, stamped-metal ceilings, ceiling fans, and even a great old elk's head. The menu lists everything from French onion soup and buffalo wings to broiled swordfish and prime rib of beef. You'll find pizza, huevos rancheros, fajitas, and popcorn shrimp. You might get intellectual indigestion if you read the entire menu, but you're certain to find something you fancy. Dessert and drink offerings are equally profuse, from mud pie to chocolate-chip-cookie pie, and from frozen daiquiris (with or without alcohol) to Dom Perignon (at the retail-store price!). You can suit your budget as well as your appetite, spending anywhere from $12 to $35 for a meal. There's a special coloring-book menu and a strolling magician most nights for kids.

L'AMERICAIN, 146 Wyllys St. (2 Hartford Sq. West). Tel. 522-6500.

Cuisine: FRENCH/NEW AMERICAN. **Reservations:** Recommended. **Directions:** Follow Main St. south, turn left on Charter Oak Ave.; from the Summit Hotel, follow Columbus Blvd. south until it becomes Wyllys St.

$ Prices: Appetizers $5–$11; main courses $14–$26; full dinner $50–$60. AE, CB, DC, MC, V.

Open: Mon–Sat 6–10pm. **Closed:** Thanksgiving and Dec 25.

Hartford's best is in a restored brick factory complex at the corner of Charter Oak Avenue in Hartford Square, about ½ mile from the Old State House. Hartford Square is a group of sedate old brick structures across the street from the Episcopal Church of the Good Shepherd. The dining rooms have been remodeled with classical inspiration along clean, modern lines. Queen Anne chairs and heavy tablecloths add to the feeling of luxury. You'll have an elegant meal prepared by chef Chris Pardue; the menu recently listed appetizers of duckling salad, veal pâté, and fresh fruit with liqueurs; or you might choose a clear lobster consommé instead. For a fish course, there was broiled Norwegian salmon filets in a sauce of white zinfandel with roasted shallots and buttered spinach. Main courses ranged from hickory-smoked turkey through pork schnitzel and Moroccan chicken to a champagne scallop, and pasta salad.

SPECIALTY DINING

IN THE CIVIC CENTER If you enter from Asylum Street near the corner of Ann Street, you'll be on the Market Level. If you enter from Trumbull Street at the corner of Asylum Street, you'll be on Level One.

Buon Appetito, at Market Level (tel. 522-4635), is open Monday through Saturday serving seafood, salads, pasta, and those huge sandwiches called grinders in New England, for about $8 to $12.

Your craving for a dinner of enchiladas, quesadillas, chili, and burritos can be satisfied at **Margarita's** (tel. 724-3331), a Mexican restaurant and watering hole that opens at 4:30pm every day and serves all sorts of Mexican food and drink until 10pm, to 11pm on Friday and Saturday. Drinks include peach margaritas and banana-rum smoothies. The surroundings are as much fun as the food, with waiters in costume and lots of dark rough wood, stucco, and brightly colored Mexican craft items. You need spend only about $12 or $14 for a meal, but the price can go up if you order a second round of drinks.

Of the full restaurants in the Civic Center, the best is **Gaetano's** (tel. 249-1629), open for lunch (Monday through Saturday from 11:30am to 2:30pm) and dinner Monday to Saturday from 4 to 10pm. The setting here is casual but stylish, and the cuisine is continental, inspired by various Italian regions. Start with a hot antipasto and go on to veal San Remo or beef Tuscadora. Of course there's pasta as well, everything from fettuccine bolognese through capellini Gaetano. A full dinner will cost about $30 per person.

7. LITCHFIELD'S LAKES & HILLS

Northwest of Hartford is tobacco country. The Connecticut River Valley has very good conditions for growing a premium wrapper leaf for cigars, the famous Connecticut Valley shade-grown tobacco. The long barns next to the fields are for drying; and part of the year the crop will be covered with gauze enclosures to protect it from too much direct sun—hence the "shade-grown" name.

A pleasant morning or afternoon can be spent driving through part of the tobacco country on the way to Litchfield, which is certainly among the most beautiful towns in New England. Litchfield County is all forest, rivers, and rolling hills—some of the prettiest country in this exceptionally pretty state.

Deeper into the northwest corner of the state you will come upon other charming towns, country inns, and resorts nestled in the Litchfield Hills (Connecticut's "Berkshires") and scattered on the shores of clear lakes. This is vacation country. In the charming old town of Salisbury, you're only 4 miles from the Massachusetts state line, 12 miles from the southern Berkshire town of South Egremont. (For the Berkshires, see Chapter 8.)

As you drive west toward the Litchfield Hills, you might want to make several attractive detours. Head out of Hartford on U.S. 44, and soon you will be in **Avon,** where there is a nice hotel and restaurant. Farther along U.S. 44, just before Winsted, turn north for **Riverton,** the charming village where Hitchcock chairs are made and Seth Thomas clocks are sold. Back on U.S. 44, just 8 miles west of Winsted, is the quiet ambience of **Norfolk,** where you'll find a lovely town green, three state parks, and Yale's Summer School of Music.

From Norfolk, you can continue west on U.S. 44 to Canaan, Salisbury, and Lakeville, or you can take U.S. 44 to Route 8 South through Torrington to U.S. 202 West, which will eventually bring you to **Litchfield.**

From Litchfield, drive along U.S. 202 south and west for 12 miles to New Preston. Then head north on Route 45, and you'll come to pretty **Lake Waramaug.** Continue north on Route 45 to Cornwall Bridge. Then head north on U.S. 7 and cross westward on Route 112 to pick up Route 41 north to **Salisbury;** or take Route 4 west from Cornwall Bridge to Sharon, then Route 41 north through Lakeville to Salisbury.

If you want to go on once up in Connecticut's northwest corner, you're very close to one of America's oldest and finest resort areas, the Berkshire Mountains of Massachusetts. The towns of South Egremont, Great Barrington, Lee, and Lenox have great charm, good restaurants, fine old inns and guesthouses, a bewildering array of cultural activities, and more antiques shops than you've ever seen before in one area at one time. For details, see Chapter 8, "Central and Western Massachusetts."

AVON

Head out of Hartford on U.S. 44 to reach Avon, 9 miles (15km) to the west.

WHERE TO STAY

AVON OLD FARMS HOTEL, Rtes. 44 and 10 (P.O. Box 961), Avon, CT 06001. Tel. 203/677-1651. Fax 203/677-0364. 160 rms (all with bath). A/C TV TEL

$ Rates: Hotel $79–$129 single or double; motel $79 single or double. AE, DC, DISC, MC, V. **Parking:** Free.

For decades, residents of Hartford have escaped to the country to find this hotel at the intersection of U.S. 44 and Conn. 10. Escaping to the country does not mean giving up the city's comforts, for the spacious rooms at the hotel are furnished with king-size, queen-size, or twin double beds, antique reproduction lamps, mirrors, tables and chairs, clock radios, original paintings, and lots of little extras like shower caps, bath oil, and mending kits. You choose from several types of rooms here. Those in the hotel are larger and more modern, and open onto a corridor; the motel-style rooms are a bit smaller, and they open (as motel rooms do) to the outside. The registration lobby is elegantly done in Georgian style, with comfy sofas and a fine marble fireplace. Guests have the use of the hotel's exercise room and sauna, hairstyling salon, and outdoor swimming pool.

The Avon Old Farms Inn was established in 1757, and a few rooms of the old inn now serve as charming dining rooms. The Forge Room is decorated with blacksmith's paraphernalia, and in chilly weather a fire in the hearth casts an appropriately mellow glow. Two other, smaller rooms near the front door are among the oldest in the inn, and are also charming. A large dining room of more recent construction is decorated with Early Americana, dark-wood beams, old pine boards, and country curtains. The menu is American with continental touches: New England seafood, roast beef with popovers, and several continental dishes which change frequently. On Sunday, brunch is an eat-all-you-like buffet. Expect to spend $35 to $40 per person for dinner, with wine, tax, and tip included. Lunch and dinner are served Tuesday through Sunday.

RIVERTON

Farther along U.S. 44, a few miles west of the vast Barkhamsted Reservoir, in lovely wooded country (much of it state forest land) lies Riverton, a fine Connecticut hill village which looks much like it did in the 1800s. Driving or strolling along the village's main street, you'll pass the Grange Hall, the Hitchcock Museum, the Village Sweet Shop, and other shops selling antiques, herbs, and contemporary crafts.

At the **Hitchcock Museum** (tel. 738-4950), look over the fine furniture in Lambert Hitchcock's original factory. Visiting hours are April through August Wednesday to Saturday 11am to 5pm and Sunday noon to 4pm; September through December, Wednesday to Saturday 11am to 4pm, Sunday noon to 4pm.

Another place you won't want to miss is the **Thomaston Clock Discount Outlet** (tel. 379-1077), selling mantel, wall, travel, and grandfather clocks from some of America's best clockmakers. The store is open Tuesday though Sunday from 10am to 5pm.

WHERE TO STAY

OLD RIVERTON INN, Rte. 20 (P.O. Box 6), Riverton, CT 06065. Tel 203/379-8678. 12 rms (all with bath).

$ Rates: (including full breakfast): $65–$100 single or double. MC, V. **Parking** Free.

Just across the Farmington River from the center of the village, on Route 20, lies the Old Riverton Inn. Originally opened in 1796 by Jesse Ives, the inn has seen many changes, modifications, and additions over the years, but it retains much of its Early American charm, with heavy wood beams in the Colonial Dining Room, and grindstones from Nova Scotia providing the paving in the Grindstone Terrace. The guest rooms are done in period style, with four-poster and canopy beds and country wallpaper; some have fireplaces.

Luncheon is served from noon to 2:30pm; dinner from 5 to 8:30pm (to 9pm on Saturday); Sunday from noon to 8pm; open Wednesday to Sunday. At dinnertime expect to pay $17 for veal française and a dollar more for broiled scallops.

WHERE TO DINE

The **Riverton General Store** in the center of the village (tel. 379-0811) can provide all the raw ingredients for a marvelous picnic, including deli sandwiches, cheese, meat, other groceries, cold beer, and hot coffee. The store also sells worms and crawlers if you happen to be interested. It's open 7 days a week from 7am to 8pm.

NORFOLK

Back on U.S. 44, just 8 miles (13km) west of Winsted, is Norfolk.

WHERE TO STAY

MANOR HOUSE, 69 Maple Ave. (P.O. Box 447), Norfolk, CT 06058. Tel. 203/542-5690, or toll free 800/488-5690. 9 rms (all with bath).
$ Rates: (including breakfast): $85–$160 single or double. AE, MC, V. **Parking:** Free.

In an area full of graceful homes-turned-bed-and-breakfast, the Manor House stands with the best. This stucco, timber, and stone inn, on 5 acres, was built in 1898 by Charles Spofford, the architect of London's underground; that helps explain the English overtones. A massive stone fireplace and authentic Tiffany windows set the tone for the common rooms. The guest rooms, most with private bath, have antique beds with down comforters; some rooms boast a fireplace or a private balcony. A full breakfast, with homemade harvested honey, is served in one of three places: in bed, in an elegant dining room, or on the sunlit porch.

LITCHFIELD

Connecticut's answer to the pretty Massachusetts towns in the Berkshires is Litchfield, which a National Park Service writer has called "probably New England's finest surviving example of a typical late 18th-century town." The town was incorporated in 1719, and in the next 100 years it grew and prospered as a center for small industry and an important way station on the Hartford-Albany stagecoach route. With this prosperity came the urge, and the wherewithal, to build very fine, graceful houses, which is what the citizens did, making sure that the houses were set well back from the roadway. Progress in the 19th century robbed Litchfield of much of its wealth—water-powered industry drove Litchfield's small-time craftpeople out of business, and the railroads bypassed the town—but the town's decline may have been a blessing in disguise. Today Litchfield retains its late 18th-century beauty, unsullied by the workers' tenements and textile mills that have changed the face of so many other New England towns.

WHAT TO SEE & DO

At a tiny **information booth** on the green, you can get a free booklet on the town's history, architecture, and activities, complete with a small map. The sightseeing is simple enough: Drive down South Street just to get the feel of the gracious neighborhood.

In addition to the following, other Litchfield curiosities include: The **Ethan Allen**

House, thought to be the one in which the famous patriot and leader of Vermont's "Green Mountain Boys" was born, is at the southern end of South Street, in the road's fork. A **milestone** dating from 1787, which informed the traveler that it was 33 MILES TO HARTFORD, 102 MILES TO NEW YORK—J. STRONG AD 1787, stands on West Street, northern side, just at the end of the town green. And the jail, right on the green at the beginning of North Street, is connected to the bank next door! Whether it's for the convenience of thieves who wish to escape or for police who may nab burglars in the bank is not clear.

TAPPING REEVE HOUSE [1773], 82 South St. Tel. 567-4501.

Stop at this house and take a look at the small, unprepossessing edifice beside it which was the nation's first school of law, established here by Tapping Reeve in 1775 (the school moved into the one-room building in 1784). North Street is as attractive as South Street, and after a drive has given you the lay of the land, park at the green and stroll along either street to see the houses more closely. The hours and admission information is for both the Tapping Reeve House and Law School.

Admission: $2 adults, free for children.
Open: Mid-May to mid-Oct, Tues–Sat 11am–4pm, Sun 1–5pm.

LITCHFIELD HISTORICAL SOCIETY, 7 South St. Tel. 567-4501.

The Litchfield Historical Society was founded in 1856 and is dedicated to preserving the history of Litchfield County. The museum has permanent exhibits in four of its five galleries, as in the Liggett Gallery, which highlights "Litchfield's Golden Age" (1780–1840), and the Nelson Gallery, which focuses on everyday life in the early 1800s. The Cunningham Gallery houses changing exhibits and community events.

Admission: $2 adults, free for children.
Open: Mid-Apr to mid-Nov, Tues–Sat 11am–5pm, Sun 1–5pm.

WHITE MEMORIAL CONSERVATION CENTER, West St. Tel. 567-0015

On West Street (U.S. 202) towards Bantam, this is the state's largest nature center with more than 35 miles of trails open year round for hiking, cross-country skiing and horseback riding. Some of the trails are interpretive nature trails that allow you to observe the bird life of a marsh pond. The Holbrook Bird Observatory is an area that has been designed specifically to attract birds in all seasons. There are sheltered viewing stations in this area. Also on the property is a museum that includes dioramas, mounted specimens, live animals, a touch center, and a 4,000-volume nature library which includes a children's room.

Admission: Trails free. Museum $1.50 adults, 75¢ children 6–12.
Open: Museum Tues–Sat 9am–5pm, Sun 11am–5pm.

HAIGHT VINEYARD, 29 Chestnut Hill Rd. Tel. 567-4045.

On Chestnut Hill Road off Route 118, a mile east of Litchfield, this quaint and inviting place prides itself on being Connecticut's first farm winery (established 1975. Besides guided winery tours and wine tastings, you can take the Vineyard Walk, a self-guided tour of the vineyards during which you can inspect the types of grapes which make Haight wines.

Some of the favorite wines here are Covertside White, the table wines, and a varietal Maréchal Foch, a chardonnay. There's even a sparkling wine made in the classic *méthode champenoise*. Prices are moderate.

Admission: Free.
Open: Mon–Sat 10:30am–5pm, Sun noon–5pm.

WHERE TO STAY & DINE

TOLLGATE HILL INN, U.S. 202 (P.O. Box 1339), Litchfield, CT 06759

Tel. 203/567-4545. 20 rms (all with bath). **Directions:** Follow U.S. 202 south from Torrington to the inn.

$ Rates: (including continental breakfast): $110–$140 single or double; $175 suite. AE, DC, MC, V. **Parking:** Free.

Just over 2 miles northeast of the village green along U.S. 202 is the Tollgate Hill Inn, a farmhouse dating from 1745. Originally it stood on the Old East Litchfield Road, where in 1789 it became a tavern to feed, quench, and house travelers on the road between Litchfield and Hartford. But in 1923 it was moved to its present site, where it continues its long tradition of offering fine food and lodging to travelers in the Litchfield Hills. Over the years the inn has been restored and renovated many times, most recently in 1983. The colonial spirit of the house was well preserved, and mated with recent improvements. You'll find a bar made of cherry to harmonize with the original paneling, a formal dining room with a fine fireplace, an arched corner cupboard, and a tavern dining room paneled in wide pine boards. In the ballroom upstairs is a large fieldstone fireplace, lots of windows, copper chandeliers, and a fiddler's loft from which music issues forth on Saturday nights.

The guest rooms are all different, with colonial furnishings, private bath, and air conditioning; some rooms with wood-burning fireplaces, private bath, and air conditioning are slightly more expensive. The suites go for $175 double—one of these has a queen-size canopy bed, bar and refrigerator, cable TV with VCR, and stereo tape cassette player, while the other is a small two-room suite with bedroom, sitting room, and color cable TV with VCR. Continental breakfast is served in your room or on the patio (in good weather).

LAKE WARAMAUG

From Litchfield, drive along U.S. 202 south and west for 12 miles to New Preston. Then head north on Route 45, and you'll come to Lake Waramaug. Attractive inns front Lake Waramaug, as does a state park with picnic and camping facilities. **Lake Waramaug State Park,** in New Preston, CT 06777 (tel. 868-0220), has 88 campsites open May 15 through Labor Day. You can reserve in advance, but only by mail. Picnic grounds and swimming are here, too.

Next door to the Hopkins Inn is the **Hopkins Vineyard,** on Hopkins Road in Warren (tel. 868-7954). The quaint red-barn winery is open for tours and tastings from 10am to 5pm 7 days a week from the beginning of May through the end of the year. From January 2 through April, you can visit on Friday, Saturday, and Sunday only, from 10am to 5pm. The winery is closed Thanksgiving and Christmas days.

Whoever heard of a vineyard in Connecticut? You'll be telling all your friends about Connecticut wines once you taste Hopkins' fine, dry Seyval Blanc, perfect for a seafood meal at the inn across the street. Wine prices are moderate and quality is high. The vineyard is not affiliated with the Hopkins Inn, although the vineyard barn was obviously part of the same estate at one time.

WHERE TO STAY

Hopkins Inn, listed under "Where to Dine," also has rooms for rent.

INN ON LAKE WARAMAUG, North Shore Rd., New Preston, CT 06777. Tel. 203/868-0563, or toll free 800/LAKEINN outside Connecticut. Fax 203/868-9173. 23 rms. A/C TV TEL

$ Rates: (including breakfast, dinner, and service): $86–$229 single or double. Children 3–14 $45, under 3 free. AE, MC, V. **Parking:** Free.

This is actually a mini-resort with all attractions. Indoor swimming pool, tennis court, air-conditioned rooms, restaurant and lounge, and water sports (rowing, canoeing, sailing) are among the many offerings. There's even a small launch designed like an old "showboat" for tours of the lake. Even so, the inn retains an antique flavor. Of the guest rooms, only five are in the original inn, while the others are in more modern but attractive guesthouses. Most rooms have working fireplaces. The inn offers many special events, like old-fashioned ice harvesting and maple sugaring, which have become traditions over the years.

WHERE TO DINE

HOPKINS INN, Hopkins Rd., New Preston, CT 06777. Tel. 203/868-7295.
    Cuisine: INTERNATIONAL. **Reservations:** Recommended; required for Sat.
    Directions: From Rte. 45, follow the shore road around Lake Waramaug to the inn.
$ **Prices:** Appetizers $3.75–$6.75; main courses $10–$18; dinner $25–$35. MC, V.
    Open: Apr–Dec, Tues–Thurs noon–2pm and 6–9pm, Fri–Sat noon–2pm and 6–10pm, Sun 12:30–8pm.

Not far from where the shore road rejoins Route 45, look for signs which point the way to this graceful old mansion set on a hill above the lake. The blackboard menus change daily, but you can be sure of finding interesting, appetizing dishes. I had a difficult choice between clams casino and smoked salmon to start, and an even harder time choosing among Backhendl (chicken) with lingonberries, steamed lobster wienerschnitzel, and live trout meunière (you can choose your own trout from the tank!). When it came to those Austrian desserts, the choice was impossible. In warm weather you can dine on the shady patio outside, with a grand view of the lake.

Hopkins Inn is most famous for its restaurant, but 10 rooms are for rent as well April through December. If you share a bath, a double room will cost $65; with private bath, prices start at $75.

EN ROUTE TO SALISBURY

Continue north on Route 45 to **Cornwall Bridge,** famous for its picturesque covered bridge. **Housatonic Meadows State Park** (tel. 672-6772) is here with camping and picnic areas, north of town on U.S. 7. Head north on U.S. 7, then cross westward on Route 112 to pick up Route 41 north to Salisbury; or take Route 4 west from Cornwall Bridge to Sharon, then Route 41 north through Lakeville to Salisbury.

SALISBURY

Salisbury is an aristocratic, historic town on the edge of the Berkshires. Late in September there's a big flea market here, and at the height of the fall foliage color the Salisbury Antiques Fair is held in the Town Hall. Come any time of year, though. The town is pretty, tranquil, surrounded by gorgeous country, and only 20 miles from the heart of the Berkshires' summer and winter activities. Stay in Cornwall Bridge on the way if you like, and consider a short trip to Lakeville for a meal.

WHERE TO STAY

CORNWALL INN AND RESTAURANT, U.S. 7, Cornwall Bridge, CT 06754. Tel. 203/672-6884. 13 rms (all with bath). AC
$ **Rates:** Inn $110 single or double; motel $76 single or double. MC, V. **Parking:** Free.

This cozy old inn has a dining room, lounge, guest rooms, and a swimming pool. The original old inn, which dates from 1810, is supplemented by tidy motel-style rooms in a neighboring red barn-style building. The rooms have all the conveniences. Note that the dining room is closed on Tuesday and Wednesday.

WHERE TO DINE

WAKE ROBIN INN, Sharon Rd., Lakeville, CT 06039. Tel. 203/435-2515.
    Cuisine: FRENCH. **Reservations:** Required.
$ **Prices:** Appetizers $3.50–$9.25; main courses $17–$25. AE, MC, V.

Open: Dinner Tues–Thurs 6–9pm, Fri–Sun 6–10pm; brunch Sun 11:30am–2pm.
A few miles down the road from Salisbury is this elegant French country inn with an excellent dining room. Start with duck pâté with green peppercorns or the soup of the day, and move on to roasted tenderloin layered with spinach, tomato, and mushrooms or swordfish in a light fennel and chervil sauce. Top it off with a delectable dessert.

The 41 rooms in this completely renovated former girls' school set on 15 acres cost $95 to $145 single or double.

LIVE FREE OR DIE says the motto on every auto license plate from New Hampshire, echoing the stirring words of Gen. John Stark, victor at the momentous Battle of Bennington (1777) and a New Hampshire native. New Hampshire folk are still very patriotic in an old-fashioned way, and committed to material progress: Modern facilities abound, and the road system is perhaps the best maintained in New England. On a vacation, "living free" in New Hampshire is a snap—mountains, beaches, lakes, amusements, special activities, and good restaurants are all available to the visitor.

SEEING NEW HAMPSHIRE

On our tour through New Hampshire, we'll look first at the state's seacoast. Yes, New Hampshire has a seacoast! Next we'll visit the charming colonial town of Portsmouth on the border with Maine. Then we'll head north into the state's heart, passing through Manchester, the state's largest city, and Concord, its capital, on our way to Lake Winnipesaukee. From this veritable inland sea, we'll head north again into the White Mountains National Forest and the skiing/hiking center of North Conway, and then even farther north to Bretton Woods. Moving west, we'll cover Franconia Notch, North Woodstock, and Waterville Valley. Finally, we'll visit Lake Sunapee and then Hanover, the hometown of Dartmouth College.

Throughout New Hampshire a rooms-and-meals tax of 8% will be added to your hotel, motel, or inn bill, and you'll also have to pay it every time you have a meal in a restaurant. Except where noted, tax is not included in the prices listed.

New Hampshire's telephone **area code** is 603.

GETTING THERE   New Hampshirites are committed to highway travel, so air links and rail lines are played down in favor of bus and car. Amtrak, in fact, has no trains in New Hampshire proper, although it does run along the New Hampshire-Vermont border for a bit, stopping in Brattleboro, Bellows Falls, Essex Junction (near Burlington), and White River Junction on the route between New York and Montréal.

By Limousine and Bus   Airport limousines run regularly from Boston's Logan airport to many points in New Hampshire. **Hudson Bus Lines' Airporter Limousine Service** (tel. 603/883-4807) goes from Logan to Manchester, Merrimack, and Nashua.

C&J Trailways runs hourly daily trips from Logan to New Hampshire's seacoast

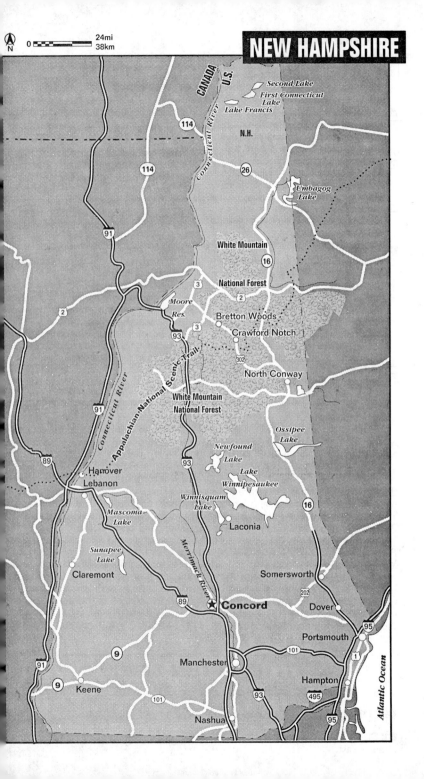

WHAT'S SPECIAL ABOUT NEW HAMPSHIRE

Museums
- ☐ Strawberry Banke, in Portsmouth, 10 acres of 18th-century buildings brought back to life and filled with working artisans.
- ☐ Manchester's Currier Gallery of Art's surprisingly good collection, beautifully displayed.
- ☐ A visit to a real Shaker village at Canterbury—you can even share in a traditional dinner.

Cool for Kids
- ☐ A cruise on the MS *Mount Washington* on Lake Winnipesaukee from Weirs Beach.
- ☐ A ride up a mountainside on the historic Mount Washington Cog Railway.
- ☐ A nostalgic train ride through the mountains on the Conway Scenic Railroad in North Conway Village.
- ☐ A visit to the Old Man of the Mountain at Franconia Notch State Park.

- ☐ Gliding through the air in a gondola of the Cannon Mountain Aerial Tramway, near Franconia Notch.

Outdoor Adventures
- ☐ Hiking up Mount Washington, the highest peak in New England.
- ☐ Swimming, boating, and fishing on Lake Winnipesaukee.
- ☐ Cross-country skiing on 90 miles (150km) of trails starting from Jackson.
- ☐ Hiking and camping along the Appalachian Trail in the White Mountains National Forest.
- ☐ Traveling the scenic Kancamagus Highway from Lincoln to Conway.
- ☐ Canoeing from Center Conway on the Saco River.
- ☐ A hot-air balloon ride along the Connecticut River Valley from Post Mills, Vt.

region and Portsmouth; call these numbers for schedules and reservations: toll free i New York and New England, 800/258-7111; in Portsmouth, 603/431-2424.

Concord Trailways, 7 Langdon St., Concord, NH 03301 (tel. 603/228-330(or toll free 800/639-3317 in New England states), has bus service from Bosto through Manchester and Concord to Laconia on Lake Winnipesaukee; from there th bus continues to Plymouth and North Woodstock, and through Franconia. Concor Trailways also has buses from Boston to Conway, North Conway, Glen, Jackso Pinkham Notch AMC Camp, Wildcat Mountain, and on to Berlin.

Vermont Transit, operating out of Boston's Greyhound terminal near the Par Plaza Hotel (tel. 617/292-4700, or toll free 800/451-3292, 800/642-3133 i Vermont), has routes from Portland, Me., to St. Johnsbury, Vt., via Boston, beside running from Logan airport in Boston to the cities of Manchester, Concord, an Hanover. Vermont Transit also runs buses from Montréal south into Vermont and few points in New Hampshire, but Montréal visitors will have to transfer at least onc to reach most of the vacation locations in the state. Vermont Transit buses depart fror the Voyageur Terminal in Montréal (tel. 514/842-2281, or toll free 800/451-3292

1. HAMPTON BEACH

45 miles (72 km) N of Boston, 11 miles (18 km) S of Portsmouth

GETTING THERE **By Bus** See the beginning of this chapter.

By Car Take I-95 north or south and exit at the Hampton toll plaza. The beach is minutes east.

ESSENTIALS   The **area code** is 603. If you have questions, contact the **Hampton Beach Area Chamber of Commerce,** 836 Lafayette Rd., P.O. Box 790, Hampton Beach, NH 03842 (tel. 603/926-8717).

Many visitors to New England forget that Vermont is the only New England state without a seacoast, and that New Hampshire is in fact a maritime state, even though its coastline is only about 20 miles long. The 20 miles are almost all beach, with some rocky headlands and coves, and four state parks with their own uncommercial stretches of beach. Hampton Beach State Park is the most southerly, and the public parking and bathing facilities here are run in the clean, well-ordered way of state park management. But just north of the state park is the town of Hampton Beach, two streets wide (north along the waterfront, south along the inland street, as far as cars are concerned). Hampton Beach is a riot of closely packed motels and cottages, ice-cream stands and hot-dog stands, penny arcades, and watering places. Lights, glitter, and throbbing crowds of the young, tanned, and adventurous make it a nonstop circus, something out of a "beach party" movie, to revel in or abhor as your taste dictates.

WHERE TO STAY

IN HAMPTON

LAMIE'S INN, 49 Lafayette St., Hampton, NH 03842. Tel 603/926-0330. Fax 603/929-0017. 33 rooms (all with bath). TV TEL
$ Rates: $79–$89 double. AE, DC, MC, V. **Parking:** Free.
This lively colonial-inspired inn was once affiliated with Omni hotels and today, under independent ownership, still welcomes seacoast guests as it has for decades. Individually decorated rooms feature some canopy beds, stenciled borders, armoires with concealed TVs, and papered baths. Friendly folk run the inn and there is a restaurant and tavern where you can spend your leisure time.

IN EXETER

About 10 miles west of Hampton Beach is a little New England town dotted with Georgian-style brick buildings. Exeter is ideal for a delightful sunny afternoon walk. Duck in for an ice cream or a cup of hot apple cider and if you have the chance, stay over at the Inn of Exeter.

INN OF EXETER, 90 Front St., Exeter, NH 03833. Tel. 603/772-5901. Fax 603/778-8757. 50 rms (all with bath), 1 suite. TV TEL
$ Rates: $75 double; $165 suite. AE, DC, DISC, MC, V. **Parking:** Free.
This Georgian inn is a wonderful romantic getaway in the trendy town that hosts a prep school with the accent on preppy. The parlor rooms have fireplaces, and the restaurant has a porchlike country atmosphere and a small cozy bar. Rooms may have four-poster beds, and the suite has a fireplace. This is an ideal overnight stop on a New England tour in autumn or any season.

FROM HAMPTON BEACH TO PORTSMOUTH

North of Hampton Beach, the state park beaches at Rye Harbor and Wallis Sands are not as bubbly with activity as Hampton, but to some tastes are all the more pleasant for that. At the state park beaches in New Hampshire, expect to pay a small parking fee, which includes use of all other facilities as well.

The drive along U.S. 1A north to Portsmouth is very pretty, winding along the coast past a succession of ever more sumptuous and meticulously maintained summer mansions, still inhabited by the wealthy and powerful of New Hampshire, Maine, and Boston.

2. PORTSMOUTH

55 miles (89km) N of Boston, 54 miles (87km) SW of Portland,
51 miles (82km) E of Manchester

GETTING THERE   By Bus   See the beginning of this chapter.

By Car   I-95, running between the Boston area and Portland, passes right by Portsmouth.

ESSENTIALS   The **area code** is 603. The **Greater Portsmouth Chamber of Commerce** maintains a visitors information center at 500 Market St. (Exit 7 off I-95), Portsmouth, NH 03801 (tel. 603/436-1118), and also an **information kiosk** in Market Square.

If the gracious maritime towns along the New England coast, Portsmouth is one of the prettiest and most interesting. A morning or afternoon spent wandering through the town's restored historic side streets, perhaps with lunch, tea, or dinner in one of its restaurants, is both relaxing and entertaining.

WHAT TO SEE & DO

STRAWBERY BANKE OUTDOOR MUSEUM, Marcy St. Tel. 433-1100.
Portsmouth's jump from wilderness to settlement started in 1630, when a group of settlers sailed into the Piscataqua River's mouth in search of fresh water and good land. As they climbed up the rise from the shore, they found not only the water and land they'd been looking for but also wild strawberries, which delighted them so much they named the place Strawbery Banke. Today that name serves to identify the center of the city's historic restoration effort, a 10-acre section of buildings dating from 1695 to 1835 brought back to life and filled with craftspeople who actually make their livings right where you see them. For the price of admission you can wander about, looking at the 42 furnished houses and buildings, exhibits, period gardens, workshops, and artisans' galleries on display.

A walk through Strawbery Banke is educational as well as entertaining, for you'll see how chairs, tables, and cabinets were made besides seeing examples of the work itself; boatbuilding, wood carving, and stoneware potting are explained, and early tools and architectural designs are spread out for your examination.

Strawbery Banke is the major part of Portsmouth's Old Harbour area, the cornerstone of which is **Prescott Park,** a waterfront park, dock, and amusement area donated to the city by the Prescott sisters in the 1930s and 1940s.

Admission: $9 adults, $8 seniors, $5 children ages 6–12, $7 ages 13–17.

Open: May–Oct, daily 10am–5pm. **Directions:** Follow the directional signs with arrows, posted throughout the town and on approach roads toward the waterfront, just south of the Rte. 1 bridge.

JOHN PAUL JONES HOUSE, Middle and State Sts. Tel. 436-8420.
No place in this pretty city is more notable than the National Historic Landmark house of John Paul Jones (1758), located right downtown. The stately house was actually a rooming house when Jones stayed in it while his frigate, the famous *Ranger,* was being built in a nearby shipyard. It is now the headquarters of the Portsmouth Historical Society, and you can visit the house and museum on a 1-hour guided tour.

Admission: $4 adults, $3 children ages 6–12.

Open: Late May to mid-Oct, Mon–Sat 10am–4pm, also Sun July–Aug noon–4pm.

WHERE TO STAY

SISE INN, 40 Court St., Portsmouth, NH 03801. Tel. 603/433-1200, or toll free 800/232-4667. 34 rms (all with bath). TV TEL
$ Rates (including continental breakfast): $99–$110 double; $125–$175 suite. AE, MC, V. **Parking:** Free.

The rooms and suites in this Queen Anne–style 1881 inn take you back to late 19th-century Portsmouth, and it's easy to imagine yourself as the guest of a wealthy Portsmouth merchant family. Guest rooms have rich carpeting, fine furniture, period pieces, but also such modern conveniences as cable TV and VCR. The inn caters to business people but off-the-road travelers won't feel out of place.

WHERE TO DINE

LIBRARY RESTAURANT, 401 State St. Tel. 431-5202.
Cuisine: CONTINENTAL. **Reservations:** Recommended.
$ Prices: Appetizers $3.75–$6.50; main courses $11–$19; dinner $30–$35. AE, DISC, MC, V.
Open: Daily 11:30am–3pm and 5–11pm; Labor Day–May, Sun brunch 11:30am–3pm.

Located in the Rockingham Hotel, in the center of town, the Library is a good choice no matter what your culinary preference. The menu lists such varied delights as Long Island duckling, rack of lamb, and veal and fish specials, along with more familiar fare and money-saving daily-special plates. The old rooms of the hotel have been preserved without overdoing the decor; books line the walls.

SZECHUAN TASTE, 54 Daniels St. Tel. 431-2226.
Cuisine: SZECHUAN. **Reservations:** Recommended.
$ Prices: Appetizers $4–$8; main courses $7.25–$14; fixed-price lunch $5–$6.50; dinner $12–$16. AE, DISC, MC, V.
Open: Mon–Fri 11:30am–10:45pm, Sat–Sun 11:30am–11pm.

This family-run place offers a refreshing change from Portsmouth's mostly seafood restaurants. The simple, dimly lit restaurant is the kind of place you go with friends, where you might not venture without a recommendation. There are many Szechuan dishes on the menu.

3. MANCHESTER

51 miles (87km) W of Portsmouth, 53 miles (85km) NW of Boston, 19 miles (31km) S of Concord

GETTING THERE **By Plane** Manchester's airport is served by Continental, Delta, Northwest, and USAir.

By Bus See the beginning of this chapter.

By Car I-93, the main route between Boston and northern New Hampshire, passes through Manchester, as does U.S. 3 (the Everett Turnpike).

ESSENTIALS The **area code** is 603. Call the **Manchester Chamber of Commerce** at 603/666-6600 with questions.

Manchester borders the Merrimack River, and the cheap waterpower brought the city wealth in the textile boom of the mid- and late 19th century. The very impressive **Amoskeag Mills** still border the river and the canals in the center of town, the brick facades stretching for almost a mile. The mills are used for various purposes today, including the manufacture of textiles and shoes (plenty of factory-outlet stores in town); continued use preserves these monuments of American architectural and industrial history.

WHAT TO SEE & DO

CURRIER GALLERY OF ART, 192 Orange St. Tel. 669-6144.

The collection of this fine museum is strong in 19th- and 20th-century European and American glass, English and American silver and pewter, and colonial and Early American furniture. It also has a nice collection of paintings and sculpture from other parts of the world. Degas, Jan Gossaert, and a follower of Meliore are represented along with other masters. A beautiful new wing shows off the collections to best advantage.

Admission: Free.

Open: Tues–Wed and Fri–Sat 10am–4pm, Thurs 10am–10pm, Sun 2–5pm.

Directions: Cross the Queen City or Amoskeag Bridge to downtown, and drive along Elm St. (Rte. 3) to Orange St. Go east on Orange 6 blocks; the museum is on your left.

ANHEUSER-BUSCH COMPANY'S MERRIMACK BREWERY, 221 Daniel Webster Hwy. (P.O. Box 610). Tel. 595-1202.

The company that offers Budweiser and Michelob is the largest brewer of beer in the world, with an annual capacity of about 86 million barrels at 12 breweries across the country. For tours, running continuously throughout the day, assemble in the special alpine-looking tour building.

After the tour there's sampling of the brew, of course, and perhaps a visit to the Clydesdale Hamlet, home for a dozen of the huge, majestic draft horses. You've probably seen them in eight-horse hitches pulling a brewer's wagon in advertisements or local parades.

Admission: Free.

Open: May–Oct, daily 9:30am–5pm. Nov–Apr, Wed–Sun 10am–4pm. **Directions:** Take the Everett Tpk. 5 miles south of Manchester to Exit 11, in the town of Merrimack.

WHERE TO STAY

HOWARD JOHNSON HOTEL, 298 Queen City Ave., Manchester, NH 03102. Tel. 603/668-2600, or toll free 800/654-2000. Fax 603/668-2600 ext. 634. 100 rms (all with bath). A/C TV TEL **Directions:** Take the Queen City Bridge exit (no. 4) from I-293.

$ Rates: Sept–Oct, $85 double. Nov–Aug, $65–$75. Children under 18 stay free in parents' room. AE, DC, DISC, MC, V. **Parking:** Free, on premises.

At this convenient motel just off I-293 you'll find king- and queen-size beds, HBO movies, an indoor pool, saunas, a lounge, and a restaurant (open from 6am to midnight).

SUSSE CHALET INN, 860 S. Porter St., Manchester, NH 03103. Tel. 603/625-2020, or toll free 800/258-1980. 102 rms (all with bath). A/C TV TEL **Directions:** Take Exit 1 from I-293/Rte. 101.

$ Rates: $45 single; $55 double. AE, CB, DC, DISC, MC, V. **Parking:** Free.

For the best value stay here, where the guest rooms are plainish but tidy and comfortable. The motel has a swimming pool, and remote-control cable TV with free movies. Location, just off I-293, is convenient.

4. CONCORD

19 miles (31km) N of Manchester, 24 miles (39km) S of Laconia,
55 miles (89km) SE of Lebanon

GETTING THERE By Bus See the beginning of this chapter.

By Car Concord is near the junction of I-89 and I-93, making it easily accessible from Boston, Manchester, central and northern New Hampshire, central and northern Vermont.

ESSENTIALS The **area code** is 603. If you have a question, call the **Concord Area Chamber of Commerce** at 603/224-2508, or contact the **New Hampshire Office of Travel and Tourism Development,** P.O. Box 856, Concord, NH (tel. 603/271-2666).

The capital of New Hampshire is a pleasant little city with an appropriate frontier-mountain feeling. First settled in 1725, the town was called Rumford for the first 40 years; the name later found its way into the title of Count Rumford, inventor of a certain sort of shallow fireplace. Since 1816 Concord has been the capital of the state. Granite, printing, electrical equipment, and leather goods, as well as a surprisingly small amount of state bureaucracy, keep the town going.

WHAT TO SEE & DO

PIERCE MANSE, 14 Penacook St. Tel. 224-9620.
Franklin Pierce, 14th president of the United States, was speaker of the New Hampshire General Court (legislature) as well as one of the town's prominent lawyers. His house, now a National Historic Site at the farthest reaches of North Main Street, was saved from demolition by a civic-minded group named the Pierce Brigade. It was his family home from 1842 to 1848. You might want to make an appointment by calling 224-9620 or 224-7668.
   Admission: $1.50 adults, 50¢ children and students.
   Open: Mid-June to mid-Sept, Mon–Fri 11am–3pm. **Closed:** Labor Day.

THE STATE HOUSE & VISITOR'S CENTER, 107 N. Main St. Tel. 271-2154.
The State Capitol, called the State House, was built in 1819 of—you guessed it—New Hampshire granite. It's the oldest state capitol in which a legislature still occupies its original chambers. Inside, the state's battle flags and portraits of its notable military commanders are proudly displayed. A statue of Daniel Webster, one of several native New Hampshire boys who made good on a national scale, stands before the building. The small size of the State House will surprise you; compared with the mammoth buildings in Providence, Hartford, and Boston, it seems barely big enough to hold just the governor's staff. But many of the tax-burdened citizens of other states are lured to New Hampshire every year by the low tax rate, kept low in part by keeping bureaucracy small. It's in the center of town.
   Admission: Free; self-guided tours.
   Open: Mon–Fri 8am–4:30pm.

CANTERBURY SHAKER VILLAGE, 288 Shaker Rd., Canterbury. Tel. 783-9511.
On the way to Laconia, you can visit a restored village founded by the Shakers in 1792. Members of the United Society of Believers in Christ's Second Appearing were called Shakers because of the religious ecstasies they sometimes experienced. Their community at Hancock, Mass., in the Berkshires (see "Stockbridge" in Chapter 8) is

the best known, but there were others, notably at Sabbathday Lake, Me., and here in Canterbury. Two of these villages are still active Shaker communities.

Besides producing the much-admired Shaker furniture and craft items, the Canterbury Shaker community specialized in producing herbs and herbal medicines which were sold throughout the country. You can still visit the herb garden, as well as the original meetinghouse (1792), an apiary (bee house), the ministry, a Sisters' shop, a laundry, horse barn, infirmary, and the schoolhouse (1826).

On the guided tour you can see dovetailed and oval box making in the carpenter's shop, and look over reproductions of Shaker designs in furniture and crafts in the carriage-house gift shop.

All year on Thursday, Friday, and Saturday evenings you can also enjoy a traditional candlelight dinner here. There is one seating (family style at long tables) at 7pm sharp. The four-course meal (choose from a poultry, meat, or fish main dish) costs $32 per person. Recipes, ingredients, and cooking methods are all true to Shaker form and philosophy. After dinner has transported you to another era, you'll be guided through the village by candlelight, or if it's off-season and the village is closed, you'll be treated to an evening of folk singing. You'll have an enjoyable evening either way. The Creamery restaurant is open for lunch daily 11:30am to 2pm and for brunch Sunday 11am to 2pm.

Admission: $7 adults, $3.50 children ages 6–12.

Open (for guided tour): May–Oct, Mon–Sat 10am–5pm, Sun noon–5pm (last tour 4pm). Apr and Nov–Dec, Fri–Sat 10am–4pm, Sun noon–4pm (last tour 3pm). **Closed:** Jan–Mar. **Directions:** Take exit 18 off I-93. Follow signs 6½ miles (10.5km) to the village.

5. LAKE WINNIPESAUKEE

Laconia: 24 miles (39km) N of Concord, 56 miles (90km) S of Franconia Notch

GETTING THERE   By Bus   See the beginning of this chapter.

By Car   I-93 is the major road to the lake; from Portsmouth, take the Spaulding Turnpike (Route 16) to Route 11.

ESSENTIALS   The **area code** is 603. The **Greater Laconia/Weirs Beach Chamber of Commerce,** 11 Veteran's Square, Laconia, NH 03246 (tel. 603/524-5531), provides information.

The largest of the lakes in New Hampshire's Lakes Region is grand indeed: 28 miles long, close to 300 miles of shoreline, 72 square miles of water to swim in or boat on, and almost 300 islands. The name has been translated as "smile of the Great Spirit," and while the lake's irregular shoreline might suggest a wry grin rather than a sunny smile, the lake's large size would certainly do the Great Spirit justice. Summer is when the lake is busiest with swimmers, boaters, water-skiers, and the like, but winter snows draw crowds to the **Gunstock** and **Alpine Ridge** ski areas near the lake's shore.

LACONIA & GILFORD

Laconia, Lake Winnipesaukee's largest town, is also its business and commercial center. Many of the area companies with large shoe factories have factory-outlet stores here where shoes sell at bargain prices. Downtown next to City Hall, the **Belknap** (*Bell*-nap) **Mill** (tel. 524-8813), a textile mill built in 1823, has been restored, and you can tour it to see the hydroelectric machinery which ran the mill from 1918 to 1969. The mill now serves as the region's center for culture and the arts. It's open from 9am to 5pm Monday through Wednesday and Friday, 9am to 9pm Thursday, and 9am to 1pm on Saturday, all year.

WHAT TO SEE & DO

BEACHES   Ellacoya State Beach, on Route 11 southeast of Glendale, is one of the nicest beaches on the lake. The entrance fee is $2 for adults and children 12 and older, there's plenty of parking, and if you go early in the day you can get one of the picnic tables. There's a snack bar, and a lifeguard is on duty all the time the beach is open. The slope of the beach is very gradual, making it ideal for small children; for more experienced swimmers, a swimming dock floats in the water farther out.

    Weirs Beach, on Route 11B near its intersection with U.S. 3, is a town beach with a similar admission charge, free parking at several lots in the town of Weirs Beach (look for the signs to the free lots—everything on the main street is metered). The town is known more for its honky-tonk penny arcades, candlepin bowling alleys, pinball machines, fortune-tellers, and fast-food stands than it is for the beauty of its beach. These amusements are open during the day and in the evening in summer, and give the town a character that differs greatly from what it once must have been: The grand old turn-of-the-century mansions around the town are some of the finest of their genre, with lots of cupolas, turrets, gables, and all the other paraphernalia that make late-Victorian architecture so intricate. You can stay overnight at Weirs Beach in one of the hotels, motels, or guesthouses, although the low lakefront situation seems to lend a mustiness to most accommodations.

BOAT RIDES   A number of large boats make tours of the lake several times daily. Most famous is the 230-foot MS *Mount Washington* (tel. 366-2628), which runs cruises from Weirs Beach between late May and late October, with the schedule varying depending on the time of year. The cruise around the lake takes 3¼ hours and costs $12 for adults, half price for children 5 to 12; under 5, free. Breakfast, luncheon buffet, a Sunday champagne brunch, drinks, and snacks are available on board. Ports of call are Centre Harbor, Wolfeboro, and Alton Bay. Shorter cruises are offered on smaller vessels operated by the same company.

WHERE TO STAY

When coming to the lake for fun, people stay in the many motels and inns on parts of the lake's shore near Laconia, or in a small, pretty town such as Wolfeboro, due east of Laconia. Skiers stay at the inns located near the slopes or in a lakefront establishment with winterized cabins.

    To get away from the hustle and bustle of the highway, drive along Route 11 and watch for signs pointing out a scenic shore road off to the left. Route 11 has been remade in recent years and is farther away from the lakeshore, while the motels are still along the old road which used to be Route 11. Most of the traffic uses the new road, leaving the old one much quieter.

BELKNAP POINT MOTEL, 107 Belknap Point Rd. (R.F.D.8), Gilford, NH 03246. Tel. 603/293-7511. 17 rms (all with bath). A/C TV TEL **Directions:** From Rte. 11, turn left on Belknap Point Rd., then go ½ mile down.

$ Rates: High season, $78–$98 double. Off-season (May to mid-June and Sept–Oct), $48–$58 double. Extra person $10. AE, MC, V. **Parking:** Free, on premises.

Those looking for quiet, luxurious accommodations with all the conveniences will enjoy the Belknap Point. It has two sections: Down on the shore of the lake, a number of modern efficiency units with kitchens and decks reach out almost over the water; and up the steep slope of the hill between the old road and the new (you can enter from either road) are a number of hotel rooms, all with ceramic tile bath, a little balcony, and gorgeous views of the lake. The owners have put a lot of thought into decorating the rooms nicely, and they work hard to make sure each guest is comfortable. The Belknap Point has its own swimming area and a grassy patio.

ESTATE MOTEL AND COTTAGES, Scenic Dr. (R.F.D. 4), Gilford, NH 03246. Tel. 603/293-7792. 10 rms (all with bath). A/C TV **Directions:** Go to end of Rte. 11 bypass, left onto Rte. 11 east, to 3.5 miles, and take left on Scenic Dr. Motel is ½ mile on left.

$ Rates: Motel $65 double; efficiency $70 double. Weekly rates available. MC, V.
Parking: Free, on premises.

Here, in another establishment along the scenic lakefront road, there are eight motel rooms and two efficiencies in white buildings. The rooms look out over a grassy lawn down to the lake; the lake boating and swimming dock are convenient. The Estate is secluded and quiet, and it's best to reserve in advance for one of its rooms. Rooms have two double beds, refrigerators, and cable TV; the efficiencies have the same, plus a sink and stove, and kitchen utensils. Three cabins are rented by the week for $350 for one bedroom, $500 for two bedrooms.

WOLFEBORO

Wolfeboro is among the prettiest and most interesting towns on the lake. It escaped the blight that hit such textile-producing towns as Laconia because Wolfeboro never industrialized; it has escaped the honky-tonk commercialism that has taken over some other lake towns, perhaps because of its "inconvenient" position at the southeastern tip of the lake. So today Wolfeboro is a fine, almost typical, New England town with the requisite historical society, white-steepled churches, gracious old houses, and some very good views of the lake.

There is less hustle and bustle in Wolfeboro than in some other lake towns, less to "see and do," but that makes it all the better for those who really want to relax. The MS *Mount Washington* stops here to pick up and discharge passengers for its tours of the lake (see above for details); and a good number of the motels and resorts in town have their own stretches of beach. Wolfeboro is proud to call itself "the oldest summer resort in America," because in 1763 Gov. John Wentworth built what is thought to be the first summer house in the United States within the town's boundaries.

WHAT TO SEE & DO

LIBBY MUSEUM, Rte. 109. Tel. 569-1035.
Dr. Henry F. Libby, a Boston dentist who was born and raised near the shores of Winnipesaukee, devoted the latter part of his life to the study and collection of natural history specimens: fish, animals, and birds. Other interests of his included early Native American lore of the region, and artifacts from the times of early settlers. All these diverse exhibits are brought together in the Libby Museum.
Admission: $1 adults, 50¢ children.
Open: Memorial Day–Sept, Tues–Sun 10am–4pm. **Directions:** Go 3 miles north of Wolfeboro on Rte. 109.

CASTLE IN THE CLOUDS, Rte. 171, Moultonboro. Tel. 476-2352.
Around the turn of the century Thomas Gustav Plant decided to build himself a retreat in the New Hampshire wilderness. While he was not alone in this—lots of rich men were building lavish estates in the region—his accomplishment is certainly among the grandest. Lucknow, as the estate was named, cost millions of dollars to build; the name comes from a castle in Scotland, and originally from a city in India, although the mansion has distinctly Central European touches to it. Today Lucknow is called Castle in the Clouds; its grounds are very beautiful, and the view of the mountains and lakes is nothing short of spectacular. Horseback trail rides are available.
Admission: $8 adults, $5.50 children ages 6–12.

Open: May to mid-June, Sat–Sun 9am–6pm. Mid-June to mid-Oct, daily 8:30am–5pm. **Directions:** Take Rte. 109 north from Wolfeboro for 17 miles, turn right (east) on to Rte. 171, and go 3 miles to the entrance.

WHERE TO STAY
In Wolfeboro

WOLFEBORO INN, 44 N. Main St., Wolfeboro, NH 03894. Tel. 603/569-3016, or toll free 800/451-2389. Fax 603/569-5375. 43 rms. A/C TV TEL
$ Rates (including continental breakfast): Summer–fall, $99–$207 double. Winter, $69–$160. AE, DISC, MC, V. **Parking:** Free, on property.
Among the most serviceable of the town's hostelries is this venerable inn, where the rooms have some antique pieces. It was built in 1812, but it has been thoroughly modernized, and prides itself on giving the "glitter-weary traveler" a comfortable and tasteful place to lodge and dine. As the inn, in the center of town, is often full in high summer, it's best to reserve in advance. In summer, enjoy the sandy beach on Lake Winnipesaukee, take a cruise in the inn's own launch, or ride one of the bicycles, canoes, or sailboards, all included in the room price. In winter, outdoor activities are cross-country skiing and iceboating.
The dining areas have wooden chairs and tables and several fireplaces, including three in Wolfe's Tavern (open 11:30am to 11:30pm) and a large brick one in the Dining Room (dinner is served from 5:30 to 10pm). The menu offers a fairly standard selection of the popular beef, seafood, and fowl dishes, but the daily specials (available at both lunch and dinner) are always interesting, and often the best values. Sandwiches at lunch are priced at $4.50 to $6. At dinner, main courses with side dishes cost $15 to $21; the daily specials are usually nearer the lower end of that range.

Nearby

PICK POINT LODGE, Windleblo Rd. (P.O. Box 220D), Mirror Lake, NH 03853. Tel. 603/569-1338. Fax 603/569-5752. 10 cottages (all with bath). TV TEL **Directions:** 4½ miles north of Wolfeboro off Rte. 109.
$ Rates (including light breakfast): Cottages, mid-July to Labor Day, $1,200–$2,400 per week. May–June and Sept–Oct, $700–$1,200 per week. Main lodge, $125 double. No credit cards. **Parking:** Free, on premises.
The Pick Point Lodge is truly unique. It was formerly a wealthy family's summer estate, and has been converted to accommodate a small number of guests in 10 large cottages (up to four bedrooms) and in two rooms in the main lodge. It's possible to fill pages with the good points of the Pick Point Lodge, but a quick sketch will give you the idea: Cottages are all very comfy and tastefully done, with fireplaces, porches, full kitchens, and, in the larger ones, two bathrooms. Much has been done to improve the facilities, including adding brass beds to all cottages, installing cable reception for TV, enlarging decks, and renovating most baths. The estates is on a 112-acre tract of forest, with several nature trails plotted for guests' use. Guests can also enjoy a ½ mile of lake frontage, indoor and outdoor tennis courts, a private beach and jetty, indoor and outdoor games, and special cookouts, cocktail parties, and such, which are "on the house" and which you can join or ignore as you wish. The hosts, the Newcomb family, are very gracious and solicitous of their guests' well-being and privacy, and they couldn't be nicer. Rates for such quality are not low, but they're reasonable for what you get. From late June to Labor Day rentals are by the week only, unless a cancellation or the like leaves a cottage or room open for several days. This could easily be the finest place on Winnipesaukee.

6. NORTH CONWAY

73 miles (118km) NE of Concord, 49 miles (79km) NE of Laconia, 39 miles (63km) E of Lincoln

GETTING THERE   By Bus   See the beginning of this chapter.

By Car North Conway is on U.S. 302 (N.H. 16A). The most beautiful way to approach is via I-93 to Lincoln, then the scenic Kancamagus Highway east. Coming from Lake Winnipesaukee, Routes 25 to 113 to 16; the more scenic approach is up the eastern shore of the lake from Alton on 28 to 109 to 25, then to 113 and 16.

ESSENTIALS The area along Route 16 between North Conway and Gorham, including the town of Bartlett on U.S. 302, is organized for tourist reasons as the **Mount Washington Valley.** The towns of North Conway and Jackson are centers for summer hiking, camping, and biking trips, and for winter skiing at the ski areas of Attitash, Mount Cranmore, Black Mountain, and Wildcat Mountain. The **Mount Washington Valley Visitors Center** (tel. 603/356-3171) has its main information office on Main Street in the center of North Conway, open during business hours and on weekends. The guides will be glad to help you with room reservations if you've had trouble finding a place to stay, and are in general very helpful. You can also write to the **Mount Washington Valley Chamber of Commerce,** P.O. Box 2300, North Conway, NH 03860 (tel. 603/356-3171, or toll free 800/367-3364), for a free 36-page booklet on any or all of these areas. You can also book reservations on the toll-free number. Office hours in the Main Street Dartmouth Bank Building are Monday to Friday 8:30am to 5pm and Saturday and Sunday 10am to 4pm.

In addition, **North Country Tours,** P.O. Box 747, North Conway, NH 03860 (tel. 603/356-3212, or toll free 800/334-7378; fax 603/356-3215), will help you to make reservations at condos, inns, resorts, and motels throughout the White Mountain area, at no charge for the service.

The **area code** is 603.

On the edge of the White Mountain National Forest and at the end of Mount Washington Valley, North Conway is the sports capital of the White Mountains. It's not a particularly large town, although the mile or two of motels and eateries along Route 16 south of town do seem to extend the boundaries. But basically one can walk to almost anything except this southern extension by parking downtown somewhere near the antique railroad station.

North Conway has taken well to its role of mountain town, and the people talk hearty and look healthy. Some of the businesses are old-time mom-and-pop affairs but a lot of shops have been citified to cater to the hiking and ski trades. But still the town has not been "taken over" by city people. Perhaps the character and charm of North Conway is best exhibited by the town library building on Main Street not far from the railroad station: Although small, it's built of massive granite blocks and has a slate roof which will last forever; it's open on weekday afternoons and Wednesday mornings.

WHAT TO SEE & DO

SHOPPING

North Conway has become synonymous with shopping and outlet stores. A spectrum of stores has opened, beckoning as many bargain hunters here as skiers. On hand you'll find such trendy names as **Ralph Lauren, Anne Klein, Banana Republic, Dansk,** and, of course **L. L. Bean.** Bean's has a good-sized factory store here that is immensely popular. There's also a shopping center adjacent to the Sheraton hotel with two dozen stores and a handful of eateries. This is the next best thing to going to Freeport or Kittery, Maine, for outlet shopping.

SKIING

The Mount Washington Valley includes five **alpine** ski areas: Attitash, Black, Cranmore, King Pine, and Wildcat. Altogether there are 94 downhill trails and 2 lifts, and the slopes range from those for the beginner to those that present a challenge even to some experienced skiers. Many of the inns recommended below under "Where to Stay" offer special ski packages that include lift fees for all five areas.

Besides the five developed ski areas in the valley, it is possible to ski in the cirque at **Tuckerman's Ravine,** where the shadows protect the snow long past the time when the cover on other slopes has begun to melt. The special excitement at Tuckerman, besides the challenge of the au naturel slopes, comes from climbing the mountain you're going to ski down, for there are no lifts. Follow the line of black dots up the mountain to the top. This is old-time skiing, with only a run or two a day, and only those with real stamina and strong legs should and will accept the challenge. But going back to the basics is exhilarating, everyone you meet here is your friend, and the fling down the mountain after the climb is a fitting way to end the season. Park in the Wildcat lot, recuperate in the cafeteria or lounge.

Every alpine ski area in the valley has some **cross-country trails,** some of which are very easy, some of which are only for experts. The center of the ski-touring activity in the valley is Jackson, where the **Jackson Ski Touring Foundation,** P.O. Box 216, Jackson, NH 03846 (tel. 603/383-9355), maintains and grooms over 157km (98 miles) of cross-country trails. The foundation is a nonprofit village organization dedicated to encouraging ski touring in and around Jackson, and it has a small office in the center of the village. Check here for passes, information, maps. There is a nominal fee for the use of the trails; a season membership is available. Clinics, tours, and rentals can all be found both in Jackson and in North Conway at the several ski shops.

OTHER WINTER SPORTS

Because of the state parks, national forest, and private reserves in the valley, lots of other winter sports are popular here. **Winter camping** is possible, using a tent or the Appalachian Mountain Club huts (see "Where to Stay," below), a few of which are open all winter. Note that many areas in the White Mountains have extremely severe weather—blizzards with temperatures of 14°F and winds gusting to 100 m.p.h. on top of Mount Washington are possible in *August.* This does not mean you will hit impossible weather, but it does mean you should check with rangers and AMC personnel, and have good equipment and a knowledge of winter camping before you go in.

Snowmobiling is also pretty big in the valley, and places in North Conway will rent you a machine by the hour or the day. Ice-skating rinks are maintained by the towns of North Conway, Conway, and Jackson. Various ponds and lakes are not bad for ice fishing—the locals will be glad to give visitors tips on the most-visited ice-fishing spots.

Tennis courts are available all year at the indoor courts of the Mount Cranmore Recreation Center (tel. 356-6301). Guest memberships are open to the public on a daily basis.

SUMMER ACTIVITIES

Besides **hiking and camping** in the state parks and national forests, Mount Washington Valley offers many other activities.

Right in North Conway Village center is the romantic old station of the **Conway Scenic Railroad** (tel. 356-5251), built in 1874 and restored to its present condition in 1974. For $7 (adults) or $4.50 (kids 4 to 12), you can buy a ticket for the scenic ride through the mountain country; choose your seat from among those in the enclosed cars or the open-air "cinder collectors." A steam locomotive and a 42-year-old and a 43-year-old diesel engine are on hand to provide the power, and if you go a little early you can visit the roundhouse to see where the locomotives are turned around. Trains run daily from mid-June through late October and on weekends only from mid-April to mid-June and late October through December. Departure times are 10am, noon, and 2 and 4pm. The trip takes about an hour. The "Sunset Special" at 6:30pm runs Tuesday, Wednesday, Thursday, and Saturday in July and August. On Friday,

Saturday, and Sunday of Thanksgiving weekend and on the first three weekends of December (with Santa aboard), the train makes special trips at 11am and 1:30pm.

The **Mount Washington Valley Theater Company,** North Conway, NH 03860 (tel. 356-5776), currently performs at the playhouse on Main Street in the Eastern Slope Inn complex. The season, from late June through Labor Day, features four lively musicals. Of course, it's most fun to see the entire series, watching the various members of the company take on different roles every other week, but even if you can't afford to stay in North Conway the entire season, you'll enjoy seeing a play here. The box office opens daily at noon, and curtain time is 8pm sharp. Tickets run $10 to $15. Group rates are available.

A considerable part of northern New Hampshire is included in the **White Mountain National Forest,** which is not to be confused with a national park. The forest does have a number of developed sites, however. Camping areas ($6 per night, cold running water, and pit toilets only) are dotted here and there, as are very pretty picnic areas. A maze of trails, some very easy and not so easy, covers a lot of the forest's vast expanse. Signs by the roadside mark the trail's beginning, but don't wander in just for a 30-minute walk if you're not familiar with the area. Instead, buy detailed maps of the trails and a trail guide from the **Appalachian Mountain Club**, 5 Joy Street, Boston, MA 02108 (tel. 617/523-0636), or from the club's Pinkham Notch Camp (tel. 603/466-2721) on Route 16 north of Jackson. The *AMC White Mountain Guide* ($15.95) will tell you all about the trail: how difficult it is, how long it is, the vertical rise, the average walking time, reference points along the way, and what to see as you walk.

Another option is to **rent a canoe** for the day or the week from **Saco Bound Inc.,** 2 miles east of Center Conway on Route 302 (tel. 447-2177). The Saco River has lots of smooth and easy areas. Overnight trips and canoe pickup service are available as well as daily canoe rental at a daily rate of $25 and pick up charge of $9.50 a canoe. The season runs April through October.

Heritage New Hampshire, on Route 16 in Glen (tel. 383-9776), has a variety of lifelike scenes and dioramas with talking figures which outline New Hampshire's history, from the docks of an English port town through the Industrial Revolution at the Amoskeag Mills in Manchester. You can walk at your own pace through the maze of displays, and costumed guides will answer any questions you may have about New Hampshire's history. The history lesson on New Hampshire passes through three centuries. And there is also a 120-foot historic mural which is New England's largest. Don't pass on the vintage trolley ride. The price is $7.50 adults, $4.50 for children 4 to 12; it's open daily from 9am to 6pm in July and August, and until 5pm in June, September, and October.

Right next to Heritage New Hampshire is **Story Land** (tel. 383-4293), a children's amusement park with rides, clowns, animals, and lots of other treats. Once you've paid the $13 admission fee, all the rides are free; children under 4 are admitted without charge. Open daily from mid-June through early September, and then weekends only until mid-October.

The **Grand Manor,** 3 miles north of North Conway on Route 16 in Glen (tel. 356-9366), is an antique and classic automobile museum with such treasures as a '51 T-bird, '57 Chevrolet Bel Air, '30 V-16 Cadillac roadster, and '34 Packard Victoria convertible. Cars range in vintage from 1910 to 1969. Hours are 9:30am to 5pm daily in the summer and on the weekends in spring and fall. Admission is $5 for adults, $ for children.

The **ski areas** at Attitash and Wildcat Mountain don't fully close down in summer. They've developed full warm-weather recreation programs to keep the visitors coming and the bills paid.

At **Attitash** (tel. 603/374-2368), the lifts keep working to take you up to the top of the Alpine Slide, a long track which you schuss down on a little cart—an exhilarating ride, and safe for all ages. You can buy a 4-hour ticket for $15 or single-ride tickets for $5.50 per adult, $4.50 per child.

At **Wildcat Mountain** the cafeteria stays open for those wanting a snack before boarding the gondolas for the 25-minute round-trip ride up the mountainside (you operation late June to early September from 10am to 6pm daily; from September 12 to October 11, it's open on weekends from 10am to 5pm). The area around Wildcat Mountain and its base camp are kept immaculate because they're within the national forest and subject to its regulation.

TWO SCENIC DRIVES

A private business, the **Mount Washington Auto Road Company,** Gorham, NH 03581 (tel. 603/466-2222 or 466-3988), operates an alpine toll road to the top of the highest peak in the Northeast, 6,288-foot Mount Washington. Start from Route 16 in Pinkham Notch. You can drive your own car (no trucks or campers) to the top of the mountain at $12 for car and driver and $5 for each passenger (kids 5 to 12, $3); vans operated by the company will take you to the top and back down again (1½ hours) for $17 per person (kids, $10) if you'd rather not drive. Hours are 7:30am to 6pm for the road, 8:30am to 5pm for the guided van tour. The season is normally from mid-May to mid-October, but remember that Mount Washington's summit has the most severe weather in the Northeast, and it's altogether possible for the road to be temporarily closed because of snow even in June or September. This, by the way, is only one of three ways to reach the Mount Washington summit, the others being on foot following the Appalachian Mountain Club trails, or by cog railway, described below.

Route 112 between Conway and Lincoln is known as the **Kancamagus Highway.** Its 33-mile length exhibits some of the finest scenery in the White Mountains, including the view from the 2,860-foot Kancamagus Pass. Almost the entire length of the road is within the boundaries of the national forest, and is therefore protected from any development more civilized than a campground (there are six along the road) or a picnic area. The drive is a must: This is White Mountains beauty in its purest form.

WHERE TO STAY

North Conway has dozens of places to stay, including a good number of motels along the southern extension of Main Street (Route 16), but I'll concentrate mainly on the small inns in the town, and on those in the neighboring towns of Jackson and Glen, most of which have excellent dining rooms. Many of the lodging establishments listed here have midweek and ski packages; be sure to inquire if you are planning an extended or active stay.

IN NORTH CONWAY

Inns & Guesthouses

THE CENTER CHIMNEY, River Rd. (P.O. Box 1220), North Conway, NH 03860. Tel. 603/356-6788. 4 rms (all with shared bath). **Directions:** Turn down River Rd. at the Texaco Station in North Conway Village.

$ Rates (including muffins and coffee): $35 single; $44–55 double. Extra bed $10. Midweek stay of 3 days, $15 off. No credit cards. **Parking:** Free, on premises.

The Center Chimney is just that: a big center-chimney Federal house built in 1787, now accepting guests. Look for the house north of town, just off Main Street, near the Saco River. There's a fireplace in the living room and cable TV and phone for guests' use. Cathedral Ledge, a popular rock-climbing spot, is just down the road.

CRANMORE INN, Kearsarge St. (P.O. Box 1349), North Conway, NH 03860. Tel. 603/356-5502, or toll free 800/822-5502. 23 rms (16 with bath). **Directions:** From Main St., turn onto Kearsarge St., and follow it 1 block to the inn.

$ Rates (including breakfast): $25–$52 single without bath, $37–$64 single with bath; $56 double without bath, $35–$67 double with bath. Add $10 per room in foliage season. AE, MC, V. **Parking:** Free. **Closed:** Christmas.

Perhaps the best for price, convenience, and pleasantness is the Cranmore Inn, just off Main Street on the street leading to the Mount Cranmore ski area, and only a few blocks from the intercity bus stop. The inn is over a century old, with guest rooms in Victorian style. Several two-bedroom suites (the two bedrooms share one bath) are available for families and friends traveling together. Meal service is family-style. There are bonuses: a huge parlor with fireplace, a games room, and a TV room; nice big lawns suitable for games and Frisbee (in summer), and a swimming pool. From the inn you can walk to the slopes of Mount Cranmore in 10 minutes, and to the center of town in 5 or less. A 5-minute walk will bring you to the Tennis and Health Club, with full privileges. Note that in winter the rate structure is a bit different: Breakfast and dinner are included in the price of the room, and rates vary depending on whether you come during the week or on the weekend.

SUNNY SIDE INN, Seavey St., North Conway, NH 03860. Tel. 603/ 356-6239. 10 rms (2 with bath). **Directions:** Turn on to Kearsarge St. at the traffic light, go right again at the top of the hill, and it's on the left.

$ **Rates** (including breakfast): $25–$50 single; $45–$65 double. MC, V. **Parking:** Free, on premises.

On a quiet back street stands the Sunny Side Inn, an affordable and cozy bed-and-breakfast place. Rooms have shared or private bath. There's a living room with fireplace and television, and also a reading nook you can use.

WILDFLOWERS, Rte. 16 (P.O. Box 802), Intervale, NH 03845. Tel. 603/356-2224. 6 rms (2 with bath). **Directions:** Go 1½ miles north of the center of North Conway on Rte. 16. You'll see the sign on the left as you head north.

$ **Rates** (including continental breakfast): $43 single; $54–$99 double. MC, V. **Parking:** Free, on site. **Closed:** Nov–Apr.

Wildflowers is another charming guesthouse—homey, simple, convenient, and friendly. With the colorful array of flowers, it is aptly named. The guesthouse is a big white house with porch posts made from peeled and painted tree trunks. The decor inside is Victorian, from marble-topped bureaus to spindle beds.

Hotels & Motels

EASTERN SLOPE INN RESORT, Main St., North Conway, NH 03860. Tel. 603/356-6321, or toll free 800/258-4708 in New England (outside New Hampshire). Fax 603/356-6189. 133 rms (all with bath). A/C TV TEL

$ **Rates:** Winter and summer, $86–$200 single or double. Children stay free in parents' room. AE, DISC, MC, V. **Parking:** Free, on premises.

For decades the Eastern Slope Inn was North Conway's posh place to stay, a stately white-pillared hotel with a genteel ambience. Today, absent of any real poshness and not particularly a resort, it remains popular with families and others who don't require fussy accommodations. Swimming pool, clay tennis courts, a restaurant and pub, a summer theater next door, and a village-center location are among the inn's advantages. Choose from rooms in the inn or in the motel like Randall House nearby, suites or efficiency suites, many of which are now condos. Half of the rooms have minibars.

RED JACKET MOUNTAIN VIEW MOTOR INN, on a slope above South Main Street, North Conway, NH 03860. Tel. 603/356-5411, or toll free 800/752-2538. Fax 603/356-3842. 164 rms (all with bath). A/C MINIBAR TV TEL

$ **Rates:** June–Oct and Dec–Mar, $105–$173 double. Nov and Apr–May, $96–$140 double. Package rates available. AE, DC, MC, V. **Parking:** Free.

North Conway's snazziest hostelry, always in great demand, is the Red Jacket Mountain View Motor Inn. At the height of the season (summer or winter) rooms go quickly because of the inn's central location and luxury accoutrements: a beautiful indoor pool covered by a dramatic wood roof, and an outdoor pool as well; saunas; a heated whirlpool; a games room with table tennis and electronic games; shuffleboard courts; tennis courts; dining room and cocktail lounge. Many rooms have views and balconies, and some rooms offer lofts so that a family can sleep more comfortably. Ceramic tile baths, two double beds to a room, air conditioning and heat, and other luxury touches add to the draw, but it's the view and the convenience that convince many people to stay here. Package plans are always available. At dinner, main courses are in the $12 to $16 range. Lunch is served in the Birchmont Tavern in the summer.

IN INTERVALE

A mile or two north of North Conway along scenic Route 16 are several inns and motels also worth considering. Although you won't be able to walk easily to town from here, these establishments have their own restaurants, and you're only a short drive from most of the hiking and ski points.

Inns

THE FOREST, A COUNTRY INN, Rte. 16A (P.O. Box 37), Intervale, NH 03845. Tel. 603/356-9772, or toll free 800/448-3534. 13 rms (10 with bath). **Directions:** Follow Rte. 16 north through North Conway. In Intervale, take Rte. 16A to inn.
$ Rates (including breakfast): $50–$102 double. Extra person $25. AE, MC, V. **Parking:** Free, on premises.
This large Victorian house, converted to take guests, has 11 rooms in the inn itself; there are also two rooms in a nearby cottage. You'll get a nice living room (with fireplace) in which to meet new friends, a heated pool in summer, and cross-country skiing in winter on groomed trails, as well as summer hiking trails.

OLD FIELD HOUSE, Rte. 16A, Intervale, NH 03845. Tel. 603/356-5478, or toll free 800/444-9245. 17 rms (all with bath). A/C TV TEL **Directions:** From North Conway on Rte. 16, bear right on Rte. 16A.
$ Rates (including continental breakfast): $74–$104 double. Stays of 3–6 nights are discounted 10%. AE, MC, V. **Parking:** Free, on premises.
The Old Field House is in a field, yes, but it is not old. It's hard to tell at first whether this hostelry is an old building redone from top to bottom or a new building made to look good and last long. Despite its sturdy granite facade and gambrel-roofed wings meant to conjure up the romantic New Hampshire past, it is quite modern. Rooms are all clean and shiny, with beamed ceilings and colonial-style furniture; beds in the rooms range from one or two doubles, a queen-size, or a tremendous king-size. Fourteen rooms have refrigerators. There's also an efficiency apartment that overlooks the pool. You get lots of extras at the Old Field House, such as a heated outdoor pool, tennis, laundry facilities, background music, a games room, and shuffleboard. A sauna and whirlpool are planned.

JACKSON

About 7 miles above North Conway on Route 16 is Jackson, right at the geographical center of the Mount Washington Valley, and the central point for cross-country skiing in the region. Besides being right in the middle of the downhill ski areas, Jackson has its own ski-touring organization (see above). It also has a collection of delightful inns open winter and summer. The **Jackson Resort Association,** P.O. Box 304, Jackson, NH 03846, will send you information, or you can contact the **Jackson Resort Association Information and Reservation Center** at 603/383-9356, or toll free 800/866-3334 daily noon to 6 pm.

Inns

CHRISTMAS FARM INN, Rte. 16B (P.O. Box CC), Jackson, NH 03846.

Tel. 603/383-4313. 35 rms (all with bath). **Directions:** Follow the road from the village toward the Black Mountain Ski Area.

$ Rates (including breakfast, dinner, and service): $136–$180 double. Children under 12 stay in parents' room for $25. AE, MC, V. **Parking:** Free.

Just outside the center of Jackson Village proper, on the road up the hill to the Black Mountain Ski Area, is the Christmas Farm Inn. Here the proprietors hold that "hospitality makes the difference," but one must admit that the resort-style facilities help: The inn has its own pool and putting green (there are two professional golf courses near Jackson), a games room, sauna, lounge, living room, shuffleboard, and a dining room done in Early American. The Christmas Inn has five separate places of accommodation, from the original inn (built in 1786) to a maple-sugaring house converted into two modern rooms, with whirlpool, good for family accommodations. Five 2-bedroom cottages with fireplaces are also on hand for two couples or families, with prices based on four adults sharing each unit. The barn has four family suites, and there's even a log cabin.

INN AT THORN HILL, Thorn Hill Rd., Jackson, NH 03846. Tel. 603/383-4242, or toll free 800/289-8990. 20 rms (18 with bath). A/C **Directions:** From Jackson Village, take Rte. 16A through covered bridge to Thorn Hill Rd., turn right and up hill to inn.

$ Rates (including breakfast and dinner): $110–$200 double. AE, MC, V. **Parking:** Free, across the street. **Closed:** Apr.

The Inn at Thorn Hill is probably our favorite place in New Hampshire. The hospitality is genuine, the surroundings gracious, and the mood romantic and appealing. Designed by Stanford White, this 1895 yellow clapboard inn is just the ticket for unwinding or rewinding after a day on the slopes or bargain-hunting in North Conway's factory outlets. The living rooms are worldly and designed with detail. The bar is just big enough for a few close friends, yet small enough to feel as though it's open just for you. The dining room is a treat: dinner may be romantic by candlelight and breakfast sumptuous as you look out at the glistening snow (usually not in summer!). Charming country rooms are in several buildings and cottages, including the roomy main inn. There's air conditioning in most rooms. Come here to eat even if you can't stay here. The whole inn is no-smoking.

VILLAGE HOUSE, Rte. 16A, Jackson, NH 03846. Tel. 603/383-6666. 10 rms (8 with bath). **Directions:** From Rte. 16 north, take Rte. 16A into Jackson.

$ Rates (including continental breakfast): $40–$100 standard double with or without bath. DISC, MC, V. **Parking:** Free, on premises.

In the center of Jackson, very near the covered bridge leading into the town from Route 16, is the Village House. The rooms here have an antique flavor. There's cable TV in the living room. Rates include use of the swimming pool, clay tennis court, outdoor spa, and also a "deluxe" continental breakfast for each person.

Old-Fashioned Resorts

EAGLE MOUNTAIN RESORT, Carter Notch Rd., Jackson, NH 03846. Tel. 603/383-9111, or toll free 800/777-1700. Fax 603/383-0854. 94 rms (all with bath). TV TEL **Directions:** Drive out of Jackson village a mile or so, past a series of cascading waterfalls to find the Eagle Mountain Resort.

$ Rates: $65–$155 double. AE, DC, DISC, ER, MC, V. **Parking:** Free, on premises.

This is one of the remaining premier grand old resorts in New England. Originally built in 1879 and completely rebuilt in 1986, the five-story white clapboard hotel commands a magnificent view of the surrounding mountains. Facilities include a heated outdoor pool, tennis courts, health club, a nine-hole golf course, playground and well-marked walking trails. The lobby is filled with rich leather sofas and the guest rooms and suites with specially made furniture. For an extra $30 per person per day you can have breakfast and dinner daily. (Sunday brunch is particularly nice.) You'll enjoy staying here.

WENTWORTH RESORT HOTELS, Jackson, NH 03846. Tel. 603/383-9700, or toll free 800/637-0013. Fax 603/383-4265. 62 rms (all with bath). TV TEL **Directions:** From Rte. 16 north, take Rte. 16A into the center of Jackson.
$ Rates: $49–$119 double; $150–$240 condominium. AE, MC, V. **Parking:** Free, on premises.

The Wentworth is a turn-of-the-century hotel, complete with rambling frame main building, lounge, elegant dining rooms, various cottages and overnight rooms, an 18-hole PGA golf course, a pool, and clay tennis courts. It's been redone from top to bottom and all is shiny and bright. The hotel is definitely of a graceful, older time. Condominium units (rentable by the day, week, or month) have been added in clusters.

A Motel

The village of Jackson is known for its country inns, and staying in one of these excellent places is a real treat. But—as you'll see—it is not inexpensive, especially when you add the 8% state room tax and the 15% "service charge," which are often found only in the fine print. For more reasonable prices in Jackson, try the motel listed below.

COVERED BRIDGE MOTOR LODGE, Rte. 16 (P.O. Box V), Jackson, NH 03846. Tel. 603/383-6630, or toll free 800/634-2911. 32 rms (all with bath). A/C TV TEL **Directions:** On Rte. 16 on the far side of the red covered bridge from the village.
$ Rates: $44–$78 double. AE, MC, V. **Parking:** Free, on premises.

S For reasonable prices in this high-priced village, try this attractive hostelry right near the red covered bridge. It has a tennis court and outdoor pool. The modern units here are designed not to clash with Jackson's forest mood, and prices are reasonable. Three efficiency apartments rent by the week, but another rents for $103 double per night with a 2-night minimum.

Mountain Hikers' Huts

The **Appalachian Mountain Club,** the organization that has done so much to preserve and maintain wilderness trails in New England, operates several lodging facilities in the White Mountain National Forest. At the **AMC's Pinkham Notch Camp** in Gorham, NH 03581 (tel. 603/466-2721), 11 miles north of Jackson on Route 16, people of all ages, whether AMC members or not, can find inexpensive bunkroom-type accommodations (106 bunks in all) and simple but hearty meals. A bunk and breakfast costs $34 per adult; bed and supper is $39; bed, breakfast, and supper is $42.25. Children 12 and under receive a discount for the beds and meals, and as a convenience the kitchen will make up trail lunches for $5 per person. Discounts are also available for AMC members. Note that you must have reservations, and they must be secured by a nonrefundable per-person per-night deposit. If you'd like a room alone, you will have to pay $20 extra for each unused bunk in the room, if others are turned away as a result. All these rules seem quite sensible. Note that the 8% **tax is already included** in these prices. MasterCard and VISA are accepted.

Besides the Pinkham Notch Camp, the AMC maintains a laudable system of **mountain huts** along its hiking trails in the mountains. Similar accommodations and meals are provided at similar prices, and with similar reservation arrangements. The huts are attended and trail meals prepared by "hutmen" and "hutwomen," a hearty breed of New England youth who pride themselves on being able to pack on their backs all the supplies needed in the huts—to a weight which would make a normal person stagger—and almost run up the mountains with the load several times a week Guided hikes are featured throughout the summer. Write for details.

7. CRAWFORD NOTCH & BRETTON WOODS

About 20 miles (32 km) NE of North Conway

GETTING THERE By Bus See the beginning of this chapter.

By Car Crawford Notch & Bretton Woods are on U.S. 302.

ESSENTIALS The **area code** is 603. If you have questions, contact the **Moun** **Washington Valley Visitors Center,** Dartmouth Bank Building, Main Street, ir North Conway (tel. 603/356-3171). Or contact the **Mount Washington Chambe** **of Commerce,** P.O. Box 2300, North Conway, NH 03860 (tel. toll free 800/367 3364); they'll send you a free 36-page booklet on the area.

North and east on U.S. 302 from Glen will take you through Crawford Notch to th **Crawford Notch State Park.** The park is a fine place for hiking and fishing and you can see two impressive waterfalls—the Flume and the Silver Cascades—fron the highway. Facilities include a 24-site campground, a picnic area, an informatio booth, and a shop featuring the products of New Hampshire artisans. The ruins o the **Willey House** hold a mystery and a story from the 1820s, when the road wa being cut and the Willey family set up house in Crawford Notch to provide for th teams that would pass through the valley. In August 1826 one of the worst storms eve to hit the White Mountains wreaked havoc in the valley, with floods, landslides, wind and rain which left the Willey House unharmed, but resulted in the death of ever member of the household.

Certainly the quaintest way to get to the top of Mount Washington is by th **Mount Washington Cog Railway** (tel. 603/846-5404, or toll free 800/922-8825) It's a 3½-mile track along a steep trestle up the mountainside. The locomotiv (powered by steam) drives a cog wheel on its undercarriage which engages with pin between the rails to pull the locomotive and train up the slope. In operation sinc 1866, the 3-hour round-trip scenic excursion is a lot of fun. At the portion of the ru known as Jacob's Ladder, the grade is a surprising 37%, but the little engine pull along trustworthily despite the steepness. At the top, the average summer temperatur is 40°F, and there may be a stiff wind. Stroll to the new visitors center for a snack drink, or souvenir, and then tour the mountaintop: See the displays highlighting th worst of Mount Washington's weather. If you pick a clear day to ascend th 6,288-foot summit, it will seem as though you can see all the way to Europe!

The base station, where you board the train, is 6 miles off U.S. 302 east of Twi Mountain, N.H. The season is Memorial Day weekend through Columbus Da (Canadian Thanksgiving), with weekends-only runs until June 10, then daily startin at 8am, and continuing hourly, with the last train leaving at 4pm. Have reservation: or try to take an early train—perhaps the 8am—to avoid having to wait in line. Fare (round-trip) are $32 for adults, $22 for children ages 6 to 12, and free for childre under 6 who sit on a parent's lap. Remember to wear a sweater or jacket, or both, fc the cool weather at the top, no matter how warm it is at the bottom.

WHERE TO STAY

MOUNT WASHINGTON HOTEL & RESORT, U.S. 302, Bretton Woods **NH 03575. Tel. 603/278-1000,** or toll free 800/258-0330. 170 rms (a with bath). **Directions:** From North Conway, follow U.S. 302 north 28 miles to Bretton Woods.

$ **Rates** (including breakfast and dinner): Mount Washington Hotel $170–$290 double; Bretton Arms $80–$155 double; Bretton Woods Motor Inn $60–$95 double without meals. AE, DC, DISC, MC, V. **Parking:** Free, on premises.

⭐ Here you'll find a downhill and cross-country ski area, several condominium developments, and three lodging establishments, the new and modern **Bretton Woods Motor Inn,** the innlike **Bretton Arms,** and the venerable rambling palace known as the **Mount Washington Hotel.** The mammoth hotel was the site of the famous Bretton Woods conference of 1944, which established the world monetary system for the postwar period. Great old hotels of this sort, with their private golf courses, riding stables, clay tennis courts, indoor and outdoor pools, live nightly entertainment, playhouses, and the like, are almost as rare as dinosaurs, so it is heartening to see that this one is still thriving. Its gracious service and accommodations are open to both the tourist and the conventioneer. The lobby is immense, with a baronial fireplace and lots of color and activity; nearby is a semicircular conservatory with a dome and many small stained-glass windows. The views of the mountains and the grounds are very fine. Rates include two meals (and tax and service). There are small fees for use of the golf course, horses from the stable, bicycles, and nursery and baby-sitting services.

If you prefer a smaller place, Bretton Arms, a restored house on the property, has 34 rooms, with no meals included in the rates. Guests are granted access to the facilities at the Mount Washington Hotel.

The Lodge at Bretton Woods out on the highway (U.S. 302) is associated with the hotel, and although the hotel operates only from late May to mid-October, the lodge stays open both winter and summer. Here the prices are for lodging only, but all privileges open to guests at the hotel are extended to guests at the lodge. Children stay free in their parents' room.

NOTCHLAND INN, Harts Location S.R., Bartlett, NH 03812. Tel. 603/ 374-6131, or toll free 800/866-6131. 11 rms (all with bath). **Directions:** From North Conway, follow U.S. 302 north 19 miles to Harts Location.

$ **Rates:** With breakfast $81–$108 double; with breakfast and dinner $126–$180 double. AE, MC, V. **Parking:** Free, on premises.

At Crawford Notch, one of the most spectacular sites on the East Coast, stands the Notchland Inn. Also quite magnificent in its own right, the granite mansion set on 400 acres has rooms with working fireplaces and antiques. Take the higher-priced room with the dinner option—the multicourse repast is served by candlelight. The hot tub sits in a gazebo by the pond. The owners, by the way, keep rare and endangered species in their sanctuary; don't be surprised to see a llama or exotic sheep grazing in the front corral. Activities include wagon- and sleigh rides, cross-country skiing, hiking, canoeing, and cycling from the inn.

---

8. WATERVILLE VALLEY

10 miles (16km) NE of I-93 at Campton Upper Village

GETTING THERE   By Car   Take I-93 to Campton Upper Village, then follow Route 49, 10 miles to Waterville Valley.

ESSENTIALS   The **area code** is 603. The **Waterville Valley Lodging Bureau** provides free reservations service; call toll free 800/468-2553, or 603/236-8371 locally. Or write to Waterville Valley Lodging Bureau, Waterville Valley, NH 03215, for information.

In 1829 a small settlement in a remote New Hampshire valley was incorporated as a town. A few farms, perhaps a small store, and a tiny public library—that was all there was to Waterville Valley. Today the little settlement is still there, in a beautiful spot deep within the White Mountains National Forest. A tasteful, tactful developer owns the valley and has dictated the shape of the new resort community. The results so far are very encouraging, almost a marvel: hotels and condominium developments under different ownership, all of striking and interesting design, furnished in good taste and staffed with competent, concerned personnel. Two ski areas are handy, a golf course and lots of tennis courts await players, and hiking, bicycling, fishing, and snowshoeing are right at a visitor's doorstep. This is a very fine resort.

WHAT TO SEE & DO

IN SUMMER

It seems as if they've thought of everything here. First and foremost, the valley is deep within the national forest, so hiking and fishing are easy to find. For tennis, there are 18 clay courts and lessons by a professional staff. The golf course in the valley is nine holes, and not too far away at White Mountains Country Club is an 18-hole course. Guests at the Valley Inn can use its paddle-tennis courts for free; the general public can use the course, day and night, for a fee. Bikes can be rented from the Golf and Tennis Club. And then, of course, there's shopping in the town square or a ride to the top of Mt. Tecumseh on the "High Country Express," the fastest gondola in the east.

IN WINTER

Although snowshoeing, hiking, skating, and general taking of country-mountain air are all possible and enjoyable in Waterville Valley, most people come to ski the trails and slopes of Mt. Tecumseh and Snow's Mountain. **Mt. Tecumseh** is the larger and more elaborate of the two, with two triple-chair lifts, five double-chair lifts, a T-bar, a J-bar, and a platter-pull lift. The vertical drop is more than 2,000 feet, and there are 3! trails and slopes. Rentals and lessons are easily available, as is a quick meal at the base cafeteria. A schuss bus takes guests from Waterville Valley hotels to Tecumseh and back. The other area, **Snow's Mountain,** is right in the valley near the hotels of the village, and has three intermediate and beginners' slopes. It's for first-timers and learners, with one double-chair lift and a vertical drop of less than 600 feet. To keep the crowds down, Mt. Tecumseh and Snow's Mountain operate on a limited-ticket basis (no more than a 15-minute wait for the lift on average). For information about snow at both areas, call 603/236-4144.

Ski packages for 2, 3, 5, or 7 nights are offered, and all facilities in the valley participate. Depending on what you want, you can get a package that includes lodging, meals, lifts, lessons, even rental equipment. Prices depend on which hotel you choose, and what options you need to do the sort of skiing you're after. Options are also offered for ski touring (trail fees, lessons, equipment, and lodging) in the packages.

WHERE TO STAY

GOLDEN EAGLE LODGE, Snowsbrook Rd., Waterville Valley, NH 03215
Tel. 603/236-4551, or toll free 800/468-2553. Fax 603/236-4174. 139 rms (all with bath). TV TEL
$ Rates: $82–$289 double. Extra person $25. Children 12 and under stay free in parents' room. AE, DC, DISC, MC, V. **Parking:** Free.
Fashioned in the style of 19th-century grand New England resorts, the Golden Eagle rises proudly to the occasion. It was designed by Graham Gund Architects, one of the most distinguished firms in the United States. The crescent-shaped six-story building

with green shutters and turrets is a mass of oversized windows, more than half of which look out on to Corcoran Pond, the namesake of the man who so carefully developed much of this valley. The 139 condominium suites vary in size from 650 to 1,050 square feet, sleeping two to eight people, and are fully furnished with understated accoutrements. Rates include use of the pool, sports center, and many other facilities in the valley.

VALLEY INN, Tecumseh Rd., Waterville Valley, NH 03215. Tel. 603/ 236-8336, or toll free 800/343-0969. Fax 603/236-4294. 51 rms (all with bath). A/C TV TEL

$ Rates: Summer/foliage season, $48–$232 double. Late spring/late fall, $48– $213 double. Children 12 and under stay free in parents' room. DISC, MC, V.
   Parking: Free, on site.

The attractive design of the Valley Inn adds to the area scenery and provides some unexpected bonuses to guests. Many rooms overlook the valley and mountains; others, the forest and settlement. All of the guest rooms have king-size bed, whirlpool bath, and pull-out sofa bed; most rooms have air conditioning. The inn's heated indoor/outdoor swimming pool is open all year: Part is enclosed by the building, but a huge window comes down just to water level, and you can swim underneath it to the outdoor portion of the pool, winter or summer. The Valley Inn has other athletic goodies: two platform (or paddle) tennis courts, an exercise room, saunas, Jacuzzi, and games room. The inn's dining room has a treetop-level view, and the lounge has live entertainment on weekends and holidays.

LONG-TERM STAYS

Several of the condominium developments in the valley have long-term (by the month or the season) rental rates for those who want an apartment rather than a hotel room. Accommodations range from one-bedroom apartments for one or two people to three-bedroom apartments that can take eight to 10 people. Each apartment is completely furnished, including kitchen utensils and dinner service, all linens, and cable color TV. There are various package and weekly plans, both for normal and holiday periods, and low-season specials are available.

   For information, contact **Windsor Hill Condominiums,** Jennings Peak Road, Waterville Valley, NH 03215 (tel. 603/236-8321, or toll free 800/343-1286 in New York, New Jersey, and New England except New Hampshire). Their apartments also rent by the day (2-day minimum) for $220 to $530 for a weekend, or $295 to $585 for a 5-night ski week. In summer you'll pay $294 to $630 per week. American Express and MasterCard are accepted.

   Another firm to contact is **Condominium Vacations,** P.O. Box 389, Waterville Valley, NH 03215 (tel. 603/236-4101, or toll free 800/468-2553). Their 40 privately owned condos have from one to four bedrooms, and may be rented by the night. Rates range from $75 for a one-bedroom condo sleeping up to four people on a midweek night in spring, to $226 per night for a four-bedroom condo sleeping eight to 10 people on a weekend night in high summer. Call for full information.

9. THE FRANCONIA NOTCH AREA

14 miles (23km) SE of Littleton, 11 miles (18km) N of Lincoln

GETTING THERE By Bus See the beginning of this chapter.

By Car Follow I-93 to U.S. 3 to Franconia Notch.

ESSENTIALS The **area code** is 603. The local **visitors center** is at the intersection of I-93 and the Kancamagus Highway (tel. 603/745-8720). It is run both by the White Mountains Association personnel and also by national forest rangers; hours of operation are Saturday to Thursday 8:30am to 5pm (to 6pm in July and August) and Friday 8:30am to 9pm.

Interstate 93 comes up from Manchester and Concord to pass through the White Mountains National Forest. The towns of North Woodstock and Lincoln form the center of the developed area within the forest, and it's here that most people come to look for a room, a meal, or any of the other services of civilization. At this point the Kancamagus Highway heads east through the most scenic 33-mile drive in the mountains; north of Lincoln and North Woodstock are several natural curiosities, including the famous **Old Man of the Mountain** at the narrow pass called Franconia Notch.

The area centered on North Woodstock and Lincoln is very rich in possibilities for outdoor activities, especially hiking, camping, picnicking, and skiing at Cannon Mountain and Mittersill in Franconia Notch itself, and at Loon Mountain near Lincoln on the Kancamagus Highway.

WHAT TO SEE & DO

SIGHTS

Franconia Notch State Park is surrounded by the **White Mountains National Forest.** The natural wonders of the park are impressive indeed, including the Notch (pass, or gap) itself, the Flume, the Basin, several lakes, and the rock outcrop in the shape of a man's profile which has all but become the state symbol of New Hampshire, the famous Old Man of the Mountain. The state park offers a wealth of outdoor activities: Lafayette Campground, the Appalachian Mountain Club's system of trails and huts, a 9-mile paved bike path, trout fishing, swimming in the mountain lakes, a number of beautiful picnic sites, and a ski area, Cannon Mountain with an aerial tramway which operates winter and summer.

THE OLD MAN The Old Man of the Mountain, also called the Great Stone Face, is one of New Hampshire's most famous features. After thousands of years in the making, it was "discovered" by white settlers at the beginning of the 19th century. The profile is formed by several ledges of granite, and in a cubist sort of way the representation is quite striking. But don't expect a mammoth image: The face is only about 40 feet high, and it's set on a cliff 1,000 feet above the valley floor. Its grandeur comes not from its size, but rather from its fidelity (it really does look like a human face in profile) and its impressive perch high in the sky, gazing out over the mountains. In recent years the state has spent a good deal of money preserving the face from the ravages of nature, for even granite formations crumble given enough wind, rain, and ice. From the highway parking lot, a path leads down to the shores of Profile Lake, and descriptive plaques tell you all about the Old Man.

South of the Old Man along U.S. 3 and to the east lies the undulant crest of Mt Liberty, which to some people resembles George Washington lying in state. Take a look, and feel free to concur or disagree!

THE BASIN & THE FLUME Also south of the Old Man along U.S. 3, signs will point to a side road and the Basin, a huge glacial pothole in the native granite, 20 feet in diameter. The hole is at the foot of a waterfall, and was presumably made by the action of small rocks and stones whirled around by the force of the water. It's a cool spot, good for contemplation.

Four miles north of North Woodstock, but still south of the Basin, is the Flume, a natural gorge or cleft in the granite. A boardwalk has been erected along the 800-foot length of the Flume, and for $6 ($3 for children) you can walk through its cool depths the granite walls rising to 60 or 70 feet above you, mosses and plants growing precariously in niches here and there. Signs explain how nature formed the Flume, and point out interesting sights along the way. Near the Flume is a covered bridge though to be one of the oldest in the state, perhaps erected as early as the 1820s. There is a seasonal information office (tel. 603/745-8391) here, which, like the Flume, is open from mid-April to mid-October.

CANNON MOUNTAIN AERIAL TRAMWAY An impressive view of Franconia Notch and the mountains is yours if you take the Cannon Mountain Aerial Tramway (tel. 823-5563) to the top of the line. The tramway operates in the summer from the end of May to October, 9am to 4:30pm, at a cost of $8 for adults, $4 for children 6 to 12, round-trip. The tramway station is just off I-93, Exit 2, and U.S. 3 north of the Old Man, and has its own parking lot. In the weathered-shingle building at the base and the summit station are cafeterias, should you be in need of a light meal, and the New England Ski Museum.

ROBERT FROST'S FARM Only a mile or two from the town of Franconia is the Frost Place, Ridge Road (tel. 823-5510), the farm that the great poet bought in the early part of this century. He lived here with his wife and children during some of the most productive and inspired years of his life, and wrote many of his best and most famous poems to describe life on this farm and the scenery surrounding it. Among these are "The Road Not Taken" and "Stopping by Woods on a Snowy Evening."

The price of admission includes a 20-minute video shown in the barn behind the house. The show explains much about Frost's early life and work, and about the countryside here. The farmhouse has been kept as faithful to the period as possible, and there are numerous interesting exhibits of Frost memorabilia, though much of the furniture is from other places. It is spare and simple, as was the rural life-style at the time. Behind the house in the forest is a ½-mile-long poetry-nature trail. Frost's poems are mounted on plaques in sites appropriate to the things they describe. In several places the plaques have been erected at the exact spots where Frost composed the poems. The various trees, shrubs, and flowers along the path are marked, though only some will be in bloom when you visit.

Admission to the site costs $3 for adults, half price for children 6 to 15, $2 for seniors. It's open on Saturday and Sunday from 1 to 5pm late May through June and early September through mid-October; in July and August, Wednesday to Monday from 1 to 5pm.

To get to the Frost Place, leave Franconia on Route 116 South, and after exactly a mile look for a sign on the right indicating Bickford Hill Road. Then turn left onto Ridge Road, a dirt road, and the Frost Place will be up a way on your right. You come to the parking lot before the house; obey the sign and park in the lot, and walk up the road to the house.

THE LOST RIVER As you travel through New Hampshire, you'll see many bumper stickers proclaiming I FOUND THE LOST RIVER. You can find it too, 6 miles west of North Woodstock on Route 112 in Kinsman Notch. Explore the narrow gorge and caverns with the help of walkways, ladders, and bridges. Like most of the attractions in this neck of the woods, it's open mid-May to mid-October. Admission costs $6 for adults and $3 for children ages 6 to 12.

CLARK'S TRADING POST Clark's on Route 3 just north of Lincoln has been a traditional shop for families traveling in the White Mountains since 1928. In addition to an old-fashioned photo parlor, water-bumper boats, a magic house, a narrow-gauge steam locomotive, and a gift shop selling moccasins, a family of native black bears performs daily. It's a bit on the campy side, but it's also part of many people's childhood.

SKIING

There are three notable ski resorts in the Franconia Notch area: Cannon Mountain and Mittersill near the Notch itself, and Loon Mountain in Lincoln at the western end of the Kancamagus Highway.

CANNON MOUNTAIN Besides the 70-passenger aerial tramway, Cannon Mountain (tel. 603/823-5563) has one triple-chair and two double-chair lifts, one quad-chair, and a pony lift, all with an hourly capacity of close to 7,000 skiers. There are 29 trails, about a quarter of them novice, another quarter expert, and the remaining half intermediate. The vertical drop is 2,145 feet, and besides having snowmaking equipment for the snowless days, the slopes are positioned so that they naturally receive and retain more than the average amount of white stuff. Cannon Mountain is operated by the state, as it is in a state park. Besides the three cafeteria and the base station and lounges nearby, you'll find a ski school, a nursery, and a ski shop where you can rent equipment.

MITTERSILL Mittersill (tel. 603/823-5511) is the junior cousin to Cannon Mountain, with a vertical drop of 1,600 feet, and one double chair and one T-bar for lifts. It's north of Cannon Mountain, off U.S. 3 on Route 18. The facility may not open this year for skiing, so you should call ahead to be sure.

LOON MOUNTAIN A drive 2 miles east of Lincoln along the Kancamagus Highway brings you to Loon Mountain (tel. 603/745-8146; for snow information 603/745-8100), a modern ski area with a gondola (four-passenger cars), two triple-chair lifts, and five double-chair lifts to take 9,600 skiers an hour up the mountain. The vertical drop is 2,100 feet, and the longest run is 3 miles. Loon has a limited-lift-lines policy (make reservations), and top-to-bottom snowmaking capacity. The Mountain Club on Loon has 240 rooms and a restaurant; other services at the base lodge include a cafeteria, lounge, nursery, ski shop, and rental shop. Lift fees are $32 on weekends, and slightly less on weekdays.

In summer and fall, Loon Mountain's gondolas operate from 9:30am to 5pm daily to take visitors on the 7,100-foot trip (1,850-foot rise) to the summit, at $8 per adult, $3 per child, free for kids 6 and under. There are cafeterias at both the base and summit stations.

Several ski areas offer package arrangements through the Ski 93 Association, named because the areas involved are all accessible by Interstate 93. Bretton Woods, Cannon Mountain, Loon Mountain, Tenney Mountain, and Waterville Valley are among the members, and you can get 3-day or 5-day cut-price lift tickets. Midweek passes good at all five areas are a real bargain. The association will be glad to help with reservations at area hotels, lodges, and inns. Write or call P.O. Box 176, North Woodstock, NH 03262 (tel. 603/745-8101).

WHERE TO STAY

You can make your base at any of several places in the area. At the southern end of Franconia Notch State Park lies North Woodstock, at the junction of U.S. 3 and Route 112, a small and fairly attractive commercial center with a few inns. Just across the Pemigewasset River where I-93 Exit 32 meets the Kancamagus Highway is the town of Lincoln, basically a commercial strip with some motels and residences.

At the northern end of the state park, near I-93 Exit 38, are the towns of **Franconia** and **Sugar Hill,** with a good number of nice inns. Finally, at I-93 Exit 42, only a few miles from the Vermont state line, is the town of **Littleton,** the largest settlement in these parts. It has two nice old inns for you to consider.

IN NORTH WOODSTOCK

WOODSTOCK INN, 80 Main St. (U.S. 3; P.O. Box 118), North Woodstock, NH 03262. Tel. 603/745-3951, or toll free 800/321-3985. Fax 603/745-3207. 6 rms (all with bath). A/C TV TEL
$ Rates (including full breakfast): High season, $60–$74 double. Off-season, $43–$59 double. AE, DISC, MC, V. **Parking:** Free.
This century-old Victorian house, very nicely redone, now has six guest rooms which share three baths. Decor is Victorian of course, except for the color TV sets and a

conditioners in some rooms. Downstairs in the inn is a full restaurant and lounge (see below). Midweek rates are slightly lower. Across the street in the 100-year-old Riverside Building are 11 rooms with private baths.

IN LINCOLN

KANCAMAGUS MOTOR LODGE, Rte. 112 (Kancamagus Hwy.), Lincoln, NH 03251. Tel. 603/745-3365, or toll free 800/346-4205 outside New Hampshire. 34 rms (all with bath). A/C TV TEL **Directions:** Take I-93 to Exit 32, then drive east on Rte. 112.
$ Rates: Summer, $63–$73 double. Winter, Sun–Thurs $46–$52 double. AE, DISC, MC, V. **Parking:** Free.

On the Kancamagus Highway a mile west of the Loon Mountain ski area is this modern motel. It has a heated outdoor pool and new rooms in a modern style furnished with private steambath and wall-to-wall carpeting. Its attraction is in its location, very close to Loon Mountain and not far at all from the attractions of Franconia Notch. The Kancamagus has a dining room, which serves a filling and well-priced breakfast ($1.89 for bacon, egg, home fries, and toast) and a cocktail lounge.

LINCOLN MOTEL, 5 Church St., Lincoln, NH 03251. Tel. 603/745-2780. 7 rms (all with bath). A/C TV TEL **Directions:** You'll see the Lincoln Motel from the Kancamagus Highway, set back from the road ½ block on the left-hand side as you go from North Woodstock east toward Loon Mountain.
$ Rates: High season, $52–$63 double. Low season, $35 double. DISC, MC, V. **Parking:** Free.

Right in town on Route 112 is an unprepossessing two-story structure with rooms that constitute one of the best bargains in the area, especially for skiers. Advantages here include good, if basic, rooms, low prices, and Loon Mountain less than 2 miles away.

IN FRANCONIA & SUGAR HILL

In the small town of Franconia, a reference point is the confluence of Routes 18 and 116. After coming from the south and meeting, the two routes head north to Littleton.

FRANCONIA INN, Easton Rd., Franconia, NH 03580. Tel. 603/823-5542, or toll free 800/473-5299. 35 rms (all with bath). **Directions:** In Franconia, turn on to Rte. 116 at Exxon Station. Inn is 2 miles down road on right.
$ Rates: $55–$88 single; $65–$97 double; from $108 suite. AE, MC, V. **Parking:** Free, on premises. **Closed:** Apr–May.

Just over 2 miles south of Franconia along Route 116 (Easton Road) is the Franconia Inn, a nice old white clapboard place built in 1868. It still provides many of the services that once brought wealthy Bostonians here: riding horses, outdoor swimming pool, four clay tennis courts, a family-size hot tub, bicycle tours, and hiking trails. Several golf courses are nearby. Right across the road from the inn is Foxfire Aviation, Inc. (tel. 823-8881), which will take you up for sailplane (glider) rides. Besides so many things to do, there is the tranquillity and beauty of the verdant Easton Valley, with fine views of Cannon Mountain, Mt. Lafayette, and the Franconia and Kinsman mountain ranges.

The guest rooms at the inn are well maintained and somewhat old-fashioned, but with clean baths. Prices depend on view and room size. An adult can have breakfast and dinner daily for $32.50; meal plans for children depend on their ages. Add taxes and tips. When you call, ask for a corner room, and also about package plans which may save you some money.

For rainy days and evenings there are movies, a games room with coin-operated games for the kids, a billiards room, an oak-paneled library with fireplace, and a screened porch set with wicker furniture. Downstairs, the Rathskeller Lounge has quiet entertainment many nights. The nice candlelit dining room adds considerably to the feeling that you've settled yourself into a huge old summer estate owned by one of your rich uncles in the heart of Robert Frost country. The "uncles" in this case are innkeepers Richard and Alec Morris. It's comfy here. Ski season, by the way, is one of the inn's best times, with trails radiating from the inn throughout the valley.

HORSE & HOUND INN, 205 Wells Rd., Franconia, NH 03580. Tel. **603/823-5501.** 10 rms (8 with bath). **Directions:** Go south out of Franconia on Rte. 18. After 2½ miles, look for Wells Rd., on the right; go ½ mile to the inn.
$ Rates (including full breakfast): $60–$80 double with bath. AE, CB, DC, MC, V. **Parking:** Free, on premises.
This is a real true-to-life country inn according to the old style. It is not plush and fancy, with priceless antiques everywhere, but rather simple, well kept, and attractive. It is well off the main roads, and blissfully, perfectly quiet except for the crackle of a fire in the fireplace on a cool day, or the murmur of conversation in the lounge. Rooms come with a double, a queen-size, or two doubles. Two units for families or couples traveling together offer two bedrooms sharing a single bath. When only one bedroom is needed, the other is locked off. The inn's dining room serves good, hearty, honest food, such as sirloin steaks and surf-and-turf; a full dinner might cost $25 to $30 per person, drinks, tax, and tip included.

SUGAR HILL INN, Rte. 117, Sugar Hill, Franconia, NH 03580. Tel. **603/823-5621,** or toll free 800/54VISIT. 11 rms (all with bath), 6 cottages (all with bath). **Directions:** Take Rte. 18 out of Franconia; turn left on to Rte. 117 for about a mile.
$ Rates (including breakfast): $94–$104 double. MC, V. **Parking:** Free, or premises.
In the village of Sugar Hill, a few miles west of Franconia along Route 117, is the Sugar Hill Inn, perched up on a hill and surrounded by grassy lawns. The original farmhouse was built in 1789, but I doubt that it then had such a commodious and welcoming front porch. In any case, the house became an inn in 1929, still with its original fireplaces (some now fitted with Franklin stoves), old board floors, and wood beams. Now the rooms have very pretty country furnishings, quilts, old paintings, rocking chairs, and hand-stenciled designs on the walls. Each of the rooms has a private bath and twin beds, a double bed, or a queen-size bed. Beside the inn are six small guest cottages with similar decor, private bath, carpeting, and TV set; they're open mid-May to mid-November only. At peak times guests will be required to take dinner here, which would add about $25 to $30 per person to the tab. At other times dinner is served by reservation, and there's usually a choice of meat, fish, and chicken, along with various soups, appetizers, and desserts. There's also a pub for lighter fare. Small, quiet, congenial, authentic—that's the Sugar Hill Inn. Jim and Barbara Quinn are your hosts.

IN LITTLETON

White clapboard churches with graceful steeples and the solid, four-square brick facades of Main Street's commercial district: This is Littleton, N.H., a fine New England town. It's neither a quaint village nor an industrial town, but something in between; Littleton may be to New Hampshire what Lake Wobegon is to Minnesota.

The local chamber of commerce and historical society have put together a pamphlet which will take you on a guided tour of the town's landmarks, including the post office and courthouse, Masonic Temple, public library, and Tilton's Opera building.

RABBIT HILL INN, Rte. 18, Lower Waterford, VT 05848. Tel. 802/748- **5168,** or toll free 800/76-BUNNY. 20 rms (all with bath). A/C **Directions:** From I-93 north, Exit 44, on to Rte. 18 north, 2 miles to inn.
$ Rates (including breakfast and dinner): $149–$219 double. 20% off winter midweek. MC, V. **Parking:** Free, on premises and on street.

Though it's actually in Vermont, the Rabbit Hill Inn is connected to Littleton, N.H., by cultural and commercial ties. Established in 1795, the inn was bought by John and Maureen Magee in April 1987. Most rooms have views of the mountains; these views are significant, as the inn is set into the side of a hill with a magnificent panorama of the mountains and the Connecticut River Valley. The plan to have breakfast and dinner here makes sense, as Lower Waterford is a tiny hamlet with few other dining opportunities.

The elegant Rabbit Hill Inn is homey in its welcome. Beautiful antique furnishings are in the dining room, pub, book nook, lounge, and guest rooms, three of which are air conditioned. Across the road from the inn is the village church, built in 1859, and next to that the small library. Besides these public-service buildings, the village of Lower Waterford has fewer than a dozen houses. The Rabbit Hill Inn sometimes accounts for fully half of the village's active population! It's idyllic and special here—"like Brigadoon," as John Magee says—and you'll love it.

WHERE TO DINE

WOODSTOCK INN, 80 Main St., North Woodstock. Tel. 745-3951.
Cuisine: AMERICAN. **Reservations:** Recommended. **Directions:** From Exit 32 off I-93, turn right on Rte. 112, then right on Rte. 3. Inn is on left.
$ Prices: Appetizers $4.50–$8; main courses $15–$21; dinner $26–$35. AE, DISC, MC, V.
Open: Mon–Sat 7am–11:30pm, Sun 7am–1pm.

The Woodstock has perhaps the best full menu in the area. For a light lunch or a drink before or after dinner there's the Woodstock Station, Lincoln's original railroad station moved to a site adjoining the inn. The favored place to sit for dinner in the inn is on the enclosed porch next to one of the large windows looking out onto Main Street, but there are other attractive Victorian dining rooms as well. Prices are moderate, because the price of your main course includes a choice of appetizer or soup, garden salad, fresh bread, rice or potato, and homemade fresh-fruit sorbet. Main courses range from sole stuffed with crabmeat and tortellini scallops Alfredo (tortellini with mushrooms and Gruyère, sautéed with fresh scallops, sauce Alfredo), through roast duckling and chicken curry with coconut and pine nuts, to tournedos au poivre, tournedos Rossini, and steak Diane. You can dine sumptuously here for a mere $20, but your dinner bill will more likely be higher when drinks, dessert, tax, and tip are included. The Woodstock Inn provides some of the best dining in the area.

10. LAKE SUNAPEE

Sunapee Harbor: 40 miles (65km) NW of Concord,
25 miles (40km) SE of Lebanon

GETTING THERE By Plane Northwest Airlines serves the airport at West Lebanon, 29 miles NW of Sunapee Harbor.

By Bus See the beginning of this chapter.

By Car Follow I-89 to N.H. Route 11 south.

ESSENTIALS The **area code** is 603. For information, contact the **Lake Sunapee Lodging Bureau,** P.O. Box 400, Sunapee, NH 03782 (tel. 603/763-2495, or toll free 800/258-3530).

Lake Sunapee is a pleasant regional vacation spot in southwestern New Hampshire, not very far from the town of Hanover, which is home to Dartmouth College. Besides summer sports such as swimming, boating, and canoeing, the area around

Lake Sunapee has its own small ski area in Mount Sunapee State Park. On a trip to Vermont or north to Hanover for a visit to Dartmouth, the shores of Lake Sunapee are a fine place to stop for a night or even a week.

Of the towns around the lake, Sunapee (sometimes called Sunapee Harbor) on the western shore is the nicest, with a good collection of inns, motels, and resorts. Although in its early days Sunapee held a tannery, gristmill, and several shops for woodworking industries, it now makes its living from summer visitors; in recent years, skiers have brought business to the town in winter as well.

The town of Mount Sunapee, on the southwestern shore, is not really a town at all, regardless of what it may say on your road map. The intersection of Routes 103 and 103B, with a motel and the state park and state beach entrance, is the "town." Don't plan to get gas there!

WHAT TO SEE & DO

To see Lake Sunapee, there is no better way than to catch the **MV _Mount Sunapee II_** (tel. 763-4030), which leaves Sunapee Harbor marina at 2:30pm on Saturday and Sunday from mid-May to mid-June for tours of the beautiful, very pure lake. From mid-June to Labor Day there are sailings at 10am and 2:30pm. And until mid-October the ship sails on weekends at 2:30pm. The tour lasts 1½ hours and costs $9 for adults. Kids under 12 pay $5; kids under 5 ride free. The _Mount Sunapee II_ holds 150 people, and the tour is narrated by the amiable captain.

In the summer, Sunapee hosts very well attended **flea markets** out on Route 103B at the blinking light (between Sunapee Harbor and Sunapee Lower Village). Both buyers and sellers flock to the intersection's roadsides, and everything from craftwork through antiques to junk is available.

The best **beach** in the area is the state park beach, near the state park entrance. The entrance fee covers use of changing rooms. Lake Sunapee is a Class A reservoir—the water is about as pure and unpolluted as you'll find anywhere.

Across the large traffic circle from the entrance road to the beach is the entrance to the state park and its chair lift to the summit of **Mount Sunapee** (tel. 603/763-2356, or toll free 800/322-3300). In summer the round-trip price in three-person chair lifts is $5.50 for adults, $2.50 for children 6 to 12. The trip takes you over 1¼ miles (1,510 feet straight up) to the summit at 2,743 feet. At the top there are walking trails (not difficult) to an overlook and to a glacial tarn named Lake Solitude. At the base of the mountain, near the gondola station, is a cafeteria; spacious lawns, hiking trails, and picnic areas are all open to the public at no charge.

For **skiing,** the Mount Sunapee area (tel. 603/763-4020, or toll free 800/322-3300 for snow information) has two double-chair lifts, three triple-chair lifts, and a pony lift. The vertical drop is 1,500 feet on 23 slopes and trails; in addition, there are 10 miles of free ski-touring trails, novice and intermediate (tel. 603/763-2356 for information). A ski school, a ski shop with rental equipment, a cafeteria, and (weekdays) a nursery are all available.

WHERE TO STAY

Though the Lake Sunapee region is perfect for vacationers, there is some spirit among the local people to limit touristic growth. Thus many of the long-standing inns here are more like self-contained mini-resorts. There are a few motels for those on a vagabond tour.

DEXTER'S INN AND TENNIS CLUB, Stagecoach Rd. (P.O. Box 703F), Sunapee, NH 03782. Tel. 603/763-5571, or toll free 800/232-5571. 1? rms (all with bath). A/C **Directions:** From I-89, Exit 12 and Rte. 11 west for 5? miles to Lefton on Winn Hill Rd. for 1½ miles.

$ Rates (including breakfast and dinner): $125–$165 double. Off-season package rates available. MC, V. **Parking:** Free, on premises.

Dexter's is hidden away on a back road, but it has a fine view of Lake Sunapee and its surrounding mountains. Built in 1801, the yellow clapboard house was renovated in he 1930s and converted to an inn in 1948. It's been owned and run by the Simpson-Durfor family for well over two decades, and has that family feel about it that makes even first-time visitors comfortable. Some of the rooms have antique pieces, including the beds; other rooms have more modern furnishings. Annex rooms have air conditioning. A cottage is available weekly. Breakfast will be delivered to your room if you like, and dinner is taken in the dining room.

Amusements include a well-equipped library and piano in the living room, a pretty outdoor swimming pool, and three professional-grade tennis courts (complete with pro and pro shop). Other games include shuffleboard, croquet, and horseshoes. Dexter's is open May through October.

HAUS EDELWEISS, 13 Maple St. (P.O. Box 609), Sunapee, NH 03782. Tel. 603/763-2100, or toll free 800/248-0713. Fax 603/763-5232. 5 rms (one with half bath). **Directions:** From I-89, Exit 12 to Rte. 11, west to Sunapee Harbor.

$ Rates (including breakfast): $32 single; $49–$59 double. MC, V. **Parking:** Free.

Out of sight from Sunapee Harbor but only a few hundred feet away is a nice and homey bed-and-breakfast with five rooms. Guests tend to gather in the living room, where TV, light snacks, and a drink are offered by the hosts. You have a choice of a traditional Bavarian, continental, or Yankee breakfast. New this year is a two-bedroom apartment suite situated over the garage on the owner's private home. The rate here is $80.

MOUNT SUNAPEE MOTEL, Rte. 103, Mount Sunapee, NH 03772. Tel. 603/763-5592. 22 rms (all with bath). TV **Directions:** From I-89 take Exit 9 and follow Rte. 103 west to motel.

$ Rates: Motel $56–$63 double; 2-room unit $55–$70 double. Credit card payments cost 5% extra. AE, DC, MC, V. **Parking:** Free.

This very popular motel is right near the entrance to Mount Sunapee State Park. It's modern, with tile bathrooms, tub-shower combinations, and at least two beds in each room. Half of the motel consists of 11 two-room units, each with a kitchenette; the outdoor swimming pool is shared by all.

---

11. HANOVER

5 miles (8km) N of Lebanon, 64 miles (100km) NW of Concord,
20 miles (32km) NE of Woodstock, Vt.

GETTING THERE By Plane Northwest Airlink and Business Express serves the airport at West Lebanon, 6 miles south of Hanover.

By Bus See the beginning of this chapter. Short-run intercity bus service is operated by Advance Transit (tel. 603/448-2815).

By Car Follow I-89 to Lebanon, then Route 120 north to Hanover; or follow I-91 in Vermont to Norwich, then go east across the Connecticut River to Hanover.

ESSENTIALS The **area code** is 603. Contact the **Hanover Chamber of Commerce,** P.O. Box A-105, Hanover, NH 03755 (tel. 603/643-3115).

---

he small town of Hanover is the home of one of the country's oldest and most prestigious colleges. **Dartmouth** (named for the earl who was colonial secretary to King George III) was founded in 1769, and its charter gives a hint of why it was located in such a remote place: It was meant primarily "for the education and instruction of Youth of the Indian Tribes," and only secondarily for the education of "English Youth and others." Today Dartmouth is more than a small undergraduate college; its graduate schools of medicine, engineering, and business administration are well respected, and the Hopkins Center for the Arts is the cultural focus of the entire region.

In many ways the college is the town and vice versa. College buildings o exceptional beauty and grace are scattered or clustered throughout Hanover, an most are shaded by trees of a prodigious height and girth. Anyone out for a driv would enjoy a walk through the campus, perhaps on one of the guided college tour (free) that leave from the college information booth during the summer; in winte tours depart from McNutt Hall. To order tickets to performances, or to find ou what's showing at the Hopkins Center, call 603/646-2422.

In winter, Dartmouth's **Winter Carnival** is the major fun and social event, wit special art shows, drama and concerts, an ice-sculpture contest, and other amuse ments.

WHAT TO SEE & DO

Everyone takes a tour of Dartmouth College, but for a more offbeat view of th campus and surrounding area take a **hot-air balloon ride.** At the Post Mills Airpor (P.O. Box 51, Post Mills, VT 05058; tel. 802/333-9254) you can take a sunrise o sunset balloon ride with trained, professional balloonists who will float you up o down the Connecticut River Valley depending on the whim of the wind. After you'v helped with the set-up process, you'll be airborne for 1 to 1½ hours, and finish with champagne reception at the touchdown site. Oh, and don't worry, they'll take yo back to the airport to pick up your car if you want. Balloons fly daily, weather an wind permitting. The cost for all this fun is $150 per person, with a minimum of tw people required for takeoff. To reach the airport from Hanover, cross the bridge t Vermont, take I-91 to exit 14, left on Route 113, go 6 miles turning east onto Rout 244. The airport is ¼-mile down the road on the right at the fork.

WHERE TO STAY & DINE
IN HANOVER

**HANOVER INN, corner of Main and Wheelock Sts., Hanover, NH 03755
Tel. 603/643-4300,** or toll free 800/443-7024. Fax 603/646-3744. 92 rms (a with bath). A/C TV TEL
$ Rates: $164 single or double; from $214 suite. AE, DC, DISC, MC, V. **Parking** Underground garage $5 per night; outdoor lot free.

Hanover's prime hostelry is right in the center of town. Some rooms have views of th lawns and buildings of the college. It fills up quickly at major college events such a matriculation, graduation, and the big football games played at home. Decor i colonial, to fit in with the rest of Hanover, but modern comfort has been given grea consideration. There are larger and slightly newer rooms in the east wing. Roor service is available 7am to 10pm.

The Hanover Inn's formal dining room and new restaurant are supplemented by lovely outdoor patio, under an awning, in summer. The feeling is very much that of a exclusive country club. At lunch, sandwiches are only about $5, but full luncheo meals (the daily specials) can be had for $8 to $10. The dinner menu offers a good an balanced selection of well-known meat, fish, and fowl dishes: Start with Norwegia gravlax and then have anything from pan-fried brook trout to native spring lamb, an the total bill will be about $35 per person. The waitresses in black uniforms wit white trim are silent, efficient, and friendly, waiting attentively at their stations whe all the diners have been served. Room service is available for all three meals.

IN LYME

LYME INN, On the Common, Lyme, NH 03768. Tel. 603/795-2222. 1 rms (12 with bath). **Directions:** From Lebanon, take Rte. 120 to Rte. 10 to Lym center.
$ Rates (including breakfast): $55–$75 single; $65–$75 double. AE, MC, V **Parking:** Free.

If Hanover is the busy college town, Lyme, N.H., 10 miles north on Route 10, is th peaceful New England village. At the center of Lyme you'll see the high-pillare facade of the inn. Built in 1809, most of the inn's rooms have bath or shower, and all have antiques and authentic decor. You should know that the inn has its own tavern, very handy in this otherwise sleepy village.

IN NORWICH, VT.

INN AT NORWICH, Main St., Norwich, VT 05055. Tel. 802/649-1143.
22 rms (all with bath). A/C TV TEL

$ Rates: $69–$99 single; $79–$109 double. AE, MC, V. **Parking:** Free, next to inn.

Just across the Connecticut River from Hanover, in Vermont, you'll find the Inn at Norwich, a nice hostelry known for its charm, dignity, and warm welcome as well as for the excellence of its dining room. The inn has been here since 1797 and its furnishings reflect its heritage, with brass and canopy beds in many rooms. The cheery lounge is called the Jasper Murdoch Tavern, after the man who opened the inn almost 200 years ago. The current innkeeper is Sally Johnson. Rates include breakfast and dinner in the pretty, formal dining room or on the porch. The cuisine is of a high order.

CHAPTER 12

MAINE

- **WHAT'S SPECIAL ABOUT MAINE**
1. **OGUNQUIT**
2. **KENNEBUNKPORT**
3. **PORTLAND**
4. **BOOTHBAY HARBOR**
5. **CAMDEN**
6. **CASTINE & BLUE HILL**
7. **BAR HARBOR**

There is something quintessentially American about this rugged and sparsely populated state, the largest in New England. It's as though the vast forests of the north and the jagged coastline of "downeast" Maine are the last American frontier, rich in natural resources but waiting for people equally rugged to tame them.

Imagine the exhilarating feeling of a cool breeze on your face while watching a tomato-orange sun rise over Acadia National Park as it kisses America with its first warmth in a new day. You might try camping and cooking on an open fire—the smell of maple-smoked bacon will rouse even the sleepiest of travelers. Little wonder the sun shines first here in Maine; it's a grand preview of what this state has to offer.

Although there are still areas of wilderness in Maine, some of the state's potential was exploited long ago, soon after its discovery by Europeans. When the French and English came to these shores, they found miles and miles of virgin growth. The tremendous white pines have been replaced by other varieties, and lumber products again yield a good deal of the state's economy.

Besides its forests, Maine has great stores of granite for building, but most are untapped as yet. Although agriculture is difficult because of the rocky soil and the short growing season, Maine potatoes are known and used throughout the eastern United States. Maine's fishers yearly pull great quantities of fish, scallops, shrimp, and the famous lobsters from the freezing Atlantic waters. But the largest industry in Maine these days is the vacation trade: campers, hikers, and fishers in the mountains and lakes, yachting and summer residents in the beautiful old coastal towns. Good food—especially the fresh seafood—and clean air draw the crowds from Boston, Montréal, and New York, and life in the southern coastal towns is lively and interesting from mid-June through Labor Day, after which the visitors become those looking for the quiet of Indian Summer and the autumn foliage season. Most resorts close up by the last week in October.

SEEING MAINE

Of the vacation areas in Maine, certainly the most popular is the southern coast where pretty towns such as Ogunquit, Kennebunkport, Boothbay Harbor, and Camden provide an atmosphere either restful or lively, cultural or natural, as you like it. Next in popularity comes the famous old resort of Bar Harbor, which is a good ways "downeast." The crowds these days come to commune with the rugged beauty of **Acadia National Park.** Finally, a smaller number of hardy souls head into the hinterland among the mountains, forests, and glacial lakes for a piece of the outdoor life.

GETTING THERE By Plane Maine's major airport is the Portland International Jetport, served by many major American air carriers. Bar Harbor Airport is served by Continental Express.

C&J Airport Limousine Service operates those long airport limousine between Boston's Logan International Airport and points along the Maine coast including Ogunquit and Kennebunk. In Ogunquit the terminal is at the Dunaway Municipal Building right in the center of town; in Kennebunk it's at the Kennebunk Inn. Places in the limousines are best reserved in advance.

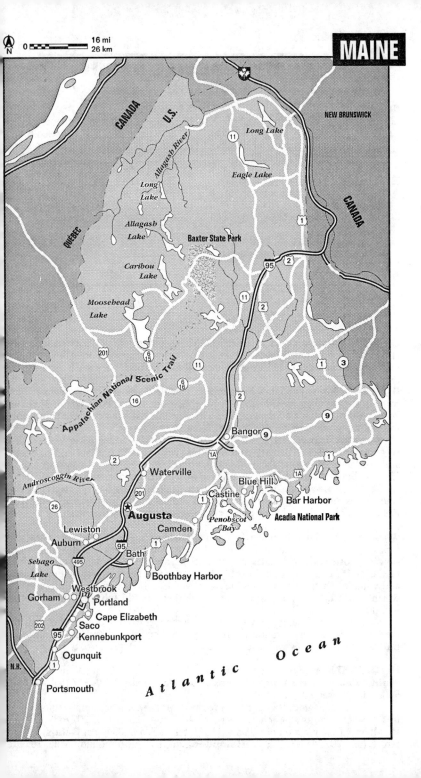

WHAT'S SPECIAL ABOUT MAINE

Seacoast

☐ The famous "rockbound coast of Maine," more than 1,000 miles long, offering an endless array of beautiful vistas and charming villages and towns.

☐ Bar Harbor National Park, one of the few national parks east of the Mississippi.

☐ Beach resort towns of Ogunquit and Kennebunkport.

☐ A cruise aboard a swift schooner in Camden, center of the sail-charter business.

Shopping

☐ Antiques shops and flea markets on both sides of U.S. 1 between Kittery and Ogunquit on Saturdays in summer.

☐ Maine's most famous store, L. L. Bean, in Freeport, open 24 hours a day, 365 days a year.

☐ Factory outlet stores in Freeport and many other coastal towns.

By Train　**Amtrak** does not operate in Maine, but its trains do connect with buses at Boston's South Station that will take you north into Maine. At press time, plans are under way to initiate rail service in Maine; call toll free 800/USA-RAIL for an update

By Bus　Greyhound Lines in conjunction with Vermont Transit operates buses from Boston to Bangor with stops in Newburyport, Mass., Portsmouth, N.H., and Portland, Brunswick, and Bangor, Me. The schedule has been cut back considerably for midway points and for connections from or to Canada.

　Vermont Transit (tel. toll free 800/451-3292, 800/642-3133 in Vermont) and **Greyhound** travel to Bangor from Montréal with stops in Burlington, Vt., Boston and Portland. In summer there are usually buses from Bangor to Ellsworth and Bar Harbor, but you should check in advance to see if they are running.

　C&J Trailways (tel. 207/828-1151, or toll free 800/639-5505) operates six daily round-trips between the Amtrak station in Boston or Logan International Airport and Portland. This is the only nonstop service available between the cities.

By Car　The Maine Turnpike (I-95) is a toll road. U.S. 1 or its scenic alternate route U.S. 1A, parallels the Maine Turnpike all the way to Brunswick, and while it's a bit slower, it costs nothing. Besides, it's more scenic, and in my opinion no other highway in the entire country could possibly have as many flea markets, antiques shops and white-elephant sales as does U.S. 1 in Maine, all the way from Kittery to Ellsworth. Weekends are the best times to catch them, but in July and August any day will do.

　Note: If you're heading for Ogunquit, take the exit from I-95 soon after you cross the state line at Kittery—follow the signs for U.S. 1 and the "shore" or "scenic" route through York, and this will save you a toll.

INFORMATION　For travel information and answers to your questions, contact the **Maine Publicity Bureau,** P.O. Box 2300, Hallowell, ME 04347 (tel. 207/582-9300, or toll free 800/533-9595).

　The State of Maine also operates **information centers** at several points of entry to the state such as at **Kittery,** between I-95 and U.S. 1 (tel. 207/439-1319); at **Houlton,** at the junction of I-95 and U.S. 1 (tel. 207/532-6346); at **Calais,** 7 Union Street (tel. 207/454-2211); at **Hampden,** on I-95 northbound, Mile 169 (tel.

207/862-6628) and southbound at Mile 172 (tel. 207/862-6638); and at **Yarmouth,** between I-95 (Exit 17) and U.S. 1 (tel. 207/846-0833).

Maine's telephone **area code** is 207. Meals and rooms in Maine are taxed at a rate of 7%, so look for this tax to be added to your bill each night, and at mealtimes.

1. OGUNQUIT

73 miles (118km) NE of Boston, Mass., 18 miles (29km) NE of Portsmouth, N.H., 35 miles (56km) SW of Portland

GETTING THERE **By Bus**   See the beginning of this chapter.

By Car   See the beginning of this chapter.

ESSENTIALS   The **area code** is 207. The Ogunquit Chamber of Commerce maintains an **information office** on U.S. 1 (P.O. Box 2289, Ogunquit, ME 03907; tel. 207/646-2939), south of the center of town, and as Main Street is U.S. 1, you will come to the office just south of the downtown area. It's open daily in season and Monday to Friday 10am to 4pm off season. Free year-round directories are available on request.

The Native American name means "beautiful place by the sea," and it holds true even today, because Ogunquit's town government has ensured that the town remains tidy and picturesque despite its tourism development. Visitors feel welcome in the town, whether they're strolling along Ogunquit's picturesque "Marginal Way," a path along the rocky coast; relaxing at the Ogunquit Beach; or dining in one of the many excellent restaurants. At Perkins Cove, a tiny peninsula is festooned with the quaint low waterfront shops and shacks from Ogunquit's fishing-village heyday. Right along U.S. 1 is the Ogunquit Playhouse (tel. 646-5511), which presents Broadway plays and musicals from late June through Labor Day. Ogunquit has been a summer resort for over a century, and it's no wonder that people come back year after year. Ogunquit is popular with and embraces the gay community in summer, much like Provincetown on Cape Cod. A handful of guesthouses, restaurants, and bars caters to a gay clientele.

WHAT TO SEE & DO

To walk **Marginal Way,** start at the town's information office, pick up a map, and you'll come out right at Barnacle Billy's in Perkins Cove, a mile or so away. The Atlantic, the rocky coast, the gulls wheeling overhead, and the smiles of the other walkers are all a treat whether the sun is shining, or it's misty, or even if there's a gale coming. The inlet at Barnacle Billy's has a drawbridge that is operated by hand. You may be called upon by yachtspeople or fishers on lobsterboats to raise the bridge for their passage!

The next thing to do is to call the **Ogunquit Playhouse** (Rte. 1; tel. 646-5511) to get seats for a performance, which will no doubt feature a star or two of national reputation. Tickets cost $19 and shows are scheduled for Monday through Saturday at 8:30pm and Wednesday and Thursday at 2:30pm.

As for **beaches,** Ogunquit's Main Beach, Little Beach, and Fottbridge Beach are ranged along a peninsula just a few minutes' walk from the center of town. Lifeguards are on duty from 8am to 5pm daily in season.

Some lazy afternoon, be sure to leave time for a stroll around the shops and galleries of Perkins Cove, the picturesque old fishing-village section of town.

You can get to know the sea in Ogunquit by going down to Perkins Cove where, next to Barnacle Billy's, the dock of the **Finestkind boats** is located. Each hour during the day, from Monday to Saturday, the lobster boats set out to cruise the Maine coast, hauling in the lobster pots and the day's catch. You can go along and have the process of lobstering explained while you view the coastline and the fishing grounds, all at $6.75 for adults, $4.75 for children. Make reservations, if you like, by calling 646-5227, or just drop down to the docks for more information. There are cocktail, starlight, and lighthouse tour cruises as well.

Auto buffs can visit the **Wells Auto Museum,** on U.S. 1 in Wells just north of Ogunquit (tel. 646-9064), where the 1907 Stanley Steamer, a rare 1912 Pathfinder roadster, a 1918 Pierce Arrow, and 75 other classics are on display. Admission costs $3 for adults, $2 for children over 6. The museum is open from mid-June through September daily 10am to 5pm; weekends only 10am to 5pm mid-May to mid-June and the first 2 weeks in October.

WHERE TO STAY

Ogunquit has a good selection of accommodations in all price ranges. It seems as though every place in town rents rooms, from the gas station to the gift shop. Many are on U.S. 1, however, which is busy with traffic. If you don't find a vacancy among the following selections, search along Shore Road toward Perkins Cove, where it's quieter.

MODERATE

CLIFF HOUSE, Bald Head Cliff (P.O. Box 2274), Ogunquit, ME 03907
   Tel. 207/361-1000. Fax 207/361-2122. 162 rms (all with bath). A/C TV TEL
   Directions: Heading north, take the York/Ogunquit exit off I-95, then take Rte.
   north 3⅓ miles to River Rd.; take a right and follow River Rd. to the end. Turn left
   onto Shore Rd. and the Cliff House will be 3½ miles ahead.
$ Rates: July–Aug, $120–$185 double. Sept to mid-Dec, and Apr–June, $85–
   $150 double. AE, MC, V. **Parking:** Free. **Closed:** Mid-Dec to Mar.
Originally guests stayed in the large old house perched on the cliff, 90 feet above the surf, but now the house is overshadowed by several large and very modern motel units, all with a view of the sea. Extensive pine-covered grounds, a heated outdoor pool, and tennis courts add to the lure of the Cliff House's remote location and its view. The rooms are luxurious, with picture windows for the sea view. Off-season, prices are somewhat lower, and special money-saving packages are offered. There's free transportation in season into town, to the beach, and to other points of interest in and around Ogunquit.

COUNTRY SQUIRE MOTEL, on U.S. 1 at Bourne's Lane, Ogunquit, ME
   03907. Tel. 207/646-3162. 34 rms (all with bath). TV
$ Rates: High season $77–$91 double. Off-season, $40–$50 double. MC, V.
   Parking: Free. **Closed:** Late Oct–late Apr.
The inspiration of this modern, attractive hotel is colonial, with an arched portico along the front of the motel, bay windows in each room, pots of plants, and colonial-style furniture. The facilities are an uncolonial matter, however, for there's a swimming pool, and each room has wall-to-wall carpeting. Fifteen rooms have cathedral ceilings and skylights. Half have telephones. Coffee and doughnuts are served each morning. The Country Squire is located just 4 blocks or so from the center of town.

SEA CHAMBERS MOTOR LODGE, 37 Shore Rd., Ogunquit, ME 03907.
   Tel. 207/646-9311. 43 rms (all with bath). A/C TV TEL **Directions:** Follow
   Shore Rd. toward the sea.
$ Rates (including continental breakfast): $125–$132 twin or double. Extra person
   $15. No credit cards. **Parking:** Free. **Closed:** Dec–Mar.

This two- and three-story motel is right down near the water and also has its own heated pool and tennis court. You can walk from your room and get right on Marginal Way, the path along the rocky coast. The whole establishment is quite modern, and all rooms have a balcony, most with good sea views.

INEXPENSIVE

COLONIAL INN RESORT, 61 Shore Rd. (P.O. Box 895), Ogunquit, ME 03907. Tel. 207/646-5191, or toll free 800/233-5191. Fax 207/646-3993. 80 rms (all with bath). A/C TV TEL **Directions:** Follow Shore Rd. toward the sea.
$ **Rates:** High season, $70–$95 single or double; $120–$130 room with kitchenette. May–June and Sept to mid-Oct, rates are 50% lower. AE, DISC, MC, V. **Parking:** Free. **Closed:** Late Oct–late Apr.
Of Ogunquit's cozy Victorian seaside hotels, the Colonial is brimming with life, having been renovated by Chet and Sheila Sawtelle. Besides the rooms in the inn, the hotel has suites with kitchen, plus some motel units with kitchenettes. The Colonial has a heated pool, whirlpool spa, a breakfast coffee shop, an elevator, and more important, a spacious veranda in the turn-of-the-century fashion, the perfect place for sitting, viewing, reading, and napping. A higher price is charged for the rooms with the best ocean views.

HAYES GUEST HOUSE, 133 Shore Rd. (R.R. 1, Box 12), Ogunquit, ME 03907. Tel. 207/646-2277. 7 rms (4 with bath). **Directions:** Follow Shore Rd. toward the sea.
$ **Rates:** $70 twin or double without bath, $73–$75 twin or double with bath. Extra person $10. No credit cards. **Parking:** Free.
Elinor Hayes is very kind and friendly and has decorated her rooms and apartments with interesting old pieces, such as a rope-frame bed made in Maine, old sea chests, and patchwork quilts. Guests have use of a refrigerator, the coffee-maker, and the swimming pool. It's a charming place, and Mrs. Hayes a charming lady, and you're within walking distance of Perkins Cove with its restaurants, shops, and galleries.

SEAFAIR INN, 14 Shore Rd. (P.O. Box 1221), Ogunquit, ME 03907. Tel. 207/646-2181. 13 rms (9 with bath), 5 efficiencies. A/C TV
$ **Rates** (including continental breakfast): $72–$128 double without bath, $104–$178 double with bath, $99 efficiency. MC, V. **Parking:** Free.
As you head down Shore Road from the main crossroads, you'll come to the Seafair Inn, on the right-hand side. Pass the two millstones at the beginning of the path, walk up through the garden, go through the sunny front porch with wicker furniture, and enter the formal parlor of this one-time Victorian summer house.

WHERE TO DINE

Perkins Cove, at the seaside end of Shore Road, has several good restaurants. In July and August it can be very difficult and expensive to park your car here, and you'd be well advised to take one of the "trolleys" (open buses) that run along Shore Road to the cove.

BARNACLE BILLY'S, Shore Rd., Perkins Cove. Tel. 646-5575.
Cuisine: LOBSTER POUND. **Reservations:** Not accepted. **Directions:** Follow Shore Rd. to Perkins Cove.
$ **Prices:** Appetizers $3.75–$7.50; main courses $8–$22. AE, MC, V.
Open: Daily 11am–10pm. **Closed:** Nov to mid-Apr.
At Barnacle Billy's you'll find good prices, good food, and good service as only you yourself could provide. The routine here is to enter, choose what you want from the blackboard menu, pay the cashier and get a slip, and submit it to the counterperson; then wander off into Barnacle Billy's waterfront dining room, done all

in pine with tables and chairs to match, and a hardwood fire going in two big stone fireplaces. The view of the marina and the cove is as good as the food: lobster, steamed clams, corn on the cob, salad, and garlic bread are all available. When the weather's fine, you can even order at a window on the brick terrace and have your meal while sitting in the sunshine, either on the terrace or on a deck a flight up; both terraces are right next to the Finestkind Boat Dock. There's free parking across the street.

CLAY HILL FARM, Agamenticus Rd. Tel. 361-2272.

> **Cuisine:** AMERICAN. **Reservations:** Recommended. **Directions:** Go south on Main St. (U.S. 1) from the blinker in the center of Ogunquit for ⅓ mile, to a blinker at a crossroads next to the Admiral's Inn; turn right—this is Agamenticus Rd.—and go 1¾ miles to the tavern, which will be on your right.

> **$ Prices:** Appetizers $5–$8; main courses $13–$23; dinner $35–$40. AE, MC, V
> **Open:** May–Oct, dinner daily 5:30pm–midnight (kitchen closes at 10pm) Nov–Mar, dinner Thurs–Sun 5:30pm–midnight (kitchen closes at 10pm).

The farmhouse has been converted into a tavern with several large dining rooms with lots of windows. Start with clam chowder or Maine crab cakes and go on to haddock stuffed with lobster. Before and after dinner you can relax in the lounge and enjoy the piano entertainment provided.

EINSTEIN'S DELI, corner of Shore Rd. and U.S. 1. Tel. 646-5262.

> **Cuisine:** DELI. **Reservations:** Not accepted.
> **$ Prices:** Main courses $3.45–$9. No credit cards.
> **Open:** Summer, 6am–midnight. Off-season, hours vary.

Ogunquit is prepared for New Yorkers who come north for the summer, or others in search of good corned beef, pastrami, bagels, and the like. Einstein's has all these delights and lots more—homemade soup and turkey club sandwiches—beside several dining areas and a take-out service. The clam chowder is true New England–style.

OLD VILLAGE INN, 30 Main St. Tel. 646-7088.

> **Cuisine:** AMERICAN/SEAFOOD. **Reservations:** Required.
> **$ Prices:** Appetizers $5–$7; main courses $8–$10 at breakfast, $13–$20 at dinner; dinner $30. AE, MC, V.
> **Open:** Breakfast daily 7:30–11:30am; dinner daily 6–10pm.

The Old Village Inn is popular because of its location, and because of its several low-ceilinged dining rooms with their heavy beams barely 6 feet from the floor, all decorated with old crockery; if the weather's fine, you'll want to dine in the inn's glassed-in conservatory amid the flowers and plants. At dinner, have the delicious lobster bisque to start, then a dish such as seafood imperial or perhaps roast duckling; the fish-of-the-day is always a good choice. A small bar provides for the thirsty. The inn has started serving breakfast from 7:30 to 11:30am but no longer offers brunch on Sunday. You might even decide to stay here as the inn offers a handful of rooms.

EASY EXCURSIONS

Just south of Ogunquit is York, or "The Yorks," as the town actually consists of Old York, York Harbor, and York Beach. York Harbor, at the mouth of the York River, is a summer resort much like Ogunquit. York Beach is more honky-tonk, with amusements and snack shops.

What you come to see is **Old York Village,** a "living history museum" operated by the Old York Historical Society (tel. 363-4974). Settled by Europeans in 1624, Old York received a royal charter in 1639, the first English town in the country to have this privilege. The historical society has preserved six historic buildings. Guides explain the details of daily community, commercial, and family life in Old York from 1740 to 1940. The tours are run from mid-June through September, Tuesday through Saturday from 10am to 4pm. Tickets cost $6 for adults, $2.50 for children 6 to 16.

Take a look at the **Old Gaol,** built as a jail in the 1700s, now a museum of colonial artifacts administered by the Old York Historical Society (tel. 363-4974). Hours are 10am to 4pm Tuesday through Saturday, mid-June through September.

Jefferds Tavern (1750) and the **Old School House** (1745) are next door to one another, providing an authentic glimpse of two aspects of life over two centuries ago. The **Emerson-Wilcox House** (1740) dates from the same era, is now a museum.

Down at the water's edge is the **John Hancock Warehouse and Wharf,** once owned by the great patriot, who signed the Declaration of Independence with a signature so large the king could read it without his glasses. It now holds exhibits on the maritime industry.

Near Sewall's Bridge on the York River is the **Elizabeth Perkins House,** built in 1730 but preserved with Colonial revival furnishings.

Finally, you may want to visit the **Old York Cemetery.** It has a fascinating collection of old New England tombstones.

KITTERY

South of York is Kittery, which is best known as the outlet center of Maine with hundreds of shops on both sides of Route 1. Kittery is more popular than Freeport for its shopping because of the abundance of stores with designer labels.

If you drive along U.S. Route 1, you might get bogged down in traffic during the summer season, but you'll also be rewarded with fine shoreline restaurants and lobster pounds.

Where to Dine

CAPE NEDDICK LOBSTER POUND, U.S. 1, Tel. 363-5471.
  Cuisine: SEAFOOD. **Reservations:** Accepted for 5 or more.
$ **Prices:** Main courses $9–$12. MC, V.
  Open: Mon–Fri 5–9pm, Sat–Sun noon–9pm.
This waterside lobster pound and restaurant is just across the street from the Cape Neddick Campground and has views of the harbor. The restaurant has decks outside where you can enjoy the view and weather. The menu lists baked stuffed lobster, broiled scallops, reef and beef kabobs, and some teriyaki dishes.

2. KENNEBUNKPORT

30 miles (48km) NE of Portsmouth, 29 miles (47km) SW of Portland

GETTING THERE By Bus See the beginning of this chapter.

By Car Coming from the south, follow I-95 (the Maine Turnpike) to Exit 2 (Wells), then U.S. 1/Route 9 north to Kennebunkport. Coming from the north, take I-95 to Exit 3 (Kennebunk), then Route 9A east to Kennebunkport. Note that there are other settlements with similar names, including Kennebunk and Kennebunk Beach.

ESSENTIALS The **area code** is 207. The **Kennebunk Kennebunkport Chamber of Commerce,** P.O. Box 740, Kennebunk, ME 04043 (tel. 207/967-0857), maintains an Information Center at the intersection of Routes 9 and 35 in Lower Village, Kennebunk. Ask for a copy of their *Guide to the Kennebunks.*

The several communities with similar names—Kennebunk, Kennebunkport, Kennebunk Beach—are clustered together on the Maine coast and constitute one of the state's most popular vacation areas, particularly since they were put on the map by President Bush and his family.

Of the towns, Kennebunkport is perhaps the most interesting. As its name implies, Kennebunkport was the waterfront part of the Kennebunk area. It's been a resort for years, drawing both the well-to-do and the student crowd living on summer earnings. Prices for rooms and meals tend to be a bit high, but for most people the price is not so important so long as they can just find a room open in this delightful Maine town.

WHAT TO SEE & DO

Shops and galleries around Dock Square draw lots of shoppers who enjoy spending their time browsing.

Gooch's Beach is right at the southern end of Beach Street, on the western shore of the Kennebunk River; Kennebunk Beach is west of Gooch's, along the coast. These beaches are good for swimming, especially on very hot days (the water tends to the chilly), and for walking, thinking, or jogging on almost any day.

Be sure to take a drive or a walk along Maine Street for a look at Kennebunkport's fine old mansions. For a look at the rocky coast, go south on Ocean Avenue to Spouting Rock.

WHERE TO STAY

EXPENSIVE

AUSTIN'S INN—TOWN HOTEL, Dock Sq. (P.O. Box 609), Kennebunk port, ME 04046. Tel. 207/967-4241, or toll free 800/227-3809. 14 rms (all with bath). A/C TV
$ Rates: High season, $73 double. Off-season, $40 double. AE, DISC, MC, V. **Parking:** Free.

Austin's is for those who want to be smack in the middle of town, right next to Dock Square, Kennebunk River, and the dock. A new and modern hostelry within an older-style building; it's possible to fit three, four, or even five people in several of the rooms, which is good for traveling families to note. Ten rooms have air conditioning. There's free parking for guests on the dock right next to the hotel. A free limo will pick up guests at the Portland or Portsmouth, N.H., airport.

BREAKWATER, Ocean Ave., Kennebunkport, ME 04046. Tel. 207/967- 3118. 20 rms (all with bath). TV **Directions:** In Kennebunkport, turn left at traffic light, then go over drawbridge. Turn right at monument on to Ocean Ave. Follow Ocean Ave. to the hotel, on the right-hand side.
$ Rates: (including full breakfast): Mid-June to Columbus Day, $90–$135 double. Columbus Day to mid-June, rates are 25%–30% lower and include continental breakfast. AE, MC, V. **Parking:** Free, on property.

The situation at the Breakwater is excellent—the open sea is right next door. Prices vary, the cheaper rooms being in the Breakwater building, the more expensive ones in the Riverside building, which is open year round and is more modern and, well preferable.

For dinner, the Breakwater has one of the best restaurants around (see below).

THE CAPTAIN JEFFERDS INN, Pearl St. (P.O. Box 691), Kennebunk port, ME 04046. Tel. 207/967-2311. 12 rms, 3 suites (all with bath). **Directions:** In Kennebunkport, turn left at traffic light, then go over drawbridge. Turn right at monument on to Ocean Ave. Go 5 short blocks, turn left on to one-way street, then another left to corner. Look for white fence.
$ Rates: (including full breakfast): $85–$125 double; $135–$145 suite for two. Minimum stay 2 nights July–Oct. MC, V. **Parking:** Free, on premises. **Closed** Nov and Jan–Mar.

This inn is one of those old sea captains' houses so immaculately restored that it made the cover of *House Beautiful;* the owners have added unusual antiques, lots of them and comfortable furnishings. There's an antique shop on the premises and another nearby under the same ownership. Children over 10 are welcome as are pets. Beside being everything a quaint inn should be, the Captain Jefferds is just off Ocean Avenue, walking distance to everything in town.

CAPTAIN LORD MANSION, at Pleasant and Green Sts. (P.O. Box 800), Kennebunkport, ME 04046. Tel. 207/967-3141, or toll free 800/522-3141. Fax 207/967-3172. 24 rms (all with bath). **Directions:** In Kennebunkport, turn left at traffic light, then over drawbridge. Turn right at monument on to Ocean Ave., and look for the mansion on the left-hand side after several blocks.

$ Rates: (including breakfast): May–Dec, $79–$199 double. Jan–Apr, rates are $20–$50 less. Children over 6 welcome. MC, V. **Parking:** Free.

Built in 1812 by a naval captain whose sailors were blockaded in Kennebunk Harbor by the British, Lord put his men to work on the mansion, and they did an impressive job. Today in this guesthouse there are antiques everywhere, and working fireplaces in most of the rooms. Driving from Dock Square down Ocean Avenue, keep glancing to your left and soon you'll see the stately yellow mansion topped by its cupola/observatory at the back of a rich greensward a block long: Captain Lord meant this first sight of the mansion to be impressive, and it certainly is.

MAINE STAY INN AND COTTAGES, 34 Maine St. (P.O. Box 500AF), Kennebunkport, ME 04046. Tel. 207/967-2117, or toll free 800/950-2117. 17 rms (all with bath). TV

$ Rates: (including full breakfast): Mid-June to mid-Oct, $85–$135 single or double. Off-season, packages available. AE, MC, V. **Parking:** Free.

Only a short walk from town, this charming place is surrounded by gardens and lofty trees. Though the rooms, including two suites, are equipped with all the modern conveniences, the spirit—and the welcome (tea is served of guests at 4pm)—befits a cozy inn. The cottages are clean, tidy, bright, and a good value; some have a working fireplace.

MODERATE

CHETWYND HOUSE, Chestnut St., Kennebunkport, ME 04046. Tel. 207/967-2235. 4 rms (2 with bath). **Directions:** Take the second left off Ocean Ave.; the street is not marked, but Chetwynd House is a short distance up on the left, and is marked clearly by a sign.

$ Rates: (including breakfast): Peak season, $110 double. Off-season, $59–$89 double. MC, V. **Parking:** Free.

Of Kennebunkport's guesthouses, certainly the most pristine is the Chetwynd, which is immaculately clean, with fine wide-board floors of a rich honey color, and very decent furnishings, including many four-poster beds. Extra pleasures at the Chetwynd House include tea and cakes; and here you're only 2 blocks from Dock Square and the center of town. This year marks the B&B's twentieth anniversary.

GREEN HERON, Ocean Ave. (P.O. Box 2578), Kennebunkport, ME 04046. Tel. 207/967-3315. 10 rms (all with bath). A/C TV **Directions:** In Kennebunkport, turn left at traffic light, then over drawbridge. Turn right at monument on to Ocean Ave., and drive until you see the house on the left-hand side.

$ Rates: (including breakfast): $64–$110 double. No credit cards. **Parking:** Free. **Closed:** Jan.

The Green Heron has been a dependable Kennebunkport hostelry for years and years. This nice old house and cottage is owned by Charles and Elizabeth Reid who have converted it into guest rooms with simple and comfortable furnishings. The beaches are within walking distance and there's a cheery breakfast room with lots of big windows overlooking the water.

WELBY INN, Ocean Ave. (P.O. Box 774), Kennebunkport, ME 04046.

Tel. 207/967-4655. 7 rms (all with bath). **Directions:** In Kennebunkport, turn lef
at traffic light, then over drawbridge. Turn right at monument on to Ocean Ave., and
continue to the inn.

$ Rates: (including breakfast): $60–$95 double. Children over 10 welcome. AE
MC, V. **Parking:** Free.

Located on Ocean Avenue, this inn can be recognized by its handsome
hand-painted tile signboard out front. One of the owners, Betsy Rogers-Knox
is the faïence artist who did the tiles for the sign, as well as those for all the
private bathrooms, and many of the paintings in this graceful old converted summer
cottage. The covered patio in front is new.

WHERE TO DINE

The cheapest way to have a lobster dinner is to wander down to the lobster pound
Although many restaurants have appropriated the name "Lobster Pound," a rea
pound is simply the place where the live lobsters are kept in saltwater vats until a
customer comes and buys them. Most lobster pounds these days have a few simpl
cooking facilities, and will boil up the lobsters, provide salad and french fries, butte
and salt and a paper plate, and charge just a little above the price of a live lobster
There are several such lobster pounds in Kennebunkport, where a cooked lobster wil
cost between $10 and $14, depending on size and season.

ARUNDEL WHARF, 43 Ocean Ave. Tel. 967-3444.
Cuisine: SEAFOOD/STEAK. **Reservations:** Required.
$ Prices: Appetizers $3–$6; main courses $9–$17; lunch $3–$9. DC, MC, V.
Open: Daily 11:30am–11:30pm. **Closed:** Nov–Mar.

As you walk across the parking lot to the restaurant, the gulls will be squealin
overhead; as you enter, you'll see a modern back deck, a beamed ceiling, an
several windows with water views, for the Arundel is indeed on a wharf by th
Kennebunk River. The staff here are young and friendly, and for lunch they mostl
serve sandwiches with a few platters offered, but for dinner you can have a boile
lobster, steak teriyaki, broiled haddock, or even lobster pie.

The restaurant's name comes from the fact that Kennebunkport was once name
Arundel, after England's earl of Arundel; in fact, it bore that name all through th
better part of its maritime prominence, changing it only in 1821.

THE BREAKWATER, Ocean Ave. Tel. 967-3118.
Cuisine: SEAFOOD/BEEF. **Reservations:** Required. **Directions:** In Kenne
bunkport, turn left at traffic light, then over drawbridge. Turn right at monument o
to Ocean Ave. Follow Ocean Ave. to the hotel, on the right-hand side.
$ Prices: Appetizers $4.25–$5.50; main courses $10–$17; meals $25–$40. AE
MC, V.
Open: May–June and Sept–Oct, dinner daily 6–9pm. July–Aug, dinner dail
5:30–10pm.

A local favorite, the dining rooms are elegant without being overly formal, and the su
porch—which is a dining room—affords a beautiful view of the sea. You can order
beef kebab or baked haddock; the broiled scallops are popular. The delicacie
proceed to swordfish and roast prime rib, with the lobster clambake priced accordin
to the day's market. Have reservations, but be sympathetic when you're told tha
specific tables can't be reserved (the ones with the sea view are the hot ones).

OLDE GRIST MILL, 1 Mill Lane. Tel. 967-4781, or toll free 800/27-GRIST.
Cuisine: SEAFOOD/STEAK. **Reservations:** Recommended on weekends.
$ Prices: Appetizers $4–$9.25; main courses $13–$27; dinner $30–$40. AE, DC
MC, V.
Open: Apr–July 4 and Labor Day–Oct, dinner Tues–Sun 5:30–9pm. Ju
4–Labor Day, dinner daily 5:30–9pm.

Dating from 1749, the Olde Grist Mill is listed in the National Register of Historic Places. It overlooks an inlet of the Kennebunk River, where it is set back from the street on its own parklike grounds. Seafood is king, of course, but for a change of pace there's also baked stuffed shrimp macadamia and sirloin steak au poivre.

WHITE BARN INN, Beach St. Tel. 967-2321.
  Cuisine: MODERN AMERICAN/REGIONAL. **Reservations:** Recommended.
$ **Prices:** Appetizers $6.50–$10; main courses $21.50–$29; meals $50–$65. AE, MC, V.
  Open: Dinner daily 6–9:30pm. **Closed:** Mon–Tues Jan–Mar.

This is one of Maine's most noted restaurants, highly respected and highly priced. The reputation is well deserved. Chef Edward Gannon prepares an array of modern American regional dishes. For starters you might have the cream of red pepper soup with diced fennel and a lemon-scented whipped crème fraîche ($6.50), or marinated tenderloin of lamb with garlic confit, a salad of assorted endives and a roasted tomato oil. Main courses include lightly grilled native salmon with sliced spring leeks, grilled onion and an orange basil oil, or steamed Maine lobster nestled on fresh fettucine with carrots and ginger in a Thai-inspired honey-and-sherry vinegar sauce. Beach Street is parallel to Ocean Avenue but across the inlet from it, to the south. If in doubt, ask for the St. Anthony Monastery; the White Barn's very near, on the other side of the street. The accommodations here are equally lovely and expensive.

AN EASY EXCURSION

Three miles northeast of Kennebunkport along Route 9, on the shore, is the village of **Cape Porpoise.** This charming little bit of Maine coastal life is a vacation haven for a small, knowledgeable few. Not fancy, not crowded, it has only a few craft shops, a few eateries, a few guesthouses, and a lot of Maine atmosphere. For pretty views of the sea, drive out and head for the pier. A brass plaque on a rock atop the sand hill there bears this legend: "August 8, 1782, a British ship of 18 guns attacked a small force of inhabitants gathered on Goat Island and was driven away by severe musket fire, losing 17 men. James Burnham of this town was killed. This tablet erected by the Maine State Council, Daughters of the American Revolution, August 8, 1921."

Well, not an awful lot exciting has happened in Cape Porpoise since that signal victory, and it's just as well, for the quiet is what makes it nice.

WHERE TO STAY

OLD GARRISON HOUSE, Pier Rd., Cape Porpoise, ME 04014. Tel. 207/967-3522. 3 rms (1 with bath).
$ **Rates:** $40 single without bath; $60 twin without bath, $65 twin with bath. No credit cards. **Parking:** Free. **Closed:** Mid-Oct to May.
This ivory-colored guest house dates back to 1730 and affords a view of the tidal cove in front and marshland in back.

WHERE TO DINE

NUNAN'S LOBSTER HUT, Mills Rd. (Rte. 9 East), Cape Porpoise. Tel. 967-4362.
  Cuisine: SEAFOOD. **Reservations:** Not accepted. **Directions:** Follow Route 9 East to the restaurant, on the right-hand side.
$ **Prices:** Dinner $12–$20. No credit cards.
  Open: Dinner daily 5–9pm.
Nunan's is an unprepossessing low-roofed shack of a place, where you can order boiled lobster, steamed clams, salads, homemade pies, beer, and wine. Some patrons return night after night. Authentic, real Maine coastal dining—that's Nunan's.

3. PORTLAND

108 miles (174km) NE of Boston, 161 miles (258km) SW of Bar Harbor

GETTING THERE   By Plane   Portland International Jetport is served by numerous national airlines.

By Bus   See the beginning of this chapter.

By Car   Follow I-95 to I-295, which makes a loop through downtown Portland.

ESSENTIALS   The **area code** is 207. The **Convention & Visitors Bureau of Greater Portland Information Center,** 305 Commercial St., Portland, ME 04101 (tel. 207/772-5800; fax 207/874-9043), on the waterfront, can fill you in on Portland life.

Cities in Maine have never had a reputation for chic or avant-garde ambience because Maine is a rural state, and it's the farmlands, woodlands, and coastal industries, such as lobstering, that count. But Portland, the state's largest city and its transportation hub and business center, may be changing all that. The Civic Center draws sports events, conventions, and big-name entertainers, and its revitalized waterfront area, known as the Old Port Exchange, is now even more attractive than it was in its Victorian heyday when the railroads, the huge sailing fleet, and the trade in lumber and fish made Portland what it is.

In Portland, you can visit the city's colonial, Early American, and Victorian landmarks, browse through the Portland Museum of Art, or take a cruise in Portland Harbor or Casco Bay. Portland is also the American end of the Prince of Fundy Cruises, which will take you and your car to Yarmouth, Nova Scotia, on an 11-hour overnight cruise.

WHAT TO SEE & DO

BOATS & CRUISES

Portland is the prime dock for Casco Bay and indeed northern New England, and you can climb aboard a boat with your car or without, for a few hours or overnight. Here are the major lines.

Casco Bay Lines, Commercial and Franklin Streets (tel. 207/774-7871), will take you (but not your car) over to Bailey's Island in summer. While on the 5½-hour cruise, you'll be told all about the island's history and its geologic features, plus lots of Portland and Casco Bay lore. On a sunny day, this is a very fine way to "take the air." The price for this cruise is $12.75 for adults, $6 for children. Other cruises are a bit shorter and a bit cheaper: There's a year-round sunset cruise to the islands (2½ hours), a seasonal music cruise around Casco Bay (3 hours), plus other seasonal runs, and the year-round cruise on the United States Mail boat, which goes to six of the Calendar Islands (3 hours).

May through October on most days, the **MS Scotia Prince** leaves Portland in the evening for Yarmouth, Nova Scotia, on an 11-hour overnight cruise. Return sailings from Yarmouth are in mid- or late morning. The ship provides satisfactory cabin accommodations, buffet and à la carte dining, mediocre live entertainment, a casino, and duty-free shopping. The ship was designed for interior use and is not built for much outdoor use. The wind on the crossing is brisk and cool, even in August, and there are no lounge chairs. The overnight crossing is a pleasant experience for those with cabins, which are at a premium in summer, so plan ahead. Day cabins (for the Yarmouth-to-Portland segment) are inexpensive and worth the extra tab. Current high season (late June to late September) prices for the cruise are from $75 per adult, half price for children ages 5 to 14 accompanied by an adult, and free for children under 5. The fare for a car is normally $98. A cabin for two costs in the range of $35 to $165. A family of four can easily spend $350 one-way. But there are several special fares that might suit your needs and will save you money. Be sure to call Prince of Fundy Cruises for latest fares, schedules, and other particulars; credit cards are accepted for passage. In Portland, call 207/775-5616; elsewhere in Maine call toll free 800/482-0955; 800/341-7540 in other states and Canada. In Yarmouth, Nova Scotia, call 902/742-3411.

SIGHTS

WADSWORTH-LONGFELLOW HOUSE, 485 Congress St. Tel. 772-1807.

This boyhood home of poet Henry Wadsworth Longfellow was built in 1785–86 by the poet's maternal grandfather, Gen. Peleg Wadsworth. The house now holds furnishings that once belonged to the famous Wadsworths and Longfellows, as well as many other period pieces. If you happen to be in town in mid-December, "Holidays at Henry's" is a warm and wonderful visit celebrating Christmas from a bygone era. There's a beautiful garden, and the Maine Historical Society, which received the bequest of the house in 1901, is located right next door.

Admission: $3 adults, $1 children under 12.

Open: June–Columbus Day weekend, Tues–Sat 10am–4pm. **Directions:** Follow Rte. 22, which leads to Congress St., to the house. **Closed:** Mid-Oct to May.

TATE HOUSE, 1270 Westbrook St. Tel. 774-9781.

The Maine forest was for a long time the prime source of masts for the British navy, and the man who managed the whole trade was George Tate, who had this house built in 1755.

Admission: $3 adults, $1 children under 12.

Open: July to mid-Sept, Tues–Sat 10am–4pm, Sun 1–4pm. May–June and mid-Sept to Oct, by appointment. **Directions:** Go southwest on Congress St. for 3¼ miles, cross the stream, and turn left on Westbrook St., very near Portland Jetport.

VICTORIA MANSION (Morse-Libby House), 109 Danforth St. Tel. 772-4841.

Built between 1858 and 1860, the Victoria Mansion has fascinating Victorian decorations and many original furnishings. It's the headquarters of the Victoria Society of Maine. If you're a Victoriana fan, this is a stop not to be missed.

Admission: $4 adults, $1.50 children 6–18.

Open: June–Labor Day, Tues–Sat 10am–4pm, Sun 1–4pm. Sept, Tues–Sat 10am–1pm, Sun 1–4pm.

PORTLAND MUSEUM OF ART, 7 Congress Sq. Tel. 773-2787.

Particularly strong are the collections of 19th- and 20th-century American art relating to Portland and to Maine, with paintings by Andrew Wyeth, Winslow Homer, and Edward Hopper. Highlights include the Joan Whitney Payson Collection featuring Renoir, Degas, Monet, Picasso, and other masters. The building was designed by I. M. Pei in 1983.

Admission: $3.50 adults, $2.50 students and seniors, $1 children 6–18, free for children under 5. Free Sat 10am–noon.

Open: Tues–Thurs 10am–9pm, Fri–Sat 10am–6pm, Sun noon–5pm.

BACK COVE, Baxter Blvd.

Here's a treat that won't cost you a cent. "The Boulevard" as it is known locally, is a popular rendezvous with its 3½-mile jogging track around Back Cove. Since the city extended the walkway over Tukey's Bridge and adjoining the interstate, walkers, joggers, cyclists, and other outdoors enthusiasts can make the circle trip as fast or as leisurely as they like. The area is well lit and scenic with the shoreline all the way around. Parking is located on one side at Payson Park and on the other by the rugby field. From April through November you'll find windsurfers in the cove and in winter cross-country skiers on the walking path. There are even exercise stations along the way.

WHERE TO STAY

The city has a few lodging places downtown, but many visitors, especially those here on business, stay in motels near Exit 8 or Exit 7 at the Maine Mall; both exits are off the Maine Turnpike.

EXPENSIVE

POMEGRANATE INN, 49 Neal St., Portland, ME 04102. Tel. 207/772-1006, or toll free 800/356-0408. 8 rms (all with bath). **Directions:** From Longfellow Square go up Pine St. to Neal St. and turn left; inn is on left.
$ Rates: (including full breakfast): $95–$125 double. AE, MC, V. **Parking:** Free on street.

In an ideal West End setting, this inn is a wonderful find for couples who appreciate warm surroundings and enjoy exploring. The fine detail work is exceptional as displayed in the faux-marbre woodwork and painted hardwood floor. Rooms feature four-poster beds, period furniture, designer fabrics, and Oriental carpets. New is a garden suite.

PORTLAND REGENCY, 20 Milk St., Portland, ME 04101. Tel. 207/774-4200, or toll free 800/727-3436. Fax 207/775-2150. 95 rms (all with bath). A/C MINIBAR TV TEL
$ Rates: $95–$140 single or double. AE, DC, DISC, MC, V. **Parking:** Valet, $5 per day.

A few steps from the port district and the commercial center of town is the Portland Regency, a new hotel located in a fine old waterfront building that was constructed in 1895 as an armory. The guest rooms are decorated in Early American reproductions not exactly accurate to the hotel's age, but very nice nonetheless. This is Portland's most luxurious downtown hostelry. Services include a revamped restaurant, bar, excellent health club with aerobics, and room service.

SONESTA PORTLAND HOTEL, 157 High St., Portland, ME 04101. Tel. 207/775-5411, or toll free 800/SONESTA. Fax 207/775-0148. 204 rms (all with bath). A/C TV TEL
$ Rates: $95–$110 single; $110–$135 double. AE, CB, DC, DISC, MC, V. **Parking:** Free.

In city center, walking distance to the museum, civic center, and Old Port district, is the renovated Eastland Hotel, a weak link in this otherwise strong chain of hotels. (It just doesn't have the pizzazz the others have.) Rates include hot buffet breakfast. Guests have use of two restaurants, two bars, and a limited fitness room. Free shuttle is provided to Jetport. Ask the hotel about weekend packages when you call for reservations.

BUDGET

SUSSE CHALET HOTEL, 340 Park Ave., Portland, ME 04102. Tel. 207/871-0611, or toll free 800/258-1980. Fax 207/871-8243. 105 rms (all with bath). A/C TV TEL **Directions:** Take Exit 5A from I-295, go right off the ramp on to Congress St., take second left onto Marston St., which leads you to Park Ave.
$ Rates: (including continental breakfast): $45–$55 single; $50–$65 double. AE, CB, DC, MC, V. **Parking:** Free.

This representative of the New England budget chain is 1 mile from downtown Portland, and has an outdoor swimming pool, as well as those familiar simple bu serviceable guest rooms with remote-control TV featuring free HBO and ESPN channels. No-smoking and wheelchair-accessible rooms are available as well.

SUSSE CHALET SAVER MOTEL, 1200 Brighton Ave. (I-95 Exit 8), Portland, ME 04102. Tel. 207/774-6101, or toll free 800/258-1980. Fax 207/772-8697. 132 rms (all with bath). A/C TV TEL **Directions:** Take Exit 8 from I-95.

$ Rates: (including continental breakfast): $45–$55 single or double. AE, CB, DC, MC, V. **Parking:** Free.

This motel also has a pool, but its highway location makes it even cheaper than its sibling establishment (see above). Continental breakfast comes with your room, restaurants are only a few steps away, and your room TV features free HBO, CNN, and ESPN channels.

WHERE TO DINE

The renaissance of Portland's waterfront district has given rise to numerous restaurants in recent years, and a short walk through the tidy and picturesque restored blocks of Fore, Exchange, Middle, and Moulton Streets will reveal interesting and moderately priced places for snacks, meals, or relaxing drinks.

BAKER'S TABLE, 434 Fore St. Tel. 775-0303.
  Cuisine: AMERICAN. **Reservations:** Recommended on weekends.
$ Prices: Appetizers $4–$9; main courses $10–$18; meals $25–$30; special lunch $13. AE, MC, V.
  Open: Lunch daily 11:30am–5:30pm; dinner Sun–Thurs 6–10pm, Fri–Sat 6–10:30pm.

At this elegant cafeteria, complete with adjoining bar, you pass through the line at lunchtime for soup and salad, and after you're seated, everything else you may need—more wine, coffee, or dessert—can be brought by a waiter. Salad here is almost a meal in itself, but with a big bowl of fish chowder it'll fill you for sure. The heartier and more expensive dinner menu (bouillabaisse, tournedos, or perhaps chicken provençale) is served amid linen-clad tables and sparkling stemware. There's soft background music, paintings by local artists, an interesting crowd, a well-stocked bar, and an espresso machine.

CAFE ALWAYS, 47 Middle St. Tel. 774-9399.
  Cuisine: NEW AMERICAN. **Reservations:** Recommended.
$ Prices: Main courses $10–$19. AE, MC, V.
  Open: Dinner Tues–Sat 5–10pm.

A colorful and stylish refuge of the designer set, Cafe Always has a menu as interesting as the clientele and the decor. Victorian wallpaper murals catch your eye; the white linen tablecloths are topped with butcher's paper. Chef-owner Cheryl Lewis might start you off with a grilled duck and wild-rice nori roll, then move on to a lobster and goat cheese burrito, followed by a salad of sun-dried tomatoes, garlic croutons, roasted pine nuts, fresh greens, and parmesan cheese. For dessert there's mocha pecan pie. All breads, desserts, ice creams, and sorbets are made right in the restaurant. The wine list, with more than 100 items, is heavy with California vintages.

PEPPERCLUB, 78 Middle St. Tel. 772-0531.
  Cuisine: AMERICAN/VEGETARIAN. **Reservations:** Not accepted.
$ Prices: Appetizers $3–$4.50; main courses $5.50–$10.95. No credit cards.
  Open: Dinner Sun–Thurs 5–9pm, Fri–Sat 5–10pm.

Imagine the look of a colorful Caribbean restaurant with the atmosphere of a San Francisco coffeehouse. That's the Pepperclub. The menu at this casual, fun restaurant is written on the blackboard and the daily specials might include vegetarian lasagne, fresh salmon, and homemade pies or cake. You can enjoy wine or beer with your meal.

THE SEAMEN'S CLUB, 1 Exchange St. Tel. 773-3333.

Cuisine: AMERICAN. **Reservations:** Required on weekends.
$ **Prices:** Appetizers $4–$9; main courses $4–$10; sandwiches $5. AE, CB, DC, MC, V.
Open: Daily 11am–11pm.

This is a good place to meet Portlanders who work in or near the waterfront, particularly at lunchtime, when sandwiches and the table d'hôte draw a crowd. Sunday brunch is good, too. At dinner, the menu is filled with the popular classics: baked stuffed shrimp, roast duckling with orange sauce, filet mignon, and lobster. Don't miss the fish or lobster chowder and roast turkey served on honey-wheat bread at lunch.

EASY EXCURSIONS SOUTH OF PORTLAND

TO CRESCENT BEACH Just south of Portland lies the charming town of **Cape Elizabeth;** about 3 miles from downtown Portland, pick up Route 77 for the speedy drive to the cape. Or you might elect to go along the Shore Road and stop at **Portland Headlight,** the first lighthouse in the United States commissioned by George Washington.

The grand headlight and park area is widely photographed, and the lawns of the old fort are a wonderful spot to have a picnic. There's also a small rocky beach for wading. On July 4th weekend, you can find the **Portland Symphony Orchestra** performing here with the magnificent headlight and beautiful Casco Bay Islands as a backdrop.

If you take Route 77, look for the Old Ocean House Road. Just down on the left is a fine old New England home with a long tree-lined drive where Bette Davis lived during her marriage to actor Gary Merrill.

About 7 miles from Portland, off Route 77, is the Two Lights Road. Drive a mile for the turnoff to **Two Lights State Park.** Another half mile down are the two lighthouses from which this area takes its name. Today, one working light is operated by the Coast Guard. The second, once owned by Gary Merrill, is a home. Don't miss the spectacular views from here; you might even go climbing on the rocks—but be careful of the high waves.

The **Lobster Shack Restaurant** is open between April and Columbus Day and provides local seafood in a rustic atmosphere. There are plenty of picnic tables outside, too. Expect a long line in summer—but it moves quickly.

Keep driving along the shore for a quick stop at **Kettle Cove,** a mile from Two Lights State Park. You can park for free here and walk along the beach into **Crescent Beach State Park.** Crescent Beach is popular with locals for romancing and is also the best nearby beach to Portland.

TO OLD ORCHARD BEACH Go to Pine Point Road, 15 minutes south of Portland, at U.S. Route 1. Less than a mile from the turnoff is the **Scarborough Marsh Nature Center,** operated by the Maine Inland Fisheries and Wildlife in conjunction with the Maine Audubon Society.

Daily programs are offered on the marshes by nature interpreters. You can even experience the marsh by canoe at night. Other programs include activities for children, wildflower lectures and tours, and canoe rentals. Call 883-5100 for more information.

Beyond the nature center is a little restaurant with fine take-out food. The **Portside Seafood Restaurant** offers clam cakes, fried clams, haddock, and fried Maine shrimp at reasonable prices.

At the bottom of the Pine Point Road (3 miles from the U.S. 1 turnoff) is the more pricey and commercial **Lobster Bake.** Here the road (also known as Route 9 west) turns south toward Old Orchard Beach. Pine Point Beach and Old Orchard melt together forming almost 7 miles of beachfront. Mid-rise condominiums are popping up these days.

You can still get a feel of decades gone by at the **Bailey's Lobster Pound** (tel 883-4571). Instead of turning right to Old Orchard, make a sharp left to Bailey's. The pound is open daily from 9am to about 6 or 7pm.

Old Orchard Beach is largely forgettable according to local folks. In the 1940s and 1950s, big bands came to play in the huge dance hall at the end of the pier. Over the years, fire claimed the pier piece by piece until it was little more than a stub. It was rebuilt but never regained its appeal.

The amusement section with rides and carnival atmosphere is popular with French Canadians who come by the thousands from Québec to soak up the sun. The beach is still in excellent condition and a popular rendezvous with teenagers from Portland to Portsmouth.

EASY EXCURSIONS NORTH OF PORTLAND

Most people head east from Portland, aiming at Camden, Boothbay, Bar Harbor, or the Canadian border. But an excursion up Routes 302 and 26, deep into Maine's forested hinterland, will bring you right up against North Woods life.

SEBAGO LAKE

Of Maine's hundreds of beautiful, clear lakes, Sebago Lake is one of the largest and most accessible. The eastern shore is somewhat developed with small villages, highway establishments, and the like; at the southern tip, the town of Sebago Lake is hardly more than a few dozen houses, two stores, and a gas station. But along the western shore in the area of the settlement called East Sebago there are a number of places that rent rooms and cabins, mingled among the larger private summer cabins and houses.

Although the roads that skirt the lake do have collections of cabins and houses here and there, it's hardly what you'd call thickly settled. You'll come across Sebago Lake State Park at the northern tip of the lake, where there's also a fine beach, picnic facilities, and a camping area. Although very busy in summer, the park is yours to enjoy with only a handful of others in early June or after Labor Day.

SABBATHDAY LAKE

Thirty miles north of Portland along Route 26 is the settlement of Sabbathday Lake, the last living Shaker community in the country. Founded in the 1700s, the Sabbathday Lake community still has a handful of active members who continue to work and live in the Shaker tradition. A shop selling community products, a museum, and a welcome center are open to visitors, though most of the other buildings are not. For more on Shaker history and beliefs, see "Stockbridge" in Chapter 8.

The spare white buildings of the village are plain but extremely well kept. Most notable is the Brick Dwelling House. In the fields near the village are several small, simple cemeteries, each with only one monument, bearing the legend "Shakers" and the dates of interment.

Up the road a few miles is the village of Poland Spring, which gained fame in the 1800s when a man was miraculously cured by its waters. The water from the spring has been bottled and shipped throughout the country since that time.

Continue north on Route 26 and you'll soon come to one of the prettiest towns in Maine, right at the edge of the White Mountains and a vast national forest.

BETHEL

Tucked away in the mountains on the western edge of Maine is the village of Bethel, on U.S. 2, the highway that heads west along the border of the White Mountains National Forest. There are two attractions: a well-known preparatory school called **Gould Academy** (founded 1836) and an excellent inn.

Should you have an extra hour to spend in Bethel, drop in at **Dr. Moses Mason House,** 15 Broad St. (tel. 824-2908), on the common, open in July and August, Monday to Friday from 10am to 4pm, weekends 1 to 4pm, and by appointment (call during business hours) the rest of the year. Moses Mason was a congressman during the Jackson administration, and had this Federal house built in 1813. Today it's furnished in antiques of the period and also holds several murals attributed to Rufus

Porter. There are research facilities, special exhibits, pictures, films, and a gift shop Admission costs $2 for adults, $1 for children.

North on Route 26, is **Grafton Notch State Park,** which has a pretty waterfal named Screw Auger. West on U.S. 2 is the White Mountains National Forest Between Gilead, Me., and Shelburne, N.H., the highway is lined with the famou: Shelburne birches. It is rare to see so many of these unusual, lovely trees in one spot For more on the national forest in New Hampshire, see Chapter 11.

Where to Stay

CHAPMAN INN, Broad and Church Sts. (P.O. Box 206), Bethel, ME 04217. Tel. 207/824-2657. 9 rms (3 with bath).
$ Rates: (including full breakfast): Winter, $75 double without bath, $85 double with bath. Summer, $55–$65 double; $25 bed in dormitory. AE, MC, V. **Parking** Free, on premises.

This has been a bed-and-breakfast place full of cheery, homey rooms since 1865. The white clapboard inn offers use of a game room, nearby pond with canoes, and private saunas as well. You can walk to golf, shops, and restaurants.

EN ROUTE TO BOOTHBAY HARBOR

North of Portland, the next major tourist destination is Boothbay Harbor. But you'l pass several interesting towns along the way, each with an attraction peculiar to Maine.

FREEPORT

This small Maine town is known all over the country and throughout the world as the headquarters of **L. L. Bean** (tel. 207/865-3111, or toll free 800/221-4221), the company that sells equipment, clothing, and supplies for outdoor activities. L. L. Bean has been in Freeport for decades, but in recent years the store's popularity ha burgeoned to epic proportions. A half dozen parking lots, administered by Bean employees, fill up quickly every day with cars bearing license plates from all over America and Canada. The large, attractive store, open 24 hours, is always mobbed during the day, and busy at night. The same shopping policy applies to the catalog—you can order 24 hours a day 7 days a week.

You're likely to find the rich and famous shopping here. Rock bands or other celebrities playing in Portland can usually be found here late at night following their performance. Don't forget to stop by Bean's trout pond in the men's department.

Bean's reputation was built by selling sturdy, good-quality items at reasonabl prices. The returns policy is absolute: If you find a Bean item unsatisfactory at an time, return it for a refund. Should you stop at Bean's, remember that the store carrie dozens of items for which there is no room in the catalog, and that there's also "factory store" for end-of-season and distressed merchandise. It's located acros Main Street in its own building. You should also know that Bean's will mail you packages home for you from the store—now with a charge. Bean's recently change the free-mailing policy. Some things do change after all. Keep it in mind if your trunk too full; take the item you've just bought to the customer service counter, and they'l take care of the rest. The store will charge $3.50 per address to ship orders both vi catalog and retail store.

The boom at Bean's has brought prosperity to Freeport, and a dozen othe shops—**Banana Republic, The Gap, Dansk, Anne Klein, Ralph Lauren Reebok,** you name it—have opened in order to profit from the press of Bean Buyers

Where to Stay

HARRASEEKET INN, 162 Main St., Freeport, ME 04032. Tel. 207/865 9377, or toll free 800/342-6423. 54 rms (all with bath).
$ Rates: $95–$185 single or double. AE, DC, DISC, MC, V. **Parking:** Free, o premises.

This is a favorite, a cheerful upscale country inn with all the modern conveniences of a hotel. Green shutters accent this white clapboard inn, well-respected for its restaurant and downstairs tavern. You'll find cozy fireplaces burning, afternoon tea, lovely rooms, and good Maine regional cooking. This is a treat for lunch of brunch even if you don't stay here. And it's a pine cone's throw from L. L. Bean.

Where to Dine

One of this town's most appealing aspects is the fact that there are almost as many restaurants as there are factory stores. They dot Main Street like umbrellas in the sand.

You'll find everything from **Ben and Jerry's** famous ice cream in the shadow of L. L. Bean's front door to the greasy spoon across the street. **McDonald's** serves up its hamburgers from inside the historic Gore House, a white clapboard house where you'll find carpeting in the dining room. Now that's progress! You might enjoy a hot pretzel from a street vendor or opt to sit on a bricked patio of a seafood takeout. This is prime real estate for people-watching.

JAMESON TAVERN, 115 Main St. Tel. 865-4196.
   Cuisine: SEAFOOD/STEAKS. **Reservations:** Recommended.
$ Prices: Appetizers $3–$7; main courses $10–$19; sandwiches $4.50. AE, DC, MC, V.
   Open: Lunch daily 11:30am–2:30pm; dinner daily 5–10pm in dining room, 11:30am–10pm or midnight, depending on season, in tavern.

Here is a colonial choice you won't want to pass up. Dating back to 1779, the inn takes pride in being the site where papers were signed separating Maine from Massachusetts. It has a colonial dining room in front and an equally inviting tavern restaurant in back. You'll find tombstone rubbings framed in the hallway. The locals love the tavern and you'll want to sample the mud pie or blackboard specials. It's local charm and easy to find—next door to Bean's.

OCEAN FARMS RESTAURANT, 23 Main St. Tel. 865-3101.
   Cuisine: SEAFOOD/STEAKS. **Reservations:** Recommended.
$ Prices: Appetizers $4–$7; main courses $4–$10 at lunch, $10–$20 at dinner. AE, MC, V.
   Open: Daily 7am–10:30pm.

The decor is knotty pine and the service is casual at breakfast and lunch but more formal at dinner. The menu is mostly seafood, but other items are always offered as well. The chef raves about the chocolate fudge cake.

BRUNSWICK

Surrounded by coastal resort towns, Brunswick is the cultural center of this part of Maine: Both Bowdoin College and Maine's only professional music theater are here. The Brunswick Music Theater (tel. 725-8769) is on the Bowdoin campus, and presents musical productions from mid-June through Labor Day each summer.

Much of Bowdoin's fame comes from the distinguished alumni who have spent their time in Brunswick and then moved on to fame and glory: Longfellow, Hawthorne, and Pres. Franklin Pierce were all Bowdoin graduates. The college is at Pine and College Streets, and free tours are available year round. While you're here, visit Bowdoin's art museum to see its collection of colonial works.

Where to Dine

STOWE HOUSE, 63 Federal St. Tel. 725-5543.
   Cuisine: STEAKS/SEAFOOD. **Reservations:** Recommended.
$ Prices: Appetizers $4–$7; main courses $10–$16.
   Open: Lunch Sun–Fri 11:30am–2:30pm; dinner daily 5:30–8:30pm.

Near Bowdoin College, this famous inn, where Marriet Beecher Stowe wrote *Uncle Tom's Cabin,* serves up regional cuisine in lovely, warm surroundings. Specialties include the broiled seafood sampler and veal médaillons sautéed with Maine crabmeat and white asparagus.

BATH

A 10-mile drive along U.S. 1 north from Brunswick brings you to Bath, a fine town of colonial and Federal houses built when Bath was a wealthy seaport and shipbuilding center.

To see these houses, take a drive down Washington Street and stop at no. 243, the headquarters of Bath's famous **Maine Maritime Museum** (tel. 443-1316). One admission ticket ($6 for adults, $2.50 for children 6 to 16, $16 for a family) admits you to the exhibit on the maritime history of Maine, the restored Percy & Small Shipyard and its buildings, the Apprentice Shop boatbuilding school, a lobstering exhibit (seasonal), and, when in port, a 142-foot fishing schooner. Just about everything you'd associate with the sea is represented in these exhibits: early fishing methods, shipbuilding, small boats, engines and steam yachts, lobstering, navigation, ship's models and paintings, sailors' memorabilia, and all sorts of coastal lore. There's even a play boat for children complete with crow's nest and a "cargo" of sand.

The 10-acre museum complex is along the river, with plenty of space for picnickers. Wear outdoor clothing and good shoes. You'll need several hours to see everything; or you can have your ticket validated for the next day also, at no extra charge. The museum is open daily from 9:30am to 5pm.

WISCASSET

Billing itself "the prettiest village in Maine," as you pass through the center of Wiscasset on U.S. 1 you can confirm this. As you cross the Sheepscot River toward Damariscotta, look south and note the two enormous hulks standing in the water. The four-masted schooners *Hesperus* and *Luther Little* once carried cargoes along the Atlantic coast. But the many-masted schooners (a few were even built with six masts!) were the last of a proud breed, replaced by the more reliable steamboats. These two relics of a romantic age sit forlorn in the mud, awaiting restoration or final destruction.

The best spot to eat here is probably **Le Garage** on Water Street (tel. 882-5409). With views of the old ships above, it sits on the Sheepscot River in a yellow clapboard building that was once a garage and before that a blacksmith's shop. Alan Dodge's eatery is open for lunch and dinner, and meals cost from $6 to $20. They are closed in January.

Directly across the street is the **Old Customs House** dating back to 1870. It houses a gift shop today with many fine items with a country flavor.

Off U.S. Route 1 on Route 27, north of Wiscasset, is **Edgecomb Pottery,** close to the Boothbay Harbor turnoff. The best pottery along the coast may be found here.

4. BOOTHBAY HARBOR

11 miles (18km) S of U.S. 1, 59 miles (95km) NE of Portland,
52 miles (84km) SW of Camden

GETTING THERE By Bus See the beginning of this chapter.

By Car Follow I-95 or U.S. 1 to Brunswick, then U.S. 1 to Bath and Wiscasset. East of Wiscasset take Route 27 south to Boothbay Harbor.

ESSENTIALS The **area code** is 207. Contact the **Boothbay Harbor Region Chamber of Commerce,** P.O. Box 356, Boothbay Harbor, ME 04538 (tel 207/633-2353), for information.

As you drive down Route 27 from U.S. 1, several miles from town you'll come to a seasonal information bureau, on the right. If it's closed, don't worry, for there's another one a bit farther along, right at the edge of town, and it's open year round.

North and east of Portland, the Maine coastline is a choppy succession of peninsulas, sea inlets, islands, and river outlets. The country here is beautiful, and vacation communities abound. Reaching many of these communities means driving down a peninsular road for quite a number of miles to the tip, and upon departure driving back up to U.S. 1—few bridges or causeways span the inlets or rivers.

Boothbay Harbor is the principal town in a region of vacation settlements that include Boothbay, Boothbay Harbor, East Boothbay, Southport, and Ocean Point. A book could be written on this region alone, and so recommendations have been limited to Boothbay Harbor itself, which is the center of the action.

WHAT TO SEE & DO

Wander down to the shore in town, and you'll see lots of signboards and ticket stands for the boats that operate on cruises out of Boothbay Harbor. Ticket prices range from about $10 to $15, and may include a search for seals, water birds, whales, and other marine life, or perhaps a clambake or a chicken bake afloat. When the moon is near full, special moonlight cruises are arranged. Cruises can be anywhere from 1 to 3 hours in length. Ask around to find a style, length, and price that's right for you. The Boothbay Harbor Region celebrates several festivals each year. Among them are the Fisherman's Festival, Windjammer Days, Antique Auto Days, Friendship Sloop Days, and the fall foliage festival.

A CLAMBAKE ON CABBAGE ISLAND

Go down to Fisherman's Wharf on Main Street, look for Pier 6, and climb aboard the MV *Argo* for a cruise out to Cabbage Island in Linekin Bay and a real Down East Maine-style clambake. Clams and lobsters are steamed amid seaweed the old-fashioned way and served up twice a day from Memorial Day through Labor Day. The *Argo* sails to the clambake Monday through Saturday at 12:45pm (returning by 3:15pm) and 5pm (returning before dark); on Sunday, departures are at 11:30am (returning by 2:45pm) and 1:30pm (returning by 4:45pm). The total cost for the clambake is $31.55 per person, and that includes the delightful round-trip boat cruise, a cup of fish chowder, two lobsters, steamed clams, corn on the cob, new Maine potatoes, and blueberry cake and coffee for dessert. The scenic island has games, paths, and sitting areas for you to enjoy as well. Call 633-7200 for clambake reservations at least ½ hour before sailing time.

MONHEGAN ISLAND

The *Balmy Days* is a sail-assisted motor craft that makes the run 16 miles out to sea to Monhegan Island, Maine's famous windswept resort-at-sea. One trip out, leaving in the morning, and one trip back from the island, leaving in mid-afternoon, are made daily. You cannot stay overnight on the island without previous hotel reservations, but the *Balmy Days*'s schedule allows you to have between 3 and 4 hours on the island if you go out and back in 1 day. Monhegan is noted for its interesting paths and walks, and that's mostly what there is to do. A one-way ticket to Monhegan Island costs $15 for adults; children under 10 are charged $15 round-trip. While it's out at Monhegan, the *Balmy Days* makes one run around the island so you can see the rugged cliffs, and this costs $1 extra. By the way, you can easily hike all there is to hike (pretty much) in the 4-hour stay on Monhegan. New this year is a supper cruise ($16 adults, $12 children), including a chicken dinner. For detailed information, call 633-2284.

A MUSEUM

BRICK HOUSE ART GALLERY, Oak St. Tel. 633-2703.
This museum has three shows of local artists each season, plus paintings on view

daily. The handsome old brick house was built in 1807 of bricks brought from England as ballast in ships which came to carry away Maine lumber—in such a forest-rich region, this brick house is a curiosity. It's in the center of the village, near McKown Hill.

Admission: Free.
Open: Mon–Sat 11am–5pm, Sun noon–5pm.

WHERE TO STAY

I've chosen mostly establishments in town or in special locations outside. The Boothbay region does have a number of bed-and-breakfast houses, most off the beaten track. For information, check (or call) the information booth.

IN TOWN

ADMIRAL'S QUARTERS INN, 105 Commercial St., Boothbay Harbor ME 04538. Tel. 207/633-2474. 8 rms (all with bath). TV
$ Rates: (including morning coffee and light breakfast): $75–$90 single or double MC, V. **Parking:** Free. **Closed:** Nov–Apr.
This large, old, white-clapboard sea captain's house built around 1820 commands marvelous views of the harbor. Upper and lower sun decks allow you to take in the view from each room.

ANCHOR WATCH BED AND BREAKFAST, 3 Eames Rd., Boothbay Harbor, ME 04538. Tel. 207/633-2284. 4 rms (all with bath), 1 suite.
$ Rates: (including continental breakfast): $65–$88 double. MC, V. **Parking:** Free.
Here is a charmer, small and intimate and run by friendly folks. Country-flavored rooms have views of the water and lawn sloping down to the shore. The coffee pot is always on and you're just a short walk to the local shops for exploring.

CAPTAIN SAWYER'S PLACE, 87 Commercial St., Boothbay Harbor, ME 04538. Tel. 207/633-2290. 10 rms (all with bath). TV
$ Rates: (including continental breakfast): Mid-May to mid-Oct, $60–$95 double MC, V. **Parking:** Free.
Run by Kim Reed-Upham and sons Nick and Aaron, this guesthouse is a classic yellow-and-white Boothbay Harbor residence—complete with rooftop "observatory." A small patio overlooks the pedestrians on Main Street, and the house's long wraparound veranda overlooks everything. The bright and tidy rooms have some period furnishings and Martha Washington bedspreads. The location couldn't be any better, nor the welcome warmer.

HILLTOP HOUSE, c/o the Mahrs, McKown Hill, Boothbay Harbor, ME 04538. Tel. 207/633-2941 or 633-3839. 5 rms (3 with bath).
$ Rates: (including breakfast): $36 double without bath, $47 double with bath $53–$74 family unit. No credit cards. **Parking:** Free.
Mrs. Mahr, a real Maine native, will rent you a homey room in her house which is located at the top of McKown Hill, in town. The porch, and its marvelous view, are yours to enjoy anytime you like. Homemade muffins and breads add a nice touch to the complimentary breakfast.

TOPSIDE, McKown Hill, Boothbay Harbor, ME 04538. Tel. 207/633-5404. 27 rms (all with bath). TEL
$ Rates: (including morning coffee): $95 single or double. MC, V. **Parking:** Free. **Closed:** Oct to mid-May.
Topside says it all about this charming hilltop house just 2 blocks from the center of town atop McKown Hill. Several fine old houses have been meticulously restored

down to the marble fireplaces (in the living rooms) and stocked with antiques for the pleasure of Topside's guests. All rooms have refrigerators, microwave ovens, and coffee percolators. And what a view—from many of the rooms or simply from a lawn chair in the midst of Topside's lush green grass, where you can take it all in as the cool breezes waft up from the harbor. Although there are other places on McKown Hill, Topside is smack at the top. As the number of rooms is limited, be sure to write or call well in advance for reservations.

NEARBY

FIVE GABLES INN, Murray Hill Rd., East Boothbay, ME 04544. Tel. 207/633-4551, or toll free 800/451-5048. 15 rms (all with bath). **Directions:** Follow Rte. 96 east to Murray Hill Rd. and the inn.
$ Rates: (including full breakfast): $80–$120 double. MC, V. **Parking:** Free. **Closed:** Dec–Apr.

All the rooms in this superbly restored old Maine costal inn have a wonderful view of Linekin Bay; five have a working fireplace. After your buffet breakfast here, enjoy the view from the large veranda, or take the sun on the lawn, or cross the road for a swim. Bustling Boothbay Harbor is 3 miles away; here in East Boothbay, it's much calmer and quieter.

LAWNMEER INN AND MOTEL, Rte. 27, Southport, ME 04569. Tel. 207/633-2544, or toll free 800/633-7645. 32 rms (all with bath). TV **Directions:** From Rte. 1, take Rte. 27 south to West Boothbay, across the bridge to Southport Island.
$ Rates: $45–$120 double. MC, V. **Parking:** Free, on property. **Closed:** Mid-Oct to mid-May.

A short drive from Boothbay Harbor, across the drawbridge in Southport, the Lawnmeer offers motel-style rooms with modern conveniences. Most rooms have water views, decks, or both. Breakfast and dinner are served during set hours. New on the menu are steamed clams and pasta dishes. In a quiet country setting, this is the place to go if you need to get away from it all.

OCEAN POINT INN, Shore Rd. (P.O. Box 409), East Boothbay, ME 04544. Tel. 207/633-4200. 61 rms (all with bath). TV **Directions:** Follow Rte. 96 east through East Boothbay to the end of the road at Ocean Point.
$ Rates: $73–$107 double. DISC, MC, V. **Parking:** Free. **Closed:** Mid-Oct to mid-May.

Way down at Ocean Point by the lighthouse, on the southern tip of a peninsula overlooking the harbor mouth is a collection of about 100 cottages, all in a serene location. Ocean Point is the only commercial establishment here, and it offers a choice of the inn, the motel, the lodge, or a number of cottages. All rooms are decorated in modern resort style with electric heat, and each guest has access to the outdoor heated swimming pool. The Ocean Point has its own restaurant open for breakfast and dinner. Meal service may vary from continental breakfast to full breakfast and from five days a week to daily service depending on the season, so check ahead. It is just over 6 miles to town, where many restaurants are situated.

WHERE TO DINE

ANDREWS' HARBORSIDE RESTAURANT, at the footbridge. Tel. 633-4074.
Cuisine: AMERICAN/SEAFOOD. **Reservations:** Recommended for large parties.
$ Prices: Appetizers $3–$14; main courses $9–$15. MC, V.
Open: May to mid-Oct, daily 7:30am–9pm.

Andrews' offers mako-shark burgers, chowders, and a lobster roll that's not gigantic but is positively stuffed with succulent lobster meat—no filler. Tables are covered in nautical blue-and-white cloths, and you have your choice of an indoor dining room with lots of windows or screened-in porch, both with fine views of the harbor. A full bar and wine list is offered. For dessert, go downstairs to the Round Top Ice Cream booth beneath the terrace. At breakfast Andrews' is known for its homemade fresh cinnamon rolls.

CHOWDER HOUSE, in the Granary, 49 Townsend Ave. Tel. 633-5761.
   Cuisine: SEAFOOD. **Reservations:** Not accepted.
$ **Prices:** Appetizers $3–$9; main courses $11–$16; dinner $20–$30. DISC, MC, V.
   Open: Mid-June to early Sept, daily 11am–9pm.
A few steps from the center of Boothbay Harbor, down near the footbridge, is the Chowder House, where you can have a drink in the Loading Dock Lounge, a woody place filled with nautical paraphernalia, then eat in the dining room with its inside waterview room and outside terrace. The clam chowder and lobster stew are made fresh daily and are served with freshly baked bread. You might choose the lobster sandwich or seafood salad, but there's meat and fowl as well. Popular choices are the native scallops sautéed in wine and butter with shallots and parsley and surf-and-turf kebabs. The Chowder House has been family owned and run for 14 years.

ROCKTIDE, 45 Atlantic Ave. Tel. 633-4455 or toll free 800/762-8433.
   Cuisine: AMERICAN/SEAFOOD. **Reservations:** See below.
$ **Prices:** Appetizers $3–$8; main courses $11–$18; dinner $25–$35. MC, V.
   Open: Dinner daily 5:30–9pm.
Located across the bay from downtown Boothbay Harbor (use the footbridge) Rocktide is a big place with four dining areas. On the Seadeck, in the Chart Room and Buoy Room, you can dress as you like, and no reservations are taken; in the Dockside and Harborside Rooms diners should observe "jacket" formality, and reservations are taken. The menu is old New England: fried Maine shrimp, ocean scallops, seafood casserole, finnan haddie, New England lobster pie, or a fisherman's platter. But there are unexpected items as well, such as a kebab of shrimp, scallops, lobster, and swordfish and sole Duxelleois and roast duck. Every main course comes with rights to the salad bar, a popover, and rice or potato.

5. CAMDEN

85 miles (137km) NE of Portland, 77 miles (124km) W of Bar Harbor

GETTING THERE   By Bus   See the beginning of this chapter.

By Car   Follow U.S. 1 to Camden.

ESSENTIALS   The **area code** is 207. The **Rockport-Camden-Lincolnville Chamber of Commerce,** P.O. Box 919, Camden, ME 04843 (tel. 207/236-4404 fax 207/236-6252), maintains an information booth on the public landing in Camden where you can get a directory of the area and also a brochure describing the walking and bike tours of Camden and Rockport outlined by the Camden Historical Society. The tours point out all the most historic places, and tell you much about the town as well.

A small coastal town wedged between the salt waters of Penobscot Bay and a range of rocky hills, Camden has a population of barely 4,000—it's small, picturesque and manageable. Edna St. Vincent Millay came from these parts, but today Camden's chief claim to fame is that it is the home port for several two-masted schooners which take eager landlubbers for cruises along the Maine coast. The hills behind the town are included in the Camden Hills State Park, with campgrounds and picnic spots, and an auto road to the top of Mt. Battie, the highest hill of the range.

WHAT TO SEE & DO

If you have a car, drive north from town along U.S. 1 and follow the signs to the entrance to **Camden Hills State Park** and the auto road to the top of Mt. Battie. Besides the town itself, the drive up will afford you a view of the rocky hills, the countryside beyond, and of Penobscot Bay.

Camden's **Windjammer fleet** of schooners provides the adventurous with a very different vacation: dipping in and out of the myriad of small harbors and inlets along the Maine coast. Cruises usually leave on Monday and last a week; they cost about $400 to $450 per person, and space must be reserved in advance. New are the half-day and one- to three-day cruises ranging in price from $25 to $300. Write to the chamber of commerce (see above) for current lists of who's sailing, and what the cost will be.

Go southeast along Bay View Street a ways and you'll come to **Laite Memorial Park and Beach,** with picnic areas and restrooms as well as a nice, chilly Maine beach.

For the rest of your time in Camden, latch onto a copy of the walking tour brochure (mentioned above) put out by the Camden Historical Society, and stroll through the town to get the flavor of it.

From Rockland Ferry Terminal (tel. 207/596-2202), you can take a car-ferry to **Vinalhaven Island,** in Penobscot Bay, for a taste of island vacation life. The *Governor Curtis* (State Ferry Service, P.O. Box 645, Rockland, ME 04841) makes the 1½-hour run to Vinalhaven three times a day, and the return trip two times a day. On Sunday there are two sailings in each direction. You can also take a car-ferry to **North Haven Island** from here. The *Everett Libby* makes the 1¼-hour trip three times a day and the return trip two times a day.

WHERE TO STAY

Camden is not packed with places to stay, and that's part of its charm. Many people stay at the motels scattered along both sides of U.S. 1, north and south of town. Here, I'll mention the best inns and guesthouses right in town, within walking distance of everything.

EXPENSIVE

CAMDEN HARBOUR INN, 83 Bay View St., Camden, ME 04843. Tel. 207/236-4200. 22 rms (all with bath). **Directions:** When U.S. 1 turns left in the center of town, turn right to reach the inn.

$ Rates: (including breakfast): Mid-June to mid-Oct, $145–$185 double. 2-night minimum in summer. AE, DISC, MC, V. **Parking:** Free.

A nice old inn (1874) with white clapboards and beautiful views of Penobscot Bay, the Camden Harbour could be a model for the typical coastal Maine inn. Breakfast is served to guests and the public and dinner is served to everyone during the summer. The tavern is a gathering spot as well. Almost all the rooms have water views, eight have fireplaces, and eight have private patios. You can have cocktails or dinner on the nice Victorian veranda, which also has a fabulous view. Children over 12 are welcome.

NORUMBEGA, 61 High St., Camden, ME 04843. Tel. 207/236-4646. 12 rms (all with bath). **Directions:** From the center of town, go north along U.S. 1.

$ Rates: (including breakfast): $135–$395 double. AE, MC, V. **Parking:** Free.

This vast stone Victorian summer cottage dates from 1886, when it was built by inventor Joseph Stearns. Having improved telegraphy, Stearns grew rich on the proceeds, and built himself a veritable castle-mansion with rich woods, worked stone, and sumptuous furnishings, many of which survive. The game room is furnished with a pool table and television. Many of the guest rooms have fine views of Penobscot Bay. Children over 7 are welcome.

WHITEHALL INN, 52 High St. (P.O. Box 558), Camden, ME 04843. Tel. 207/236-3391. Fax 207/236-4427. 50 rms (45 with bath). TEL **Directions:** On Rte. 1, go just north of town center.

$ Rates: (including breakfast and dinner): High season, $128–$160 double. MC, V
Parking: Free, private lot.

The graceful old inn has been Camden's prime place to stay for almost a century, and is easily recognizable by its pillared porches. Camden's most famous daughter, Edna St. Vincent Millay, gave a reading here when she was just a girl. The decor is refined in both the public rooms and guest rooms. The mood in the dining room is semiformal (jackets for dinner). The hotel offers sport-fishing parties (the kitchen prepares fish caught by guests), a tennis court, shuffleboard, and Aqua sport boat.

MODERATE

BLUE HARBOR HOUSE, 67 Elm St., Camden, ME 04843. Tel. 207/236-3196, or toll free 800/248-3196. Fax 207/236-6523. 10 rms (all with bath).
$ Rates: (including full breakfast): $85–$125 double. AE, MC, V. **Parking:** Free
This friendly bed-and-breakfast guesthouse just a few blocks' walk south of the center of town, on U.S. 1, serves a full breakfast on the sun porch. Dinner is available by reservation only for $20 per person. In the separate carriage house (built 1806) are two suites for rent.

EDGECOMBE-COLES HOUSE, 64 High St., Camden, ME 04843. Tel. 207/236-2336. 6 rms (all with bath).
$ Rates (including breakfast): $105–$160 double. AE, DISC, MC, V. **Parking:** Free.
This huge turn-of-the-century summer cottage retains its earlier glory, with period furnishings filling the rooms and lovely views of the garden. The room with the king-size bed has a fireplace. Three rooms have ocean views and three have TVs.

GOODSPEED'S GUEST HOUSE, 60 Mountain St., Camden, ME 04843. Tel. 207/236-8077. 5 rms (1 with bath).
$ Rates: $45–$49 single; $72–$85 double; $135 suite for four. No credit cards.
Parking: Free.
This house, ½ mile up the hill on Route 52, has been beautifully redone and furnished with antiques by its owners, who provide a warm welcome and rooms with shared bath. Four rooms have sinks in the bedroom and one room has a private bath. A tiny deck, set with umbrella-shaded tables and chairs, allows you to enjoy the quiet of this location.

HAWTHORN INN, 9 High St., Camden, ME 04843. Tel. 207/236-8842. 10 rms (all with bath).
$ Rates: (including breakfast): $70–$110 single or double; $110–$225 suite. MC, V. **Parking:** Free.
This big Victorian house with a view of Camden Harbor is just a few minutes' walk north of the commercial district on U.S. 1, and has been carefully and lovingly restored—the large, airy rooms are furnished with antiques and there are Jacuzzis in the carriage-house rooms. You might enjoy breakfast on the outdoor deck while your children play nearby in the playground. Afternoon tea is served at 4pm.

MAINE STAY, 22 High St., Camden, ME 04843. Tel. 207/236-9636. rms (3 with bath).

$ Rates: (including full breakfast and afternoon tea): $47–$87 single; $57–$97 double. MC, V. **Parking:** Free, next to inn.

This big white house built in 1802 has very charming rooms with antiques and Oriental rugs, some of which share baths, and two pretty living rooms and a deck that overlooks the backyard. Located in the center of the historic district, the inn is about a 5-minute walk to the town center.

THE OWL AND THE TURTLE, 8 Bay View St., Camden, ME 04843. Tel. 207/236-9014. 3 rms (all with bath). A/C TV TEL **Directions:** Entering the commercial center northbound on U.S. 1, turn right onto Bay View St. when U.S. 1 turns left.

$ Rates: (including continental breakfast): $65–$70 single; $75–$80 double. MC, V. **Parking:** Free.

This is perhaps the strangest name for a guesthouse, but it is explained when one realizes that the building that houses the Owl and the Turtle Bookshop also houses a few very nice motel-type rooms, each with a marvelous view of the inner harbor. The Owl's rooms are nicely decorated, but there are so few of them you must reserve in advance by phone or mail.

SWAN HOUSE, 49 Mountain St., Camden, ME 04843. Tel. 207/236-8275. 6 rms (all with bath).

$ Rates: (including full breakfast): $80–$110 double. MC, V. **Parking:** Free, next to inn.

The fine Victorian house dates from 1870 and has six guest rooms, all with baths, in the house and the Cygnet Annex. It specializes in generous breakfasts. Nestled at the foot of Mt. Battie, the inn is next to a state park trail that leads to the summit.

WINDWARD HOUSE BED AND BREAKFAST, 6 High St., Camden, ME 04843. Tel. 207/236-9656. 6 rms (all with bath), 1 apartment.

$ Rates: (including breakfast): $65–$125 double. MC, V. **Parking:** Free.

Personal service and beautiful accommodations are a hallmark here. It is a delightful atmosphere with flowers and shrubs all around. Inside, fireplaces, Oriental rugs on hardwood floors, and antiques combine to make a stay here everything a Maine B&B experience should be. The room overlooking the garden in the back has a four-poster bed and skylights, and is particularly fine. Children over 10 are welcome.

WHERE TO DINE

CAPPY'S CHOWDER HOUSE, 1 Main St. Tel. 236-2254.
Cuisine: AMERICAN/SEAFOOD. **Reservations:** Not accepted.
$ Prices: Appetizers $6–$10; main courses $10–$18 at lunch, $18–$26 at dinner. MC, V.
Open: Daily 7:30am–midnight.

The two dining levels (the upstairs one with a water view and raw bar) have a rich nautical decor and an eclectic menu. The seafood—clam, fish, and lobster chowders, plates, salads—is excellent, plus there are burgers, daily fish specials, stir-fries, and steaks. You can get breakfast here as well. Downstairs is the bakery with fresh breads, doughnuts, and sandwiches. Management prides itself on the desserts, especially the crunch-a-nutter pie. Liquor is served at the bar, which provides a social center and quick-lunch place for many of the local yacht crews; tables and booths are for serious diners.

AN EASY EXCURSION TO ROCKPORT

A few minutes south of Camden is Rockport, a charming seaside town with a lovely harbor and the **Sail Loft Restaurant** (tel. 236-2330). Lunch and dinner are offered daily, and its reputation of more than 30 years stems in part from its blueberry muffin and clam chowder. The Sail Loft has a small bar tucked into one corner and views of the harbor from many tables in the restaurant.

6. CASTINE & BLUE HILL

These little villages, set apart on a peninsula in the Penobscot Bay, are gems. With only a few places to stay and to dine, these towns draw a steady crowd of summer regulars who come for the beauty, the seclusion, the quiet, the easy summer life. At the end of the section, I've also mentioned Deer Isle, which is south of Blue Hill.

CASTINE
20 miles (32km) S of Bucksport, 20 miles (32km) W of Blue Hill

GETTING THERE **By Bus** See the beginning of this chapter.

By Car Turn right onto Route 175 at Orland, east of Bucksport, and continue on Routes 166 and 166A to Castine.

ESSENTIALS The **area code** is 207. The **Castine Town Office** (tel. 207/326 4502) may be able to answer your questions.

In the winter of 1613, Sieur Claude de Turgis de la Tour founded a small trading post here among the Tarrantine people. The struggle for North America's forest, natural and maritime wealth was already beginning, and the French Fort Pentagoet founded by Turgis de la Tour would be conquered by the English in 1628. Treaty returned Pentagoet to France in 1635, and during the tumultuous period until 1676, the place changed hands many times. The British took it and called it Penobscot Fort; the French retook it and built the formidable Fort Saint Peter. At one time the village was the capital of all French Acadia (the lands in what is now Atlantic Canada). Even the Dutch coveted the fort, and ruled here from 1674 to 1676. In the latter year Baron de Saint Castin recaptured the town for France, and opened a trading station. Fortifications were strengthened, and despite raids by the British, the family of Baron de Saint Castin ruled over the town (now called Bagaduce) even after the wealthy baron himself returned to France, in 1703. By 1760, however, the fate of French North America was sealed, and Castin's Fort, or Bagaduce, was to be held by the British after that year.

English settlers brought new life to Bagaduce during the 1760s, and dissatisfaction boiled in the English colonies at this period. Some of the townspeople were loyal to the king, others sympathized—actively and passively—with the American revolutionaries. But in 1779 a British naval force came from Nova Scotia, intent on making the town safe for British Loyalists (and thereby influencing the negotiations that would determine the fledgling United States' northern border). The British built Fort George to defend the town.

The challenge to American sovereignty was taken up by the General Court (legislature) of Massachusetts, which governed the territory at the time, and the ill-fated Penobscot Expedition was outfitted and launched at an ultimate cost of $7 million. Bad luck and bad commanding resulted in the destruction of most of the American force, almost bankrupting the Commonwealth of Massachusetts. Fort George was enlarged and strengthened over the years, and the town thrived until the border between the U.S. and Canada was determined. Unhappily for residents of

Bagaduce, the boundary was to be the St. Stephen River (the present boundary), and not the Penobscot. Those loyal to the British Crown put their houses on boats and sailed them to sites along the coast of what is today New Brunswick at St. Andrews. Some of the houses moved still stand in St. Andrews.

In 1796 the name of Bagaduce was changed to Castine, and although it was occupied by British forces during the War of 1812, there was never again to be much military action. But in the 350 years of Castine's history, its forts—Fort Pentagoet, Fort George, and the American Fort Madison—saw a surprising amount of attack and defense.

WHAT TO SEE & DO

Visit the sites of the forts: **Fort Pentagoet,** near the Wilson Museum on Perkins Road; **Fort George,** near the entrance to town; and **Fort Madison.** Fort George is now a State Memorial, kept up by the Bureau of Parks and Recreation.

Historical signboards placed around the village outline Castine's fascinating history. For a closer look, visit the **Wilson Museum,** on Perkins Street, 3 blocks from Main Street to the southwest. Open Tuesday through Sunday, late May through September, from 2 to 5pm (admission free), the museum has exhibits explaining the rich local history, and prehistoric artifacts from the Americas, concentrating on the growth of the human ability to fashion tools. On Sunday and Wednesday afternoons in July and August, you can also visit the museum's authentic, working blacksmith shop, see Castine's century-old hearses, and take a guided tour (for a nominal fee) of the John Perkins House (1763–83).

WHERE TO STAY & DINE

CASTINE INN, Main St. (P.O. Box 41), Castine, ME 04421. Tel. 207/ 326-4365. 20 rms (all with bath).
$ Rates: (including breakfast): $70–$105 single; $75–$110 double. Extra person $20. MC, V. **Parking:** Free. **Closed:** Nov to mid-Apr.
The Castine Inn is a three-story 1898 clapboard summer hotel filled with antiques and fireplaces. Many rooms and the broad porch offer views of the deep harbor and inn's gardens. Dinner is served nightly between 5:30pm and 8:30pm, and includes traditional and regional cuisine.

PENTAGOET INN, Main St. (P.O. Box 4), Castine, ME 04421. Tel. 207/326-8616, or toll free 800/845-1701. 16 rms (all with bath).
$ Rates: (including half-board): $169 double. MC, V. **Closed:** Nov–Apr.
This beautiful, old, gabled-and-turreted, pale-yellow house with dark-green trim, is right in the center of the village. Interior decoration harks back to Castine's fascinating Revolutionary period, although the inn building dates from Victoria's time, 1894. The comforts are modern and drinks are served on the porch daily in the summer. The five-course evening meal offers several choices, usually including Maine lobster. Lindsey and Virginia Miller have a charming place, and we recommend it for those who want a quiet getaway to a beautiful town. Parking is available on the street.

BLUE HILL

20 miles (32km) E of Castine, 14 miles (23km) SE of Ellsworth

GETTING THERE By Bus See the beginning of this chapter.

By Car Coming from the west and south, take U.S. 1 to Orland, then Route 175 south to South Penobscot, then follow signs eastward to Blue Hill. Coming from the east and north, take U.S. 1 to Ellsworth, then Route 172 south and west to Blue Hill.

ESSENTIALS The **area code** is 207. The **Blue Hill Chamber of Commerce**, P.O. Box 520, Blue Hill, ME 04614 (no phone), is helpful. **Liros Gallery** on Main Street is acting as the chamber for now and can be reached at 207/374-5370.

Blue Hill is a town of majestic elm trees, with prim white clapboard homes and churches. It attracts visitors because its most outstanding "attractions" are peace, quiet, and an easy pace.

Blue Hill was settled in 1762 by colonists from Andover, Mass., and by 1792 it was turning Maine's forests into ships, and was sending these ships around the world. In 1816 granite quarries were opened, and stonecutting complemented shipping, and from 1879 to 1881, there was also a copper mine.

Today, if you're not coming to Blue Hill on vacation, you're probably coming to enroll your child in the George Stevens Academy (1803), a preparatory school. Or perhaps you've arrived to attend a chamber music concert in Kneisel Hall, performed by students and faculty of the summer music school twice weekly in July and August at 8pm.

You may want to visit the **Holt House** (1815), home of the Blue Hill Historical Society, open in July and August Tuesday through Friday from 1 to 4pm. The stocky but dignified four-chimney home remains much as it did during Federal days. Take a look also at the pretty stained-glass windows in the **First Congregational Church.** Also worth visiting is the 1814 **Parson Fisher House.**

WHERE TO STAY

ARCADY DOWN EAST, South St., Blue Hill, ME 04614. Tel. 207/374-5576. 7 rms (5 with bath). **Directions:** Go 1 mile south along Rtes. 172 and 175.
$ Rates: (including breakfast): $85–$110 double. AE, MC, V. **Parking:** Free.
As you drive up, you'll see a fantastic shingled castle of a place, looking as though it really belongs in Bar Harbor. If a summer cottage could be called "baronial," it would be this one run by Bertha and Gene Wiseman, with lots of public rooms, views of Cadillac Mountain in the distance, and a great variety of guest rooms, one with a fireplace. All the rooms have been repapered and come with robes and fresh fruit.

BLUE HILL FARM, Rte. 15 (P.O. Box 437), Blue Hill, ME 04614. Tel. 207/374-5126. 14 rms (7 with bath). **Directions:** Go 2 miles from the center of the village on Rte. 15 (turn at the Exxon station).
$ Rates: (including breakfast): $63–$73 single; $73–$83 double. No credit cards. **Parking:** Free.
It's quiet here, with ducks cruising serenely on the pond, and you'll think you're visiting some comfortably established country cousins. This is an authentic Maine farm now run as a bed-and-breakfast place by Jim and Marcia Schatz. Rooms in the converted farmhouse and barn have private or semiprivate bath (two rooms to a bath).

BLUE HILL INN, Union St. (P.O. Box 403), Blue Hill, ME 04614. Tel. 207/374-2844. 11 rms (all with bath).
$ Rates: High season, $110–$160 double with breakfast, $147–$195 double with half-board. Off-season, rates are about 25% lower. MC, V. **Parking:** Free.
This has served as the town's prime hostelry since about 1840, and is an even better place to stay and dine since innkeepers Mary and Don Hartley took over in 1987. Four of the inn's rooms have working fireplaces and furnishings authentic to the period. Dinner is served by candlelight each evening in summer and on weekends and holidays in the off-season.

WHERE TO DINE

FIREPOND RESTAURANT, Main St. Tel. 374-2135.

Cuisine: AMERICAN GOURMET. **Reservations:** Recommended.
$ **Prices:** Appetizers $4–$8; main courses $15–$19; dinner $25–$35. DC, MC, V.
Open: Memorial Day–Nov, daily 5–9:30pm.
Right in the center of Blue Hill, this cozy dining room fills up quickly in the evenings, especially on weekends, as diners order roast duckling with mangoes and ginger, or tournedos with Roquefort and lingonberries.

JONATHAN'S, Main St. Tel. 374-5226.
Cuisine: NEW ENGLAND. **Reservations:** Recommended.
$ **Prices:** Appetizers $3–$7; main courses $9–$16; dinner $20–$25. MC, V.
Open: June–Oct, dinner daily 5–9:30pm. Nov–May, dinner Wed–Sun 5–8pm (but call first to double-check).
The fare here is moderately priced and varied, and includes everything from New American cuisine to Szechuan stir-fried beef to braised rabbit dijonnaise. Diners have more than 200 wines to choose from.

AN EASY EXCURSION

You can continue southward, taking Route 15 to Deer Isle and Stonington, its southernmost town. Just after you cross the humpback bridge onto Deer Isle proper, you'll see a little chamber of commerce **information booth,** open in summer. Shortly after passing the booth, you'll enter the village of Deer Isle.
Stonington is a fishing village, summer resort, and former granite-quarrying town. Beyond Stonington is **Isle au Haut,** part of Acadia National Park. A mail boat (tel. 207/367-2468) will take you over to the island in less than an hour, and you can hike along the park trails. Call ahead to be sure it is running.

Where to Stay

PILGRIM'S INN, Deer Isle, ME 04627. Tel. 207/348-6615. 13 rms (8 with bath).
$ **Rates:** (including half-board): $136–$146 double without bath, $160–$170 double with bath. No credit cards. **Parking:** Free. **Closed:** Mid-Oct to mid-May.
The inn, dating from 1793, is furnished with many antiques, Laura Ashley fabrics, and nice country touches. Each evening, hors d'oeuvres are served in the common room, with its 8-foot-wide fireplace, and dinner follows in the dining room, a converted barn. Innkeepers Jean and Dud Hendrick will lend you a bicycle so you can explore on your own, or will give you advice about local excursions, including to Isle au Haut, and to the Haystack School of arts and crafts.
Note that no smoking is allowed in guest rooms or in the dining room and that a 2-night stay is encouraged. Should you want to stay for a full week, you can take advantage of special rates.

7. BAR HARBOR

161 miles (260km) NE of Portland, 20 miles (32km) SE of Ellsworth

GETTING THERE **By Plane** Continental Express serves Bar Harbor Airport, 8 miles northeast of the town.

By Bus See the beginning of this chapter.

By Car Follow U.S. 1 to Ellsworth, then Route 3 south to Bar Harbor.

ESSENTIALS The **area code** is 207. The **Bar Harbor Chamber of Com-**

merce, 93 Cottage St. (P.O. Box 158), Bar Harbor, ME 04609 (tel. 207/288-5103), maintain **information booths** at their Cottage Street office and at the *Bluenose* Ferry Terminal on Route 3 (tel. 207/288-3393).

When a Yankee talks about a "Down-Easter," he's talking about somebody from Maine, but when somebody from Maine talks about a Down-Easter, he means somebody from the region of Bar Harbor or even farther east. Most of us think of the Maine coastline as running its ragged way north, but a quick look at the map will show that Bar Harbor is at about the same longitude as San Juan, Puerto Rico, and that indeed the Maine coastline heads more directly east than it does north at this point. These are the wilder shores of Maine and the settlements are fewer, the vegetation not so lush, and the climate a bit harsher than in other parts of the state, but at the same time the scenery is more dramatic, the air is charged with life, and there is a sense of wild nature.

The French influence was for a long time paramount in these parts, and many Down-Easters today speak French as a second language. In fact, it was Samuel de Champlain who gave Mount Desert Island its name, in the form of "L'lle des Monts-Deserts," and even today the local pronunciation is "dez-*zert*", following the French style.

When steamships and railroads were opening up America in the 1800s, they also opened up Down East Maine, and by the end of the century, Bar Harbor, a small town on rocky Mount Desert Island, boasted almost as many palatial summer homes as Newport, although the ones here were perhaps not quite so lavish—but pretty close. In any case, only a small number of the original dozens of mansions are still standing, for a great number were wiped out in the Great Fire of 1947.

Today Bar Harbor is a nice town with a wonderful collection of nice little inns also lots of motels, most lining the roads into town from Ellsworth. The big attractions in the area, for which so much housing must be provided, are the town itself, the cruise boats to Yarmouth, Nova Scotia, and of course Acadia National Park. The park takes up something like half of the land of Mount Desert Island and much of that on the smaller surrounding islands, and is one of the few national parks in the eastern United States and the only National Park in New England.

WHAT TO SEE AND DO

BICYCLING

Should you want to rent a bike for trips around town or into Acadia National Park check with **Bar Harbor Bicycle Shop** at 141 Cottage St. (tel. 288-3886), corner o Eden Street, Route 3 (Cottage Street is parallel to West Street but 1 block south of it away from the water). Rates are $9 for up to 4 hours, $14 for up to 12 hours, plus deposit.

CRUISES

The **Frenchman Bay Boating Company** (tel. 288-3322) organizes all sorts o boat trips: sightseeing, sailing, whale watching, lobstering, and deep-sea fishing. The *Friendship III* motors out to the Gulf of Maine twice daily in search of the leviathan of the deep; the 4-hour whale watch costs $28 for adult, $18 for kids 5 to 11, free fo the little ones. If sail power is your preference, hop aboard the schooner *Bay Lady* fo one of its four daily 2-hour cruises in Frenchman Bay, the saltwater shushing along it hull, the wind singing in the rigging, and nary a motor's chug or growl.

For sightseeing cruises, the diesel-powered *Acadian* is the boat to take. Cruise th shores of Bar Harbor and Acadia National Park to a detailed narration of the sights Cruises last 1 or 2 hours and cost $9.75 to $12.75 for adults, $8.75 to $9.75 for kids to 11, and are free for kids under 5. Prehaps the most thoroughly authentic cruis offered is aboard the 40-passenger *Katherine,* which the captain takes out as a lobster boat to check his traps. Along the way, he'll introduce you to the local seals as well. Fares are $14 for adults, $9 for kids 5 to 11, and free for those under 5. As for fishing, morning and afternoon trips aboard the *Dolphin* cost $30 for adults, $22 for kids 5 to 12 (under 5 not allowed); the price includes rod, reel, and bait.

You can sail aboard a traditional three-masted schooner, the *Natalie Todd.* This 101-foot historic wooden vessel offers 2-hour sails from the Bar Harbor Inn Pier for $16 per adult, $10 for children under 12. The *Natalie Todd* sails three times a day at 10am, 2pm, and 6pm. Tickets are available at the pier or at the *Natalie Todd* ticket office at 27 Main St. (tel. 288-4585). For information in the off-season call 207/546-2927 or write Capt. Steven F. Pagels, P.O. Box 8, Cherryfield, ME 04622.

A HARBOR-VIEW WALK

If you're willing to walk for 30 to 45 minutes, you can enjoy one of Bar Harbor's nicest little hikes. Follow Main Street (Route 3) south out of town, past the park on the right, and about a mile down the road (15 to 25 minutes' walk) is a pull-off spot for cars (capacity: four vehicles). If you reach the Ocean Drive Motor Inn, you've gone too far. Walk down the dirt road, closed by a chain, near the little metal sign marking the boundary of U.S. government land, posted on a tree. It's less than a 10-minute walk to Rocky Harbor along the dirt road through the fragrant forests. When you come to a fork, bear left with the road (a path goes off straight). When you reach the viewing point, you'll find a grassy clearing furnished with litter barrels for picnickers (no tables). If you've brought a picnic, you can share it with the gulls and ducks. It's secluded, beautiful, quiet, and in walking distance from town—a fine place.

ACADIA NATIONAL PARK

The rugged terrain of Mount Desert Island has attracted lovers of natural beauty for over a century, and soon after summer visitors began to arrive here in numbers, preservation efforts were begun. By the end of World War II, Acadia National Park was well along to its present size of more than 30,000 acres, or something like half the land on the island (the other half is still in private hands). Focal point of park activities is **Cadillac Mountain,** at 1,530 feet the highest point on America's Atlantic coast. The thing to do at Cadillac Mountain is to hike (or drive) to the top of it for the views. In fact, local people have recognized that those who see the sun break forth on the horizon from Cadillac Mountain are the first people in the United States to greet the new day, so there's a "Sunrise from Mount Cadillac Club." You can join by picking up a blank from the Bar Harbor information bureau, and filling it out with the help of your hotel manager the night *before* you plan to see the sunrise. Then, if you follow through, you get to be a member of this exclusive club.

Besides Cadillac Mountain, the first thing to do in the park is drive the Loop Road, a one-way scenic ocean drive which takes you past many of the most interesting scenic, topographic, and geologic features of the island. Admission to the park is $5 per car; this pass is good for 7 days. Stop at **Thunder Hole** when the surf's up to feel the bashing and pushing of the waves, or at **Sand Beach** for a chilly ocean swim. There's national park camping at **Black Woods** (follow the signs). This is the only campground where you can reserve ahead; call your local Mistix outlet as early as the spring for reservations.

On the island's western peninsula, **Echo Lake** is the park's freshwater swimming area; there's a lookout tower atop **Beech Mountain,** and a park campground is down near the peninsula's southern tip at **Seawall.** And throughout the park are 100 miles of hiking trails (maps sold at park headquarters), and lots of "carriage roads" good for bike trips or horseback riding.

Not far from the town of Bar Harbor, in the park at Sieur des Monts Spring, is the **Abbe Museum of Stone Age Antiquities,** a wildflower garden, and a nature center. Entrance to the park is $5 per vehicle for a 7-day pass.

The beach at **Seal Harbor** is very fine, and open to the public for free. It is one of Mount Desert Island's poshest summer resorts, with all sorts of famous and wealthy people inhabiting the big houses secluded along the forested streets of the village. Park in the lot across the street.

A visit to Acadia National Park wouldn't be complete without tea and popovers ($5) at the **Jordan House** (tel. 276-3116). A tradition for almost 100 years, the restaurant serves lunch on the porch from 11:30am to 2:30pm, afternoon tea on the lawn from 2:30 to 5:30pm, and dinner by the fireside from 5:30 to 9pm. You can get snacks and beverages on the overlook throughout the day from 9am to 6pm. Whether you dine or not, you are invited to stroll around the gardens and spacious grounds; the view of the lake and mountains from the lawn is stunning. It's open late May to late October.

TOURS

National Park Tours (tel. 207/288-3327) runs two tours daily from Bar Harbor beginning from Testa's Restaurant, 53 Main St. The cost is $12 per adult, $6 per child under 12. The tour takes you through the town of Bar Harbor past many of the mansions left from its heyday, and stops at Cadillac Mountain, Sieur des Mont Spring, and Thunder Hole. Traditionally the tours have left at 10am and 2pm, but call in advance to check the times, and to make a reservation.

If you have a car, you can rent a cassette tape recorder with a prerecorded tour narration from **Sightseeing Tapes, Inc.** You pay the $11 rental fee for the tape and player ($8 if you only rent the tape), and start out to follow the description of many interesting points in the national park. The advantage here is that this tour is cheaper overall if you have several people in your car, and you can turn off the tape at any time should you want to spend a while at some point. Tapes and machines are for rent at the National Park Visitor Center at Hulls Cove, the first park entrance you come to when approaching Bar Harbor from the north on Route 3.

A FERRY TO NOVA SCOTIA

The Marine Atlantic ship MV *Bluenose* sails from Bar Harbor to Yarmouth, Nova Scotia, and back again daily in summer between late June and late September. It's a car-ferry with room for 1,000 passengers and 250 cars, a sun deck, buffet, dining room, cafeteria, bar, casino, and duty-free shop. The *Bluenose* leaves Bar Harbor every morning in summer and returns from Yarmouth in late afternoon, arriving back in Bar Harbor at night. The trip takes about 6 hours each way, and costs $45 per adult, $22.50 per child 5 to 13 years; cars cost $75; trailers and campers cost $155 up to 30 feet long, with a summertime minimum charge of the normal car's fare. You can rent a day-use cabin for an extra $40. Off-season schedules are such that the ferry leaves Bar Harbor one day and returns the next; fares are about 25% lower. The vehicle fees do not include the driver's ticket, so a car-and-driver crossing in summer would pay over $100, and a family of four with a car would pay over $350 for the journey round-trip. Note that you must make reservations in advance. Write to the Marine Atlantic Reservations Bureau, P.O. Box 250, North Sydney, NS, B2A 3M3, Canada; or call toll free 800/341-7981 in the continental United States. The number in Bar Harbor is 207/288-3395; in Yarmouth, call 902/742-3513.

WHERE TO STAY

While there are plenty of rooms to handle the thousands of visitors each year, the problem is to get the room you want rather than one you're forced to take. Reservations are advisable in all recommended places, and as these are some of the choicer spots, I'd suggest that you reserve early.

If you arrive without a reservation, make your way to Mount Desert Street, which was a favorite locale of those who built palatial "summer cottages," and which today has an abundance of wonderful old inns.

EXPENSIVE

BAR HARBOR INN, Newport Dr. (P.O. Box 7), Bar Harbor, ME 04609. Tel. 207/288-3351, or toll free 800/248-3351. 130 rms (all with bath). TV TEL
$ Rates: $59–$199 double. AE, DISC, MC, V. **Parking:** Free.

Set amid its own lush grounds on a point overlooking Frenchman Bay, this was once a private club, that has been converted, expanded, and renovated to take in visitors year round, and the feeling is that of a posh resort in the 1920s. White pillars frame the front porch; attendants pad quietly here and there. The inn's large heated swimming pool is next to a little copse of trees and only a few yards from the waters of the Atlantic, and here, as everywhere else at the inn, the views are magnificent. The rooms are not old-fashioned, however, with lots of windows looking onto either the bay or the inn's lush grounds; in 1988, new rooms were added, each with private terrace and oversized beds. The atmosphere is formal but friendly. One dresses well for dinner, served in the semicircular dining room that overlooks the bay.

CLEFTSTONE MANOR, Rte. 3 (Eden St.), Bar Harbor, ME 04609. Tel. 207/288-4951, or toll free 800/962-9762. 16 rms (all with bath).
$ Rates: (including breakfast and evening refreshments): $95–$180 double. DISC, MC, V. **Parking:** Free. **Closed:** Nov–Mar.

Farther from the center of town, 500 yards from the *Bluenose* dock, up on a hillside, is the Cleftstone Manor, one of Bar Harbor's finest inns. A Victorian summer house in the grand manner, the inn has spacious public rooms, good views from many of the guest rooms, and many elegant touches. No smoking is allowed in the manor. Breakfasts are of home-baked breads and pastries. Afternoon tea and evening refreshments are served. Repeat guests will likely notice all the changes taking place here such as repapered guest rooms, some with fireplaces, and other nice touches.

HOLBROOK HOUSE, 74 Mount Desert St., Bar Harbor, ME 04609. Tel. 207/288-4970. 10 rms (all with bath), 2 cottages.
$ Rates: (including breakfast and afternoon refreshments): High season, from $110 single or double. Off-season, from $100 single or double. MC, V. **Parking:** Free.

Built in 1880, the Holbrook House, in the center of town, has rooms that provide enough space for even the most enormous Victorian family. Also on hand are two cottage suites decorated in chintz and with period furnishings. Now the family in residence—hardly of Victorian size—is that of Dorothy and Mike Chester, who will welcome you and make sure you're comfortable.

LEDGELAWN INN, 66 Mount Desert St., Bar Harbor, ME 04609. Tel. 207/288-4596, or toll free 800/274-5334. Fax 207/288-9968. 33 rms (all with bath). TV TEL
$ Rates: (including continental breakfast): $95–$250 double. AE, MC, V. **Parking:** Free, on premises. **Closed:** Dec–Mar.

Having escaped destruction in the Great Fire of 1947, the "cottage" built for Boston shoe magnate John Brigham has been fully converted to a fine inn. The public rooms are positively grand in scale, the lawns and trees elaborate, the guest rooms elegant. Many rooms have working fireplaces and private sauna-and-whirlpool baths. The Ledgelawn has a widow's walk on top, open for the view or the warm rays of the sun until 6pm. The inn has a swimming pool and hot tub. Guests also have access to clay tennis courts and an Olympic-size pool at Bar Harbor Club.

MANOR HOUSE INN, 106 West St., Bar Harbor, ME 04609. Tel. 207/288-3759, or toll free 800/437-0088. 14 rms (all with bath)
$ Rates: (including breakfast): Late June to mid-Oct, $85–$153 single or double.

Off-season, $85–$125 single or double. AE, MC, V. **Parking:** Free. **Closed:** Mid-Nov to mid-Apr.

Period furnishings fill all the guest rooms of this huge Victorian home. The Chauffeur's Cottage, two guest cottages, and five gardens also occupy the acre of grounds, which is listed in the National Register of Historic Places. Guests can eat breakfast in a lovely garden.

MIRA MONTE INN, 69 Mount Desert St., Bar Harbor, ME 04609. Tel. 207/288-4263, or toll free 800/553-5109. 11 rms (all with bath). A/C TV TEL

$ Rates: (including continental breakfast): $102–$152 single or double. AE, MC, V. **Parking:** Free. **Closed:** Late Nov–early May.

Mira Monte Inn is a fine old Victorian house (1864) lovingly restored and maintained by Bar Harbor native Marian Burns, who will happily give you advice on nature trails and local activities. All rooms come with period furnishings and each room has something different: a canopy bed, brass bed, fireplace, porch, or bay window. Four fireplaces are new.

MODERATE

ANCHORAGE MOTEL, 51 Mount Desert St., Bar Harbor, ME 04609. Tel. 207/288-3959. 48 rms (all with bath). TV TEL

$ Rates: High season, $44–$84 single or double. Off-season, from $53 single or double. AE, CB, DC, MC, V. **Parking:** Free.

This is a tidy two-story motel set back from Mount Desert Street, the street with all the inns. The standard modern motel comforts cost a bit more here because this is Bar Harbor, and the location is good.

HEARTHSIDE B&B, 7 High St., Bar Harbor, ME 04609. Tel. 207/288-4533. 9 rms (all with bath). **Directions:** Stay on Rte. 3 as it becomes Mount Desert St. and take the third left (High St.), a one-way street, before the Episcopal church.

$ Rates: (including full breakfast): $75–$110 single or double. MC, V. **Parking:** Free.

Run by Susan and Barry Schwartz, on a quiet street close to town, the living room of this inn has a fireplace and other touches of past Bar Harbor elegance. Afternoon tea is served. Three rooms have a fireplace and one has a whirlpool tub. The inn has a no-smoking policy.

STRATFORD HOUSE INN, 45 Mount Desert St., Bar Harbor, ME 04609. Tel. 207/288-5189. 10 rms (8 with bath). TV

$ Rates: (including continental breakfast): $70–$80 double without bath, $85–$135 double with bath. AE, MC, V. **Parking:** Free. **Closed:** Mid-Oct to mid-May.

Stratford House looks like Queen Elizabeth I's-own summer cottage, for it has everything you could imagine in the way of Tudor domestic architecture—it's gabled and half-timbered. Though built by a publishing magnate, this inn was the summer home of musical greats Fritz Kreisler and Jan Paderewski. The music room is appointed with a grand piano and an organ. Some guest rooms have a fireplace and each is furnished with a four-poster mahogany or brass bowbottom bed.

THORNHEDGE INN, 47 Mount Desert St., Bar Harbor, ME 04609. Tel. 207/288-5398. 13 rms (all with bath). TV

$ Rates: (including breakfast): High season, $80–$140 single or double. AE, MC, V. **Parking:** Free. **Closed:** Mid-Oct to mid-May.

In 1900 a retired Boston publisher named Lewis Roberts built himself a "cottage" in Bar Harbor. It has gone through several hands since then, lately having been owned by a former dean of Harvard Medical School, and today it is among Bar Harbor's most desirable places to stay. The aim of its owners is to "recapture the spirit of Bar Harbor at the turn of the century," and they have done so by arranging to purchase many of the house's original furnishings. Today the large, sunny, gracious master bedroom on the second floor is done in the turn-of-the-century style; adjoining is the original bathroom, which is a good deal larger than the standard motel room today. Many rooms have working fireplaces, in which fire laws allow artificial logs to be burned. You can tell that I like Thornhedge, and when you stay there, you'll know why. As you're driving or walking along Mount Desert Street, you can't miss Thornhedge, for it's painted a bright, cheery yellow.

VILLAGER MOTEL, 207 Main St., Bar Harbor, ME 04609. Tel. 207/288-3211 or 288-3011. 63 rms (all with bath). A/C TV TEL **Directions:** Take Rte. 3 heading south out of town.

$ Rates: July–Aug, $70–$90 single or double. Sept–Oct, $45–$72 single or double. May–June, $39–$59 single or double. AE, MC, V. **Parking:** Free. **Closed:** Nov–Mar.

The Villager is a very neat two-story motel of moderate size and the usual comforts: a heated outdoor pool, modern rooms, and a convenient location which still leaves you within walking distance of the sights, shops, and restaurants in town. All of these advantages, plus the moderate rates, assure that the Villager is often full, so it's good to make reservations in advance.

BUDGET

ACADIA MOTEL-HOTEL, 20 Mount Desert St., Bar Harbor, ME 04609. Tel. 207/288-5721. 10 rms (all with bath). TV

$ Rates: $45–$58 single or double. AE, DISC, MC, V. **Parking:** Free. **Closed:** Nov–Apr.

Rooms here are in the budget class, tidy but simple. Some rooms have air conditioners and private entrances (the "motel" rooms), while others are entered through the hall ("hotel"). The wraparound porch is new. Add $5 per child.

BASS COTTAGE IN THE FIELD, "The Field," Main St., Bar Harbor, ME 04609. Tel. 207/288-3705. 10 rms (6 with bath).

$ Rates: $37 single; $52–$89 double. No credit cards. **Parking:** Free. **Closed:** Mid-Oct to mid-May.

One of the most centrally located and inexpensive, authentic cottages in Bar Harbor, Bass Cottage has been operated and run by sisters in the Maddocks family since it was purchased in 1928. Most rooms in this inn, built in 1885, have private baths, and some have an ocean view. Walk to one of the many restaurants less than a block away, then relax on the wicker-furnished, glass-enclosed porch. This is a real find!

MCKAY LODGING, 243 Main St., Bar Harbor, ME 04609. Tel. 207/288-3531, or toll free 800/86-MCKAY. Fax 207/288-5772. 23 rms (17 with bath). MINIBAR TV TEL

$ Rates: (including breakfast): $60–$69 double without bath, $69–$110 double with bath. AE, MC, V. **Parking:** Free. **Closed:** Nov–Apr.

The McKay Cottages are a mere 1½ blocks from the park and the center of town life. They offer simple but comfortable and fairly homey accommodations at an unbeatable price. Rooms in the main house are air conditioned.

MOUNT DESERT ISLAND YWCA, 36 Mount Desert St., Bar Harbor, ME 04609. Tel. 207/288-5008. 35 rms (none with bath).

$ Rates: Weekly rates $80 single; $140 double. No credit cards. **Parking:** Free. Individual women travelers can stay at the YWCA, where rooms rent by the night and by the week and include clean bed linens, use of the laundry room, and kitchen privileges. Weekly rates are available only if paid in full at the beginning of your stay. Upon arrival, you will be charged a membership fee of $10 (for stays of a week or more) and a $25 returnable security deposit. Rooms are hard to come by in the summer, so write ahead for reservations. Open year round.

WHERE TO DINE

As you drive toward Bar Harbor from Ellsworth, the road is lined with little shacks and stores bearing the magic word **LOBSTERS.** Outside each is a strange arrangement of backyard barbecues in a row, with large pots or drums on them and stovepipes (in some cases very rickety ones) shooting up. These contraptions are used to prepare a traditional lobster clambake. The drums or kettles are filled with lobsters, clams, corn on the cob, and seaweed, and then saltwater is poured in, the fire is started, and the whole business is cooked up and served to the droves of motorists. Some places have tables where you can sit to consume your feast, at others you take the goodies home with you, but in any case this is the way to get the most seafood for your dollar, and the eating couldn't be better! This is the real Maine experience, and shouldn't be missed.

How does one pick the right place to stop? Every single one seems to have a signboard out front giving the price-per-pound of lobster, and you can go by this to some degree. But the price and poundage depend on how the lobster is stored: The best places will store the live lobsters on ice, and not in seawater, as the seawater can add a great deal of weight to the lobster when it's put on the scale. In any case, make sure the lobster is alive, not dead and limp.

MODERATE

BRICK OVEN RESTAURANT, 21 Cottage St. Tel. 288-3708.
Cuisine: SEAFOOD/STEAKS. **Reservations:** Recommended.
$ Prices: Appetizers $2.50–$6; main courses $8–$17; dinner $25. AE, MC, V.
Open: Mid-May to late Oct, dinner daily 4 or 5–10pm.

The Brick Oven is almost as proud of its decor as it is of its cuisine. Owner Freddie Pooler has re-created the '50s and '60s here, with an astounding variety of memorabilia. Upstairs is a surprisingly evocative replica of a drugstore soda fountain from that time. Freddie's Burger World, next door, is a convincingly authentic 1950s burger joint, jukebox and all. The menu this year is more formal though the casual atmosphere remains. Liquor is served and wine is now available by the glass or bottle

OPERA HOUSE, 27 Cottage St. Tel. 288-3509.
Cuisine: ECLECTIC. **Reservations:** Not accepted.
$ Prices: Fixed-price dinner $25. AE, DC, MC, V.
Open: July–Aug, dinner daily 5:30–9pm or later. Sept–June, dinner Tues–Sun 5:30–9pm or later.

Opera aficionados and lovers of fine food will be delighted by this unique restaurant Although the restaurant is only open at night, the "Listening Room" is open throughout the day and everyone is invited to wander through the gallery and listen to a portion of the 90-minute taped program of the day while paying homage to the opera greats whose pictures grace the walls. A placard at the entrance advises DINING FOR ADULTS and YOU ARE WELCOME DRESSED AS YOU ARE. The à la carte menu includes crawfish étouffée ($21.95). The fixed-price menu features roast duck in cognac or Cajun blackened halibut. If you've dined elsewhere, at least have dessert and a cordial or coffee; the rich crème brûlée is a wonderful way to end an evening

INEXPENSIVE

ISLAND CHOWDER HOUSE, 38 Cottage St. Tel. 288-4905.
Cuisine: SEAFOOD. **Reservations:** Recommended.
$ Prices: Appetizers $4–$7; main courses $10–$17; dinner $18. AE, MC, V.
Open: May–Oct, daily 11am–10pm or later.

Have a table in the attractive, woody dining room and order the shore dinner of clam chowder, steamed clams, lobster, french fries, and coleslaw, and the bill will be a reasonable $18, tax and tip included. Fish-and-chips is a third of that price.

MIGUEL'S, 51 Rodick St. Tel. 288-5117.
Cuisine: MEXICAN. **Reservations:** Not accepted.
$ Prices: Appetizers $4–$6.25; main courses $6–$12.75; dinner $12–$20. MC, V

Open: Dinner daily 5–10pm. **Closed:** Mid-Nov to Mar; Mon off-season.
Located behind the firehouse, this quaint, attractive storefront eatery offers delicious quesadillas, burritos, tacos, chilis rellenos, even shrimp fajitas and carne asada. For an appetizer, try the chimitas for $3.50. Huge frozen margaritas (and other liquor) are served, and on summer evenings you can dine on the patio.

BUDGET

BUBBA'S, 30 Cottage St. Tel. 288-5871.
Cuisine: AMERICAN. **Reservations:** Not accepted.
$ Prices: Sandwiches and light meals $4–$10.
Open: Daily 11:30am–1am.
This is a favorite sandwich-and-drinks place for many of the more interesting people in Bar Harbor on vacation. Soups, salads, and sandwiches make up the bill of fare all day, but sipping and socializing are what it's all about. The choice of 10 kinds of burgers is noteworthy. The big bar and the bentwood make it all upbeat and enjoyable.

EVENING ENTERTAINMENT

At **Geddy's** (tel. 288-5077), on Main Street near the corner of West Street, every night in summer is witness to some sort of live performance. Jazz, Dixieland, pop, and rock all issue forth from its sidewalk windows. Check the playbill out front and then walk in. There's no cover or minimum, and beer is $1.50 to $3, or a bit more (for Heineken and the like). Happy hour, from 3 to 7pm, sees all drinks reduced to about half price.

AN EASY EXCURSION FROM BAR HARBOR

Besides Bar Harbor, Mount Desert Island is home to **Seal Harbor, Southwest Harbor,** and **Northeast Harbor.** Take Route 3 around the island for a look at each of these harbors, all distinctive areas. Mount Desert Island hosts many summer homes of old-money families, such as the Rockefellers.

Just outside Northeast Harbor is Somes Sound and **Abel's Lobster Pound** (tel. 276-5827). Open between May 25 and October 15, Abel's is well-known for its shore dinners. The lobster pound is an open-air hut arrangement down the hill from the restaurant. The rustic-inspired dining room is on a split level and provides views of the Sound. The staff takes your lobster order and runs it down to the pound, where the lobster is cooked. The food isn't fancy, but the atmosphere is real New England.

WHERE TO STAY

GREY ROCK INN, Northeast Harbor, ME 04662. Tel. 207/276-9360. 9 rms (7 with bath).
$ Rates: (including breakfast): $115–$165 double. No credit cards. **Parking:** Free.
Closed: Nov to mid-May.
This small and lovely inn is run by a mother and son who take pride in the 1911-vintage clapboard and fieldstone house. Afternoon tea is served in the cozy living room warmed by a fireplace. Three guest rooms also have fireplaces. Breakfast might be served on the porch or in the dining room.

FROM BAR HARBOR TO CANADA

The coastal highway, U.S. 1, winds east and north from Ellsworth. You might want to wander south along Route 186 for views of the scenic **Schoodic Peninsula.** If not, head ever northeastward, toward the Canadian frontier.

When you get to Cobscook Bay, you will have reached the easternmost limits of the United States. Cobscook Bay can boast two state parks, **Cobscook Bay State**

Park and **Quoddy Head State Park.** However, the following park is even more interesting.

ROOSEVELT CAMPOBELLO INTERNATIONAL PARK A Canadian island with an Italian-sounding name on which an American president spent his summers. These little mysteries are not at all as difficult to solve as one might suppose. Campobello Island is officially part of Canada, even though the major access road comes from Lubec, Me. (You must pass through Customs.) And the "Italian" name is nothing more than the name of a former Nova Scotian governor, William Campbell, with two "o's" added for exotic flavor. When the island was granted to Capt. William Owen by Governor Campbell in 1767, it was still part of the Canadian province of Nova Scotia. (The province of New Brunswick was not formed until 1784, when large numbers of United Empire Loyalists fled New England to live in King George III's still-loyal dominions to the north.)

Franklin Delano Roosevelt's father, James, bought some land on the island in 1883, at a time when lots of important city people were building vast "summer cottages" at Bar Harbor, Passamaquoddy Bay, and other northern coastal locations. Young Franklin—to solve that last little mystery—came here long before he was president of the United States, and spent many a teenaged summer rowing, paddling and sailing on the waters, and hiking through the woods.

In 1920 FDR ran for the vice presidency—and lost. Taking on a a banking job instead, he looked forward to a relaxing summer at Campobello in 1921. On August 10 of that year, the first signs of illness showed, and 2 weeks later the doctor diagnosed the crippling disease as polio. When he left the island in September, he had no way of knowing that the few more times he would see the summer cottage and his Campobello friends would be brief weekend visits—as president of the United States.

The day-to-day lives of the great and powerful are fascinating to explore in detail, and a visit to the Roosevelt house on Campobello Island gives one a peek at the early years of this incredibly courageous man who went on to become governor of New York and president of the United States after having been crippled by polio. It is no less intriguing to see how a well-to-do family spent its summers at the turn of the century, with long and leisurely days filled by sports, games, and family fun. Servants saw to the chores, and even they must have enjoyed getting away from the city to such a beautiful spot.

The Roosevelt Cottage is now part of Roosevelt Campobello International Park, a joint American-Canadian effort open the Saturday prior to Memorial Day through Columbus Day from 9am to 5pm eastern standard time. Guides at the reception center will point out the path to the Roosevelt Cottage, show you movies about the island, and map out the various walks and drives in the 2,600-acre nature preserve. There is no charge for admission.

CALAIS–ST. STEPHEN Residents of Maine and New Brunswick, while the best of friends, cling to memories of their ancestors' fervent support for, respectively, George Washington and George III. With the success of the American Revolution, United Empire Loyalists flocked across the frontier into Canada so as not to be disloyal to the monarch. The "Loyalist" and "Revolutionary" towns preserve the good-natured rivalry.

But things are different in Calais, Me. (pronounced "callous"), and its neighboring city, St. Stephen, N.B. Folks in these two towns, cheek-by-jowl on the St. Croix River, make a point of telling visitors how they ignored the affinities of *both* sides during the War of 1812, and St. Stephen even supplied powder-poor Calais with gunpowder for its Fourth of July celebrations! In fact, by the time the war came, families in the twin towns were so closely intermarried that no one wanted to take the time to sort out who should be loyal to whom.

These days residents celebrate this unique plague-on-both-their-houses philosophy with an International Festival in the first week of August. The two bridges over the river between the towns are thronged with merrymakers moving back and forth—through the watchful but benevolent eye of Customs, of course—and Canadian and American flags fly everywhere.

Despite its interesting history, there's little to detain you in Calais, and soon you'll be heading onward, into Canada (see Frommer's *Canada*), or back down U.S. 1 to points south and west. When you return home, however, you'll know what the maritime forecasters mean when they predict weather for the coastline "from Eastport (on Cobscook Bay) to Block Island (Rhode Island)." And you'll be able to say that you've been at the easternmost point in the United States.

The Green Mountain State is one of the nation's most rural, with lots of trees and very few people—only about half a million in the whole state. But the greenery is Vermont's glory, and green is even the color of the state's auto license plates. To protect the sylvan beauty of the state, and to keep the roads from becoming cluttered with "off-site advertising," the state government has devised a plan whereby participating stores, restaurants, lodging places, and attractions put information on their establishments in a little book called the *Vermont Visitors' Handbook,* yours for free by writing to the Vermont Development Agency, Montpelier, VT 05602. The establishments in the handbook have numbers, and an attractive green sign out on the highway nearby will direct you to the store, restaurant, or motel, and will also bear its number.

Only in Vermont would some enterprising citizens come up with a promotion to support the dairy industry and its hardworking farmers in an effort to preserve the small dairy farms of the state. Nowhere but in Vermont can you adopt a cow. With one cow for every two residents, Vermont has almost 2,400 dairy farms. The "Adopt a Cow" program lets you support a cow and his farmer while receiving an "Info-Pak" and T-shirt. It's just one of the glories of visiting the Green Mountain State.

Skiing is another of Vermont's glories, and resorts in this state are usually more winter- than summer-oriented. Heavy precipitation gives many ski areas a good, long season, and the mountain scenery and imported "alpine" architecture help get one into the spirit of winter fun. No Vermont lodge would think of opening without its fireplace stocked with logs to give the glow to an après-ski cocktail and conversation.

Don't be too surprised by Yankee humor, especially during mud season, as some of the locals may refer to Vermont as the state with four seasons: early winter, mid-winter, late winter, and next winter. They'll be pleased to show you around and show off all the wonderful features that beckon visitors any time of year.

Although winter is its prime season, Vermont is also beautiful in summer. Room rates are lower, many ski resorts run their chair and gondola lifts for sightseers, and the state parks do a booming business with campers, hikers, and picnickers. And winter or summer, most places in Vermont have the distinct advantage of being quite accessible, whether you plan to come by car, bus, train, or air.

SEEING VERMONT

GETTING THERE   By Plane   Burlington is served by several major air carriers and their regional commuter subsidiaries, such as Business Express (Delta Connec-

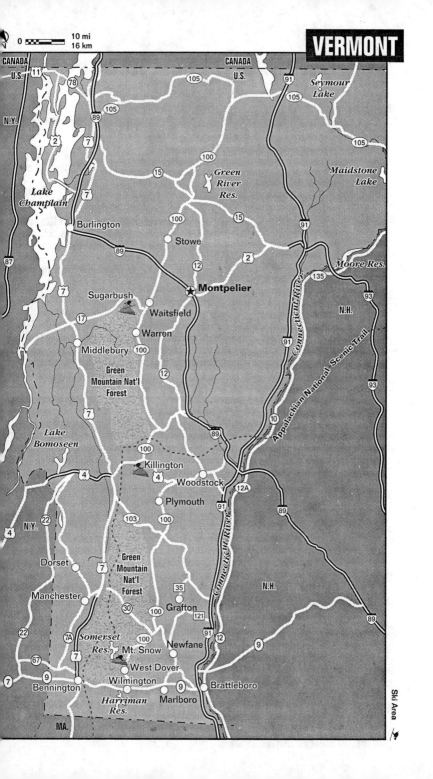

WHAT'S SPECIAL ABOUT VERMONT

Museums

- ☐ The Bennington Museum, with its excellent Revolutionary and Early American collection, as well as a superb exhibit of paintings by Grandma Moses.
- ☐ Shelburne Museum, south of Burlington, a huge complex of more than 37 historic buildings, a steamboat, and art galleries, holding the fullest collection of Americana ever assembled.
- ☐ Hildene, in Manchester, the former gracious country mansion of Robert Todd Lincoln, Abraham's son.

Shopping

- ☐ The Vermont State Craft Center at Frog Hollow in Middlebury—a gallery of Vermont artisans' achievements.
- ☐ Small factories in Grafton and Plymouth selling delicious locally made Vermont Cheddar.

Cool for Kids

- ☐ Alpine slides at Manchester and Stowe, adding an outdoor thrill to a summer vacation.
- ☐ The elevator ride to the top of the Bennington Battle Monument and the panoramic view.
- ☐ The magnificent steeds at the Morgan Horse Farm in Middlebury.

Beautiful Towns & Villages

- ☐ Grafton, Dorset, Woodstock, Manchester, Newfane, and many other small Vermont settlements—all picture-perfect New England towns.

Resorts

- ☐ Vermont's ski resorts in summer—vacation resorts featuring playhouses, hiking, mountain biking, and many other indoor and outdoor pursuits.

---

tion), Metro Airlines (Trans World Express), and Continental Express. In addition USAir, United Airlines, and Continental Airlines have direct flights to Burlington in large aircraft. Direct flights go to Burlington from Atlanta, Boston, Buffalo, Chicago Cleveland, New York City, Orlando, Philadelphia, Pittsburgh, and Washington, D.C.

By Train Two Amtrak trains serve Vermont, and both run between New York City and Montréal. The *Montrealer* runs daily between Washington, D.C., via New York City to Montréal, stopping in Brattleboro (for Mount Snow), Bellows Falls White River Junction (for Woodstock and Killington), Montpelier, Waterbury (fo Stowe), Essex Junction (for Burlington), and St. Albans. The *Montrealer* is a night train.

The *Adirondack* runs daily between New York City and Montréal, skirting Vermont as it runs up the Hudson. Stops at Whitehall (for Rutland), Port Henry, and Port Kent (for Burlington) are the most convenient for reaching points in Vermont although there are lots of other stops. The *Adirondack* is a day train.

By Bus Vermont has its own large bus line, **Vermont Transit Lines** (tel 802/864-6811, 212/971-6300 in New York City; or toll free 800/451-3292 800/642-3133 in Vermont), which operates from New York (in conjunction with Greyhound), Montréal (in conjunction with Voyageur), and Boston to virtually al points of interest in Vermont. Other services run from Portsmouth, N.H., Portland Me., and Concord, N.H., to points in Vermont.

By Car Take the Interstates: I-95 from New York City and Connecticut, I-93 t I-89 from Boston, and Canada 10 to 133 to I-89 if you're driving from Montréal Vermont's Route 100, which winds through the center of the state from north t south, links most of the resort areas.

NFORMATION State information booths are maintained on the major access oads to the state; stop at one for a map and for the *Vermont Visitors' Handbook* mentioned above.

Vermont has a law that prohibits skis from sticking out beyond the normal width of the car. Roads are very well maintained in Vermont in winter, but remember that the roads into the mountains are gradients, so it's best to have snow tires. Dry gas, to prevent your fuel lines from freezing, isn't a bad idea either.

The Vermont **tax on rooms and meals** is 8%, and the **area code** for the entire state is 802.

1. BRATTLEBORO

8 miles (13km) W of Marlboro

GETTING THERE   By Train   There's one train nightly between New York and Montréal (see the beginning of this chapter).

By Bus   Vermont Transit Lines (tel. 802/864-6811, or toll free 800/451-3292, 800/642-3133 in Vermont) serves Brattleboro.

By Car   Follow I-91, the major north-south route along the Connecticut River Valley, or Route 9 (east-west) in Vermont and New Hampshire.

ESSENTIALS   The **area code** is 802. The Brattleboro Chamber of Commerce **information office** is at 180 Main St., right in the center of town (tel. 802/254-4565), and is open during business hours.

The first town you are likely to encounter if you come from New York or Boston is Brattleboro, and in a way this is as it should be, for Brattleboro was the site of Vermont's first colonial settlement. In 1724 a small fortress was built at the spot now marked by a granite commemoration stone, and named Fort Dummer. There had been white settlers in the area before that, but the fort became the focal point of a community as well as its principal defense against the Native Americans.

Today Brattleboro is one of the state's larger towns, with a population around 13,000, and industries that range from printing and book manufacture to furniture making and the manufacture of optical products. As for famous sons, the great Mormon leader Brigham Young was born (1801) nearby in Windham County, and Rudyard Kipling married a Brattleboro woman in 1892, and they lived near the town for some time.

If you have an hour to spend in town before you rush off to the music festival at Marlboro, or the hiking and skiing at surrounding resorts, check out the **Brattleboro Museum & Art Center** (tel. 257-0124), in the town's old Union Railroad Station down near the intersection of Routes 119, 142, and U.S. 5, only a few steps from the center of town. It's open Tuesday through Sunday from 12 to 6pm. Admission is $2 adults, $1 seniors and college students; children under 18 free.

WHERE TO STAY

There is one interesting downtown hotel. Otherwise, Brattleboro's lodgings are motels on the outskirts. Most motels are on U.S. 5 north of Brattleboro on the way to Putney (Exit 3N from I-95); another collection of places to stay and to dine is on Route 9 west of Brattleboro (I-95 Exit 2).

LATCHIS HOTEL, 50 Main St., Brattleboro, VT 05301. Tel. 802/254-6300. 35 rms (all with bath). A/C MINIBAR TV TEL

$ Rates: $34–$52 single; $40–$62 double; higher in foliage season. AE, MC, V
   Parking: Free.

The small downtown hotel where lumber traders stayed in the 1930s has bee
renovated and given new life. Now a pleasant monument to the local expression of th
art deco style, the Latchis offers comfortable accommodations with period deco
within walking distance of everything downtown. The grill restaurant is new and ther
is even a brewery that produces ales and lager for the inn. The restaurant serves lunc
and dinner every day and brunch on Sunday. Deluxe rooms are larger than standar
rooms, and come with continental breakfast, cinema passes, and minibars.

WHERE TO DINE

COMMON GROUND, 25 Elliot St. Tel. 257-0855.
   Cuisine: INTERNATIONAL. **Reservations:** Recommended.
$ Prices: Appetizers $3; main courses $3–$11; lunch $3–$5; dinner $16–$18. N
   credit cards.
   Open: Summer, Mon and Wed–Sat 11:30am–9pm, Sun 10:30am–2pm. Winte
   Sun–Thurs 11:30am–8pm.

The location of Brattleboro's oldest natural-foods restaurant also serves as a popula
coffeehouse (live music on weekends) and gallery for local artists. Its second-floc
location allows it to utilize a glassed-in patio terrace where diners may sit throughou
the year. The menu is interesting and international, with dishes from Italy, China
Mexico, the Middle East, India, the Caribbean, Japan, and the USA, to name but
few. The prices are certainly reasonable, the food delicious, and the staff friendly.

2. MARLBORO & WILMINGTON

West of Brattleboro are some of Vermont's—and all New England's—lovelie
unspoiled villages, worthy of a few days' stay, or at least a meal or a rest sto
Marlboro and Wilmington are on Route 9, west of Brattleboro, in the direction c
Bennington.

MARLBORO

8 miles (13km) W of Brattleboro, 10 miles (16km) E of Wilmington

GETTING THERE   By Car   Follow Route 9 west from Brattleboro.

ESSENTIALS   The **area code** is 802. The nearest **visitors center** is o
Interstate 91 in Guilford (tel. 802/254-4593), about 8 miles away.

The town's name brings to mind immediately the summertime **Marlboro Musi
   School and Festival,** directed by Rudolf Serkin for many years. The festiv
brings together dozens of the most talented musicians in the country, some famou
and some soon to be famous, for 2 months' practice, consultation, and tutorial. C
weekends from mid-July to mid-August the school is opened to concert audience
most of whom have ordered their tickets weeks or months in advance and have als
made early lodging reservations. The auditorium at Marlboro College seats few
than 700 people, and to keep the spirit of the chamber music, directors ar
performers resist demands for a larger hall.

   If you're interested in attending weekend festival concerts, write early to Marlbo
Music, Marlboro, VT 05344 (tel. 802/254-2394); this is the address to use from la

June through mid-August. From September through mid-June, write to Marlboro Music, 135 South 18th Street, Philadelphia, PA 19103 (tel. 215/569-4690). Or you can phone the box office at 802/254-2394, and ask for schedules, prices, and purchase forms. Then, when you've got your tickets, make a reservation either in Marlboro, or nearby Brattleboro or Wilmington, or even in Bennington—that city is only a 45-minute drive away through the forests of southern Vermont.

WHERE TO STAY

Marlboro is a location more than a bustling town, and when you drive to the dot on the map you will find a church, a small town office building, and several houses. But that's about all, and so for many products and services you must drive to Brattleboro. Several inns and restaurants in the area, however, provide well for travelers year round, as well as for festival visitors. Both of the inns recommended below have excellent dining rooms.

LONGWOOD INN, Rte. 9 (P.O. Box 86), Marlboro, VT 05344. Tel. 802/257-1545. 15 rms (13 with bath).
$ Rates: High season, $91–$144 double with breakfast, $136–$187 double with breakfast and dinner. AE, MC, V. **Parking:** Free. **Closed:** Early Apr.
Ten miles west of Brattleboro and 15 miles east of Mount Snow, only a short drive from Marlboro College and the music festival, is the Longwood Inn, a fine old Vermont clapboard dwelling over two centuries old. The inn's rooms are pretty and country-comfortable. It is the dining room, however, that is the center of inn life. The cuisine is up-to-date American regional; the menu changes weekly. During the summer season, when the music festival is running, and also during foliage season (to Columbus Day), the inn serves all three meals every day. At other times of the year, breakfast is provided for inn guests, and dinner is served to all Wednesday through Sunday.

OLD WHETSTONE INN, South St., Marlboro, VT 05344. Tel. 802/254-2500. 12 rms (8 with bath).
$ Rates: $35–$80 single; $60–$85 double; 3-night minimum stay required in summer. No credit cards. **Parking:** Free.
The Whetstone has been an inn for close to two centuries: The upstairs was once a "ballroom" where the local gentry could stage their get-togethers; the downstairs was a tavern along the stagecoach route between Boston and Albany. In winter, cross-country ski trails start at the inn's back door. The inn's pond (the reservoir in case of fire) is right out back. As there's no great activity in the town, nothing will disturb you unless you take to your feet or your bicycle to go to the music festival, 2 miles away. During the Marlboro Music Festival, a 3-night weekend stay is required. Higher rates are for rooms with a private bath or a kitchenette and meals are not included, but you can get breakfast each morning (waffles, pancakes, popovers, and home-baked muffins and biscuits), dinners on concert nights during the summer and on weekends and certain weekdays at other times in the year.

WILMINGTON

10 miles (16km) W of Marlboro, 21 miles (34km) E of Bennington

GETTING THERE By Car   Route 9 meets Route 100 in Wilmington.

ESSENTIALS   The **area code** is 802. **Mount Snow/Haystack Region Chamber of Commerce,** P.O. Box 3, Wilmington, VT 05363 (tel. 802/464-8092), can answer your questions.

Almost equidistant between Brattleboro and Bennington is Wilmington, a cross-roads town where Route 9 meets Route 100. Many people pass through Wilmington as they begin their journey northward along Vermont's central scenic artery, Route 100. There are many good inns here, partly because it's a crossroads and partly because it is close to the ski slopes of Mount Snow.

WHERE TO STAY

HERMITAGE INN, Coldbrook Rd. (P.O. Box 457), Wilmington, VT 05363. Tel. 802/464-3511. Fax 802/464-2688. 15 rms (all with bath). **Directions:** Follow Rte. 100 north about 2½ miles, turn left onto Coldbrook Rd.; the inn is about 3 miles.

$ Rates (including breakfast and dinner): $180–$200 double. AE, DC, MC, V. **Parking:** Free.

When you see the inn, you'll understand why it's named Hermitage: Jim raises his own game birds, makes his own maple syrup and jam, and has a vast and well-selected wine cellar. If he ever wanted to be a hermit, he'd be set for life. You can become a hermit in this plentiful hideaway, which was once the home of the editor of the *Social Register*. The main house is over a century old, has some of the original furnishings and many others from the same period, and most of the guest rooms have working fireplaces. The inn's other attractions include fine views of Haystack Mountain and a shop. It's a real country experience, not a citified country inn.

As you might expect from the bounty described above, the dining here is superb and exceptional, with lots of game fowl, trout, and fresh home-grown vegetables, plus wines from that venerable cellar, which has been abuilding for almost three decades. Lunch is sometimes served during the busy summer season, at an extra charge. The inn's other attractions include cross-country ski trails, ski rentals, tennis court, and a trout pond. Golf and ski packages are offered.

TRAIL'S END, Smith Rd., Wilmington, VT 05363. Tel. 802/464-2727. 14 rms (all with bath). TV **Directions:** About 5 miles from Mount Snow, 4 miles north of the traffic light in Wilmington, ½ mile east of Rte. 100.

$ Rates (including breakfast): $85–$100 single, $85–$130 double. MC, V. **Parking:** Free.

Despite its woodland location, Trail's End is no backwoods establishment, for it has a swimming pool, clay tennis court, and trout pond, and a dining room in which remarkably delicious meals are the rule. Three rooms have TV sets. Four rooms have fireplaces in addition to the two fireplace suites. Trail's End is certainly one of Mount Snow's most attractive, architecturally interesting, congenial places to stay.

THE WHITE HOUSE OF WILMINGTON, Rte. 9, Wilmington, VT 05363. Tel. 802/464-2135, or toll free 800/541-2135. Fax 802/464-5222. 12 rms (all with bath).

$ Rates (including breakfast and dinner): $190 double. AE, DC, MC, V. **Parking:** Free.

This could well be this area's most elegant and gracious inn. Housed in an imposing turn-of-the-century (1914) mansion with lofty porticoes and high-ceilinged public rooms with elegant furniture, it has charming, spacious guest rooms; five of which have a fireplace. The White House is a complete resort, with a lovely rose garden complete with fountain. The dining room, which is very well regarded, serves breakfast and dinner daily. On Sunday, there's brunch and, in winter, a special skiers' lunch.

Facilities include a 60-foot outdoor swimming pool, an indoor swimming pool, a sauna, a whirlpool, and lots of hiking and cross-country ski trails. Children over 10 welcome.

WHERE TO DINE

ROADHOUSE, Rte. 100 at Old Ark Rd. Tel. 464-5017 or 464-5694.
   Cuisine: AMERICAN. **Reservations:** Recommended.
$ Prices: Dinner MC, V.
   Open: Dinner daily 6–10pm; Sun brunch (in winter only) 11am–2pm.
The Roadhouse, just north of the center, is what its name implies, not a fancy place, but a good place to come for solid country-casual eating and full bar at a reasonable price. Standard old-time favorites such as steaks, chicken, and simple seafood fill the menu; the bread is baked right here. Prices include soup, salad, breads, main course, and dessert.

3. BENNINGTON

21 miles (34km) W of Wilmington; 14 miles (22.5km) N of Williamstown,
Mass.; 140 miles (226km) NW of Boston, Mass.

GETTING THERE By Car U.S. 7 is the main north-south route, Route 9 the main east-west one.

ESSENTIALS The **area code** is 802. The **Bennington Area Chamber of Commerce** (tel. 802/447-3311 or 447-1162) is at Veteran's Memorial Drive (Route 7 North), about a mile from the intersection of Main and North/South streets. Open during business hours, the chamber can give you a good, detailed map of the town and lots of information on both the town and the surrounding region.

"Vermont's most historic area" is how the citizens of Bennington tout their town.
   The reason for this civic pride is that the revolutionary war's Battle of Bennington was fought near here (the actual site is now in neighboring Walloomsac, N.Y.) in 1777. The battle is looked upon as a turning point in the war, since the British troops expected to encounter little resistance at Bennington and instead were forced to retreat after having lost a good number of casualties and prisoners to the Revolutionaries. Soon afterward, at the Battle of Saratoga, the British soldiers thus weakened were forced to surrender, giving the Americans their first great victory of the war.
   Although the Battle of Bennington was certainly influential in the winning of the war, it is doubtless remembered so well today because of a 300-foot-high obelisk that was built in 1891 to commemorate it. Both the monument (which has an observation platform) and the well-known Bennington Museum's collection of Americana are open to visitors.

WHAT TO SEE & DO

The historic sights of the town are mostly grouped along West Main Street, in the section called **Old Bennington.** You can buy a single ticket which admits you to the town's three most important sights: the Bennington Museum, the Bennington Battle Monument, and the Park-McCullough House, for $8.50 per adult, $6.50 per senior, $6 for a child aged 12 to 17, or $5 for a child aged 6 to 11 (under 6 get in free). The ticket represents a small savings over the price of three individual admission tickets. Pick yours up at the Bennington Area Chamber of Commerce, the Bennington Museum, or the Park-McCullough House.
   While you're at the Park-McCullough House in North Bennington, drive or walk through the campus of **Bennington College,** the unique loosely structured 4-year college, which stresses artistic creation and an acquaintance with nature. The situation of the college is particularly beautiful and is particularly well adapted for the creative efforts of the students. It is located on 550 acres dotted with biking trails, playing fields, tennis courts, and a spring-fed lake. The college is respected for its summer programs, including its summer writing workshops. Call 802/442-5401 for more information.

THE BENNINGTON MUSEUM

⭐ The Bennington Museum, West Main Street (Route 9; tel. 447-1571), has a collection dominated by Revolutionary and Early American history. Paintings glass items (molded, blown, and pressed), American-made furniture and carvings, arms, toys, and costumes are all included, and there are considerable numbers of very attractive treasures. The Bennington pottery, for instance, is more like china with its gold or colored trim; it was made here for wealthy customers for over 100 years. Of the paintings, the most fascinating are the ones in the Grandma Moses collection. Anna Mary Moses (1860–1961) was a farm girl in nearby New York State, and later as a farmer's wife she did all the heavy, hard work that life on a farm demands, yet still found time to paint. After she was 70 years old and could no longer keep up with the heavy farm work, her paintings took on such a charming and primitive character, and such spirit, that one of her paintings now hangs in the Metropolitan in New York, and many others are here in the Bennington Museum. At the age of 100 she was still at work, and she died at 101. You can look back into what life was like for her in the exhibit called "And Life Is What You Make It" in the Grandma Moses Schoolhouse Museum, also in the Bennington Museum.

The museum is open daily from 9am to 5pm. Admission costs $5 for adults, $4 for young people 12 to 17 and seniors, free for children under 12, and $12 per family. The museum closes Thanksgiving Day and Christmas week.

THE BENNINGTON BATTLE MONUMENT

The impressive obelisk is more than 306 feet tall, which makes it the tallest structure in Vermont. It took 4 years (1887–91) to build, and when it was finished one could walk to the top by means of an interior staircase. Today the staircase is closed and an elevator hums up and down. Buy your ticket ($1) in the souvenir shop to the west of the monument entrance, and pick up a copy of the free leaflet describing the battle and the monument. The monument is open daily April through October.

This was not the site of the battle, but of the colonists' arsenal which was the object of the British advance. His supplies depleted by the action at Fort Ticonderoga, "Gentleman Johnny" Burgoyne sent two of his units toward Bennington to capture the Revolutionaries' arms stores. But General Burgoyne misjudged the size of the rebel force, and was unaware that Gen. John Stark, who had fought at Bunker Hill and under Washington at Trenton and Princeton, commanded the Americans. Stark cleverly headed off the British advance at Walloomsac (New York), 6 miles west of the arsenal. Stark is said to have exclaimed, "There are the Redcoats! They will be ours tonight or Molly Stark sleeps a widow."

The pitched battle on August 16, 1777, lasted 2 hours, and when the smoke cleared, the American forces were victorious. On the way back to Bennington, Stark's troops were surprised by British reinforcements, but Col. Seth Warner and his Green Mountain Boys arrived in time to save the day for the Americans. The losses at Bennington and lack of supplies weakened the British force, and Burgoyne surrendered his entire command in October following the Battle of Saratoga.

The view from the monument is very fine. Though you wouldn't recognize it, you can look west to where the battle actually took place, less than 6 miles away. For a closer view, follow "Bennington Battlefield" signs from the monument through covered bridge to North Bennington, then west on Route 67 to the Bennington Battlefield Historic site near Walloomsac, N.Y. Plaques describe the battle, and shaded picnic tables provide a good place for a rest and a snack.

PARK-McCULLOUGH HISTORIC HOUSE MUSEUM

Of Bennington's outstanding Victorian mansions, one is exceptionally well kept. The Park-McCullough House (tel. 442-5441), just off Route 67A at the corner of West an

Park streets in North Bennington, is open for guided tours through the house daily, early May through October from 10am to 4pm (last tour leaves at 3pm). Adults pay $3; seniors pay $2.50; students 12 to 17 pay $1.50; children 11 and under accompanied by an adult, free. Besides the house, still stuffed with period furnishings and personal effects, there's a pint-size "manor" for a children's playhouse and a cupola-topped carriage house complete with century-old carriages.

WHERE TO STAY

Bennington has dozens of motels on the highways that approach it, but as is my custom I will concentrate most heavily on the establishments right in town. However, one of the following inns, the Hill Farm Inn, is in the village Arlington, about 15 miles north of Bennington, which has a number of its own hostelries, in the town proper and on Route 7A between Bennington and Arlington.

MODERATE

FOUR CHIMNEYS RESTAURANT & INN, 21 West Rd. (Rte. 9 West), Old Bennington, VT 05201. Tel. 802/447-3500. 12 rms (all with bath). A/C TV TEL **Directions:** Follow Route 9 west to the inn, on the right-hand side.
$ Rates (including continental breakfast): $100–$115 double. AE, CB, DC, MC, V. **Parking:** Free.

Noted mostly for its restaurant (see below), Four Chimneys does have several pleasant, comfortable guest rooms. The inn is set on spacious grounds good for walks, reading and just sitting. If you decide to dine here as well, you'll feel right at home.

HILL FARM INN, R.R. 2, Box 2015, Arlington, VT 05250. Tel. 802/375-2269, or toll free 800/882-2545. 13 rms (8 with bath). **Directions:** Go north of Bennington, and 4 miles north of Arlington, just off Rte. 7A.
$ Rates (including breakfast): $65 double without bath, $80 double with bath. AE, DISC, MC, V. **Parking:** Free.

This inn has been receiving guests since 1905, but was actually built as two farmhouses in the early 1800s. Of the 11 guest rooms and two suites, seven are in the inn proper, and six in the 1790 guesthouse next door.

BUDGET

BENNINGTON MOTOR INN, 143 W. Main St., Bennington, VT 05201. Tel. 802/442-5479, or toll free 800/359-9900. 16 rms (all with bath). A/C MINIBAR TV TEL
$ Rates: $52–$62 1 queen bed; $58–$68 2 beds. Extra person $5. Extra bed $5. AE, DC, MC, V. **Parking:** Free.

The little extras at this motor inn, located 3½ blocks west of the Route 7 intersection, include coffee-makers in the rooms, color TV (with cable and in-room movies), and individual thermostats. Some of the larger rooms, designated family units, can sleep up to six people, and these rooms also have little refrigerators. During the foliage-season rates are higher.

BEST WESTERN NEW ENGLANDER MOTOR INN, 220 Northside Dr., Bennington, VT 05201. Tel. 802/442-6311, or toll free 800/528-1234. Fax 802/442-6311. 58 rms (all with bath). A/C TV TEL
$ Rates: $67–$107 double and twin bed; $67–$91 double bed. Extra person $7. AE, CB, DC, DISC, MC, V. **Parking:** Free.

Between Bennington and North Bennington is the New Englander, a fairly large motel of 58 rooms arranged around a central court with a swimming pool and the motel's restaurant, which helps block noise from the busy street. As this is Bennington, the rooms have been done with Early American inspiration, although all

furnishings are modern. In the clutter and strip development of Northside Drive, th
New Englander is a very pleasant oasis, complete unto itself, and rooms ar
moderately priced. The New Englander's rooms are comfortable and pleasant an
contain coffee-makers.

KIRKSIDE MOTOR LODGE, 250 W. Main St., Bennington, VT 05201
   Tel. 802/447-7596. 23 rms (all with bath). A/C TV TEL
$ Rates: $44 double bed; $52 queen-size bed; $56 king-size bed. AE, MC, V
   Parking: Free.
Off-season, prices here are about 15% less, but during foliage season they're a fev
dollars higher. The rooms come with cable color TV and the usual motel comfort:
There's little problem with street noise because of the motel's position and locatio
on Route 9 West just 1½ blocks from Routes 7 and 9. If you stay here, you'll be righ
beside the handsome Gothic-style church, and about equidistant from the center c
town and the museum and monument.

WHERE TO DINE

ALLDAYS & ONIONS, 519 Main St. Tel. 447-0043.
   Cuisine: AMERICAN. **Reservations:** Recommended.
$ Prices: Appetizers $2–$6; main courses $11–$19; lunch $5–$8. MC, V.
   Open: Mon–Wed 7am–5:30pm, Thurs–Sat 7am–5:30pm and 6–8pm.
Bennington's purveyor of the daily fresh and delicious is a combination country store
delicatessen, gourmet food shop, restaurant, and bistro. Drop by and join th
assortment of locals and travelers, Bennington College students and professors fc
freshly baked morning muffins and Colombian coffee, a wonderful create-your-ow
sandwich, or a cool pasta salad. Evening suppers often feature enticing pasta dishes c
fish. They have a small but good eclectic wine selection.

BRASSERIE, 324 Country St. Tel. 447-7922.
   Cuisine: NEW AMERICAN. **Reservations:** Not accepted. **Directions:** Tur
off Main St. by the Dunkin' Donuts (460 Main) and go straight; the street ends a
Country St. at Potters' Yard, a complex that includes the restaurant.
$ Prices: Appetizers $3.50–$8; main courses $10–$17. MC, V.
   Open: Daily 11:30am–8pm.
In Bennington there is a place called the Potters' Yard, a complex of shops an
galleries in which local works of art and craft are displayed and sold, and in th
same complex at School and Country streets is the Brasserie. As the nam
might suggest, the Brasserie is fashioned on a French tavern restaurant, with beer an
wine and delicious dishes, such as the pâté maison with French bread or chicke
curry. A chef's salad or Greek salad and a variety of sandwiches or omelets ar
similarly good choices. The patio is the choice place to dine in good weather.

FOUR CHIMNEYS RESTAURANT, 21 West Rd. (Rte. 9 West), Ol
Bennington. Tel. 447-3500.
   Cuisine: FRENCH. **Reservations:** Recommended. **Directions:** Follow Rout
9 West to the inn, on the right-hand side.
$ Prices: Appetizers $5–$11; main courses $14–$24; lunch $5.50–$12.50; dinne
$25–$35. AE, CB, DC, MC, V.
   Open: Lunch Tues–Sun 11:30am–2pm; dinner Mon–Sat 5pm–10pm, Su
2–9pm.
Only ½ mile west of the Bennington Museum, this imposing and many
chimneyed white mansion shaded by huge old trees set in spacious, well-tende
grounds was once the home of a prominent Bennington businessman. Now i
formal salons, informal solarium, patio, and terraces are set up for elegant dinin
Chef Alex Koks's English-language menu is admirably straightforward: What woul
be "maigret de canard, sauce framboise" in a more pretentious place is "broiled brea
of duck with raspberry vinegar sauce" at the Four Chimneys—and just as deliciou
Classics, such as beef Wellington, rack of lamb, and roast Cornish game hen, come i
preparations that are interesting and original without being hyperexotic. The food

xcellent, the service the same, and luncheon, on a pleasant summer's day, is a special reat. House wines are under $15 per bottle, several good selections cost $20 or less, nd most bottles are under $35.

4. WEST DOVER & MOUNT SNOW

West Dover: 6 miles (10km) N of Wilmington;
3 miles (5km) SE of Mount Snow ski area

GETTING THERE By Car   Follow Route 100.

ESSENTIALS   The **area code** is 802. **Mount Snow/Haystack Region Chamber of Commerce,** P.O. Box 3, Wilmington, VT 05363 (tel. 802/464-8092), an answer your questions.

Because of its southern Vermont location within driving distance of the metropolitan centers of Boston, Hartford, Providence, and New York, Mount Snow is one of Vermont's most popular ski resorts. The ski resort encouraged the inn trade, and the inns began playing host to summer travelers, and now this area is as popular in the warm months as in the cold.

The ski area is immense, with three different faces of the mountain covered with trails and lifts—13 lifts in all, including two enclosed, skis-on gondolas. The highest vertical drop is almost 2,000 feet, and you could take the same lift a dozen times and never come down the same trail or slope. It's crowded, yes, because it's close to the cities, and is a good mountain for beginners and intermediate skiers, but it's also got a lot of variety, and certainly a lot of activity. A resort this big has all the facilities: a "Pumpkin Patch" nursery for small children, a bar, a cafeteria, and equipment rentals, a ski school, and 40 miles of cross-country trails.

WHERE TO STAY

About 100 inns, lodges, hotels, and motels are clustered near the ski area, on the approach roads, or in the villages near Mount Snow. From this bewildering assortment of choices, several stand out.

THE INN AT SAWMILL FARM, Rte. 100 (P.O. Box 367), West Dover, VT 05356. Tel. 802/464-8131. Fax 802/464-8131. 21 rms (all with bath). A/C
$ Rates (including breakfast and dinner): $240–$350 double. No credit cards.
  Parking: Free at main entrance.
Here is a deluxe country inn that began as an inn with an attitude but has developed into a warm venue set amid romantic surroundings. It appears regularly in designer magazines with lavish spreads of photos showing the guest rooms—Victorian, Federal, turn-of-the-century—in the inn's various buildings. The dining rooms are particularly wonderful, providing the perfect ambience for cozy, romantic dinners of elegant, carefully prepared dishes from a positively sumptuous menu. In the evening even in summer the public rooms are all aglow with a multitude of candles—trays of them set on antiques here and there—adding a soft warm mood everywhere. Be sure to note the temperature-controlled wine cellar with more than 36,000 bottles of wine and over 500 labels.

On the inn's carefully tended grounds are a swimming pool, two trout ponds, and a tennis court. The inn proper, and old farmhouse and barn, houses 11 guest rooms, and in other buildings there are 10 rooms, each with a fireplace; 16 rooms have air conditioning. Prices may be a bit higher in foliage season, and between Christmas and New Year's. Children under 10 cannot be lodged at the inn.

KITZHOF, Rte. 100, West Dover, VT 05356. Tel. 802/464-8310, or toll free 800/388-8310. 25 rms (all with bath). TV **Directions:** Go about 10 miles north of Wilmington on Rte. 100; inn is on right just beyond West Dover.

$ Rates (including breakfast and dinner): Winter, $128–$139 double; $54 quad pe person. AE, DISC, MC, V. **Parking:** Free. **Closed:** Apr to mid-May.

Kitzhof is a particularly nice alpine-style lodge set back from the highway, chargin; quite moderate prices. No two rooms are alike except in their comfort and sparklin; cleanliness. Most rooms have TV sets. Knotty-pine boards and logs and rusti emphasis; a Finnish-style sauna and a whirlpool bath are added luxuries open to al guests. An outdoor pool is heated for summer use. There's a BYOB bar with setups Reductions are in order for lots of things, such as 5-day economy ski weeks ane coming early or late in the ski season. The Kitzhof takes bus tours in summer and cai provide lodging for transient guests when there's room.

WHERE TO DINE

BRUSH HILL RESTAURANT, Rte. 100. Tel. 896-6100.
Cuisine: CONTEMPORARY. **Reservations:** Required.
$ Prices: Appetizers $6–$7.25; main courses $16.25–$22; dinner $45–$50. MC V.
Open: Dinner Wed–Sun 6–10pm.

North of West Dover is Brush Hill, a late 18th-century post-and-beam barn that' been restored and turned into a romantic dining spot. A 12-foot-long brick fireplac takes the chill off in foliage season; all diners enjoy it, as there are fewer than a doze tables. Chef Mike Sylva apprenticed at Jaspers in Boston, and while he's in the kitche creating New American cuisine treats, his wife, Lee, acts as hostess (and she als makes the desserts). The menu changes monthly, but recently dinner started with a unusual antipasto of grilled artichokes, shallots, red pepper, and smoked scamonza and was followed by a rack of lamb with mint essence, grilled leeks, and garlic Dessert may be the dieter's to-order-or-not dilemma, with pastry puffs filled wit French vanilla ice cream topped by a chocolate rum sauce.

5. NEWFANE & GRAFTON

Newfane and Grafton are two of Vermont's most picture-perfect towns, with tall ol trees, white churches with high steeples, and gracious old houses designed wit classical touches. Come early in spring when they're "sugaring off," and see tow children tap the maple trees along village streets. Come in summer and explore fo yard and antiques sales. Come in autumn for the blazing color. Or come in winter t hide away in a comfy inn and dine each night from a superb menu.

NEWFANE

14 miles (23km) NW of Brattleboro, 16 miles (26km) NE of West Dover,
15 miles (24km) S of Grafton

GETTING THERE   By Car   Follow Route 30 north from Brattleboro; from Wes Dover, follow unnumbered roads via East Dover, Brookside, South Newfane an Williamsville to Route 30, then north.

ESSENTIALS   The **area code** is 802. The nearest **visitors center** is o Interstate 91 in Guilford (tel. 802/254-4593).

WHERE TO STAY & DINE

FOUR COLUMNS INN, West St. (P.O. Box 278), Newfane, VT 05345
Tel. 802/365-7713. 15 rms (all with bath). A/C TEL
$ Rates (including breakfast): $100–$170 double. AE, MC, V. **Parking:** Free.

You can come here for dinner Wednesday through Monday from 6 to 9pm. Find a table in the cozy dining room, which recalls a hunting lodge in Europe with its rough-hewn beams, large fireplace, and spindle-backed chairs. Then get ready for such delicacies as a cold salmon mousse, followed by venison or rack of lamb, duck, or steak, finishing up with fancy pastries. The wine list has vintages priced from $15 to $50, and a full dinner for two here might cost $80 to $125.

As for the guest rooms, they are as charming as the inn and the town, with private bath, air conditioning, and breakfast included. The inn also has a pool, and hiking trails pass near the front door.

GRAFTON

15 miles (24km) N of Newfane, 7 miles (11km) S of Chester

GETTING THERE By Car Follow Route 35 north from Newfane, or south from Chester; from I-91 northbound, take Exit 5, then Route 121 west to Grafton; from I-91 southbound, take Exit 6, then U.S. 5 south to Bellows Falls and North Westminster, then Route 121 west to Grafton.

ESSENTIALS The **area code** is 802. The nearest **visitors center** is on Interstate 91 in Guilford (tel. 802/254-4593).

Like Newfane, Grafton is a piece of old New England, but there is a nobility about this town—something like Woodstock—that makes it special. Carefully preserved houses and public buildings from a century or two ago are joined unobtrusively by more modern structures on the outskirts. Summer or winter, Grafton is a place bewitching in its beauty. Stop for a cup of coffee, a drink or a meal, or even for overnight. Be careful, though—one overnight easily leads to week-long stays here.

WHAT TO SEE & DO

Grafton is perfect just for relaxing walks and sitting by the fireplace, but there are lots of other things to do as well. Start with a **horse-and-carriage ride** (in summer) around town. You'll see the driver, the steed, and the buggy at the stand in front of the Old Tavern Monday through Saturday between mid-June and the end of October. The ride is not just for fun—you'll get a complete narrative tour of Grafton as you trot along.

Grafton harbors a number of antiques shops, artists' galleries, a village store, and the **Grafton Village Cheese Company** (tel. 843-2221). The Cheese Company makes Cheddar, and you can see it being made and buy samples or supplies by following the Townshend Road about ½ mile south of the village. Hours are 8:30am to 4pm weekdays all year, 10am to 4:30pm on Saturday from June through October.

By now no doubt you are completely enchanted with the town. To delve into its history, pay a visit to the **Grafton Historical Society Museum** (tel. 843-2584), on Main Street just down from the post office. The exhibits of Grafton memorabilia, old photographs, history, and genealogical files are open from 2:30 to 4:30pm on Saturday and Sunday from June through mid-October, on Sunday July through September, and on holiday weekends and holiday Mondays.

WHERE TO STAY & DINE

THE OLD TAVERN AT GRAFTON, Rte. 35, Grafton, VT 05146. Tel. 802/843-2231. 35 rms (all with bath). TV TEL

$ Rates: $70–$150 single or double. AE, MC, V. **Parking:** Free.

The center of Grafton's social life since it was built in 1801 as a way station on the stagecoach road, the Old Tavern is also a town landmark. In its long history as a place to stay the night, the Old Tavern has played host to General Grant, Woodrow Wilson, Rudyard Kipling, and even woodsman-philosopher Henry David

Thoreau. With its annexes, the inn can lodge about 100 people. Its rooms have private baths and modern conveniences, but the ambience is still old New England. The Old Tavern is not what one would call "quaint," but it is an authentic landmark, charming, hospitable, and very comfortable. Facilities include a pond for swimming, two tennis courts, and a games room.

You have a choice of dining rooms. For a drink before dinner, make your way to the Barn, with its own separate bar, several fireplaces, and a TV room. Lunch is served at the Old Tavern from noon to 2pm, and dinner from 6:30 to 9pm, by reservation. A dinner, main courses range from $18 to $27.

---

6. MANCHESTER

24 miles (39km) N of Bennington, 7 miles (11km) S of Dorset

GETTING THERE By Bus See the beginning of this chapter.

By Car Follow U.S. 7 north from Bennington or south from Rutland.

ESSENTIALS The **area code** is 802. The Manchester and the Mountain Chamber of Commerce (tel. 802/362-2100) maintains an **information office** on U.S. 7A in Manchester Center for your convenience.

The town of Manchester was once a summer resort on the order of the Berkshire towns. Settled before the Revolution, the town has a wide main street and handsome houses that retain the charm of the early Federal period.

As the county seat of Bennington County, Manchester was an important place long before Mt. Equinox (3,800 ft.), to the west, drew crowds of hikers and skiers. The sprawling Equinox Hotel right in the center of town has undergone another face-lift.

In the modern town of Manchester Center, just a few miles north along U.S. 7, all is bustle and activity, with traffic lights, filling stations, shopping centers, supermarkets, restaurants, and motels.

As the story is told, in the early days, the Village of Manchester wanted to attract business and visitors but decided folks would not come to a town without sidewalks. The local quarry of the only stone available was enlisted to provide the necessary materials for sidewalks. As a result, today the Village of Manchester enjoys the distinction of having 17 miles of *Marble* sidewalks.

WHAT TO SEE & DO

What do you do in winter? That's easy: You **ski**. Big Bromley, Snow Valley, Magic Mountain, Stratton Mountain, and numerous ski-touring centers are located within a few miles of Manchester Center. Right in Manchester is the ski-touring center at Hildene.

As for **summer activities,** you can play golf, swim, hike, or ride a bike. Rent a bike from Battenkill Sports, in the stone house 1¼ miles east of U.S. 7A along Route 11/30, Manchester Center (tel. 362-2734). Three-speed, 10-speed, men's, women's, and children's bikes are available.

At the Bromley ski area on Route 11, 6 miles east of Manchester, an Alpine Slide (tel. 824-5522) draws downhill racers in summer. You take the ski lift to the top, and then choose among the three alpine slide tracks, two-thirds of a mile long, controlling the speed of your little cart as you travel to the bottom. The slide is open late May to mid-October from 9am to 5pm, if the weather's good. The slide is fun, and the chair-lift ride that takes you up over the verdant hills is equally enjoyable.

Abraham Lincoln had four sons, but only one of them lived to adulthood. When President Lincoln was assassinated in 1865, Robert Todd Lincoln was an officer serving under General Grant in the Union Army. Later a successful lawyer and businessman, Lincoln came to Manchester in 1902, bought 412 acres of land, and began construction of **Hildene.** The mansion was completed in 1904, and Lincoln spent the summers there until his death in 1926. The estate was inherited by his wife, and then his granddaughter, who left it to the Church of Christ, Scientist, in 1975. It's now owned and maintained by a nonprofit group, the Friends of Hildene (tel. 362-1788).

Robert Todd Lincoln built more than a house here. Hildene's 22 buildings include a dairy barn, horse barn, sugar house, greenhouse, even a small observatory. You can roam the grounds, tour the 22-room Georgian Revival mansion, inspect Lincoln family heirlooms any day of the week, mid-May through October from 9:30am to 4pm (last tour). Admission costs $6 for adults, $2 for children. In winter, Hildene is the site of a ski-touring center. To find it, go 2 miles south along U.S. 7A from the intersection with Route 11/30—the intersection is the main crossroads in Manchester Center.

WHERE TO STAY

Christmas tours and a June food-and-wine fest are featured at some of the historic inns of Manchester.

1811 HOUSE, Manchester Village, VT 05254. Tel 802/362-1811, or toll free 800/432-1811. 14 rms (all with bath). A/C
Rates (including full breakfast): $110–$180 double. AE, MC, V. Children 16 and older welcome. **Parking:** Free.

Think of someone special you'd like to spend a romantic, fun time with, and picture yourselves here at the 1811 House. This historic 1770s house (the name came from when the inn first started taking guests) sits on seven acres of lawns and gardens, and you can cool off in the pond. If you sit in the tartan-clad pub (usually on the honor system, even to nonguests), you can see out the back door across the gardens right up to the Equinox's new golf course. Bravo on the food. Oh yes, the inn has so many single malt liquors that the folks at the liquor store usually direct inquiries and samplers here for a taste test. The rooms are exquisite. Six have fireplaces and three are contained in a separate carriage house. This is my favorite historic inn in Vermont.

EQUINOX HOTEL, RESORT & SPA, Rte. 7A, Manchester, VT 05254. Tel. 802/362-4700, or toll free 800/362-4747. Fax 802/362-1595. 164 rms (all with bath). A/C TV TEL
Rates (including breakfast): $170–$315 double. AE, DC, DISC, MC, V. **Parking:** Free, behind hotel.

The Equinox saw its heyday in Victorian times, with four presidents as guests over the years. (It was almost five: Lincoln had reservations for 1865, but was assassinated.) As the inn's fame and clientele grew, wings and additions were added to the original building, making at last a vast, rambling wonder of a place. With its recent face-lift, the Equinox is better than ever, and again ready to welcome the best. The Equinox has all the facilities of a luxury hotel, and then some: 18-hole golf course, heated swimming pool, three tennis courts, a health fitness center, lounge, and restaurant. The hotel came under new ownership last year and closed for extensive renovations. All guest rooms were redone, the lounge and restaurants expanded, and the lobby moved and expanded upward with a new fireplace added. The result is a magnificent and splendid facility of a bygone era.

INN AT MANCHESTER, Rte. 7A (P.O. Box 41), Manchester, VT 05254. Tel. 802/362-1793. 20 rms (13 with bath). A/C

$ Rates (including breakfast): $65–$100 double; $115–$130 suite. AE, DISC, MC V. **Parking:** Free, on premises.

This restored Vermont Victorian inn between Manchester Village and Mancheste Center has plenty of room for guests in 16 rooms and suites in the inn, and four mor in the restored carriage house, where there's a separate lounge. The rooms bear th names of delightful mountain and meadow flowers, such as primrose, black-eye Susan, and blue phlox. Antiques are placed carefully in all the rooms, and eac bedroom has a different style of coordinated linens and comforters. Old print paintings, and posters, picked up by innkeepers Stan and Harriet Rosenberg durin their travels, are found on walls throughout the inn. The inn has a pool and offer wine and cheese to guests.

RELUCTANT PANTHER INN, West Rd., Manchester Village, VT 05254
Tel. 802/362-2568, or toll free 800/822-2331. Fax 802/362-2586. 16 rms (a with bath). A/C TEL TV

$ Rates (including full breakfast and à la carte dinner): $160–$280 double. MC, V

This lavender clapboard inn sitting on a marble foundation and surrounded by marble sidewalks and a marble terrace has a longstanding reputation in the villag The restaurant is wonderful and a good reason to stay put for dinner. The bar area quaint and inviting and the parlor room at the entry has real ash and maple leave woven into the wallcovering. Rooms are equally as original and may feature a fireplac in the superior category or suite.

VILLAGE COUNTRY INN, Rte. 7A, Manchester Village, VT 05254. Te
802/362-1792, or toll free 800/370-0300. 15 rms (all with bath). TV

$ Rates (including full breakfast and dinner): $130–$195 double. AE, DISC, MC, V
Parking: Free.

This historic 1889 inn has a big front porch that beckons you to come and linge Inside is a stone fireplace, a tavern, and garden-style dining room. The rooms a country-inspired with French overtones with all the frilly details such as lace an down pillows. Rooms include all bed arrangements, even twins, to accommoda most needs. You can request an air conditioner and a telephone.

7. DORSET

7 miles (11km) N of Manchester

GETTING THERE   By Car   Follow Route 30 north from Manchester.

ESSENTIALS   See "Manchester," above.

Settled in 1768, Dorset is one of the many villages in New England that is older tha the American Republic. It's a gem of a village, having kept its rural spirit and fir buildings intact over the centuries, and any new structures were required to add to tl harmony of the village and its setting.

For a number of years Dorset was an artists' and writers' summer resort, but the: days it is usually only the successful in those fields who can afford to stay in one Dorset's few charming old inns; rather, the village now caters to those who ha become successful in the city, and who need to get away to the peace of tl countryside for a few days or weeks.

In Dorset the sidewalks are marble, and so is a nice church with Gothic touch not far from the town green. There's a marble quarry about a mile south of town, ar besides supplying the soft, easily cut stone for a myriad of uses in Dorset, the quar supplied most of the marble for the New York Public Library building.

For recreation, Dorset has the **Dorset Playhouse** (tel. 802/867-5777), down past the church just past the end of the town green on Cheney Road. Plays are performed by professional actors June through August and community players September through May.

The **J. K. Adams Company Factory Store,** on Route 30 a mile south of town, makes fine wood products—carving boards, butcher blocks, kitchen worktables, even kitchen organizers like a spice block that holds 16 glass jars and revolves on a lazy Susan. All the items are available at a reduced price, and the "seconds" are sold at prices up to 40% off the norm, but compared to other outlet prices in New England, these are not too special.

WHERE TO STAY & DINE

BARROWS HOUSE, Dorset, VT 05251. Tel. 802/867-4455. 28 rooms (all with bath). A/C TV

$ Rates: (including breakfast and dinner): $160–$215 double. MC, V.

Besides loving the town of Dorset, you'll love the Barrows House with its main inn dating back to 1784 and the seven other white clapboard buildings on the property. There's an outdoor pool and two tennis courts, not to mention the fancy gardens to walk through. We even found fiddleheads growing in one patch outside the front door. Guest rooms are a mix of country inn and modern appointments. There are a handful of rooms upstairs in the main inn but the ground floor is used mostly for dining. Small groups enjoy this place to hold their powwows and executive think-tank sessions. It's located 6 miles north of Manchester in the center of town.

DORSET INN, Church St., Dorset, VT 05251. Tel. 802/867-5500 or 867-9392. Fax 802/867-5542. 31 rms (all with bath). A/C

$ Rates: (including breakfast): $70 single; $100–$150 double. AE, MC, V.
Parking: Free on premises.

The inn, which claims to be Vermont's oldest continuously operated inn, has several older rooms in the original building, and a larger number of rooms in an artfully disguised modern addition which blends in well with the older part. Twenty rooms are air conditioned. Dorset Inn guests enjoy privileges at the Field Club, which is virtually next door. The inn has a dining room with lunch ranging from $5 to $9 and dinner courses, $17 to $22.

---

8. WOODSTOCK

16 miles (26km) W of White River Junction, 20 miles (32km) E of Sherburne Center (Killington), 14 miles (23km) NE of Plymouth

GETTING THERE By Car   From I-89 or I-91, follow U.S. 4 west.

ESSENTIALS   The **area code** is 802. From late June through the foliage season, there is a town **information booth** (tel. 802/457-1042) in service on the village green, where you can get a free village map and list of town businesses. Otherwise, contact the **Woodstock Area Chamber of Commerce,** P.O. Box 468, 18 Central St., Woodstock, VT 05091 (tel. 802/457-3555).

Woodstock was chartered in 1761, and within 5 years it had been designated the shire town (county seat) of Windsor County. The particular significance of these little facts is that they explain why the town is so beautiful today, why so many lovely buildings survive, and why the town escaped the ravages (and riches) brought by 19th-century industry. The industry here was government, the only pollutant from which is hot air, and this rises out of sight at once.

Besides its fine buildings, Woodstock boasts no fewer than four church bells made by Paul Revere. Three are still in service, but one cracked after two centuries of use and is now on display on the south porch of the Congregational church.

Woodstock is particularly well situated, in a beautiful valley of the Ottauquechee River with mountains all around. In winter, skiers can be put up in the town while they spend the day on the slopes of Mount Tom or Suicide Six.

WHAT TO SEE & DO

SIGHTS

The Woodstock Historical Society's **Dana House Museum,** on Elm Street (tel 457-1822), just around the corner from the green, is open for visits Monday through Saturday, early May through late October, from 10am to 5pm, on Sunday 2 to 5pm Admission costs $3.50 for an adult, $2.50 for a senior citizen, $1 for a child over 12 The collections include furniture, decorative arts, antique toys, paintings, textiles historic clothing, and local artifacts. There is a research library and museum gift shop on premises.

In your walks around town, you might want to look for the **three covered bridges** across the Ottauquechee, including one built in 1969 and rebuilt 5 years later—Middle Bridge, just off the green in the middle of town.

On the far side of the Ottauquechee from the town green is a cemetery, and at the east edge of the cemetery is the beginning of a walking trail. The **Billings Park Trails** are maintained by the town, and are yours to enjoy for free.

SKIING

Woodstock was the site of the first ski tow in the United States—a rope on a pulley that pulled skiers up the slopes in a farmer's field. Today a well-known ski area is close by, called **Suicide Six.** In addition, the **Woodstock Ski Touring Center,** at the Woodstock Country Club, Route 106, Woodstock, VT 05091 (tel. 802/457-2114, or toll free 800/448-7900), has nearly 50 miles of marked trails for skating and classic technique, plus equipment rental, cross-country ski shop, restaurant and lounge lessons, ski tours, and midweek ski-free plans with the Woodstock Inn (tel. toll free 800/448-7900). A new indoor sports center is located a mile away and connects to cross-country trails.

Suicide Six (despite the terrifying name) is a fine, midsized, family ski area with two double-chair lifts, and a free J-bar on the beginners' slope. Located 3 miles north of Woodstock on Route 12, it also offers midweek ski-free plans with the Woodstock Inn. Package plans are available through the inn; there is 50% snowmaking capability and lessons and equipment can be had on the spot in a new base lodge which also houses a ski-rental shop, restaurant, and lounge (tel. 802/457-1666).

You can stay in Woodstock and ski elsewhere, of course, and the Killington and Pico ski areas, just a short drive away, present all the challenge and facilities a skier could want.

A NEARBY ATTRACTION

While in Woodstock, take a spin over to **Quechee Gorge,** 8 miles to the east. The highway bridge carries U.S. 4 right across the picturesque gorge; below, the Ottauquechee River slips swiftly between boulders and jagged rock walls. The Grand Canyon it's not, but pretty? Definitely.

For the best view, follow the signs to the viewpoint north of the highway. Or enter Quechee State Park, on the east side of the gorge, and take the short hiking trail down to the edge of the gorge. The walk will take 15 minutes, one-way. By the way, there's camping and picnicking at Quechee State Park.

WHERE TO STAY

JACKSON HOUSE AT WOODSTOCK, Rte. 4, Woodstock, VT 05091. Tel. 802/457-2065. 12 rms (all with bath).
$ **Rates:** (including full breakfast): $120–$160 double. Children over 14 welcome. No credit cards. **Parking:** Free.

The Jackson House vies for the top spot in my heart as Vermont's best inn (and best-kept secret) along with the 1811 House of Manchester Village and the Inn at the Round Barn Farm in Waitsfield. Come here if you want to be enveloped by country warmth. The inn was the home of a lumber baron who artfully decorated each room in different woods from maple to cherry. The room Gloria Swanson used to stay in is popular today and is furnished with old photos; other rooms may have a cannonball bed, Victorian pieces, or French Empire appointments. Three rooms are suites. Breakfasts are an event and feature such items as a Santa Fe omelet or baked apples stuffed with mincemeat. Hors d'oeuvres and wine and champagne are offered evenings while a harpist plays in the library. You'll find Jackson House 1½ miles west of oval in the center of Woodstock.

SHIRE MOTEL, 46 Pleasant St., Woodstock, VT 05091. Tel. 802/457-2211. 26 rms (all with bath). A/C MINIBAR TV TEL
$ **Rates:** $58–$88 double. AE, MC, V. **Parking:** Free.

If you want a fancy place to stay, try the Woodstock Inn. But if you want comfortable and convenient lodgings at a good price, head straight for the Shire Motel, just east of the center. I've found the proprietors to be particularly helpful and friendly. It is well kept and has the advantage of being within walking distance of the village green.

WOODSTOCK INN AND RESORT, no. 14 The Green, Woodstock, VT 05091. Tel. 802/457-1100, or toll free 800/448-7900. Fax 802/457-3824. 143 rms (all with bath). A/C TV TEL
$ **Rates:** $128–$243 single; $130–$245 double. AE, MC, V. **Parking:** Free, on premises.

This place is well known as Laurence Rockefeller's little baby, a distinguished inn as popular with others as it is to its owner. This stately clapboard inn with a bricked townhouse addition faces South street on one side and the town's oval green in front. The service is attentive, the food very well prepared with the accent on regional fare, and the accommodations first rate. The premiere rooms are in the townhouse section artfully adjoining the original inn, where rooms have colonial-inspired appointments, luxury baths, VCRs, cable TVs, alcoves with book shelves, and fine linens and window treatments. The courtyard features a Paul Revere bell as its focal point. There's an extensive health facility owned by the inn down the road about 2 miles, with everything from swimming to aerobics and a Robert Trent Jones championship golf course.

WHERE TO DINE

BENTLEYS OF WOODSTOCK, 3 Elm St. Tel. 457-3232.
Cuisine: CONTINENTAL. **Reservations:** Required in peak season.
$ **Prices:** Appetizers $3–$8; main courses $12–$19; lunch $10–$14; dinner $25–$35. AE, MC, V.
Open: Sun–Fri 11:30am–2:30am, Sat 11:30am–1:30am. **Closed:** Thanksgiving.

In its various dining rooms, Bentleys, in the center of town, has captured the spirit of a Victorian tavern but without the heaviness: a pillared bar with potted palms, bentwood chairs, and Victorian sofas. The crowd is eclectic but tends to the young and sophisticated, the prices are moderate, and the food is good and simple or good and fancy. Lunch is burgers and sandwiches, light lunch plates, and salads; for dinner, these same dishes are on order, or you can indulge in a wheel of baked Brie, maple mustard chicken, shrimp and scallop stir-fry, or creative pasta dishes. There's live entertainment some evenings. The new chef is earning rave reviews, and if you're here Friday or Saturday night at 10pm you'll see the ceiling roll back to transform the dining room into a dance club replete with sophisticated light show. Bentley's is just a few steps across the village green.

THE PRINCE AND THE PAUPER, 24 Elm St. Tel. 457-1818.
  Cuisine: CONTINENTAL. **Reservations:** Recommended.
$ Prices: Fixed-price dinner $28. MC, V.
  Open: Dinner daily 6–9:30pm.
The Prince and the Pauper is down an alley named Dana Lane, which runs alongside the Woodstock Historical Society's building in the center of town. Low-beamed ceilings, candle lanterns casting a golden aura onto the small tables, a worldly clientele, and good conversation are what make the mood here, but the exotic array of dishes and delicacies add to it: Where else would you find calamari in beer batter as an appetizer, or main courses like salmon in pastry? Roast duckling is on the menu too, which changes frequently, of course, but the intimate atmosphere and the international flair remain. A lighter tavern or bistro menu is offered for $9.95 to $12.95 and you can order à la carte from the main menu, too. The lounge opens at 5pm.

9. PLYMOUTH

14 miles (23km) SW of Woodstock, 36 miles (58km) N of Grafton,
10 miles (16km) S of Sherburne Center (Killington)

GETTING THERE   By Car   Follow U.S. 4 west from Woodstock, then Route 100A; Route 100, the main north-south road through central Vermont, passes 1 mile west of Plymouth.

ESSENTIALS   See "Woodstock," above.

Calvin Coolidge was born in this tiny Vermont hamlet not far from the intersection of Routes 100 and 100A, and you can visit the **Coolidge Homestead** and the **Calvin Coolidge Birthplace** (tel. 672-3773). The former president's early history is interesting, but the story of his "inauguration" is full of fascination. While he was vice president, Mr. Coolidge came to Plymouth for a vacation in August 1923. Before he could even unwind, news came that President Harding was dead, and that he, Calvin Coolidge, was the 30th president of the United States. But he had to take the oath of office! The local notary public in the tiny town was none other than the new president's own father, Col. John Coolidge, and it was Colonel John who—as the only judicial official handy—administered the oath to his son by the light of a kerosene lamp at 2:47am, August 3, 1923.

You can visit the Homestead, the Birthplace, the **Wilder Barn** (a farmer's museum), the village church, the cemetery where President Coolidge is buried, and Wilder House, once the home of Coolidge's mother. Wilder House today holds a small restaurant and lunch counter.

The historic site is open daily Memorial Day through Columbus Day from 9:30am to 5:30pm. Admission for adults costs $3.50, children under 14 years of age enter for free, and a family ticket costs $12.

Don't miss Plymouth's outstanding attraction, the **Plymouth Cheese Company,** P.O. Box 1, Plymouth, VT 05056 (tel. 802/672-3650). The company's president, Mr. John Coolidge, is a scion of the famous village clan. Come to see the delicious Vermont granular-curd cheese being made on weekdays from 11:30am to 1pm, or come to sample and purchase the cheese Monday through Saturday from 8am to

5:30pm, on Sunday from 9am to 5:30pm. The cheese comes cut to order by the ounce or the pound, or in 3- and 5-pound wheels, and it is aged 3, 6, or 12 months to produce mild, medium, or sharp Cheddar. Cheeses are also available flavored with sage, caraway, garlic, dill, or pimiento. By the way, watching the cheese-making costs nothing; a 5-pound wheel costs $19.

---

10. KILLINGTON

10 miles (16km) N of Plymouth, 20 miles (32km) W of Woodstock,
12 miles (19km) E of Rutland

GETTING THERE By Car Follow U.S. 4 or Route 100 to Killington Road.

ESSENTIALS The **area code** is 802. The whole Killington area, which is part of the town of Sherburne, is organized with the **Killington Lodging Bureau** in charge of making room reservations for you. You can call or write to a lodge or motel directly, or you can call the lodging bureau to see what's available at 802/773-1330, or toll free 800/621-6867. The Killington and Pico Areas Association, P.O. Box 114, Killington, VT 05752 (tel. 802/775-7070), also maintains an **information booth** at the junction of U.S. 4 and Route 100 in Sherburne, at the Lothlorien Gift Shop; the booth is open during business hours.

With many skiers, Killington is the only word they have to hear before they begin thinking snow. The resort is one of Vermont's prime ski areas, and is especially noted for its progressive approach to development of its facilities (for instance, the addition of "gladed" ski trails, which give one the feeling of skiing right in the forest) and its snowmaking and grooming capabilities. But in recent years Killington has expanded its breadth of activities so that now you can go there for skiing in winter, organized backpacking and camping trips in the summer, tennis practice and lessons, a golf course, or for the summer playhouse and the Hartford Ballet. The resort is booming, but it is laid out so well on the side of the mountain that there is plenty of room for all the activities and the visitors.

WHAT TO SEE & DO

SKIING AT KILLINGTON & PICO Well, here you have it: one of the best-managed ski areas in the United States, with a good snowmaking capability, a variety of trails, a well-organized ski school, a very accessible location, lots of parking, three lounges, quick food service or a nice restaurant, several bars, and a long skiing season—what more can I say? The vertical drop is more than 3,000 feet, there are six chair lifts, a gondola said to be the longest in the world, and four Poma lifts, all with a total capacity of 10,000 skiers per hour. If that sounds like a mob scene, I must admit that it does get crowded, but also that it's a big mountain, and there does seem to be room for everyone.

If you don't choose a package plan which includes room, meals, and lift tickets, Killington Resort has various packages just for the slopes, including special rates on lifts for 2 to 7 days, or plans with which you get lifts and lessons for 2 to 7 days at reduced rates, or all three—lifts, lessons, and equipment rentals—for one price.

At Pico (*pie*-ko) Peak near Killington, there are five chair lifts, two T-bars, a vertical drop of 2,000 feet, and plenty of easy parking. It's a good, challenging area. Killington and Pico have a **ski report phone** for up-to-date information of ski conditions. With the resort's powerful snow-making capabilities, the Killington area traditionally has the longest ski season in the east, operating about 7 months, from October to mid-June. Call 800/545-5449 for information.

SUMMER AT KILLINGTON   Everyone coming to the Killington area will want to take the **Killington Gondola & Chairlift** (tel. 802/422-3333, or toll free 800/432-0100) to reach the 4,241-foot summit of Mount Killington. They say that this was the point from which the territory of "Verdmont" (green mountain) was christened in 1763. At the top you'll find a cafeteria, cocktail lounge, observation deck, and a self-guiding nature trail.

You can take either the chair lift or the gondola. The chair lift operates all summer, the gondola only in foliage season.

The base station for the chair lift is at the top of Killington Road; it runs daily from early July through Labor Day, and mid-September to early October, from 10am to 4pm. Round-trip tickets cost $9 for adults, $5 for children 6 to 12; free for kids 5 and under.

The gondola base station is on U.S. 4, 1 mile west of the junction with Route 100. It operates daily in foliage season only (mid-September through Columbus Day), from 10am to 4pm. Tickets cost $14 round-trip for adults, $8 for children 6 to 12; free for those 5 and under.

Killington Playhouse is at the Snowshed Vacation Center, Killington, VT 05751 (tel. 802/422-3333), and has performances of Broadway musicals from the beginning of July through early September, Tuesday through Sunday at 8pm. Tickets are $15 for adults; under 12 and over 65, $12. You can buy tickets at the door, but reservations are requested.

WHERE TO STAY

Killington is a well-organized resort community, and so virtually all activities here are organized around various package plans which are designed to save visitors money over the normal daily rates. A package usually includes lodging, meals, and the price of the activity: lift tickets, tennis lessons, horseback riding, backpacking trips. In ski season most inns operate on the Modified American Plan (MAP), in which you are required to take breakfast and dinner with your room. Call the **lodging bureau** at 800/621-6867 or 802/773-1330 to ask about the package plans, or to make reservations; or send a card to **Killington Ski Area,** Killington, VT 05751, asking for information on ski, hiking, or tennis package plans.

TRAILSIDE LODGE AT KILLINGTON, Coffee House Rd., Killington, VT 05751. Tel. 802/422-3532, or toll free 800/447-2209. 28 rooms (all with bath).

$ **Rates:** (including breakfast and dinner): $54–$120 double. MC, V. **Parking:** Free.

This former farmhouse, near Route 100 about 2½ miles off Route 4, is youthful and energetic and the best of its type in Killington. You won't find friendlier folks than Fred and Susan Field anywhere. Imagine Club Med on the cheap sans the beach atmosphere, and you'll understand the atmosphere here. Bike tours make this popular in summer and skiers love it in winter, especially the family table servings in the dining room where you'll always have plenty to eat. There is a full-service bar and a whirlpool for socializing or maybe even late-in-the-evening romancing. Accommodations are dormitory-like—some come with several twin beds and a double arrangement, but most with bunk styling. Don't be dismayed! If you book a double, there will only be two of you, no matter how many beds the room takes! And there's cross-country skiing at your doorstep to boot.

WHERE TO DINE

HEMINGWAY'S RESTAURANT, Rte. 4. Tel. 422-3886.
   Cuisine: CONTINENTAL. **Reservations:** Recommended.
$ **Prices:** Appetizers $6–$10; main courses $21–$26; fixed-price 4-course dinner $38. AE, CB, DC, MC, V.

Open: Dinner Wed–Sun 6–10pm. **Closed:** Mid-Apr to mid-May.
Established in a restored Vermont farmhouse, the restaurant has won several awards for its dishes. You might start dinner (the only meal served) by ordering hand-rolled fettuccine with smoked trout and scallions, or consommé of rabbit; then go on to shrimp with dark rum and currants, or grilled pheasant with Beaujolais. There's also a tasting menu which includes wine. The wine list is full and well balanced, everything from Château Lafitte-Rothschild ($185) to Sutter Home white zinfandel ($12).

11. MIDDLEBURY

32 miles (52km) N of Rutland, 34 miles (55km) S of Burlington

GETTING THERE   By Car   Several highways converge at Middlebury, including U.S. 7, and Vermont Routes 23, 30, and 125.

ESSENTIALS   The **area code** is 802. The Addison County Chamber of Commerce, 2 Court St., Middlebury, VT 05753 (tel. 802/388-7951), has an **information office** in the center of town, on the left-hand side as you come into Middlebury from the south (on U.S. 7) or the east (Route 125). The office is open during business hours.

Like its more famous counterpart of Hanover, N.H., the town of Middlebury is replete with beautiful old Georgian and 19th-century buildings, a small college of a high quality, and a pretty town green. Hanover has Dartmouth, and Middlebury has Middlebury College, but only Middlebury has the Vermont State Craft Center at Frog Hollow and the University of Vermont's Morgan Horse Farm—but more of that later.

WHAT TO SEE & DO

Once you've settled in and taken a stroll around this charming town, wander over to **Middlebury College** for a look at its exceptionally pretty campus and old granite buildings. Those in need of information about the college can get it by dropping in at the admissions office in Emma Willard House on Main Street (Route 30). Middlebury was founded by local people in the 19th century and went on to become a high-quality school. Robert Frost's participation in the Breadloaf Writers' Conference held in Middlebury's mountain campus close to nearby Ripton) spread the college's reputation even further.

Robert Frost wasn't the only person of renown to tramp the streets of Middlebury. A man named John Deere was an apprentice here from 1821 to 1825, after which he moved to Illinois and invented the world's first steel moldboard plow, making his name a household word in farms across the nation.

Deere's apprenticeship took place at Frog Hollow, which is down the hill from Court House Square, across the river bridge, and down Frog Hollow Lane on the right. The **Vermont State Craft Center at Frog Hollow** (tel. 388-3177) has fascinating craft exhibitions all year, not to mention craft classes and a gallery of Vermont crafts. Gallery hours are 9:30am to 5pm Monday through Saturday year round, and noon to 5pm on Sunday from June through December. They have a new gallery in Burlington now too.

To see the magnificent steeds at the University of Vermont's **Morgan Horse Farm** (tel. 388-2011), head west on Route 125 from Middlebury, turn right onto Route 23 (Weybridge Street), and follow signs to the farm for about 2½ miles. Admission to the farm is $3.50 per adult, $2 for teens (kids under 12 get in for free), 9am to 4pm daily, May through October. Once on this working farm, you'll get a guided tour of the stables, an audiovisual presentation about the farm and the Morgan horse, and the chance to roam the farm's spacious grounds to see the Morgans in training or playing and perhaps have a picnic at the picnic area.

WHERE TO STAY & DINE

The **Addison County Chamber of Commerce,** 2 Court St., Middlebury, VT 05753 (tel. 802/388-7951), maintains a list of homeowners who rent rooms to visitors. When crowds of parents swell the town for graduation, or alums return for homecoming, the town's lodging places are always filled. The "Homeowners Listing" is a very useful service. Drop by the chamber's information office at the same address or call.

MIDDLEBURY INN AND MOTEL, 20 Court House Sq., Middlebury, VT 05753. Tel. 802/388-4961, or toll free 800/842-4666. 65 rms (all with bath). A/C TV TEL

$ Rates: $68–$134 single; $75–$144 double. Children under 18 stay free in parents' room. Pets $6 per day. AE, DISC, MC, V. **Parking:** Free.

The great old inn dominates the square even more than the red-brick courthouse just up the hill from it. Guest rooms are in several locations: 45 in the inn itself, 5 in the Hubbard House attached to the inn, 5 in the Victorian-style Porter Mansion, and 10 in a modern motel annex. Price is determined by the size and location (and thus the views) of the room. The inn has its own dining room, which serves breakfast, lunch, and dinner.

WAYBURY INN, Rte. 125, East Middlebury, VT 05740. Tel. 802/388-4015, or toll free 800/348-1810. 14 rms (all with bath).

$ Rates: (including breakfast): Summer, $85–$115 double. Children get their own room at half the room price. AE, DISC, MC, V. **Parking:** Free.

As soon as you come up the front walk you'll recognize the Stratford Inn, or rather the Waybury Inn. You see the Waybury Inn is the real-life inspiration for the hit television comedy "Newhart," set in a Vermont country inn. You won't find Bob Newhart or Mary Frann tending the front desk, but you'll find lots of other familiar connections with the show. Rooms in the cozy, quaint (1810) inn have been refurbished in period style; five rooms are air conditioned. The inn provides guests with bikes and croquet equipment. The Waybury's dining room serves dinner and Sunday brunch at moderate prices. At dinnertime, a full-course meal of juice, main course, vegetables, potato, and bread made right in the inn, and dessert will cost between $25 and $30. There's also a fully licensed tavern.

12. SUGARBUSH, WARREN & WAITSFIELD

Waitsfield: 20 miles (32km) SW of Montpelier, 22 miles (35.5km) S of Stowe, 6 miles (10km) N of Warren

GETTING THERE   By Car   Both Warren and Waitsfield are on Route 100.

ESSENTIALS   The **area code** is 802. The **Sugarbush Chamber of Commerce** will help you out with information regarding lodging, dining, events, and activities if you write to P.O. Box 173, Waitsfield, VT 05673, or if you call 802/496-3409, or toll free 800/828-4748.

The area centered on Warren, Vt., along Route 100, can boast three well-known ski resorts: Sugarbush Valley, Mad River Glen, and Sugarbush North. Although much of the crowd here comes to stay in its own condominiums, a number of inns, motels, and guesthouses amply provide for the rest.

WHAT TO SEE & DO

Sugarbush has lots of opportunities for **good skiing,** and although the resort is not so highly ramified as those at Mount Snow, Killington, or Stowe, well, perhaps that's part of the charm here—an absence of big-time crowds. That doesn't mean you'll have no wait for the lift lines, though. Short lift lines these days are only at places with reserved-seat lift tickets, or at places not worth skiing, and Sugarbush, Sugarbush North, and Mad River Glen are not among them.

SUGARBUSH VALLEY At Sugarbush proper, the slopes and trails come down almost 2,500 feet from top to bottom, and they're laid out so that close to half of them are rated as suitable for expert skiers. Lifts include a gondola almost 2 miles long, four chair lifts, and a Poma. Rentals, instruction, and cross-country ski trails are all part of the establishment. The ski school offers a ski-week "saturation skiing workshop," which claims to instruct students in centeredness and energy awareness as well as techniques on the slopes. Lots of package plans are up for grabs—call the information numbers given at the beginning of this section.

MAD RIVER GLEN Mad River Glen is an easy drive from Waitsfield center on Route 17. This is a smaller area than Sugarbush, but still a good size, with four chair lifts all radiating out from one base area. The vertical drop is 2,000 feet, and the preponderance of trails (three-quarters of them) are for moderately well trained or expert skiers. Mad River Glen has a ski shop, rental shop, a ski school, and a nursery. For information, contact Mad River Glen, Waitsfield, VT 05673 (tel. 802/496-3551). Call the ski and snow line toll free in Vermont at 800/696-2001, or 802/496-2001.

SUGARBUSH NORTH & SOUTH Sugarbush consists of two mountains, Sugarbush South and North. Together they provide 80 trails and 16 lifts, the majority rated intermediate and expert. Equipment and lessons are yours at the base stations for the appropriate fees.

Sugarbush South rises to two peaks nearly 4,000 feet high. Below nine lifts whisk you around the rolling ridges. **Sugarbush North's** trails and slopes descend 2,600 feet from top to bottom, and about half the runs are classed as good for the median-level skier. But a look at the mountain trail plan will show you that taking the four-person chair lift to the top of Mt. Ellen will start you on some very long and pretty tricky runs. Sugarbush North has 36 trails and slopes in all, and usually a good amount of cover for a long season. For lodging information, call 802/583-2381, or toll free 800/53SUGAR.

The air currents around Sugarbush make it good for soaring or gliding, and the **Sugarbush Soaring Association,** P.O. Box 123, Warren, VT 05674 (tel. 496-2290), can fill you in on getting airborne. Call or write for details. Just so you'll know: You can qualify for solo glider flight in less than 2 weeks of good, full daily lessons and flights.

WHERE TO STAY & DINE

INN AT THE ROUND BARN FARM, East Warren Rd., Waitsfield, VT 05673 Tel. 802/496-2276. 11 rms (all with bath). A/C TEL TV
$ Rates: (including breakfast): $90–$130 double. AE, MC, V. **Parking:** Free.

This is one of our favorite places to be. From the outside it looks typical of the rural Vermont countryside; inside is a delightful, cheerful, and designer atmosphere. Five ponds dot the landscaped backyard on this 85-acre former dairy farm. The library has wide pine floors, a fireplace, and compact disc player. The breakfast room is French-inspired and overlooks the ponds in rear. A game room is in the daylight basement. The round barn has been restored and has an indoor pool; it is used mostly for functions. The rooms and suites are luxurious, especially the latter, and may be the best inn rooms in the state. Five rooms have four-poster beds and three have private whirlpools and some new ones also have fireplaces. You'll be hard-pressed to find better anywhere in New England. It's about 1½ miles off Route. 100 at Bridge Street.

SUGARBUSH INN, Sugarbush Access Rd., Warren, VT 05674. Tel 802/583-2301, or toll free 800/451-4213. 46 rms (all with bath). A/C TV TEL
$ Rates: $111–$160 double. AE, MC, V. **Parking:** Free.

With its own pools (indoor and outdoor), batteries of tennis courts, golf course, and nature paths through the woods, the Sugarbush Inn, 2 miles north of Warren, is the area's most posh resort inn. Rooms are tasteful and very comfy. The inn became part of the Sugarbush ski resort in 1990, but does not enjoy the reputation it once had

EASY EXCURSIONS

The reason to take a detour and visit **Montpelier,** the state capital of Vermont, is to take a look at the capitol building, a comely classical structure modeled on the Grecian Temple of Theseus. It's made of granite from nearby Barre, of course, but the dome is of wood covered in copper and then gilded. The State House will surprise you: It's so small, but then you'll notice that the capital city, Montpelier, is pretty small too; and thus you realize that you are in the midst of the most rural state in the Union, 48th in population (only about a half million Vermonters in all, spread through almost 10,000 square miles). In fact, a Vermont schoolchild once wrote, in Vermont "the trees are close together and the people are far apart."

The first thing you must know about **Barre** is that its name is pronounced like the name "Barry," and not like a drinking place. The next thing to know is that Barre is the granite capital of the world, having the world's largest quarry for the stone, and also a good number of the world's finest craftspeople to work it. Guided tours of the quarries and the workshops are offered daily, and prove a fascinating way to spend a few hours; but even more fascinating is a visit to the Hope Cemetery, eight-tenths of a mile north of the U.S. 302/Vt. 14 intersection, on Vt. 14. The cemetery has two gates and is open until sunset. We speak of making "monuments to survive ourselves," and in Barre the phrase is literal! Stonecutters here create the monument of their dreams for their own resting places. You'll see a balanced granite cube resting precariously on one corner, self-portraits and statues, a ponderous granite armchair, even a relief of a husband and wife sitting up in bed, hands joined in eternal friendship. Hope Cemetery is more like a sculpture garden, a touching memorial to artisans and artists who came here from many parts of the world.

The Rock of Ages quarry is open from the beginning of May through October with tours every day from 8:30am to 5pm, free. You can take a tram ride from 10am to 3pm Monday through Friday, June through September, for $2 per adult, $1 per child.

13. STOWE

22 miles (35.5km) N of Waitsfield, 36 miles (58km) E of Burlington

GETTING THERE By Bus See the beginning of this chapter.

By Car Stowe is on Route 100, 10 miles north of I-89 Exit 10.

ESSENTIALS The **area code** is 802. Businesses in the area are organized in the **Stowe Area Association,** P.O. Box 1320, Stowe, VT 05672 (tel. 802/253-6617 or toll free 800/24-STOWE). The information office, in the center of Stowe very near the intersection of Routes 100 and 108 (the Mountain Road), is open daily in ski season from 9am to 9pm; to 6pm the rest of the year. If you don't have a reservation when you arrive in Stowe, drop in here for help.

For information on snow conditions in the area, call toll free 800/63-STOWE in the winter.

The lodges and inns around Stowe adopt alpine or Central European names, and although the terrain here is hardly "alpine," somehow the names make sense. The village is dominated by Vermont's highest mountain, Mount Mansfield (4,393 ft.), certainly no Matterhorn; but there is definitely a European feeling in Stowe, the feeling one has in some tiny Austrian village amid emerald-green rolling hills, winding roads, and steep slopes. Perhaps it is the lushness (in summer) of the lawns, forests, and wildflowers, or perhaps it is the rain and mists—Lamoille County is said to have the greatest amount of precipitation in the state—which make everything so lush. Whatever, there is certainly an especially attractive air about Stowe.

The frequent rain is not a liability, either, for local people learn to plan on it, and the earth scents after the rain are part of the pleasure of Stowe. And besides, it's all this precipitation which makes Stowe one of the best skiing areas in the East, with plenty of deep cover and a long season.

Winter or summer, the narrow rocky mountain defile known as Smuggler's Notch is a dramatic place for a hike or a drive, and is just another one of those things that make Stowe special.

WHAT TO SEE & DO

Much of the territory around Stowe is part of Vermont's **Mount Mansfield's State Forest and Park,** and for summer visitors that means hiking trails (especially the Long Trail from Massachusetts to Canada), camping areas, and picnicking. Winter visitors will want to note the state ski area, and Spruce Peak ski area.

SKIING STOWE   The trails are down both Mount Mansfield and Spruce Peak, the mountains on either side of the Smuggler's Notch defile, and the variety of trails is such that there's plenty of adventure for everyone, no matter what your ability. In fact, the mountains, the staff in charge of trail maintenance, and especially the Sepp Ruschp Ski School have all worked hard over many years to earn for Stowe the high regard it has among skiers. The vertical drop is more than 2,000 feet, and the lifts include five chairs, three T-bars, and a gondola with four-passenger cars. Beginners will want to start off at the Toll House Slopes, near the base of the toll road up Mount Mansfield; the next logical step is to Spruce Peak; and after you've mastered that, go on to the more difficult among the Mount Mansfield trails and slopes. Lessons and rentals are available, and there are restaurants at **Cliff House** (top of the Mansfield gondola) and **Octagon** (top of the toll road), as well as at the base camps.

A big event of the winter season at Stowe is the annual **Winter Carnival,** held during the second week in January, when special races, church suppers, square dances, hockey and skating matches, a snow-sculpture contest, and even a Queen's Ball are held—hotel rates are not raised for this event. Check with the Stowe Area Association for a carnival schedule.

SUMMER AT STOWE   Some of Stowe's pleasures are best appreciated during warm weather. The breathtaking ride to the top of Vermont's highest mountain in a **gondola** (tel. 253-7311) costs $9.50 round-trip for adults, $5 for children. One child rides free for each paying adult. Or you can drive to the top of Mount Mansfield on the toll road, climbing even higher into the mist, past bunches of exotic wildflowers, feeling the air get cooler. The toll-road base station is near the ski areas just south of Smuggler's Notch; you pay for your car ($10) and then proceed up the road, which is paved only for ¼ mile—the rest is stabilized dirt. (But the ¼ mile at the bottom is so perfect for skateboarding that the management has had to erect a sign prohibiting the fast and fancy rollers from monopolizing this stretch of its land!) Both the gondola and the toll road are open daily from mid-June through mid-October, weather permitting. The gondola is new and expanded by 700 feet. It is also the fastest in the world.

It's hardly less exciting just to make the drive through Smuggler's Notch. You approach the mountains and the defile, and start turning the sharp bends in the road as you meet a sign saying SHIFT TO LOW GEAR NOW—and it means it. The road begin to twist among tremendous boulders fallen from the steep sides of the defile over th eons; the foliage gets very thick, the trees block much of the sun's light, and as yo grind along up the switchback slope, a sense of wildness and excitement takes ove Just over the pass is a stopping place (you dare not stop unless you can pull off th road) with benches, toilets, a snack stand, and several impromptu trails that invite on to clamber—at least for a few hundred feet—into the rocks.

It's no exaggeration to say that something's always happening in Stowe in June July, and August: Antique-car rallies, horse and dog shows, a craft fair, even a fiddler meeting, and a surprisingly authentic Oktoberfest (in October, natch) crowd into th schedule. **Topnotch,** that posh resort on Mountain Road near Mount Mansfield, the place to rent horses by the hour or for a trail ride: Call 253-8585 and ask for th stables. The going rate is $20 per hour.

Stowe has an **Alpine Slide,** operated by the Mount Mansfield Company (te 253-7311). You start by taking a cool and scenic ride up a chair lift. At the top, yo mount a small sled and begin your descent along a concrete runway which weaves an turns like a bobsled run all the way to the bottom of the mountain slope. The ide (and the Alpine Slide design) came from Germany. The slide is open daily mid June t September and on weekends and holidays only from Memorial Day and throug mid-October; on rainy days, the slide closes down. Rides cost $6 per adult, $4 pe child, and five-ride ticket books are available. Take your slide-ride between 10am an 5pm, weather permitting. The Alpine Slide is 6 miles north of Stowe village on Rou 108 at Spruce Peak.

The more familiar summer pastimes are well covered, too. **Stowe Country Clu** has an 18-hole golf course; tennis courts abound (many hotels and lodges have the own); hiking, bicycling, fishing, and photographing can fill whole weeks.

Lastly, the **Green Mountain Guild of White River Junction** brings summe theater to Stowe during July and August, every week Tuesday through Saturday Performances are at Stowe High School on Barrows Road. Contact the Stowe Are Association for current schedules, reservations, and prices.

A CINEMA Stowe now has a movie house, in the complex called Stowe Cente which is exactly a mile north of Stowe village along Mountain Road. Call 253-4678 t see what's playing. When you get there, you can choose a regular theater seat or comfy corner of the Projection Room—a cocktail lounge—from which to see th film.

WHERE TO STAY

Stowe has a good variety of lodging places, posh or modest, dauntingly expensive surprisingly cheap. In summer, there is no problem finding exactly the room you wa at the price you want to pay. But on busy winter weekends you'd be well advised t reserve in advance. Just give the **Stowe Area Association** a ring (see above) an reservations will be made for you. In winter, the toll-free number is in operation; summer, call on the regular line.

Most hostelries in Stowe require winter visitors to have breakfast and dinner; in th jargon this is called the Modified American Plan. Smaller places generally have BYO bars or lounges, which helps greatly in reducing the expense of an after-ski glow. F supplies, trundle down to the Vermont State Liquor Store on Route 100 south town, open from 9:15am to 6pm; to 8pm on Friday; closed Sunday.

What follows is a selection of my favorite places to stay in Stowe, summer winter. Bus service along Route 100 (the Mountain Road) connects the ski slopes Stowe Village during the busy winter season.

VERY EXPENSIVE

STOWEHOF INN, Edson Hill Rd. (P.O. Box 1108), Stowe, VT 05672. Te **802/253-9722,** or toll free 800/422-9722. Fax 802/253-7513. 48 rms (all wi bath). A/C MINIBAR TV TEL **Directions:** It's about 3½ miles northeast of Stowe village, off the Mountain Rd. (Rte. 108).

$ Rates: (including half-board): $120–$210 double. Weekly rates and special package deals available. AE, MC, V. **Parking:** Free.

This is my first choice in Stowe. The inspiration of the bold, unusual, and exciting place is definitely alpine, and the public rooms give a sense of coziness and charm such as one might get in a small European Schloss. Architect Larry Hess's masterful planning of spaces—split levels, strange angles, nooks, crannies, high ceilings, and low ceilings—has resulted in a truly delightful place to spend time. There's a sunken fireplace pit, a cardplayers' nook decorated with giant playing cards (a royal flush, no less), a library seating area, and a living room with panoramic view of the valley. One motif used throughout the inn, from the main entrance to the dining and living rooms, is that of support "columns" of massive tree trunks stripped of bark and dried to a silvery, ringing hardness. All this sounds wild, but it's so well done that Stowehof is truly a delight to be in, plus the grounds are lovely.

Each of the guest rooms is decorated differently, and each has a private balcony or patio. Some "demi-suites" have extra Murphy beds, or fireplaces or kitchenette. There are several dining rooms, but one in particular is among the area's best, with a full, wonderful dinner plus wine costing about $120 for a couple. Guests also enjoy the downstairs pub.

Additional attractions at the Stowehof Inn include a heated swimming pool, tennis courts, shuffleboard, pitch-and-putt green, sauna, library, a games room and horseback riding.

TRAPP FAMILY LODGE, Luce Hill Rd., Stowe, VT 05672. Tel. 802/253-8511, or toll free 800/826-7000. 93 rms (all with bath). TV TEL **Directions:** Take Rte. 108 (Mountain Rd.) from the center of Stowe 2 miles to a fork by a white church. Rte. 108 bears right, but you bear left and follow this side road up the mountain slope, following the signs to the lodge.

$ Rates: (including breakfast and dinner): $130–$235 double. AE, CB, DC, DISC, MC, V. **Parking:** Free.

The singing Trapp family of *Sound of Music* fame left the mountains of their native Austria before World War II and settled here in Stowe, later using this as home base for their worldwide concert tours. Members of the family still are involved in operating the resort. The Main Lodge, destroyed by fire in 1980, has been rebuilt; there's also a Lower Lodge. All the rooms come with private bath, and many have balconies as well. Other facilities include indoor and outdoor swimming pools, a sauna, and a fitness room. Maria von Trapp is buried here.

MODERATE

ANDERSEN LODGE, 3430 Mountain Rd., R.R. 1, Box 1450, Stowe, VT 05672. Tel. 802/253-7336, or toll free 800/336-7336. 17 rms (all with bath). A/C TV

$ Rates: (including half-board): $108–$156 double. AE, MC, V. **Parking:** Free.

This small, friendly Tyrolean inn between Mount Mansfield and Stowe has an authentic European ambience lent by its Austrian proprietors, Trude and Dietmar Heiss. Mr. Heiss is an Austrian-trained chef as well, and so the meals (which come with your room in ski season) are particularly hearty and "alpine." You can play tennis, the piano, bumper pool, and swim in the pool, or use the sauna and Jacuzzi, or just sit in front of the fire. Some rooms have telephones and refrigerators.

GABLES INN, 1457 Mountain Rd., Stowe, VT 05672. Tel. 802/253-7730, or toll free 800/GABLES-1. 17 rms (all with bath).

$ Rates: Summer, $64–$80 double; $117 queen-size bed. Winter, $90–$220 double with breakfast, après-ski snacks, and dinner. AE, MC, V. **Parking:** Free.

This homey, congenial inn several miles northwest of Stowe has some large rooms with a queen-size bed, fireplace, and hot tub; some rooms have air conditioning and

TV. The Gables also has a swimming pool, picnic area, hot tub, and a front porch where you can have breakfast (to noon) while gazing at Mount Mansfield.

GOLDEN EAGLE RESORT MOTOR INN, Mountain Rd., Stowe, VT 05672. Tel. 802/253-4811, or toll free 800/626-1010. 65 rms (all with bath). A/C TV TEL

$ Rates: $69–$129 double; $99–$205 apartment. AE, DC, DISC, MC, V. **Parking:** Free.

You can bed down in a comfortable room, suite, efficiency unit, or vacation apartment; such amenities as fireplaces, balconies, refrigerators, and private whirlpool baths are available in some accommodations. The Golden Eagle, ½ mile north of Stowe Village, has many facilities, including a hot tub, indoor and outdoor swimming pools, fitness room, sauna, whirlpool bath, tennis court, and even two stocked trout ponds for fishing buffs. There are three restaurants. Service here is friendly, experienced, and dependable. Weekly and monthly rates can bring the apartment prices down somewhat.

SCANDINAVIA INN, Mountain Rd., Stowe, VT 05672. Tel. 802/253-8555, or toll free 800/544-4229. 18 rms (all with bath). TV TEL

$ Rates: (including breakfast): Summer, $55–$90 double. Fall, $65–$95 double. AE, DISC, MC, V. **Parking:** Free.

Keeping close to the spirit of its name, this inn, two miles northwest of Stowe Village, is a dark-wood building with peaked gables and white trim, decked with Scandinavian flags. In summer there are lounge chairs on the front porch, flower boxes that provide splashes of color, and picnic tables. This inn has a surprising range of services, including a sauna, hot tub, swimming pool, whirlpool bath, fitness room, game room, barbecue grills, and bicycles.

THE SKI INN, Mountain Rd., Stowe, VT 05672. Tel. 802/253-4050. 10 rms (5 with bath). TV

$ Rates: Winter, with half-board, $90–$110 double with bath. Summer, with breakfast, $40–$50 double with bath. AE. **Parking:** Free.

This inn specializes in good food and good conversation. Very near the ski areas (both downhill and cross-country), the Ski Inn is a large white country inn with a big living room/BYOB lounge with a fireplace, a pine-paneled game room in the basement, and simple but bright and pleasing rooms with a twin and double bed. Mrs. Heyer, who operates the Ski Inn, shares her conversation, helpful hints, and friendly atmosphere with all her guests, and particularly lucky ones may even get some of her wild-berry preserves.

STOWEFLAKE INN, Mountain Rd., Stowe VT. Tel. 802/253-7355, or toll free 800/253-2232. 95 rms (all with bath), 25 town houses. A/C TV TEL

$ Rates: $48–$120 double. DC, DISC, MC, V. **Parking:** Free.

The Stoweflake is a long-standing favorite in Stowe, a family-run operation that has grown steadily over the years and today provides some of the best accommodations and service around. There are two tennis courts, outdoor pool, indoor pool, putting green, 370-yard driving range, nearby golf, and health club with saunas, whirlpool, and some fitness equipment. The restaurant is well regarded locally. Come in the summer and you might just see the Stoweflake's hot air balloon. Rooms have all the comforts of a first-class hotel, and the town houses are even bigger.

WHERE TO DINE

During ski season, of course, most people will want to eat at their inns, or will be obliged to do so. Stowehof, the Golden Eagle, and the Yodler, are some of the preferred dining places in the valley. Almost every other inn serves meals as well.

14. BURLINGTON

225 miles (363km) NW of Boston, Mass.; 98 miles (158km)
S of Montréal, P.Q.; 36 miles (58km) W of Stowe

GETTING THERE   By Plane   Burlington is served by several major air carriers and their regional commuter subsidiaries, including Business Express (Delta Connection), Metro Airlines (Trans World Express), and Continental Express. In addition, USAir, United Airlines, and Continental Airlines have direct flights to Burlington in large aircraft. Direct flights go to Burlington from Atlanta, Boston, Buffalo, Chicago, Cleveland, New York City, Orlando, Philadelphia, Pittsburgh, and Washington, D.C.

By Train   Amtrak's day-train *Adirondack* runs daily between New York City and Montréal, skirting Vermont as it runs up the Hudson. It stops at Port Kent, N.Y., from which you can take a cross-lake ferryboat to Burlington. The train runs mid-May to mid-Oct.

By Bus   Vermont has its own large bus line, **Vermont Transit Lines,** 135 St. Paul St., Burlington, VT 05401 (tel. 802/864-6811, or toll free 800/451-3292, 800/642-3133 in Vermont, in New York City call 212/971-6300), which operates from New York City (in conjunction with Greyhound), Montréal (in conjunction with Voyageur), and Boston to virtually all points of interest in Vermont, including its home base at Burlington. Burlington's Vermont Transit bus station (tel. 802/864-6811) is at the southeastern end of Church Street Marketplace across City Hall Park.

By Car   Follow I-89, which runs between Boston and the U.S.-Canadian border north of Burlington.

ESSENTIALS   The **area code** is 802. In the midst of Church Street Marketplace, near the corner with Bank Street, is an **information gallery** (no phone) with brochures and maps. For more elaborate or detailed information, contact the **Lake Champlain Regional Chamber of Commerce,** 209 Battery St. (P.O. Box 453), Burlington, VT 05402 (tel. 802/863-3489).

The largest city in Vermont is a town of only about 50,000 population, but in this state, small is beautiful. Burlington's situation on the shores of Lake Champlain brings it extra attractiveness and aquatic-sports opportunities as well. The town is the seat of the University of Vermont, and student activities and cultural events add an extra dimension to Burlington's daily life. Of the city's native sons, the educator and philosopher John Dewey is the most famous, and Ethan Allen, while not born here, chose Burlington as his home in his later years. Today part of his farm is encompassed by Ethan Allen Park.

Besides being a college town, Burlington is industrial: Weapons, data-processing equipment, textiles, and consumer products are all made here, and Burlington's medical facilities serve the northern part of the state. Burlington is one of two termini for Lake Champlain ferryboat crossings (the other is Port Kent, N.Y.).

Downtown Burlington is a fairly compact area easily negotiated on foot. The heart of town for visitors and locals alike is Church Street Marketplace, a 4-block stretch of Church Street from Pearl Street to College Street closed to vehicular traffic, beautified with trees, benches, and sidewalk cafés, and busy with strollers, street vendors, shoppers, lovers, performers, and sidewalk-bench conversationalists. At the northwestern end of Church Street stands the pretty Unitarian church, built in 1816.

WHAT TO SEE & DO

Much of Burlington's cultural life centers on the **University of Vermont** campus, and on the campuses of the other three colleges in the area: **St. Michael's, Trinity,** and **Champlain.**

The University of Vermont stages an annual summer **Champlain Shakespeare Festival,** held at the Royall Tyler Theatre (tel. 656-2094), on the Main Street side of the campus. A **Mozart Festival** is held in summer as well. See below for information on the university's museum.

Much of the lakefront land in Burlington is encompassed by parks, including **Oak Ledge Park** and **Red Rocks Park** in South Burlington, **Battery Park** near Burlington's center and only 5 blocks from the ferries, and **Burlington Municipal Beach** on Institute Road north of the ferry dock along the lake shore. **Ethan Allen Park** is north of the center of town; take North Avenue (Route 127) starting at Battery Park.

MUSEUMS

ROBERT HULL FLEMING MUSEUM, Colchester Ave. Tel. 656-0750.

The University of Vermont's museum, on its campus not far from downtown Burlington, has a good collection of archeological and ethnographic holdings (including some good Pre-Columbian objects), as well as gems such as a Kang Hsi vase, Wei terra-cotta, a Cole painting, 17th-century Persian miniatures, early Roman glass, Coptic carvings, and a bona-fide Egyptian mummy.

Admission: Free.

Open: Tues–Fri 9am–4pm, Sat–Sun 1–5pm. **Directions:** From the center of town, go east on Pearl St., which merges with Colchester Ave.; look for the museum on the right-hand side.

SHELBURNE MUSEUM, Rte. 7, Shelburne. Tel. 985-3346.

Visitors to Burlington must make a detour to the town of Shelburne to see the Shelburne Museum, a gala festival of Americana collected into 37 historic buildings arranged on 45 acres, including an authentic one-room schoolhouse, six fully furnished early New England homes, a jail complete with stocks, an Adirondack hunting lodge, a print shop, and a lighthouse that once guided ships on Lake Champlain. The buildings you see date from the 17th, 18th, and early 19th centuries; each was moved here from its original location in Vermont, New Hampshire, New York, or Massachusetts, and all are now filled with the artifacts of earlier American life. The museum is said to have about the best and fullest collection of Americana ever assembled. Among the artifacts are a 1920s carousel, a round dairy barn (1901), and even the huge 220-foot side-wheel steamship SS *Ticonderoga* docked here after its last run on the lake. Four art galleries feature paintings and sculpture by European and American artists (Andrew Wyeth, Grandma Moses, Ogden Pleissner, Rembrandt, Monet, Manet, Degas), and other buildings hold displays of folk art both charming and authentic: quilts, decoys, glassware, and furniture, plus the tools used to make these items. The museum has a cafeteria and snack bars, picnic tables, a bookshop, stores, and free parking.

Admission: Ticket good for 2 consecutive days $15 adults; $6 children 6 to 14; free for kids under 6.

Open: Mid-May to mid-Oct, daily 10am–5pm. Guided tours offered off-season at 1pm. **Directions:** Go 7 miles south of the city along U.S. 7.

LAKE CHAMPLAIN FERRIES

One of the favorite things to do in Burlington is to take the ferry over to Port Kent, N.Y., whether you're actually interested in getting to Port Kent or not. Ferries, leaving from the King Street Dock in Burlington, operate in spring, summer, and fall, leaving each terminus at about 1-hour intervals from 8 or 9:20am to 5:30 or 6:30pm, a bit more frequently in summer, with 14 trips a day in each direction. You can take your car across if you're going somewhere: Price for car and driver, one-way, is $12; each extra adult pays $3 one-way; children 6 to 12 pay $1. The trip, a marvelous way to get to know Lake Champlain, takes about an hour each way. This ferry doesn't run in winter, but ferries between Grand Isle, Vt., and Plattsburgh, N.Y., operate year round. You'll also find a ferry chugging between Charlotte, Vt., and Essex, N.Y., from early April through early January.

WHERE TO STAY

EXPENSIVE

RADISSON BURLINGTON HOTEL, 60 Battery St., Burlington, VT 05401. Tel. 802/658-6500, or toll free 800/333-3333. Fax 802/658-4659. 255 rms (all with bath). A/C TV TEL

$ Rates: $72–$135 double. Extra person or bed $10. Children under 18 stay free in parents' room. AE, CB, DC, DISC, ER, MC, V. **Parking:** Free.

The Radisson bills itself as "Vermont's most luxurious hotel," and although many other hotels may dispute the claim, there's no disputing the Radisson's quality. Tropical plants bring freshness to an enclosed Garden Court next to the pool and whirlpool bath. Many of the rooms have gorgeous views of Lake Champlain, while others open onto the indoor swimming pool. The more expensive rooms are those with a lake-and-mountain view, and the Plaza rooms have extra amenities. The two restaurants serve American and French cuisine. Facilities include an indoor swimming pool, a whirlpool, and fitness room.

SHERATON-BURLINGTON HOTEL AND CONFERENCE CENTER, 870 Williston Rd., Burlington, VT 05403. Tel. 802/862-6576, or toll free 800/677-6576, or 800/325-3535. Fax 802/862-5137. 310 rms (all with bath). A/C TV TEL

$ Rates: Summer, $84–$137 double. AE, DC, DISC, ER, MC, V. **Parking:** Free, next to hotel.

Located only 1½ miles from the airport, at the intersection of U.S. 2 and I-89, this is the prime choice of business travelers. The heart of the hotel is the Summerhouse, a four-story space with translucent ceiling sheltering fountains, plants, and many hotel services. Higher prices are for the new Concierge Level rooms, which have marvelous views of Mount Mansfield. There is a restaurant and a pub/lounge with live entertainment. The hotel provides a free airport shuttle service, a fitness center, and an indoor swimming pool.

MODERATE

ECONO LODGE, 1076 Williston Rd., Burlington, VT 05403. Tel. 802/ 863-1125, or toll free 800/55ECONO. Fax 802/658-1296. 177 rms (all with bath). A/C TV TEL

$ Rates: $49–$67 single; $56–$77 double. AE, CB, DC, ER, MC, V. **Parking:** Free, at motel.

At the Econo Lodge, at the intersection of U.S. 2 and I-89, in addition to a health spa, you get the usual, expected motel comforts—rooms with one or two double beds, color TV, free HBO, full bath, even an outdoor swimming pool.

HOWARD JOHNSON MOTOR LODGE, 1 Dorset St. (P.O. Box 993), Burlington, VT 05402. Tel. 802/863-5541, or toll free 800/654-2000. Fax 802/862-2755. 89 rms (all with bath). A/C TV TEL

$ Rates: May–Oct, $58–$70 single; $70–$80 double. Children under 18 stay free in parents' room. AE, MC, V. **Parking:** Free.

Prices are on the order of the other chain hotels, but there are several advantages to staying at Hojo's, at the intersection of U.S. 2 and I-89 (Exit 14E). You get an indoor-outdoor pool, fitness room, hot tub, saunas, tennis courts, and cable color TV. Lots of rooms are equipped with two double beds. The familiar HoJo restaurant operates 24 hours.

WHERE TO DINE

Though not bursting with restaurants, Burlington has good dining possibilitie
Several of the best places are located in the area of Church Street Marketplace, right i
the center of town.

ALFREDO'S RESTAURANT, Church Street Marketplace. Tel. 864-0854
Cuisine: ITALIAN. **Reservations:** Recommended for large parties.
$ Prices: Appetizers $2–$8; main courses $10–$15; lunch $10; dinner $15–$25
AE, DC, MC, V.
Open: Mon–Fri 11:30am–9:30pm, Sat–Sun 11:30am–10:30pm.

In the alley across from City Hall on Church Street Marketplace are three simple bu
cozy and charming storefront dining rooms with lace curtains, red-and-white-checke
tablecloths, and live lobsters in a tank by the door. In good weather, food is serve
under an open air awning in the back. With its latest expansion, the decor has move
toward café styling, with a row of French windows running along one side. Pasta in a
its variations—fettuccine, capellini, vermicelli, manicotti, ravioli, linguine, lasagne—
is a strong suit here, but there's also delicious veal sorrentino (veal with eggplant an
mozzarella in a marsala sauce), chicken in garlic with peppers and mushrooms, an
many other Italian delights. Prices are good: On Thursday evening, some veal dishe
are priced at only $10. Friday is lobster night with the chef's special appetizer include
in the price of lobster dishes.

BOURBON STREET GRILL, 213 College St. Tel. 865-2800.
Cuisine: AMERICAN/CAJUN. **Reservations:** Recommended. **Directions**
Follow College St. to the corner of S. Winooski.
$ Prices: Appetizers $2.50–$7.50; main courses $5–$17; full lunch $10; full dinne
$20. AE, DC, MC, V.
Open: Mon–Sat 11:30am–midnight, Sun brunch 10:30am–3pm.

At South Winooski, this is a tidy little storefront bistro with whirling ceilin
fans, and a menu for any time of day. Soups, salads, burgers, and sandwiche
share space on the menu with jambalaya, Cajun flank steak, and shrim
étouffée. For a little Louisiana thrill, preface your meal by ingesting an authenti
Louisiana Hurricane, a powerful rum-based concoction which calms you down i
you're in the midst of a storm, or starts a storm if you aren't.

CARBUR'S, 117 St. Paul St. Tel. 862-4106.
Cuisine: AMERICAN. **Reservations:** Not accepted.
$ Prices: Appetizers $2–$5; main courses $7–$13; lunch $10. AE, DC, DISC, MC
V.
Open: Mon–Thurs 11am–11pm, Fri 11am–midnight, Sat 11:30am–midnigh
Sun 11:30am–11pm.

Carbur's is done in heavy mod-Victoriana and tends to the quietly outrageous: A sig
in the window says FAMOUS SINCE 1974. The dining room has a tremendously hig
ceiling equipped with ceiling fans that spin slowly even on cool days, just fc
atmosphere. The menu is a book 16 pages long, filled with sandwiches, soups, sala
plates, almost all—with a few exceptions like the monster five-decker sandwich—fc
around $8. The menu, by the way, is laden with enough drawings and amusing patte
to keep you entertained all through your meal. Come for lunch or dinner any day. I
faces City Hall Park at the southeastern end of Church Street Marketplace. They hav
another restaurant in Portland, Me., too.

DEJA VU CAFE, 185 Pearl St. Tel. 864-7917.
Cuisine: FRENCH. **Reservations:** Required.
$ Prices: Appetizers $3.50–$7.25; main courses $4–$24. AE, DC, MC, V.
Open: Daily 11:30am–midnight.

Dark, cool, and restful inside, the Déjà Vu Café, near the corner of South Winoosk
Street, around the corner from the northeastern end of Church Street Marketplac
has a high-peaked roof and ornate trim that hint at Gothic style. Cozy booths an
simple tables on three levels provide plenty of dining space; in summer, there a

ables on the courtyard as well. The menu is short but varied and well balanced with nteresting appetizers (including escargots en croûte), soups, salads, elaborate sandwiches, and light main-course dishes, such as fettuccine Alfredo, an "American cassoulet," and chicken with corn and achiote. Breton crêpes, those large, thin pancakes, are served filled with smoked salmon, sausage and cheese, ham and chicken. n the evening, more substantial plates (veal, steaks, etc.) are added to the menu. The wine list is decent, the beer list long and interesting. Come for lunch, tea (4 to 6pm), dinner, or a late-night snack.

INDEX

GENERAL INFORMATION

DESTINATIONS

Key to abbreviations: *B* = Budget; *B&B* = Bed & Breakfast; *E* = Expensive; *GH* = Guest House; *Hs* = Hostel; *I* = Inexpensive; *M* = Moderate; *VE* = Very Expensive; * = Author's favorite; *$* = Super-value choice.

Now Save Money on All Your Travels by Joining
FROMMER'S ™ TRAVEL BOOK CLUB
The World's Best Travel Guides at Membership Prices

FROMMER'S TRAVEL BOOK CLUB is your ticket to successful travel! Open up a world of travel information and simplify your travel planning when you join ranks with thousands of value-conscious travelers who are members of the FROMMER'S TRAVEL BOOK CLUB. Join today and you'll be entitled to all the privileges that come from belonging to the club that offers you travel guides for less to more than 100 destinations worldwide. Annual membership is only $25 (U.S.) or $35 (Canada and all foreign).

The Advantages of Membership

1. Your choice of three free FROMMER'S TRAVEL GUIDES. You can pick two from our FROMMER'S COUNTRY and REGIONAL GUIDES (listed under Comprehensive, $-A-Day, and Family) and one from our FROMMER'S CITY GUIDES (listed under City and City $-A-Day).
2. Your own subscription to **TRIPS & TRAVEL** quarterly newsletter.
3. You're entitled to a **30% discount** on your order of any additional books offered by FROMMER'S TRAVEL BOOK CLUB.
4. You're offered (at a small additional fee) our **Domestic Trip Routing Kits.**

Our quarterly newsletter **TRIPS & TRAVEL** offers practical information on the best buys in travel, the "hottest" vacation spots, the latest travel trends, world-class events and much, much more.

Our **Domestic Trip Routing Kits** are available for any North American destination. We'll send you a detailed map highlighting the best route to take to your destination—you can request direct or scenic routes.

Here's all you have to do to join:
Send in your membership fee of $25 ($35 Canada and foreign) with your name and address on the form below along with your selections as part of your membership package to **FROMMER'S TRAVEL BOOK CLUB, P.O. Box 473, Mt. Morris, IL 61054-0473.** Remember to check off 2 FROMMER'S COUNTRY and REGIONAL GUIDES and 1 FROMMER'S CITY GUIDE on the pages following.

If you would like to order additional books, please select the books you would like and send a check for the total amount (please add sales tax in the states noted below), plus $2 per book for shipping and handling ($3 per book for all foreign orders) to:

FROMMER'S TRAVEL BOOK CLUB
P.O. Box 473
Mt. Morris, IL 61054-0473
1-815-734-1104

[ ] **YES**. I want to take advantage of this opportunity to join FROMMER'S TRAVEL BOOK CLUB.

[ ] **My check is enclosed**. Dollar amount enclosed _____*
(all payments in U.S. funds only)

Name_____

Address_____

City_____ State_____ Zip_____

To ensure that all orders are processed efficiently, please apply sales tax in the following areas: CA, CT, FL, IL, NJ, NY, TN, WA, and CANADA.

*With membership, shipping and handling will be paid by FROMMER'S TRAVEL BOOK CLUB for the three free books you select as part of your membership. Please add $2 per book for shipping and handling for any additional books purchased ($3 per book for all foreign orders).

Allow 4-6 weeks for delivery. Prices of books, membership fee, and publication dates are subject to change without notice.

Please Send Me the Books Checked Below

FROMMER'S COMPREHENSIVE GUIDES

(Guides listing facilities from budget to deluxe, with emphasis on the medium-priced)

	Retail Price	Code		Retail Price	Code
☐ Acapulco/Ixtapa/Taxco 1993–94	$15.00	C120	☐ Jamaica/Barbados 1993–94	$15.00	C105
☐ Alaska 1990–91	$15.00	C001	☐ Japan 1992–93	$19.00	C020
☐ Arizona 1993–94	$18.00	C101	☐ Morocco 1992–93	$18.00	C021
☐ Australia 1992–93	$18.00	C002	☐ Nepal 1992–93	$18.00	C038
☐ Austria 1993–94	$19.00	C119	☐ New England 1993	$17.00	C114
☐ Austria/Hungary 1991–92	$15.00	C003	☐ New Mexico 1993–94	$15.00	C117
☐ Belgium/Holland/ Luxembourg 1993–94	$18.00	C106	☐ New York State 1992–93	$19.00	C025
			☐ Northwest 1991–92	$17.00	C026
☐ Bermuda/Bahamas 1992–93	$17.00	C005	☐ Portugal 1992–93	$16.00	C027
			☐ Puerto Rico 1993–94	$15.00	C103
☐ Brazil, 3rd Edition	$20.00	C111	☐ Puerto Vallarta/Manzanillo/ Guadalajara 1992–93	$14.00	C028
☐ California 1993	$18.00	C112			
☐ Canada 1992–93	$18.00	C009	☐ Scandinavia 1993–94	$19.00	C118
☐ Caribbean 1993	$18.00	C102	☐ Scotland 1992–93	$16.00	C040
☐ Carolinas/Georgia 1992–93	$17.00	C034	☐ Skiing Europe 1989–90	$15.00	C030
☐ Colorado 1993–94	$16.00	C100	☐ South Pacific 1992–93	$20.00	C031
☐ Cruises 1993–94	$19.00	C107	☐ Spain 1993–94	$19.00	C115
☐ DE/MD/PA & NJ Shore 1992–93	$19.00	C012	☐ Switzerland/Liechtenstein 1992–93	$19.00	C032
☐ Egypt 1990–91	$15.00	C013	☐ Thailand 1992–93	$20.00	C033
☐ England 1993	$18.00	C109	☐ U.S.A. 1993–94	$19.00	C116
☐ Florida 1993	$18.00	C104	☐ Virgin Islands 1992–93	$13.00	C036
☐ France 1992–93	$20.00	C017	☐ Virginia 1992–93	$14.00	C037
☐ Germany 1993	$19.00	C108	☐ Yucatán 1993–94	$18.00	C110
☐ Italy 1993	$19.00	C113			

FROMMER'S $-A-DAY GUIDES

(Guides to low-cost tourist accommodations and facilities)

	Retail Price	Code		Retail Price	Code
☐ Australia on $45 1993–94	$18.00	D102	☐ Mexico on $50 1993	$19.00	D105
☐ Costa Rica/Guatemala/ Belize on $35 1993–94	$17.00	D108	☐ New York on $70 1992–93	$16.00	D016
			☐ New Zealand on $45 1993–94	$18.00	D103
☐ Eastern Europe on $25 1991–92	$17.00	D005			
			☐ Scotland/Wales on $50 1992–93	$18.00	D019
☐ England on $60 1993	$18.00	D107			
☐ Europe on $45 1993	$19.00	D106	☐ South America on $40 1993–94	$19.00	D109
☐ Greece on $45 1993–94	$19.00	D100			
☐ Hawaii on $75 1993	$19.00	D104	☐ Turkey on $40 1992–93	$22.00	D023
☐ India on $40 1992–93	$20.00	D010	☐ Washington, D.C. on $40 1992–93	$17.00	D024
☐ Ireland on $40 1992–93	$17.00	D011			
☐ Israel on $45 1993–94	$18.00	D101			

FROMMER'S CITY $-A-DAY GUIDES

(Pocket-size guides with an emphasis on low-cost tourist accommodations and facilities)

	Retail Price	Code		Retail Price	Code
☐ Berlin on $40 1992–93	$12.00	D002	☐ Madrid on $50 1992–93	$13.00	D014
☐ Copenhagen on $50 1992–93	$12.00	D003	☐ Paris on $45 1992–93	$12.00	D018
			☐ Stockholm on $50 1992–93	$13.00	D022
☐ London on $45 1992–93	$12.00	D013			

FROMMER'S TOURING GUIDES
(Color-illustrated guides that include walking tours,
cultural and historic sights, and practical information)

	Retail Price	Code		Retail Price	Code
☐ Amsterdam	$11.00	T001	☐ New York	$11.00	T008
☐ Barcelona	$14.00	T015	☐ Rome	$11.00	T010
☐ Brazil	$11.00	T003	☐ Scotland	$10.00	T011
☐ Florence	$ 9.00	T005	☐ Sicily	$15.00	T017
☐ Hong Kong/Singapore/	$11.00	T006	☐ Thailand	$13.00	T012
Macau			☐ Tokyo	$15.00	T016
☐ Kenya	$14.00	T018	☐ Venice	$ 9.00	T014
☐ London	$13.00	T007			

FROMMER'S FAMILY GUIDES

	Retail Price	Code		Retail Price	Code
☐ California with Kids	$17.00	F001	☐ San Francisco with Kids	$17.00	F004
☐ Los Angeles with Kids	$17.00	F002	☐ Washington, D.C. with Kids	$17.00	F005
☐ New York City with Kids	$18.00	F003			

FROMMER'S CITY GUIDES
(Pocket-size guides to sightseeing and tourist accommodations
and facilities in all price ranges)

	Retail Price	Code		Retail Price	Code
☐ Amsterdam 1993–94	$13.00	S110	☐ Miami 1993–94	$13.00	S118
☐ Athens, 9th Edition	$13.00	S114	☐ Minneapolis/St. Paul, 3rd	$13.00	S119
☐ Atlanta 1993–94	$13.00	S112	Edition		
☐ Atlantic City/Cape May	$ 9.00	S004	☐ Montréal/Québec City	$13.00	S125
1991–92			1993–94		
☐ Bangkok 1992–93	$13.00	S005	☐ New Orleans 1993–94	$13.00	S103
☐ Barcelona/Majorca/	$13.00	S115	☐ New York 1993	$13.00	S120
Minorca/Ibiza 1993–94			☐ Orlando 1993	$13.00	S101
☐ Berlin 1993–94	$13.00	S116	☐ Paris 1993–94	$13.00	S109
☐ Boston 1993–94	$13.00	S117	☐ Philadelphia 1993–94	$13.00	S113
☐ Cancún/Cozumel/Yucatán	$ 9.00	S010	☐ Rio 1991–92	$ 9.00	S029
1991–92			☐ Rome 1993–94	$13.00	S111
☐ Chicago 1993–94	$13.00	S122	☐ Salt Lake City 1991–92	$ 9.00	S031
☐ Denver/Boulder/Colorado	$ 8.00	S012	☐ San Diego 1993–94	$13.00	S107
Springs 1990–91			☐ San Francisco 1993	$13.00	S104
☐ Dublin 1993–94	$13.00	S128	☐ Santa Fe/Taos/Albuquerque	$13.00	S108
☐ Hawaii 1992	$12.00	S014	1993–94		
☐ Hong Kong 1992–93	$12.00	S015	☐ Seattle/Portland 1992–93	$12.00	S035
☐ Honolulu/Oahu 1993	$13.00	S106	☐ St. Louis/Kansas City	$13.00	S127
☐ Las Vegas 1993–94	$13.00	S121	1993–94		
☐ Lisbon/Madrid/Costa del	$ 9.00	S017	☐ Sydney 1993–94	$13.00	S129
Sol 1991–92			☐ Tampa/St. Petersburg	$13.00	S105
☐ London 1993	$13.00	S100	1993–94		
☐ Los Angeles 1993–94	$13.00	S123	☐ Tokyo 1992–93	$13.00	S039
☐ Madrid/Costa del Sol	$13.00	S124	☐ Toronto 1993–94	$13.00	S126
1993–94			☐ Vancouver/Victoria 1990–	$ 8.00	S041
☐ Mexico City/Acapulco	$ 9.00	S020	91		
1991–92			☐ Washington, D.C. 1993	$13.00	S102

Other Titles Available at Membership Prices

SPECIAL EDITIONS

	Retail Price	Code		Retail Price	Code
☐ Bed & Breakfast North America	$15.00	P002	☐ Where to Stay U.S.A.	$14.00	P015
☐ Caribbean Hideaways	$16.00	P005			
☐ Marilyn Wood's Wonderful Weekends (within a 250-mile radius of NYC)	$12.00	P017			

GAULT MILLAU'S "BEST OF" GUIDES
(The only guides that distinguish the truly superlative
from the merely overrated)

	Retail Price	Code		Retail Price	Code
☐ Chicago	$16.00	G002	☐ New England	$16.00	G010
☐ Florida	$17.00	G003	☐ New Orleans	$17.00	G011
☐ France	$17.00	G004	☐ New York	$17.00	G012
☐ Germany	$18.00	G018	☐ Paris	$17.00	G013
☐ Hawaii	$17.00	G006	☐ San Francisco	$17.00	G014
☐ Hong Kong	$17.00	G007	☐ Thailand	$18.00	G019
☐ London	$17.00	G009	☐ Toronto	$17.00	G020
☐ Los Angeles	$17.00	G005	☐ Washington, D.C.	$17.00	G017

THE REAL GUIDES
(Opinionated, politically aware guides for youthful budget-minded travelers)

	Retail Price	Code		Retail Price	Code
☐ Able to Travel	$20.00	R112	☐ Kenya	$12.95	R015
☐ Amsterdam	$13.00	R100	☐ Mexico	$11.95	R016
☐ Barcelona	$13.00	R101	☐ Morocco	$14.00	R017
☐ Belgium/Holland/ Luxembourg	$16.00	R031	☐ Nepal	$14.00	R018
			☐ New York	$13.00	R019
☐ Berlin	$11.95	R002	☐ Paris	$13.00	R020
☐ Brazil	$13.95	R003	☐ Peru	$12.95	R021
☐ California & the West Coast	$17.00	R121	☐ Poland	$13.95	R022
☐ Canada	$15.00	R103	☐ Portugal	$15.00	R023
☐ Czechoslovakia	$14.00	R005	☐ Prague	$15.00	R113
☐ Egypt	$19.00	R105	☐ San Francisco & the Bay Area	$11.95	R024
☐ Europe	$18.00	R122			
☐ Florida	$14.00	R006	☐ Scandinavia	$14.95	R025
☐ France	$18.00	R106	☐ Spain	$16.00	R026
☐ Germany	$18.00	R107	☐ Thailand	$17.00	R119
☐ Greece	$18.00	R108	☐ Tunisia	$17.00	R115
☐ Guatemala/Belize	$14.00	R010	☐ Turkey	$13.95	R027
☐ Hong Kong/Macau	$11.95	R011	☐ U.S.A.	$18.00	R117
☐ Hungary	$14.00	R118	☐ Venice	$11.95	R028
☐ Ireland	$17.00	R120	☐ Women Travel	$12.95	R029
☐ Italy	$13.95	R014	☐ Yugoslavia	$12.95	R030